WEBSTER'S NEW WORLD™

JAPANESE DICTIONARY

POCKET EDITION

Fujihiko Kaneda
EDITOR

Bruce Rogers
SUPERVISING EDITOR

MACMILLAN • USA

Macmillan General Reference
A Simon & Schuster Macmillan Company
1633 Broadway
New York, NY 10019-6785

A Webster's New World™ Book

MACMILLAN is a registered trademark of Macmillan, Inc.
WEBSTER'S NEW WORLD DICTIONARY is a
registered trademark of Simon & Schuster, Inc.

Originally published in Japan i 1983 by Yohan Publications,
Inc., as *Yohan English-Japanese, Japanese-English Dictionary*

ISBN: 0-02-861411-9

Manufactured in the United States of America

10   9   8   7   6   5   4   3   2   1

EDITOR'S PREFACE

A good teacher and a good dictionary are, needless to say, the most necessary elements for mastering a foreign language.

For those who are beginning to study the Japanese language, and especially those who live outside Japan, a great difficulty is that there are few teachers with whom they can work. Some are fortunate in finding good teachers, but most must grapple with this rather difficult language without help. Therefore, a good dictionary is of vital importance.

This little dictionary was compiled with the aim of presenting the beginner and the intermediate student with as many useful words as possible, with as many meanings as possible, and in as small a volume as practical. The editor has attempted to include as many important idioms and derivatives as space permitted, and since it is presumed that most users will be adults, the most useful words occurring in daily conversation and appearing in popular magazines and newspapers have been given.

It is hoped that this dictionary will serve as a helpful companion to students of the Japanese language.

The editor wishes to thank Bruce Rogers for helpful supervision.

Fujihiko Kaneda

Parentheses and Brackets

1. Parentheses ( )

a. English words in parentheses before the translated words are clarifying explanations.

Example: **act** *n.* (deed) kōi; (main division of a play) maku

b. Italicized English words in parentheses before the translated words show supplemental explanations as "in the field of," or category of special use.

Example: **article** *n.* (thing) shinamono; (*newspaper*) kiji; (*gram.*) kanshi

c. Translated words in parentheses can be omitted.

Example: **anchor** *n., v.* ikari (o orosu) = *n.* ikari ―― *v.* ikari o orosu

2. Brackets [ ]

Words or letters in brackets can replace the word or letter preceding the brackets.

Example: **irregular** *adj.* fukisoku na [no] = fukisoku na, fukisoku no
jōhin na [ni] elegant [ly], graceful [ly]
= jōhin na elegant, graceful
jōhin ni elegantly, gracefully

A NOTE ON PRONUNCIATION

The user of the dictionary, especially if a native speaker of English, should take care not to let the appearance of the romanized syllable or word lead him astray. This is particularly true of the romanized syllable with an "e" in it. For instance, *she* is not the English word "she"; nor is *he* the English word "he." The *she* in romanization is pronounced as in *she*pherd; the *he* in romanization is pronounced as in *he*lp. The Japanese word *sake* (rice wine) is very often mispronounced to become the English word "sake." One remedy for this has been to use an accent mark to make the romanized word appear saké. However, it was found that in this dictionary, the use of such an accent mark would be too extensive and would tend to confuse the user rather than clarify the pronunciation.

Guide to
PRONUNCIATION OF JAPANESE

The pronunciation of Japanese vowels is the same as in Italian or Spanish; that of consonants is as in English:

Short Vowels

a as in *father, alms*
e as in *pen, red*
i as in *ink, machine*
o as in *open, ocean*
u as in *true, cruel*

Vowel Combinations

All combined vowels are pronounced in full; for examples:

ei = *e* + *i* sounded as in *day*
ai = *a* + *i* sounded as in *alive*
ou = *o* + *u* sounded as in *float*
au = *a* + *u* sounded as in *out*

Long Vowels

The long vowels are indicated in this dictionary by macrons; they are pronounced as the short vowels, but the sound is double in length: *a*, *e*, *i*, *o*, *u*,. For example:

o in *hato* (*pigeon*) is like the *o* in *oil*.
o in *tōtō* (*at last*) is like the *o* in *torch*.

An *n* occuring before *b*, *m*, and *p* changes

to an *m* in sound and is so written when romanized; ie.,

> *shin+ bun= shimbun* (*newspaper*)
> *shin+ pai= shimpai* (*worry*)
> *an+ ma= amma* (*massage*)

The initial *g* in a word is usually glottal as the *g* in *get*, the mid-word *g* is often nasalized as the *ng* in *king*. There are exceptions to this and the distinctions are rather vague and unimportant.

Doubled consonants should be given full value in pronunciation, a doubled *c* is usually written and always pronounced as *tc*; ie.,

> *yatta* (*gave*) = *yat+ ta*
> *kitta* (*cut*) = *kit+ ta*
> *matchi* (*match*) = *mat+ chi*
> *kotchi* (*here*) = *kot+ chi*

The *u* is nearly mute in Japanese except where it is the initial syllable. Particularly where *u* follows an *s*, it is not articulated. Thus *desu* as in *"Dare desu ka?"* (*Who is it?*) is pronounced as *des* in *desparate*; *sutēki* (*steak*) is near to *"steiki"*.

Other consonantal sounds about which there may be doubt in the learner's mind are:

> *ch* as in *child*
> *sh* as in *shine*
> *ts* as in *pets*, *cats*

The *r* is pronounced with the tip of the tongue; a sound midway between *l* and *r*, never rolled.

In this dictionary, an apostrophe after an *n* indicates that the *n* is pronounced separately from the following letter:

shin'nyū = shin-nyū
han'ei = han-ei

Accent indications are not given as they vary with geographical areas and this lack of standard will confuse the learner. Students who wish to make a more thorough study of the language can consult **the Nihongo Akusento Jiten** (Dictionary of Japanese Accents) published by the Japan Broadcasting Corporation.

Rōmaji (Romanization)

There are three systems for writing Japanese in the Latin alphabet: 1) *Hepburn* (*Hebon-shiki*), most generally used, 2) *Official* (*Kunrei-shiki*), now almost obsolete, and 3) *Japanese* (*Nihon-shiki*). Basically, the three systems are alike; the Hepburn system is used throughout this dictionary as it is considered the easiest to use insofar as pronunciation is concerned. Where considered useful, the official romanization has been given in parentheses.

The following chart shows the two Japanese phonetic writing systems (syllabaries); the cursive symbols to the left are *hiragana*; the angular symbols to the right are *katakana*. *Hiragana* is used for prefixes and suffixes to the Chinese characters (*kanji*) and for purely Japanese words; *katakana* is used for words of foreign origin and on official documents. *Hiraga-*

na is the first system learned by school children, although *katakana* is considered easier because of its simplicity of form.

a	i	u	e	o
あ ア	い イ	う ウ	え エ	お オ
ka	**ki**	**ku**	**ke**	**ko**
か カ	き キ	く ク	け ケ	こ コ
sa	**shi**	**su**	**se**	**so**
さ サ	し シ	す ス	せ セ	そ ソ
ta	**chi**	**tsu**	**te**	**to**
た タ	ち チ	つ ツ	て テ	と ト
na	**ni**	**nu**	**ne**	**no**
な ナ	に ニ	ぬ ヌ	ね ネ	の ノ
ha	**hi**	**fu**	**he**	**ho**
は ハ	ひ ヒ	ふ フ	へ ヘ	ほ ホ
ma	**mi**	**mu**	**me**	**mo**
ま マ	み ミ	む ム	め メ	も モ
ya	**i**	**yu**	**e**	**yo**
や ヤ	い イ	ゆ ユ	え エ	よ ヨ
ra	**ri**	**ru**	**re**	**ro**
ら ラ	り リ	る ル	れ レ	ろ ロ
wa	**i**	**u**	**e**	**o**
わ ワ	い イ	う ウ	え エ	を ヲ
ga	**gi**	**gu**	**ge**	**go**
が ガ	ぎ ギ	ぐ グ	げ ゲ	ご ゴ
za	**ji**	**zu**	**ze**	**zo**
ざ ザ	じ ジ	ず ズ	ぜ ゼ	ぞ ゾ
da	**ji**	**zu**	**de**	**do**
だ ダ	ぢ ヂ	づ ヅ	で デ	ど ド

ba	bi	bu	be	bo
ば バ	び ビ	ぶ ブ	べ ベ	ぼ ボ

pa	pi	pu	pe	po
ぱ パ	ぴ ピ	ぷ プ	ぺ ペ	ぽ ポ

kya	kyu	kyo
きゃ キャ	きゅ キュ	きょ キョ

gya	gyu	gyo
ぎゃ ギャ	ぎゅ ギュ	ぎょ ギョ

sha	shu	she	sho
しゃ シャ	しゅ シュ	しぇ シェ	しょ ショ

ja	ju	je	jo
じゃ ジャ	じゅ ジュ	じぇ ジェ	じょ ジョ

cha	chu	che	cho
ちゃ チャ	ちゅ チュ	ちぇ チェ	ちょ チョ

nya	nyu	nyo
にゃ ニャ	にゅ ニュ	にょ ニョ

hya	hyu	hyo
ひゃ ヒャ	ひゅ ヒュ	ひょ ヒョ

bya	byu	byo
びゃ ビャ	びゅ ビュ	びょ ビョ

pya	pyu	pyo
ぴゃ ピャ	ぴゅ ピュ	ぴょ ピョ

fa	fi	fu	fe	fo
ふぁ ファ	ふぃ フィ	ふ フ	ふぇ フェ	ふぉ フォ

mya	myu	myo
みゃ ミャ	みゅ ミュ	みょ ミョ

rya	ryu	ryo
りゃ リャ	りゅ リュ	りょ リョ

n
ん ン

ENGLISH-JAPANESE

A

a *adj.* (*indef. art.*) (one) hitotsu no ひとつの;
(a certain) aru ある

abacus *n.* soroban そろばん

abandon *v.* (desert) suteru 捨てる; (give up)
akirameru あきらめる

abbey *n.* sōin 僧院; shūdōin 修道院

abbreviate *v.* shōryaku suru 省略する

abdomen *n.* onaka おなか; hara 腹

abhor *v.* hidoku kirau ひどくきらう

ability *n.* nōryoku 能力; shuwan 手腕

able *adj.* dekiru できる; jōzu na 上手な
    be able to (suru koto ga) dekiru (することが)
できる

abnormal *adj.* (unusual) ijō na 異常な; (unnatural) fushizen na 不自然な

aboard *adv., prep.* (on board a ship) jōsen shite
乗船して; (on board a train) jōsha shite 乗車
して

abolish *v.* (do away with) haishi suru 廃止する

about *adv., prep.* (*time*) (approximately) koro こ
ろ; goro ごろ; (*quantity*) kurai くらい; gurai
ぐらい; (*amount*) yaku 約; oyoso およそ;
(concerning) ...ni tsuite ...について

above *adv., prep.* ...no ue ni ...の上に; ...yori
ue ni ...より上に

abroad *adv.* (foreign country) gaikoku ni 外国
に; (overseas) kaigai ni 海外に

abrupt *adj.* totsuzen no 突然の; kyū na 急な

absent *adj.* kesseki no [shite iru] 欠席の [して
いる] *absent-minded* bon'yari shite ぼんやり
して

absolute *adj.* (positive) zettai no 絶対の; (perfect) kanzen na 完全な

absorbent cotton *n.* dasshimen 脱脂綿

accelerator *n.* akuseru アクセル

accept *v.* (receive) ukeru 受ける; (agree) shō-daku suru 承諾する

access *n.* (approach) sekkin 接近; (admittance) mensetsu 面接

accessory *n.* fuzoku-hin 付属品; akusesarī アクセサリー

accident *n.* (unexpected or unlucky event) jiko 事故; sainan 災難 *car accident* jidōsha jiko 自動車事故

accommodate *v.* (adapt) tekiō saseru 適応させる; (harmonize) chōwa saseru 調和させる

accompany *v.* (go along with) ...to issho ni iku といっしょに行く; (co-exist with) fuzui suru 付随する

accomplish *v.* (carry out) shitogeru しとげる; (fulfill) kansei suru 完成する

accord *v.* (be consistent) itchi suru 一致する; (give) ataeru 与える; (grant) yurusu 許す

according *adj.* *according to* ... ni yoru to ... によると; ... ni yore ba ... によれば; ... ni shita-gatte ... に従って

accordingly *adv.* shitagatte 従って; dakara だから

account *v.* (consider) to omou と思う; (explain) setsumei suru 説明する; (count) kanjō suru 勘定する —— *n.* (calculation) keisan 計算; (business record) kanjō 勘定; yokin kōza 預金口座; (reason) riyū 理由

accountant *n.* kaikei-gakari 会計係

accumulate *v.* (pile up) chikuseki suru 蓄積する; (heap up) tsumi-ageru 積み上げる

accurate *adj.* seikaku na 正確な

accuse *v.* ... o hinan suru ... を非難する; semeru せめる

accustom *v.* narasu 慣らす *be accustomed to* ... ni nareru に慣れる

ache *v.* (pain) itamu 痛む —— *n.* itami 痛み

achieve *v.* (accomplish) yaritogeru やりとげる; (attain) mokuteki o tassuru 目的を達する

acid *n.* san 酸 ——*adj.* sui すい; suppai すっ
ぱい

acknowledge *v.* (admit) mitomeru 認める; (appreciate) kansha suru 感謝する

acquaint *v.* (let know) shiraseru 知らせる; (make familiar) seitsū saseru 精通させる
be acquainted with ...o shitte iru ...を知って
いる

acquire *v.* (gain) uru 得る; te ni ireru 手に
入れる; (learn) narau 習う

across *adv.* (on the other side of) ... no mukō-gawa ni ...の向こう側に ——*prep.* yokogitte
横切って

act *v.* (behave) furumau ふるまう; okonau 行な
う ——*n.* (deed) kōi 行為; (major division
of a play) (geki no) maku (劇の)幕

action *n.* (doing) hataraki はたらき; (activity) ka-tsudō 活動

active *adj.* katsudō-teki na 活動的な

actor *n.* haiyū 俳優; dan'yū 男優

actress *n.* joyū 女優

actual *adj.* genjitsu no 現実の

acute *adj.* (sharp) surudoi 鋭い; (of disease) kyū-sei no 急性の

adapt *v.* (adjust to) tekiō saseru 適応させる;
(modify) shūsei suru 修正する

add *v.* kuwaeru 加える; tasu たす

addition *n.* tashizan たし算; *in addition to* ...ni
kuwaete ...に加えて

address *n.* jūsho 住所; atena 宛名

addressee *n.* jushin-nin 受信人

addresser *n.* hasshin-nin 発信人

adequate *adj.* tekitō na 適当な; jūbun na じゅう
ぶんな

adhere *v.* kuttsuku くっつく; nebaritsuku ねばり
つく

adhesive plaster *n.* bansōkō ばんそうこう

adjective *n.* keiyō-shi 形容詞

adjust *v.* (arrange) totonoeru 整える; (put in

order) seiri suru 整理する

administration *n.* (government) gyōsei 行政; (management) keiei 経営; kanri 管理

admiral *n.* kaigun-taishō 海軍大将; shireichōkan 司令長官

admire *v.* kanshin suru 感心する; homeru ほめる

admission *n.* nyūjō 入場
  admission fee nyūjō-ryō 入場料
  admission free nyūjō muryō 入場無料
  admission ticket nyūjō-ken 入場券

admit *v.* (let in) ireru 入れる; (accept) mitomeru 認める; (confess) barasu ばらす; (allow) yurusu 許す

adolescence *n.* seinen-ki 青年期; seishun 青春

adopt *v.* saiyō suru 採用する *adopted child* yōshi 養子

adore *v.* akogareru あこがれる

adult *n.* otona おとな; seijin 成人

advance *n., v.* (move forward) zenshin (suru) 前進(する); susumu 進む; (progress) shimpo (suru) 進歩(する); (payment beforehand) sakibarai (suru) 先払い(する)
  in advance of …yori mo susunde よりも進んで; yori mo mae ni よりも前に

advantage *n.* (superiority) yūri 有利; (benefit) rieki 利益 *take advantage of* …o riyō suru …を利用する

adventure *n.* (risk) bōken 冒険; adobenchā アドベンチャー; (danger) kiken 危険

adversary *n.* (enemy) teki 敵; (opponent) aite 相手

adverse *adj.* (opposed) hantai no 反対の; (unfavorable) furi na 不利な

advertise *v.* kōkoku suru 広告する

advertisement *n.* kōkoku 広告

advice *n.* (counsel) chūkoku 忠告; (news) shirase 知らせ

advise *v.* (give advice to) chūkoku suru 忠告する; (inform) shiraseru 知らせる

affair *n.* (matter) jiken 事件; (things) mono 物

affect *v.* (influence) eikyō suru 影響する; (move) kandō saseru 感動させる

affection *n.* (love) aijō 愛情; (influence) eikyō 影響

affirm *v.* (assert) dangen suru 断言する; (confirm) kakunin suru 確認する; (say "yes") kōtei suru 肯定する

afflict *v.* (torment) kurushimeru 苦しめる; (distress) nayamaseru 悩ませる

afford *v.* (give) ataeru 与える *(negative)* ...o kau [motsu] yoyū ga aru ... を買う[持つ]余裕がある; (supply) kyōkyū suru 供給する

afraid *adj.* (in fear) osorete 恐れて; kowai こわい; (apprehensive) shimpai shite 心配して

after *prep.* (behind) ...no ato ni ...の後に —— *conj.* (later) nochi ni 後に *after all* kekkyoku 結局

afternoon *n.* gogo 午後

afterward(s) *adv.* (later) ato de 後で; (subsequently) tsugi ni 次に

again *adv.* (once more) mata また; futatabi ふたたび; mō ichido もう一度

against *prep.* ...ni hantai shite ...に反対して; ni mukatte に向かって; ...ni motarete ...にもたれて

age *n.* (years) nenrei 年齢; (period) jidai 時代

agent *n.* dairi-nin[-ten] 代理人[店]

aggressive *adj.* kōgeki-teki na 攻撃的な

agitate *v.* (disturb) dōyō saseru 動揺させる; (excite) kōfun saseru 興奮させる

ago *adv.* izen ni 以前に; mae ni 前に *10 years ago* jū-nen mae 10年前

agony *n.* (great suffering) hageshii kurushimi はげしい苦しみ

agree *v.* (consent) sansei suru 賛成する; (be in accord) itchi suru 一致する

agriculture *n.* nōgyō 農業

ahead *adv.* (before) mae ni 前に; (in front of)

zempō ni 前方に; (forward) mae e 前へ

aid *v.* tasukeru 助ける; enjo suru 援助する
—— *n.* enjo 援助; tetsudai 手伝い

aim *v.* mezasu めざす; nerau ねらう —— *n.*
(purpose) mokuteki 目的

air *n.* (atmosphere) kūki 空気; (sky) sora 空;
(manner) yōsu 様子

airplane *n.* hikōki 飛行機; kōkūki 航空機

airport *n.* kūkō 空港

alarm *n.* (warning of danger) keihō 警報; (surprise) odoroki おどろき —— *v.* (surprise)
bikkuri saseru びっくりさせる; odorokasu
おどろかす

alarm clock mezamashi-dokei 目覚時計

album *n.* arubamu アルバム

alcohol *n.* arukōru アルコール

ale *n.* bīru ビール

alert *adj.* (watchful) chūi-bukai 注意深い; (vig-
ilant) yudan no nai ゆだんのない; nukeme no
nai 抜目のない

alien *adj.* (foreign) gaikoku(-jin) no 外国(人)の
—— *n.* (foreigner) gaikoku-jin 外国人

alien registration booklet gaikoku-jin tōroku
shōmeisho 外国人登録証明書

all *adj.* subete no すべての; zembu no ぜんぶの
—— *pron.* minna みんな; zembu ぜんぶ

all at once totsuzen 突然

allergic *adj.* arerugī-sei no アレルギー性の

alley *n.* (narrow passage) komichi 小道; roji
路地; (back lane) ura-dōri 裏通り

alliance *n.* dōmei 同盟

alligator *n.* wani (-gawa) わに(皮)

allot *v.* (assign) wariateru 割りあてる; (distribute) bumpai suru 分配する

allow *v.* (permit) yurusu 許す; kyoka suru 許可
する; (admit) mitomeru 認める; (give) ataeru
与える

allowance *n.* (permission) kyoka 許可; (grant)
kyūyo 給与

allusion *n.* (hint) anji 暗示; (indirect mention) honomekashi ほのめかし; (meaningful mention) atetsuke あてつけ

ally *v.* (unite) dōmei suru 同盟する ——*n.* (allied state) dōmei-koku 同盟国

almanac *n.* (calendar) koyomi 暦; (annual publication) nenkan 年鑑

almighty *adj.* zen'nō no 全能の

almost *adv.* hotondo ほとんど; taitei たいてい

alone *adj., adv.* tada hitori (de) ただひとり (で); hitori dake ひとりだけ

along *prep.* (by the length) ...ni sotte ...に沿って ——*adv.* (in company) issho ni いっしょに

alongside *adv., prep.* ...no katawara ni ...のかたわらに; ni yokozuke ni ...に横づけに

aloud *adv.* (loudly) ō-goe de 大声で; koe o dashite 声を出して

already *adv.* sude ni すでに; mō もう

also *adv.* (too) ...mo mata ...もまた; (besides) nao なお; katsu かつ

alter *v.* kaeru 変える; henkō suru 変更する

alternate *adj.* (occuring by turns) kōgo no 交互の; (every other) hitotsu oki no ひとつおきの ——*v.* (perform by turns) kōtai ni suru 交代にする

alternative *adj.* dochira ka ippō no どちらか一方の

although *conj.* dakeredomo だけれども; dewa aruga ではあるが

altitude *n.* (vertical height) takasa 高さ; (height above sea-level) kaibatsu 海抜

altogether *adv.* (wholly) mattaku まったく; (completely) kanzen ni 完全に; (totally) sukkari すっかり; (on the whole) zentai to shite 全体として

always *adv.* tsune ni 常に; itsumo いつも

a. m. gozen 午前 *cf.* p. m. gogo 午後

amateur *n.* shirōto しろうと; amachua アマチュア

amaze *v.* bikkuri saseru びっくりさせる；odoro-kasu 驚かす

ambassador *n.* taishi 大使

ambition *n.* (aspiration) yashin 野心；taimō 大望

ambulance *n.* kyūkyū-sha 救急車

amend *v.* (change for the better) aratameru 改める；(correct) teisei suru 訂正する

America *n.* (the U. S. A.) Amerika-gasshūkoku アメリカ合衆国；Beikoku 米国

American *n., adj.* Amerika-jin [no] アメリカ人 [の]；Beikoku-jin [no] 米国人 [の]；(American English) Amerika-eigo アメリカ英語；Beigo 米語

amid *prep.* (in the middle of) ...no mannaka ni [de] ...のまん中に [で]

among *prep.* (in the middle of) ...no naka ni [de] ...の中に [で]；(between) ...no aida ni ...の間に

amount *v.* (add up to) sōgaku [sōkei] ...ni naru 総額 [総計]...になる ―― *n.* (sum total) sō-kei 総計；gōkei 合計；(quantity) ryō 量

ample *adj.* (spacious) hiroi 広い；(quite enough) jūbun na 十分な

amuse *v.* (entertain) tanoshimaseru 楽しませる；omoshirogaraseru 面白がらせる；(divert) nagu-sameru なぐさめる

amusement *n.* (delight) tanoshimi 楽しみ；yoro-kobi 喜び；(diversion) goraku 娯楽

analyze *v.* bunkai suru 分解する；bunseki suru 分析する

ancestor *n.* senzo 先祖；sosen 祖先

anchor *n., v.* ikari (o orosu) 錨 (をおろす)

ancient *adj.* mukashi no 昔の；kodai no 古代の

and *conj.* soshite そして；to と

angel *n.* tenshi 天使；enzeru エンゼル

anger *n.* ikari 怒り ―― *v.* okoraseru 怒らせる

angle¹ *n.* (corner) kado 角；sumi 隅；(standpoint) kenchi 見地

angle² *v.* (fish) sakana o tsuru 魚を釣る

angler tsuri-bito 釣人

angry *adj.* okotta 怒った; hara o tateta 腹を立てた   *angrily* okotte 怒って

animal *n.* dōbutsu 動物; kedamono けだもの

ankle *n.* ashi-kubi 足首; kurubushi くるぶし

annex *n.* bekkan 別館; shinkan 新館

anniversary *n.* kinen-bi 記念日; kinen-sai 記念祭

announce *v.* (inform) shiraseru 知らせる; (publish) happyō suru 発表する·

annoy *v.* (trouble) komaraseru 困らせる; nayamaseru 悩ませる; ira-ira saseru イライラさせる

annual *adj.* (reckoned by the year) ichi-nen no 一年の; (recurring yearly) mainen no 毎年の —— *n.* (year book) nenkan 年鑑

another *adj., pron.* (one more) mō hitotsu no もう一つの; (different) betsu no 別の; (some other) hoka no 外の *one another* tagai ni 互いに *one after another* zoku-zoku to 続々と

answer *n.* (reply) kotae 答; henji 返事 —— *v.* kotaeru 答える; henji o suru 返事をする

ant *n.* ari あり

antarctic *adj.* (cf. arctic) nankyoku no 南極の —— *n.* (the A-) nankyoku 南極

anticipate *v.* (expect) yoki suru 予期する

antique *adj.* kodai no 古代の; mukashi no 昔の —— *n.* kottō-hin 骨とう品

antonym *n.* (cf. synonym) han'igo 反意語

anxious *adj.* (troubled in mind) shimpai na 心配な; (earnestly desirous) setsubō shite 切望して; tsuyoku nozomu 強く望む

any *adj., pron.* (*interrogative sentence*) nani ka なにか; dare ka だれか; ikura ka いくらか; (*negative sentence*) nani mo なにも; dare mo だれも; sukoshi mo 少しも; (*affirmative sentence*) (whatever) nan demo なんでも; (whichever) dore demo どれでも; (every) dare demo だれでも; minna みんな —— *adv.* sukoshi wa 少しは; sukoshi demo 少しでも; sukoshi mo 少しも

anybody *pron.* dare ka だれか; dare, demo だれ

でも

anyhow *adv.* (nevertheless) tonikaku とにかく;
(by any means) dōshite mo どうしても; zehi-
tomo ぜひとも

anyone *pron.* dare demo だれでも; dare ka だれ
か

anything *pron.* (*interrogative*) nani ka なにか;
(*negative*) nani mo なにも; (*affirmative*) nan demo なんでも —— *adv.* sukoshi wa 少しは; sukoshi demo 少しでも; (*negative*) sukoshi mo 少
しも

anyway *adv.* (at all events) tonikaku とにかく;
(by all means) dōshite mo どうしても

anywhere *adv.* doko demo どこでも; dokoka e
[ni] どこかへ [に]; (*negative*) doko nimo どこ
にも

apart *adv.* (remote from) hanarete 離れて; (separately) betsu-betsu ni 別々に

apartment *n.* (room) heya 部屋; apāto アパート
apartment house manshon マンション

ape *n.* (monkey) saru 猿

apiece *adv.* hitotsu-zutsu 一つずつ; hitori zutsu
一人ずつ; mei-mei ni めいめいに

apologize *v.* ayamaru あやまる; shazai suru 謝罪
する

apology *n.* (acknowledgement) shazai 謝罪; (explanation) benkai 弁解

apparatus *n.* sōchi 装置; kigu 器具

apparel *n.* (clothing) ifuku 衣服 —— *v.* (dress)
kiseru 着せる

apparent *adj.* (obvious) akiraka na 明らかな;
(plain) meiryō na 明瞭な

appeal *v.* (have recourse to) uttaeru 訴える; (request) yōkyū suru 要求する; (be attractive)
kyōmi o sosoru 興味をそそる

appear *v.* (be visible) mieru 見える; (come out)
arawareru 現われる; (seem) rashii らしい

appearance *n.* (occurrence) shutsugen 出現; (sem-
blance) gaiken 外見

appendicitis *n*. mōchō-en 盲腸炎

appendix *n*. (supplement) furoku 付録; tsuika 追加 *(anat.)* mōchō 盲腸

appetite *n*. shokuyoku 食欲

applaud *v*. hakushu suru 拍手する

apple *n*. ringo リンゴ

applicant *n*. (candidate) shigan-sha 志願者

application *n*. (request) mōshikomi(-sho) 申し込み(書); shigan 志願; tekiyō 適用; ōyō 応用

apply *v*. (practice) tekiyō suru 適用する; ōyō suru 応用する; (make request) yōkyū suru 要求する; (use) mochiiru 用いる

appoint *v*. (fix) shitei suru 指定する; sadameru 定める

appointment *n*. (engagement) yakusoku 約束; (assignment) shitei 指定

appreciate *v*. (judge correctly) tadashiku handan suru 正しく判断する; (value) hyōka suru 評価する; (be grateful for) kansha suru 感謝する; (enjoy) ajiwau 味わう; kanshō suru 鑑賞する

apprehend *v*. (arrest) tsukamaeru つかまえる; (understand) rikai suru 理解する; (dread) shimpai suru 心配する

approach *v., n*. chikazuku (koto) 近づく(こと); sekkin (suru) 接近(する)

appropriate *v*. (take possession of) sen'yū suru 占有する; (make one's own) jibun no mono ni suru 自分のものにする ——*adj*. (fit) tekitō na 適当な

approval *n*. kyoka 許可; shōnin 承認; sansei 賛成

approve *v*. (consent) sansei suru 賛成する; (think well of) mitomeru 認める

approximate *adj*. (be similar to) daitai no 大体の; (nearly exact) gaisan no 概算の

April *n*. shi-gatsu 四月

apron *n*. epuron エプロン; maekake 前掛け

apt *adj*. (likely to) ...shigachi na ...しがちな; (suitable) tekitō na 適当な

arc *n.* ko 弧; yumi-gata 弓形

arch *n.* āchi アーチ —— *adj.* yumi-gata no 弓形の

architect *n.* kenchiku-ka 建築家; sekkei-sha 設計者

architecture *n.* kenchiku 建築

arctic *adj.* (cf. antarctic) hokkyoku no 北極の —— *n.* (the A-) hokkyoku 北極

area *n.* (space) menseki 面積; (region) chiiki 地域

argue *v.* (discuss) giron suru 議論する; (prove) shōmei suru 証明する; (persuade) tokifuseru 説き伏せる

aristocrat *n.* kizoku(no ichi-in) 貴族(の一員)

arithmetic *n.* sansū 算数; keisan 計算

arm *n.* ude 腕; *pl.* (weapon) buki 武器

armament *n.* gumbi 軍備

armistice *n.* kyūsen 休戦

armor *n.* yoroi よろい

army *n.* rikugun 陸軍; guntai 軍隊

around *adv., prep.* (round about) mawari ni [no] まわりに[の]; (on every side) shihō ni 四方に; (all round) gururi to[ni] ぐるりと[に]; (about) yaku 約; daitai 大体
all around itaru-tokoro ni いたる所に

arrest *v.* (seize) taiho suru 逮捕する; (stop) tomeru 止める

arrival *n.* tōchaku 到着; (appearance) shutsugen 出現; tōjō 登場

arrive *v.* tōchaku suru 到着する; tsuku 着く

arrow *n.* ya 矢; (direction sign) ya-jirushi 矢印

art *n.* geijutsu 芸術; bijutsu 美術; (craft) gijutsu 技術

article *n.* (thing) shinamono 品物; (*newspaper*) kiji 記事; (*gram.*) kanshi 冠詞

artificial *adj.* jinkō no 人工の; mozō no 模造の

as *conj.* (because) ...dakara ...だから; ...nanode ...なので; (when, while) ...no toki wa ...の時は; ...nagara ...ながら; ...no yō ni ...のよう

に —— *prep.* ...toshite ...として —— *adv.*
onaji kurai ni 同じ位に

as ... as possible dekiru dake ...suru できる
だけ...する

as far as (*...be concerned*) ...ni kansuru
kagiri wa ...に関する限りは

as for [*to*] ...ni kanshite wa ...に関しては

as if marude ...no yō ni まるで...のように

as it were iwaba いわば; chōdo ちょうど

as much dōryō no 同量の

as regards ...ni tsuite ...について; ...ni
kanshite ...に関して

as soon as ...to dōji ni ...と同時に

as yet mada まだ; ima no tokoro wa 今の
ところは

ascend *v.* (go up) agaru 上がる; (climb) noboru
登る

ascent *n.* (upward path) nobori-zaka 登り坂; (upward movement) jōshō 上昇

ash *n.* hai 灰 *ashtray* hai-zara 灰皿

ashamed *adj.* haji te 恥じて *be ashamed of...*
...o hazukashii to omou ...を恥ずかしいと思
う

ashore *adv.* (on land) rikujō ni 陸上に; (to shore)
kishi ni 岸に; umibe ni 海辺に

go ashore jōriku suru 上陸する

Asia *n.* Ajia アジア

aside *adv.* (to or on one side) soba e [ni] そばへ
[に] ; (apart from) hanarete 離れて

ask *v.* (inquire) shitsumon suru 質問する; tazuneru たずねる; (request) tanomu 頼む; (beg) o-
negai suru お願いする; (require) motomeru 求
める; (invite) shōtai suru 招待する

asleep *adv., adj.* (in sleep) nemutte (iru) 眠って
(いる)

aspiration *n.* taimō; netsubō 熱望

aspire *v.* netsubō suru 熱望する; tsuyoku nozomu
強く望む

ass *n.* (donkey) roba ろば; (fool) baka ばか

assemble *v.* (gather) atsumeru 集める；(come together) atsumaru 集まる；(put together) kumitateru 組み立てる

assembly *n.* (meeting) shūkai 集会；kaigi 会議

assent *v.* (agree) dōi suru 同意する；(consent) sansei suru 賛成する

assert *v.* (maintain) shuchō suru 主張する；(declare) dangen suru 断言する

assist *v.* (help) tetsudau 手伝う；enjo suru 援助する；(aid) tasukeru 助ける

assistant *n.* joshu 助手；ashisutanto アシスタント

associate *v.* (combine) kumiawaseru 組み合わせる；(join) nakama ni suru 仲間にする；(participate in) sanka suru 参加する；(keep company) kōsai suru 交際する —— *n.* (partner) kumiai-in 組合員；(colleague) dōryō 同僚；(companion) nakama 仲間

association *n.* (union) kumiai 組合；(society) kyōkai 協会；(fellowship) kōsai 交際

assorted *adj.* (classified) kumiawaseta 組み合わせた；iro-iro na 色々な

assume *v.* (undertake) hikiukeru 引き受ける；(take for granted) katei suru 仮定する

assurance *n.* (positive assertion) hoshō 保証；(self-confidence) jishin 自信

life assurance seimei hoken 生命保険

assure *v.* (insure) hoshō suru 保証する；(make sure) tashikameru 確かめる；(state positively) dangen suru 断言する

astonish *v.* odorokaseru 驚かせる；bikkuri saseru びっくりさせる

be astonished at bikkuri suru びっくりする

astonishment *n.* odoroki 驚き

astronaut *n.* uchū-hikōshi 宇宙飛行士

astronomer *n.* temmongaku-sha 天文学者

astronomy *n.* temmon-gaku 天文学

at *prep.* ...ni に；...ni oite ...において；...de ...で

at first saisho wa 最初は

at home uchi ni iru うちにいる

at last tsui ni ついに; tō tō とうとう

at random detarame ni でたらめに; teatari shidai ni 手当り次第に

athlete *n.* kyōgi-sha 競技者; senshu 選手; undō-ka 運動家 ——*adj.* undō kyōgi no 運動競技の

Atlantic *adj.* Taiseiyō no 大西洋の ——*n.* (the Atlantic Ocean) Taiseiyō 大西洋

atlas *n.* chizu-chō 地図帳

atmosphere *n.* (air) kūki 空気; taiki 大気; (environment) fun'iki 雰囲気; kankyō 環境

atom *n.* genshi 原子

atomic bomb *n.* genshi bakudan 原子爆弾

attach *v.* (fasten) (tori) tsukeru (とり)付ける; tsuku つく; (seize) tsukamaeru つかまえる *attached to* fuzoku no 付属の

attachment *n.* (attaching) fuzoku-hin 付属品; (affection) aijō 愛情

attack *v.* (assail) kōgeki suru 攻撃する; semeru 攻める *be attacked by a disease* byōki ni kakaru 病気にかかる ——*n.* kōgeki 攻撃; (fit of illness) (byōki no) hossa (病気の) 発作

attain *v.* (achieve) yaritogeru やり遂げる; (gain) uru 得る; (reach) tassuru 達する

attempt *v.* (try) tamesu 試す; kokoromiru 試みる; yattemiru やってみる ——*n.* kokoromi 試み

attend *v.* (be present at) …ni shusseki suru …に出席する; (go to) kayou 通う; (escort) tsukisou 付き添う; (accompany) dōhan suru 同伴する; (care for) sewa o suru 世話をする; (listen) kiku 聴く; (pay attention) chūi suru 注意する

attendant *adj.* (waiting upon) tsukisoi no 付き添いの; (present) resseki no 列席の ——*n.* (follower) tsukisoi-nin 付添い人; (attendant) shusseki-sha 出席者; (gasorin-sutando no) jūgyōin (ガソリンスタンドの) 従業員

attention *n.* (notice) chūi 注意; (consideration)

hairyo 配慮; kokoro-zukai 心づかい; (care) sewa 世話 ***pay attention to*** ...ni chūi o harau ...に注意を払う

attic *n.* yaneura-beya 屋根裏部屋

attire *n.* ifuku 衣服; fukusō 服装 ―― *v.* yoso'ou 装う; kikazaru 着飾る

attitude *n.* (manner) taido 態度; (posture) shisei 姿勢

attorney *n.* (lawyer) bengo-shi 弁護士; (agent) dairi-nin 代理人

attract *v.* (draw to oneself) hiku 引く; hikitsu-keru 引き付ける; (charm) miwaku suru 魅惑する

attraction *n.* (allurement) hikitsukeru koto 引き付けること; (attracting power) inryoku 引力; (charm) miryoku 魅力; (feature) yobimono 呼び物

attribute *v.* (put down to) ...no kekka de aru ...の結果である; ...no sei ni suru ...のせいにする ―― *n.* (characteristic quality) tokushitsu 特質; (symbol) shōchō 象徴

auction *n.* kyōbai 競売; seri-uri せり売り

audible *adj.* (yoku) kikoeru (よく)聞こえる

audience *n.* chōshū 聴衆; kankyaku 観客

aunt *n.* oba おば

author *n.* chosha 著者; sakka 作家

authority *n.* ken'i 権威; ōsoritī オーソリティー

authorize *v.* (sanction) ninka suru 認可する; (justify) seitō to mitomeru 正当と認める; (give authority to) kengen o ataeru 権限を与える

authorized *adj.* kentei-zumi no 検定済みの; kōnin no 公認の

autobiography *n.* jijoden 自叙伝

automatic *a.* jidō no 自動の; ōtomachikku オートマチック

automobile *n.* jidōsha 自動車

autumn *n.* aki 秋

avail *v.* (profit by) riyō suru 利用する; (be of use) yaku ni tatsu 役に立つ ―― *n.* (profit) rieki

利益

available *adj.* (usable) yaku ni tatsu 役に立つ; (obtainable) te ni irerareru 手に入れられる

avenge *v.* fukushū suru 復しゅうする; kataki o utsu かたきを討つ

avenue *n.* (broad street) ō-dōri 大通り; (tree-lined road) namiki-michi 並木道

average *n.* (medium) heikin 平均 —— *adj.* heikin no 平均の; futsū no 普通の —— *v.* heikin …de aru 平均…である

　on the average heikin shite 平均して

aviation *n.* hikō 飛行; kōkū 航空

avoid *v.* (shun) sakeru 避ける; nogareru 逃れる

avoidable *adj.* sakerareru 避けられる

await *v.* (wait for) matsu 待つ; (expect) kitai suru 期待する

awake *v.* (cease to sleep) mezameru 目覚める —— *adj.* (not sleeping) nemuranai 眠らない

award *n.* (prize) shō 賞 —— *v.* (give after examination) (shinsa shite) ataeru (審査して) 与える

aware *adj.* (knowing) shitte 知って; (conscious) kizuite 気付いて; (informed) shōchi shite 承知して　*be aware of* …o shitte iru …を知っている; kizuite iru 気付いている

away *adv.* (at a distance from) hanarete 離れて; (to a distance) tōku e 遠くへ; (to another place) achira e あちらへ

awe *n.* osore 恐れ —— *v.* osore saseru 恐れさせる

awful *adj.* (dreadful) osoroshii 恐ろしい; (fearful) kowai こわい; (terrible) monosugoi ものすごい; (sublime) sōgon na 壮厳な; (*colloq.*) (considerable) hijō na 非常な

awfully *adv.* (terrible) osoroshiku 恐ろしく; (very) hidoku ひどく

awkward *adj.* (clumsy) migurushii 見苦しい; bukakkō na ぶかっこうな; (unskilful) bukiyō na 無器用な; (hard to handle) yakkai na やっ

かいな；(inconvenient) fuben na 不便な
ax n. ono おの
axis n. jiku 軸；jiku-sen 軸線
axle n. shimbō 心棒；jiku 軸；shajiku 車軸
azalea n. tsutsuji つつじ

B

baby n. akambō 赤ん坊；(colloq.) aka-chan 赤ちゃん

bachelor n. (otoko no) hitori-mono（男の）独り者；(dansei no) dokushin-sha（男性の）独身者

back n. (rear) ushiro 後ろ；(rear of the human body) se 背；senaka 背中；(behind) ura 裏 ——adj. ushiro no 後ろの ——v. modoru 戻る；(move backward) kōtai suru 後退する **back up** (kuruma ga) bakku suru（車が）バックする；(support) shiji suru；支持する —— adv. ushiro e 後ろへ

background n. haikei 背景

backward adv. ushiro ni 後ろに；(reversed) gyaku ni 逆に ——adj. (retarded) chie no okureta 知恵の遅れた

bacteria n. baikin ばい菌；bakuteria バクテリア

bad adj. warui 悪い；furyō no 不良の；kusatte iru 腐っている

badge n. kishō 記章；bajji バッジ；shirushi しるし

bag n. (sack) fukuro 袋；(satchel) kaban かばん；(hand-bag) hando-baggu ハンドバッグ

baggage n. te-nimotsu 手荷物

bait n. (lure) esa えさ；(temptation) yūwaku 誘惑 ——v. esa o tsukeru[de tsuru] えさをつける[でつる]

bake v. yaku 焼く **baking powder** bēkingu paudā ベーキングパウダー

bakery n. pan-ya パン屋

balance n. (scales) hakari はかり；(counterpoise)

tsuriai 釣り合い; (account) sashihiki-zandaka 差引き残高 —— v. (match) tsuriawasu 釣り合わす; (compare) hikaku suru 比較する; (settle) kessan suru 決算する

bald *adj.* hageta はげた

ball[1] *n.* bōru ボール; mari まり; tama 玉; (sphere) kyū 球

ball[2] *n.* (dance) butō-kai 舞踏会

ballad *n.* min'yō 民謡

balloon *n.* kikyū 気球; fūsen 風船

ballot *n., v.* tōhyō (suru) 投票(する)

bamboo *n.* take 竹

ban *n., v.* kinshi (suru) 禁止(する)

band *n.* obi 帯; himo ひも; bando バンド; (troop) tai 隊; (musical band) gakudan 楽団

bandage *n., v.* hōtai (o suru) 包帯 (をする)

bang *n., v.* don (to utsu) ドン (と打つ); zudon (to naru) ズドン (と鳴る)

banish *v.* tsuihō suru 追放する; oiharau 追い払う

bank[1] *n. (establishment)* ginkō 銀行

bank[2] *n. (geographical)* dote 土手; teibō 堤防; kishi 岸

bankrupt *n.* hasan-sha 破産者 —— *adj.* hasan no 破産の

banner *n.* (flag) hata 旗; (standard) gunki 軍旗

banquet *n., v.* enkai (o moyo'osu) 宴会(を催す)

bar *n.* (stick) bō 棒; (place for servicing liquor) sakaba 酒場; bā バー

barbarian *n.* yaban-jin 野蛮人 —— *adj.* yaban na 野蛮な

barber *n.* rihatsu-shi 理髪師; toko-ya 床屋

bare *adj.* (naked) hadaka no 裸の; (empty) kara no 空の

bargain *n.* (agreement) baibai keiyaku 売買契約; (goods offered cheap) horidashi-mono 掘出し物; kakuyasu-hin 格安品

bark *v.* (*of dog, etc.*) hoeru ほえる

barn *n.* naya 納屋; mono'oki 物置

barometer *n.* seiu-kei 晴雨計

barrack *n.* *(army)* heisha 兵舎; barakku バラック

barrel *n., v.* taru (ni tsumeru) 樽 (に詰める)

barren *adj.* (unproductive) fumō no 不毛の

barrier *n.* (fence) saku 柵; bōheki 防壁; (hindrance) shōgai 障害

base *n.* (foundation) kiso 基礎; dodai 土台; (mil.) kichi 基地 *air base* kūgun-kichi 空軍基地

baseball *n.* yakyū 野球

basin *n.* tarai たらい; semmenki 洗面器

basis *n.* (foundation) kiso 基礎

basket *n.* kago かご

bat¹ *n., v.* (*baseball*) batto(de utsu) バット (で打つ)

bat² *n.* (flying mammal) kōmori こうもり

bath *n.* (o-)furo (お)ふろ *bathroom* furoba ふろ場 *take a bath* furo ni hairu ふろに入る

bathe *n., v.* nyūyoku(suru) 入浴 (する); (immerse in water) suiyoku (suru) 水浴(する) *take a bathe* (*in the sea*) kaisuiyoku o suru 海水浴をする

battery *n.* chikudenchi 蓄電池; batterī バッテリー

battle *n.* (war) sentō 戦闘; tatakai 戦い —— *v.* tatakau 戦う

bay *n.* (*geog.*) wan 湾

be *v.* ...de aru ...である; ...desu ...です; iru いる; imasu います

beach *n.* kaigan 海岸; hama 浜

bead *n.* bīzu ビーズ; *pl.* (rosary) juzu じゅず

beak *n.* kuchibashi くちばし

beam *n.* (light) kōsen 光線; (*archit.*) hari はり —— *v.* (shine) kagayaku 輝く

bean *n.* mame 豆

bear¹ *n.* (*mammal*) kuma くま

bear² *v.* (carry) hakobu 運ぶ; (support) sasaeru 支える; (endure) gaman suru がまんする; (give birth to) umu 産む; (hold) motsu 持つ *bear in mind* kioku suru 記憶する; kokoro ni tomeru 心に留める

beard n. ago-hige あごひげ

bearing n. (attitude) taido 態度; (endurance) nintai 忍耐; (relation) kankei 関係; *(mech.)* bearingu ベアリング

beast n. dōbutsu 動物; kedamono けだもの

beat v. (strike repeatedly) (tsuzukete) utsu (続けて) 打つ; (defeat) uchiyaburu 打ち破る; makasu 負かす

beautiful adj. utsukushii 美しい; kirei na きれいな *beautifully* utsukushiku 美しく

beauty n. utsukushisa 美しさ; bi 美

because prep. (for) naze naraba なぜならば; (since) ...dakara ...だから *because of* ...ga gen'in de ...が原因で

become v. (come to be) ...ni naru ...になる; niau 似合う; fusawashii ふさわしい

bed n. beddo ベッド; shindai 寝台

bedroom n. shinshitsu 寝室

bee n. mitsubachi みつばち

beef n. gyūniku 牛肉 *beefsteak* bifuteki ビフテキ

beer n. bīru ビール *draft beer* nama bīru 生ビール

beetle n. *(insect)* kabutomushi かぶと虫

before adv. (ahead) mae ni 前に; (in front of) zemmen ni 前面に; (previously) izen ni 以前に —— prep., conj. ...yori mae ni ...より前に *before long* mamonaku まもなく

beg v. (ask) tanomu 頼む; (entreat) negau 願う

beggar n. kojiki 乞食

begin v. hajimeru 始める *begin with* ...kara hajimeru ...から始める

beginner n. shoshinsha 初心者

beginning n. hajime 初め; saisho 最初

behalf n. rieki 利益 *in behalf of* ...no tame ni ...のために *on behalf of* ...ni kawatte ...に代って

behave v. (conduct) furumau ふるまう *Behave*

yourself! O-gyōgiyoku shinasai! お行儀よくしなさい.

behavior *n.* (manners) hinkō 品行; (conduct) kōi 行為; (way of behaving) furumai ふるまい; (attitude) taido 態度

behind *adv.* (to or at the rear) ushiro ni 後ろに; …no ato ni …の後に; (late) okurete 遅れて
behind time chikoku suru 遅刻する
behind times jisei ni okurete 時勢に遅れて

being *n.* (existence) jitsuzai 実在; (living thing) seibutsu 生物 *human being* jinrui 人類

belief *n.* (confidence) shin'nen 信念; (faith) shinjin 信心; (reliance) shinrai 信頼

believe *v.* (trust) shinjiru 信じる; (think) omou 思う

bell *n.* kane 鐘; beru ベル; suzu 鈴

belong *v.* zoku suru 属する

belongings *n.* (possessions) shoyū-butsu 所有物; (luggage) nimotsu 荷物

beloved *adj.* (much loved) saiai no 最愛の; itoshii いとしい ——*n.* (darling) aijin 愛人

below *adv.* (on the earth) shita ni 下に ——*prep.* (lower than) …yori shita ni …より下に

belt *n.* (band) obi 帯; bando バンド; (zone) chitai 地帯

bench *n.* benchi ベンチ; nagaisu 長いす

bend *vt.* (curve) mageru 曲げる; kagameru かがめる ——*vi.* magaru 曲がる; (stoop) kagamu かがむ ——*n.* magari 曲がり

beneath *prep.* (below) …yori shita ni …より下に; (inferior) …yori otoru …より劣る; (lower) …yori hikui …より低い

benefit *n.* (profit) rieki 利益; (favor) onkei 恩恵 ——*v.* (do good to) tame ni naru ためになる; (receive benefit) rieki o ukeru 利益を受ける

berry *n.* (small fleshy fruit, as of strawberry) (ichigo nado no) mi (いちごなどの) 実

berth *n.* (*on a ship or vehicle*) shindai 寝台; teihaku-ichi 停泊位置 ——*v.* teihaku suru 停泊

する

beside *prep.* (at or by the side of) …no soba ni …のそばに; (close to) …no chikaku ni …の近くに

besides *prep.* (in addition to) …no hoka ni …の外に; (except) …o nozoite …を除いて ——— *adv.* (moreover) sara ni さらに; (else) sono hoka ni その外に

best *adj.* ichiban yoi いちばんよい; saijō no 最上の ——— *n.* saizen 最善; saikō 最高

bet *v.* kakeru 賭ける ——— *n.* kake(-kin) 賭け（金） *I bet you!* Tashikani! たしかに; Machigai naku! 間違いなく

betray *v.* (be a traitor to) uragiru 裏切る; (reveal) mikkoku suru 密告する

better *adj.* motto yoi もっとよい; yori yoi よりよい ——— *v.* (improve) yokunaru よくなる; kaizen suru 改善する

between *prep., adv.* …no aida ni [o] …の間に[を] *between ourselves* koko dake no hanashi desu ga …ここだけの話ですが…

beverage *n.* nomimono 飲み物; inryō 飲料

beware *v.* ki o tsukeru 気をつける; yōjin suru 用心する

bewilder *v.* komaraseru 困らせる

beyond *prep.* (position) …no mukō ni …の向うに; (more than) …ijō ni …以上に; …o koete …を越えて; (time) …o sugite …を過ぎて

bias *n.* (oblique line) shasen 斜線; (prejudice) henken 偏見

Bible *n.* seisho 聖書; baiburu バイブル

bicycle *n.* jitensha 自転車

bid *v.* (command) meijiru 命じる; (utter a greeting) (aisatsu o) noberu （あいさつを）述べる; (offer as a price) nyūsatsu suru 入札する *bid off* seri-otosu せり落とす

big *adj.* (large) ōkii 大きい; (great) erai えらい

bill[1] *n.* (note of charges for goods, work, etc.) kanjōgaki 勘定書; tsuke つけ; seikyūsho 請求書;

(note) tegata 手形; (bank-note) shihei 紙幣;
satsu 札

bill² *n.* (beak of a bird) kuchibashi くちばし

billion *n.* (*U.S.*) (a thousand million) jū-oku
10億; (*Br.*) (a million million) itchō 1兆

bind *v.* (tie) musubu 結ぶ; shibaru しばる;
(book) seihon suru 製本する; (oblige) gimu o
owaseru 義務を負わせる

biography *n.* denki 伝記

biology *n.* seibutsu-gaku 生物学

bird *n.* tori 鳥

birth *n.* tanjō 誕生; shussei 出生

birthday *n.* tanjōbi 誕生日

biscuit *n.* bisuketto ビスケット

bishop *n.* sōjō 僧正

bit *n.* (small amount) sukoshi 少し; wazuka わ
ずか; (small piece) kakera かけら
a bit of sukoshi no 少しの
bit by bit sukoshi-zutsu 少しずつ

bite *v.* kamu かむ; kamitsuku かみつく ——*n.*
(a mouthful) hitokuchi 一口

bitter *adj.* *(taste)* nigai 苦い; (severe) kibishii
厳しい; (hard) tsurai つらい

black *adj.* kuroi 黒い; (dark) kurai 暗い ——
n. (*color*) kuro(-iro) 黒(色); (negro) kokujin
黒人

blackboard *n.* kokuban 黒板

blade *n.* (grass) ha 葉; *(metal)* ha 刃

blame *v.* (accuse) hinan suru 非難する; togameru
とがめる ——*n.* (responsibility for bad result) sekinin 責任

blank *n., adj.* (not written or printed on) hakushi
(no) 白紙 (の); (empty) kūhaku (no) 空白
(の)

blanket *n.* mōfu 毛布

blast *n.* (violent gust of wind) tsuyoi hito-fuki no
kaze 強い一吹きの風; toppū 突風 ——*v.*
(explode) bakuhatsu suru 爆発する

blaze *n.* (bright flame) hono'o 炎 ——*v.* (burn)

moeru 燃える

bleach *v.* (make white) hyōhaku suru 漂白する

bleed *v.* (emit blood) shukketsu suru 出血する；
chi ga deru 血が出る

blend *v.* kongō suru 混合する；mazeru まぜる

bless *v.* (praise) (kami o) tataeru（神を）たた
える；(confer a blessing upon) (kami ga) megu
mi o tareru（神が）恵みをたれる；(invoke
God's favor on) kami no megumi o inoru 神の
恵みを祈る

blessed *adj.* shinsei na 神聖な；shiawase na 幸
せな

blessing *n.* (benediction) shukufuku 祝福；(mercy)
(kami no) megumi（神の）恵み

blind *adj.* (sightless) me no mienai 目の見えない；
mekura no めくらの；mōmoku no 盲目の
——*n.* (*window*) hiyoke 日よけ；buraindo
ブラインド

blink *v.* (wink) matataki suru またたきする；
(twinkle) kira-kira hikaru きらきら光る

block *n.* (large piece of wood or stone) (ki ya
ishi no) katamari（木や石の）かたまり；(a
portion of a city) ichi-kukaku 一区画

blond *n.*, *adj.* kimpatsu (no) 金髪（の）；buron-
do (no) ブロンド（の）

blood *n.* chi 血；ketsueki 血液；(descent) kettō；
血統　***blood pressure*** ketsuatsu 血圧

bloom *n.* (flower) hana 花；(florescence) kaika
開花　——*v.* saku 咲く

blossom *n.*, *v.* hana (ga saku) 花（が咲く）　***in
full blossom*** mankai de 満開で

blot *n.* (stain) yogore 汚れ；shimi しみ；(blemish)
ketten 欠点

blotter *n.* suitori-gami 吸い取り紙

blouse *n.* burausu ブラウス

blow[1] *v.* (kaze ga) fuku（風が）吹く　***blow out***
fuki kesu 吹き消す　***blow the nose*** hana o kamu
はなをかむ　***blow down*** fuki taosu 吹き倒す
blow up bakuha suru 爆破する

blow² *n.* (hard stroke with fist, hammer) kyōda 強打; dageki 打撃

blue *adj.* aoi 青い ── *n.* ao 青

bluff *n.* (cliff) zeppeki 絶壁; dangai 断崖

blunt *adj.* nibui 鈍い; donkan na 鈍感な

blush *v.* (kao o) akarameru (顔を) 赤らめる ── *n.* sekimen 赤面

boar *n.* (pig) osu-buta 雄豚; (wild boar) inoshishi いのしし

board *n.* (thin plank) ita 板; (food served) tabemono 食べ物 *go on board* jōsen [jōsha] suru 乗船 [乗車] する ── *v.* (lodge) geshuku suru [saseru] 下宿する[させる]

boarder *n.* geshuku-nin 下宿人

boarding-house *n.* geshuku-ya 下宿屋

boat *n.* (oared vessel) bōto ボート; (small ship) kogata no fune [kisen] 小型の船 [汽船]

bob *n.* (float) uki うき; (pendulum) furiko 振子; (short hair) dampatsu 断髪

body *n.* (human body) karada 体; (corpse) shitai 死体

bog *n.* numa(-chi) 沼(地); sawa 沢

boil¹ *vi.* waku 沸く; nieru 煮える ── *vt.* wakasu 沸かす; niru 煮る

boil² *n.* (*on the body*) odeki おでき; dekimono できもの

bold *adj.* (audacious) daitan na 大胆な; (brave) yūkan na 勇敢な; (impudent) atsukamashii 厚かましい

bolt *n.* (headed metal pin) boruto ボルト; (sliding bar) kan'nuki かんぬき; (thunderbolt) denkō 電光; inazuma 稲妻; (escape) tōsō 逃走

bomb *n.* bakudan 爆弾; (attack with bombs) bakugeki suru 爆撃する

bond *n. pl.* (restraints) sokubaku 束縛; (obligation) gimu 義務; (securities) yūkashōken 有価証券 ── *n.* (bonded warehouse) hozei sōko 保税倉庫

bone *n.* hone 骨

book *n.* hon 本; shoseki 書籍; *pl.* (account-books) chōbo 帳簿 ——*v.* (enter) chōbo ni kinyū suru 帳簿に記入する; (reserve) yoyaku suru 予約する *booking office* kippu uriba 切符売場

bookkeeper *n.* boki-gakari 簿記係; kaikei-gakari 会計係

bookstore *n.* hon-ya 本屋; shoten 書店

boom *n.* (deep resonant sound) gōon 轟音; (time of prosperity) niwaka-keiki にわか景気; būmu ブーム

boot *n. pl.* nagagutsu 長靴; būtsu ブーツ

booth *n.* (shed) koya 小屋; (stall) baiten 売店; būsu ブース

border *n.* (boundary) kyōkai 境界; (frontier) kokkyō 国境; (edge) heri へり ——*v.* (adjoin) sessuru 接する; (edge) fuchi o tsukeru 縁を付ける

bore¹ *v.* ana o akeru [horu] 穴をあける [掘る]

bore² *n., v.* (dull) taikutsu (saseru) 退屈 (させる); unzari (saseru) うんざり(させる)

born *adj.* umare-nagara no 生れながらの; tensei no 天性の; umareta 生れた

borrow *v.* kariru 借りる

borrower *n.* shakuyōnin 借用人; karite 借り手

bosom *n.* (breast) mune 胸; (heart) kokoro 心; (interior) naibu 内部

boss *n.* (manager, master) bosu ボス; oyabun 親分; oyakata 親方

both *pron., adj.* ryōhō (no) 両方(の) ——*adv.* ryōhō tomo 両方共
both A and B A mo B mo AもBも

bother *v.* (annoy) nayamasu 悩ます; (worry) shimpai saseru 心配させる ——*n.* (trouble) meiwaku 迷惑; mendō 面倒

bottle *n., v.* bin (ni tsumeru) びん(に詰める)
bottle opener sen'nuki 栓抜き

bottled *adj.* binzume no びん詰めの

bottleneck *n.* airo あい路; nankan 難関

bottom *n.* (lowest part) soko 底; (base) kiso 基

礎 *at* (*the*) *bottom* hontō wa 本当は

bough *n.* ō-eda 大枝

bounce *v.* (rebound) hane-kaeru [-agaru] 跳ね
かえる[あがる]; hazumu はずむ; (leap sud-
denly) tobi-agaru とびあがる

bound[1] *n. pl.* (boundary) kyōkai 境界; *pl.* (lim-
itations) genkai 限界 —— *v.* (limit) seigen
suru 制限する

bound[2] *v.* (leap) haneru 跳ねる; (jump) tobi-
haneru とびはねる; (bounce) hazumu はずむ

bound[3] *adj.* (headed for) ...iki no ...行きの

boundary *n.* (border) kyōkai 境界; (limiting
line) kyōkaisen 境界線; (extreme edge) genkai
限界

bouquet *n.* hanataba 花束

bow[1] *n., v.* (salutation) ojigi (suru) おじぎ
(する)

bow[2] *n.* (*weapon*) yumi 弓; yumi gata no mono
弓形のもの; (*knot*) chō-musubi 蝶結び

bow[3] *n.* (*of a ship*) senshu 船首; hesaki へさき

bowl[1] *n.* hachi 鉢; domburi どんぶり; bōru ボー
ル

bowl[2] *n., v.* tama (o korogasu) 球(をころがす)

box[1] *n., v.* hako(zume ni suru) 箱(づめにする)

box[2] *v.* hirate de utsu 平手で打つ; (fight with the
fists) kentō o suru 拳闘をする

boy *n.* shōnen 少年; otoko no ko 男の子

brace *n.* (clamp) kasugai かすがい; shichū 支柱
—— *v.* (support) sasaeru 支える; (strain) kinchō saseru 緊張させる; (encourage) genki zu-
keru 元気づける

bracelet *n.* udewa 腕輪; buresuretto ブレス
レット

bracket *n.* (kaku-)kakko (角) かっこ —— *v.*
kakko ni ireru かっこに入れる

brag *n., v.* jiman(suru) 自慢(する)

braid *n.* kumihimo 組ひも; amihimo 編ひも
—— *v.* kumu 組む; amu 編む

brain *n.* nō 脳; *pl.* zunō 頭脳; *pl.* (intelligence)

chiryoku 知力

brake *n., v.* burēki(o kakeru) ブレーキ(をかける)

branch *n.* (bough of tree) eda 枝; (small stream) shiryū 支流; (branch office) shiten 支店

brand *n.* (trade mark) shōhyō 商標; torēdo-māku トレードマーク; (owner's mark) yaki-in 焼印

brass *n.* shinchū しんちゅう

brave *adj.* yūkan na 勇敢な; isamashii 勇ましい

bravery *n.* yūki 勇気; yūkan 勇敢

bread *n.* pan パン; (living) seikei 生計

breadth *n.* (width) hirosa 広さ; haba 幅

break *vi.* kowareru こわれる; wareru 割れる; kudakeru 砕ける; yabureru 破れる ―― *vt.* kowasu こわす; waru 割る; kudaku 砕く; yaburu 破る; (interrupt) chūdan suru 中断する
break away nogareru 逃れる
break even gobu-gobu ni naru 五分五分になる
break in (force in) shin'nyū suru 侵入する; (tame) narasu ならす
break into (force in) oshiiru 押し入る; (burst) niwaka ni…shidasu にわかに…し出す
break into laughter dotto warau どっと笑う
break into tears watto naki-dasu わっと泣き出す
break out okoru 起こる; boppatsu suru 勃発する; hassei suru 発生する
break through toppa suru 突破する; kiri-nuke-ru 切り抜ける
break up sankai suru 散会する; (*school*) kyūka ni naru 休暇になる
―― *n.* (crack) wareme 割れ目; (interruption) chūdan 中断

breakable *adj.* kowareyasui こわれ易い

breakfast *n.* chōshoku 朝食; asagohan 朝ごはん

breast *n.* (chest) mune 胸; chichi 乳; (heart) kokoro 心

breath *n.* iki 息; kokyū 呼吸

breathe *n., v.* iki (o suru) 息(をする); kokyū (suru) 呼吸(する)

breed *v.* (raise) shiiku suru 飼育する; (produce) umidasu 生み出す —— *n.* (strain) hinshu 品種; shurui 種類

breeze *n.* (light wind) bifū 微風; soyokaze そよ風

brew *n., v.* jōzō(suru) 醸造(する)

bribe *n., v.* wairo(o tsukau) わいろ(を使う)

brick *n.* renga れんが; *pl.* (*Br.*) (wooden toy) tsumiki 積み木

bride *n.* hanayome 花嫁; shimpu 新婦

bridegroom *n.* hanamuko 花むこ; shinrō 新郎

bridge *n.* hashi 橋; (*card game*) burijji ブリッジ

brief *adj.* (short) mijikai 短い; (concise) kantan na 簡単な —— *n.* (summary) yōyaku 要約
in brief yōsuru ni 要するに

brier *n.* ibara いばら

bright *adj.* (shining) kagayaku 輝く; (light up) akarui 明るい; (fine) hareta 晴れた; (clever) rikō na 利口な; (cheerful) kaikatsu na 快活な

brilliant *adj.* (shining) kagayaku 輝く; (splendid) rippa na 立派な; (clever) saiki no aru 才気のある

brim *n.* fuchi 縁; heri へり; (of hat) tsuba つば

bring *v.* (fetch) motte-kuru 持って来る; (cause to come with one) tsurete-kuru 連れて来る; (carry) motarasu もたらす
bring about hikiokosu 引き起こす
bring in mochikomu 持ち込む
bring out ōyake ni suru 公にする; (publish) shuppan suru 出版する
bring up (rear) sodateru 育てる; (educate) kyōiku suru 教育する

brink *n.* (edge) gakeppuchi がけっぷち; (border of water) mizugiwa 水ぎわ

brisk *adj.* (active) kappatsu na 活発な; (quick) hayai 速い

British *adj.* Igirisu no イギリスの; Eikoku no 英国の —— *n.* (the B-) Igirisu-jin イギリス人; Eikoku-jin 英国人

brittle *adj.* moroi もろい；kowareyasui こわれ
易い

broad *adj.* (wide) haba no hiroi 幅の広い；(liberal) kandai na 寛大な

broadcast *n., v.* hōsō(suru) 放送(する)
broadcasting station hōsōkyoku 放送局

broil *v.* yaku 焼く；aburu あぶる

broken *adj.* (shattered) kowareta こわれた；(rent)
yabureta 破れた

bronze *n., adj.* seidō (no) 青銅(の)；buronzu
(no) ブロンズ(の)

brood *n.* (bird) hitokaeri no hina ひとかえりの
ひな ——*v.* tamago o daku 卵を抱く；(think
deeply) kangae-komu 考え込む

brook *n.* ogawa 小川

broom *n.* (sweeping implement) hōki ほうき；
(bot.) enishida えにしだ

brother *n.* (elder) ani 兄；niisan 兄さん；(younger)
otōto 弟；pl. kyōdai 兄弟
brother-in-law giri no kyōdai 義理の兄弟

brow *n.* (forehead) hitai 額；odeko おでこ；pl.
(eyebrow) mayuge まゆ毛

brown *n., adj.* chairo (no) 茶色 (の)；kasshoku
(no) かっ色 (の)

bruise *n.* dabokushō 打撲傷；uchimi 打ち身

brush *n., v.* burashi(o kakeru) ブラシ(をかける)；
hake 刷毛；(for writing) fude 筆 *brush up* (burashi de) migaki ageru (ブラシで)磨き上げる

brute *n.* yajū 野獣；kemono けもの ——*adj.*
(brutal) yaban na 野蛮な

bubble *n.* shabon-dama しゃぼん玉；(archit.) dōmu ドーム

bucket *n.* baketsu バケツ；teoke 手桶

buckle *n.* bakkuru バックル；shimegane 締め金
——*v.* (fasten) shimeru 締める

bud *n.* me 芽；tsubomi つぼみ ——*v.* megumu
芽ぐむ；tsubomi o motsu つぼみを持つ

Buddhism *n.* bukkyō 仏教

Buddhist *n.* bukkyōto 仏教徒

budget *n.* yosan(-an) 予算(案) —— *v.* yosan o tateru 予算を立てる

buffalo *n.* yagyū 野牛; baffarō バッファロー *water buffalo* suigyū 水牛

buffet *n.* (side-board) shokki todana 食器戸棚; (refreshment room) byuffe ビュッフェ

bug *n.* (insect) konchū 昆虫; mushi 虫; (beetle) kabutomushi かぶと虫

bugle *n., v.* rappa (o fuku) ラッパ (を吹く)

build *v.* tateru 建てる; kenchiku suru 建築する

building *n.* tatemono 建物; biru(dingu) ビル(ディング)

building blocks *n.* (wooden toy) tsumiki 積み木

bulb *n.* (*plant*) kyūkon 球根; (electric bulb) denkyū 電球

bulge *n.* (protruding part) (oke, taru no) dō (おけ、たるの) 胴; (outward swelling) fukurami ふくらみ —— *v.* (swell out) fukureru ふくれる

bulk *n.* (volume) yōseki 容積; kasa かさ; (size) ōkisa 大きさ; (cargo) funani 船荷; (great part) daibubun 大部分

bull *n.* o-ushi 雄牛

bullet *n.* tama たま; dangan 弾丸

bulletin *n.* keiji 掲示; kōhō 公報 *bulletin board* keiji-ban 掲示板

bump *v.* (collide) tsukiataru 突き当る; (strike) butsukeru ぶつける —— *n.* shōtotsu 衝突

bunch *n.* (cluster) fusa 房; taba 束 —— *v.* (tie together) tabaneru 束ねる

bundle *n.* (package) tsutsumi 包み; (bunch) taba 束 —— *v.* (wrap) tsutsumu 包む; (tie together) tabaneru 束ねる

burden *n.* (heavy load) omoni 重荷; (obligation) futan 負担 —— *v.* (load heavily) ni o owaseru 荷を負わせる; (oppress) kurushimeru 苦しめる

bureau *n.* kyoku 局; bu 部; (chest of drawers) ishōdansu 衣装だんす

burglar *n.* dorobō 泥棒; gōtō 強盗

burial *n.* (interment) maisō 埋葬; (funeral) sōshiki

葬式

burn *vt.* moyasu 燃やす；yaku 焼く；(scorch) kogasu 焦がす ── *vi.* moeru 燃える；yakeru 焼ける；kogeru 焦げる ── *n.* (injury from burning) yakedo やけど

burst *v.* (fly in pieces) haretsu suru 破裂する；(explode) bakuhatsu suru 爆発する；(rush suddenly) totsuzen...suru 突然...する *burst into tears* watto nakidasu わっと泣き出す *burst out laughing* dotto waraidasu どっと笑い出す

bury *v.* (put into the ground) uzumeru 埋める；(interment) maisō suru 埋葬する

bush *n.* (thicket) yabu やぶ；(clump of shrub) kusamura 草むら；shigemi 茂み

business *n.* shokugyō 職業；shigoto 仕事；shōbai 商売

bust *n.* (sculpture) kyōzō 胸像；(woman's bosom) (josei no) mune (女性の)胸

busy *adj.* isogashii 忙しい；tabō na 多忙な ── *v.* isogashiku suru 忙しくする

but *conj.* (however) shikashi しかし；keredomo けれども ── *adv.* (only) tada ただ；...nomi ...のみ；(except) ...o nozoite wa ...を除いては *but for* (without) ...ga nakattara ...がなかったら

butcher *n.* nikuya 肉屋

butter *n.* batā バター

butterfly *n.* chō ちょう；chōchō ちょうちょう

button *n., v.* botan (o tsukeru, de tomeru) ボタン (を付ける，で止める)

buy *v.* kau 買う；kōnyū suru 購入する ── *n.* kaimono 買物

buzz *n., v.* bun-bun (iu) ぶんぶん(言う)；būn(to unaru) ぶーん(とうなる)；zawameku ざわめく

by *prep.* (aside) ...no soba ni ...のそばに；no chikaku ni ...の近くに；(along) ...ni sotte ...に沿って；(each separately) zutsu ずつ；(by means of) ...ni yotte ...によって；(past) ...o tōtte ...を通って；(not later than) made niwa までには；

(during) no aida の間　*by and by* yagate やが
て; mamonaku 間もなく　*by chance* gūzen 偶
然; tamatama たまたま　*by day* hiru wa 昼は
by oneself hitori de ひとりで　*by the way*
tsuide dakeredo ついでだけれど; toki ni 時に

C

cab *n.* takushī タクシー

cabbage *n.* kyabetsu キャベツ

cabin *n.* (hut) koya 小屋; (a room in a ship)
senshitsu 船室

cabinet *n.* (furniture) yōdansu 用だんす; kazari-
dana 飾り棚; (body of ministers) naikaku 内閣;
(private room) shishitsu 私室

cable *n.* (rope) ōzuna 大綱; (submarine cable)
kaitei densen [denshin] 海底電線 [電信]; kaigai dempō 海外電報 —— *v.* gaiden o utsu
外電を打つ

café *n.* kissaten 喫茶店; kōhī コーヒー

cage *n.* torikago 鳥かご; ori おり —— *v.* kago
[ori] ni'ireru かご [おり] に入れる

cake *n.* kēki ケーキ; kashi 菓子

calamity *n.* sainan 災難; fukō na dekigoto 不幸
な出来事

calculate *v.* keisan suru 計算する

calendar *n.* karendā カレンダー; koyomi 暦

calf[1] *n.* (a young cow) ko-ushi 子牛

calf[2] *n.* (*of leg*) fukurahagi ふくらはぎ

call *v.* yobu 呼ぶ; (speak loudly) sakebu 叫ぶ;
(make a call) hōmon suru 訪問する; (telephone)
denwa o kakeru 電話をかける —— *n.* (cry)
yobigoe 呼び声; (visit) hōmon 訪問; (demand)
yōkyū 要求
call at hōmon suru 訪問する
call for (demand) yōkyū suru 要求する; (go
to pick up) tori ni iku 取りにいく
call back (recall) yobi-kaesu 呼びかえす

call in (ask to come) yobu 呼ぶ; kite-morau 来てもらう

call on (visit) hōmon suru 訪問する

call up (ring up) denwa o kakeru [suru] 電話をかける［する］

calm *adj.* (quiet) shizuka na 静かな; (tranquil) odayaka na 穏やかな

calmly *adv.* shizuka ni 静かに; ochitsuite 落ちついて

camel *n.* rakuda らくだ

camellia *n.* tsubaki つばき

camera *n.* kamera カメラ; shashinki 写真機

camp *n.* kyampu キャンプ; yaei 野営; tento seikatsu テント生活

campaign *n.* (*mil.*) sentō 戦闘; sen'eki 戦役; undō 運動

election campaign senkyo undō 選挙運動

campus *n.* kōtei 校庭; kōnai 構内; kyampasu キャンパス

can¹ *v. aux.* (be able) dekiru できる; (may) shitemoyoi してもよい

can² *n.* kan 缶 —— *v.* kanzume ni suru 缶詰めにする   ***can opener*** kan-kiri 缶切り

canal *n.* unga 運河; horiwari 掘り割り

cancel *v.* torikesu 取り消す; mukō ni suru 無効にする —— *n.* torikeshi 取り消し

cancer *n.* gan がん

candidate *n.* shigansha 志願者; kōhosha 候補者

candle *n.* rōsoku ろうそく

candy *n.* kyandē キャンデー; ame あめ

cane *n.* (walking-stick) tsue 杖; (whip) muchi むち

canyon *n.* (fukai) kyōkoku (深い) 峡谷

cap *n.* bōshi 帽子

capable *adj.* dekiru できる; shiuru しうる; yūnō na 有能な

capacity *n.* (ability) sainō 才能; nōryoku 能力; (cubic content) yōseki 容積; (relative character) shikaku 資格

cape[1] *n.* misaki 岬

cape[2] *n.* (sleeveless outdoor garment) kēpu ケープ; manto マント

capital *n.* (chief city) shufu 首府; (capital letter) ō-moji 大文字; (funds) shihon 資本 —— *adj.* omo na 主な; shuyō na 主要な

capitalism *n.* shihon-shugi 資本主義

capsule *n.* (pill) kapuseru カプセル

captain *n.* (chief, leader)-cho ...長; kyaputen キャプテン; (the master of a ship) senchō 船長; (*army*) taii 大尉; (*navy*) taisa 大佐

captive *n.* horyo 捕虜; toriko とりこ —— *adj.* torawareta 捕らわれた

capture *n.* hokaku 捕獲; bundori 分捕り —— *v.* bundoru 分捕る; (take by force) toraeru 捕らえる; hokaku suru 捕獲する

car *n.* jidōsha 自動車; kuruma 車

card *n.* kādo カード; torampu トランプ; (business card) meishi 名刺

cardinal *adj.* (fundamental) kihon-teki na 基本的な; (vermillion) hi-iro no 緋色の; shinku no 深紅の —— *n.* (*church*) sūkikei 枢機卿; (*bird*) kōkanchō 紅冠鳥

care *n.* (concern) kigakari 気掛かり; (anxiety) shimpai 心配; (charge) sewa 世話; (attention) chūi 注意 —— *v.* shimpai suru 心配する; sewa o suru 世話をする *take care of* ...no sewa o suru ...の世話をする *care for* ...o konomu ...を好む; hoshigaru ほしがる

career *n.* (profession) shokugyō 職業; (course through life) keireki 経歴; rireki 履歴

careful *adj.* (watchful) chūi-bukai 注意深い; (prudent) yōjin-bukai 用心深い *Be careful!* Ki o tsukete! 気を付けて.

careless *adj.* (thoughtless) fuchūi na 不注意な; buyōjin na 不用心な

caress *n.* (gentle touch) aibu 愛撫; (kiss) kissu キッス

cargo *n.* (freight of a ship) funani 船荷; nimotsu

荷物　*cargo boat* kamotsusen 貨物船

carpenter *n.* daiku 大工

carriage *n.* kuruma 車；(conveying) umpan 運搬；unsō 運送

carrot *n.* ninjin にんじん

carry *v.* (convey) hakobu 運ぶ；(bring) motte iku 持って行く
　carry on tsuzukeru 続ける
　carry out jikkō suru 実行する

cart *n.* niguruma 荷車

carton *n.* bōru-gami ボール紙；bōru-bako ボール箱

cartoon *n.* manga 漫画

cartridge *n.* kātorijji カートリッジ

carve *v.* (cut) kiru 切る；kiritsukeru 切り付ける；(produce by cutting) chōkoku suru 彫刻する

case[1] *n.* hako 箱；kēsu ケース

case[2] *n.* (situation) baai 場合；tachiba 立場；(event) jiken 事件；(state) jijō 事情；(example) rei 例；(question) mondai 問題；(patient) kanja 患者
　in any case donna baai demo どんな場合でも
　in case of need masaka no toki niwa まさかの時には

cash *n.* genkin 現金 —— *v.* genkin ni suru 現金にする

cashier *n.* genkinsuitō-gakari 現金出納係；reji-gakari レジ係

cask *n.* taru たる

cast *v.* (throw) nageru 投げる；(assign, as an actor's part) haiyaku suru 配役する —— *n.* (actors in the play) haiyaku 配役

castle *n.* shiro 城

casual *adj.* (accidental) gūzen no 偶然の；(unexpected) omoi-gakenai 思いがけない；fui no 不意の；(occasional) rinji no 臨時の；(informal wear) fudangi no ふだん着の

cat *n.* neko 猫

catalog(ue) *n.* katarogu カタログ；mokuroku 目

録 —— *v.* mokuroku o tsukuru 目録を作る

catastrophe *n.* (denouement) (geki no) ōzume (劇の) 大詰め; (ruin) hametsu 破滅; (disastrous ruin) hisan na saigo 悲惨な最後

catch *v.* (seize) toraeru 捕らえる; tsukamaeru 捕まえる; (grasp) rikai suru 理解する; (be in time for) ma ni au 間に合う
I have caught cold. Kaze o hiki mashita. かぜを引きました.

caterpillar *n.* (larva) kemushi 毛虫; aomushi 青虫; (tractor) kyatapirā キャタピラー

cathedral *n.* daiseidō 大聖堂; daigaran 大がらん; daijiin 大寺院

cattle *n.* (farm animals) kachiku 家畜; (oxen, cows) ushi 牛

cause *n.* (power producing anything) gen'in 原因; (reason) riyū 理由; (motive) dōki 動機 —— *v.* (bring about) hikiokosu 引き起こす; (be the cause of) gen'in to naru 原因となる; (make) saseru させる

caution *n.* (carefulness) yōjin 用心; (warning) keikoku 警告

cautious *a.* (careful) yōjin-bukai 用心深い; (prudent) shinchō na 慎重な

cave *n.* horaana ほら穴

cease *v.* (end) owaru 終わる; oeru 終える; (stop) yameru やめる

cedar *n.* himaraya-sugi ヒマラヤ杉; sugi(-zai) 杉(材)

ceiling *n.* tenjō(-ita) 天井(板)

celebrate *v.* (commemorate) iwau 祝う; (perform) shiki o okonau 式を行なう

celebrated *adj.* (famous) yūmei na 有名な

celery *n.* serorī セロリー

cell *n.* (small room) ko-beya 小部屋; (ultimate element of organic structures) saibō 細胞

cellar *n.* (underground room) chikashitsu 地下室; (wine-cellar) sakagura 酒蔵

cement *n.* semento セメント

cemetery *n.* (kyōdō) bochi （共同）墓地

censure *v.* hinan suru 非難する；togameru とがめる

census *n.* kokusei chōsa 国勢調査；jinkō chōsa 人口調査

cent *n.* sento セント

center *n.* chūshin 中心；man'naka まん中；sentā センター —— *v.* (concentrate) shūchū suru 集中する

central *adj.* chūshin no 中心の；chūō no 中央の；(principal) omo na 主な

century *n.* (group of hundred) hyaku-nen 百年；seiki 世紀

cereal *n.* kokurui 穀類；kokumotsu 穀物

ceremony *n.* gishiki 儀式；reigi 礼儀

certain *adj.* (sure) tashika na 確かな；kakujitsu na 確実な；(some, one) aru ある；tashō no 多少の

certainly *adv.* tashika ni 確かに；kanarazu 必ず

certificate *n.* (testimonial) shōmeisho 証明書；(license) menkyo 免許

certify *v.* shōmei suru 証明する；menkyo o ataeru 免許を与える

chain *n.* kusari 鎖；(connected series) renzoku 連続 —— *v.* (connected with chain) kusari de tsunagu 鎖でつなぐ

chair *n.* isu 椅子 *take a chair* chakuseki suru 着席する

chairman *n.* (president) gichō 議長；kaichō 会長

chamber *n.* (room) heya 部屋；(House) gikai 議会

champion *n.* (winner) champion チャンピオン；(fighter) senshu 選手

chance *n.* (accident) gūzen 偶然；(luck) kōun 幸運；(opportunity) kikai 機会；chansu チャンス —— *adj.* gūzen no 偶然の *by any chance* man'ichi 万一 *by chance* gūzen ni 偶然に

change *v.* (vary) kaeru 変える；(alter) kaeru 代える；(exchange an article) kōkan suru 交換

する; (exchange money) ryōgae suru 両替する —— *n.* (variation) henkō 変更; henka 変化; (small money) kozeni 小銭; (the balance of money) o-tsuri おつり

channel *n.* kaikyō 海峡; (water-course) suiro 水路; (*TV*) channeru チャンネル

chant *n.* uta 歌 —— *v.* utau 歌う

chaos *n.* konton 混とん; (utter confusion) muchitsujo 無秩序

chapel *n.* reihaidō 礼拝堂; chaperu チャペル

chapter *n.* (main division of a book) shō 章; (branch office) shisha 支社

character *n.* (symbol) kigō 記号; fugō 符号; (letter) moji 文字; (distinctive mark) tokuchō 特徴; (essential quality) tokusei 特性; (reputation) meisei 名声 *Chinese character* kanji 漢字

characteristic *n.* tokuchō 特徴; tokushoku 特色 —— *adj.* dokutoku no 独特の

charcoal *n.* mokutan 木炭; sumi 炭

charge *v.* (fill) mitasu 満たす; (entrust with a duty) sekinin o owaseru 責任を負わせる; daika o seikyū suru 代価を請求する; tsuke ni suru つけにする; (command) meirei suru 命令する —— *n.* (load) nimotsu 荷物; (electrification) jūden 充電; (responsibility) sekinin 責任; (duty) gimu 義務; (price) nedan 値段 *in charge of* ...no kakari ...の係り; no sekinin-in-sha ...の責任者

charity *n.* (benevolence) jihi 慈悲; (almsgiving) jizen 慈善; (Christian love) ai 愛; (kindness) shinsetsu 親切

charm *n.* (attractiveness) miryoku 魅力; (on a bracelet) chāmu チャーム; omamori お守り —— *v.* miwaku suru 魅惑する; uttori saseru うっとりさせる

charming *adj.* miryoku-teki na 魅力的な; suteki na 素敵な

chart *n.* zuhyō 図表; gurafu グラフ; (navigator's sea map) kaizu 海図

charter *n*. (license) tokkyojō 特許状; menkyojō 免許状 —— *v*. (hire for exclusive use) karikiru 借り切る

chase *v*. (pursue) oikakeru 追いかける; (run after) tsuiseki suru 追跡する

chatter *v*. (jabber) (becha-becha) shaberu (べちゃべちゃ) しゃべる; saezuru さえずる —— *n*. oshaberi おしゃべり; mudabanashi むだ話

chauffeur *n*. untenshu 運転手

cheap *adj*. (nedan no) yasui (値段の) 安い; (of little account) yasuppoi 安っぽい

cheat *v*. damasu だます; azamuku 欺く

check *v*. (prevent) soshi suru 阻止する; (examine accuracy of) shōgō suru 照合する; kensa suru 検査する —— *n*. kogitte 小切手; (checkmate) ōte 王手; (test) kensa 検査; (plaid pattern) chekku チエック

cheek *n*. hoho ほほ; hoppeta ほっぺた

cheer *n*. (frame of mind) kigen きげん; (encouragement) hagemashi はげまし; (applause) kassai かっさい; (vigor) genki 元気; (fare) gochisō ごちそう —— *v*. (get encouraged) genki-zukeru 元気づける; (incite) hagemasu はげます; (applaud) kassai suru かっさいする *cheer on* seien suru 声援する *cheer up* nagusameru 慰める

cheerful *adj*. genki no ii 元気のいい; (pleasant) tanoshii 楽しい

cheese *n*. chīzu チーズ

chemical *adj*. kagaku no 化学の

chemistry *n*. kagaku 化学

cherry *n*. (cherry-tree) sakura no ki 桜の木; (fruit) sakurambo さくらんぼ

chest *n*. (box) hako 箱; (treasury) kinko 金庫; (funds) shikin 資金; (breast) mune 胸; *chest of drawers* tansu たんす

chestnut *n*. kuri no ki [mi] 栗の木 [実]; (*color*) kuri-iro 栗色

chew *v*. kamu かむ; kamikudaku かみくだく

chicken *n*. hiyoko ひよこ; (fowl) niwatori にわ

とり；toriniku 鳥肉

chief *n.* (leader) chō 長；kashira 頭 —— *adj.*
(principal) saikō no 最高の；(important) shuyō
na 主要な

child *n.* kodomo 子供；jidō 児童；yōji 幼児

childhood *n.* yōshō 幼少；yōnen jidai 幼年時代

childish *adj.* (puerile) kodomoppoi 子供っぽい；
adokenai あどけない；(simple) tanjun na 単純
な

chill *n.* (coldness) hie 冷え；reiki 冷気；(feverish
shivering) okan 悪感；(coldness) reitan 冷淡
—— *adj.* (cold) samui 寒い；tsumetai つめたい
—— *v.* (make cold) hiyasu 冷やす；(cool) hieru
冷える **catch a chill** samuke ga suru 寒気が
する

chimney *n.* entotsu 煙突

chin *n.* ago あご

chip *n.* (ki no) kirehashi (木の)切れ端；kakera
かけら；hahen 破片；(*electronics*) chippu チップ
—— *v.* (cut) kiru 切る；kezuru 削る；(break) waru 割る

chocolate *n.* chokorēto チョコレート

choice *n.* (selection) sentaku 選択；(preference)
yorigonomi より好み —— *adj.* (well-chosen)
erinuki no えり抜きの；(excellent) jōtō na 上
等な

choke *v.* (stop the breathing of) iki o tomeru
息をとめる；(smother) chissoku saseru 窒息
させる；(block up) fusagu ふさぐ

choose *v.* (select) erabu 選ぶ；(pick out) sentaku
suru 選択する；(decide) kimeru 決める

chopsticks *n.* hashi はし

chronic *adj.* (continuous) keizoku suru 継続
する；(inveterate) mansei no 慢性の

chronicle *n.* nendaiki 年代記；(record) kiroku
記録

chrysanthemum *n.* kiku (no hana) 菊(の花)

church *n.* kyōkai 教会；(church service) reihai
礼拝

cigar *n.* hamaki (tabako) 葉巻(たばこ)

cigarette *n.* (kamimaki) tabako (紙巻)たばこ

cinema *n.* eiga 映画

circle *n.* en 円; (circumference) enshū 円周; (group) nakama 仲間; sākuru サークル

circuit *n.* (distance round) shūi 周囲; (round about journey) junkai 巡回; (path of current) kairo 回路

circular *adj.* (round) marui 丸い; (circulating) junkai no 巡回の; kairan no 回覧の —— *n.* (handbill) bira ビラ; chirashi チラシ

circulate *v.* (move about) mawaru 回る; (send around) junkan saseru 循環させる; (go around) junkan suru 循環する; (pass current) ryūtsū saseru [suru] 流通させる[する]

circumstance *n.* (conditions) jijō 事情; jōtai 状態; (environment) kyōgū 境遇; kankyō 環境

circus *n.* sākasu サーカス

citizen *n.* (civilian) shimin 市民; (inhabitant) jūmin 住民

city *n.* toshi 都市; tokai 都会; shi 市
  city office shiyakusho 市役所

civil *adj.* shimin no 市民の; minkan no 民間の; ippanjin no 一般人の; (polite) teinei na ていねいな *civil law* mimpō 民法 *the Civil War* (*U. S.*) namboku sensō 南北戦争

civilization *n.* bummei 文明; bunka 文化

claim *n.* (demand) yōkyū 要求; (assertion) seikyū 請求; shuchō 主張 —— *v.* yōkyū suru 要求する; seikyū suru 請求する; shuchō suru 主張する

clam *n.* hamaguri はまぐり

clamor *n.* (shouting) sawagi さわぎ; (din) wameki わめき —— *v.* wai-wai sawagu わいわいさわぐ

clang *n.* kachin [kān, garan] to iu oto カチン[カーン, ガラン]という音 —— *v.* garan garan to naru [narasu] ガランガランと鳴る[鳴らす]

clap *v.* (applaud) te o tataku 手を叩く; hakushu suru 拍手する

clash v. (collide) shōtotsu suru 衝突する；kachiau かちあう —— n. (conflict) shōtotsu 衝突；gachin gachin [jan-jan] to iu oto ガチンガチン［ジャンジャン］という音

clasp v. (grasp) nigirishimeru 握りしめる；(embrace) dakishimeru 抱きしめる；(fasten with a clasp) (tomegane de) tomeru （止め金で）止める；(shake hands) akushu suru 握手する —— n. (buckle) tomegane 止め金；(hook) hokku ホック；(handshake) akushu 握手；(embrace) hōyō 抱擁

class n. kyū 級；kumi 組；kurasu クラス；(social division) kaikyū 階級

classic adj. koten no 古典の；(of the highest excellence) ichiryū no 一流の；kessaku no 傑作の —— n. koten 古典

classify v. (arrange in classes) bunrui suru 分類する；(assign to a class) tōkyū ni wakeru 等級に分ける

classroom n. kyōshitsu 教室

clause n. (single proviso) jōkō 条項；kajō 箇条；(short sentence) tambun 短文

claw n. (sharp nail) (tori, kemono no) tsume （鳥，けものの）爪；(kani, ebi no) hasami （かに，えびの）はさみ —— v. (scratch) hikkaku 引っかく；kakimushiru かきむしる

clay n. nendo 粘土；(earth) tsuchi 土

clean adj. seiketsu na 清けつな；kirei na きれいな

cleanly adv. kirei ni きれいに

clear adj. (uncloudy) hareta 晴れた；(limpid) tōmei na 透明な；(bright) akarui 明るい；(plain) akiraka na 明らかな —— v. (remove) torinozoku 取り除く；(become clear) hareru 晴れる
clear away (remove) torinozoku 取り除く；(vanish) kiri ga hareru 霧がはれる
clear up (grow clear) hareru 晴れる；(solve) kaiketsu suru 解決する

clergyman n. bokushi 牧師

clerk *n.* (scribe) shoki 書記; (office clerk) jimuin 事務員; (salesman) ten'in 店員

clever *adj.* (intelligent) rikō na 利口な; atama no ii 頭のいい; (skillful) kiyō na 器用な

client *n.* irainin 依頼人; kyaku 客; tokui とくい

cliff *n.* gake がけ; zeppeki 絶壁; dangai 断がい

climate *n.* kikō 気候; fūdo 風土

climax *n.* chōten 頂点; kuraimakkusu クライマックス

climb *v.* noboru 登る; yojinoboru よじ登る

clip *v.* (snip) hasami kiru はさみ切る; (trim) karikomu 刈り込む —— *n.* kamibasami 紙ばさみ; kurippu クリップ

clipper *n. pl.* barikan バリカン; *pl.* (shears) tsumekiri 爪切り; (fast sailing ship) kaisoku hansen 快速帆船

cloak *n.* (mantle) (sode-nashi) gaitō (袖なし) 外とう; manto マント —— *v.* gaitō o kiru [kiseru] 外とうを着る [着せる]

cloakroom *n.* kurōku クローク; keitaihin azukarisho 携帯品預り所

clock *n.* kake-dokei 掛時計

clockwise *adj., adv.* migi-mawari no [ni] 右回りの [に]

close *adj.* (shut) tojita 閉じた; (near) chikai 近い; (intimate) shimmitsu na 親密な —— *adv.* (near) sekkin shite 接近して —— *v.* (shut) tojiru 閉じる; (finish) owaru 終る

closely *adv.* pittari to ぴったりと; sekkin shite 接近して

closet *n.* (cupboard) todana 戸棚; oshiire 押入れ; (study) shosai 書斎; (private room) shishitsu 私室

cloth *n.* nuno 布; nunogire 布切れ

clothe *v.* kimono o kiseru [kiru] 着物をきせる [きる]

clothes *n.* kimono 着物; ifuku 衣服

cloud *n.* kumo 雲 —— *v.* (grow cloudy) kumoru 曇る; kumoraseru 曇らせる

cloudy *adj.* kumotta 曇った

club *n., v.* kurabu クラブ; (cudgel) kombō [de utsu] こん棒 [で打つ]

clue *n.* itoguchi 糸口; tegakari 手がかり

clumsy *adj.* (unskillful) bukiyō na 不器用な; (ill-contrived) heta na へたな

cluster *n.* (group) mure 群れ; (bunch) fusa 房 —— *v.* muragaru 群がる

clutch *v.* tsukamu つかむ; nigiru 握る —— *n.* tsukamu koto つかむこと; kuratchi クラッチ

coach *n.* (stage-coach) yonrin ōgata basha 四輪大型馬車; (trainer) kōchi コーチ —— *v.* kōchi suru コーチする; shidō suru 指導する

coal *n.* sekitan 石炭

coarse *adj.* (rude) soya na 粗野な; sozatsu na 粗雑な; (rough in texture) kime no arai きめのあらい

coast *n.* kaigan 海岸; engan 沿岸; hamabe 浜辺

coat *n.* uwagi 上着; kōto コート

coax *v.* (wheedle) iikurumeru 言いくるめる; nadameru なだめる; odateru おだてる

cockroach *n.* abura-mushi 油虫; gokiburi ゴキブリ

cocoa *n.* kokoa ココア

code *n.* (system of laws) hōten 法典; (set of rules) kisoku 規則; (system of signals) angō 暗号; fugō 符号

coffee *n.* kōhī コーヒー

coffin *n.* kan 棺; hitsugi ひつぎ

coin *n.* kahei 貨幣; kōka 硬貨

coincide *v.* itchi suru 一致する; fugō suru 符合する

cold *adj.* samui 寒い; (indifferent) reitan na 冷淡な —— *n.* samusa 寒さ; (*sickness*) kaze 風邪 *have a slight cold* kazegimi desu 風邪ぎみです

collapse *v.* (fall down) tsubureru つぶれる; hōkai suru 崩壊する; (fail) shippai suru 失敗する; (lose courage) kujikeru くじける —— *n.*

(utter failure) shippai 失敗; (break down) hōkai 崩壊; (prostration) suijaku 衰弱; (loss of courage) ikishōchin 意気消沈

collar *n.* (neckband) eri えり; kubiwa 首輪; karā カラー

colleague *n.* dōryō 同僚

collect *v.* atsumeru 集める; matomeru まとめる

collector *n.* shūshūka 収集家; (rent collector) shūkin'nin 集金人

college *n.* daigaku 大学; karejji カレッジ

colony *n.* shokuminchi 植民地

color *n.* iro 色; karā カラー; *pl.* (paints) enogu 絵具

column *n.* (pillar) enchū 円柱; hashira 柱; (feature article) (shimbun no) ran （新聞の）欄

comb *n.* kushi 櫛 —— *v.* kushi de tokasu 櫛でとかす; kushikezuru くしけずる

combat *n.* (fight) sentō 戦闘; (struggle) kakutō 格闘 —— *v.* tatakau 戦う; funtō suru 奮闘する

combination *n.* (join together) ketsugō 結合; kumiawase 組合せ —— *v.* ketsugō suru 結合する; rengō suru 連合する; (co-operate) kyōryoku suru 協力する

come *v.* kuru 来る; (happen) okoru 起こる; shōjiru 生じる; ...ni naru ...になる
  come across deau 出会う
  come out deru 出る; hatsubai suru 発売する
  come home kitaku suru 帰宅する
  come along yattekuru やって来る
  come back kaeru 帰る
  come from ...no umare de aru ...の生れである

comedy *n.* kigeki 喜劇

comfort *n.* nagusame 慰め; (pleasant) tanoshimi 楽しみ —— *v.* nagusameru 慰める

comfortable *adj.* (pleasant) kimochi no yoi 気持ちのよい; kiraku na 気楽な

command *v.* meijiru 命じる; shiki suru 指揮する —— *n.* meirei 命令; shiki 指揮

commemorate v. kinen suru 記念する; (celebrate) iwau 祝う

commence v. hajimeru 始める; hajimaru 始まる

comment n. (criticism) rompyō 論評; (annotation) chūshaku 注釈; kaisetsu 解説 —— v. chūshaku suru 注釈する; hihyō suru 批評する

commerce n. shōgyō 商業; tsūshō 通商; bōeki 貿易; torihiki 取引き *commercial* komāsharu no コマーシャルの; shōgyō no 商業の

commission n. (allowance) tesūryō 手数料; (trust) inin 委任; (charge) itaku 委託; iin 委員

commit v. (do something wrong) okasu 犯す; (entrust) itaku suru 委託する *commit a crime* tsumi o okasu 罪を犯す

committee n. iinkai 委員会; (guardian) kōken'nin 後見人

commodity n. (goods) shōhin 商品; nichiyōhin 日用品

common adj. (joint) kyōtsū no 共通の; (usual) tsūjō no 通常の; (ordinary) futsū no 普通の; (general) ippan no 一般の *common sense* jōshiki 常識

communicate v. (hold intercourse) tsūshin suru 通信する; (transmit) tsutaeru 伝える

communication n. (correspondence) tsūshin 通信; dentatsu 伝達; kōtsūkikan 交通機関; hōdō 報道

communism n. kyōsan-shugi 共産主義

community n. kyōdō-seikatsu-tai 共同生活体; shakai 社会

compact n. (contract) keiyaku 契約 —— adj. (dense) chimitsu na 緻密な; (concise) kanketsu na 簡潔な

companion n. (associate) nakama 仲間; hanashi-aite 話し相手; tomo 友

company n. (association) kōsai 交際; (companions) nakama 仲間; tomodachi 友だち; (firm) kaisha 会社

compare v. hikaku suru 比較する; kuraberu 比

べる；(liken) tatoeru たとえる

compass *n.* (range) han'i 範囲；(circuit) shūi 周囲；(*ship*)rashimban 羅針盤；(*drawing*) kompasu コンパス

compensate *v.* tsugunau 償う；benshō suru 弁償する

compete *v.* kyōsō suru 競争する；arasou 争う

competent *adj.* (capable) yūnō na 有能な；(adequate) tekinin no 適任の

competition *n.* kyōsō 競争

competitor *n.* kyōsōsha 競争者

complain *v.* fuhei o iu 不平を言う；guchi o kobosu ぐちをこぼす；nageku 嘆く

complete *v.* (finish) kansei suru 完成する；mitasu 満たす ―― *adj.* (perfect) kanzen na 完全な；(entire) jūbun na 十分な

complexion *n.* (appearance of the face) kaoiro 顔色；(general appearance) yōsu 様子

complicate *v.* (intricate) fukuzatsu ni suru 複雑にする；konran saseru 混乱させる

complicated *adj.* fukuzatsu na 複雑な

compliment *n. pl.* (greetings) aisatsu あいさつ；(flattery) oseji お世辞；(praise) sanji 賛辞

comply *v.* (agree) ōjiru 応じる；shōdaku suru 承諾する

compose *v.* (make up) kumitateru 組み立てる；(compose a poem) shi o tsukuru 詩を作る；(set to music) sakkyoku suru 作曲する

comprehend *v.* rikai suru 理解する

compromise *n.* (mutual concession) dakyō 妥協 ―― *v.* dakyō suru 妥協する

compute *v.* keisan suru 計算する **computer** kompyūtā コンピューター：keisan-sha [-ki] 計算者［器］

comrade *n.* nakama 仲間；dōshi 同志

conceal *v.* kakusu 隠す；himitsu ni suru 秘密にする

concede *v.* (grant) yuzuru ゆずる；(admit to be true) mitomeru 認める

conceive v. (imagine) kokoro ni idaku 心に抱く; kangaeru 考える; (become pregnant) ninshin suru 妊娠する

concentrate v. shūchū suru 集中する; sen'nen suru 専念する

conception n. (general notion) gainen 概念; (invention) chakusō 着想; (impregnation) ninshin 妊娠

concern v. (relate to) kankei suru 関係する; (affect) eikyō suru 影響する; (be concerned) shimpai suru 心配する —— n. (company) kaisha 会社; (relation) kankei 関係; (anxiety) shimpai 心配 *be concerned with*[*in*] ...ni kankei ga aru に関係がある *be concerned about*[*for*] ...ni kanshin o motsu に関心を持つ

concerned adj. (employed in) jūji suru 従事する; (interested) rigai kankei no aru 利害関係のある; (anxious) shimpai suru 心配する

concerning prep. ...ni kanshite に関して; ...ni tsuite について

concert n. ensōkai 演奏会; konsāto コンサート

conclude v. (bring to an end) oeru 終える; (decide) kettei suru 決定する; (come to an end) ketsuron suru 結論する

conclusion n. (termination) ketsumatsu 結末; (end) shūketsu 終結; ketsuron 結論

concrete adj. (definite) gutai-teki na 具体的な; (physical) yūkei no 有形の —— n. (building material) konkurīto コンクリート —— v. (harden) katameru 固める; (become hard) katamaru 固まる; (give shape to) gutaika suru 具体化する

condemn v. (blame) togameru とがめる; hinan suru 非難する; (sentence) senkoku suru 宣告する

condense v. (compress) gyōshuku saseru 凝縮させる; (epitomize) yōyaku suru 要約する; (concentrate) shūchū suru 集中する

condition *n.* (prerequisite) jōken 条件; (state) jōtai 状態

conduct *n.* (behavior) kōi 行為; (management) un'ei 運営; (leading) shidō 指導 ―― *v.* (guide) an'nai suru 案内する; (behave) furumau ふるまう

conductor *n.* (leader of an orchestra) shikisha 指揮者; (tour conductor) tenjōin 添乗員; (*train*) shashō 車掌

confectioner *n.* kashi-ya 菓子屋

confer *v.* (grant) ataeru 与える; juyo suru 授与する; (take counsel) sōdan suru 相談する

conference *n.* (meeting) kaigi 会議; (consultation) sōdan 相談

confess *v.* (tell one's faults) kokuhaku suru 告白する; hakujō suru 白状する; (admit) mitomeru 認める

confession *n.* kokuhaku 告白; zange ざんげ

confidence *n.* (firm trust) shin'yō 信用; (reliance) shinrai 信頼; (self-reliance) jishin 自信; (secret) himitsu 秘密

confine *v.* (limit) seigen suru 制限する; (shut up) tojikomeru 閉じ込める

confirm *v.* tashikameru 確かめる; kakunin suru 確認する

conflict *n.* (struggle) tōsō 闘争; arasoi 争い; (collision) shōtotsu 衝突 ―― *v.* (fight) tatakau 戦う; (clash) shōtotsu suru 衝突する

conform *v.* (adapt) itchi saseru 一致させる; tekigō saseru 適合させる; (obey) shitagau 従う

confuse *v.* (throw into disorder) konran saseru 混乱させる; (perplex) tōwaku saseru 当惑させる

confusion *n.* konran 混乱

congratulate *v.* (felicitate) iwau 祝う; omedetō to iu おめでとうと言う

congress *n.* (assembly) kaigi 会議; (legislature) gikai 議会; kokkai 国会

connect *n.* (join) tsunagu つなぐ ―― *v.* (unite)

setsuzoku suru 接続する
   be connected with kankei suru 関係する

connection *n.* (relation) kankei 関係; (union) renketsu 連結

conquer *v.* seifuku suru 征服する; uchikatsu 打ち勝つ

conquest *n.* (subjugation) seifuku 征服; (aquisition) kakutoku 獲得

conscience *n.* ryōshin 良心; dōgishin 道義心

conscious *adj.* (aware) ishiki shite iru 意識している; (sensible) kizuite iru 気付いている

consciousness *n.* ishiki 意識; jikaku 自覚

consent *n., v.* dōi (suru) 同意(する); shōdaku (suru) 承諾(する)

consequence *n.* (result) kekka 結果; (importance) jūyōsa 重要さ

conservative *adj.* hoshu-teki na 保守的な —— *n.* hoshushugi-sha 保守主義者

considerable *adj.* (worthy of consideration) kōryo subeki 考慮すべき; (important) jūyō na 重要な; (rather large) taryō no 多量の; kanari no かなりの

consideration *n.* kōryo 考慮; shiryo 思慮
   in consideration of ...o kōryo shite を考慮して

consist *v.* (be consistent) itchi suru 一致する; (be composed of) naritatsu 成り立つ
   consist of ...de kōsei sarete iru ...で構成されている

consistent *adj.* (compatible) itchi shita 一致した; (harmonized) chōwa shita 調和した

conspicuous *adj.* (attracting notice) medatsu 目立つ; (clearly visible) hakkiri mieru はっきり見える

conspire *v.* kyōbō suru 共謀する; imbō o takuramu 陰謀をたくらむ

constant *adj.* (invariable) kawaranai 変らない; (continuous) taema nai 絶え間ない; (resolute) kenjitsu na 堅実な

constitute *v.* (compose) kōsei suru 構成する; soshiki suru 組織する; (appoint) nimmei suru 任命する

constitution *n.* (structure) kōsei 構成; (form) soshiki 組織; (physical nature) taikaku 体格; (*government*) kempō 憲法

construct *v.* kenzō suru 建造する; kensetsu suru 建設する

consul *n.* ryōji 領事

consulate *n.* ryōjikan 領事館

consult *v.* (take counsel) sōdan suru 相談する; (seek advice from) shinsatsu o ukeru 診察を受ける; (refer to) (jisho) o shiraberu (辞書) を調べる

consume *v.* (use up) shōhi suru 消費する; (destroy) horobosu 滅ぼす

contact *n.* (touching) sesshoku 接触; (connection) renraku 連絡

contagious disease *n.* densembyō 伝染病

contain *v.* (include) fukumu 含む; (hold) ireru 入れる; irete iru 入れている

container *n.* iremono 入れ物; yōki 容器

contemplate *v.* (gaze upon) jitto nagameru じっと眺める; (meditate) jitto kangaeru じっと考える; (expect) kitai suru 期待する; (intend) shiyō to omou しようと思う

contemporary *adj.* (of the day) gendai no 現代の; (contemporaneous) dōjidai no 同時代の

content *n.* (capacity) yōryō 容量; (what is contained) naiyō 内容; (table of contents) mokuji 目次; (satisfaction) manzoku 満足 —— *adj.* (satisfied) manzoku shita 満足した

contest *n.* (competition) kyōsō 競争; (debate) ronsō 論争

continent *n.* tairiku 大陸; rikuchi 陸地

continue *v.* tsuzukeru 続ける; keizoku suru 継続する

contract *n.* keiyaku 契約; ukeoi 請負

contrary *adj.* (opposite) hantai no 反対の; gyaku

no 逆の ── *n.* hantai 反対　***on the contrary***
kore ni hanshite これに反して
contrast *n., v.* taishō(suru) 対照(する)
contribute *v.* (aid) kōken suru 貢献する; (give)
kifu suru 寄付する
contribution *n.* kōken 貢献; kifu 寄付
control *n.* shihai (ryoku) 支配 (力); kanri 管理;
kontorōru コントロール ── *v.* (govern) shihai suru 支配する; (direct) kanri suru 管理す
る; (have control over) seigyo suru 制御する
controversy *n.* ronsō 論争; ronsen 論戦
convenient *adj.* (opportune) benri na 便利な;
tsugō no yoi 都合のよい; (suitable) tekisetsu
na 適切な
convention *n.* (assembly) shūkai 集会; (rule)
kanrei 慣例
conversation *n.* kaiwa 会話; danwa 談話
convey *v.* (carry) hakobu 運ぶ; (transmit) tsutaeru 伝える; (communicate) shiraseru 知らせる
convince *v.* (make [feel] sure) kakushin saseru
確信させる; (persuade) nattoku saseru 納得
させる
cook *v.* ryōri suru 料理する ── *n.* ryōri-nin
料理人; kokku コック
cool *adj.* (moderately cold) suzushii 涼しい;
tsumetai 冷たい; (calm) ochitsuita 落ち着いた;
(cold-hearted) reitan na 冷淡な
cooperate *v.* kyōryoku suru 協力する; kyōdō
suru 協同する
copper *n.* dō 銅; (copper coin) dōka 銅貨
copy *n.* (reproduction) fukusha 複写; kopī コ
ピー; utsushi 写し; (one of a number of the
same books) satsu 冊; bu 部 ── *v.* (make a
copy of) utsusu 写す; fukusha suru 複写する
cord *n.* tsuna 綱; himo ひも; obi 帯
cordial *adj.* (hearty) kokoro kara no 心からの;
(friendly) shinsetsu na 親切な ── *n.* (*drink*)
kajitsu-shu 果実酒
core *n.* (central part) shin しん; chūshimbu 中心

部; (the heart) kakushin 核心

corn[1] *n.* (cereals) kokumotsu 穀物; (wheat) komugi 小麦; ōmugi 大麦; (maize) tōmorokoshi とうもろこし

corn[2] *n.* (horny thickening of the skin) uo-no-me 魚の目

corner *n.* kado 角; sumi 隅; (crossing) kōsaten 交差点

corporation *n.* kaisha 会社; dantai 団体

corpse *n.* shitai 死体

correct *a.* seikaku na 正確な; tadashii 正しい —— *v.* (amend) teisei suru 訂正する

correction *n.* teisei 訂正

correctly *n.* seikaku ni 正確に; machigai naku 間違いなく

correspond *v.* (be similar) ni sōtō suru に相当する; (agree) itchi suru 一致する; (communicate) buntsū suru 文通する

correspondence *n.* buntsū 文通; tsūshin 通信

corrupt *adj.* (rotten) kusatta くさった; (depraved) daraku shita 堕落した —— *v.* kusaru くさる; daraku suru 堕落する

cost *v.* (be priced at) (hiyō ga) kakaru (費用が)かかる; (require) yōsuru 要する —— *n.* (price) nedan 値段; (expense) hiyō 費用

costly *adv.* kōka na 高価な

costume *n.* fukusō 服装; ishō 衣装

cottage *n.* (small house) koya 小屋; (small country residence) inakaya 田舎家

cotton *n.* momen 木綿; wata 綿
   absorbent cotton dasshimen 脱脂綿
   cotton thread momen-ito 木綿糸

cough *n., v.* seki (o suru) せき(をする)
   cough drop sekidome doroppu せきどめドロップ

council *n.* kaigi 会議

counsel *n.* (consultation) sōdan 相談; kyōgi 協議; (advice) chūkoku 忠告 —— *v.* (advise) chūkoku suru 忠告する; (consult) sōdan suru 相談

する *counselor* kaunserā カウンセラー

court *n.* (palace) kyūtei 宮廷; (court of justice) saibansho 裁判所; (*tennis*) kōto コート

courtesy *n.* (polite behavior) reigi 礼儀; (politeness) teinei ていねい
courtesy of ...no kōi ni yotte の好意によって

cousin *n.* itoko いとこ

cover *v.* (overlay) o'ou 覆う; kakusu 隠す; (enclose) tsutsumu 包む —— *n.* (*book*) hyōshi 表紙; kabā カバー; (lid) futa ふた

cow *n.* me-ushi め牛

coward *n.* okubyō-mono おくびょう者 —— *adj.* okubyō na おくびょうな

crab *n.* kani かに

crack *n.* (fissure) wareme 割れ目; (fault) ketten 欠点 —— *vi.* (open into fissures) hibi ga hairu ひびが入る; (break) wareru 割れる —— *vt.* waru 割る

cracker *n.* (fire cracker) kanshakudama かんしゃく玉; (biscuit) kurakkā クラッカー

cradle *n.* (little baby's bed on rockers) yurikago 揺りかご; (place of origin) hasshōchi 発祥地

craft *n.* (cleverness) kōmyō 巧妙; (handicraft) kōgei 工芸

craftsman *n.* shokunin 職人; (artisan) kōgeika 工芸家

crane *n.* (*bird*) tsuru 鶴; (machine hoisting heavy objects) kijūki 起重機; kurēn クレーン

crank *n.* (*machine*) kuranku クランク; (eccentric person) kimuzukashiya 気むずかし屋

crash *v.* (make a crash) gara-gara [gachan] to iu oto o tateru ガラガラ [ガチャン] と言う音を立てる; (break in pieces) kudakeru 砕ける; (collide) shōtotsu suru 衝突する

crave *v.* (ask earnestly) kongan suru 懇願する; (desire) setsubō suru 切望する; (demand) motomeru 求める

crawl *v.* (creep) hau はう; (walk slowly) yukkuri aruku ゆっくり歩く —— *n.* (*swimming*) kurōru クロール

crazy *adj.* kichigai no 気違いの; kichigai-jimita 気違いじみた

cream *n.* kurīmu クリーム

create *v.* (produce) sōzō suru 創造する

creation *n.* (production) sōzō 創造; (universe) tenchi 天地 *the Creation* tenchi-sōzō 天地創造

credit *n.* (trust) shin'yō 信用; (honor) meiyo 名誉; (*bookkeeping*) kashikata 貸方

creep *v.* (crawl) hau はう; (come on stealthily) kossori shinobikomu こっそり忍び込む

crew *n.* norikumi-in 乗組員

cricket *n.* (*insect*) kōrogi こおろぎ; (*open-air game*) kuriketto クリケット

criminal *adj.* tsumi no 罪の; hanzai no 犯罪の —— *n.* hanzaisha 犯罪者; han'nin 犯人

cripple *n.* bikko びっこ; fugusha 不具者

crisis *n.* kiki 危機

crisp *adj.* (firm but easily broken) pari-pari suru パリパリする; kari-kari suru カリカリする; (lively) kibi-kibi shita きびきびした; (fresh) sawayaka na さわやかな; (curly) kami no chijireta 髪のちぢれた

critic *n.* hihyōka 批評家

criticism *n.* hihyō 批評; hyōron 評論

crocodile *n.* wani わに

crooked *adj.* (bend) magatta 曲った; (wicked) fusei no 不正の

crop *n.* (yield) sakumotsu 作物; shūkaku 収穫 —— *v.* (reap) shūkaku suru 収穫する; (gather) karu 刈る

cross *n.* jūjika 十字架; jūjikei 十字形 —— *adj.* (lying or being across) kōsa shita 交差した; (annoyed) fukigen na ふきげんな —— *v.* (go or walk across) yokogiru 横切る; (obstruct) jama o suru じゃまをする

crossing *n.* (*railroad*) fumikiri 踏切; (*street*) kōsaten 交差点

crow *n.* karasu からす —— *v.* (make a rooster's

cry) (ondori ga) toki o tsukuru （おんどりが）
時をつくる

crowd *n.* (dense multitude) gunshū 群集; (large
number) ōzei 大勢 —— *v.* (collect in a crowd)
muragaru 群がる; atsumeru 集める

crowded *adj.* zattō shita 雑踏した

crown *n.* (diadem) ōkan 王冠; (throne) ōi 王位

crude *adj.* (natural state) ten'nen no mama no
天然のままの; (rude) somatsu na 粗末な;
(raw) nama no 生の

cruel *adj.* (inhuman) zankoku na 残酷な; mugoi
むごい

cruise *v.* (sail to and fro) junkō suru 巡航する;
(*taxicab*) nagasu 流す —— *n.* (cruise ship) jun-
kōsen 巡航船

crumb *n.* pan-kuzu パンくず; pan-ko パン粉

crumble *vi.* kudakeru 砕ける —— *vt.* kona-gona
ni suru こなごなにする

crush *v.* (press) oshitsubusu 押しつぶす; kudaku
砕く

cry *v.* (shout) sakebu 叫ぶ; (weep) naku 泣く
—— *n.* sakebi 叫び

crystal *n.* (rock-crystal) suishō 水晶; kesshō 結
晶 —— *adj.* (transparent) tōmei na 透明な

cub *n.* (young fox, wolf, lion etc.) (kitsune, ōkami,
raion nado no) （狐, 狼, ライオンなどの）子;
yōjū 幼獣

cucumber *n.* kyūri きゅうり

cuff[1] *n.* (wristband) sode-guchi 袖口; kafusu カフ
ス

cuff[2] *v.* (slap) hirate de utsu 平手で打つ

culture *n.* (intellectual development) bunka 文化;
(tillage) kōsaku 耕作; (refinement) kyōyō 教養

cup *n.* koppu コップ; chawan 茶わん

cupboard *n.* shokki todana 食器戸棚

cure *v.* (restore to health) (byōki o) naosu （病気
を）治す; (heal) chiryō suru 治療する —— *n.*
(medical treatment) chiryō 治療

curio *n.* kottō(-hin) 骨とう（品）

curiosity *n.* kōkishin 好奇心

curious *adj.* fushigi na 不思議な；kimyō na 奇妙な

curl *n.* chijire-ge ちぢれ毛；maki-ge 巻き毛 —— *v.* kami o chijiraseru 髪をちぢらせる；kāru saseru カールさせる

currency *n.* (circulation) ryūtsū 流通；tsūyō 通用；(current money) tsūka 通貨

current *n.* (stream) nagare 流れ；(electric current) denryū 電流 —— *adj.* (in general circulation) ryūkō no 流行の；tsūyō shite iru 通用している

curtain *n.* kāten カーテン；(*stage*) maku 幕

curve *n.* magari 曲がり；kābu カーブ；(curved line) kyokusen 曲線 —— *v.* magaru 曲がる；mageru 曲げる

cushion *n.* kusshon クッション；zabuton 座布団

custom *n.* (habit) fūshū 風習；shūkan 習慣 —— *pl.* (import duties) kanzei 関税；zeikan 税関

customer *n.* o-kyaku お客；tokui-saki 得意先

cut *v.* kiru 切る；tatsu 断つ —— *n.* tachikata 裁ち方
　cut away kakedasu 駆け出す；nigeru 逃げる
　cut down kiritaosu 切り倒す
　cut in warikomu 割り込む
　cut short mijikaku suru 短くする

cute *adj.* (clever) rikō na 利口な；(pretty) kawaii 可愛い

cycle *n.* junkan 循環；(bicycle) jitensha 自転車；(motorcycle) ōtobai オートバイ；(current cycle) saikuru サイクル

cylinder *n.* entōkei 円筒形；shirindā シリンダー

D

dad *n.* otōchan お父ちゃん；papa パパ

daily *adj.* mainichi no 毎日の；hibi no 日々の —— *adv.* mainichi 毎日

dairy *n.* sakunyū-jō 搾乳場；rakunō-jō 酪農場；(milk shop) gyūnyū-ya 牛乳屋

daisy *n.* hinagiku ひな菊

dam *n.* damu ダム；seki せき

damage *n.* higai 被害；songai 損害

damn *v.* (curse) norou のろう

damp *adj.* shimetta 湿った ——*v.* shimerasu 湿らす ——*n.* (moisture) shikki 湿気

dance *n.* dansu ダンス；butō 舞踏 ——*v.* odoru 踊る；mau 舞う

dandelion *n.* tampopo タンポポ

dandruff *n.* fuke ふけ

Dane *n.* Demmāku-jin デンマーク人

danger *n.* kiken 危険；shōgai 障害

dangerous *adj.* kiken na 危険な；abunai 危ない

Danish *adj.* Demmāku no デンマークの ——*n.* Demmāku-go デンマーク語

dare *v.* omoikitte …suru 思い切って …する；aete …suru あえて …する；suru yūki ga aru する勇気がある
I dare say osoraku 恐らく；tabun 多分

dark *adj.* kurai 暗い；kuroi 黒い

darling *adj.* (much loved) kawaii かわいい ——*n.* kawaii hito かわいい人

darn *v.* tsukurou つくろう；kagaru かがる

dart *n.* (javelin) nage-yari 投げ槍；(arrow) nage-ya 投げ矢；(rush) tosshin 突進

date *n.* hizuke 日付；nengappi 年月日；dēto デート

daughter *n.* musume 娘

dawn *n.* yoake 夜明け；akegata 明け方 ——*v.* yo ga akeru 夜が明ける

day *n.* hi 日；hiru 昼；jidai 時代
all day long ichi-nichi-jū 一日中
day by day mainichi 毎日
every other day ichi-nichi oki ni 一日おきに
the other day senjitsu 先日；
some day itsuka いつか
the day after tomorrow asatte あさって；myō-

go-nichi 明後日

the day before yesterday issaku-jitsu 一昨日;
ototsui おととい

daybreak *n.* yoake 夜明け

daylight *n.* hiruma 昼間; nikkō 日光

daytime *n.* hiruma 昼間

dead *adj.* shinde iru 死んでいる

deadly *adj.* inochi ni kakawaru 命にかかわる;
chimeiteki na 致命的な

deaf *n., adj.* tsumbo (no) つんぼ(の)

deal *v.* (manage) toriatsukau 取り扱う; (distribute) bumpai suru 分配する; (do business)
torihiki suru 取り引きする ——*n.* (quantity)
ryō 量; (bargain) torihiki 取り引き

dealer *n.* shōnin 商人; ...shō ...商

dear *adj.* shin'ai na 親愛な; shitashii 親しい;
(costly) kōka na 高価な ——*n.* (one's cher-
ished) aijin 愛人

death *n.* shi 死; shibō 死亡

debt *n.* shakkin 借金; fusai 負債; saimu 債務

deceive *v.* (delude) damasu だます; azamuku 欺
く; (betray) uragiru 裏切る

December *n.* jūni-gatsu 十二月

decide *v.* (settle) kettei suru 決定する; kimeru
決める; (determine) kesshin suru 決心する

decision *n.* (settlement) kettei 決定; (determination) kesshin 決心

deck *n.* (*ship*) kampan 甲板; dekki デッキ ——
v. (adorn) kazaru 飾る

declare *v.* (proclaim) sengen suru 宣言する;
(affirm) dangen suru 断言する

decline *v.* (bend) katamuku 傾く; (refuse) kotowaru 断る ——*n.* (inclination) katamuki 傾
き; (decay) otoroe 衰え

decrease *vi.* heru 減る; genshō suru 減少する
——*vt.* herasu 減らす

decree *n.* (order) meirei 命令; (edit) fukoku 布
告; (ordinance) hōrei 法令

dedicate *v.* (devote) sasageru 捧げる; (consecrate)

hōnō suru 奉納する

deep *adj.* fukai 深い; (*color*) koi 濃い —— *adv.* fukaku 深く —— *n.* fukami 深み

deer *n.* shika 鹿

defeat *n.* (rout) haiboku 敗北; (frustration) zasetsu 挫折 —— *v.* makasu 負かす

defect *n.* (fault) ketten 欠点; (shortcoming) tansho 短所; jakuten 弱点

defend *v.* (protect) fusegu 防ぐ; mamoru 守る; (vindicate) bengo suru 弁護する

defense *n.* bōgyo 防御; shubi 守備; bengo 弁護

defer *v.* (postpone) nobasu 延ばす; enki suru 延期する

defile *v.* (make dirty) yogosu 汚す; (pollute) kegasu 汚す

define *v.* (make clear in outline) teigi suru 定義する; (explain) setsumei suru 説明する

definite *adj.* (precise) meikaku na 明確な; ittei no 一定の; hakkiri shita はっきりした

degree *n.* teido 程度; dankai 段階; (rank) tōkyū 等級; do 度

delay *vt.* (put off) nobasu 延ばす; (make later) okuraseru 遅らせる —— *vi.* temadoru てまどる; guzu-guzu suru ぐずぐずする —— *n.* enki 延期; chitai 遅滞

delegate *v.* (depute) haken suru 派遣する; (entrust) inin suru 委任する

delegation *n.* haken-iin 派遣委員; daihyō-dan 代表団

deliberate *v.* (ponder) kangae nuku 考え抜く; (take counsel) sōdan suru 相談する —— *adj.* (careful) shiryo-bukai 思慮深い; shinchō na 慎重な; (done on purpose) koi no 故意の

delicate *adj.* (exquisite) bimyō na 微妙な; sensai na 繊細な; (highly wrought) seikō na 精巧な

delicious *adj.* oishii おいしい; umai うまい

delight *vt.* (please) ureshigaraseru 嬉しがらせる; yorokobaseru 喜ばせる; tanoshimaseru 楽しませる —— *vi.* (take delight) tanoshimu 楽しむ;

yorokobu 喜ぶ —— *n.* (great pleasure) yorokobi 喜び

delightful *adj.* tanoshii 楽しい; ureshii 嬉しい

deliver *v.* (distribute) haitatsu suru 配達する;
todokeru 届ける; (save) sukuu 救う; (release)
kaihō suru 解放する

delivery *n.* (distribution) haitatsu 配達; (deliverance) kyūjo 救助

demand *v.* (call for) yōkyū suru 要求する; seikyū suru 請求する —— *n.* (request) yōkyū
要求; juyō 需要

democracy *n.* minshushugi 民主主義

demonstrate *v.* (prove) shōmei suru 証明する;
(show) arawasu 現わす

demonstration *n.* (logical proving) shōmei 証明;
(act of making evident) jiiundō 示威運動

denial *n.* (negation) hitei 否定; (rejection) kyozetsu 拒絶

denounce *v.* (accuse publicly) (kōzen to) hinan
suru (公然と) 非難する; (charge) kokuhatsu
suru 告発する

dense *adj.* (thick) koi 濃い; (crowded together)
shigetta 茂った; fukai 深い; mitsu na 密な

dentist *n.* ha-isha 歯医者; shika-i 歯科医

denture *n.* ire-ba 入歯

deny *v.* hitei suru 否定する; (refuse) kyozetsu
suru 拒絶する

depart *v.* shuppatsu suru 出発する; (leave) saru
去る; (die) shinu 死ぬ
   departure time shuppatsu jikan 出発時間

department *n.* bu 部; bumon 部門; shō 省;
kyoku 局 *department store* hyakkaten 百貨店;
depāto デパート

depend *v.* (rely) tayori ni suru 頼りにする;
shinrai suru 信頼する; (be contingent) …ni
yoru による

deposit *n.* (deposit money) yokin 預金; (security)
hoshōkin 保証金 —— *v.* azukeru 預ける

depress *v.* (press down) sageru 下げる; (lower)

hikuku suru 低くする; (discourage) genki o nakusu 元気をなくす; (weaken) yowameru 弱める

depression *n.* (dejection) iki-shōchin 意気消沈; yūutsu 憂うつ; (dullness) fukeiki 不景気

depth *n.* fukasa 深さ; fukami 深み

deputy *n.* dairi (-nin) 代理(人)

derive *v.* (draw) hikidasu 引き出す; (got from) ...kara uru から得る; (come) yurai suru 由来する

descend *v.* kudaru 下る; oriru 降りる

descendant *n.* shison 子孫

describe *v.* (tell or write about) byōsha suru 描写する; noberu 述べる

desert *n.* (arid, sandy region) sabaku 砂漠

deserve *v.* (be worthy of) ni atai suru に価する; (be worthy to have) ...o ukeru kachi ga aru ...を受ける価値がある

design *n.* dezain デザイン; (plan) sekkei 設計 —— *v.* (plan) kuwadateru 企てる; keikaku suru 計画する

desire *v.* negau 願う; nozomu 望む —— *n.* negai 願い; nozomi 望み; (craving) yokubō 欲望

desk *n.* tsukue 机

despair *v.* (lose hope) zetsubō suru 絶望する; (give up) akirameru あきらめる

despatch *v.* (send off) kyūsō suru 急送する; haken suru 派遣する

desperate *adj.* (hopeless) zetsubō-teki na 絶望的な; (reckless) hisshi no 必死の

despise *v.* keibetsu suru 軽べつする; sagesumu さげすむ

despite *prep.* (in spite of) ...nimo kakawarazu ...にもかかわらず

dessert *n.* dezāto デザート

destination *n.* (place of destination) mokutekichi 目的地; ikisaki 行き先

destiny *n.* ummei 運命; shukumei 宿命

destroy *v.* (pull down) hakai suru 破壊する; (ruin) horobosu 滅ぼす; (kill) korosu 殺す

destruction *n.* (ruin) hakai 破壊; metsubō 滅亡

detach *v.* (separate) bunri suru 分離する; (dispatch) haken suru 派遣する

detail *n.* (particulars) shōsai 詳細; (item) saibu 細部 —— *v.* kuwashiku hanasu 詳しく話す

detailed *adj.* shōsai na 詳細な; kuwashii 詳しい

detain *v.* hikitomeru 引き留める; temadoraseru 手間取らせる

detect *v.* (discover) mitsukeru 見付ける; miyaburu 見破る

detective *n.* tantei 探偵; (police detective) keiji 刑事

detergent *n.* senzai 洗剤

determination *n.* kesshin 決心; kettei 決定

determine *v.* (make up one's mind) kesshin suru 決心する; (decide) kettei suru 決定する

detour *n.* mawari-michi 回り道

develop *v.* (make or become larger) hattatsu saseru [suru] 発達させる [する]; hatten saseru [suru] 発展させる [する]; (*photo.*) genzō suru 現像する

device *n.* (plan) kufū 工夫; kōan 考案; (design) ishō 意匠

devil *n.* akuma 悪魔; oni 鬼

devise *v.* (contrive) kufū suru 工夫する; (invent) hatsumei suru 発明する

devote *v.* (consecrate) sasageru 捧げる; ateru あてる

devoted *adj.* kenshinteki na 献身的な; nesshin na 熱心な; chūjitsu na 忠実な

devotion *n.* (piety) shinjin 信心; (zeal) nesshin 熱心; (intense loyalty) kenshin 献身

diabetes *n.* tōnyō-byō 糖尿病

diamond *n.* daiyamondo ダイヤモンド

diaper *n.* omutsu おむつ; oshime おしめ

diarrhea *n.* geri 下痢

diary *n.* nikki 日記; nisshi 日誌

dictate *v.* kaki toraseru 書き取らせる; (reading aloud for writing) kōjutsu suru 口述する; (give orders for) sashizu suru 指図する

dictator *n.* dokusaisha 独裁者; shireisha 指令者

dictionary *n.* jisho 辞書; jiten 辞典

die *v.* shinu 死ぬ; nakunaru なくなる; shibō suru 死亡する

diet *n.* (usual fare) shokuji 食事; (Diet) kokkai 国会

differ *v.* (be different) chigau 違う; (disagree) iken ga awanai 意見が合わない

difference *n.* chigai 違い; sōi 相違

different *adj.* chigatta 違った; kotonatta 異なった

difficult *adj.* kon'nan na 困難な; muzukashii むずかしい

dig *v.* horu 掘る

dignity *n.* (calm stateliness) igen 威厳; (nobleness) kihin 気品

diligent *adj.* kimben na 勤勉な

dim *adj.* (obscure) usugurai うす暗い; (indistinct) mōrō to shita もうろうとした

dimension *n.* (measurement) sumpō 寸法; (size) ōkisa 大きさ; (capacity) yōseki 容積; (bulk) kasa かさ

diminish *v.* (lessen) herasu 減らす; (become less) heru 減る; sukunaku suru 少なくする

dimple *n.* ekubo えくぼ

dine *v.* seisan [bansan] o toru 正さん[晩さん]をとる; shokuji o suru 食事をする

dining-car *n.* shokudō-sha 食堂車

dinner *n.* seisan 正さん; bansan 晩さん

diplomacy *n.* gaikō 外交

diplomatic *adj.* gaikō no 外交の

direct *adj.* (immediate) chokusetsu no 直接の; (straight) massugu no まっすぐの —— *adv.* (directly) chokusetsu ni 直接に; massugu ni まっすぐに —— *v.* (give direction) shiji suru 指示する; (order) meijiru 命じる

direction *n.* (course) hōkō 方向; (management) kanri 管理

director *n.* shihai-nin 支配人; jūyaku 重役

dirt *n.* (dust) gomi ごみ; hokori ほこり; (mud) doro どろ

dirty *adj.* kitanai きたない; fuketsu na 不潔な; yogoreta よごれた

disagree *v.* sō wa omowanai そうは思わない

disappear *v.* (go out of sight) mienaku naru 見えなくなる; (vanish) kieru 消える

disappoint *v.* gakkari saseru がっかりさせる; shitsubō saseru 失望させる

disaster *n.* (calamity) saigai 災害; tensai 天災; (misfortune) fukō 不幸

disc (=disk) *n.* (quoit) emban 円盤; (record) rekōdo レコード

discharge *v.* (shoot) hassha suru 発射する; (dismiss) kaiko suru 解雇する; (pay out) shiharau 支払う; (perform one's duty) (gimu o) hatasu (義務を) 果たす —— *n.* hassha 発射; kaiko 解雇

discipline *n.* (training) kunren 訓練; (order) fūki 風紀 —— *v.* kunren suru 訓練する; shitsukeru しつける

discontinue *v.* (stop) chūshi suru 中止する; (cease) yameru 止める

discord *n.* (disagreement) fuitchi 不一致; (strife) fuwa 不和; nakatagai 仲たがい

discount *n.*, *v.* waribiki (suru) 割引(する)

discourse *n.* kōen 講演; ronsetsu 論説

discover *v.* hakken suru 発見する; mitsukeru 見つける; ...to [ga] wakaru ...と [が] わかる

discovery *n.* hakken 発見

discuss *v.* tōron suru 討論する; rongi [giron] suru 論議 [議論] する; sōdan suru 相談する

discussion *n.* rongi 論議; tōgi 討議

disdain *v.* keibetsu suru 軽べつする

disease *n.* byōki 病気; yamai 病

disgrace *n.* fumeiyo 不名誉; fumemboku 不面目

disgust v. fukai ni suru 不快にする; mukatsuka-seru むかつかせる ——— n. (nausea) mukatsuki むかつき; (loathing) hidoku kirau koto ひどくきらうこと

dish n. sara 皿; (food served in a dish) (sara ni motta) ryōri (皿に盛った)料理
dishcloth fukin ふきん
dishrack mizukiri 水切り

disinfectant n. shōdokuzai 消毒剤

dismay n. (fright) osore 恐れ; rōbai ろうばい ——— v. (terrify) odorokasu 驚かす; osore saseru 恐れさせる

dismiss v. (allow to leave) saraseru 去らせる; (discharge) kaiko suru 解雇する

disobey v. (not obey) shitagawanai 従わない; (violate) somuku 背く

disorder n. (confusion) konran 混乱; ranzatsu 乱雑; (lack of order) muchitsujo 無秩序

disperse v. (scatter) chirasu 散らす; chiru 散る; chirijiri ni naru ちりぢりになる

display v. (show) shimesu 示す; (show off) mise-birakasu 見せびらかす ——— n. (exhibition) ten-ran 展覧; chinretsu 陳列

dispose v. (regulate) shobun suru 処分する; (arrange) haichi suru 配置する
disposed to ...suru ki ga aru する気がある

dispute n., v. ronsō (suru) 論争 (する); kōron (suru) 口論 (する)

dissolve v. (decompose) bunkai saseru [suru] 分解させる [する]; (liquefy) tokasu とかす; tokeru とける

distant adj. tōi 遠い; hanareta 離れた

distinct adj. (clear) hakkiri shita はっきりした; meiryō na 明瞭な; (different) kotonatta 異なった; niteinai 似ていない

distinguish v. (make a distinction) kubetsu suru 区別する; (characterize) medataseru 目立たせる; tokuchō-zukeru 特徴づける

distinguished adj. yūmei na 有名な

distribute v. (deal out) bumpai suru 分配する; haikyū suru 配給する

district n. chiku 地区; chihō 地方; chiiki 地域

ditch n. mizo みぞ; dobu どぶ

dive v. moguru もぐる; sensui suru 潜水する

divert v. (turn aside) sorasu そらす; (amuse) nagusameru 慰める

divide v. (separate into parts) wakeru 分ける; bunkatsu suru 分割する; (be separated) waru 割る

divine adj. (of God) kami no 神の; (sacred) shinsei na 神聖な

division n. (separation) bunkatsu 分割; (boundary) kyōkai 境界

divorce n., v. rikon (suru) 離婚 (する)

do v. suru する; nasu なす; okonau 行なう

dock n. dokku ドック; pl. (wharf) hatoba 波止場; gampeki 岸壁

doctor n. hakase 博士; (physician) ishi 医師

document n. shorui 書類; bunsho 文書

dodge v. (avoid by twisting aside) (hirari to) mi o kawasu (ひらりと) 身をかわす; yokeru よける; (evade) ...o ii nukeru ...を言い抜ける

dog n. inu 犬; -ken ...犬

doll n. ningyō 人形

dolphin n. iruka いるか

dome n. marutenjō 丸天井; dōmu ドーム

domestic adj. (of the home) katei no 家庭の; (home-made) jikasei no 自家製の; (internal) kokunai no 国内の —— n. (household servant) meshitsukai 召使

dominate v. (rule) tōji suru 統治する; shuken ga aru 主権がある

dominion n. (sovereignty) shuken 主権; (power of rule) tōchiken 統治権; (territory) ryōdo 領土

donkey n. roba ろば

doom n. (fate) ummei 運命; (death) shi 死 —— v. ummei o sadameru 運命を定める

door n. doa ドア; tobira 扉; to 戸

dot *n.* ten 点 ―― *v.* ten o utsu 点を打つ

double *adj.* ni-bai no 2 倍の; kasanatta 重なった ―― *adv.* ni-bai ni 2 倍に ―― *n.* bai 倍

doubt *n.* utagai 疑い; giwaku 疑惑 ―― *v.* utagau 疑う

doubtful *adj.* utagawashii 疑わしい

doubtless *adv.* utagainaku 疑いなく; tashika ni 確かに

dough *n.* neriko 練り粉; nama-pan 生パン

doughnut *n.* dōnatsu ドーナツ

dove *n.* hato はと

down *adj.* shita ni [e] 下に[へ] ―― *prep.* no shita ni の下に ―― *adj.* kudari no 下りの *down train* kudari ressha 下り列車

downstairs *adv.* ikkai no [ni, de] 一階の [に, で]

downtown *n., adv.* shōgyōchiku(e, de) 商業地区 (へ, で) ―― *n., adj.* hankagai(no) 繁華街 (の)

dozen *n.* dāsu ダース

draft *n.* (rough copy) sōkō 草稿; (plan) sekkei-zu 設計図; (rough sketch) shitae 下絵; (bill of exchange) tegata 手形

dragon *n.* ryū 竜

dragonfly *n.* tombo とんぼ

drain *n.* (drain-pipe) haisui-kan 排水管; (sewer) gesui 下水 ―― *v.* (draw off) haisui suru 排水する; (drink up) nomihosu 飲み干す

drama *n.* geki 劇; gikyoku 戯曲; dorama ドラマ

draw *v.* (pull) hiku 引く; hipparu 引っ張る; (draw breath) iki o suru 息をする; (attract) hikitsukeru 引き付ける; (sketch out) e o kaku 絵をかく; (leave a game undecided) hikiwake ni suru 引き分けにする

drawer *n.* (cf. drawee) tegata furidashi-nin 手形振出人; *pl.* (underpants) shitabaki 下ばき; (a boxlike compartment in furniture) hikidashi 引出し

dread *v.* (fear) osoreru 恐れる; kowagaru こわが

る　　*dreadful* osoroshii 恐ろしい

dream *n.* yume 夢; gensō 幻想 ——*v.* yume o miru 夢をみる

dreary *adj.* wabishii わびしい; monosabishii 物寂しい

dress *v.* (clothe) kiseru 着せる; (put on clothes) kiru 着る ——*n.* doresu ドレス; ifuku 衣服

drift *v.* tadayou 漂う; hyōryū suru 漂流する ——*n.* hyōryū 漂流

drill *n.* (tool for boring holes) kiri きり; doriru ドリル ——*v.* (train) kunren suru 訓練する; (bore with drill) ana o akeru 穴をあける

drink *v.* nomu 飲む; kampai suru 乾杯する

drip *v.* shitataru したたる; potari-potari ochiru ぽたりぽたり落ちる ——*n.* shitatari したたり; shizuku しずく

drip-dry nō-airon ノーアイロン

drive *v.* (urge on) ou 追う; (operate a vehicle) unten suru 運転する; doraibu suru ドライブする

drop *n.* shitatari したたり; shizuku しずく ——*v.* (let fall in drops) shitatarasu したたらす; (let fall) otosu 落す

drown *vt.* oboresaseru おぼれさせる ——*vi.* oboreru おぼれる

drug *n.* kusuri 薬; yakuhin 薬品

drugstore *n.* kusuri-ya 薬屋; doraggu-sutoa ドラッグストア

drum *n.* doramu ドラム; taiko 太鼓

dry *adj.* kawaita 乾いた; kansō shita 乾燥した; (*of wine*) karakuchi no 辛口の

duck *n.* (*domestic*) ahiru あひる; (*wild*) kamo かも

due *adj.* tekitō no [na] 適当の [な]; (appropriate) seitō na 正当な; (payable) shiharau-beki 支払うべき　*due to* …ni yoru による

dull *adj.* (stupid) nibui 鈍い; fukappatsu na 不活発な; inki na 陰気な

dumb *adj.* oshi no おしの; mugon no 無言の

duplicate *n.* utsushi 写し; (reproduction) fukusha 複写 —— *v.* (copy) utsushi o toru 写しを取る *duplicate key* aikagi 合かぎ

during *prep.* no aida ni [wa] の間に[は]; -jū 中

dust *n.* chiri ちり; hokori ほこり; (earth) tsuchi 土 *duster* fukin ふきん

duty *n.* gimu 義務; hombun 本分

dye *v.* someru 染める —— *n.* senryō 染料

dynamic *adj.* dōteki na 動的な; dainamikku na ダイナミックな; chikarazuyoi 力強い

E

each *adj.* sore-zore no それぞれの; ono-ono no 各々の *each other* tagai ni 互いに

eager *adj.* nesshin na 熱心な *eagerly* nesshin ni 熱心に; shikiri ni しきりに

ear *n.* mimi 耳; (spike) ho 穂

early *adj.* hayai 早い; shoki no 初期の; wakai 若い *early or late* osokare hayakare 遅かれ早かれ

earn *v.* (gain by work) (doryoku shite) uru (努力して) 得る; kasegu かせぐ; mōkeru もうける

earnest *adj.* (serious) majime na まじめな; (zealous) nesshin na 熱心な

earth *n.* chikyū 地球; (ground) jimen 地面; tochi 土地

earthquake *n.* jishin 地震

ease *n.* (comfort) kiraku 気楽; anraku 安楽; kutsurogi くつろぎ; (facility) yōi 容易 *at ease* kiraku ni 気楽に

easily *adv.* yōi ni 容易に; tayasuku たやすく; raku ni 楽に

east *n., adj.* higashi (no) 東 (の); tōhō (no) 東方 (の) [the E-] Tōyō 東洋

Easter *n.* Fukkatsusai 復活祭

eat *v.* taberu 食べる; kuu 食う

echo *n.* hankyō 反響; kodama こだま; yamabiko

山びこ

economics *n.* keizai-gaku 経済学

economy *n.* keizai 経済; (frugality) setsuyaku 節約

edge *n.* (cf. blade) ha 刃; (margin) fuchi 縁; heri へり

edit *v.* henshū suru 編集する

edition *n.* han 版; (edited copy) kankō-bon 刊行本

editor *n.* henshū-sha 編集者; shuhitsu 主筆

editorial *adj.* henshū no 編集の —— *n.* (leading article) shasetsu 社説; ronsetsu 論説

educate *v.* kyōiku suru 教育する; (train) kunren suru 訓練する

eel *n.* unagi うなぎ

effect *n.* (efficacy) kōka 効果; (result) kekka 結果; (influence) eikyō 影響

effective *adj.* kōka-teki na 効果的な

efficient *adj.* nōritsu-teki na 能率的な; (capable) yūnō na 有能な; (having an effect) yūkō na 有効な

effort *n.* doryoku 努力; honeori 骨折り

egg *n.* tamago 卵 *egg beater* awadate-ki 泡立て器 *egg white* (tamago no) shiromi (卵の)白身 *egg yolk* (tamago no) kimi (卵の)黄身

eight *n., adj.* hachi (no) 8 (の); yattsu 八つ

either *adj.* dochira ka no どちらかの; dochira mo どちらも; sōhō 双方 —— *prep.* ...ka matawa かまたは —— *pron.* dochira ka どちらか; (*negative*) dochira mo どちらも

elaborate *adj.* (complicated) nen'iri no 念入りの; tan'nen na 丹念な; (highly finished) seikō na 精巧な

elastic *adj.* (springy) danryoku no aru 弾力のある; hazumu はずむ
elastic band gomu-himo ゴムひも

elbow *n.* hiji ひじ

elect *v.* (choose) erabu 選ぶ; (choose by vote) senkyo suru 選挙する

election *n.* (choosing by vote) senkyo 選挙; (choice) sentaku 選択

electric *adj.* denki no 電気の
electric fan sempū-ki 扇風機
electric shaver denki-kamisori 電気かみそり

electricity *n.* denki 電気

elegant *adj.* yūbi na 優美な; jōhin na 上品な

element *n.* (factor) yōso 要素; genso 元素

elementary *adj.* shoho no 初歩の
elementary school shō-gakkō 小学校

elephant *n.* zō 象

elevate *v.* (raise) ageru 上げる; (lift up) takameru 高める

elevator *n.* erebētā エレベーター

eleven *n., adj.* jū-ichi (no) 11, 十一 (の)

eliminate *v.* (take out) nozoku 除く; sakujo suru 削除する

else *adv.* sono hoka ni その外に; samo nakereba さもなければ

elsewhere *adv.* dokoka hoka no tokoro de [ni] どこか外の所で [に]; yoso ni [de] よそに [で]

embarrass *v.* komaraseru 困らせる; nayamasu 悩ます

embassy *n.* taishi-kan 大使館

embrace *v.* dakishimeru 抱きしめる; hōyō suru 抱擁する

emergency *n.* hijōji 非常時; kinkyū 緊急; kikyū 危急

emigrate *v.* (kaigai ni) ijū suru (海外に) 移住する

eminent *adj.* (notable) chomei na 著名な; (distinguished) sugureta すぐれた

emotion *n.* (feeling) kanjō 感情; (excited mental state) kandō 感動; kangeki 感激

emperor *n.* kōtei 皇帝; ten'nō 天皇; teiō 帝王

emphasis *n.* kyōchō 強調; kyōsei 強勢

empire *n.* teikoku 帝国

employ *v.* (engage) yatou 雇う; (use) tsukau 使

う; shiyō suru 使用する

employee *n.* shiyō-nin 使用人; jūgyō-in 従業員

employer *n.* yatoi-nushi 雇主

empty *adj.* kara no 空の ―― *v.* kara ni suru 空にする; akeru 空ける

enclose *v.* dōfū suru 同封する; (fence in) kakoi o suru 囲いをする; tsutsumu 包む

encounter *v.* deau 出合う; sōgū suru 遭遇する

end *n.* (cf. beginning) owari 終り; saigo 最後; (tip) hashi 端; (object) mokuteki 目的

endeavor *n.*, *v.* doryoku (suru) 努力(する)

endless *adj.* mugen no 無限の; hateshinai 果てしない

endure *v.* gaman suru がまんする; shinobu 忍ぶ; taeru 耐える

enema *n.* kanchō 浣腸

enemy *n.* teki 敵

energy *n.* (power) seiryoku 精力; kakki 活気; enerugī エネルギー

engage *v.* (promise) yakusoku suru 約束する; (occupy) jūji saseru 従事させる; (hire) yatou 雇う; (betroth) kon'yaku suru 婚約する

engagement *n.* (promise) yakusoku 約束; (betrothal) kon'yaku 婚約; (occupation) yōji 用事

engine *n.* kikan 機関; enjin エンジン

engineer *n.* gishi 技師

England *n.* Eikoku 英国; Igirisu イギリス

English *adj.* Eikoku no 英国の ―― *n.* Eikoku-jin 英国人; Eigo 英語

engrave *v.* (carve) chōkoku suru 彫刻する

enjoy *v.* tanoshimu 楽しむ

enormous *adj.* kyodaina 巨大な; bakudai na 莫大な

enough *adj.* jūbun no [na] 十分の [な]; ...ni taru に足る ―― *n.* jūbun 十分; takusan たくさん

enter *v.* (ni) hairu (に)入る; (ni) kuwawaru (に)加わる

enter into o hajimeru を始める

enterprise *n.* jigyō 事業; kigyō 企業

entertain *v.* (have as a guest) motenasu もてなす; (amuse) tanoshimaseru 楽しませる

enthusiasm *n.* nekkyō 熱狂; netsu 熱

entire *adj.* (whole) zentai no 全体の; (complete) mattaku no 全くの

entrance *n.* iriguchi 入口; genkan 玄関; nyūjō 入場; nyūgaku 入学

entry *n.* (front door) iriguchi 入口; (act of entering) nyūjō 入場; (registry) kinyū 記入

envelope *n.* fūtō 封筒

environment *n.* shūi 周囲; kankyō 環境

envy *n.* sembō せん望; urayami うらやみ; netami ねたみ

episode *n.* sōwa 挿話; episōdo エピソード

equal *n.* ...ni hitoshii ...に等しい; (evenly matched) dōtō no 同等の

equipment *n.* jumbi 準備; sōchi 装置

era *n.* jidai 時代; kigen 紀元

erase *v.* (rub out) nugui-kesu ぬぐい消す; suri-kesu すり消す; sakujo suru 削除する

eraser *n.* (*blackboard use*) kokuban-fuki 黒板ふき; (rubber) keshigomu 消しゴム

erect *adj.* chokuritsu shita 直立した; massugu no まっすぐの —— *v.* massugu ni suru まっすぐにする

err *v.* (mistake) ayamaru 誤る; machigaeru 間違える

errand *n.* tsukai 使い; tsukaiaruki 使い歩き; (mission) shimei 使命

error *n.* ayamari 誤り; machigai 間違い

escape *v.* nogareru 逃れる; nigeru 逃げる —— *n.* tōbō 逃亡; tōsō 逃走

escort *v.* goei suru 護衛する; tsukisou 付添う; okutte iku 送って行く —— *n.* tsukisoi 付添い; (guard) goei 護衛

essay *n.* zuihitsu 随筆; essei エッセイ —— *v.* (attempt) kokoromiru 試みる; tamesu ためす

essence *n.* honshitsu 本質; seizui 精髄; essensu

..

エッセンス

essential *adj.* (of the greatest importance) jūyō na 重要な; (intrinsic) honshitsu-teki na 本質的な; (indispensable) zettai ni hitsuyō na 絶対に必要な

essentially *adv.* honshitsu-teki ni 本質的に; honrai 本来

establish *v.* (found) setsuritsu suru 設立する; (settle) hiraku 開く

establishment *n.* setsuritsu 設立

estate *n.* (rank) mibun 身分; kaikyū 階級; (property) zaisan 財産

estimate *v.* (calculate approximately) mitsumoru 見積る; (evaluate) hyōka suru 評価する

eternal *adj.* eikyū no 永久の; eien no 永遠の

Europe *n.* Yōroppa ヨーロッパ

evaporate *v.* jōhatsu suru 蒸発する

eve *n.* zen'ya 前夜; zenjitsu 前日

even *adj.* (flat) taira na 平らな; (level) suihei no 水平の; (equal in degree) dōtō no 同等の; (cf. odd) gūsū no 偶数の —— *adv.* ...de saemo ...でさえも; ...sura ...すら *even if* [*though*] tatoe...demo たとえ...でも —— *v.* taira ni suru 平らにする

evening *n.* yūgata 夕方; ban 晩

event *n.* jiken 事件; dekigoto 出来事 *at all events* dōshitemo どうしても; tonikaku とにかく

eventual *adj.* (final) kekkyoku no 結局の

ever *adv.* katsute かつて; (always) itsumo いつも *ever since* irai 以来; sono go zutto その後ずっと *ever so* hijō ni 非常に; don'na ni...demo どんなに...でも

every *adj.* (each without exception) subete no すべての; (each) sore-zore no それぞれの; ...goto ...ごと *every day* mainichi (no) 毎日(の) *every month* maitsuki 毎月 *every week* maishū 毎週 *every other day* ichi-nichi oki ni 一日おきに; kakujitsu ni 隔日に

everybody *pron.* daredemo (mina) だれでも (みな)

everything *pron.* banji 万事; subete no mono すべての物

everywhere *adv.* doko ni demo どこにでも; itaru tokoro ni いたる所に

evidence *n.* shōko 証拠; keiseki 形跡

evident *adj.* akiraka na 明らかな; meihaku na 明白な

evil *adj.* (bad) warui 悪い; (wicked) yokoshima na よこしまな

evolution *n.* shinka 進化; hatten 発展

exact *adj.* (accurate) seikaku na 正確な; (strict) genkaku na 厳格な

exaggerate *v.* kochō suru 誇張する

examination *n.* shiken 試験; kensa 検査; kentō 検討

examine *v.* shiken suru 試験する; kentō suru 検討する

example *n.* rei 例; jitsurei 実例; mihon 見本

exceed *v.* masaru 勝る; koeru こえる

excellent *adj.* sugureta すぐれた

except *prep.* nozoite 除いて; no hoka wa の外は —— *v.* nozoku 除く

exception *n.* reigai 例外

excess *n., adj.* yobun (no) 余分(の); kado (no) 過度 (の); chōka 超過 —— *v.* chōka suru 超過する

exchange *v.* torikaeru 取りかえる; kōkan suru 交換する; (change) ryōgae suru 両替する —— *n.* kōkan 交換; (bill of exchange) kawase 為替; ryōgae 両替

excite *v.* kōfun saseru 興奮させる; shigeki suru 刺激する

excitement *n.* shigeki 刺激; kōfun 興奮

exclaim *v.* (cry out) sakebu 叫ぶ

exclude *v.* (shut out) shimedasu しめ出す; (cf. include) jogai suru 除外する

exclusive *adj.* haita-teki na 排他的な; dokusen-

teki na 独占的な

excuse *v.* (forgive) yurusu 許す; kamben suru かんべんする; (make an excuse) …no iiwake o suru …の言い訳をする; benkai o suru 弁解をする

Excuse me. Gomen nasai. ごめんなさい; Shitsurei desu ga. 失礼ですが

execute *v.* (carry out) jikkō suru 実行する; hatasu 果たす

executive *adj.* jikkō no 実行の; jikkōryoku no aru 実行力のある —— *n.* (one having administrative authority in an organization) keiei-sha 経営者; (branch of government) gyōsei-bu 行政部

exercise *n.* undō 運動; taisō 体操; kunren 訓練; renshū 練習 —— *v.* undō suru 運動する; (train) renshū suru 練習する

exert *v.* (use) hatarakaseru 働かせる; mochiiru 用いる

exhaust *v.* (empty) kara ni suru 空にする; (use up) tsukai-tsukusu 使い尽す; (tire out) shōmō suru 消耗する; tsukare-hateru 疲れ果てる

exhibit *v.* (show) shimesu 示す; (display) tenji suru 展示する; shuppin suru 出品する

exhibition *n.* hakuran-kai 博覧会; tenran-kai 展覧会; tenji-kai 展示会

exist *v.* sonzai suru 存在する; jitsuzai suru 実在する; seizon suru 生存する; aru ある

exit *n.* (way out) deguchi 出口; (act of going out) taijō 退場

expand *vt.* (dilate) fukuramaseru ふくらませる; (spread out) hirogeru 広げる; (develop) hatten saseru 発展させる —— *vi.* fukuramu ふくらむ; hirogaru 広がる

expect *v.* yoki suru 予期する; (look forward to) kitai suru 期待する; (think) omou 思う

expedition *n.* ensei 遠征; tanken(-tai) 探険(隊)

expel *v.* (turn out) oidasu 追い出す; tsuihō suru 追放する; hassha suru 発射する

expense *n*. (outlay) shuppi 出費; (cost) hiyō 費用; (sacrifice) sonshitsu 損失
  at the expense of ...no hiyō de ...の費用で; ...o gisei ni shite ...を犠牲にして

expensive *adj*. hiyō no kakaru 費用のかかる; (nedan ga) takai (値段が) 高い; kōka na 高価な

experience *n*. keiken 経験; taiken 体験 —— *v*. (undergo) keiken suru 経験する; (meet with) sōgū suru 遭遇する

experiment *n*. jikken 実験; shiken 試験; kokoromi 試み

expert *n*. ekisupāto エキスパート; semmon-ka 専門家

expire *v*. (come to an end) owaru 終わる; (terminate) manki ni naru 満期になる; (die) shinu 死ぬ; (breathe out) iki o haku 息を吐く

explain *v*. setsumei suru 説明する

explode *v*. bakuhatsu suru 爆発する; haretsu suru 破裂する

explore *v*. tanken suru 探険する; chōsa suru 調査する

export *n., v.* yushutsu (suru) 輸出(する)

expose *v*. (sun) hi ni ateru 日にあてる; (subject to light) (hi ni) sarasu (日に) さらす; (reveal) abaku あばく

exposure *n*. (*photo*) roshutsu 露出; (display) chinretsu 陳列

express *v*. happyō suru 発表する; hyōgen suru 表現する; (utter) noberu 述べる —— *adj*. (specific) tokubetsu no 特別の; (clear) meihaku na 明白な; (urgent) shikyū no 至急の —— *n*. (express train) kyūkō ressha 急行列車

expression *n*. hyōgen 表現; happyō 発表

exquisite *adj*. (delicately beautiful) hijō ni utsukushii 非常に美しい; (elaborate) seikō na 精巧な

extend *vt*. (stretch out) hirogeru 広げる; (stretch forth) nobasu のばす —— *vi*. hirogaru 広が

る; nobiru のびる

extent n. (area) hirosa 広さ; ōkisa 大きさ; (scope) han'i 範囲; (degree) teido 程度

exterior n., adj. gaibu (no) 外部(の)

external adj. gaimen no 外面の ―― n. gaibu 外部; gaikan 外観

extinguish v. (put out) kesu 消す; (annihilate) zetsumetsu suru 絶滅する
　　extinguisher shōkaki 消火器

extra adj. (additional) yobun no 余分の; (special) tokubetsu no 特別の

extract v. (pull out) nukitoru 抜き取る; shiboridasu しぼり出す; (pick out) bassui suru 抜粋する ―― n. bassui 抜粋; (essence) ekisu エキス

extraordinary adj. (unusual) ijō na 異常な; hijō na 非常な

extreme adj. kyokutan na 極端な; kyokudo no 極度の

eye n. me 目

eyebrow n. mayu(ge) まゆ(毛)
　　eyebrow pencil mayuzumi まゆ墨

eyedrops (= eye lotion) n. megusuri 目薬

eyelash n. matsuge まつげ

eyelid n. mabuta まぶた

eyesight n. shiryoku 視力; shikai 視界

F

fable n. otogi-banashi おとぎ話; gūwa 寓話

fabric n. (textile) orimono 織物

face n. kao 顔; kaotsuki 顔つき; (surface) hyōmen 表面 ―― v. (front on) ...ni men suru ...に面する *face to face* mukaiatte 向かい合って *face powder* oshiroi おしろい

facility n. (easiness) yōi 容易; (dexterity) takumi 巧み; pl. (convenience) bengi 便宜; (equipment) setsubi 設備

fact *n.* jijitsu 事実；shinjitsu 真実
  in fact jissai wa 実際は；jitsu ni 実に

faction *n.* (party) tōha 党派；(clique) (shō-)haba-tsu (小)派閥

factor *n.* yōso 要素；yōin 要因

factory *n.* kōjō 工場

faculty *n.* (ability) sainō 才能；nōryoku 能力；
  (division of learning at a university) gakubu 学部；(instructors within such a division) (ga-kubu-)kyōju-dan (学部)教授団

fade *v.* (lose color) iro ga sameru 色がさめる；
  (dim) hikari ga usureru 光が薄れる；(disappear gradually) shidai ni kiete iku しだいに消えていく

Fahrenheit *n.* kashi 華氏

fail *v.* shippai suru 失敗する；shisokonau し損なう；fusoku suru 不足する

failure *n.* shippai 失敗

faint *adj.* (feeble) yowa-yowa-shii 弱々しい；
  suijaku shita 衰弱した；(slight) kasuka na かすかな —— *v.* (swoon) kizetsu suru 気絶する；(become weak) yowaku naru 弱くなる

fair *adj.* (beautiful) utsukushii 美しい；(fine) hareta 晴れた；(just) kōhei na 公平な —— *n.* (exhibition) hakuran-kai 博覧会

fairy *n., adj.* yōsei (no yōna) よう精(のような)

faith *n.* (reliance) shinrai 信頼；shin'nen 信念；(re-ligious belief) shinkō 信仰；(fidelity) chūjitsu 忠実

faithful *adj.* chūjitsu na 忠実な

fall *v.* (drop) ochiru 落ちる；(cf. stand) taoreru 倒れる；sagaru 下がる —— *n.* (drop) rakka 落下；(decline) metsubō 滅亡；(autumn) aki 秋
  fall ill byōki ni naru 病気になる
  fall on (attack) kōgeki suru 攻撃する；(begin) ...o hajimeru ...を始める

false *adj.* (erroneous) ayamatta あやまった；(un-true) itsuwari no 偽りの；(counterfeit) nise no 偽の *false eyelashes* tsuke-matsuge つけまつ

げ **false teeth** ireba 入れ歯

fame n. meisei 名声; meiyo 名誉

familiar adj. (intimate) shitashii 親しい; shimmitsu na 親密な; (closely acquainted) yoku shitte
iru よく知っている

family n. kazoku 家族; ikka 一家

famine n. kiga 飢餓; ue 飢え

famous adj. yūmei na 有名な; nadakai 名高い

fan n. ōgi 扇; sensu 扇子; (ardent admirer) fan
ファン

fancy n. (unfounded belief) kūsō 空想; (capricious idea) kimagure 気まぐれ; (taste) shumi
趣味 ——— v. (imagine) kūsō suru 空想する;
(think) omou 思う; (like) konomu 好む

fantastic adj. (capricious) kimagure na 気まぐれ
な; (eccentric) fūgawari na 風変りな; (imaginary) gensō-teki na 幻想的な

fantasy n. (imagination) kūsō 空想; (illusion)
gensō 幻想

far adv. tōku (ni) 遠く(に); haruka na はるか
な

fare n. (transportation charge) unchin 運賃;
(food) inshokubutsu 飲食物 ——— v. (get on)
kurasu 暮らす; yatte iku やって行く; (go) iku
行く

farewell int. sayōnara さようなら; gokigen'yō
ごきげんよう ——— n. (leave-taking) wakare
別れ; itomagoi いとまごい

farewell meeting sōbetsu-kai 送別会

farewell present sembetsu せん別

farm n. nōjō 農場; nōen 農園; hatake 畑

farther adv. motto tōi もっと遠い; mukō ni
[no] 向こうに[の]

fascinate v. miwaku suru 魅惑する

fashion n. ryūkō 流行; fasshon ファッション;
(style) kata 型

fast adj. hayai 速い; (watch) (tokei ga) susunde
iru (時計が)進んでいる ——— adv. hayaku
速く ——— n., v. danjiki (suru) 断食(する)

fasten *v.* (attach securely) shikkari tomeru しっかり止める; (make secure) shimeru 締める

fat *adj.* (obese) futotta 太った —— *n.* (grease) shibō 脂肪; aburami 脂身

fatal *adj.* (fateful) ummei no 運命の; (deadly) chimei-teki na 致命的な

fate *n.* shukumei 宿命; (destruction) hametsu 破滅; (death) shi 死 —— *v.* ummei-zukeru 運命づける

father *n.* (male parent) chichi 父; (male ancester) senzo 先祖; (priest) shimpu 神父

fatigue *n.*, *v.* hirō(saseru) 疲労(させる); tsukare (saseru) 疲れ(させる)

fault *n.* (error) kashitsu 過失; (mistake) ayamari あやまり; (defect) ketten 欠点

favor *n.* (goodwill) kōi 好意; (good graces) onkei 恩恵; hikitate 引き立て
ask a favor of (a person) (hito ni) sewa o tanomu (人に) 世話を頼む; onegai o suru お願いをする
in favor of ...ni sansei shite ...に賛成して

favorable *adj.* (well-disposed) kōi aru 好意ある; (convenient) tsugō no yoi 都合のよい; (advantageous) yūri na 有利な

favorite *adj.* (preferred above others) ki-ni-iri no 気に入りの —— *n.* (preference) kōbutsu 好物

fear *n.* (dread) kyōfu 恐怖; (anxiety) fuan 不安; shimpai 心配

feast *n.* (banquet) shukuen 祝宴; enkai 宴会; (religious festival) matsuri 祭り; shukusai-jitsu 祝祭日

feat *n.* (achievement) kōseki 功績; (trick) hayawaza 早業

feather *n.* hane 羽

feature *n.* (face) kao 顔; mehanadachi 目鼻立ち; (distinguished characteristic) tokuchō 特徴; tokushoku 特色

February *n.* ni-gatsu 二月

fee *n.* (remuneration) tesūryō 手数料; (admission)

nyūjō-ryō 入場料

feeble *adj.* yowai 弱い; byōjaku na 病弱な

feed *v.* (give food to) shokumotsu o ataeru 食物を与える; (make grow) sodateru 育てる; (nourish) yashinau 養う; kau 飼う —— *n.* (food for animals) esa えさ; (food) shokumotsu 食物

feel *v.* (perceive) kanjiru 感じる; (touch) sawaru さわる —— *n.* kanji 感じ; tezawari 手ざわり

feeling *n.* kankaku 感覚; kanji 感じ; kimochi 気持; kanjō 感情

fellow *n.* (companion) nakama 仲間; (man) otoko 男; (*colloq.*) yatsu やつ

felt *n.* feruto フェルト; mōsen 毛せん

female *n., adj.* josei(no) 女性(の); (*animal*) mesu(no) 雌(の)

feminine *adj.* josei no 女性の; josei-teki na 女性的な; on'na rashii 女らしい

fence *n.* kaki 垣; saku さく; hei へい

fern *n.* shida (-rui) しだ(類)

ferry *n.* watashi-bune 渡し(船); renraku-sen 連絡船; ferī フェリー

fertile *adj.* hiyoku na 肥よくな

festival *n.* matsuri 祭り; saijitsu 祭日

fetch *v.* itte motte[tsurete] kuru 行って持って[連れて]来る

fever *n.* netsu 熱; netsubō 熱望

few *adj.* sukunai 少ない; shōsū no 少数の —— *n.* shōsū no hito [mono] 少数の人 [物]

fiber *n.* sen'i 繊維

fiction *n.* shōsetsu 小説; tsukuri-banashi 作り話

field *n.* (open country) nohara 野原; (piece of arable land) hatake 畑; (battlefield) senjō 戦場

fierce *adj.* hageshii 激しい; mōretsu na 猛烈な

fifteen *n., adj.* jūgo(no) 15, 十五(の)

fifth *n., adj.* dai-go(no) 第五(の)

fifty *n., adj.* go-jū (no) 50, 五十(の)

fig *n.* ichijiku いちじく

fight *n.* (battle) sentō 戦闘; (combat) kakutō

figure 88

格闘; (fighting spirit) tōshi 闘志 —— *v.* (contend with) tatakau 戦う

figure *n.* (form) katachi 形; (bodily shape) sugata 姿; (person) jimbutsu 人物; (number) sūji 数字

file *n.* fairu ファイル; kami-basami 紙ばさみ

fill *v.* (make full) mitasu 満たす; ippai ni suru いっぱいにする; (occupy) ..o shimeru ...を占める —— *n.* (full supply) jūbun 十分

film *n.* firumu フィルム

filter *n.* roka-ki ろ過器; firutā フィルター

final *adj.* (last) saigo no 最後の; (decisive) kettei-teki na 決定的な

finance *n.* zaisei 財政; zaisei-gaku 財政学

find *v.* mitsukeru 見付ける; miidasu 見出す; ...to wakaru ...とわかる

fine *n.* (excellent) rippa na 立派な; (handsome) utsukushii 美しい; (of superior quality) sugureta すぐれた; (cloudless) hareta 晴れた —— *n.* (penalty) bakkin 罰金

finger *n.* yubi 指 *fingerprint* shimon 指紋

finish *v.* oeru 終える; sumasu すます; kansei suru 完成する

fir *n.* momi no ki もみの木

fire *n.* hi 火; taki-bi たき火

fire alarm *n.* kasai keihō 火災警報; kasai hōchi-ki 火災報知器

fire department *n.* shōbō-sho 消防署

fire engine *n.* shōbō-sha 消防車

firefly *n.* hotaru ほたる

fireman *n.* shōbōshi 消防士

fireplace *n.* danro 暖炉

fireworks *n.* hanabi 花火

firm *adj.* (solid) shikkari shita しっかりした; katai 固い —— *n.* (business company) shōsha 商社; kaisha 会社

first *adj.* dai-ichi no 第一の; saisho no 最初の *first name* namae 名前 *for the first time* hajimete 初めて

first aid *n.* ōkyū teate 応急手当

fish *n*. sakana 魚; uo 魚 ——*n*., *v*. tsuri (o suru) 釣り(をする)

fisherman *n*. ryōshi 漁師; gyofu 漁夫

fist *n*. kobushi こぶし; genkotsu げんこつ

fit *adj*. ni tekitō na に適当な ——*v*. au 合う; niau 似合う ——*n*. (spasm) hossa 発作

five *n*., *adj*. go (no) 5, 五(の); itsutsu (no) 五つ (の)

fix *v*. (make firm) kotei saseru 固定させる; (fasten) toritsukeru 取り付ける; (determine) kimeru 決める; (put in order) seiton suru 整とんする

flag *n*. hata 旗; (national flag) kokki 国旗

flake *n*. (flat thin piece) hakuhen 薄片; ippen 一片

flame *n*. hono'o 炎; kaen 火炎; (passion) jōnetsu 情熱

flap *v*. (slap) karuku utsu 軽く打つ; (motion of wing) habataki suru はばたきする

flare *n*. yurameku hono'o ゆらめく炎; (*skirt*) fureā フレアー ——*v*. mera-mera moeru めらめら燃える

flash *n*. senkō 閃光; hirameki ひらめき; (flashlight) kaichū-dentō 懐中電灯

flat *adj*. (level and smooth) hiratai 平たい; taira na 平らな ——*n*. heimen 平面
flat tire panku パンク

flatter *v*. oseji o iu おせじを言う; kobi-hetsurau こびへつらう

flavor *n*. fūmi 風味; aji 味 ——*v*. ...ni fūmi o tsukeru ...に風味をつける

fleet *n*. kantai 艦隊; sentai 船隊

flesh *n*. niku 肉; nikutai 肉体; mi 身

flexible *adj*. (pliant) mageyasui 曲げやすい; shinayaka na しなやかな; (adaptable) yūzū no kiku 融通のきく

flicker *v*. (quiver) soyogu そよぐ; yurameku ゆらめく; (flash and die away by turns) chirachira suru ちらちらする

flight *n.* hikō 飛行; (run away) tōsō 逃走

flint *n.* (*for lighter*) ishi 石

flip *v.* (fillip) hajiku はじく; (strike lightly) karuku utsu 軽く打つ

float *v.* (get afloat) uku 浮く; (set afloat) ukaberu 浮かべる

flock *n.* (herd) mure 群れ; (crowd) gunshū 群集 —— *v.* muragaru 群がる

flood *n.* kōzui 洪水; ōmizu 大水 —— *v.* (overflow) hanran suru はんらんする

floor *n.* (lower surface of a room) yuka 床; (story) kai 階

florist *n.* hana-ya 花屋

flour *n.* (fine meal) kona 粉; (wheat meal) komugiko 小麦粉

flourish *v.* (thrive) sakaeru 栄える; hanjō suru 繁盛する; (grow vigorously) shigeru 茂る

flow *n.* (stream) nagare 流れ; (rise of tide) ageshio 上げ潮 —— *v.* nagareru 流れる

flower *n.* hana 花 *flower arranging* ikebana 生け花

flu *n.* infuruenza インフルエンザ; ryūkan 流感

fluid *n.* ekitai 液体 —— *adj.* ryūdōsei no 流動性の

flush *v.* (dotto) nagareru (どっと) 流れる; (be flooded) mizubitashi ni naru 水浸しになる; (blush) kao ga akaku naru 顔が赤くなる —— *n.* (vigor) genki 元気 —— *adj.* (abundant) hōfu na 豊富な

flute *n.* furūto フルート; yokobue 横笛

flutter *v.* (flap with the wings) habataki suru はばたきする

fly[1] *v.* tobu 飛ぶ; (flee from) nigeru 逃げる

fly[2] *n.* (*insect*) hae はえ

foam *n., v.* awa (datsu) 泡(立つ)

focus *n.* shōten 焦点; (center) chūshin 中心 —— *v.* (concentrate) shūchū suru 集中する

fog *n.* kiri 霧; moya もや

foil *n.* haku はく; (*cooking*) kukkingu-foiru ク

ッキングフォイル

fold *v.* (double up) orikasaneru 折り重ねる；tatamu たたむ ——*n.* (*in garment*) hida ひだ
folding chair oritatami-isu 折りたたみいす

folk *n.* (people) hitobito 人々；(nation) minzoku 民族 *folk song* min'yō 民謡

follow *v.* ...ni tsuzuku ...に続く；ni shitagau に従う；ni tsuite iku について行く

following *adj.* tsugi no 次の；ika no 以下の

fond *adj.* (liking) sukide 好きで；(tender) yas·· 優しい

food *n.* tabemono 食べ物；shokumotsu 食物
food poisoning shokuchūdoku 食中毒

fool *n.* baka ばか；(clown) dōkemono 道化者 ——*v.* baka ni suru ばかにする

foot *n.* ashi 足；(bottom) fumoto ふもと；soko 底
on foot aruite 歩いて
at the foot of no fumoto ni のふもとに

footprint *n.* ashi-ato 足跡

footstep *n.* ayumi 歩み；(tread) ashi-oto 足音；

for *prep.* (on behalf of) no tame ni のために；
(against) ni mukatte に向って；(*time*) no aida の間；(in place of) no kawari ni の代りに
——*conj.* (because) to iu nowa というのは；
no riyū de の理由で
for all nimo kakawarazu にもかかわらず
for ever eien ni 永遠に；eikyū ni 永久に
for example tatoeba たとえば
for oneself jibun de 自分で；dokuryoku de 独力で
for one's age toshi no wari ni 年のわりに

forbid *v.* (prohibit) kinjiru 禁じる；(prevent) samatageru 妨げる

force *n.* (power) chikara 力；wanryoku 腕力；*pl.*
(troops) guntai 軍隊 ——*v.* (press) shi'iru 強いる

forceful *adj.* chikara-zuyoi 力強い；kyōryoku na 強力な

fore *adj.* mae no 前の；zempō no 前方の；saki no

先の

forecast *n., v.* yosō(suru) 予想(する); (predict) yohō(suru) 予報(する)

forefinger *n.* hitosashi-yubi 人差し指

forehead *n.* hitai ひたい

foreign *adj.* gaikoku no 外国の; gaijin no 外人の
　foreign language gaikokugo 外国語
　The Ministry of Foreign Affairs gaimu-shō 外務省

foreigner *n.* gaikokujin 外国人

forest *n.* mori 森; shinrin 森林

forget *v.* (not remember) wasureru 忘れる; (mislay) okiwasureru 置き忘れる

forgive *v.* yurusu 許す; menjo suru 免除する

fork *n.* fōku フォーク

form *n.* (shape) katachi 形; (figure of body) sugata 姿; (mode) keishiki 形式; (formula) shoshiki 書式 ——— *v.* katachizukuru 形づくる

formal *adj.* (regular) seishiki no 正式の; (of the nature of form) keishiki-teki na 形式的な

former *adj.* (earlier) izen no 以前の; mukashi no 昔の; (previous) zensha no 前者の; saki no 先の

formerly *adv.* mukashi 昔; izen 以前

formidable *adj.* (terrifying) osoroshii 恐ろしい; (hard to overcome) tegowai 手ごわい

formula *n.* kōshiki 公式; shiki 式

formulate *v.* kōshiki ni suru 公式にする

forth *adv.* mae e 前へ; zempō e 前方へ; soto e 外へ

fortnight *n.* ni-shūkan 2週間 ——— *adv.* kakushū no[ni] 隔週の[に]

fortunate *adj.* (lucky) kōun na 幸運な; un no yoi 運のよい

fortune *n.* (good luck) un 運; kōun 幸運

forty *n., adj.* yon-jū(no) 40, 四十-(の)

forward *adv.* mae ni 前に; kongo 今後; saki ni 先に ——— *adj.* zempō no 前方の

foul *adj.* (dirty) fuketsu na 不潔な; kitanai 汚い; (vulgar) hiwai na 卑わいな ——— *adv.* (unfairly) fusei ni 不正に

found v. sōritsu suru 創立する; kisozukeru 基礎
づける

foundation n. (base) dodai 土台; kiso 基礎; (establishment) kensetsu 建設; (fund) kikin 基金

fountain n. izumi 泉; (jet of water) funsui 噴水

four n., adj. yon 4; yottsu (no) 四つ (の); shi 4

fourteen n., adj. jū-shi(no) 14, 十四(の)

fowl n. niwatori にわとり; pl. kakin 家きん

fox n. kitsune きつね

fraction n. bunsū 分数; hasū 端数; (fragment) kakera かけら

fracture n., v. kossetsu (suru) 骨折 (する); funsai
suru 粉砕する —— v. kujiku くじく

fragment n. hahen 破片; dampen 断片; kakera
かけら

fragrance n. kaori 香り; kōki 香気; hōkō 芳香

frail adj. yowai 弱い; hakanai はかない

frame n. (construction) kōzō 構造; honegumi 骨
組み; waku わく; (picture) gakubuchi 額縁

frank adj. sotchoku na 卒直な; shōjiki na 正直
な

free adj. jiyū na 自由な —— adv. jiyū ni 自由
に

freeze v. kōru 凍る; kōri ga haru 氷が張る; hieru 冷える

freight n. (transportation) yusō 輸送; (transported
goods) kamotsu 貨物; (charge for transporting
goods) unchin 運賃

French adj. Furansu(-jin) no フランス(人)の
—— n. Furansu-go フランス語; Furansu-jin フ
ランス人

frequent adj. tabi-tabi no 度々の; shiba-shiba
okoru しばしば起こる; himpan na ひんぱんな

fresh adj. (new) atarashii 新しい; (not stale)
shinsen na 新鮮な; (raw) nama no 生の; (vivid)
sōkai na そう快な

Friday n. kin'yō-bi 金曜日

friend n. yūjin 友人; tomodachi 友だち

fright *n.* odoroki 驚き；(terror) kyōfu 恐怖

fringe *n.* fusaberi 房べり；fuchi 縁

frock *n.* (gown or dress) uwagi 上着；(frock-coat) furokku-kōto フロックコート

frog *n.* kaeru かえる

from *prep.* kara から；de で
from door to door ie kara ie e to 家から家へと
from place to place achi-kochi あちこち
from time to time tokidoki 時々

front *n.* mae 前；zempō 前方；shōmen 正面
in front of no mae ni の前に ──*v.* ni men suru に面する

front door *n.* toguchi 戸口；genkan 玄関

frontier *n.* kokkyō 国境

frost *n.* shimo 霜

frown *v.* mayu o hisomeru 眉をひそめる；kao o shikameru 顔をしかめる ──*n.* shikamet-tsura しかめっ面；shibui-kao 渋い顔

frozen food *n.* reitō-shokuhin 冷凍食品

fruit *n.* kudamono 果物

fry *v.* abura de ageru 油で揚げる；furai ni suru フライにする

fuel *n.* nenryō 燃料 *fuel oil* tōyu 灯油

fulfill *v.* (complete) hatasu 果たす；togeru 遂げる；(satisfy) mitasu 満たす

full *adj.* (filled) michite iru 満ちている；ippai no いっぱいの；(complete) kanzen na 完全な ──*n.* jūbun 十分；ippai いっぱい ──*adv.* jūbun ni 十分に

fun *n.* tawamure たわむれ；nagusami なぐさみ

function *n.* kinō 機能；hataraki はたらき；(office) yakume 役目；(duty) nimmu 任務

fund *n.* shikin 資金；kikin 基金；*pl.* zaigen 財源

fundamental *adj.* kompon no 根本の；kiso no 基礎の

funeral *n., adj.* sōshiki (no) 葬式 (の)

funny *adj.* okashii おかしい；omoshiroi 面白い

fur *n.* kegawa (seihin) 毛皮 (製品)

furious *adj.* mōretsu na 猛烈な；ikari kurutta 怒

り狂った

furnish *v.* (provide) sonae tsukeru 備え付ける；
(supply) kyōkyū suru 供給する

furniture *n.* kagu 家具

further *adv.* sara ni さらに；sono ue ni その上に

fury *n.* (rage) gekidō 激動；(violence) mōretsu 猛
烈

fuse *n.* hyūzu ヒューズ；dōkasen 導火線

future *n., adj.* mirai (no) 未来 (の)；shōrai (no)
将来 (の)
　in the future kongo 今後；kore-kara これから

G

gain *v.* (get) te ni ireru 手に入れる；(win) katsu
勝つ；(*watch*) (tokei ga) susumu (時計が) 進む；
(profit) mōkeru もうける ―― *n.* (profit) rieki
利益；(increase) zōka 増加

gallery *n.* (place for art exhibits) garō 画廊；gya-
rarī ギャラリー；(corridor) horō 歩廊；kairō
回廊；(*theater*) tenjō-sajiki 天井さじき

gallon *n.* garon ガロン

gallop *n.* gyaroppu ギャロップ；shissō 疾走
　―― *v.* hayaku hashiru はやく走る

gamble *n., v.* gyamburu(o suru) ギャンブル(を
する)；tobaku(o suru) とばく(をする)；baku-
chi(o suru) ばくち(をする)

game *n.* gēmu ゲーム；kyōgi 競技；shiai 試合

gap *n.* (break) wareme 割れ目；(opening) sukima
すきま；(blank space) kūhaku 空白

garage *n.* garēji ガレージ

garbage *n.* (waste parts of food) nama-gomi
生ごみ　*garbage bag* gomi-bukuro ごみ袋

garden *n.* niwa 庭；teien 庭園

gardener *n.* ueki-ya 植木屋

gardening *n.* engei 園芸

gargle *n., v.* ugai (o suru) うがい (をする)

garlic *n.* nin'niku にんにく

garment *n.* irui 衣類; *pl.* kimono 着物; ishō 衣装

garter *n.* kutsushita-dome 靴下どめ; gātā ガーター; (the G-) gātā kunshō ガーター勲章

gas *n.* gasu ガス; (gasoline) gasorin ガソリン
gas station gasorin-sutando ガソリンスタンド

gasoline *n.* gasorin ガソリン

gasp *v.* aegu あえぐ; iki o kirasu 息を切らす

gate *n.* mon 門; deiriguchi 出入口

gather *vt.* (bring together) atsumeru 集める —— *vi.* (come together) atsumaru 集まる

gauge *n.* hyōjun sumpō 標準寸法; (device for measuring) keiki 計器 —— *v.* (measure) hakaru はかる; (estimate) hyōka suru 評価する

gay *adj.* kaikatsu na 快活な; yōki na 陽気な

gaze *v.* mitsumeru 見詰める —— *n.* chūshi 注視; gyōshi 凝視

gear *n.* haguruma 歯車; giya ギヤ

gem *n.* hōseki 宝石

general *adj.* ippan no 一般の; zentai no 全体の —— *n.* (high-ranking army officer) rikugun taishō 陸軍大将
in general ippan ni 一般に; futsū 普通

generation *n.* ichi-dai 一代; issedai 一世代

generous *n.* kedakai 気高い; kandai na 寛大な

genius *n.* tensai 天才

gentle *adj.* (mild) onwa na 温和な; yasashii 優しい; (kindly) shinsetsu na 親切な

gentleman *n.* shinshi 紳士; otoko 男

genuine *adj.* hommono no 本物の; hontō no 本当の

geography *n.* chiri (-gaku) 地理 (学)

germ *n.* saikin 細菌; baikin ばい菌

German *n., adj.* Doitsu (no) ドイツ (の); Doitsu-jin (no) ドイツ人 (の); Doitsu-go (no) ドイツ語 (の)

gesture *n.* miburi 身ぶり; jesuchā ジェスチャー; temane 手まね

get *v.* (earn) uru 得る; (receive) uketoru 受け取

る；(buy) kau 買う；(bring) motte kuru 持って来る；(catch) byōki ni kakaru 病気にかかる

get about aruki-mawaru 歩き回る

get along susumu 進む；(manage) umaku yatte iku うまくやって行く

get away nigeru 逃げる

get home uchi ni kaeru うちに帰る

get over (recover from) kaifuku suru 回復する

get through (finish) shūryō suru 終了する；shitogeru しとげる；(survive) ikinagaraeru 生きながらえる

get together (assemble) atsumeru 集める；atsumaru 集まる；(reach an agreement) (iken ga) itchi suru (意見が) 一致する

get up (rise) okiru 起きる；kishō suru 起床する

ghost *n.* yūrei 幽霊；bōrei 亡霊；bakemono 化け物

giant *n.* kyojin 巨人；ō-otoko 大男 ——*adj.* kyodai na 巨大な

gift *n.* okurimono 贈り物；gifuto ギフト；(o-) miyage (お) みやげ

gigantic *adj.* kyodai na 巨大な

gild *v.* kimmekki suru 金めっきする

ginger *n.* shōga しょうが

giraffe *n.* kirin キリン

girdle *n.* obi 帯；gādoru ガードル

girl *n.* shōjo 少女；on'na no ko 女の子；musume 娘

give *v.* ageru あげる；ataeru 与える

give off hanatsu 放つ；dasu 出す

give out happyō suru 発表する；haifu suru 配布する

give up yameru 止める；akirameru あきらめる

give way shirizoku 退く；kuzureru 崩れる

glacier *n.* hyōga 氷河

glad *adj.* yorokonde 喜んで；ureshii 嬉しい；yorokobashii 喜ばしい

glance *v.* (look briefly) chirari to miru ちらりと見る；hitome miru 一目見る；(glint) hirameku

ひらめく ──*n.* (quick look) ikken 一見；
(flash) senkō せん光

glare *v.* (shine with a dazzling light) gira-gira
hikaru ぎらぎら光る；(stare fiercely) niramitsu-
keru にらみつける ──*n.* (blinding light)
mabushii hikari まぶしい光；(fierce stare) nira-
mi にらみ

glass *n.* garasu ガラス；koppu コップ；(mirror)
kagami 鏡；*pl.* (spectacles) megane めがね

glaze *v.* (fit with glass) garasu o hameru ガラス
をはめる；(coat with a glassy layer) uwagusuri
o kakeru 上薬をかける

gleam *n.* (faint glow) kasukana hikari かすかな
光；(flash) kirameki きらめき ──*v.* (glitter)
kirameku きらめく

glee *n.* ōyorokobi 大喜び；kanki 歓喜

glide *v.* suberu 滑る；kūchūkassō suru 空中滑走
する *glider* guraidā グライダー

glimmer *v.* chira-chira hikaru ちらちら光る

glimpse *n.* (momentary look) ikken 一見；
(glance) hitome 一目 ──*v.* chirari to miru
ちらりと見る

glisten *v.* kira-kira hikaru きらきら光る

glitter *v.* pika-pika [kira-kira] hikaru ぴかぴか
[きらきら]光る

globe *n.* (ball) kyū 球；(the earth) chikyū 地球；
(terrestrial globe) chikyūgi 地球儀；(heavenly
body) tentai 天体

gloom *n.* (partial darkness) usukuragari 薄暗
がり；(melancholy) yū'utsu 憂うつ；inki 陰気
──*v.* (grow dark) kuraku naru 暗くなる

glory *n.* (renown) homare ほまれ；(honor) eikō
栄光；kōei 光栄

glossary *n.* (list of technical or special words
with definitions) yōgo-kaisetsu 用語解説；
(dictionary of special words) yōgo-jiten 用語辞
典

glove *n.* tebukuro 手袋；gurōbu グローブ

glow *v.* (be incandescent) hakunetsu suru 白熱

する；(flush) hoteru ほてる

glue *n.* nikawa にかわ

go *v.* iku 行く；(turn out) ...ni naru ...になる
  go about aruki-mawaru 歩き回る
  go back on (*colloq.*) (break, as a promise)
  (yakusoku o) yaburu（約束を）破る
  go by (pass) (toki ga) keika suru（時が）経過
  する
  go on (continue) tsuzuku 続く
  go out (be extinguished) kieru 消える
  go over (examine) yoku shiraberu よく調べる；
  (do again) ...o kurikaesu ...を繰り返す
  go through (search) yoku ...o chōsa suru よく
  ...を調査する；(endure)...ni taeru ...に耐える
  go through with ...o saigo made yari togeru
  ...を最後までやり遂げる
  be going to ...shiyō to shiteiru ...しようとし
  ている

goal *n.* kesshōten 決勝点；gōru ゴール

goat *n.* yagi 山羊

god *n.* kami 神

goddess *n.* megami 女神

gold *n.* kin 金；kin-iro 金色；ōgon 黄金
  the golden age ōgon jidai 黄金時代

goldfish *n.* kingyo 金魚

golf *n.* gorufu ゴルフ

good *adj.* yoi 良い；zenryō na 善良な；jōtō na
  上等な；(right) tadashii 正しい；(kind) shinsetsu
  na 親切な —— *n.* (what is good) zen 善；
  (merchandise) shōhin 商品；(profit) rieki 利益

good-by(e) *int.* sayōnara さようなら —— *n.*
  itomagoi いとまごい

goose *n.* gachō が鳥

gorge *n.* (deep narrow ravine) kyōkoku 峡谷
  —— *v.* (eat greedily) gatsu-gatsu taberu がつ
  がつ食べる

gorgeous *adj.* karei na 華麗な；gōka na 豪華な

gossip *n.* goshippu ゴシップ；mudabanashi
  むだ話

govern *v.* osameru 治める; shihai suru 支配する

government *n.* seiji 政治; seifu 政府

gown *n.* gaun ガウン; uwagi 上着

grab *v.* (snatch suddenly) hittakuru ひったくる; tsukamu つかむ

grace *n.* (favor) megumi 恵み; onkei 恩恵; (elegance) yūbi 優美; shitoyakasa しとやかさ; jōhin 上品

grade *n.* tōkyū 等級; (*school*) gakunen 学年

gradual *adj.* dankai-teki na 段階的な; yuruyaka na 緩やかな
gradually shidai ni 次第に; jojo ni 徐々に

graduate *v.* sotsugyō suru 卒業する ——*n.* sotsugyōsei 卒業生

grain *n.* kokumotsu 穀物; tsubu 粒

grammar *n.* bumpō 文法

grand *adj.* sōdai na 壮大な; yūdai na 雄大な; dōdō taru 堂々たる

granddaughter *n.* mago-musume 孫娘

grandfather *n.* sofu 祖父; ojii-san おじいさん

grandmother *n.* sobo 祖母; obā-san おばあさん

grandson *n.* otoko no mago 男の孫

grant *v.* yurusu 許す; mitomeru 認める ——*n.* kyoka 許可

grape *n.* budō ぶどう

grasp *v.* (seize upon) shikkari tsukamu しっかりつかむ; (understand) rikai suru 理解する; wakaru 分かる ——*n.* (control) tōgyo 統御; (grip) tsuyoi nigiri 強い握り

grass *n.* kusa 草; shiba 芝

grateful *adj.* arigataku omou ありがたく思う; ureshii 嬉しい

gratify *v.* manzoku saseru 満足させる; yorokobaseru 喜ばせる

gratitude *n.* kansha (no kimochi) 感謝 (の気持)

grave¹ *adj.* (important) jūdai na 重大な; (solemn) majime na まじめな; (dignified) igen no aru 威厳のある

grave² *n.* (burial place) haka (ana) 墓 (穴)

gravel *n.* jari 砂利

gravity *n.* (terrestrial gravitation) jūryoku 重力; inryoku 引力; (importance) jūdaisa 重大さ

gravy *n.* gureibī グレイビー; nikujiru 肉汁

gray *n.* hai-iro 灰色; nezumi-iro ねずみ色; gurei グレイ

grease *n.* yushi 油脂; gurisu グリス

great *adj.* (big) ōkii 大きい; idai na 偉大な; (important) jūdai na 重大な

Greece *n.* Girisha ギリシャ

green *n., adj.* (grassy) midori-iro (no) 緑色 (の); (green vegetables) yasai 野菜
green pepper pīman ピーマン

greet *v.* aisatsu suru あいさつする; mukaeru 迎える

grief *n.* fukai kanashimi 深い悲しみ

grieve *vt.* kanashimaseru 悲しませる —— *vi.* nageku 嘆く

grill *n.* (gridiron) yakiami 焼き網; yakiniku 焼き肉; (grill-room) guriru グリル

grind *v.* (crush into bits) hiku ひく; kona ni suru 粉にする; (sharpen) togu 研ぐ

grip *v.* shikkari tsukamu しっかりつかむ —— *n.* nigiri 握り; gurippu グリップ

groan *n.* umeki-goe うめき声 —— *v.* umeku うめく; kurushimu 苦しむ

grocery *n.* shokuryōhin-ten 食料品店

groom *n.* hanamuko 花婿

groove *n., v.* mizo (o horu) 溝(を掘る)

gross *adj.* (big) ōkii 大きい; (coarse) somatsu na 粗末な; hidoi ひどい —— *n.* (twelve dozen) gurosu グロス; (gross sum) sōkei 総計

ground *n.* (land) tochi 土地; (surface of earth) jimen 地面; gurando グランド; *pl.* (cause or basis) riyū 理由; konkyo 根拠

group *n.* shūdan 集団; dantai 団体; gurūpu グループ

grove *n.* komori 小森; kodachi 木立ち

grow *v.* seichō suru 成長する; ōkiku naru 大き

くなる;...ni naru ...になる **grown-up** otona (no) 大人 (の); seijin (no) 成人 (の)

growl *n.* unari うなり —— *v.* unaru うなる; (complain) gami-gami iu がみがみ言う

growth *n.* (process of growing) seichō 成長; hatsuiku 発育; (development) hattatsu 発達

grumble *v.* (mutter) butsu-butsu iu ぶつぶつ言う; (complain) fuhei o iu 不平を言う —— *n.* tsu-buyaki つぶやき

guarantee *n., v.* hoshō (suru) 保証 (する); hoshō-nin 保証人

guard *n.* (watchman) ban'nin 番人; gādoman ガードマン —— *v.* (protect) mamoru 守る; (take precautions) yōjin suru 用心する

guess *v.* suiryō suru 推量する; kentō o tsukeru 見当をつける; (suppose) ...to omou ...と思う —— *n.* suisoku 推測

guest *n.* kyaku 客

guide *n.* an'naisha 案内者; gaido ガイド

guilt *n.* yūzai 有罪; tsumi 罪

guilty *adj.* tsumi no aru 罪のある; yūzai no 有罪の

gulf *n.* wan 湾

gulp *v.* hito-nomi ni suru ひとのみにする; gutto nomu ぐっと飲む

gum¹ *n.* gomu ゴム; (adhesive) gomunori ゴムのり)

gum² *n. pl.* (flesh around the teeth) haguki 歯茎

gun *n.* (rifle) teppō 鉄砲; jū 銃

gutter *n.* (eaves) toi とい; (small channel) komizo 小溝

guy *n.* otoko 男; yatsu やつ

gymnasium *n.* taiikukan 体育館; jimu ジム

gynecologist *n.* fujinka-i 婦人科医

H

habit *n.* shūkan 習慣; shūsei 習性
in the habit of ...suru kuse ga aru ...するくせ

がある；…shigachi de aru …しがちである

hail¹ *n.* arare あられ；hyō ひょう ―― *v.* arare ga furu あられが降る

hail² *n.* (greeting) aisatsu あいさつ；(shout of applause) kanko 歓呼 ―― *v.* (cheer) (kanko shite) mukaeru (歓呼して)迎える；(shout to) ōgoe de yobu 大声で呼ぶ

hair *n.* ke 毛；kami no ke 髪の毛

half *n.* hambun 半分；ni bun no ichi 2分の1 ―― *adj.* hambun no 半分の；nakaba no 半ばの *half an hour* han-jikan 半時間

halfway *adj.* nakaba no 半ばの；chūto no 中途の

hall *n.* kaikan 会館；ōhiroma 大広間；hōru ホール

halt *v.* tomaru 止まる；teishi suru 停止する；(rest) kyūsoku suru 休息する ―― *n.* kyūshi 休止；teishi 停止

ham *n.* hamu ハム

hammer *n.* kanazuchi 金づち；hammā ハンマー

hand *n.* te 手；(pointer on a clock) tokei no hari 時計の針；(penmanship) hisseki 筆跡

handicap *n.* handikyappu ハンディキャップ

handkerchief *n.* hankachi ハンカチ

handle *n.* handoru ハンドル；e 柄 ―― *v.* (deal with) toriatsukau 取り扱う

handsome *adj.* (good-looking) utsukushii 美しい；hansamu na ハンサムな；(fine) rippa na 立派な

handwriting *n.* hisseki 筆跡；shuseki 手跡

handy *adj.* chōhō na 重宝な；tegoro na 手ごろな

hang *v.* kakeru かける；tsurusu つるす

happen *v.* okoru 起る；tama-tama…suru たまたま…する

happy *adj.* kōfuku na 幸福な；shiawase na 幸せな；tanoshii 楽しい

harbor *n.* minato 港 ―― *v.* (give shelter to) kakumau かくまう

hard *adj.* (rigid) katai 固い；(difficult to do) muzukashii むずかしい；(severe) kibishii 厳しい ―― *adv.* (with energy) hageshiku 激しく；

isshōkemmei ni 一生けんめいに；(firmly) kataku 固く

harden *vt., vi.* (make or become hard) kataku suru [naru] 固くする[なる]

hardly *adv.* hotondo …de nai ほとんど … でない

hardly…when [*before*] …suru to hotondo dōji ni …するとほとんど同時に

hardship *n.* kon'nan 困難

hardware *n.* kanamono 金物

harm *n.* gai 害；shōgai 障害 —— *v.* gai suru 害する

harmful yūgai na 有害な

harmless mugai no 無害の

harmony *n.* chōwa 調和；itchi 一致

harness *n.* bagu 馬具 —— *v.* bagu o tsukeru 馬具をつける

harp *n.* tategoto たて琴；hāpu ハープ

harsh *adj.* (rough to touch) ara-ara-shii 荒々しい；(rough to the ear) mimi-zawari na 耳障りな；(severe) hidoi ひどい

harvest *n.* kari-ire 刈入れ；shūkaku 収穫

haste *n.* (hurry) isogi 急ぎ；awateru koto あわてること —— *v.* isogu 急ぐ

in haste isoide 急いで

hasten *vi.* isogu 急ぐ —— *vt.* isogaseru 急がせる

hat *n.* bōshi 帽子

hatch *v.* (bring or come forth from an egg) (tamago o) kaesu (卵を) かえす；(tamago ga) kaeru (卵が) かえる；(contrive) anshutsu suru 案出する —— *n.* (hatchway) hatchi ハッチ

hatchet *n.* teono 手おの；ono おの

hate *v.* nikumu 憎む；kirau きらう —— *n.* ken'o 嫌悪

haughty *adj.* ōhei na 横柄な；gōman na ごうまんな；kōman na 高慢な

haul *v.* hipparu ひっぱる；hikizuru ひきずる

have *v.* (possess, own, hold) motte iru 持ってい

る; ...ga aru ...がある; (eat) taberu 食べる;
(cause to be done) shite morau してもらう; saseru させる; (be wearing) kiteiru 着ている

have a good time tanoshiku sugosu 楽しく過ご
す

have got motsu 持つ

have to (be obliged) shinakereba naranai しな
ければならない

have ...to do with ...to kankei ga aru ...と
関係がある

hawk *n.* taka たか

hay *n.* hoshikusa 干し草; magusa まぐさ

hazard *n.* (danger) kiken 危険; (risk) bōken
冒険; (chance) un 運

he *pron.* kare ga 彼が; kare wa 彼は

head *n.* atama 頭; zunō 頭脳; (chief) chō 長

headache *n.* zutsū 頭痛

headline *n.* midashi 見出し

headmaster *n.* kōchō 校長

headquarters *n.* hombu 本部; shireibu 司令部

health *n.* kenkō 健康　*healthful* kenkō ni yoi
健康によい　*healthy* kenkō na 健康な; kenzen
na 健全な

heap *n.* (pile) tsumi-kasane 積み重ね; (mass) shūdan 集団 ──── *v.* tsumi-kasaneru 積み重ねる

hear *v.* kiku 聞く; kikoeru 聞える

hear about ...ni tsuite komakani kiku ...につ
いて細かに聞く

hear from ...kara tayori ga aru ...から便りが
ある

hear of ...no uwasa o kiku ...のうわさを聞く

heart *n.* shinzō 心臓; (mind) kokoro 心; (love)
ai 愛; (*figure*) hāto-gata ハート型

by heart sora de 空で; kioku de 記憶で

take to heart kokoro ni tomeru 心にとめる;
fukaku kanashimu 深く悲しむ

broken heart shitsuren 失恋

heat *n.* netsu 熱; atsusa 暑さ

heater hītā ヒーター; dambō sōchi 暖房装置

heave *v.* (lift) (omoi mono o) mochiageru (重い 物を）持ち上げる

heaven *n.* ten 天; sora 空; tengoku 天国; (god) kami 神

heavy *adj.* (weighing much) omoi 重い; (severe) hidoi ひどい

hedge *n.* ikegaki 生垣; kakine 垣根

heel *n.* kakato かかと

height *n.* takasa 高さ; *pl.* kōchi 高地; takadai 高台

heir *n.* sōzoku-nin 相続人

hell *n.* jigoku 地獄

hello *int.* moshi-moshi もしもし; yā やあ

helmet *n.* kabuto かぶと; herumetto ヘルメット

help *v.* tetsudau 手伝う; tasukeru 助ける

helpful *adj.* tasuke ni naru 助けになる; yaku ni tatsu 役に立つ

helpless *adj.* tayorinai 頼りない

hem *n.* heri へり —— *v.* fuchi o toru 縁をとる

hen *n.* mendori めんどり; mesudori 雌鳥

hence *adv.* (from now) ima-kara 今から; kongo 今後; (therefore) sore dakara それだから; (from here) koko-kara ここから

her *pron.* kanojo no 彼女の; kanojo ni [o] 彼女に［を］

herb *n.* kusa 草; (medical herb) yakusō 薬草

here *adv.* koko (e) ここ（へ）; koko (ni) ここ (に)

hereafter *adv.* kongo wa 今後は

hereby *adv.* kore ni yotte これによって

heritage *n.* isan 遺産; sōzoku-butsu 相続物

hero *n.* eiyū 英雄; yūshi 勇士; hīrō ヒーロー; shujinkō 主人公

heroine *n.* joketsu 女傑; on'na shujinkō 女主人公; hiroin ヒロイン

herring *n.* nishin にしん
　kippered herring kunsei nishin くん製にしん

hers *pron.* kanojo no mono 彼女のもの

herself *pron.* kanojo-jishin 彼女自身

hesitate *v.* chūcho suru ちゅうちょする；tamerau ためらう

hide[1] *vt.* kakusu 隠す ―― *vi.* kakureru 隠れる

hide[2] *n.* (animal skin or pelt) kemono no kawa けものの皮

hideous *adj.* (horrible) osoroshii おそろしい；nikumubeki 憎むべき

high *adj.* takai 高い；kōkyū no 高級の

highland *n.* kōchi 高地；kōgen-chihō 高原地方

highly *adv.* takaku 高く；(in high degree) kōdo ni 高度に；(very) ōini 大いに；(honorably) rippa ni 立派に
speak highly of... ...o homeru ...をほめる

highway *n.* dōro 道路；haiuei ハイウエイ

hike *n., v.* haikingu (o suru) ハイキング（をする）

hill *n.* koyama 小山；oka 丘

hillside *n.* sampuku 山腹

hilltop *n.* oka no chōjō 丘の頂上

him *pron.* kare o [ni] 彼を [に]

himself *pron.* kare-jishin 彼自身

hinder *v.* samatageru 妨げる；jama o suru 邪魔をする

hinge *n.* chōtsugai ちょうつがい；(central principle) kaname かなめ；chūshin 中心 ―― *v.* chōtsugai de ugoku ちょうつがいで動く

hint *n.* hinto ヒント；anji 暗示 ―― *v.* honomekasu ほのめかす

hip *n.* shiri しり；koshi 腰

hire *n.* (rent) chintai-ryō 賃貸料；chinshaku-ryō 賃借料 ―― *v.* (employ for wages) yatou 雇う；chingari suru 賃借りする；chingashi suru 賃貸しする

his *pron.* kare no 彼の；kare no mono 彼のもの

history *n.* rekishi 歴史

hit *v.* utsu 打つ；ateru 当てる ―― *n.* dageki 打撃；anda 安打；hitto ヒット

hive *n.* mitsubachi no su みつばちの巣

hobby *n.* shumi 趣味；dōraku 道楽

hold *v.* (have) motsu 持つ; nigiru 握る; (keep in general condition) tamotsu 保つ; (observe) kai o hiraku 会を開く; moyo'osu 催す

hold on (seize) shikkari motsu しっかり持つ; (continue) tsuzukeru 続ける

hold out (stretch) nobasu 伸ばす; (endure) mochikotaeru 持ちこたえる

hold up (raise) ageru 上げる; (stop and rob) oihagi suru 追はぎする

hold one's breath iki o korosu 息を殺す

holder *n.* (possessor) shoyū-sha 所有者; iremono 入れ物; hōrudā ホールダー

hole *n.* ana 穴

holiday *n.* kyūjitsu 休日; shukusai-jitsu 祝祭日

Holland *n.* Oranda オランダ

hollow *adj.* (concave) kubonda くぼんだ; (validity) utsuro na うつろな ——*n.* kubomi くぼみ; utsuro うつろ; (hole) ana 穴

holy *adj.* shinsei na 神聖な; shinjin-bukai 信心深い

home *n.* katei 家庭; uchi うち; wagaya わが家

at home kiraku ni 気楽に

homely *adj.* uchitoketa 打ち解けた; katei-teki na 家庭的な

home-made *adj.* jikasei no 自家製の

honest *adj.* shōjiki na 正直な; jitchoku na 実直な; (sincere) seijitsu na 誠実な

honey *n.* hachimitsu はちみつ

honeybee *n.* mitsu-bachi みつばち

honeymoon *n.* shinkon-ryokō 新婚旅行

honor *n.* (high respect) sonkei 尊敬; (glory) eiyo 栄誉

hood *n.* fūdo フード; zukin ずきん

hoof *n.* hizume ひずめ

hook *n.* kagi かぎ; (fish hook) tsuri-bari つり針; hokku ホック ——*v.* (curved as a hook) magaru 曲がる; (crook) mageru 曲げる

hoop *n.* (oke no) taga (おけの)たが; (ring) wa 輪

hop *v.* pyon-pyon tobu ぴょんぴょん跳ぶ

hope *n.* kibō 希望; nozomi 望み ——*v.* nozomu
望む; kibō suru 希望する; kitai suru 期待する

horizon *n.* chiheisen 地平線; suiheisen 水平線

horn *n.* tsuno 角; rappa ラッパ; tsuno-bue 角笛

horrible *adj.* osoroshii おそろしい; zotto suru
ぞっとする

horror *n.* kyōfu 恐怖; senritsu 戦りつ

horse *n.* uma 馬

hose *n.* (stocking) sutokkingu ストッキング;
(flexible tube) hōsu ホース

hospital *n.* byōin 病院

hospitality *n.* motenashi もてなし; kantai 歓待

hostile *adj.* (enemy) teki no 敵の; (unfriendly)
teki'i no aru 敵意のある

hot *adj.* atsui 暑い

hotel *n.* hoteru ホテル; ryokan 旅館

hound *n.* ryōken 猟犬 ——*v.* tsuiseki suru 追跡
する

hour *n.* jikan 時間; jikoku 時刻

house *n.* ie 家; (the H-) gi'in 議院

household *n., adj.* kazoku (no) 家族(の)

housekeeper *n.* (housewife) shufu 主婦; (head
female servant) jochū-gashira 女中頭; (lady
help) kaseifu 家政婦

housekeeping *n.* kaji 家事; kasei 家政

housewife *n.* shufu 主婦

how *adv.* dōshite どうして; don'na hōhō de
どんな方法で
How do you do? Gokigen ikaga desuka? ごき
げんいかがですか; Kon'nichi wa. 今日は.
How much? Ikura desuka?　いくらですか.
How about...? ...ni tsuite wa dō desuka ...
についてはどうですか.

however *conj.* (nevertheless) nimo kakawarazu
にもかかわらず; (though) dakeredomo だけれ
ども ——*adv.* (by whatever means) don'na
ni ...tomo (demo) どんなに ...とも (でも);
ikura ...demo いくら ...でも

howl *v.* tōboe suru 遠ほえする ――*n.* hoe-goe ほえ声

hug *v.* dakishimeru 抱き締める

huge *adj.* kyodai na 巨大な; bakudai na ばく大 な

hum *v.* bun-bun iu ぶんぶんいう; hanauta o utau 鼻歌をうたう

human *adj.* ningen no 人間の *human being* ningen 人間; hito 人

humble *adj.* (lowly) iyashii 卑しい; (modest) tsutsumashii つつましい; (not proud) tsutsu-mashii つつましい

humid *adj.* shikki'no aru 湿気のある; shimeppoi しめっぽい

humility *n.* kenson 謙そん

humor *n.* yūmoa ユーモア

hundred *n., adj.* hyaku (no) 100, 百(の)

hunger *n.* kūfuku 空腹; ue 飢え ――*vt.* ue saseru 飢えさせる ――*vi.* ueru 飢える; (strong desire) setsubō suru 切望する

hungry *adj.* kūfuku na 空腹な; onaka ga suita おなかが空いた

hunt *v.* kari o suru 狩をする; (search) sagasu 探す ――*n.* kari 狩; shuryō 狩猟; (chase) tsuiseki 追跡

hurrah *int.* furē フレー ――*n.* (shout of joy) banzai 万歳; kanko 歓呼

hurry *v.* isogu 急ぐ; sekasu せかす ――*n.* isogi 急ぎ
Hurry up! Hayaku! 早く!
in a hurry isoide 急いで

hurt *v.* (injure) kizutsukeru 傷つける; (distress) kanjō o gaisuru 感情を害する ――*n.* (wound, harm) kizu 傷; fushō 負傷; (damage) gai 害; (pain) kutsū 苦痛

husband *n.* otto 夫; shujin 主人; teishu 亭主

hush *vt.* (make silent) shizuka ni saseru 静かに させる; damaraseru 黙らせる ――*vi.* (become silent) damaru 黙る *Hush! Hush!* Shi' shi'

しっしっ

hustle *n.* genki 元気; hassuru ハッスル ——*v.*
     genki yoku yaru 元気よくやる; hassuru suru
     ハッスルする

hut *n.* koya 小屋

hydrogen *n.* suiso 水素

hymn *n.* sambika 賛美歌

I

I *pron.* watakushi wa (ga) 私は (が); watashi
     wa (ga) わたしは (が)

ice *n.* kōri 氷; aisu アイス ——*vt.* kōraseru
     凍らせる ——*vi.* kōru 凍る
     iced hiyashita 冷やした

ice cream *n.* aisu-kurīmu アイスクリーム

icicle *n.* tsurara つらら

idea *n.* aidea アイデア; gainen 概念; kangae
     考え; chishiki 知識; iken 意見
     have no idea zen-zen wakaranai 全然わからな
     い; (towa) omoi mo yoranai (とは) 思いもよら
     ない

ideal *n.* risō 理想 ——*adj.* risō-teki na 理想的な

identical *adj.* dōitsu no 同一の

identify *v.* dōitsushi suru 同一視する; itchi suru
     一致する

idiot *n.* hakuchi 白痴; baka ばか

idle *v.* namakeru 怠ける; asonde kurasu 遊んで
     暮らす ——*adj.* taida na 怠惰な; (useless)
     mueki na 無益な

idol *n.* gūzō 偶像; aidoru アイドル

if *conj.* (in case that) moshi …naraba もし …な
     らば; (even if) toshite mo としても; (whether)
     de aruka dōka であるかどうか

ignorant *adj.* mugaku no 無学の; muchi no 無知
     の

ignore *v.* mushi suru 無視する; kaeriminai 顧み
     ない

ill *adj*. (sick) byōki de 病気で; (bad) warui 悪い —— *n*. (evil) aku 悪

illegal *adj*. fuhō no 不法の; ihō no 違法の

illness *n*. byōki 病気

illuminate *v*. akaruku suru 明るくする; terasu 照らす

illusion *n*. (deceptive appearance) gen'ei 幻影; gensō 幻想; (misconception) sakkaku 錯覚; (false impression) genkaku 幻覚

illustrate *v*. (make clear) akiraka ni suru 明らかにする; (explain) setsumei suru 説明する; (provide with pictures) sashie o ireru 挿絵を入れる **illustrated** e-iri no 絵入りの; zukai no 図解の

illustration *n*. zukai 図解; sashi-e 挿絵; irasuto イラスト

image *n*. zō 像; imēji イメージ

imagine *v*. (form mental image of) sōzō suru 想像する; (guess) omou 思う

imitate *v*. maneru まねる; mohō suru 模倣する

imitation *n*. mane まね; mohō 模倣; imitēshon イミテーション; nisemono 偽物

immediate *adj*. (direct) chokusetsu no 直接の; jika no じかの; (without delay) sokuji no 即時の

immediately *adv*. sugu ni すぐに; tadachi ni 直ちに

immense *adj*. (unlimited) mugen no 無限の; (infinite) musū no 無数の; (very great, vast, huge) kyodai na 巨大な; bakudai na ばく大な

immerse *v*. (mizu ni) tsukeru (水に)つける; hitasu 浸す; (sink) shizumeru 沈める

immigrate *vi*. (come as a settler) ijū suru 移住する —— *vt*. (bring in as a settler) ijū saseru 移住させる

immortal *adj*. fushi no 不死の; fumetsu no 不滅の

imperial *adj*. teikoku no 帝国の; kōshitsu no 皇室の

implement *n.* (tool) dōgu 道具; kigu 器具; yōgu 用具

imply *v.* (mean) imi suru 意味する; (suggest) anji suru 暗示する; honomekasu ほのめかす

import *v.* yunyū suru 輸入する; (mean) imi suru 意味する ——*n.* yunyū 輸入

important *adj.* jūyō na 重要な; taisetsu na 大切な

impose *v.* (put on) ka suru 課する; owaseru 負わせる

impossible *adj.* fukanō na 不可能な; arienai ありえない

impress *v.* (fix indelibly) inshōzukeru 印象づける; (influence deeply) kandō saseru 感動させる

impression *n.* inshō 印象

improve *v.* kairyō suru 改良する; kaizen suru 改善する

impulse *n.* (impetus) shōdō 衝動; hazumi はずみ; (sudden wish) dekigokoro 出来心

in *prep.* ...no naka ni ...の中に; ...no tame ni ...のために

Is Mr. Jones in? Jones san wa gozaitaku desuka? ジョーンズさんはご在宅ですか.

inaugurate *v.* (induct into office formally) shūnin saseru 就任させる; (celebrate the public use formally) ōyake ni kōkai suru 公に公開する; (begin, open) hajimeru 始める; kaishi suru 開始する

incessant *adj.* taemanai 絶え間ない

inch *n.* inchi インチ

incident *n.* dekigoto 出来事; jiken 事件

incline *v.* (lean) katamukeru 傾ける; (bend) (karada o) mageru (体を) 曲げる; (tend) ...shitai ki ga suru ...したい気がする *be inclined to* ...suru keikō ga aru ...する傾向がある ——*n.* (slope) saka 坂; keisha 傾斜; shamen 斜面

include *v.* (comprise) fukumu 含む; (embrace) hōkatsu suru 抱括する

income *n.* shūnyū 収入; shotoku 所得 *income tax* shotokuzei 所得税

inconvenient *adj.* fuben na 不便な

increase *v.* masu 増す; fuyasu 増やす; zōka suru 増加する

incredible *adj.* shinjirarenai 信じられない

indeed *adv.* hontō ni 本当に; jissai 実際

indefinite *adj.* fumeiryō na 不明瞭な; futei no 不定の; aimai na あいまいな

independent *adj.* (standing by itself) dokuritsu no 独立の; (not dependent) shihai [eikyō] o u-kenai 支配 [影響] を受けない

index *n.* sakuin 索引; indekkusu インデックス

indicate *v.* (point out) sashi-shimesu 指し示す; shiji suru 指示する

indigestion *n.* fushōka 不消化; shōka furyō 消化不良

indirect *adj.* kansetsu no 間接の; tōmawashi no 遠回しの

indispensable *adj.* kakukoto no dekinai 欠くことのできない; nakutewa naranai なくてはならない

individual *adj.* koko no 個々の; kojin no 個人の —— *n.* kojin 個人; hito 人

indulge *vi.* (give oneself to) fukeru ふける —— *vt.* (yield to the desire of) kimama ni saseru 気ままにさせる; (humor) amayakasu 甘やかす

industrious *adj.* kimben na 勤勉な; yoku hataraku よく働く

industry *n.* (diligence) kimben 勤勉; doryoku 努力

inevitable *adj.* sakerarenai 避けられない

infant *n.* yōji 幼児; shōni 小児

infect *v.* densen saseru 伝染させる; kansen saseru 感染させる; utsusu うつす *be infected with* kansen shite iru 感染している

inferior *adj.* kai no 下位の; yori ottota より劣った —— *n.* meshita no mono 目下の者

infinite *adj.* (boundless) mugen no 無限の; (immense) bakudai na ばく大な; obitadashii おびただしい

influence *n., v.* eikyō(o oyobosu) 影響(を及ぼす); kanka(suru) 感化(する)

inform *v.* shiraseru 知らせる; hōkoku suru 報告する

information *n.* chishiki 知識; jōhō 情報

ingenious *adj.* (skilled) kiyō na 器用な; (skillfully contrived) takumi na 巧みな

ingredient *n.* (component) seibun 成分; (element) yōso 要素

inherit *v.* (receive as an heir) sōzoku suru 相続する; (have by heredity) iden suru 遺伝する

inheritance *n.* (succession) sōzoku 相続; (heredity) iden 遺伝; (heritage) isan 遺産; sōzoku-zaisan 相続財産

inheritor *n.* (heir) sōzoku-nin 相続人

initial *adj.* saisho no 最初の

initiative *n.* (lead) sossen 率先; inishiachibu イニシアチブ

injure *v.* (hurt) kega o saseru けがをさせる; (harm) gai o suru 害をする

injustice *n.* (unfairness) fusei 不正; fukōhei 不公平

ink *n.* inki インキ

inland *adj.* naichi no 内地の; nairiku no 内陸の —— *n.* (interior of a country) naichi 内地; (domestic) kokunai 国内

inn *n.* yadoya 宿屋; ryokan 旅館

innocent *adj.* (simple) mujaki na 無邪気な; (not guilty) muzai no 無罪の; (harmless) mugai no 無害の

inquire *v.* kiku 聞く; tou 問う; tazuneru 尋ねる

inquiry *n.* toiawase 問い合せ; shitsumon 質問

inscribe *v.* (write in or on) kaku 書く; shirusu しるす; (engrave) kizamu 刻む; horu 彫る

insect *n.* konchū こん虫

insert *v.* sashikomu 差し込む; sōnyū suru 挿入する

inside *n.* uchigawa 内側; naibu 内部 ——*adj.* naibu no 内部の ——*adv.* naibu ni 内部に; uchigawa ni 内側に

insist *v.* iiharu 言い張る; shuchō suru 主張する; koshitsu suru 固執する

inspect *v.* (examine officially) kensa suru 検査する; (look closely into) chōsa suru 調査する

inspire *v.* (breathe) suikomu 吸い込む; (infuse by breathing) fukikomu 吹き込む; (animate) hagemasu 励ます; kangeki saseru 感激させる

install *v.* (instate) shūnin saseru 就任させる; nimmei suru 任命する; (set up) suetsukeru すえ付ける; setsubi suru 設備する

installment *n.* geppukin 月賦金; bunkatsu-barai 分割払い

instance *n.* rei 例; jitsurei 実例 *for instance* tatoeba 例えば

instant *adj.* (urgent) kinkyū no 緊急の; (immediate) sokuji no 即時の ——*n.* sokkoku 即刻; (precise moment) shunkan 瞬間

instead *adv.* kawari ni 代りに *instead of...* ...no kawari ni ...の代りに

instinct *n.* hon'nō 本能

institute *v.* setsuritsu suru 設立する; mōkeru 設ける ——*n.* kyōkai 協会; gakkai 学会

institution *n.* (established law) seido 制度; (establishment) setsuritsu 設立; (established society) kyōkai 協会

instruct *v.* (teach) oshieru 教える; (direct) sashizu suru 指図する

instruction *n.* (teaching) kyōju 教授; (direction) sashizu 指図; (commands) shirei 指令

instrument *n.* (tool) kikai 器械; (means) shudan 手段

insult *n., v.* bujoku (suru) 侮辱(する)

insurance *n.* hoken 保険
　　car insurance jidōsha hoken 自動車保険
　　fire insurance kasai hoken 火災保険
　　life insurance seimei hoken 生命保険

insure *v.* hoken o tsukeru 保険をつける; (guarantee) hoshō suru 保証する

intelligence *n.* (faculty of understanding) chiryoku 知力; (knowledge) chishiki 知識; (sagacity) sōmei そう明; (information) jōhō 情報

intelligent *adj.* chiteki na 知的な; riseiteki na 理性的な

intend *v.* ...suru tsumori de aru ...するつもりである; shiyō to omou しようと思う

intent *n.* ishi 意志; (intention) ikō 意向; (purpose) mokuromi もくろみ —— *adj.* (eager) nesshin na 熱心な; isshin ni natte 一心になって

intention *n.* ishi 意志; ikō 意向; ito 意図; (purpose) mokuteki 目的

intercourse *n.* (social communication) shakō 社交; (communication between individuals) kōsai 交際; (commerce) tsūshō 通商

interest *n.* (feeling of curiosity or concern) kyōmi 興味; kanshin 関心; (profit) rieki 利益 —— *v.* (excite curiosity of) kyōmi o motaseru 興味を持たせる
 be interested in... ...kyōmi ga aru 興味がある
 interesting omoshiroi 面白い

interfere *v.* (meddle) kanshō suru 干渉する; (interrupt) bōgai suru 妨害する

interior *n., adj.* naibu (no) 内部(の); uchigawa (no) 内側(の)

internal *adj.* naibu no 内部の; (domestic) kokunai no 国内の

international *adj.* kokusai-teki na 国際的な

interpret *v.* (explain, tell the meaning of) setsumei suru 説明する; kaishaku suru 解釈する; (translate) tsūyaku suru 通訳する *interpreter* tsūyaku 通訳

interrupt *v.* jama o suru じゃまをする; saegiru さえぎる; (cut off) chūdan suru 中断する

interval *n.* ma 間; aima 合間; kankaku 間隔
 at intervals ma o oite 間をおいて

interview *n.* kaiken 会見; mensetsu 面接; intabyū

インタビュー

intimate *adj.* (close) shimmitsu na 親密な; shitashii 親しい ―― *n.* (intimate friend) shin'yū 親友

into *prep.* ...no naka ni [e] の中に [へ]

introduce *v.* (insert) ireru 入れる; (lead in) michibiku 導く; (usher in) an'nai suru 案内する; (make acquainted with) shōkai suru 紹介する

invade *v.* shinryaku suru 侵略する; shinkō suru 侵攻する

invalid *adj.* (feeble) byōjaku no 病弱の; (not valid) mukō no 無効の ―― *n.* (sick person) byōnin 病人; mukō 無効

invaluable *adj.* hijō ni kichō na 非常に貴重な; hyōka dekinai hodo no 評価できないほどの

invariable *adj.* henka shinai 変化しない; ittei no 一定の

invent *v.* (produce a new device) hatsumei suru 発明する; (think up) kōan suru 考案する

invest *v.* (clothe) kiseru 着せる; (put money into business) tōshi suru 投資する

invisible *adj.* me ni mienai 目に見えない

invitation *n.* shōtai(jō) 招待(状)

invite *v.* sasou 誘う; maneku 招く

iron *n.* tetsu 鉄; (device used for pressing cloth) airon アイロン

irregular *adj.* fukisoku na [no] 不規則な [の]

irritate *v.* (provoke) okoraseru 怒らせる; (vex) ira-ira saseru いらいらさせる

island *n.* shima 島

isolate *v.* (place apart) hanasu 離す; kakuri suru 隔離する; (place alone) koritsu saseru 孤立させる

issue *n.* (result) kekka 結果; (outflow) ryūshutsu 流出; (publishing) hakkōbutsu 発行物; gō 号 ―― *v.* (publish) hakkō suru 発行する; (emerge) arawareru 現れる

it *pron.* sore wa [ga] それは [が]

itch *n.* kayui koto かゆいこと ―― *v.* kayui か

ゆい; muzu-gayui むずがゆい

item *n.* (single detail) kajō 箇条; kōmoku 項目;
(detail of news) kiji 記事

its *pron.* sore no それの; sono その

ivory *n., adj.* zōge (no) 象牙 (の)

J

jab *n.* fui ni tsuku [utsu, sasu] koto 不意に突く
[打つ, 刺す] こと; jabu ジャブ

jacket *n.* jakketto ジャケット; uwagi 上着

jade *n.* hisui ひすい

jail *n.* keimusho 刑務所; rōgoku ろう獄

jam *n.* jamu ジャム

January *n.* ichi-gatsu 一月

japan *n.* urushi 漆; shikki 漆器

Japan *n.* Nippon 日本; Nihon 日本

Japanese *n., adj.* Nippon [Nihon] no 日本の;
Nippon [Nihon]-jin (no) 日本人 (の); Nihon-go
(no) 日本語(の)

jar *n.* tsubo つぼ; bin びん

jaw *n.* ago あご

jazz *n.* jazu ジャズ

jealous *adj.* netamibukai ねたみ深い; shitto-bukai しっと深い; yakimochiyaki no 焼もちやき
の

jeans *n. pl.* jīnzu ジーンズ; jīpan ジーパン

jelly *n.* zerī ゼリー

jest *n., v.* jōdan (o iu) 冗談 (を言う); share (o iu)
しゃれ (を言う)

Jesus *n.* Iesu Kirisuto イエス・キリスト

jet *n.* (jet-propelled aircraft) jetto-ki ジェット機;
(spouting) funsha 噴射 ——*v.* (emit) funshutsu suru 噴出する

Jew *n.* Yudaya-jin ユダヤ人

jewel *n.* hōseki 宝石

job *n.* shigoto 仕事; shokugyō 職業

jockey *n.* kishu 騎手

join v. (unite) ketsugō suru 結合する; (put together) issho ni suru いっしょにする; (unite with) sanka suru 参加する

joint n. (juncture) tsugime 継ぎ目; (articulation) kansetsu 関節 —— adj. (combined) gōdō no 合同の

joke n. jōdan 冗談; jōku ジョーク

jolly adj. (gay) yōki na 陽気な; (merry) yukai na 愉快な

journal n. (daily account) nikki 日記; (daily newspaper) nikkan shimbun 日刊新聞; (magazine) zasshi 雑誌

journey n., v. tabi (o suru) 旅(をする); ryokō (suru) 旅行 (する)

joy n. yorokobi 喜び; kanki 歓喜

judge n. saibankan 裁判官; hanji 判事 —— v. (decide by judgement) handan suru 判断する; (try) saiban suru 裁判する; shinsa suru 審査する

jug n. mizusashi 水差し; jokki ジョッキ

juice n. jūsu ジュース; shiru 汁; eki 液

July n. shichi-gatsu 七月

jump n., v. chōyaku (suru) 跳躍(する); jampu (suru) ジャンプ(する)

junction n. (joining) rengō 連合; (joining-point) setsugō-ten 接合点; (connecting station) renraku-eki 連絡駅

June n. roku-gatsu 六月

jungle n. mitsurin 密林; janguru ジャングル

junior n. nenshōsha 年少者; junia ジュニア

jury n. baishin-in 陪審員

just adj. (right) tadashii 正しい; seigi no 正義の; (just) kōhei na 公平な —— adv. (exactly) chōdo 丁度 *just now* tatta ima たった今

justice n. seigi 正義; kōhei 公平; seitō 正当

justify v. (prove to be just) tadashii to suru 正しいとする; (vindicate) bemmei suru 弁明する

juvenile adj. jidō no 児童の; shōnen no 少年の

K

keen *adj.* surudoi 鋭い；(eager) nesshin na 熱心な；(intense) hageshii 激しい

keep *v.* (observe) tamotsu 保つ；(protect) mamoru 守る；(support) yashinau 養う；(maintain) kau 飼う；(continue) …shi tsuzukeru …し続ける

keep away chikazukenai 近付けない

keep good time (tokei ga) kichin to au (時計が) きちんと合う

keep in mind kioku suru 記憶する

keep off fusegu 防ぐ；…o sakeru …を避ける

keep on tsuzukeru 続ける

keep up …o sasaeru …を支える

kerosene *n.* tōyu 灯油

kettle *n.* yuwakashi 湯沸かし；(tea kettle) yakan やかん

key *n.* kagi 鍵；kī キー

kick *n.* keru ける

kidnap *v.* yūkai suru 誘かいする；sarau さらう

kidney *n.* jinzō 腎臓

kill *v.* korosu 殺す；massatsu suru まっ殺する

kin *n.* (relatives, family) ketsuzoku 血族；shinzoku 親族；iegara 家柄

kind *adj.* shinsetsu na 親切な；(gentle) yasashii 優しい

king *n.* ō 王；kokuō 国王

kiss *n.* kisu キス；seppun 接ぷん

kit *n.* (set of tools) dōgu 道具；(box for tools) dōgu-bako 道具箱

kitchen *n.* daidokoro 台所；kitchin キッチン

kite *n.* tako たこ；(kind of hawk) tobi とび

kitten *n.* ko-neko 子ねこ

knee *n.* hiza ひざ；hiza-gashira ひざ頭

kneel *v.* hizamazuku ひざまずく

knife *n.* naifu ナイフ；kogatana 小刀

knit *v.* amu 編む

knob *n.* (*of door*) totte 取っ手; nigiri 握り; (lump) kobu こぶ

knock *v.* tataku たたく; utsu 打つ ―― *n.* nokku ノック

knot *n.* musubi(me) 結び(目); (nautical mile) kairi 海里

know *v.* shiru 知る; shitte iru 知っている

knowledge *n.* (information) chishiki 知識; (scholarship) gakumon 学問

knuckle *n.* (joint of finger) yubi no kansetsu 指の関節; (fist) genkotsu げん骨

Korea *n.* Chōsen 朝鮮; Kankoku 韓国

L

label *n.* raberu ラベル; retteru レッテル

labor *n.* rōdō 労働; rōryoku 労力; shigoto 仕事

laboratory *n.* jikkenshitsu 実験室; kenkyūsho 研究所

lace *n.* rēsu レース

lack *n.* ketsubō 欠乏; fusoku 不足 ―― *v.* ... ga nai ...がない; ...o kaite iru ...を欠いている

ladder *n.* hashigo はしご

lady *n.* kifujin 貴婦人; shukujo 淑女; redī レディー

lake *n.* mizu'umi 湖

lamb *n.* ko-hitsuji 子羊; (flesh of the lamb as food) ko-hitsuji no niku 子羊の肉

lame *adj.* bikko no びっこの ―― *v.* bikko o hiku びっこをひく

lament *v.* nageku 嘆く; kanashimu 悲しむ ―― *n.* hitan 悲嘆

lamp *n.* rampu ランプ

land *n.* riku 陸; tochi 土地; kuni 国 ―― *v.* jōriku suru 上陸する

landlord *n.* (innkeeper) (ryokan no) shujin (旅館の) 主人; (landowner) jinushi 地主; (owner of a house) yanushi 家主

landmark *n.* rikuhyō 陸標; mokuhyō 目標; (boundary mark) kyōkaihyō 境界標; (epoch-making event) kakki-teki na dekigoto 画期的な出来事

landscape *n.* keshiki 景色; fūkei 風景

language *n.* kotoba 言葉; gengo 言語

lantern *n.* chōchin ちょうちん; rantan ランタン

lap¹ *n.* hiza ひざ

lap² *v.* (fold) oritatamu 折りたたむ; (bend and lay) orikasaneru 折り重ねる; (wrap up) tsutsumikomu 包み込む —— *n.* (overlapping part) kasanatte iru bubun 重なっている部分; (one circuit of a race track) kyōgijō no isshū 競技場の一周

lap³ *v.* (take into the mouth with the tongue) nameru なめる; (wash, flow against) (nami ga kishi o) utsu [arau] (波が岸を) 打つ [洗う]

lapse *n.* (small error) chottoshita machigai [ayamachi] ちょっとした間違い [過ち]; (passing, as of time) (toki no) keika (時の) 経過; (fall) daraku 堕落 —— *v.* (pass) toki ga sugiru [tatsu] 時が過ぎる [たつ]; (flow) nagareru 流れる

lard *n.* buta no shibō 豚の脂肪; rādo ラード

large *adj.* ōkii 大きい; ōkina 大きな; hiroi 広い; daikibo na 大規模な

lark *n.* hibari ひばり

last *adj.* (after all others) saigo no 最後の; (most recent) saikin no 最近の; kono-mae no この前の —— *v.* (continue) tsuzuku 続く

at last tsui ni ついに; tōtō とうとう

last evening yūbe ゆうべ; sakuban 昨晩

last month sengetsu 先月

last night sakuya 昨夜

last time kono-mae この前

last week senshū 先週

last year kyonen 去年; sakunen 昨年

late *adj.* osoi 遅い; okureta 遅れた; (recent) saikin no 最近の; (recently dead) ko 故 *lately* saikin 最近; chikagoro 近ごろ

later *adj.* (subsequently) nochi no 後の —— *adv.* (by and by) yagate やがて

latitude *n.* ido 緯度

latter *adj.* (second of two) kōsha no 後者の; ato no 後の; (more recent) motto saikin no もっと最近の

laugh *v.* warau 笑う —— *n.* warai 笑い

laughter *n.* warai (-goe) 笑い(声)

launch *v.* (send a newly-made ship into water) shinsui saseru 進水させる; (send out) okuridasu 送り出す; (set out) chakushu suru 着手する —— *n.* shinsui 進水; (large motor boat) ranchi ランチ

laundry *n.* sentaku-ya 洗たく屋; kurīningu-ya クリーニング屋

laurel *n.* gekkei-ju 月桂樹; gekkei-kan 月桂冠

lavatory *n.* semmenjo 洗面所; toire トイレ; keshōshitsu 化粧室; benjo 便所

law *n.* hōritsu 法律; hōsoku 法則

lawn *n.* shibafu 芝生

lawyer *n.* hōritsuka 法律家; bengoshi 弁護士

lay *v.* (make lie) yokotaeru 横たえる; (put down) oku 置く; (produce) tamago o umu 卵を生む
lay by [*up*] takuwaeru 貯える
lay out sekkei suru 設計する

layer *n.* (single thickness) ichi-mai 一枚; (stratum) sō 層

lazy *v.* namakeru 怠ける —— *adj.* bushō na 不精な; taida na 怠惰な

lead¹ *v.* (conduct) michibiku 導く; (guide) an'nai suru 案内する; (pass) sugosu 過ごす —— *n.* (position at the front) sendō 先導; (command) shiki 指揮; (measure of precedence) kachikoshi 勝ち越し; (leadership) rīdāshippu リーダーシップ

lead² *n.* namari 鉛

leader *n.* shidōsha 指導者; rīdā リーダー

leaf *n.* ko no ha 木の葉; (sheet of paper) ichi-mai 一枚

league *n.* remmei 連盟; dōmei 同盟; rīgu リーグ

leak *n.* mizumore 水漏れ; moreguchi 漏れ口
—— *vi.* moreru 漏れる　—— *vt.* morasu 漏らす

lean[1] *v.* (incline) katamuku 傾く; (bend) magaru まがる; motareru もたれる; yorikakaru 寄り掛かる　—— *n.* katamuki 傾き

lean[2] *adj.* (thin) yaseta やせた

leap *v.* (jump) tobu 跳ぶ; haneru 跳ねる

learn *v.* (gain knowledge) manabu 学ぶ; narau 習う; (acquire information about) shiru 知る; (hear) kiku 聞く　*learn by heart* anki suru 暗記する

lease *n.* (contract for letting land or building for rent) shakuchi [shakuya] keiyaku 借地 [借家]契約　—— *v.* (rent) chingashi [chingari] suru 賃貸[賃借]する

least *adj.* saishō no 最小の; mottomo sukunai 最も少ない

leather *n.* kawa 皮; nameshi-gawa なめし皮

leave[1] *v.* (go away) ...o saru ...を去る; (depart) shuppatsu suru 出発する; (let stay behind) nokosu 残す; (let remain) ...no jōtai ni shite oku ...の状態にしておく
leave off yameru 止める
leave out habuku 省く

leave[2] *n.* (permission) kyoka 許可; (permitted absence from duty) kyūka 休暇; (farewell) itomagoi いとまごい

lecture *n., v.* kōgi (suru) 講義 (する); kōen (suru) 講演 (する)

left *n., adj.* hidari (no) 左 (の)　*left-handed* hidari-kiki no 左利きの

leg *n.* ashi 足; (long support pole) shichū 支柱

legal *adj.* hōritsu no 法律の; (lawful) gōhō no 合法の

legend *n.* (traditional tale) densetsu 伝説; (myth) shinwa 神話

leisure *n.* hima 暇; yoka 余暇

lemon *n.* remon レモン

lend *v.* kasu 貸す

length *n.* nagasa 長さ; tate 縦; (extent in space, or time) han'i 範囲 *at length* tsui'ni ついに; tōtō とうとう

lengthen *vt.* (prolong) nagaku suru 長くする; nobasu 伸ばす —— *vi.* nagaku naru 長くなる; nobiru 伸びる

lens *n.* renzu レンズ

less *adj.* yori sukunai より少ない; yori chiisai より小さい

lesson *n.* gakka 学課; jugyō 授業; ressun レッスン

let *v.* (allow) …saseru …させる; suru koto o yurusu することを許す; (lease) kasu 貸す
let alone hōnin suru 放任する
let down sageru さげる

letter *n.* (alphabetical character) moji 文字; (written message) tegami 手紙; (literature) bungaku 文学

lettuce *n.* retasu レタス; sarada-na サラダ菜

level *n., adj.* taira (na) 平ら (な); suihei (no) 水平 (の); (horizontal plane, line) suihei-men 水平面; suihei-sen 水平線

liable *adj.* (apt) …shigachi na …しがちな; suru noga tōzen no するのが当然の

liar *n.* usotsuki うそつき

liberal *adj.* jiyū na 自由な; kandai na 寛大な

liberty *n.* jiyū 自由; hōmen 放免; (one's own way) katte 勝手

library *n.* tosho-shitsu 図書室; tosho-kan 図書館; (collection of books) zōsho 蔵書

license *n.* menkyo 免許; kyoka 許可; raisensu ライセンス

lick *v.* (lap) nameru なめる; (overcome) makasu 負かす —— *n.* hito-name ひとなめ

lid *n.* (cover) futa ふた; (eyelid) mabuta まぶた

lie¹ *n., v.* uso (o tsuku) うそ (をつく)

lie[2] v. yokotawaru 横たわる；neru 寝る；(be) aru ある；(be situated) ichi suru 位置する

life n. seimei 生命；inochi 命；jinsei 人生；(way of living) seikatsu 生活　*for life* isshōgai 一生涯

lift v. ageru 上げる；mochiageru 持ち上げる —— n. (*Br.*) (elevator) erebēta エレベータ

light n. hikari 光；akari 明かり —— adj. akarui 明るい；(not heavy) karui 軽い；(easy) yōi na 容易な

lightly adv. karugaru to 軽々と；keikai ni 軽快に

lightning n. denkō 電光；inazuma 稲妻

like[1] v. (be fond of) konomu 好む；suku 好く；(disposed to) shitai したい —— n. konomi 好み　*I like it.* Sukidesu. 好きです.

like[2] adj. (similar) nite iru 似ている —— prep. ...ni nita ...に似た；(such, so) ...no yō na ...のような；(have appearance of) rashii らしい；(suitable) ...ni fusawashii ...にふさわしい

likely adj. (credible) hontō rashii 本当らしい；shinjiru ni taru 信じるに足る；(probable) rashii らしい；arisō na ありそうな

lily n. yuri (no hana) ゆり（の花）

limb n. (leg or arm) teashi 手足；(wing) tsubasa 翼；(bough) eda 枝

lime n. raimu ライム

limit n. (utmost extent) gendo 限度；(boundary) kyōkai 境界；(termination) genkai 限界 —— v. seigen suru 制限する

limp[1] n., v. bikko (o hiku) びっこ（をひく）

limp[2] adj. (flexible) jūnan na 柔軟な；(flaccid) gunya-gunya no ぐにゃぐにゃの

line n. sen 線；rain ライン；(rope) tsuna 綱 —— v. (take position in a line) narabu 並ぶ；seiretsu suru 整列する；(mark with a line) sen o hiku 線を引く

linen n. rin'neru リンネル

linger v. guzu-guzu suru ぐずぐずする：temadoru

手間どる

lining *n.* fuku no ura(-ji) 服の裏(地)

lion *n.* raion ライオン; shishi しし

lip *n.* kuchibiru くちびる   *lip stick* kuchi-beni 口紅

liquid *n., adj.* (fluid) ryūdō-tai (no) 流動体 (の); ekitai (no) 液体 (の)

liquor *n.* arukōru inryō アルコール飲料; sakerui 酒類

list *n.* hyō 表; risuto リスト; mokuroku 目録

listen *v.* kiku 聞く; mimi o katamukeru 耳を傾ける

liter *n.* rittoru リットル

literal *adj.* (not exaggerated) mojidōri no 文字通りの; kochō no nai 誇張のない; (accurate) seikaku na 正確な

literature *n.* bungaku 文学; bungei 文芸

little *adj.* chiisai 小さい; sukoshi no 少しの; sukunai 少ない

live *v.* (be alive) ikiru 生きる; (dwell) sumu 住む; seikatsu suru 生活する —— *adj.* ikite iru 生きている

livelihood *n.* seikei 生計; kurashi 暮し

lively *adj.* yōki na 陽気な; genki no yoi 元気のよい

liver *n.* kanzō 肝臓; rebā レバー

lizard *n.* tokage とかげ

load *n.* ni 荷; tsumini 積荷 —— *v.* ni o tsumu 荷を積む

loaf *n.* (pan no) hito-katamari (パンの) 一塊

loan *n.* (act of lending) kashitsuke 貸し付け; (something lent esp. money at interest) kashitsuke-kin 貸付金; (government loan) kōsai 公債 —— *v.* (lend) kasu 貸す

lobby *n.* robī ロビー; hikae no ma 控えの間; rōka 廊下

lobster *n.* ise-ebi いせえび

local *adj.* (of a particular place) chihō no 地方の; (of only one part) kyokubu no 局部の; tochi no 土地の

locate *v.* (find the place of) no ichi o mitsukeru の位置を見付ける; (show the position of) ichi o sadameru 位置を定める; (establish in a certain place) setsuritsu suru 設立する

location *n.* (situation) ichi 位置; (place of residence) shozaichi 所在地

lock *n., v.* jō (o orosu) 錠 (をおろす)

locomotive *n.* kikansha 機関車

locust *n.* inago いなご; batta ばった; (cicada) semi せみ

lodge *vi.* tomaru 泊まる; geshuku suru 下宿する —— *vt.* tomeru 泊める; geshuku saseru 下宿させる —— *n.* (hut) koya 小屋 *lodger* geshuku-nin 下宿人

lodging *n.* shukuhaku 宿泊; geshuku 下宿; *pl.* (rented room) kashima 貸間 *lodging-house* geshuku-ya 下宿屋

log *n.* maruta 丸太

logic *n.* ronri (-gaku) 論理 (学)

lone *adj.* kodoku na 孤独な; sabishii 寂しい

lonely *adj.* kodoku na 孤独な; sabishii 寂しい; hitori-botchi no ひとりぼっちの

long *adj.* nagai 長い —— *adv.* nagaku 長く —— *v.* (wish earnestly) setsubō suru 切望する; (yearn) shitau 慕う

long ago mukashi 昔

long for …o setsubō suru …を切望する

long-distance call chōkyori-denwa 長距離電話

so long sayōnara さようなら

longitude *n.* keido 経度; keisen 経線

look *v.* miru 見る; nagameru 眺める; (take care) chūi suru 注意する; ki o tsukeru 気を付ける; (expect) kitai suru 期待する; (anticipate) yoki suru 予期する

look about mimawasu 見回す

look after …no sewa o suru …の世話をする

look for sagasu 探す; motomeru 求める

look forward to …o kitai suru …を期待する

look into chōsa suru 調査する

look like …rashii …らしい; ni nite iru に似ている

Look out! Ki o tsukete! 気を付けて; Abunai! 危ない.

loop *n., v.* wa(ni suru) 輪(にする)

loose *adj.* (lax) yurui ゆるい; (not fastened) jiyū na 自由な; (not strict) darashi no nai だらしのない ——*v.* (untie) toku 解く; (become loose) yurumu ゆるむ

lose *v.* (unable to find) ushinau 失う; funshitsu suru 紛失する; (mislay) okiwasureru 置き忘れる; (*watch*) okureru 遅れる; (fail to catch) (kisha ni) nori-okureru (汽車に) 乗り遅れる; (defeat) makeru 負ける *lose one's way* michi ni mayou 道に迷う *loser* haisha 敗者

loss *n.* sonshitsu 損失; (damage) songai 損害; (forfeiture) funshitsu 紛失; (failure) shippai 失敗; (defeat) haiboku 敗北 *at a loss* mayotte 迷って; komatte 困って

lost *adj.* (missing) nakunatta なくなった; ushinatta 失った; (strayed) mayotta 迷った; (ruined) horobita 滅びた

lost article ishitsu-butsu 遺失物

report on lost property ishitsu-todoke 遺失届

lost and found office ishitsu-butsu toriatsukai-sho 遺失物取扱所

lot *n.* kuji くじ; (destiny) ummei 運命; (*colloq.*) (great amount) takusan たくさん *a lot of* takusan no たくさんの

lotion *n.* rōshon ローション; keshōsui 化粧水

lotus *n.* hasu はす

loud *adj.* ōgoe no 大声の; yakamashii やかましい

lounge *n.* (pass time in a relaxed way) nora-kura shite sugosu のらくらして過ごす; (comfortably furnished waiting room) kyūkei-shitsu 休憩室

love *n., v.* ai (suru) 愛 (する); aijō (o motsu) 愛情(を持つ); suki(de aru) 好き(である)

lovely *adj.* utsukushii 美しい; airashii 愛らしい

low *adj.* (having little height) hikui 低い; (cheap) yasui 安い —— *adv.* hikuku 低く; yasuku 安く

lower *v.* sageru 下げる; hikuku suru 低くする

loyal *adj.* chūgi na 忠義な; chūjitsu na 忠実な

luck *n.* un 運; kōun 幸運

luggage *n.* te-nimotsu 手荷物

lumber *n.* (timber) zaimoku 材木

luminous *adj.* kagayaku 輝く; akarui 明るい

lump *n.* (irregularly shaped mass) katamari 塊; (abnormal swelling in the body) kobu こぶ

lunch *n.* chūshoku 昼食; bentō 弁当

lung *n.* hai 肺

lure *v.* (allure) yūwaku suru 誘惑する —— *n.* (allurement) yūwaku suru mono 誘惑するもの; miryoku 魅力; (artificial bait for fish) giji-bari 擬似針

luxury *n.* zeitaku ぜいたく; zeitaku-hin ぜいたく品

lyric *adj.* jojō-teki na 叙情的な —— *n.* jojōshi 叙情詩

M

machine *n.* kikai 機械

machinery *n.* kikai-sōchi 機械装置; kikai-rui 機械類

mackerel *n.* saba さば

mad *adj.* ki no Kurutta 気の狂った; kichigai no 気違いの

madam *n.* fujin 夫人; okusama 奥様; madamu マダム

magazine *n.* zasshi 雑誌

magic *n.* mahō 魔法; kijutsu 奇術; tejina 手品

magnet *n.* jishaku 磁石

magnificent *adj.* sōrei na 壮麗な; sōdai na 壮大な; rippa na 立派な

maid *n.* (young girl) shōjo 少女; (virgin) otome おとめ; (female servant) jochū 女中

mail *n.* yūbin(-butsu) 郵便(物) *mail order* tsūshin-hambai 通信販売

mailbox *n.* (*receiving*) yūbimbako 郵便箱; (*sending*) posuto ポスト

main *adj.* (principal) shuyō na 主要な; (most important) mottomo jūyō na 最も重要な —— *n.* (chief pipe in a system) honkan 本管 *main street* ō-dōri 大通り

maintain *v.* (keep) tamotsu 保つ; sasaeru 支える; (support) shiji suru 支持する

maize *n.* tōmorokoshi とう.もろこし

majesty *n.* igen 威厳; songen 尊厳; (M-) heika 陛下

major *adj.* omo na 主な; ōkiihō no 大きい方の; tasū no 多数の

majority *n.* daitasū 大多数; kahansū 過半数

make *v.* (form, shape) tsukuru 作る; koshiraeru こしらえる; (develop into) …ni naru …になる; (do, act) suru する
make away with mochinige suru 持ち逃げする
make up for… …no tsugunai o suru …の償いをする
make up one's mind kesshin suru 決心する
make out (find out) mitsukeru 見付ける; (understand) rikai suru 理解する
make use of (utilize) riyō suru 利用する
make sure (*of*) … …o tashikameru …を確かめる

make-up *n.* mēkyappu メーキャップ

male *n.* otoko 男; osu 雄 —— *adj.* dansei no 男性の

man *n.* (human being) hito 人; (adult male) otoko 男

manage *v.* (handle) toriatsukau 取り扱う; (control) kanri suru 管理する

management *n.* (control) keiei 経営; (treatment) sōjū 操縦; (handling) toriatsukai 取扱い

manager *n.* shihainin 支配人; manējā マネージャー

manifest *v.* (show clearly) meiji suru 明示する; (display) hyōmei suru 表明する ——*adj.* (evident) akiraka na 明らかな

mankind *n.* ningen 人間; jinrui 人類

manner *n.* (way of acting) hōhō 方法; yarikata やり方; (outward bearing) taido 態度; *pl.* (polite social behavior) gyōgi 行儀; sahō 作法; manā マナー **in a manner** iwaba いわば; aru imi dewa ある意味では

mantle *n.* manto マント

manual *adj.* te no 手の; te de suru 手でする ——*n.* (handbook) handobukku ハンドブック

manufacture *n.* seizō 製造; *pl.* (manufactured goods) seihin 製品

manuscript *n.* (document written by hand) genkō 原稿; (written or typed book) shahon 写本

many *adj.* ōku no 多くの; tasū no 多数の; takusan no たくさんの
How many? Ikutsu? いくつ

map *n.* chizu 地図

maple *n.* kaede かえで; momiji もみじ

marble *n.* dairiseki 大理石

march *n.* kōshin 行進; (*musical composition*) kōshin-kyoku 行進曲; māchi マーチ

March *n.* san-gatsu 三月

margin *n.* (border) fuchi 縁; heri へり; (blank) yohaku 余白; (blank border of a printed page) rangai 欄外; (difference) rizaya 利ざや; (extra amount) yojō 余剰

marine *adj.* (of the sea) umi no 海の; kaiyō no 海洋の; (of shipping) sempaku no 船舶の; kaiji no 海事の

mark *n.* (sign) shirushi 印; māku マーク; (score) tensū 点数; (target) mato 的; (symbol) kigō 記号; (scratch) ato 跡 ——*v.* (put a mark on) shirushi o tsukeru 印をつける

market *n.* ichiba 市場; māketto マーケット

marmalade *n.* māmarēdo マーマレード

marriage *n.* kekkon 結婚

marry *v.* kekkon suru [saseru] 結婚する [させる]

Mars *n.* kasei 火星

marsh *n.* numachi 沼地；shitchi 湿地

marvel *n.* odoroku-beki mono [hito] 驚くべき物 [人]；kyōi 驚異 —— *v.* odoroku 驚く

marvelous *adj.* fushigi na 不思議な；odoroku-beki 驚くべき

mascot *n.* masukotto マスコット；mamori-gami 守り神

mash *v.* suritsubusu すりつぶす

mask *n.* kamen 仮面；masuku マスク

mason *n.* ishiya 石屋；renga-kō れんが工

mass¹ *n.* (lump) katamari 塊；(great part) daibubun 大部分；(group) shūdan 集団
the masses ippan taishū 一般大衆
mass communication masukomi マスコミ
mass production tairyō seisan 大量生産

mass² *n.* misa ミサ；gishiki 儀式

massacre *n., v.* gyakusatsu (suru) 虐殺 (する)

mast *n.* masuto マスト；hobashira 帆柱

master *n.* shujin 主人；sensei 先生 —— *v.* shūtoku suru 修得する
master of ceremonies shikaisha 司会者

mat *n.* mushiro むしろ；goza ござ；tatami 畳

match¹ *n.* matchi マッチ *match-box* matchi-bako マッチ箱

match² *n.* (one equal or similar to another) kōtekishu 好敵手；(game) shiai 試合；(marriage) kekkon 結婚 —— *vi.* (be equal to) ...ni hitteki suru ...に匹敵する；(harmonize) chōwa suru 調和する —— *vt.* (marry) kekkon saseru 結婚させる

material *n.* zairyō 材料；genryō 原料 —— *adj.* (physical) busshitsu-teki na 物質的な

mathematics *n.* sūgaku 数学

matter *n.* (substance) busshitsu 物質；(affair)

jiken 事件；(question) mondai 問題；(case)
kotogara 事柄；(thing) mono 物
as a matter of fact jijitsu wa 事実は
no matter how... tatoe don'na ni ...demo た
とえどんなに …でも

mature *adj.* (ripe) seijuku shita 成熟した ───
v. seijuku suru 成熟する

maximum *adj.* (greatest) saidai no 最大の；(highest) saikō no 最高の

may *v. aux.* (*permission*) shite mo yoi してもよ
い；(*possibility*) kamo shirenai かもしれない；
(*wish*) ...suru yō ni ...するように；(*concession*)
...shiyō tomo ...しようとも；(can) dekiru で
きる

May *n.* go-gatsu 五月

maybe *adv.* tabun 多分

me *pron.* watashi o [ni] わたしを [に]；wata-
kushi o [ni] わたくしを [に]

meal *n.* (food served in one sitting) shokuji 食事；
(coarsely ground grain) hikiwari ひき割り

mean[1] *v.* (intend) suru tsumori するつもり；(signify) imi suru 意味する

mean[2] *n., adj.* (middle point) chūkan(no) 中間
(の)；(average) heikin(no) 平均(の)；(moderate)
tekido no 適度の

mean[3] *adj.* (humble) iyashii 卑しい；(low in quality) geretsu na 下劣な

meaning *n.* imi 意味；shushi 主旨

means *n.* (method) shudan 手段；hōhō 方法；
(wealth) shiryoku 資力；tomi 富
by all means kanarazu 必ず；zehitomo 是非とも
by any means dōnika shite どうにかして
by means of ...ni yotte ...によって
by no means kesshite...de nai 決して...でない

meantime *n., adv.* (meanwhile) sono aida (ni) そ
の間(に)；sono-uchi (ni) そのうち(に)；aima
(ni) 合間 (に)

measurement *n.* sokutei 測定；sokuryō 測量

meat *n.* niku 肉

mechanic *n.* shokkō 職工; kikaikō 機械工

mechanical *adj.* kikai no 機械の; kikai-teki na 機械的な

medal *n.* medaru メダル; kunshō 勲章

medicine *n.* igaku 医学; (drug) kusuri 薬

Mediterranean *n., adj.* (the M-) Chichūkai (no) 地中海(の)

medium *adj.* (intermediate) chūkan no 中間の; (moderate) nami no 並の ——*n.* (means) shudan 手段; (mediation) baikai (-butsu) 媒介(物)

meet *v.* (come upon) deau 出会う; (be present at the arrival of) mukaeru 迎える; (come together) atsumaru 集まる

meeting *n.* shūkai 集会; kai 会; mītingu ミーティング

melody *n.* merodī メロディー; senritsu 旋律

melon *n.* meron メロン

melt *vi.* (become liquid by heat) tokeru 溶ける ——*vt.* (liquify by heat) tokasu 溶かす; (soften) yawarageru 和らげる

member *n.* kaiin 会員; membā メンバー; (member of legislature) giin 議員

memorial *adj.* kinen no 記念の ——*n.* kinembutsu 記念物

memory *n.* (faculty of remembering) kioku (-ryoku) 記憶(力); (recollection) tsuioku 追憶; omoide 思い出 *in memory of...* ...no kinen ni ...の記念に

mend *v.* (repair) naosu 直す; shūzen suru 修繕する; (reform) aratameru 改める

mental *adj.* (of the mind) seishin no 精神の; (intellectual) chiteki na 知的な; zunō no 頭脳の

mention *v.* noberu 述べる; ...ni tsuite hanasu ...について話す *not to mention* iu made mo naku 言うまでもなく

menu *n.* menyū メニュー

merchandise *n.* shōhin 商品

merchant *n.* shōnin 商人; kouri shōnin 小売商人

mercury *n.* (quicksilver) suigin 水銀; (M-) suisei 水星

mercy *n.* jihi 慈悲; awaremi 哀れみ; nasake 情
け   *at the mercy of...* ...no nasu ga mama ni
...のなすがままに

merit *n.* (value) kachi 価値; (goodness) chōsho
長所; (meritorious deed) tegara 手柄

mermaid *n.* (on'na no) ningyo （女の）人魚

merry *adj.* yōki na 陽気な; kaikatsuna 快活な;
yukai na 愉快な

mesh *n.* ami no me 網の目; *pl.* ami 網

message *n.* messēji メッセージ; dengon 伝言

messenger *n.* shisha 使者; tsukai 使い

metal *n.* kinzoku 金属

meter *n.* mētoru メートル; (instrument for
measuring) mētā メーター

method *n.* hōhō 方法; (order) junjo 順序

microscope *n.* kembikyō 顕微鏡

middle *adj.* (equally distant from extremes) mannaka no 真ん中の; (central) chūō no 中央の;
(medium) chūgurai no 中位の ——*n.* (middle
area or point) chūō(-bu) 中央(部) *middle
age* chūnen 中年 *middle class* chūsan kaikyū
中産階級

midnight *n.* mayonaka 真夜中; yahan 夜半

might *n.* (great physical strength) chikara 力;
(great power) kenryoku 権力

mild *adj.* onwa na 穏和な; odayaka na 穏やかな

mile *n.* mairu マイル

military *adj.* rikugun no 陸軍の; guntai no 軍隊の

milk *n.* miruku ミルク; gyūnyū 牛乳

million *n., adj.* hyaku-man (no) 百万 (の); (indefinite large number) musū no 無数の

millionaire *n.* hyaku-man chōja 百万長者; daifu-
gō 大富豪; ōganemochi 大金持ち

mind *n.* (spirit) kokoro 心; seishin 精神; (memory)
kioku 記憶; (attention) chūi 注意 ——*v.* chūi
suru 注意する; ki o tsukeru 気を付ける; (concern oneself) shimpai suru 心配する
Never mind. Dō itashi mashite. どういたしまし

て；Ki ni shinaide kudasai. 気にしないで下さい

mine¹ *pron.* watakushi [watashi] no mono わたく
し [わたし] のもの

mine² *n.* kōzan 鉱山　*coal mine* tankō 炭鉱

mineral *n., adj.* kōbutsu (no) 鉱物(の)；kōseki
(no) 鉱石 (の)

mingle *vt.* mazeru 混ぜる；kongō suru 混合する
—— *vi.* mazaru 混ざる

miniature *n.* (very small model) minichua ミニチ
ュア；(very small painting) shōgazō 小画像；
(very small copy) shukuzu 縮図　—— *adj.* kogata no 小型の

minimum *n., adj.* saishōgendo (no) 最小限度 (の)；
saishōryō 最小量

minister *n.* (head of a governmental department)
daijin 大臣
Prime Minister sōri-daijin 総理大臣

minor *adj.* chiisai hō no 小さい方の；shōsū no
少数の　—— *n.* miseinen-sha 未成年者

mint¹ *n.* (*aromatic plant*) hakka はっか

mint² *n.* (M-) (place where coins are manufactured)
zōhei-kyoku 造幣局　—— *v.* (produce coins)
(kahei o) chūzō suru (貨幣を)鋳造する　——
adj. (unused) mishiyō no 未使用の

minus *adj.* mainasu no マイナスの；…o hiita …
を引いた

minute *n.* fun [pun] 分；(a moment) shunkan 瞬間

miracle *n.* kiseki 奇跡；kyōi 驚異

mirror *n.* kagami 鏡

mirth *n.* (merriment) yōki 陽気；(gaiety) yukai 愉
快；(gladness) ōyorokobi 大喜び

mischief *n.* (prank) itazura いたずら；(harm) gai
害；kigai 危害

misery *n.* fukō 不幸；fu'un 不運

miss *v.* (fail to hit) atesokonau 当て損う；hazusu
外す；(fail to find) mitsukaranai 見付からない；
(fail to hear) kiki-morasu 聞きもらす；(fail to
catch) (kisha ni) noriokureru 乗り遅れる；(o-
mit) habuku 省く；(avoid) sakeru 避ける；(find

the absence of) …ga nai noni ki ga tsuku …が
ないのに気が付く;(feel the want of) …ga nai
no'o sabishiku omou …がないのを寂しく思う

Miss *n.* (*after surname*) …san …さん

mission *n.* (person's vocation) shimei 使命;(a
body of envoys to foreign country) shisetsu 使
節;(missionary vocation) dendō 伝導

missionary *adj.* dendō no 伝導の ―― *n.* dendō-
shi 伝導師;senkyōshi 宣教師

mist *n.* kiri 霧;kasumi かすみ ―― *v.* kiri ga kakaru 霧がかかる

mistake *v.* machigaeru 間違える ―― *n.* machigai 間違い

mitten *n.* futamata-tebukuro 二また手袋;miton
ミトン

mix *v.* mazeru 混ぜる;kongō suru 混合する
  mix-up konran 混乱;rantō 乱闘

moan *v.* umeku うめく;unaru うなる ―― *n.*
umeki うめき;unari-goe うなり声

mob *n.* (crowd) gunshū 群集;yajiuma 野次馬;(ri-
oters) bōto 暴徒

mock *v.* (ridicule) azakeru あざける;baka ni suru
ばかにする;(mimic in derision) mane o shite
karakau まねをしてからかう

mode *n.* (method) hōhō 方法;hōshiki 方式;(style)
yōshiki 様式

model *n.* mokei 模型;moderu モデル;(example)
mohan 模範

moderate *adj.* (avoiding extremes) tekido no 適度
の;(reasonable) muri no nai 無理のない;(*price*)
takaku nai 高くない

modern *adj.* kindai no 近代の;gendai no 現代の;
modan na モダンな

modest *adj.* (humble) kenson na けんそんな;
(unpretentious) hikaeme na 控え目な

modify *v.* (moderate) aratameru 改める;shūsei suru 修正する;(qualify) shūshoku suru 修飾する

moist *adj.* shimeppoi 湿っぽい;jime-jime shita
じめじめした

mold[1] *n.* (cast, moulding) kata 型; igata 鋳型; (character) seishitsu 性質

mold[2] *n., v.* kabi (ga haeru) かび (が生える)

mole *n.* mogura もぐら

moment *n.* (brief interval of time) shunkan 瞬間; (importance) jūyō 重要 *in a moment* tadachi ni 直ちに; tachimachi たちまち

Monday *n.* getsuyō-bi 月曜日

money *n.* kinsen 金銭; kane 金
Time is money. Toki wa kane nari. 時は金なり

monkey *n.* saru さる

monopoly *n.* sembai 専売; dokusen 独占

monotonous *adj.* tanchō na 単調な; taikutsu na 退屈な

monster *n.* kaibutsu 怪物; bakemono 化け物

month *n.* tsuki 月; ikkagetsu 1か月

monthly *adj.* maitsuki no 毎月の; tsuki ikkai 月1回 —— *n.* (monthly magazine) gekkan zasshi 月刊雑誌

monument *n.* kinen-butsu [-hi] 記念物 [碑]

mood[1] *n.* (state of mind or feeling) kibun 気分; kokochi 心地

mood[2] *n.* (verb form to express a fact, wish, order) hō 法

moody *adj.* (changing in mood) kibun no kawari yasui 気分の変りやすい; (gloomy) yū'utsu na 憂うつな; inki na 陰気な

moon *n.* tsuki 月

moonlight *n.* gekkō 月光 —— *adj.* tsukiyo no 月夜の

mop *n.* zōkin ぞうきん

moral *adj.* dōtoku no 道徳の; dōtoku-teki na 道徳的な —— *n.* (moral teaching) kyōkun 教訓; (ethics) rinri 倫理

more *adj.* yori ōi より多い; motto tasū [taryō] no もっと多数 [多量] の —— *adv.* motto もっと —— *n.* sara ni tasū [taryō] さらに多数 [多量]
a little more mō sukoshi もう少し

more and more masu-masu ますます; dan-dan だんだん

all the more naosara なおさら

no more (not…any more) mō…de nai もう…でない; mō jūbun de aru もう十分である

not more than seizei せいぜい

the more…the more sureba suru hodo masu-masu すればするほどますます

once more mō ichido もう一度

one more mō hitotsu (no) もう一つ (の)

still more naosara なおさら

some more mō sukoshi (no) もう少し (の)

moreover *adv.* nao なお; sono-ue ni その上に; sara ni さらに

morning *n.* asa 朝; gozen 午前 *Good morning!* Ohayō(gozai masu). おはよう(ございます).

mortal *adj.* (causing death) shinu-beki ummei no 死ぬべき運命の; (fatal) chimei-teki na 致命的な; (human being) ningen 人間

mortar *n.* morutaru モルタル; shikkui しっくい

mosquito *n.* ka か

moss *n.* koke こけ

most *adj.* mottomo ōi 最も多い; mottomo tasū [taryō] no 最も多数 [多量] の —— *adv.* mottomo 最も; hijō ni 非常に *at the most* seizei せいぜい

moth *n.* ga が

mother *n.* haha(-oya) 母(親); okā-san お母さん *mother-in-law* gibo 義母; shūtome しゅうとめ

motion *n.* (act of moving) undō 運動; (gesture) dōsa 動作; miburi 身振り *motion picture* eiga 映画

motive *n.* dōki 動機; dōin 動因

motor *n.* mōtā モーター

motto *n.* hyōgo 標語; mottō モットー

mound *n.* dote 土手; tsuka 塚; (small hill) ko-oka 小丘 —— *v.* dote o kizuku 土手を築く

mount *n.* yama 山; …san …山 *Mt. Fuji* Fuji-san 富士山 —— *v.* …ni agaru …に上がる;

(ni) noboru （に）登る

mountain *n.* yama 山; *pl.* sammyaku 山脈

mourn *v.* kanashimu 悲しむ; (grieve) nageku 嘆く

mouse *n.* hatsuka-nezumi 二十日ねずみ

moustache *n.* kuchi-hige 口ひげ

move *vt.* (change position) ugokasu 動かす; (affect deeply) kandō saseru 感動させる —— *vi.* (take some action) ugoku 動く; (change one's residence) hikkosu 引っ越す

movement *n.* (act of moving) undō 運動; (action) dōsa 動作; (transfer) idō 移動

movie *n.* eiga 映画

Mr. *n.* -shi …氏; -san …さん; -kun …君

Mrs. *n.* -fujin …夫人; -san …さん; okusama 奥様

much *adj.* ōku no 多くの; taryō no 多量の —— *n.* taryō 多量; takusan たくさん —— *adv.* ōini 大いに
make much of... …o omonjiru …を重んじる
not ...so much as …hodo …de nai …ほど…でない
much less naosara …de nai なおさら…でない
much more mashite まして; naosara なおさら
not so much ...as …yori mushiro …よりむしろ

muffler *n.* mafurā マフラー; erimaki 襟巻

mug *n.* dai-kappu 大カップ; magu マグ

multiply *v.* (increase in number) masu 増す; fuyasu 増やす; (cf. divide) jōjiru 乗じる; kakeru かける

multitude *n.* (large number) tasū 多数; (crowd) gunshū 群集; minshū 民衆

municipal *adj.* shi no 市の; shiei no 市営の; shisei no 市政の

murder *n.* satsujin 殺人; hitogoroshi 人殺し —— *v.* hito o korosu 人を殺す; satsugai suru 殺害する

murmur *n.* (softly spoken word) sasayaki ささやき; (indistinct complaint) tsubuyaki つぶやき; (low, indistinct, and continuous sound) zawameki ざわめき

muscle *n.* kin'niku 筋肉; kinryoku 筋力; wanryoku 腕力

museum *n.* hakubutsu-kan 博物館; bijutsu-kan 美術館

music *n.* ongaku 音楽

must *v. aux.* (have to) shinakereba naranai しなければならない; (certain) ... ni chigai nai ...に違いない ―― *n.* (absolute requirement) zettai ni hitsuyō na koto ぜったいに必要なこと *must not* shitewa ikenai してはいけない

mustard *n.* karashi からし

mute *adj.* (silent) mugon no 無言の; (not able to speak) oshi no おしの

mutter *v.* (speak in low, indistinct tones) sasayaku ささやく; (complain) butsu-butsu iu ぶつぶつ言う

mutton *n.* maton マトン; hitsuji no niku 羊の肉

mutual *adj.* sōgo no 相互の; otagai no お互いの

muzzle *n.* (snout) hana-zura 鼻面; (open end of gun) jūkō 銃口

my *pron.* watashi no わたしの; watakushi no 私の

myself *pron.* watashi [watakushi] jishin わたし [わたくし]自身

mystery *n.* shimpi 神秘; himitsu 秘密; fushigi 不思議

myth *n.* shinwa 神話

mythology *n.* (myths) shinwa 神話; shinwa-gaku 神話学

N

nail *n.* (fingernail or toenail) tsume つめ; (cf. spike) kugi 釘 *nail clipper* tsume-kiri つめ切り

naked *adj.* hadaka no 裸の; mukidashi no むきだしの

name *n.* namae 名前; seimei 姓名 —— *v.* (give a name to) ...to nazukeru ...と名付ける

namely *adv.* sunawachi すなわち

napkin *n.* napukin ナプキン

narcissus *n.* suisen 水仙

narrate *n.* hanasu 話す; monogataru 物語る; noberu 述べる

narrative *n., adj.* monogatari (no) 物語(の); hanashi (no) 話(の)

narrow *adj.* semai 狭い; hosoi 細い
narrow-minded kokoro no semai 心の狭い

nasty *adj.* (dirty) hidoku kitanai ひどく汚い; (unpleasant) kimochi no warui 気持ちの悪い

nation *n.* (cf. people) kokumin 国民; (race) minzoku 民族; (state) kuni 国; kokka 国家

nationalism *n.* (devotion to the nation) kokkashugi 国家主義; (patriotic feelings) aikokushin 愛国心

native *adj.* (of one's birth place) umare no 生れの; shōkoku no 生国の; (inborn) umaretsuki no 生れつきの; (indigenous) dochaku no 土着の —— *n.* (one born in a place) ...umare no hito ...生れの人; (original inhabitant of a place) genjūmin 原住民

natural *adj.* (existing in or by nature) shizen no 自然の; ten'nen no 天然の; (innate) umaretsuki no 生れつきの

naturally *adv.* (spontaneously) shizen ni 自然に; (without exaggeration) ari no mama ni ありのままに; (of course) mochiron もちろん; tōzen 当然

nature *n.* (basic quality) honshitsu 本質; (kind, sort) shurui 種類; (physical universe) busshitsukai 物質界; (natural scenery) shizen 自然

naught *n.* zero ゼロ; mu 無

naughty *adj.* itazura na いたずらな; wampaku na 腕白な; gyōgi no warui 行儀の悪い

naval *adj.* kaigun no 海軍の

navigate *v.* kōkai suru 航海する；sōjū suru 操縦する；kōkō suru 航行する

navy *n.* kaigun 海軍

near *adv.* chikaku 近く ——— *prep.* ...no chikaku ni ...の近くに ——— *adj.* chikai 近い
near at hand (close at hand) sugu chikaku ni すぐ近くに；(not far in the future) chikai uchi ni 近いうちに *near-sighted* kinshi no 近視の

nearly *adv.* (almost) hotondo ほとんど；yaku 約

neat *adj.* (tidy) kichin to shita きちんとした；(trim) kogirei na こぎれいな；(skillful) tegiwa no yoi 手際のよい

necessary *adj.* (needful) hitsuyō na 必要な；(inevitable) hitsuzen-teki na 必然的な；sakegatai 避けがたい ——— *n.* (requisite) hitsuju-hin 必需品 *necessaries of life* seikatsu hitsuju-hin 生活必需品

neck *n.* kubi 首；eri 襟

necklace *n.* kubi-kazari 首飾り；nekkuresu ネックレス

necktie *n.* nekutai ネクタイ

need *n.* (necessity) hitsuyō 必要；(something needed) hitsuyō-hin 必要品 ——— *v.* hitsuyō to suru 必要とする；(must) shinakereba naranai しなければならない

needle *n.* hari 針

needless *adj.* fuhitsuyō na 不必要な *needless to say* iu mademo naku 言うまでもなく

negative *adj.* (saying "no") hitei-teki na 否定的な；(not positive) shōkyoku-teki na 消極的な ——— *n.* hitei 否定；(*photographic film*) inga 陰画；nega ネガ

neglect *v.* (be remiss about) okotaru 怠る；(ignore) mushi suru 無視する ——— *n.* taiman 怠慢；mushi 無視

negotiate *v.* kōshō suru 交渉する

Negro *n.*, *adj.* kokujin (no) 黒人(の)

neighbor *n.* rinjin 隣人；kinjo no hito 近所の人

neighborhood *n.* kinjo 近所; fukin 付近

neither *adv.* **neither ... nor** demonaku ...demo nai でもなく ...でもない; ...mo mata ...de nai ...もまた ...でない; dochira mo ...de nai どちらも ...でない; dochira mo ...shinai どちらも ...しない

nerve *n.* shinkei 神経; (mental strength) kiryoku 気力

nervous *adj.* shinkei no 神経の; shinkei-shitsu na 神経質な

nest *n.* (birdnest) su 巣; sumika すみか ——*v.* su o tsukuru 巣を作る

net¹ *n.* ami 網; netto ネット

net² *n., adj.* (net amount) shōmi no 正味の; jun 純 *net profit* jun'eki 純益

Netherland *n.* Oranda オランダ

network *n.* (chain of TV stations) hōsōmō 放送網; nettowāku ネットワーク; (netting) amizaiku 網細工

neurotic *n.* noirōze ノイローゼ

neutral *adj.* chūritsu no 中立の; chūsei no 中性の

never *adv.* kesshite ...shinai 決して ...しない
Never mind! Goshimpai naku. ご心配なく; Dō itashi mashite. どういたしまして.
Never! Tondemo nai. とんでもない.

nevertheless *adv.* sore nimo kakawarazu それにもかかわらず

new *adj.* atarashii 新しい ——*adv.* atarashiku 新しく *new year* shin'nen 新年

news *n.* nyūsu ニュース; tayori 便り

newspaper *n.* shimbun 新聞

next *adj.* tsugi no 次の
next door tonari 隣
next month raigetsu 来月
next time kono tsugi この次
next week raishū 来週

nice *adj.* yoi 良い; ii いい; rippa na 立派な

nickel *n.* nikkeru ニッケル; (coin worth five

cents) go-sento no hakudōka 5 セントの白銅貨

niece *n.* mei めい

night *n.* yoru 夜; yo 夜; ban 晩

 all night hito-ban-jū 一晩中; yodōshi 夜通し

 every night maiban 毎晩

 Good night! Oyasumi nasai. おやすみなさい.

 last night sakuya 昨夜; sakuban 昨晩; yūbe ゆうべ

 tomorrow night myōban 明晩

nightcap *n.* nezake 寝酒

nightfall *n.* higure 日暮れ; yūgata 夕方

nine *n., adj.* ku (no) 9, 九 (の); kyū (no) 9, 九 (の); kokonotsu (no) 九つ (の)

nineteen *n., adj.* jūku (no) 19, 十九 (の); jūkyū (no) 19, 十九 (の)

ninety *n., adj.* kyū-jū (no) 90, 九十 (の)

ninth *n., adj.* dai-ku(no) 第9 (の)

nip *v.* tsuneru つねる; hasamu 挟む

no *adj., adv.* (sukoshimo) nai (少しも) ない; iie いいえ; …de nai …でない

 No thank you. Kekkō desu. 結構です.

noble *adj.* (showing greatness of character) tōtoi 貴い; kedakai 気高い; (illustrious) rippa na 立派な; (of high hereditary rank) kōki no 高貴の

nobody *pron.* dare mo …de nai だれも …でない

nod *v.* unazuku うなずく; (be drowsy) uto-uto suru うとうとする; (nemukute) kokkuri kokkuri suru (眠くて) こっくりこっくりする

noise *n.* mono'oto 物音; sō'on 騒音; sawagi 騒ぎ

nominate *v.* shimei suru 指名する; nimmei suru 任命する

none *pron.* dare mo …nai だれも …ない; sukoshimo …nai 少しも …ない; kesshite …nai 決して …ない

nonsense *n.* muimi 無意味; tawagoto たわごと; nansensu ナンセンス

noodle *n.* nūdoru ヌードル; hoshi-udon 干うどん

noon *n.* shōgo 正午; mahiru 真昼

nor *conj.* mo mata …(de) nai もまた …(で) ない; mata …demo nai また …でもない

normal *adj.* seijō no 正常の; hyōjun no 標準の

north *n., adj.* kita (no) 北 (の); hoppō (no) 北方 (の)

northeast *n., adj.* hokutō (no) 北東(の); hokutō (e) 北東(へ)

northwest *n., adj.* hokusei (no) 北西(の); hokusei (e) 北西(へ)

nose *n.* hana 鼻 *nosebleed* hanaji 鼻血

not *adv.* …de nai …でない; shinai しない
  not a little sukunakarazu 少なからず
  not always kanarazushimo 必ずしも
  not at all sukoshimo …de nai 少しも …でない
  Not at all. Dō itashi-mashite. どういたしまして.
  not yet mada …nai まだ …ない

notable *adj.* (outstanding) sugureta すぐれた; yūmei na 有名な; (remarkable) ichijirushii 著しい; chūmoku subeki 注目すべき —— *n.* chomeijin 著名人.

note *n.* (brief written record) oboegaki 覚え書; (commentary) chū 注; (promissory note) yakusoku tegata 約束手形; (musical tone) ompu 音符; (notice) chūi 注意; (short letter) mijikai tegami 短い手紙 —— *v.* (write down) kakitomeru 書き留める; (remark) chūi suru 注意する

noted *adj.* yūmei na 有名な; chomei na 著名な

nothing *n.* (not anything) nani mo nai koto 何もないこと; (naught) mu 無; (something of no value) toru ni tarinai koto 取るに足りないこと
  nothing but …igai niwa nani mo nai …以外には何もない; tada…dake ただ…だけ
  for nothing (without payment) tada de ただで; (in vain) muda ni むだに
  come to nothing muda ni owaru むだに終る

notice *n.* (attention) chūi 注意; (observation) chūmoku 注目; (information) shirase 知らせ —— *v.* (observe) chūmoku suru 注目する; (be aware of) ki ga tsuku 気が付く

take notice of... ...o kokoro ni tomeru ...を心に留める

without notice yokoku nashi de 予告なしで; mudan de 無断で

notify *v.* ...ni tsūkoku suru ...に通告する

notion *n.* (opinion) kangae 考え; iken 意見; (conception) gainen 概念

notorious *adj.* akumei takai 悪名高い; naute no 名うての

noun *n.* meishi 名詞

novel *n.* shōsetsu 小説

novelty *n.* meatarashii mono [koto] 目新しい物 [事]

November *n.* jūichi-gatsu 十一月

now *adv.* ima 今; mō もう *just now* chōdo ima ちょうど今 *now and then* tokidoki 時々

nowadays *adv.* konogoro dewa このごろでは; chikagoro 近ごろ

nowhere *adv.* doko nimo...nai どこにも...ない

nucleus *n.* kaku 核; genshikaku 原子核

nude *n., adj.* (bare) hadaka (no) 裸 (の); arino mama no ありのままの

number *n.* kazu 数; sūji 数字; bangō 番号; nambā ナンバー —— *v.* (count) kazoeru 数える; bangō o utsu 番号を打つ

telephone number denwa bangō 電話番号

a number of tasū no 多数の

numerous *adj.* tasū no 多数の

nun *n.* shūdō-jo 修道女; nisō 尼僧

nurse *n.* (wet nurse) uba 乳母; (sick-nurse) kangofu 看護婦 —— *v.* (suckle) chichi o nomaseru 乳を飲ませる

nursery *n.* kodomo-beya 子供部屋; ikuji-shitsu 育児室 *nursery rhyme* dōyō 童謡

nut *n.* ko no mi 木の実; nattsu ナッツ

nymph *n.* ninfu ニンフ; josei 女性

O

oak *n.* kashi かし

oar *n.* kai かい; ro ろ

oatmeal *n.* ōtomīru オートミール

obedience *n.* fukujū 服従; jūjun 従順

obey *v.* shitagau 従う; fukujū suru 服従する

object *n.* (material thing) mono 物; buttai 物体; (purpose) mokuteki 目的; taishō(-butsu) 対象 (物) —— *v.* (make an objection) hantai suru 反対する; igi o tonaeru

oblige *v.* (force) yoginaku saseru 余儀無くさせる; (make grateful) arigatagaraseru 有り難がらせる

(*be*) *obliged to* (put under necessity) sezaru o enai せざるをえない; (thank) arigataku omou 有難く思う

oblong *n., adj.* (rectangular) chōhō-kei (no) 長方形 (の); (prolate) daen-kei (no) だ円形 (の)

obscure *adj.* (vague) aimai na あいまいな; bonyari shita ぼんやりした; (not clear) fumeiryō na 不明瞭な; (dim) usugurai 薄暗い

observe *v.* (watch) kansatsu suru 観察する; (perceive) kizuku 気付く; (keep) mamoru 守る; (remark) noberu 述べる

obstacle *n.* shōgai(-butsu) 障害(物); (hindrance) bōgai 妨害

obstinate *adj.* (stubborn) ganko na 頑固な; gōjō na 強情な

obstruct *v.* (hinder) bōgai suru 妨害する; (block up) fusagu ふさぐ

obtain *v.* uru 得る; te ni ireru 手に入れる

obvious *adj.* akirakana 明らかな; wakarikitta 分り切った

occasion *n.* (case) ba'ai 場合; (chance) kikai 機会; (reason) riyū 理由; (cause) gen'in 原因 —— *v.* (cause) hikiokosu 引き起す

occasionally *adv.* tokiori 時折; tokidoki 時々

occupation *n.* (vocation) shokugyō 職業; (occupying) senryō 占領

occupy *v.* (seize possession of) senryō suru 占領する; (reside in) sumu 住む; (engage oneself) jūji suru 従事する; (keep busy) isogashiku suru 忙しくする

occur *v.* (happen) okoru 起る; (come into one's mind) (kokoro ni) ukabu (心に) 浮かぶ

ocean *n.* taiyō 大洋; kaiyō 海洋; umi 海
Pacific Ocean Taiheiyō 太平洋
Atlantic Ocean Taiseiyō 大西洋

o'clock *n.* ...ji ...時

October *n.* jū-gatsu 十月

odd *adj.* (not even) kisū no 奇数の; (fragmentary) hampa na 半端な; (strange) kimyō na 奇妙な; (extra) yobun no 余分の

odds *n.* (difference) yūretsu no sa 優劣の差; (advantage) handikyappu ハンディキャップ; (balance of advantage) shōsan 勝算; (betting ratio) kakeritsu かけ率 *odds and ends* garakuta がらくた

odor *n.* (perfume) kaori 香り; (smell) nioi におい

of *prep.* (belonging to) ...no ...の; (from) ...kara ...から; (concerning, about) ...ni tsuite ...について; (which is called) ...to iu ...と言う
of course mochiron もちろん

off *adv.* (away) hanarete 離れて; satte 去って; achira e あちらへ
Off limits. Tachiiri kinshi. 立入り禁止

offend *v.* (make angry) okoraseru 怒らせる; (displease) kanjō o gaisuru 感情を害する; (commit an offense) tsumi o okasu 罪を犯す
offender ihansha 違反者

offense *n.* (crime) tsumi 罪; hanzai 犯罪; (insult) burei 無礼; (anger) rippuku 立腹; (attack) kōgeki 攻撃

offer *v.* (present) teikyō suru 提供する; (propose) mōshideru 申し出る; (suggest) teian suru 提案

する —— *n.* (proposal) mōshikomi 申し込み；(presentation) teikyō 提供；(suggestion) teian 提案

office *n.* jimusho 事務所；kaisha 会社；ofisu オフィス

officer *n.* (one who holds an office) kōmuin 公務員；shokuin 職員；(commissioned officer) shōkō 将校

official *n.* (officer) kōmuin 公務員 —— *adj.* (public) ōyake no 公の；kōshiki no 公式の *official documents* kōbunsho 公文書

often *ad.* shiba-shiba しばしば

oh *int.* ō おー；oya おや

oil *n.* abura 油；(petroleum) sekiyu 石油

O. K. *adj. adv.* yoroshii よろしい；shōchi 承知；ōkē オーケー

old *adj.* (aged) toshitotta 年取った；(ancient) mukashi no 昔の；(cf. new) furui 古い *old-fashioned* kofū na 古風な；kyūshiki no 旧式の

olive *n.* orību オリーブ

omit *v.* (leave out) shōryaku suru 省略する；habuku 省く；(fail to do) okotaru 怠る

on *prep.* no ue ni「de」の上に「で」；(toward) …ni mukatte …に向かって；(concerning) …ni tsuite …について；(near to) …no soba …のそば；(kawa no) hotori ni (川の) ほとりに

once *adv.* (one time only) ichido 一度；(formerly) katsute かつて *at once* sugu ni すぐに *once more* mō ichido もう一度 *once upon a time* mukashi-mukashi 昔々

one *adj.* (single) hitotsu no 一つの；(a certain) aru ある —— *n.* (lowest number) ichi 1, 一；(single person or thing) hitori 一人；hitotsu 一つ —— *pron.* (person) hito 人；(thing) mono 物 *one after another* tsugi-tsugi to 次々と *one another* tagai ni 互いに *one by one* hitotsu-zutsu 一つずつ；hitori zutsu ひとりずつ

onion *n.* tamanegi 玉ねぎ

only *adj.* (sole) tada hitotsu no ただ一つの
—— *adv.* (merely) dake だけ; tada ただ; tan ni
単に; hon'no ほんの
not only . . . but dake de naku . . . mo mata だけ
でなく …もまた

onward *adj.* zenshin suru 前進する; zenshin-teki
na 前進的な —— *adv.* zempō e 前方へ; saki
e 先へ; susunde 進んで

open *adj.* (not closed) hiraite iru 開いている;
aite iru あいている; (having no cover) o'oi no
nai 覆いのない; (free for the public) kōkai no
公開の; (not fenced in) hirobiro to shita 広々
とした; (frank) sotchoku na 率直な —— *v.*
(begin) hajimeru 始める; (make open) akeru
あける; hiraku 開く —— *n.* (the outdoors)
kogai 戸外
bottle opener sen'nuki せん抜き
open air kogai 戸外
opener kankiri かん切り

operate *v.* (perform) hataraku 働く; (influence)
sayō suru 作用する; (perform an operation)
shujutsu suru 手術する; (manage) keiei suru
経営する

operator *n.* denwa-kōkanshu 電話交換手

opinion *n.* iken 意見; setsu 説

opponent *n.* (adversary) aite 相手; (foe) teki 敵;
hantaisha 反対者 —— *v.* (opposing) taikō suru 対抗する; (resist) teikō suru 抵抗する

opposite *adj.* hantai no 反対の; (facing) mukai
gawa no 向かい側の

oppress *v.* appaku suru 圧迫する; shiitageru
虐げる

optical *adj.* me no 目の; shiryoku no 視力の

optimism *n.* rakuten-shugi 楽天主義; rakkan 楽
観

or *conj.* matawa または; aruiwa あるいは; sunawachi すなわち; samonaito さもないと

oral *adj.* kōtō no 口頭の; kōjutsu no 口述の

orange *n.* mikan みかん

orator *n.* kōensha 講演者; enzetsusha 演説者; benshi 弁士

orbit *n.* kidō 軌道; (eye-socket) ganka 眼か —— *v.* kidō ni notte mawaru 軌道に乗って回る **orbiter** jinkō-eisei 人口衛星

orchard *n.* kajuen 果樹園

orchestra *n.* ōkesutora オーケストラ

orchid *n.* ran らん —— *adj.* usu-murasaki-iro no 薄紫色の

order *n.* (command) meirei 命令; (sequence) junjo 順序; (itemized request) chūmon 注文; (order) chitsujo 秩序; seiton 整とん —— *v.* (command) meijiru 命じる; (arrange) seiton suru 整とんする
in order junjo tadashiku 順序正しく
in order to …suru tame ni …するために
out of order koshō shiteiru 故障している; kurutte iru 狂っている

orderly *adv.* seizen to shita 整然とした

organ *n.* (musical instrument with keys, pipes etc.) paipu-orugan パイプオルガン; (special part of the body) kikan 器管 *digestive organ* shōka-ki 消化器

organization *n.* (system) soshiki 組織; kikō 機構; (association) dantai 団体

organize *v.* soshiki suru 組織する

orient *n.* (the O-) Tōyō 東洋

oriental *adj.* Tōyō no 東洋の; Tōyō-jin no 東洋人の

origin *n.* kigen 起源; hajimari 始まり; okori 起り

original *adj.* (first in order) hajime no 初めの; (creative) dokusō-teki na 独創的な —— *n.* (original work) gembun 原文; gembutsu 原物

originate *v.* (create) kōan suru 考案する; (begin) hajimeru 始める; okoru 起る

ornament *n.* sōshoku(-butsu) 装飾(物)

orphan *n., adj.* koji (no) 孤児 (の)

orphan asylum kojiin 孤児院

ostrich *n.* dachō だちょう

other *adj.* hoka no 外の; ta no 他の
each other tagai no 互いの
the other day senjitsu 先日
in other words iikaereba 言い換えれば

otherwise *adv.* (in a different way) sō de naku そうでなく; hoka no 外の; (if not) sō de nakereba そうでなければ

ought *v. aux.* subeki de aru すべきである; suru noga tōzen de aru するのが当然である; no hazu de aru のはずである

our *pron.* wareware no 我々の; watakushi-tachi no 私たちの; watashi-tachi no わたしたちの

ours *pron.* wareware no mono 我々のもの; watakushi-tachi no mono 私たちのもの; watashi-tachi no mono わたしたちのもの

out *adv.* soto ni「e」外に「へ」 ── *adj.* soto no 外の
out of …kara …から
out of breath iki ga kireru 息が切れる

outbreak *n.* boppatsu ぼっ発; hassei 発生

outdoor *adj.* kogai no 戸外の; soto no 外の

outdoors *adv.* kogai de「ni」戸外で「に」; soto de「ni」外で「に」

outer *adj.* soto no 外の; gaibu no 外部の

outfit *n.* (set of equipment) shitaku (-hin) 支度 (品); jumbi 準備; (articles forming an equipment) yōgu (-rui) 用具 (類)

outlet *n.* (way out) deguchi 出口; (market for goods) hanro 販路; (*electrical*) konsento コンセント

outline *n.* (contour) rinkaku 輪郭; (quick sketch) ryakuzu 略図; (summary) kōgai こう概; autorain アウトライン

output *n.* (yield) seisandaka 生産高; (*electrical*) shutsuryoku 出力

outside *n., adj.* gaibu (no) 外部 (の); sotogawa (no) 外側 (の)

outsider *n.* kyokugaisha 局外者; autosaidā アウトサイダー

outstanding *adj.* medatsu 目立つ; kencho na 顕著な

oval *adj.* (egg-shaped) tamago-gata no 卵形の; (elliptical) daenkei no だ円形の

oven *n.* tempi 天火; (small furnace) kamado かまど

over *prep.* (above) …no ue o …の上を; (across) yokogitte 横切って; (more than) ijō ni 以上に
——— *adv.* koete 越えて; mukō ni 向うに; (ended) owatte 終って; sunde すんで; (once again) kurikaeshite 繰り返して; (too much) kado ni 過度に
overtime zangyō 残業
over there achira あちら

overcoat *n.* gaitō 外とう; ōbā オーバー

overcome *v.* uchikatsu 打ち勝つ; uchimakasu 打ち負かす

overhear *v.* futo kiku ふと聞く; tachi-giki suru 立ち聞きする

overlook *v.* miorosu (look down upon) 見下ろす; (watch over) kantoku suru 監督する; (fail to notice) miotosu 見落とす; (tolerate) ōme ni miru 大目に見る

overseas *adj.* kaigai no [kara no] 海外の [からの]; gaikoku no [kara no] 外国の [からの]

overtake *v.* (come up with) oitsuku 追い付く; (come up suddenly) totsuzen osou 突然襲う

overthrow *v.* (overturn) kutsugaesu くつがえす; hikkuri-kaesu 引っくり返す; (defeat) makasu 負かす; (upset) taosu 倒す

overwhelm *v.* (overcome completely) attōsuru 圧倒する; (engulf) (umi ga) makikomu (海が) 巻き込む

overwork *n.* karō 過労; ōbāwāku オーバーワーク
——— *v.* hataraki sugiru 働き過ぎる

owe *v.* …ni ou …に負う; …ni kari [gimu] ga aru …に借り [義務] がある

owing to …no tame ni …のために
owl *n.* fukurō ふくろう
own *adj.* jibun no 自分の; dokuji no 独自の
—— *v.* (possess) shoyū suru 所有する **owner**
shoyūsha 所有者
ox *n.* o-ushi 雄牛
oxygen *n.* sanso 酸素
oyster *n.* kaki かき

P

pace *n.* ayumi 歩み; hochō 歩調; pēsu ペース
pacific *adj.* heiwa na [no] 平和な [の]; (the P-)
Taiheiyō 太平洋
pacify *v.* (appease) nadameru なだめる; (calm)
shizumeru 静める; (establish peace) heitei suru
平定する; shizumeru 静める
pack *n.* tsutsumi 包み; (burden) nimotsu 荷物;
(set) hito-soroi 一揃い —— *v.* tsutsumu 包む;
nizukuri suru 荷造りする
package *n.* (parcel) tsutsumi 包み; hōsō 包装;
pakkēji パッケージ; kozutsumi 小包
packet *n.* (small bundle) chiisana taba 小さな束;
(small package) kozutsumi 小包; (*cigarettes*)
hito-hako 一箱 *postal packet* yūbin-kozutsumi
郵便小包
pad *n.* (pillow) makura 枕; (stuffing) tsumemono
詰物; paddo パッド; (bundle) taba 束; (*paper*)
hito-tsuzuri 一つづり *writing pad* binsen 便
せん
page *n.* (leaf of a book) pēji ページ; (boy servant)
hoteru no bōi ホテルのボーイ
pageant *n.* yagai-geki 野外劇; pējento ページェ
ント
pain *n.* (bodily or mental suffering) kutsū 苦痛;
pl. (labor) honeori 骨折り; (trouble) kushin
苦心
paint *n.* enogu 絵具; penki ペンキ —— *v.* egaku

描く; penki o nuru ペンキを塗る

pair *n.* ittsui 一対; hitokumi 一組; itchaku 一着

pal *n.* nakama 仲間

palace *n.* (monarch's residence) kyūden 宮殿; (magnificent building) dai-teitaku 大邸宅

pale *n.* (whitish) aojiroi 青白い; (faint) iro no usui 色の薄い

palm *n.* te no hira 手の平; (cf. date-palm) shuro しゅろ

pamphlet *n.* panfuretto パンフレット

pan *n.* (dish) sara 皿; (cf. frying pan) hira-nabe 平なべ

pane *n.* (ita-) garasu (板)ガラス; (window-pane) mado-garasu 窓ガラス

panel *n.* kagami-ita 鏡板; paneru パネル; hame 羽目

panic *n.* kyōkō 恐慌; panikku パニック

pants *n.* (trousers) zubon ズボン; (drawers) pantsu パンツ; pantī パンティー; zubon-shita ズボン下

paper *n.* kami 紙; (newspaper) shimbunshi 新聞紙   *sheet of paper* ichi-mai no kami 一枚の紙

parade *n., v.* parēdo (suru) パレード (する); kōshin (suru) 行進 (する)

paradise *n.* rakuen 楽園; tengoku 天国

paragraph *n.* (bunshō no) setsu (文章の) 節; kiji 記事

parallel *adj.* heikō no 平行の   —— *n.* heikō-sen 平行線

paralyze *v.* mahi saseru 麻ひさせる; muryoku ni suru 無力にする

parcel *n.* kozutsumi 小包

pardon *v.* (forgive) yurusu 許す; yōsha suru 容赦する   *I beg your pardon.* Gomen nasai. ごめんなさい; Shitsurei desu ga. 失礼ですが.

parent *n.* oya 親; *pl.* ryōshin 両親

park *n.* (public land for recreation) kōen 公園   —— *v.* (leave a vehicle temporarily) chūsha suru 駐車する

parliament *n.* gikai 議会

parlor *n.* (sitting room) ima 居間; (drawing room) ōsetsuma 応接間

parrot *n.* ōmu オウム —— *v.* monomane o suru 物まねをする

part *n.* (a portion of a whole) bubun 部分; …bun no ichi …分の1; (duty) hombun 本分; (role) yakuwari 役割; (*play*) yaku 役; (side) gawa 側 —— *v.* (divide) wakeru 分ける; (leave each other) wakareru 別れる

for my part watashi to shitewa わたしとしては
part from …to wakareru …と別れる
take part in sanka suru 参加する

participate *v.* sanka suru 参加する

particle *n.* ryūshi 粒子; biryūshi 微粒子; bunshi 分子

particular *adj.* (specific) tokushu no 特殊の; (special) tokubetsu no 特別の; (detailed) shōsai na 詳細な; (individual) dokuji no 独自の; (hard to please) yakamashii やかましい; (distinguished from others) ichijirushii 著しい —— *n.* (item) jikō 事項; kajō 箇条 *in particular* toku ni 特に

particularly *adv.* toku ni 特に; ichijirushiku 著しく; kuwashiku 詳しく

partition *n.* (dividing line) shikiri 仕切り; (division) bunkatsu 分割; bumpai 分配

partner *n.* (companion) nakama 仲間; aite 相手; (a wife or a husband) haigūsha 配偶者

party *n.* kai 会; pātī パーティー; (political party) tō 党; seitō 政党

pass *v.* (move) ugoku 動く; (make one's way) tōru 通る; (go by) tsūka suru 通過する; (go forward) zenshin suru 前進する; (elapse) toki ga tatsu 時がたつ; (spend) sugosu 過ごす; (pass an examination) gōkaku suru 合格する; (be transferred) wataru 渡る —— *n.* (free pass) muryō jōsha「nyūjō」ken 無料乗車「入場」券
pass away (die) shinu 死ぬ

pass by tōri-sugiru 通り過ぎる

pass for (be taken for) ...to minasareru ...とみなされる

pass over ...o koeru ...を越える; (overlook) ...o miotosu ...を見落とす

passenger *n.* jōkyaku 乗客; ryokaku 旅客; tsū-kōnin 通行人

passion *n.* (zeal) jōnetsu 情熱; (violent emotion) gekijō 激情; (rage) gekidō 激動

passport *n.* ryoken 旅券; pasupōto パスポート

past *adj.* (cf. present) kako no 過去の; sugisatta 過ぎ去った —— *n.* kako 過去

paste *n.* nori のり; pēsuto ペースト

pastime *n.* kibarashi 気晴らし; goraku 娯楽

pastor *n.* bokushi 牧師

pastry *n.* neriko-gashi 練り粉菓子; pai パイ

pasture *n.* bokujō 牧場; bokusō-chi 牧草地

pat *v.* karuku tataku 軽くたたく; naderu なでる

patch *n.* (piece to mend a hole) tsugihagi つぎはぎ; (spot) hanten はん点; (piece of plaster) kōyaku こう薬; (small piece of ground) shōji-men 小地面 —— *v.* tsugi o ateru つぎを当てる; tsukurou つくろう

patent *n.* sembai tokkyo 専売特許 —— *v.* tokkyo o ukeru 特許を受ける

path *n.* ko-michi 小道; hoso-michi 細道

patience *n.* nintai 忍耐; gaman 我慢

patient *adj.* gaman-zuyoi 我慢強い; shimbō-zuyoi 辛抱強い —— *n.* (sick person) kanja 患者

patriot *n.* aikokusha 愛国者; shishi 志士

patrol *n.* junsatsu 巡察; patorōru パトロール

patron *n.* kōensha 後援者; hogosha 保護者; patoron パトロン

pattern *n.* (fine example) mohan 模範; tehon 手本; (paper pattern) katagami 型紙; (design) moyō 模様

pause *n.* kyūshi 休止; kugiri 区切り

pave *v.* shiku 敷く; hosō suru 舗装する

pavement *n.* hodō 舗道; shiki-ishi 敷石

pay *v.* (give money to one for goods or services) shiharau 支払う; harau 払う; (make up for) tsugunau 償う ——*n.* (salary) kyūryō 給料; (wages) chingin 賃銀 *pay a call* hōmon suru 訪問する

payment *n.* (act of paying) shiharai 支払い; (requital) shikaeshi 仕返し

pea *n.* endō-mame えんどう豆

peace *n.* heiwa 平和; heian 平安

peaceful *adj.* heiwa na 平和な; heion na 平穏な *peacefully* heiwa ni 平和に; heion ni 平穏に

peach *n.* momo (no ki) 桃 (の木)

peacock *n.* kujaku くじゃく

peak *n.* (top of a mountain) sanchō 山頂; mine 峰; (the highest point) chōten 頂点

peanut *n.* pīnatsu ピーナツ

pear *n.* nashi なし

pearl *n.* shinju 真珠; pāru パール

pebble *n.* koishi 小石

peculiar *adj.* (special) dokutoku no 独特の; tokushu na 特殊な; (strange) hen na 変な

pedal *n.* ashifumi 足踏み; pedaru ペダル

peddler *n.* gyōshōnin 行商人

pedestrian *adj.* hokō no 歩行の; toho no 徒歩の ——*n.* hokōsha 歩行者

peel *vt.* kawa o muku 皮をむく ——*vi.* kawa ga mukeru 皮がむける ——*n.* kawa 皮

peep *v.* nozoku のぞく; sotto miru そっと見る; (chirp) piyo-piyo [chū-chū] naku ぴよぴよ [ちゅうちゅう] 鳴く

peer[1] *n.* dōryō 同僚; nakama 仲間; (nobleman) kizoku 貴族

peer[2] *v.* sukashite jitto miru 透してじっと見る; gyōshi suru 凝視する

pelican *n.* perikan ペリカン

pen *n.* pen ペン *penholder* penjiku ペン軸

penalty *n.* batsu 罰; bakkin 罰金; iyakukin 違約金

pencil *n.* empitsu えんぴつ

penetrate *v.* (pierce through) tsuranuku 貫く; fukaku hairikomu 深く入り込む; kantsū suru 貫通する; (permeate) shimikomu しみ込む

penguin *n.* pengin ペンギン

peninsula *n.* hantō 半島

penny *n.* ichi-penī 1 ペニー

pension *n.* nen-kin 年金; onkyū 恩給; (cheap hotel) penshon ペンション

people *n.* kokumin 国民; minzoku 民族; jimmin 人民; hitobito 人々

pepper *n.* koshō こしょう

per *prep.* (for every) ...ni tsuki ...につき; (by means of) ...ni yori ...により

perceive *v.* mitomeru 認める; ki ga tsuku 気が付く

percent *n.* pāsento パーセント

perform *v.* shitogeru し遂げる; hatasu 果たす; jikkō suru 実行する

performance *n.* jikkō 実行; suikō 遂行

perfume *n.* (fragrant liquid) kōsui 香水; (pleasant odor) yoi kaori よい香り

perhaps *adv.* tabun たぶん; osoraku おそらく

peril *n., v.* kiken (ni sarasu) 危険 (にさらす)
in peril of ...no kiken o okashite ...の危険を冒して

period *n.* kikan 期間; jiki 時期; jidai 時代; (full stop) piriodo ピリオド

permanent *adj.* (lasting) eikyū no 永久の; (constant) kawaranai 変らない

permit *v.* yurusu 許す *permission* kyoka 許可

perpendicular *adj.* suichoku no 垂直の; kiritatta 切り立った; chokuritsu no 直立の

perpetual *adj.* (eternal) eikyū no 永久の; (constant) taema nai 絶え間ない

perpetually *adv.* eikyū ni 永久に

persecute *v.* hakugai suru 迫害する; kurushimeru 苦しめる

persevere *v.* shimbō suru 辛抱する; gaman suru

我慢する

persist v. iiharu 言い張る; koshitsu suru 固執
する

person n. (human being) hito 人; ningen 人間;
(body) karada 体; (personality) jinkaku 人格

personal adj. (individual) koko no 個々の;
(private) jiko no 自己の; isshinjō no 一身上の
personal effects mi no mawari hin 身の回り品

personality n. kosei 個性; jinkaku 人格

perspiration n. ase 汗; hakkan 発汗

persuade v. tokitsukeru 説きつける; settoku
suru 説得する; nattoku suru 納得する
persuade oneself kakushin suru 確信する

pet n. aigan-dōbutsu 愛がん動物; petto ペット;
(favorite) okini'iri お気に入り

petal n. kaben 花弁; hanabira 花びら

petrol n. gasorin ガソリン

petroleum n. sekiyu 石油

phase n. kyokumen 局面; keisei 形勢; jōtai 状態

phenomenon n. genshō 現象

philosophy n. tetsugaku 哲学

phone n., v. denwa (o kakeru) 電話 (をかける)

photograph n., v. shashin (o toru) 写真 (をとる);
satsuei (suru) 撮影 (する)

phrase n. ku 句; jukugo 熟語; furēzu フレーズ

physical adj. (material) busshitsu-teki 物質的;
(external) gaiteki no 外的の; (bodily) karada
no 体の; nikutai no 肉体の; (natural) shizen
no 自然の; (physics) butsurigaku no 物理学の
physical education taiiku 体育
physical examination shintai kensa 身体検査

physician n. isha 医者; naika-i 内科医

physicist n. butsuri-gakusha 物理学者

piano n. piano ピアノ

pick v. tsuku 突く; tsutsuku つつく; (make a
hole by picking) tsutsuite ana o akeru つつい
て穴をあける
pick at (try to pull) tsumamō to suru つまも
うとする; (find fault with continually) ara o

sagashi-mawaru あらを探し回る

pick out (select) erabu 選ぶ

pick up horu 掘る; (lay hold of and take up) tsukande hiroi-ageru つかんで拾い上げる; (discover by chance) gūzen mitsukeru 偶然見付ける; (take up) noseru 乗せる

pickle *n.* tsukemono つけ物; pikurusu ピクルス

picnic *n.* pikunikku ピクニック

picture *n.* (painting) e 絵; (photograph) shashin 写真; (motion picture) eiga 映画 —— *v.* (represent in picture) egaku 描く

pie *n.* pai パイ *piecrust* pai-no kawa パイの皮

piece *n.* ippen 一片; ikko 一個; (*music*) ikkyoku 一曲; kakera かけら; (coin) kahei 貨幣

a piece of hitotsu no 一つの

pier *n.* sambashi 桟橋; bōhatei 防波堤; hatoba 波止場

pierce *v.* sasu 刺す; tsuranuku 貫く; tsukitōsu 突き通す

pig *n.* buta 豚 *pigskin* butagawa 豚皮

pigeon *n.* hato はと

pile *n.* (heap) taiseki 堆積; ...no yama ...の山; (stake) kui くい —— *v.* (heap up) tsumi-kasaneru 積み重ねる; (drive piles into) kui o uchikomu くいを打ち込む

pilgrim *n.* junreisha 巡礼者 —— *adj.* junrei no 巡礼の —— *v.* junrei suru 巡礼する

pill *n., v.* gan'yaku(o nomaseru) 丸薬 (をのませる); (birth control pill) piru ピル

pillar *n.* hashira 柱; enchū 円柱

pillow *n.* makura 枕 —— *v.* (rest) noseru のせる; ...o makura ni suru ...を枕にする

pilot *n.* (one who operates an aircraft) sōjūshi 操縦士; (one who operates a ship) mizusaki-an'nainin 水先案内人; (guide) an'nainin 案内人 —— *adj.* (experimental) jikken-teki na 実験的な; (trial) shiken-teki na 試験的な

pin *n.* pin ピン; tome-bari 留め針

pinch *v.* (squeeze between two hard edges) hasa-

mu 挟む; (squeeze with thumb and forefinger)
tsuneru つねる; (press so as to give pain) shi-
metsukeru 締め付ける; (distress) komaraseru
困らせる ——*n.* tsuneru koto つねること;
(emergency) kikyū 危急; (strait) kukyō 苦境;
(bit) shōryō 少量

pine[1] *n.* matsu 松   *pine cone* matsukasa 松かさ

pine[2] *v.* (suffer intense longing) omoi-nayamu 思
い悩む; (yearn) omoi-kogareru 思いこがれる

pineapple *n.* painappuru パイナップル

ping-pong *n.* takkyū 卓球; pin-pon ピンポン

pink *n.* (*plant*) sekichiku 石竹 ——*n., adj.* mo-
moiro(no) 桃色(の); pinku (no) ピンク(の)

pint *n.* painto パイント

pioneer *n.* kaitakusha 開拓者; paionia パイオニ
ア ——*v.* kaitaku suru 開拓する

pipe *n.* kan 管; kuda 管; paipu パイプ

pirate *n.* kaizoku 海賊

pistol *n.* kenjū けん銃; pisutoru ピストル

pit *n.* ana 穴; kubomi くぼみ

pitch[1] *v.* (throw) nageru 投げる; tōkyū suru 投球
する; (put up, as a tent) tento o haru テントを
張る; (rise and fall, as a ship) fune ga tate ni
yureru 船が縦に揺れる ——*n.* (top) chōten
頂点; (degree) do 度; (*musical tone*) onshoku
no kōtei 音色の高低; (*boat race*) pitchi ピッチ;
(*baseball*) tōkyū 投球

pitch[2] *n.* (dark, sticky substance obtained from
coal tar) pitchi ピッチ; tāru タール; (*pine*)
matsu-yani 松やに

pitcher[1] *n.* (*baseball*) tōshu 投手

pitcher[2] *n.* (cf. jug) mizu-sashi 水差し

pity *n.* (compassion) awaremi 哀れみ; (sympathy)
dōjō 同情; (regret) zan'nen 残念 ——*v.* awa-
remu 哀れむ; kinodoku ni omou 気の毒に思
う

place *n.* basho 場所; ichi 位置; (social rank) chii
地位 ——*v.* (put) oku 置く
   in place of ...no kawari ni ...の代りに

out of place futekitō na 不適当な
take place okoru 起る
take the place of …ni kawaru …に代る

plain *adj.* (clear) meihaku na 明白な; (easy) yasashii 易しい; (simple) shisso na 質素な; jimi na 地味な; muji no 無地の; (frank) sotchoku na 率直な

plan *n., v.* keikaku(suru) 計画(する); (drawing) sekkei(suru) 設計(する); puran(o neru) プラン(を練る)

plane[1] *n., v.* (*tool*) kan'na (o kakeru) かんな(をかける)

plane[2] *n.* (flat surface) heimen 平面; (horizontal plane) suiheimen 水平面; (level) suijun 水準; (grade) dankai 段階 —— *adj.* taira na 平らな

plane[3] *n.* (airplane) hikōki 飛行機

planet *n.* yūsei 遊星; wakusei 惑星

plank *n.* atsuita 厚板; ita 板

plant *n.* (cf. vegetable) shokubutsu 植物; (herb) sōmoku 草木; (apparatus) setsubi 設備; (factory) shisetsu 施設

plantation *n.* (large farm) dai-nōen 大農園; (grove or wood of planted trees) shokurin 植林

plaster *n.* (*for coating walls*) shikkui しっくい; (medical plaster) harigusuri 張り薬; (gesso) sekkō 石こう

plastic *n.* purasuchikku プラスチック; gōsei-jushi 合成樹脂

plate *n.* (thin, flat sheet of metal) ita 板; (shallow dish) sara 皿; (name plate) hyōsatsu 表札

plateau *n.* kōgen 高原; daichi 台地

platform *n.* dan 壇; endan 演壇; (pulpit) kyōdan 教壇; purattohōmu プラットホーム *platform ticket* (eki no) nyūjō-ken (駅の) 入場券

play *v.* (amuse oneself) asobu 遊ぶ; (perform music) ensō suru 演奏する; (act on a stage) shibai o suru 芝居をする —— *n.* (sport) yūgi 遊戯; (drama) gikyoku 戯曲

player *n.* (actor) haiyū 俳優; (performer on a musical instrument) ensōsha 演奏者; (one skilled in a game) senshu 選手

playground *n.* undōjō 運動場

playmate *n.* asobi-tomodachi 遊び友だち、

pleasant *adj.* kokochi yoi 心地よい; tanoshii 楽しい; yukai na 愉快な

please *v.* yorokobaseru 喜ばせる; ki ni iru 気に入る; dōzo どうぞ *Please come in.* Dōzo o-hairi kudasai. どうぞお入り下さい、

pleasure *n.* tanoshimi 楽しみ; yukai 愉快; jiyū 自由 *with pleasure* yorokonde 喜んで

plenty *n.* takusan たくさん; hōfu 豊富 —— *adv.* tappuri たっぷり *in plenty* hōfu ni「na」豊富に「な」

pliers *n.* penchi ペンチ

plot *n.* (small piece of ground) shōjimen 小地面; (secret plan) imbō 陰謀; takurami たくらみ; (plan or essential facts of tale) suji 筋 —— *v.* (conspire) takuramu たくらむ

plow *n.* suki すき —— *v.* (plough land) suku すく; tagayasu 耕す

pluck *v.* (pull off) hikinuku 引き抜く; mushiru むしる; (summon up to do) yūki o furuiokosu 勇気を奮い起す

plug *n.* (stopper) sen 栓; (*electric*) puragu プラグ; sashikomi 差込み

plum *n.* sumomo すもも; puramu プラム

plump *adj.* futotta 太った; yoku koeta よく肥えた

plunge *v.* (dive) tobikomu 飛び込む; (thrust violently) tsukkomu 突っ込む

plural *adj.* fukusū no 複数の

plus *prep.* (added to) …o kuwaete …を加えて —— *adj.* (*mathematics*) sei no 正の; (*electric*) purasu no プラスの; (extra) yobun no 余分の

ply[1] *v.* (engage in a task) sesse to hagemu せっせと励む; (traverse a route regularly) teiki-teki ni ōfuku suru 定期的に往復する; (use) tsukau

使う

ply[2] *n.* (one layer, as of cloth, yarn) hida ひだ; (ito no) yori (糸の)より *plywood* gōban 合板; beniya-ita ベニヤ板

p. m. *n.* gogo 午後

pneumonia *n.* haien 肺炎

poached egg *n.* otoshi-tamago 落とし卵

pocket *n.* poketto ポケット ——*adj.* kogata no 小型の

poem *n.* (ippen no) shi (一編の) 詩

poet *n.* shijin 詩人

poetry *n.* shiika 詩歌; imbun 韻文

point *n.* (cf. line) ten 点; (tapering sharp end) sentan 先端; (essential part) yōten 要点 —— *v.* (indicate) shiji o suru 指示をする; (sharpen) togaraseru とがらせる
  on the point of masa ni ...shiyō to shite まさに ...しようとして
  point out shiteki suru 指摘する
  to the point tekisetsu ni 適切に
  point of view kenchi 見地

poison *n.* doku 毒; dokuyaku 毒薬 ——*v.* dokusatsu suru 毒殺する

poisoning *n.* chūdoku 中毒

poke *v.* tsuku 突く; tsutsuku つつく; (stir the fire) hi o kakitateru 火をかき立てる

poker *n.* (*tool*) hikakibō 火かき棒; (card game) pōkā ポーカー

polar *adj.* kyokuchi no 極地の *polar bear* shi-rokuma 白くま *polar star* (Polaris) hokkyoku-sei 北極星

pole[1] *n.* (long, slender piece of wood) bō 棒; sao さお; hashira 柱; (flag pole) hata-zao 旗ざお

pole[2] *n.* (extremity of the earth's axis) kyokuchi 極地
  North Pole hokkyoku 北極
  South Pole nankyoku 南極

Pole[3] *n.* Pōrando-jin ポーランド人

police *n.* keisatsu 警察; (the p-) keikan 警官

police station keisatsu-sho 警察署

police box kōban 交番; junsa-hashutsusho 巡査
派出所

policeman keikan 警官; junsa 巡査; omawari-
san おまわりさん

policy *n.* seisaku 政策; hōshin 方針

polish *v.* migaku みがく; hikaraseru 光らせる

polite *adj.* teinei na 丁寧な; jōhin na 上品な

politic *adj.* seiji no 政治の; seisaku no 政策の

politics *n.* seiji 政治; (political science) seiji-gaku
政治学; (political principles) seisaku 政策

poll *n., v.* tōhyō (suru) 投票(する)

pond *n.* ike 池

pony *n.* ko-uma 小馬

pool *n.* mizutamari 水たまり; koike 小池; pūru
プール

poor *adj.* bimbō na 貧乏な; mazushii 貧しい;
awarena 哀れな; hinjaku na 貧弱な

pop *n.* (small, sharp explosive report) pan ぱん,
pon ぽん, pachi-pachi ぱちぱち, zudon ずどん
―― *v.* pon to oto ga suru ぽんと音がする;
(burst open) hajikeru はじける   *popcorn* pop-
pu-kōn ポップコーン

Pope *n.* Rōma hō'ō ローマ法王

poppy *n.* (cf. opium-poppy) keshi けし; (scarlet)
makka 真っ赤; shinkōshoku 深紅色

popular *adj.* ninki no aru 人気のある; ryūkō no
流行の; taishū-teki na 大衆的な

population *n.* jinkō 人口

porcelain *n.* (cf. china) jiki 磁器

pork *n.* buta-niku 豚肉

port *n.* (harbor) minato 港; (left side of a ship)
fune no sagen 船の左げん

portable *adj.* keitaiyō no 携帯用の; pōtaburu ポ
ータブル

porter *n.* (gatekeeper) momban 門番; (carrier)
umpan'nin 運搬人; (redcap) akabō 赤帽

portion *n.* (part of whole) ichi-bubun 一部分;
(share) wakemae 分け前   ―― *v.* (divide) bun-

katsu suru 分割する; (distribute) bumpai suru 分配する

portrait *n.* shōzō 肖像; shashin 写真

portray *v.* (show by a picture) egaku 描く; (picture in words) byōsha suru 描写する; (make a portrait of) ...no shōzō o kaku ...の肖像を描く

Portugal *n.* Porutogaru ポルトガル

pose *n., v.* shisei (o toru) 姿勢 (をとる); pōzu (o suru) ポーズ (をする)

position *n.* (right place) ichi 位置; (social rank) mibun 身分; chii 地位; (office) shoku 職; (attitude) shisei 姿勢

positive *adj.* meikaku na 明確な; kettei-teki na 決定的な

possess *v.* shoyū suru 所有する (*be*) *possessed of* ...o yū suru ...を有する; motte iru 持っている

possibility *n.* kanōsei 可能性

possible *adj.* kanō na 可能な; dekiru できる

possibly *adv.* (perhaps) arui wa あるいは; tabun たぶん; (by any possible means) dekiru dake できるだけ

post[1] *n.* (pillar) hashira 柱

post[2] *n.* (mail) yūbimbutsu 郵便物 —— *v.* (mail a letter) yūsō suru 郵送する; (inform) shiraseru 知らせる

post[3] *n.* (position) chii 地位

postage *n.* yūzei 郵税 *postage stamp* yūbin kitte 郵便切手

postcard *n.* (yūbin-) hagaki (郵便)はがき

poster *n.* posutā ポスター; harigami はり紙

postman *n.* yūbin-haitatsu(-nin) 郵便配達(人)

postmark *n., v.* keshi'in (o osu) 消印(を押す); shōin (o suru) 消印 (をする)

postmaster *n.* yūbinkyoku-chō 郵便局長

post office *n.* yūbin-kyoku 郵便局

postpone *v.* (put off) enki suru 延期する

pot *n.* tsubo つぼ; bin びん; (*cooking*) fuka-nabe 深なべ; (flower pot) ueki-bachi 植木鉢

potato *n.* jagaimo じゃがいも *sweet potato* satsumaimo さつまいも

potential *adj.* (possible) kanō na 可能な; (latent) senzai-teki na 潜在的な

poultry *n.* tori-niku 鳥肉; *pl.* kakin 家きん

pound[1] *n.* (unit of weight) pondo ポンド

pound[2] *v.* (strike heavily) tsuyoku utsu 強く打つ; (crush) tsuki-kudaku 突き砕く

pour *v.* (flow) sosogu 注ぐ; (cause to flow in a stream) ryūshutsu suru 流出する; (rain heavily) ame ga zā-zā furu 雨がざあざあ降る

poverty *n.* hinkon 貧困; ketsubō 欠乏; bimbō 貧乏

powder *n.* (dust) kona 粉; (face powder) o-shiroi おしろい; (powdered medicine) konagusuri 粉薬; (gunpowder) kayaku 火薬 ―― *v.* kona ni suru 粉にする; o-shiroi o tsukeru おしろいを付ける

power *n.* (strength) chikara 力; (ability) nōryoku 能力; (energy) enerugī エネルギー; (authority) kenryoku 権力

powerful *adj.* kyōryoku na 強力な

practical *adj.* jissai-teki na 実際的な; jitsuyō muki no 実用向きの

practice *n.* (exercise) renshū 練習; (actual performance) jisshi 実施; jikkō 実行 ―― *v.* renshū suru 練習する
in practice jissaijō 実際上
put in practice jikkō ni utsusu 実行に移す

prairie *n.* dai-sōgen 大草原

praise *n.* shōsan 称賛 ―― *v.* homeru 褒める; shōsan suru 称賛する

prawn *n.* kuruma-ebi 車えび

pray *v.* inoru 祈る; negau 願う

prayer *n.* inori 祈り; kitō 祈とう; inoru-hito 祈る人

preach *v.* sekkyō suru 説教する; toku 説く

precaution *n.* yōjin 用心; keikai 警戒; yobō-shudan 予防手段

precede *v.* ...ni sakidatsu ...に先立つ

precedent *n.* senrei 先例 —— *adj.* izen no 以前の

preceding *adj.* senkō suru 先行する; mae no 前の; saki no 先の; zenjutsu no 前述の

precious *adj.* tōtoi 貴い; kichō na 貴重な

precise *adj.* seikaku na 正確な; seimitsu na 精密な

precisely *adv.* seikaku ni 正確に

predecessor *n.* zen'ninsha 前任者; sempai 先輩; (ancestor) senzo 先祖

preface *n.* jobun 序文; hashigaki 端書き

prefecture *n.* ken 県; fu 府

prefer *v.* (like better) yori...no hō o konomu より...の方を好む; (choose) yoi to omou よいと思う

pregnant *adj.* ninshin shite iru 妊娠している

prejudice *n.* henken 偏見; higami ひがみ —— *v.* henken o idakaseru 偏見を抱かせる; kirawaseru 嫌わせる

preliminary *adj.* (introductory) yobi-teki na 予備的な; (previous) maeoki no 前置きの —— *n. pl.* (preliminary arrangements) jumbi 準備

premier *n.* (prime minister) shushō 首相; sōri-daijin 総理大臣 —— *adj.* (foremost) shui no 首位の

preparation *n.* jumbi 準備; yoshū 予習

prepare *v.* yōi suru 用意する; jumbi suru 準備する

prescription *n.* (rule) kitei 規定; (*medical*) shohō (-sen) 処方(せん)

presence *n.* sonzai 存在; shusseki 出席 *in the presence of* ...no me no mae de ...の目の前で; ...ni chokumen shite ...に直面して

present[1] *adj.* (cf. absent) aru ある; iru いる; shusseki shite iru 出席している; sonzai suru 存在する; (now existing) genzai no 現在の *at present* genzai dewa 現在では

present[2] *n.* (gift) okurimono 贈り物; purezento

プレゼント ——*v.* (give) okuru 贈る; sashi-dasu 差し出す; (introduce) shōkai suru 紹介する; (show) shimesu 示す; arawasu あらわす

presently *adv.* (soon) yagate やがて; mamonaku 間もなく

preserve *v.* (keep safe) hogo suru 保護する; (maintain) iji suru 維持する ——*n. pl.* (fruit cooked with sugar) satōzuke 砂糖づけ; chozō-butsu 貯蔵物

president *n.* daitōryō 大統領; (chairman of company) shachō 社長; (head of university) gakuchō 学長

press *v.* (push against) osu 押す; appaku suru 圧迫する; (iron clothing) puresu suru プレスする; (urge on) shikiri ni unagasu しきりに促す ——*n.* (machine that applies pressure) assakuki 圧搾機; (printing machine) insatsuki 印刷機; (printing establishment) insatsujo 印刷所; (the P-) shimbun 新聞

pressure *n.* atsuryoku 圧力; appaku 圧迫; kyōsei 強制 *atmospheric pressure* kiatsu 気圧

presume *v.* (suppose) to omou と思う; sōzō suru 想像する

pretend *v.* ...o yoso'ou ...を装う; furi o suru ふりをする; itsuwaru 偽る

pretty *adj.* (fine) kirei na きれいな; (attractive) kawaii 可愛い ——*adv.* (fairly) kanari かなり; sōtō ni 相当に

prevail *v.* (be current) ryūkō suru 流行する; (gain the mastery) katsu 勝つ; yūsei de aru 優勢である

prevent *v.* (hinder) samatageru 妨げる; jama suru じゃまする; (keep safe from) yobō suru 予防する

prevention *n.* yobō 予防; bōshi 防止; (obstruction) bōgai 妨害; jama じゃま

previous *adj.* izen no 以前の; saki no 先の ——*adv.* izen ni 以前に; arakajime あらかじめ

prey *n.* ejiki え食; gisei 犠牲 ——*v.* hoshoku

suru 捕食する

price n. (cost) kakaku 価格; (sacrifice) gisei 犠牲; daishō 代償 —— v. nedan o tsukeru 値段を付ける

at any price don'na gisei o harattemo どんな犠牲を払っても

prick v. (make a thrust) tsuki sasu 突き刺す; (pain sharply) chiku-chiku itamu チクチク痛む; (raise the ears) kikimimi o tateru 聞き耳を立てる —— n. (thorn) toge とげ; (wounded by a sharp point) sashikizu 刺し傷; (sharp pain) tōtsū とう痛 *prick of conscience* ryōshin no kashaku 良心のかしゃく

pride n. hokori 誇り; jiman 自慢; jifu 自負 *take pride in* jiman suru 自慢する

priest n. sō 僧; bokushi 牧師

primary adj. (original) kompon no 根本の; (elemental) honrai no 本来の; (first in order of time) saisho no 最初の; (chief) omo na 主な; (elementary) shoho no 初歩の

prime adj. dai-ichi no 第一の; shuyō na 主要な —— n. (beginning) hajime 初め; saisho 最初 *prime minister* shushō 首相

primitive adj. (original) genshi no 原始の; (ancient) mukashi no 昔の; (earliest in time) shoki no 初期の; (not highly developed) mikai no 未開の; yōchi na 幼稚な

primitive age genshi-jidai 原始時代

primitive man genshi-jin 原始人

prince n. ōji 王子; kōtaishi 皇太子; shin'nō 親王; kōshaku 公爵

princess n. kōjo 皇女; ōjo 王女; ōhi 王妃; kōshaku fujin 公爵夫人

principal adj. (main) shuyō na 主要な; dai-ichi no 第一の —— n. (head of school) kōchō 校長 *principal sum* gankin 元金

principle n. genri 原理; gensoku 原則; shugi 主義 *in principle* gensoku to shite 原則として

print n., v. insatsu (suru) 印刷 (する); (photo.)

yakitsuke (suru) 焼き付け (する); (engraved plate) hanga 版画 ***printer*** insatsu-gyōsha 印刷業者; insatsuki 印刷機

prior *adj.* mae no 前の; saki no 先の; (earlier in time) yori mae no より前の; (superior in importance) yori jūyō na より重要な ***prior to*** yori mae ni より前に

prison *n.* keimusho 刑務所; kankin 監禁 ***prisoner*** jukeisha 受刑者; shūjin 囚人

private *adj.* kojin no 個人の; watakushi no 私の ***in private*** naisho de 内緒で

priviledge *n.* tokken 特権; tokuten 特典

prize *n.* hōbi 褒美; shō(-hin) 賞(品) —— *v.* (value highly) taisetsu ni suru 大切にする

probable *adj.* arisō na ありそうな; ...shisō na ...しそうな

probably *adv.* tabun たぶん; osoraku wa おそらくは

problem *n.* mondai 問題; gimon 疑問; nammon 難問

procedure *n.* tetsuzuki 手続き; shochi 処置

proceed *v.* (go on) susumu 進む; omomuku おもむく; tsuzukeru 続ける; (be carried on) okonawareru 行われる; okoru 起る

process *n.* (course) keika 経過; (ongoing movement) shinkō 進行; (method) hōhō 方法 *in process of* ...no shinkō-chū de ...の進行中で; ...no saichū de ...の最中で

procure *v.* (obtain) te ni ireru 手に入れる; uru 得る; kakutoku suru 獲得する

produce *v.* (yield) seisan suru 生産する; seizō suru 製造する; (play) jōen suru 上演する

producer *n.* seisansha 生産者; seizōsha 製造者; prodyūsā プロデューサー

product *n.* sambutsu 産物; seisambutsu 生産物; seihin 製品; (result) seika 成果

production *n.* seisan 生産; seisaku 製作

profession *n.* shokugyō 職業; semmon 専門

professional *adj.* shokugyō no 職業の; semmon

no 専門の; honshoku no 本職の ── *n.* kurōto 玄人; puro プロ

professor *n.* kyōju 教授

profit *n.* rieki 利益; mōke もうけ

profitable *adj.* yūri na 有利な

program *n.* puroguramu プログラム; bangumi
番組; yoteihyō 予定表

progress *n.* (advance) shinkō 進行; (improvement) shimpo 進歩; (development) hattatsu
発達 *make progress* shimpo suru 進歩する;
hakadoru はかどる

prohibit *v.* (forbid) kinjiru 禁じる; (hinder)
samatageru 妨げる

prohibition *n.* kinshi 禁止; kinrei 禁令

project *v.* (plan) keikaku suru 計画する; (protrude) tsukidasu 突き出す; (cause an image to
fall upon a surface) tōsha suru 投射する; eisha
suru 映写する

prominent *adj.* (standing out) tsukideta 突き出
た; (well-known) chomei na 著名な; (important) jūyō na 重要な

promise *n., v.* yakusoku (suru) 約束 (する); (like-
lihood) mikomi (ga aru) 見込み (がある)

promote *v.* (help forward) sokushin suru 促進
する; zōshin suru 増進する; (raise in rank)
shōshin saseru 昇進させる

promotion *n.* zōshin 増進; sokushin 促進; shōshin 昇進

prompt *adj.* (quick) binsoku na 敏速な; tekipaki
shita てきぱきした; (ready) sokuza no 即座の;
(incite) sosonokasu そそのかす; (dictate) shirei
suru 指令する

pronounce *v.* (utter a word) hatsuon suru 発音
する; (declare) dangen suru 断言する

pronunciation *n.* hatsuon 発音

proof *n.* (convincing evidence) shōko 証拠; shōmei 証明; (test) shiken 試験; (alcoholic strength
of a liquor) (arukōru bun no) tsuyosa (アルコ
ール分の) 強さ; (proof-sheet) kōsei-zuri 校正

刷り ——*adj.* ...ni taeru ...に耐える ——
adj. bō- 防; tai- 耐
fireproof bōka no 防火の; taika no 耐火の
waterproof bōsui no 防水の

propaganda *n.* senden 宣伝; senden-katsudō 宣
伝活動

proper *adj.* (fit) tekitō na 適当な; (correct) seitō
na 正当な; tadashii 正しい

properly *adv.* tekitō ni 適当に; tadashiku 正しく

property *n.* zaisan 財産; shoyū-butsu 所有物

prophet *n.* yogensha 予言者

proportion *n.* (comparative) wariai 割合; (ratio)
hiritsu 比率; (harmonious relation) chōwa 調
和
in proportion to... ...ni hirei shite ...に比例
して

propose *v.* mōshikomu 申し込む; teigi suru 定義
する

proprietor *n.* mochinushi 持ち主; shoyūsha 所有
者; keieisha 経営者

prose *n.* sambun 散文

prosecute *v.* (carry on) okonau 行う; (persist in
so as to complete) suikō suru 遂行する; (take
legal action against) kiso suru 起訴する

prospect *n.* (outlook) miharashi 見晴らし;
(chance for success) mikomi 見込み; (looking
forward) senken 先見

prospective *adj.* (relating to the future) mirai no
未来の; (expected) yoki sareru 予期される

prosper *v.* sakaeru 栄える; hanjō suru 繁盛する

protect *v.* (keep from harm) hogo suru 保護する;
(guard) fusegu 防ぐ

protest *v.* (object) kōgi suru 抗議する; (assert)
shuchō suru 主張する; (affirm) dangen suru
断言する ——*n.* (dissent) igi 異議; (remon-
strance) kōgi 抗議; (disapproval) fufuku 不服

proud *adj.* (arrogant) kōman na 高慢な; (showing pride) tokui no 得意の; (splendid) rippa
na 立派な; (imposing) dōdō to shita 堂々と

した; (feeling satisfaction) hokorashii 誇らしい

prove *v.* (demonstrate) shōmei suru 証明する; (try out) shinsa suru 審査する; (turn out) ...de aru koto ga wakaru ...であることが分かる

proverb *n.* kotowaza ことわざ

provide *v.* (prepare) sonaeru 備える; yōi suru 用意する; (supply) kyōkyū suru 供給する

provided *prep.* (if) moshi ...naraba もし...ならば; (on condition) ...to iu jōken de ...という条件で

province *n.* (division of a country) shū 州; ryōdo 領土; ken 県; kuni 国; *pl.* (area outside cities) inaka 田舎; chihō 地方

provision *n.* (preparation) jumbi 準備; (supply) kyōkyū 供給; (statement making a condition) kitei 規定; jōkō 条項; *pl.* (stock of food) shokuryō 食糧; ryōshoku 糧食

provoke *v.* (irritate) okoraseru 怒らせる; (displease) nayamasu 悩ます; kurushimeru 苦しめる; (incite) sosonokasu そそのかす

prudent *adj.* shiryo-bukai 思慮深い; shinchō na 慎重な

prune[1] *v.* (cut branches from a tree) ki o karikomu 木を刈り込む; eda o orosu 枝を下ろす

prune[2] *n.* (dried plum) hoshi-sumomo 干しすもも

pry[1] *v.* (look curiously) jiro-jiro miru じろじろ見る; (peep) nozoku のぞく; (snoop) sensaku suru せんさくする

pry[2] *v.* (move with a lever) teko de ugokasu てこで動かす ——*n. pl.* teko てこ

psychology *n.* shinri-gaku 心理学

public *adj.* ōyake no 公の; kōshū no 公衆の
public opinion seron 世論
in public kōzen to 公然と

publication *n.* shuppan(-butsu) 出版(物)

publicity *n.* (announcement) kōhyō 公表; (public attention) kōji 公示; (advertisement) kōkoku 広告

publish v. (announce) happyō suru 発表する；(issue a printed work for sale) shuppan suru 出版する

publisher n. shuppansha 出版社；hakkōsha 発行者

pudding n. pudingu プディング；purin プリン

puff n. (powder puff) pafu パフ ——n., v. (whiff) pū to fuku (oto) プーと吹く(音)

pull v. (draw) hiku 引く；hipparu 引っ張る；(row) kogu こぐ ——n. hiku koto 引くこと；hito-kogi ‥こぎ

pull in (*train*) tōchaku suru 到着する

pull off (*garment*) nugu 脱ぐ

pull on (*garment*) kiru 着る；haku はく

pull out (*tooth*) nuku 抜く；(*train*) hassha suru 発車する

pulp n. (wood-pulp) parupu パルプ；(soft, moist part of fruit) kaniku 果肉

pulse n. (beating of the heart) myakuhaku 脈はく；(vibration) shindō 振動 ——v. myaku o utsu 脈を打つ

pump n., v. pompu (de kumu) ポンプ (でくむ)

punch[1] v. (perforate or mark with a punch) ana o akeru 穴をあける；(*ticket*) (kippu o) kiru (キップを)切る；(hit) naguru 殴る ——n. (blow with the fist) panchi パンチ；(tool for piercing or stamping) ana'ake-ki 穴あけ器；panchi パンチ

punch[2] n. (fruit drink) panchi パンチ；ponchi ポンチ

punctual adj. jikan o mamoru 時間を守る；kichōmen na きちょうめんな

punctuate v. kutō o kiru 句読を切る；kutōten o tsukeru 句読点をつける

punish v. bassuru 罰する；korashimeru 懲らしめる

punishment n. (punishing) batsu 罰；(penalty) keibatsu 刑罰；(chastisement) chōbatsu 懲罰

pupil[1] n. seito 生徒；deshi 弟子

pupil² *n.* (black center of the eye) hitomi ひとみ; dōkō どう孔

puppet *n.* chiisai ningyō 小さい人形

puppy *n.* ko-inu 小犬; inukoro 犬ころ

purchase *v.* (buy) kau 買う; (acquire) kakutoku suru 獲得する ——*n.* kaiire 買入れ; kōnyū 購入

pure *adj.* junsui na 純粋な; junketsu na 純血な; keppaku na 潔白な

purple *n., adj.* murasaki-iro (no) 紫色(の)

purpose *n.* (aim) mokuteki 目的; (design) ishi 意志

for the purpose of no mokuteki de の目的で; …no tame ni …のために

on purpose koi ni 故意に; wazato わざと

purse *n.* (small bag for money) saifu 財布; (prize money) shōkin 賞金 ——*v.* (pucker) (kuchi o) subomeru (口を) すぼめる

pursue *v.* (chase) tsuiseki suru 追跡する; tsuikyū suru 追求する; (carry out) suikō suru 遂行する; (follow) tadoru たどる

pursuit *n.* (following) tsuiseki 追跡; (carrying out) suikō 遂行

in pursuit of …o tsuiseki shite …を追跡して; …o motomete …を求めて

push *v.* (press forward) osu 押す; (impel) oshi-susumu 押し進む

put *v.* (place) oku 置く; (cause) saseru させる; (express) hyōgen suru 表現する; (rate) hyōka suru 評価する; (entrust) yudaneru ゆだねる; (proceed) susumu 進む; (throw) nageru 投げる

put aside [*away*] katazukeru 片付ける

put by totte oku とっておく; takuwaeru 蓄える

put in naka ni ireru 中に入れる; sashikomu 差し込む

put in order seiton suru 整とんする

put off (take off) nugu 脱ぐ; torisaru 取り去る; (postpone) enki suru 延期する; (set out) shuppatsu suru 出発する

put on (clothe oneself with) kiru 着る; (*pants, shoes*) haku はく; (place on) ue ni noseru 上に載せる

put out (turn out) kesu 消す; (drive out) oidasu 追い出す; (publish) shuppan suru 出版する

put up with (endure) shimbō suru 辛抱する; gaman suru 我慢する

puzzle *n.* nammon 難問; (riddle) nazo なぞ ——*n., v.* (perplexity) tōwaku (saseru) 当惑 (させる)

pyramid *n.* piramiddo ピラミッド

Q

quack *n., v.* gā-gā (naku) があがあ (鳴く)

quail[1] *n.* (*game bird*) uzura うずら

quail[2] *v.* (lose courage) ojikeru おじける; (shrink) hirumu ひるむ

quaint *adj.* (agreeably odd) fūgawari na 風変りな; kimyō na 奇妙な

quake *v.* (shake) shindō suru 震動する; (tremble) furueru 震える

qualification *n.* shikaku 資格; seigen 制限; menkyo 免許

qualify *v.* (competent for a position) shikaku o ataeru 資格を与える; (describe as) minasu 見なす; (limit) seigen suru 制限する; (modify) shūshoku suru 修飾する

quantity *n.* ryō 量; gaku 額; *pl.* tasū 多数; taryō 多量

quarrel *n., v.* kenka(suru) けんか(する); kōron (suru) 口論(する)

quarter *n.* (a fourth part) yombun no ichi 4分の 1, ¼; (fourth of an hour) jū-go-fun 15分; (region) chiiki 地域; (district) chiku 地区

quaver *v.* (tremble) furueru 震える; (utter with quavers) koe o furuwaseru 声を震わせる

quay *n.* hatoba 波止場; gampeki 岸壁

queer *adj.* (odd) myō na 妙な; hen na 変な; (doubtful) utagawashii 疑わしい

query *n., v.* shitsumon (suru) 質問（する）; (inquire into) tazuneru 尋ねる

question *n.* (inquiry) shitsumon 質問; (problem) mondai 問題

queue *n., v.* gyōretsu 行列; retsu(o tsukuru) 列（を作る）

quick *adj.* (rapid) hayai 速い; (alert) kibin na 機敏な; (clever) rikō na 利口な; (keen) surudoi 鋭い ―― *adv.* hayaku 速く *as quick as lightning* denkō-sekka ni 電光石火に

quiet *adj.* (still) shizuka na 静かな; (gentle) odayaka na 穏やかな; (peaceful) heisei na 平静な ―― *n.* (tranquillity) heisei 平静; (stillness) seijaku 静寂

quilt *n.* kake-buton 掛けぶとん; kiruto キルト; sashiko 刺し子

quit *v.* (give up) suteru 捨てる; (stop) yameru やめる; (go away) tachisaru 立ち去る

quite *adv.* mattaku まったく; kanzen ni 完全に

quiver *vi.* (tremble) furueru 震える; (shake) yureru 揺れる ―― *vt.* (cause to shake) furue saseru 震えさせる ―― *n.* (vibration) shindō 震動

quiz *n.* kuizu クイズ; (question) shitsumon 質問

quote *v.* (cite) in'yō suru 引用する

R

rabbit *n.* usagi うさぎ

race[1] *n.* (contest of speed) kyōsō 競走; (horse racing) keiba 競馬; (contest for supremacy) kyōsō 競争 ―― *v.* kyōsō suru 競走する

race[2] *n.* (tribe) minzoku 民族; (division of mankind) jinshu 人種

rack *n.* ami-dana 網だな; rakku ラック

racket[1] *n.* (light bat with a netted hoop, used in

games) raketto ラケット

racket² *n.*, *v.* (noisy talk and play) ōsawagi (suru) 大騒ぎ (する); bakasawagi (suru) ばか騒ぎ (する)

radar *n.* rēdā レーダー

radiant *adj.* (bright) kagayaku 輝く; kagayaita 輝いた; akarui 明るい

radiator *n.* dambō-sōchi 暖房装置; rajiētā ラジエーター

radical *adj.* (fundamental) kompon-teki na 根本的な; kiso no 基礎の; (of radicals in politics) kyūshin-teki na 急進的な; (extreme) kageki na 過激な

radio *n.* rajio ラジオ; musen-denshin 無線電信

radish *n.* hatsuka-daikon 二十日大根

radius *n.* hankei 半径

raft *n.* (floating platform) ikada いかだ

rag *n.* boro ぼろ; kuzumono くずもの

rage *n.* (violent anger) hageshii ikari 激しい怒り; (great enthusiasm) nekkyō 熱狂; (fad) ryūkō 流行 —— *v.* (show violent anger) hageshiku okoru 激しく怒る

raid *n.*, *v.* (sudden attack) shūgeki (suru) 襲撃 (する)   *raider* shin'nyū-sha [-ki] 侵入者 [機]

rail *n.* rēru レール; (handrail) tesuri 手すり

railroad *n.* tetsudō 鉄道

rain *n.*, *v.* ame (ga furu) 雨 (が降る)
  rain cats and dogs doshaburi ni ame ga furu 土砂降りに雨が降る
  rain or shine seiu ni kakawarazu 晴雨にかかわらず

raincoat *n.* reinkōto レインコート

raindrop *n.* amadare 雨だれ

rainfall *n.* kōu 降雨; uryō 雨量

rainy *adj.* ame no ōi 雨の多い; ame no furu 雨の降る

raise *v.* (lift up) ageru 上げる; (take into higher position) takaku suru 高くする; (make stand up) okosu 起こす; (build up) tateru 立てる; (encour-

age) genki-zukeru 元気づける；(breed) kau 飼
う；(increase) fuyasu 増やす；(collect) atsumeru
集める；(promote) shōshin saseru 昇進させる；
(make grow) saibai suru 栽培する

raisin *n.* hoshi-budō 干しぶどう

rake *n., v.* kumade (de kaku) くま手 (でかく)

rally *v.* (gather again) futatabi yobi-atsumeru
再び呼び集める；(regain health) kaifuku suru
回復する；(reassembly) shūgō 集合；(mass meeting) taikai 大会；(*tennis*) rarī ラリー

ram *n.* (male sheep) o-hitsuji 雄羊

ranch *n.* nōjō 農場；bokujō 牧場

random *adj.* detarame no でたらめの；teatari
shidai no 手当たりしだいの　*at random* detarame ni でたらめに

range *n.* (extent) han'i 範囲；(chain of mountains)
sammyaku 山脈；(line) retsu 列；(cooking stove)
renji レンジ ―― *v.* (extend) ...ni wataru
...にわたる；(arrange in rows) naraberu 並べ
る

rank *n.* (row) retsu 列；(social class) kurai 位；
chii 地位；kaikyū 階級 ―― *vi.* (form a row)
narabu 並ぶ ―― *vt.* (place in a row) naraberu 並べる

ransom *n.* (money paid to set a captive free) mi-
noshiro-kin 身の代金；(compensation) baishō-
kin 賠償金

rapid *adj.* hayai 早い；kyūsoku na 急速な

rapidly *adv.* hayaku 速く；kyūsoku ni 急速に

rare *adj.* mare na まれな；mezurashii 珍しい

rarely *adv.* mare ni まれに；mezurashiku 珍しく

rascal *n.* akkan 悪漢；warumono 悪者

rash[1] *adj.* (reckless) mukōmizu no 向こう見ずの；
(imprudent) mufumbetsu na 無分別な；(hasty)
sekkachi no せっかちの

rash[2] *n.* hasshin 発疹；fukidemono 吹出物

rat *n.* nezumi ねずみ；nonezumi 野ねずみ

rate *n.* (fixed ratio) wariai 割合；(proportional
amount) ritsu 率；(class) tōkyū 等級；(price

per unit) tanka 単価; nedan 値段 —— *v.* (calculate the value of) mitsumoru 見積もる; hyōka suru 評価する

at any rate tonikaku とにかく; sukunakutomo 少なくとも

rather *adv.* (preferably) mushiro むしろ; (somewhat) ikubun いくぶん; (on the contrary) soredokoroka それどころか; (of course) mochiron もちろん

ratio *n.* wariai 割合; hiritsu 比率

ration *n.* haikyū(-ryō) 配給(量); wariate(-ryō) 割当て(量) —— *v.* wariateru 割り当てる

rational *adj.* risei-teki na 理性的な; gōri-teki na 合理的な

rave *v.* (talk wildly) wameku わめく; (praise greatly) gekishō suru 激賞する; (storm) arekuru'u 荒れ狂う

rave oneself hoarse donari-chirashite koe o karasu 怒鳴り散らして声をからす

raw *adj.* (uncooked) nama no 生の; (raw material) genryō no 原料の; (inexperienced) mijuku na 未熟な; (untrained) funare no 不慣れの; (unprocessed) mikakō no 未加工の; (sore) kawa ga muketa 皮がむけた; hiri-hiri suru ひりひりする; (cold and damp) usura-samui 薄ら寒い

ray *n.* kōsen 光線; hōsha-sen 放射線

razor *n.* kamisori かみそり

reach *v.* (arrive at) tsuku 着く; tōchaku suru 到着する; todoku 届く; (amount) tassuru 達する; (extend the hand) te o nobasu 手を伸ばす —— *n.* (the act of stretching out a bodily part) nobasu koto 伸ばすこと; (extent something can reach) todoku han'i 届く範囲

react *v.* (act in return) handō suru 反動する; (act in response to) han'nō suru 反応する

read *v.* yomu 読む; dokusho suru 読書する *reading* dokusho 読書

reader *n.* dokusha 読者

readily *adv.* (easily) yōi ni 容易に; (willingly) susunde 進んで; kokoroyoku 快く; (promptly) sumiyaka ni 速やかに

ready *adj.* (prepared) yōi no dekita 用意のできた; (willing) yorokonde…suru 喜んで…する; sugu…suru すぐ…する; (about to do) sugu ni…shiyō to suru すぐに…しようとする; (prompt) binsoku na 敏速な

ready-made *adj.* kisei no 既製の; redī-mēdo レディーメード

real *adj.* (actual) jissai no 実際の; (true) hontō no 本当の

reality *n.* genjitsu 現実; jitsuzai 実在; shinjitsu 真実 *in reality* jissai wa 実際は; (in fact) jitsu ni 実に

realize *v.* (make real) jitsugen suru 実現する; (understand) (hakkiri to) rikai suru (はっきりと)理解する; (achieve) nashitogeru なし遂げる; (gain) kane o mōkeru 金をもうける

really *adv.* hontō ni 本当に; jissai 実際; mattaku まったく

realm *n.* (region) ryōbun 領分; (kingdom) ōkoku 王国; (division) kai 界; bumon 部門

reap *v.* karu 刈る; kariireru 刈り入れる

rear¹ *adj.* ushiro no 後ろの; haigo no 背後の ── *n.* kōhō 後方; kōbu 後部
at the rear of …no haigo ni …の背後に
in the rear of kōhō ni 後方に

rear² *v.* (bring up) sodateru 育てる; (breed) shiiku suru 飼育する; (build) tateru 建てる; (rise on the hind legs, as a horse) ato-ashi de tatsu 後足で立つ

reason *n.* (cause) riyū 理由; gen'in 原因; (motive) dōki 動機; (right) seitō 正当 *by reason of* …no riyū de …の理由で

reasonable *adj.* dōri ni kanatta 道理にかなった; risei no aru 理性のある; tekitō na 適当な; (fair) seitō na 正当な

reasonably *adv.* gōriteki ni 合理的に; seitō ni

正当に

rebel *n.* muhon-nin 謀反人；hangyakusha 反逆者
—— *v.* muhon suru 謀反する；somuku 背く

recall *v.* (call back) yobi-kaesu 呼び返す；(remember) omoidasu 思い出す；(revoke) torikesu
取り消す —— *n.* yobimodoshi 呼び戻し；rikōru リコール *beyond [past] recall* torikaeshi no tsukanai 取り返しのつかない

receipt *n.* ryōshūsho 領収書；reshīto レシート

receive *v.* uketoru 受け取る；ukeru 受ける；
(greet) mukaeru 迎える；(welcome) kangei suru
歓迎する

receiver *n.* (*person*) uketorinin 受取人；(*apparatus*) juwaki 受話器；reshībā レシーバー

recent *adj.* chikagoro no 近ごろの；saikin no
最近の

reception *n.* (act of receiving) uketoru koto 受
け取ること；(formal social function) kangeikai
歓迎会；resepushon レセプション *wedding reception* kekkon hirōen 結婚披露宴

recess *n.* (break from work) yasumi (-jikan) 休
み (時間)；(hollow in a wall) kabe no kubomi
壁のくぼみ —— *v.* (take recess) kyūkei suru
休憩する

recipe *n.* (cooking) chōrihō 調理法；tsukurikata
作り方

recital *n.* risaitaru リサイタル；dokusōkai 独奏
会；dokushōkai 独唱会

reckless *adj.* (rash) mukōmizu no 向こう見ず
の；(careless) fuchūi na 不注意な

reckon *v.* (count) keisan suru 計算する；(suppose) omou 思う；(regard as) …to minasu
…とみなす；(rely upon) ate ni suru 当てにす
る

recognition *n.* (act of recognition) ninshiki 認識；
(acknowledgment) shōnin 承認

recognize *v.* (know again) mitomeru 認める；
(identify) mioboe ga aru 見覚えがある

recollect *v.* (remember) omoidasu 思い出す；

kaisō suru 回想する

recommend *v.* (suggest as suited for) suisen suru 推薦する; (advise) susumeru 勧める

record *n.* kiroku 記録; rekōdo レコード *break the record* kiroku o yaburu 記録を破る

recover *v.* (get back) torimodosu 取り戻す; (regain health) kaifuku suru 回復する

recreation *n.* rekuriēshon レクリエーション; kibarashi 気晴らし; goraku 娯楽

red *n.* (color like blood) aka-iro 赤色 —— *adj.* akai 赤い; (communist) kyōsanshugi (-sha) no 共産主義 (者) の

redeem *v.* (buy back) kaimodosu 買い戻す; (pay off) shōkan suru 償還する; (recover) kaifuku suru 回復する; (atone for) tsumi no tsugunai o suru 罪の償いをする

reduce *v.* (diminish) chijimeru 縮める; herasu 減らす; (change) ...ni kaeru ...に変える; (lower) sageru 下げる

reduction *n.* (diminution) shukushō 縮小; (discount) waribiki 割引

reel[1] *n.* (spool or frame with thread, film) ito-maki 糸巻き; rīru リール; ito-guruma 糸車 —— *v.* ito-maki [rīru] ni maku 糸巻き [リール] に巻く

reel[2] *v.* (stagger) yoromeku よろめく; (walk unsteadily) yoro-yoro aruku よろよろ歩く —— *n.* yoromeki よろめき *drunken reel* chidori ashi 千鳥足

refer *v.* (allude) ...ni tsuite noberu ...について述べる; (try to get information) sanshō suru 参照する; sankō ni suru 参考にする; (direct for help or action) sashimukeru 差し向ける; (relate) kankei suru 関係する; (submit) yudaneru ゆだねる; makaseru 任せる

reference *n.* (being referred) sankō 参考; (source of information) shōkai 照会

refine *vt.* (make fine) jōhin ni suru 上品にする; senren suru 洗練する; (make pure) seisei suru

精製する；junka suru 純化する ──── *vi.* (become fine or pure) jōhin ni naru 上品になる；senren sareru 洗練される；junka suru 純化する
refined jōhin na 上品な；seisei sareta 精製された

reflect *v.* (throw back light or heat) hansha suru 反射する；(mirror) utsusu 映す；han'ei suru 反映する；(think seriously) kangaeru 考える；hansei suru 反省する；(recollect) kaisō suru 回想する；omoi okosu 思い起こす

reflection *n.* (reflecting) hansha 反射；han'ei 反映；(contemplation) jukkō 熟考

reform *n., v.* kairyō (suru) 改良 (する)；kaizen (suru) 改善 (する)

refrain *v.* (hold oneself back) sashi-hikaeru 差し控える；enryo suru 遠慮する；(forbear) gaman suru 我慢する

refresh *v.* (make fresh or stronger) genki-zukeru 元気づける；sōkai ni suru そう快にする；(revive, as with food, drink, etc.) (tabetari, nondari shite) genki o kaifuku suru （食べたり，飲んだりして）元気を回復する

refreshment *n.* genki kaifuku 元気回復；tsukare-yasume 疲れ休め；(food, or drink) inshoku-butsu 飲食物

refrigerator *n.* reizōko 冷蔵庫

refuse[1] *v.* (reject) kyozetsu suru 拒絶する；koto-waru 断る

refuse[2] *n.* (rubbish) kuzu くず；haibutsu 廃物

regard *v.* (observe closely) chūmoku suru 注目する；miru 見る；mitsumeru 見詰める；(consider) ...to kangaeru ...と考える；(esteem) sonchō suru 尊重する ──── *n.* (attention) chūi 注意；kanshin 関心；(relation) kankei 関係；(respect) sonkei 尊敬；(gaze) chūmoku 注目
as regards ...ni tsuite wa ...については；...ni kanshite wa ...に関しては
with [in] regards to (regarding) ...ni tsuite ...について；ni kanshite に関して

regiment *n., v.* rentai (ni hensei suru) 連隊 (に編成する)

region *n.* (area) chihō 地方; chitai 地帯; ryōiki 領域

register *v.* (record) tōroku suru 登録する; (register mail) kakitome ni suru 書留にする; (indicate) shimesu 示す —— *n.* regisutā レジスター

regret *n., v.* kōkai (suru) 後悔 (する); zan'nen (ni omou) 残念 (に思う)

regrettable *adj.* zan'nen na 残念な; oshimareru 惜しまれる

regular *adj.* (orderly) kisoku-teki na 規則的な; (formal) seishiki no 正式の; (usual) tsūjō no 通常の

regularly *adj.* kisoku tadashiku 規則正しく; teiki-teki ni 定期的に

regulate *v.* (put in order) totonoeru 整える; (adjust) chōsetsu suru 調節する; (restrict) seigen suru 制限する

regulation *n.* (control) torishimari 取締り; (adjustment) chōsei 調整; (rule) kisoku 規則

rehearsal *n.* keiko けいこ; renshū 練習; rihāsaru リハーサル

reign *n.* (exercise of sovereign power) tōji 統治; (sway) shihai 支配; (term of a sovereign's rule) miyo 御代; chisei 治世 —— *v.* (rule with sovereign power) kunrin suru 君臨する; tōji suru 統治する

reject *v.* (refuse) kyozetsu suru 拒絶する; kyohi suru 拒否する; kotowaru 断わる; (throw away) suteru 捨てる

rejoice *vi.* yorokobu 喜ぶ —— *vt.* yorokobaseru 喜ばせる

relate *vt.* (tell) noberu 述べる; hanasu 話す; (narrate) monogataru 物語る; (bring into relation) kankei saseru 関係させる —— *vi.* (stand in some relation) kankei suru 関係する

relation *n.* kankei 関係 *in relation to* ...ni tsuite …について；…ni kanren shite …に関連して

relative *n.* (one related by kinship) shinrui 親類；(*gram.*) (relative word) kankeishi 関係詞 —— *adj.* (related) kankei no aru 関係のある

relax *vt.* yurumeru 緩める —— *vi.* yurumu 緩む —— *n.* rirakkusu リラックス

release *v.* (unfasten) hanasu 放す；(set free) kaihō suru 解放する；(relieve) suku'u 救う —— *n.* (discharge) kaihō 解放

reliable *adj.* shinrai dekiru 信頼できる

reliance *n.* shinrai 信頼

relief[1] *n.* (comfort) ian 慰安；(ease) anshin 安心；anraku 安楽；(deliverance) kyūjo 救助；(relay) kōtai 交代

relief[2] *n.* (*archit.*, *sculpture*) ukibori-zaiku [-moyō] 浮彫細工 [模様]

relieve *v.* (help) suku'u 救う；kyūjo suru 救助する；(free from pain or anxiety) anshin saseru 安心させる；yawarageru 和らげる；(relay) kōtai suru 交代する

religion *n.* shūkyō 宗教

relish *n.* (seasoning) ajitsuke 味付け；(cf. condiment) chōmiryō 調味料；(flavor) aji 味；fūmi 風味 —— *v.* (give a relish to) ajitsuke o suru 味付けをする；(enjoy) shōmi suru 賞味する；oishiku taberu おいしく食べる

rely *v.* shinrai suru 信頼する；ate ni suru 当てにする；tanomi ni suru 頼みにする

remain *v.* (be left after part is gone) nokoru 残る；(stay) todomaru とどまる；(continue) …no mama de aru …のままである —— *n. pl.* (part left over) nokori 残り；(dead body) shitai 死体

remark *v.* (say) noberu 述べる；hanasu 話す；(notice) chūmoku suru 注目する；(perceive) kanjiru 感じる；(observe) kansatsu suru 観察する；(make comment) hihyō suru 批評する —— *n.* (mention) hatsugen 発言；chūi 注意；hihyō 批評

remarkable *adj.* ichijirushii 著しい; chūmoku-subeki 注目すべき

remedy *n.* (cure) chiryō (-hō) 治療 (法); (healing medicine) kusuri 薬 —— *v.* (relieve) suku'u 救う; (cure) chiryō suru 治療する

remember *v.* (recall) omoidasu 思い出す; (have in mind) oboete iru 覚えている

remembrance *n.* (memory) kioku 記憶; (memorial) kinen 記念

remind *v.* omoi-dasaseru 思い出させる; kizuka-seru 気付かせる

remit *v.* (send money) sōkin suru 送金する; (pardon) yurusu 許す

remittance *n.* sōkin 送金

remote *adj.* tōi 遠い; empō nō 遠方の; hanareta 離れた

remove *vt.* (move to another place) utsusu 移す; (take away) torisaru 取り去る; katazukeru 片付ける —— *vi.* (change one's house) tenkyo suru 転居する; hikkoshi suru 引っ越しする

renew *v.* (make or become new) atarashiku suru [naru] 新しくする [なる]; (revive) fukkatsu suru 復活する; (continue after intermission) futatabi hajimeru 再び始める; (replenish) motodōri ni hojū suru 元通りに補充する

renounce *v.* (abandon) suteru 捨てる; hōki suru 放棄する; kiken suru 棄権する; (give up) aki-rameru あきらめる

renown *n.* (fame) meisei 名声; yūmei 有名 **renowned** yūmei na 有名な

rent *n.* yachin 家賃; heyadai 部屋代; jidai 地代; (payment for hire) chinshaku-ryō 賃借料 —— *v.* (let for rent) chingashi suru 賃貸しする; (hire) chingari suru 賃借りする

repair *v.* (mend) shūzen suru 修繕する; shūri suru 修理する; naosu 直す; (restore) kaifuku suru 回復する

repay *v.* (pay back) harai-modosu 払い戻す; shakkin o kaesu 借金を返す; (recompense) mukuiru 報いる

repeal *v.* (recall, revoke) haishi [haiki, tekkai] suru 廃止 [廃棄, 撤回] する; (annul) mukō ni suru 無効にする

repeat *v.* (say or do over again) kurikaesu 繰り返す; (recite) anshō suru 暗唱する

repent *v.* kōkai suru 後悔する; kuiru 悔いる

repetition *n.* kurikaeshi 繰り返し

replace *v.* (take place of) ...ni kawaru ...に代わる; (put back in place) moto e modosu 元へ戻す

reply *v.* kotaeru 答える; henji suru 返事する

report *n., v.* (tell about) hōkoku (suru) 報告 (する); (tell as news) hōdō (suru) 報道 (する); repōto (suru) レポート (する) ——*n.* (rumor) uwasa うわさ; (explosive noise) bakuon 爆音

repose *vi.* (take rest) kyūsoku suru 休息する ——*vt.* (give rest to) yasumaseru 休ませる ——*n.* (rest) kyūsoku 休息; (sound sleep) suimin 睡眠; (quiet) heisei 平静

represent *v.* (express by description) hyōgen suru 表現する; (stand for) daihyō [dairi] suru 代表 [代理] する; (portray) egaki dasu 描き出す; (symbolize) shōchō suru 象徴する

representation *n.* hyōgen 表現; daihyō 代表

reproach *v.* semeru 責める; hinan suru 非難する

reproduce *v.* (produce again) saisei suru 再生する; (make a copy) fukusha suru 複写する

reprove *v.* (censure) hinan suru 非難する; togameru とがめる; (scold) shikaru しかる

reptile *n.* hachūrui-dōbutsu は虫類動物

republic *n.* kyōwa-koku 共和国; kyōwa-seitai 共和政体

repulse *v.* (drive back) gekitai suru 撃退する; (reject) kyozetsu suru 拒絶する

reputation *n.* (repute) hyōban 評判; (good fame) meisei 名声

request *v.* (beg for) negau 願う; (ask for) tanomu 頼む; irai suru 依頼する; (demand) yōkyū

suru 要求する ―― n. (expressed desire) negai 願い; (asking) yōkyū 要求

require v. (need) hitsuyō to suru 必要とする;
(demand) yōkyū suru 要求する **requirement**
yōkyū 要求; hitsuyō 必要

rescue n., v. kyūjo (suru) 救助 (する); kaihō
(suru) 解放 (する)

research n., v. (scientific study) kenkyū (suru)
研究 (する); (investigation) chōsa (suru) 調査
(する)

resemble v. ...ni niteiru ...に似ている; ruiji
suru 類似する

reserve v. (keep back for future use) totte oku
取っておく; (set aside) torinokete oku 取りの
けておく; rizābu suru リザーブする; yoyaku
suru 予約する
reservation yoyaku 予約; horyū 保留
reserved yoyaku-zumi no 予約済みの

reside v. (live) sumu 住む; kyojū suru 居住する

residence n. (apartment) teitaku 邸宅; (house)
jūtaku 住宅; (living) kyojū 居住

resign v. (give up) dan'nen suru 断念する; aki-
rameru あきらめる; (give up an office) jishoku
suru 辞職する

resist v. teikō suru 抵抗する; hankō suru 反抗
する

resolute adj. (determined) kesshin shita 決心し
た; danko to shita 断固とした

resolution n. kesshin 決心; ketsui 決意

resolve vi. (make up one's mind) kesshin suru
決心する; (break up) bunkai suru 分解する;
(dissolve) tokeru 溶ける ―― vt. (cause to
determine) kesshin saseru 決心させる; (solve)
toku 解く; (settle) kettei suru 決定する ――
n. (resolution) kesshin 決心

resort n. (place for vacation) asobi-basho 遊び
場所; sakari-ba 盛り場; kōraku-chi 行楽地;
(means) shudan 手段 ―― v. (frequent)shiba-
shiba kayou しばしば通う; (have recourse to)

…ni tasuke o motomeru …に助けを求める

resource *n.* (property) shisan 資産; (new sources of supply) shigen 資源; (funds) shikin 資金; (means) shudan 手段

respect *n., v.* (honor) sonkei (suru) 尊敬 (する); (esteem) sonchō (suru) 尊重 (する); (relate) kankei (suru) 関係 (する); (point, regards) ten 点; (concern) kankei 関係
in respect of (= *with respect to*) …ni kanshite …に関して
in all [*many*] *respects* subete [ōku] no ten de すべて [多く] の点で
in this respect kono ten de この点で

respectable *adj.* (worthy of respect) sonkei subeki 尊敬すべき; rippa na 立派な; (fairly good) kanari no かなりの

respective *adj.* sore-zore no それぞれの; ono-ono no 各々の

response *n.* kotae 答え; (reply) henji 返事; (reaction) han'nō 反応 *in response to* …ni kotaete …に答えて; …ni ōjite …に応じて

responsibility *n.* sekinin 責任; gimu 義務

responsible *adj.* (obliged to do) sekinin no aru 責任のある; (trustworthy) shinrai dekiru 信頼できる

rest¹ *n.* (inactivity) kyūsoku 休息; (peace) ansei 安静 —— *vt.* (give repose to) yasumaseru 休ませる —— *vi.* (take rest) yasumu 休む; (be still) seishi suru 静止する; (depend) shinrai suru 信頼する; (lean) yorikakaru 寄り掛かる; (place) oku 置く

rest² *n.* (the r-) (remainder) nokori 残り; zambu 残部; *pl.* sono hoka no mono [hitotachi] その外のもの [人たち]

restaurant *n.* ryōriten 料理店; shokudō 食堂; resutoran レストラン

restless *adj.* ochitsukanai 落ち着かない *restlessly* sowa-sowa shite そわそわして

restore *v.* (recover) kaifuku suru 回復する; (es-

tablish again) fukkō suru 復興する; (put back)
(moto e) modosu (元へ) 戻す

restrain *v.* (hold back) yokusei suru 抑制する;
(check) sokubaku suru 束縛する; (limit) seigen
suru 制限する

restrict *v.* (limit) seigen suru 制限する; (confine)
sokubaku suru 束縛する

result *n.* (effect) kekka 結果; seiseki 成績 ——
v. (kekka to shite) okoru (結果として) 起こる;
…ni owaru …に終る

as a result of …no kekka to shite …の結果と
して

in result sono kekka その結果

in the result kekkyoku 結局

result in …ni owaru …に終る

without result muda ni 無駄に

resume *v.* (begin again) futatabi hajimeru 再び始
める; (continue) tsuzukete yaru 続けてやる;
(summarize) yōyaku suru 要約する

retail *v.* kouri suru 小売りする —— *n., adj.* kouri (no) 小売り (の)

retain *v.* (keep) tamotsu 保つ; horyū suru 保留す
る; (remember) kioku suru 記憶する; (hire) ya-
totte oku 雇っておく

retire *v.* (go back) shirizoku 退く; (withdraw) taikyaku suru 退却する; (go into retreat) intai suru 引退する; (go to bed) nedoko ni hairu 寝床
に入る

retort *v.* (reply) iikaesu 言い返す; (present a coun-
terargument) hanron suru 反論する; hambaku
suru 反ばくする —— *n.* (quick, incisive reply)
kuchigotae 口答え; sakaneji さかねじ; hambaku
反ばく

retreat *n., v.* taikyaku (suru) 退却 (する) ——
n. (place of seclusion) intaijo 隠退所

return *vi.* (come or go back) kaeru 帰る —— *vt.*
(bring back) kaesu 返す; (repay) hempō suru 返
報する; (respond) henji suru 返事する; (yield
profit) rieki o ageru 利益をあげる —— *n.* ka-

eri 帰り; fukki 復帰; kikan 帰還; *pl.* (profit) rieki 利益; *pl.* (official report) hōkokusho 報告書
in return (*for*) …no hempō ni…の返報に; hen-
rei to shite 返礼として; …no kawari ni …の代
りに
return ticket ōfuku kippu 往復切符
by return of post orikaeshi 折り返し

reveal *v.* (disclose) arawasu 現わす; (show) shimesu 示す

revenge *n., v.* fukushū (suru) 復しゅう (する)

revenue *n., v.* (state's annual income) sainyū 歳入;
(income) shūnyū 収入

reverse *v.* (turn to or in the opposite direction)
gyaku ni suru [naru] 逆にする[なる]; hantai
ni suru [naru] 反対にする[なる] ―― *n., adj.*
(contrary) gyaku (no) 逆 (の); (opposite) hantai
(no) 反対 (の); (back or rear) ura (no) 裏 (の);
(defeat) haiboku 敗北; (failure) shippai 失敗

review *n., v.* (study again) fukushū suru 復習する;
(look back on) kaiko suru 回顧する; (criticize)
hyōron suru 評論する

revise *v.* kaitei suru 改訂する; shūsei suru 修正す
る

revive *vi.* (come back to life) ikikaeru 生き返る;
fukkatsu suru 復活する; (recover) kaifuku suru
回復する; (regain vigor) genki-zuku 元気づく
―― *vt.* (bring to life) ikikaeraseru 生き返らせ
る; (make fresh) genki o kaifuku saseru 元気を
回復させる

revolt *n., v.* hanran (o okosu) 反乱 (を起こす);
hangyaku (suru) 反逆 (する); muhon (o okosu) 謀反 (を起こす); (fill or be filled with
disgust) fuyukai ni omou 不愉快に思う; mukatsuku むかつく

revolution *n.* (revolving) kaiten 回転; (complete
change) kaikaku 改革; (overthrow of a government) kakumei 革命

revolve *vi.* (rotate) kaiten suru 回転する; mawaru 回る; (move in an orbit) unkō suru 運行す

る —— *vt.* mawasu 回す; (think over) omoi-
megurasu 思い巡らす

revolver *n.* rempatsushiki pisutoru 連発式ピス
トル; reborubā レボルバー

reward *n.* hōshū 報酬; hōbi ほうび; sharei 謝礼
—— *v.* mukuiru 報いる; sharei suru 謝礼する

rhyme *n.* in 韻; shi 詩

rhythm *n.* rizumu リズム

rib *n.* rokkotsu ろっ骨; abara-bone あばら骨;
(rib of an umbrella) kasa no hone かさの骨

ribbon *n.* ribon リボン; himo ひも

rice *n.* kome 米; meshi 飯; (rice plant) ine 稲

rich *adj.* (wealthy) kanemochi no 金持の; (abundant) hōfu na 豊富な; (thick) nōkō na 濃厚な
—— *n. pl.* (wealth) tomi 富; zaisan 財産

rid *v.* (free) nogare saseru 逃れさせる; (remove)
…kara torinozoku …から取り除く
get [*be*] *rid of* …kara torinozoku …から取り
除く; katazukeru 片付ける; oi-harau 追い払う

riddle *n., v.* (puzzle) nazo (o kakeru) なぞ (を掛
ける); (solve) nazo (o toku) なぞ (を解く)

ride *v.* noru 乗る; (be carried in or on a vehicle)
notte iku 乗って行く; (sit on and manage a
horse) uma ni noru 馬に乗る —— *n.* (*horse*)
jōba 乗馬; (*vehicle*) jōsha 乗車

ridge *n.* (top) itadaki 頂; chōjō 頂上; (cf. crest)
one 尾根; mine 峰; (ridge in ploughed ground)
une うね *ridge of nose* hana-suji 鼻筋

ridicule *n.* azakeri あざけり; chōshō 嘲笑 ——
v. azakeru あざける; baka ni suru ばかにする

ridiculous *adj.* okashii おかしい; bakageta ばか
げた

rifle *n.* shōjū 小銃; raifuru-jū ライフル銃

right *adj.* (just) tadashii 正しい; (true) hontō no
本当の; (proper) tekitō na 適当な; (cf. left) migi no 右の; (straight) massugu na 真っすぐな
—— *n.* (privilege) kenri 権利; (justice) seigi 正
義
All right. Yoroshii. よろしい。

right away sugu ni すぐに; tadachi ni 直ちに

right-hand *adj*. migite no 右手の; migigawa no 右側の

rightly *adj*. tadashiku 正しく; seitō ni 正当に

rigid *adj*. (stiff) katai 堅い; (strict) genjū na 厳重な

rim *n*. (edge) fuchi 縁; heri へり

ring[1] *n*. wa 輪; (finger ring) yubiwa 指輪; (*boxing*) ringu リング

ring[2] *vt*. narasu 鳴らす ―― *vi*. naru 鳴る
　ring off denwa o kiru 電話を切る
　ring up denwa o kakeru 電話をかける

rinse *v*. yusugu ゆすぐ; susugu すすぐ

riot *n*., *v*. sōdō (o okosu) 騒動 (を起こす); bōdō (o okosu) 暴動 (を起こす)

rip *vt*. saku 裂く; yaburu 破る ―― *vi*. sakeru 裂ける; yabureru 破れる

ripe *adj*. (mature) jukushita 熟した; enjuku shita 円熟した; minotta 実った

rise *v*. (get up) okiru 起きる; tachi-agaru 立ち上がる; (come or go up, ascend) noboru 昇る; (increase) masu 増す

risk *n*. kiken 危険; bōken 冒険
　at the risk of ...o toshite ...を賭して
　run risks kiken o okasu 危険を冒す

rite *n*. (ceremony) gishiki 儀式; (general custom) kanshū 慣習; shūkan 習慣

rival *n*. (competitor) kyōsōsha 競争者; raibaru ライバル ―― *v*. (be comparable to) ...ni hitteki suru ...に匹敵する; (vie with) kyōsō suru 競争する

river *n*. kawa 川　*riverside* kawabe 川辺

road *n*. (way) michi 道; (means) shudan 手段; hōhō 方法

roar *v*. (make a deep, loud cry) hoeru ほえる; (bawl) donaru 怒鳴る; (resound) todoroku とどろく ―― *n*. hoegoe ほえ声; unari うなり

roast *v*. aburu あぶる; mushiyaki ni suru 蒸焼きにする

rob *v.* ubau 奪う；gōtō o suru 強盗をする

robber *n.* gōtō 強盗

robe *n.* rōbu ローブ；*pl.* ifuku 衣服

robin *n.* komadori 駒鳥

rock[1] *n.* iwa 岩；ishi 石

rock[2] *v.* (move gently to and fro) (zengo ni) yuri-ugokasu (前後に) 揺り動かす；(sway from side to side) (yoko ni) yuri-ugokasu (横に) 揺り動かす ——*n., v.* dōyō (suru) 動揺 (する)

rocket *n.* roketto ロケット；noroshi のろし

rod *n.* (stick) sao さお；(fishing rod) tsuri-zao 釣りざお；(switch) muchi むち

role *n.* (character played by an actor) yaku 役；(function) yakume 役目；nimmu 任務

roll *v.* (move by turning) korogasu 転がす；(wrap round upon itself) maite tsutsumu 巻いて包む；(flatten with a roller) (rōrā de) narasu (ローラーで) ならす；(wind into a ball or tube) marumeru 丸める；maku 巻く ——*n.* (rolling) kaiten 回転；(cf. pitch) (fune no) yokoyure (船の) 横揺れ；(scroll) makimono 巻物；(list of names) meibo 名簿；(*bread*) rōrupan ロールパン；(peal) (kaminari ga) goro-goro naru oto (雷が) ゴロゴロ鳴る音

romance *n.* romansu ロマンス；ren'ai shōsetsu 恋愛小説

roof *n.* yane 屋根

room *n.* heya 部屋；(space) basho 場所；yochi 余地

root *n.* (*plant*) ne 根；(origin) kompon 根本；kigen 起源 ——*v.* (take root) nezuku 根付く

rope *n.* tsuna 綱；nawa なわ；rōpu ロープ ——*v.* musubu 結ぶ；shibaru 縛る

rose *n.* bara (-iro) ばら(色) ——*adj.* bara-iro no ばら色の

rot *vt.* kusaraseru 腐らせる ——*vi.* kusaru 腐る ——*n.* fuhai 腐敗

rotary *v.* (turning round) kaiten suru 回転する ——*adj.* kaiten-shiki no 回転式の ——*n.* rōtarī ロータリー

rotate *v.* (revolve) kaiten suru [saseru] 回転する [させる]; (alternate) kōtai suru [saseru] 交代する[させる]; (circulate) junkan suru [saseru] 循環する[させる]

rotten *adj.* (decayed) kusatta 腐った; (corrupt) daraku shita 堕落した; (disagreeable) iyana いやな

rouge *n.* beni 紅; kuchi-beni 口紅

rough *adj.* (coarse in texture) arai 粗い; (not level) deko-boko no でこぼこの; (not smooth) zara-zara no ざらざらの; (coarse) soya na 粗野な; rambō na 乱暴な ——*n.* (rough draft, sketch) sōan 草案; gairyakuzu 概略図

round *adj.* (circular) marui 丸い; enkei no 円形の; (spherical) kyūkei no 球形の; (go round) isshū suru 一周する ——*n.* (circle) en 円; (globe) kyū 球; (ring) wa 輪 ——*adv.* ...no mawari ni ...の回りに; ...o mawatte ...を回って; gururi to ぐるりと ——*v.* maruku naru [suru] 丸くなる [する]
   all the year round ichinen-jū 一年中
   round trip shūyū 周遊; ōfuku 往復

roundabout *adj.* (circuitous) tōmawari no 遠回りの; mawarimichi no 回り道の; (indirect) kanse-tsu-teki na 間接的な; tōmawashi no 遠回しの ——*n.* (merry-go-round) kaiten mokuba 回転木馬

rouse *v.* (waken) me o samasaseru 目を覚まさせる; (excite) genki-zuku [-zukeru] 元気付く[付ける]; funki suru [saseru] 奮起する[させる]

route *n.* (road) michi 道; rosen 路線; rūto ルート; (line) kōro 航路

routine *n.* (prescribed procedure) kimarikitta shigoto 決まりきった仕事 ——*adj.* (unvary-ing) okimari no お決まりの; (everyday) nichi-jō no 日常の

row[1] *n.* (rank) retsu 列; (line) gyō 行; (row of houses) yanami 家並 *in rows* retsu o nashite

列をなして

row²*v.* (propel a boat with oars) fune o kogu 舟をこぐ

row³*n.* (disturbance) sōdō 騒動; (noise) sawagi 騒ぎ; (dispute) ronsō 論争; (noisy quarrel) kenka けんか —— *v.* sawagu 騒ぐ; kenka suru けんかする

royal *adj.* ō no 王の; ōshitsu no 王室の; ōritsu no 王立の

rub *v.* kosuru こする; masatsu suru 摩擦する; suri-tsukeru 擦り付ける

rubber *n.* gomu ゴム; (eraser) keshigomu 消しゴム

rubbish *n.* kuzu くず; gomi ごみ; garakuta がらくた

rucksack *n.* ryukkusakku リュックサック

rudder *n.* (fune no) kaji (舟の) かじ

rude *adj.* (impolite) shitsurei na 失礼な; burei na 無礼な; (crude) soya na 粗野な

ruffle *v.* (make rough) kakimidasu かき乱す; (ripple) sazanami o tateru さざ波を立てる; (disturb) magotsukaseru まごつかせる —— *n.* (ripple) sazanami さざ波; (narrow, pleated cloth trimming) hida-kazari ひだ飾り

rug *n.* (floor covering) jūtan じゅうたん; (lap robe) hizakake mōfu ひざ掛け毛布

ruin *n.* (destruction) hametsu 破滅; *pl.* (remains of a destroyed house or city) haikyo 廃きょ; iseki 遺跡 —— *v.* hametsu saseru 破滅させる

ruined *adj.* arehateta 荒れ果てた; botsuraku shita 没落した

rule *n.* (regulation) kisoku 規則; (habitual practice) shūkan 習慣; (government) shihai 支配 —— *v.* (govern) shihai suru 支配する; (draw with a ruler) jōgi de sen o hiku 定規で線を引く

ruler *n.* (governor) shihaisha 支配者; tōjisha 統治者; (cf. foot-rule) jōgi 定規

rum *n.* ramu-shu ラム酒; sake 酒

run *v.* hashiru 走る; kakeru 駆ける; (flee) nigeru

逃げる; (flow) (kawa ga) nagareru (川が) 流れ
る; (manage) keiei suru 経営する; (make a quick
trip) isoide ryokō suru 急いで旅行する; (be
worded) kaite aru 書いてある; (operate) (kikai
o) ugokasu (機械を) 動かす —— *n.* (point
scored in baseball) tokuten 得点
run after oikakeru 追いかける
run against butsukaru ぶつかる
run away nigeru 逃げる
run down tomaru 止まる
run over (pass over) hiku 引く; (review hastily)
zatto yomu ざっと読む; (overflow) afureru あ
ふれる
run short of ...ga ketsubō suru ...が欠乏する
in the long run kekkyoku 結局; tsuiniwa つい
には

rural *adj.* inaka no 田舎の; inaka-fū no 田舎風の
rush *n., v.* (dash) tosshin (suru) 突進 (する); sattō
(suru) 殺到 (する); (hurry) isogaseru 急がせる
rust *n.* sabi さび —— *v.* sabiru さびる *rusty*
sabita さびた
rye *n.* raimugi ライ麦; kuromugi 黒麦 *rye bread*
raimugi pan ライ麦パン *rye whisky* rai-uisukī
ライウイスキー

S

sack *n.* fukuro 袋; sakku サック —— *v.* fukuro
ni ireru 袋に入れる
sacred *adj.* (holy) shinsei na 神聖な; (dedicated)
sasagerareta ささげられた
sacrifice *n., v.* gisei (ni suru) 犠牲 (にする)
sad *adj.* kanashii 悲しい; mijimena 惨めな *sadly*
kanashiku 悲しく; itamashiku 痛ましく
saddle *n., v.* kura (o oku) 鞍 (を置く)
sadness *n.* kanashimi 悲しみ; hiai 悲哀
safe *adj.* anzen na 安全な; buji na 無事な ——
n. (strongbox) kinko 金庫 *safely* anzen ni 安

全に；buji ni 無事に

safety *n.* anzen 安全；buji 無事

sage *n.* (venerable wise man) seijin 聖人；kenjin 賢人；tetsujin 哲人 —— *adj.* kashikoi 賢い；kemmei na 賢明な

sail *n.* (canvas) ho 帆；(small ship) fune 船 —— *v.* (move or travel by means of a sail) hansō suru 帆走する；(navigate) kōkai suru 航海する

sailor *n.* suifu 水夫；sen'in 船員

saint *n.* (holy person) seijin 聖人；(S-) sei 聖

sake *n.* (purpose) ...no tame ...のため；mokuteki 目的；(benefit) rieki 利益

for the sake of ...no tame ni ...のために

for God's sake dōka どうか；onegai dákara お願いだから

salad *n.* sarada サラダ

sale *n.* hambai 販売；ureyuki 売れ行き；(bargain) bāgen sēru バーゲンセール

salesgirl *n.* joten'in 女店員

salesman *n.* ten'in 店員；hambai'in 販売員；sērusuman セールスマン

salmon *n.* sake さけ；shake しゃけ

saloon *n.* (large public room) ō-hiroma 大広間；saron サロン；(better class bar) sakaba 酒場

salt *n.* shio 塩 —— *adj.* shioke no aru 塩気のある —— *v.* shio-zuke ni suru 塩づけにする

salute *n., v.* aisatsu (suru) あいさつ（する）；keirei (suru) 敬礼（する）

salvage *n., v.* kainan kyūjo (suru) 海難救助（する）

salve *n.* (medicinal ointment) kōyaku こう薬；nankō 軟こう —— *v.* (soothe) nagusameru 慰める

same *adj.* onaji 同じ；dōyō no 同様の；dōitsu no 同一の

all the same (nevertheless) それでも；yahari onajiku やはり同じく

sample *n.* mihon 見本；sampuru サンプル；hyōhon 標本

sand *n.* suna 砂

sandal *n.* sandaru サンダル

sand-glass *n.* suna-dokei 砂時計

sandpaper *n.* kami-yasuri 紙やすり

sandwich *n.* sandoitchi サンドイッチ

sanitary *adj.* eisei-jō no 衛生上の; eisei-teki na 衛生的な

sardine *n.* iwashi いわし

sash¹ *n.* (ornamented band) obi 帯; kazari-obi 飾り帯

sash² *n.* (sliding frame for window glass) mado-waku 窓枠; sasshi サッシ

satellite *n.* (small planet) eisei 衛星　*man-made satellite* jinkō-eisei 人工衛星

satin *n.* shusu しゅす; saten サテン

satire *n.* fūshi 風刺; hiniku 皮肉

satisfaction *n.* manzoku 満足

satisfy *v.* (content) manzoku saseru 満足させる; (convince) nattoku saseru 納得させる

Saturday *n.* doyō-bi 土曜日

sauce *n.* sōsu ソース

saucepan *n.* shichū-nabe シチューなべ

saucer *n.* uke-zara 受け皿; dai-zara 台皿　*flying saucer* sora-tobu emban 空飛ぶ円盤

sausage *n.* sōsēji ソーセージ

savage *adj.* (uncivilized) yaban na 野蛮な; (cruel) zankoku na 残酷な ——*n.* yabanjin 野蛮人

save *v.* (rescue) suku'u 救う; (keep for future use) takuwaeru 蓄える; (spare) setsuyaku suru 節約する ——*prep.* (except)…o nozoite…を除いて
saving (rescue) kyūjo 救助; *pl.* (money saved) chokin 貯金
save for…igai wa…以外は

say *v.* (utter) iu 言う; noberu 述べる; oi おい; chotto ちょっと; ne ね　*to say nothing of* iu made mo naku 言うまでもなく

saying *n.* kakugen 格言; kotowaza ことわざ

scale[1] *n.* (set of graded marks) memori 目盛；(ruler) monosashi 物指し；(proportion) wariai 割合；kibo 規模

scale[2] *n. pl.* (balance) tembin-bakari てんびんばかり —— *v.* hakari ni kakeru はかりにかける

scale[3] *n.* (fish) uroko うろこ；kokera こけら；(scab) kasabuta かさぶた —— *v.* uroko o otosu うろこを落とす；kara [saya] o muku から[さや]をむく

scandal *n.* shūbun 醜聞；sukyandaru スキャンダル

scarce *adj.* (scanty) toboshii 乏しい；(rare) mare na まれな　*scarcely* hotondo…nai ほとんど…ない；yatto やっと

scare *v.* (frighten) odorokaseru 驚かせる；bikkuri saseru びっくりさせる —— *n.* (fright) kyōfu 恐怖；odoroki 驚き

scarf *n.* eri-maki 襟巻；sukāfu スカーフ

scatter *v.* baramaku ばらまく；makichirasu まき散らす

scene *n.* (place, setting) bamen 場面；(view) fūkei 風景；keshiki 景色

scenery *n.* keshiki 景色；fūkei 風景

scent *n.* (perfume) kaori 香り；(odor) nioi におい；(sense of smell) kyūkaku 嗅覚 —— *v.* (smell) kagu かぐ；(perfume) kaoraseru 香らせる

schedule *n.* sukejūru スケジュール；yotei 予定；ichiranhyō 一覧表

scheme *n., v.* keikaku (suru) 計画 (する)

scholar *n.* (learned person) gakusha 学者；(student) gakusei 学生；(student given scholarship aid) shōgakusei 奨学生

scholarship *n.* shōgakukin 奨学金

school *n.* gakkō 学校；(schoolhouse) kōsha 校舎；(school hours) jugyō-jikan 授業時間；(sect) ryūha 流派

schoolboy *n.* danshi-seito 男子生徒

schooldays *n.* gakusei-jidai 学生時代

schoolgirl *n.* joshi-seito 女子生徒

school hours *n.* jugyō-jikan 授業時間

schoolhouse *n.* kōsha 校舎

science *n.* kagaku 科学

scissors *n. pl.* hasami はさみ

scold *v.* shikaru しかる; gami-gami iu がみがみ言う

scoop *n.* (small, shovel-like utensil) kogata no sukoppu 小形のスコップ; (cf. ladle) shakushi しゃくし; hishaku ひしゃく; (*newspaper*) (beat) tokudane 特種; sukūpu スクープ ——*v.* (hollow out) kurinuku くりぬく; eguru えぐる; (ladle out) suku'u すくう; kumidasu くみ出す

scope *n.* (range) han'i 範囲; (range of view or action) genkai 限界; (room) yochi 余地; (opportunity to function) kikai 機会; hakeguchi はけ口

scorch *vt.* kogasu 焦がす ——*vi.* kogeru 焦げる ——*n.* yakekoge 焼け焦げ

score *n.* (record of points made) tokuten (-kiroku) 得点 (記録); sukoa スコア; (notch) kizamime 刻み目; (twenty) ni-jū 20; (result of a test) shiken no kekka 試験の結果; (debt) shakkin 借金; (account) kanjō 勘定; (wound) kirikizu 切り傷; (*music*) gakufu 楽譜 ——*v.* (make a score or scores) tokuten suru 得点する; (keep score) tokuten o kiroku suru 得点を記録する

scorn *n., v.* keibetsu(suru) 軽べつ(する); azawarau あざ笑う

scout *n.* (one sent in advance to gather information) sekkō 斥候; (boy [girl] scout) bōi [gāru] sukauto ボーイ [ガール] スカウト; (talent scout) sukauto スカウト ——*v.* (reconnoiter) teisatsu suru 偵察する; sekkō ni iku 斥候に行く

scowl *v.* kao o shikameru 顔をしかめる ——*n.* shikame-tsura しかめ面

scramble *v.* (climb or crawl with the hands and feet) hau はう; yojinoboru よじ登る; (struggle for something) ubai-au 奪い合う; (mix confusedly) gochamaze ni suru ごちゃまぜにする
scrambled eggs iritamago いり卵

scrap *n.* (fragment) kirehashi 切れ端; (discarded material) kuzu くず; (newspaper cuttings) (shimbun no) kirinuki (新聞の) 切抜き

scrape *v.* (rub forcefully) kosuru こする; (scratch) kaku かく; (polish) migaku 磨く; (remove by rubbing) kosuri otosu こすり落とす; (shave) soru そる

scratch *v.* (rub the skin to relieve itching) kaku かく; (wound with nails or claws) hikkaku 引っかく; (write roughly) hashiri-gaki suru 走り書きする —— *n.* (slight cut or wound) kaki-kizu かき傷; kasuri-kizu かすり傷

scream *v.* kyā to iu キャーと言う; himei [kanakiri-goe] o ageru 悲鳴 [金切り声] をあげる

screen *n.* (thing used to conceal) tsuitate つい立; shikiri 仕切り; (window insertion of framed mesh) amido 網戸; (surface for showing movies) sukurīn スクリーン
folding screen byōbu びょうぶ
sliding screen shōji 障子; fusuma ふすま

screw *n.* (nail-like fastener with a spiral groove) neji ねじ; (propeller) sukuryū スクリュー —— *v.* (fasten with a screw) neji de tomeru ねじで止める *screwdriver* neji-mawashi ねじ回し; doraibā ドライバー

script *n.* (handwriting) tegaki 手書き; (scenario) kyakuhon 脚本

sculptor *n.* chōkoku-ka 彫刻家

sculpture *n., v.* chōkoku (suru) 彫刻 (する)

sea *n.* umi 海; ...kai ...海
The Sea of Japan Nihon-kai 日本海
by sea fune de 船で; kairo de 海路で
go to sea funanori ni naru 船乗りになる
put to sea shuppan suru 出帆する; shukkō suru 出航する

seabed *n.* (the s-) kaitei 海底

seabird *n.* umidori 海鳥

seaboard *n.* kaigan-sen 海岸線; umibe 海辺; engan (chihō) 沿岸 (地方)

seacoast *n*. kaigan 海岸; engan 沿岸

seafood *n*. kaisan-shokuhin 海産食品

seal[1] *n*. azarashi あざらし

seal[2] *n*. (stamped emblem or design) han 判; in-shō 印章; (device for closing envelopes or packages) fūin 封印 —— *v*. (affix a seal to) han o osu 判を押す; (close) fū o suru 封をする

sea level *n*. kaisuimen 海水面

sea lion *n*. ashika あしか

seam *n*. nuime 縫い目 —— *v*. nuiawaseru 縫い合わせる　*seamless* shīmuresu シームレス

seaman *n*. sen'in 船員; funanori 船乗り

sea mile *n*. kairi 海里

search *v*. (look through) sagasu 捜す; (investigate) shiraberu 調べる —— *n*. (examination) chōsa 調査; (searching) sōsa 捜査　*in search of* …o sagashite …を捜して; …o motomete …を求めて

seashell *n*. kai(-gara) 貝(殻)

seashore *n*. kaigan 海岸; umibe 海辺

seasick *adj*. fune ni yotta 船に酔った; funayoi no 船酔いの

seaside *n*. (the s-) umibe 海辺; hamabe 浜辺; kaigan 海岸

season *n*. (any of four divisions of the year) kisetsu 季節; shiki 四季; (special time of year) jisetsu 時節; jiki 時期; kikan 期間 —— *v*. (give relish to) aji「fūmi」o tsukeru 味「風味」を付ける

seasoning *n*. (condiment) chōmiryō 調味料; yakumi 薬味

seat *n*. (surface or place for sitting) zaseki 座席; isu いす; (center, capital) chūshinchi 中心地; shozaichi 所在地; (buttocks) shiri 尻; (location) basho 場所; ichi 位置
take a seat seki ni tsuku 席に着く
Take a seat, please. Dōzo okake kudasai. どうぞお掛けください.

seaweed *n*. kaisō 海藻; mo 藻; nori のり

second[1] *adj.* dai-ni no 第二の; ni-ban me no 二番目の; (another) betsu no 別の

second[2] *n.* (1/60 a minute) byō 秒; (moment) shunkan 瞬間

secret *adj.* (kept from being generally known) himitsu no 秘密の; (kept hidden from others) kakureta 隠れた —— *n.* (kcy) hiketsu 秘けつ *in secret* naisho de 内緒で; himitsu ni 秘密に

secretary *n.* hisho 秘書; shokikan 書記官; jimukan 事務官; (*U.S.*) (S-) chōkan 長官 *the Secretary of State* kokumu-chōkan 国務長官

sect *n.* (religious order) shūha 宗派; kyōha 教派

section *n.* (part) bubun 部分; (district) chiku 地区; (division) ka 課; (*book*) setsu 節 —— *v.* (divide into parts) kuwake suru 区分けする; bunkatsu suru 分割する

secure *adj.* (safe) anzen na 安全な; (certain) kakujitsu na 確実な; (stable) kengo na 堅固な —— *v.* (make safe) anzen ni suru 安全にする; (make firm) kakujitsu ni suru 確実にする *securely* anzen ni 安全に; kakujitsu ni 確実に

security *n.* (safety) anzen 安全; (guarantee) hoshō 保証; *pl.* (stocks and bonds) kabu 株; saiken 債券

seduce *v.* sosonokasu そそのかす; yūwaku suru 誘惑する

see *v.* (look at) miru 見る; (meet) au 会う; (understand) wakaru わかる; (consider) kangaeru 考える; (take care) ki o tsukeru 気をつける; (undergo) keiken suru 経験する; (find out) mitsukeru 見付ける; (make sure) tashikameru 確かめる *see off* miokuru 見送る *see through* miyaburu 見破る; minuku 見抜く *I see.* Wakarimashita. 分りました.

seed *n., v.* tane (o maku) 種(をまく)

seek *v.* (search for) sagasu 捜す; (try to obtain) motomeru 求める; (attempt) ...shiyō to suru ...しようとする

seem *v.* (appear) ...no yōni mieru ...のように見える; rashii らしい

seize *v.* (grasp) tsukamu つかむ; (catch) toraeru 捕らえる; (understand) rikai suru 理解する

seldom *adv.* metta ni...(shi) nai ...めったに...(し) ない; (rarely) tama ni たまに; mare ni まれに

select *v.* erabu 選ぶ —— *adj.* eranda 選んだ; e-rinuki no えり抜きの　*selection* sentaku 選択

self-confidence *n.* jishin 自信

self-control *n.* jisei 自制

selfish *adj.* riko-teki na 利己的な; wagamama na 我ままな

sell *v.* uru 売る; ureru 売れる

semester *n.* gakki 学期; han-gakunen 半学年

senate *n.* jōin 上院　*senator* jōin-giin 上院議員

send *v.* (cause to be conveyed) okuru 送る; (direct to go) ikaseru 行かせる
send away oidasu 追い出す
send for ...o okuridasu ...を送り出す; mukae ni yaru 迎えにやる

senior *adj.* (older) toshiue no 年上の; jōkyū no 上級の —— *n.* (student in his fourth year of high school or college) (kōkō, daigaku no) yo-nensei (高校、大学の) 四年生

sensation *n.* (sense) kankaku 感覚; (feeling) kanji 感じ; (emotion) kandō 感動; (excitement) sen-sēshon センセーション

sense *n.* (power to see, etc.) kankaku 感覚; (feeling) kanji 感じ; (perception) ninshiki 認識; ishi-ki 意識; (meaning) imi 意味; (sound judgement) fumbetsu 分別

senseless *adj.* mukankaku no 無感覚の; mufum-betsu na 無分別な

sensible *adj.* (judicious) fumbetsu no aru 分別のある; (perceptible) kanjirareru hodo no 感じられるほどの; kanari no かなりの; (aware) kan-zuite [kizuite] iru 感づいて [気付いて] いる

sensitive *adj.* kanji yasui 感じやすい; binkan na

敏感な

sentence *n., v.* bunshō 文章; bun 文; (punishment) hanketsu (o kudasu) 判決 (を下す)

sentiment *n.* (feeling) kanjō 感情; (maudlin emotion) kanshō 感傷

sentimental *adj.* kanshō-teki na 感傷的な; namida moroi 涙もろい

separate *adj.* (set apart) wakareta 別れた; (individual) koko no 個々の ―― *v.* (divide) wakeru 分ける; (come apart) wakareru 別れる

separately *adv.* betsu-betsu ni 別々に

September *n.* ku-gatsu 九月

sequence *n.* (continuous series) renzoku 連続; (order of occurrence) junjo 順序

sergeant *n.* (*army*) gunsō 軍曹; (*police*) keibu 警部

series *n.* (sequence) renzoku 連続; shirīzu シリーズ

serious *adj.* (earnest) majime na まじめな; (thoughtful) honki no 本気の; (important) omoomo shii 重々しい; taisetsu na 大切な; jūdai na 重大な

seriously *adj.* majime ni まじめに; hidoku ひどく

sermon *n.* sekkyō 説教

serpent *n.* hebi 蛇

servant *n.* meshitsukai 召使い

serve *v.* (work for) …ni tsukaeru …に仕える; (avail) …ni yakudatsu …に役立つ; (offer food, etc. to) (shokutaku ni) dasu 食卓に出す; kubaru 配る ―― *n.* (*tennis*) sābu サーブ

service *n.* (act of serving) hōshi (-katsudō) 奉仕 (活動); sewa 世話; (system for supplying public needs) kōkyō-jigyō 公共事業; (maintenance and repair) afutā-sābisu アフターサービス; (religious meeting) reihai 礼拝

sesame *n.* goma ごま

session *n.* (sitting) kaikai 開会; kaitei 開廷; kaiki 会期; (term) gakki 学期

set *v.* (put) oku 置く；(place) sueru 据える；(impose) kasuru 課する；(adjust) tadasu 正す；totonoeru 整える；(fix) kimeru 決める；(disappear below the horizon) (hi ga) shizumu（日が）沈む；(establish) tateru 建てる；(sit on eggs) mendori ga tamago o daku めん鳥が卵を抱く

set about torikakaru 取り掛かる；chakushu suru 着手する

set aside soba ni oku そばに置く；(reserve) totte oku 取って置く；(disregard) mushi suru 無視する

set free kaihō suru 解放する

set in hajimaru 始まる；…ni naru …になる

set off [*out*] (start) shuppatsu suru 出発する

set up (erect) tateru 立てる；(build) tateru 建てる

—— *adj.* (fixed) kotei shita 固定した；(determined) fudō no 不動の —— *n.* (group, collection) kumi 組；setto セット

settle *v.* (arrange) torikimeru 取り決める；(fix in one place) ochitsukeru 落着ける；(pay up) shiharau 支払う；seisan suru 清算する；(fix) sadamaru 定まる *settle down* eijū suru 永住する

seven *n., adj.* shichi (no) 7，七 (の)；nanatsu (no) 7，七つ (の)

seventeen *n., adj.* jū-shichi (no) 17，十七 (の)

seventy *n., adj.* shichi-jū (no) 70，七十 (の)；nana-jū (no) 70，七十 (の)

several *adj.* ikutsuka no 幾つかの；sūko no 数個の；(various) shuju no 種々の；(individual) kakuji no 各自の —— *n.* sūnin 数人；sūko 数個

severe *adj.* (strict) kibishii 厳しい；genkaku na 厳格な；(violent) hageshii 激しい

sew *v.* nuu 縫う *sewing* saihō 裁縫

sex *n.* sei 性；sekkusu セックス

shade *n.* hikage 日陰；monokage 物陰

shadow *n.* (shade) kage 影; hitokage 人影; (darkness) kuragari 暗がり; yami やみ

shaft *n.* (slender stem of an arrow) yagara 矢柄; (arrow) ya 矢; (spear) yari やり; (axle) jiku 軸; (spindle) shimbō 心棒; (stalk) e 柄

shake *v.* furi-ugokasu 振り動かす; (tremble) furueru 震える; yureru 揺れる —— *n.* shindō 震動; furue 震え

shall *v. aux.* ...darō ...だろう; saseru させる

shallow *adj.* (not deep) asai 浅い —— *n.* (shoal) asase 浅瀬

shame *n.* haji 恥 *shameful* hazubeki 恥ずべき *shameless* atsukamashii 厚かましい

shampoo *n., v.* shampū (de arau) シャンプー (で洗う)

shape *n.* (form) katachi 形; (appearance) gaikan 外観 —— *v.* katachi-zukuru 形造る

share *n.* (portion) wakemae 分け前; (stocks) kabu 株 —— *v.* wakachi-au 分かち合う; bumpai suru 分配する

shark *n.* same さめ; fuka ふか

sharp *adj.* (keen) surudoi 鋭い; eibin na 鋭敏な; (steep) kewashii 険しい; (pointed) togatta とがった

shatter *v.* (smash) uchi-kudaku 打ち砕く; funsai suru 粉砕する; kujiku くじく

shave *v.* soru そる; (pare) kezuru 削る

shawl *n.* shōru ショール; katakake 肩掛け

she *pron.* kanojo wa [ga] 彼女は [が]

shear *v.* (clip) hasami-kiru はさみ切る; karu 刈る —— *n. pl.* (scissors) ō-basami 大ばさみ

shed¹ *n.* (hut) koya 小屋; mono'oki 物置

shed² *v.* (cause to flow) nagasu 流す; (pour out) kobosu こぼす; (radiate) (hikari o) hanatsu (光を) 放つ

sheep *n.* hitsuji 羊

sheer¹ *adj.* (pure) junsui no 純粋の; (thin and transparent) sukitōru 透き通る; goku usui ごく薄い; (very steep) kewashii 険しい —— *adv.*

(utter) mattaku no 全くの; (completely) kanzen ni 完全に

sheer [2] v. (swerve) hōkō o kaeru 方向を変える; (waki e) soreru (わきへ) それる

sheet n. (cf. bedclothes) shikifu 敷布; shītsu シーツ; (broad thin piece, as of paper, glass) ichi-mai no kami [garasu] 一枚の紙 [ガラス]; ...mai ...枚

shelf n. (cf. bookshelf) tana 棚; (sandbank) sasu 砂州; (ledge) iwadana 岩棚; anshō 暗礁

shell n. kara 殻; (seashell) kaigara 貝殻; (*turtle*) (kame no) kō (かめの) 甲 —— v. kara o toru 殻をとる

shelter n. (refuge) kakureba 隠れ場; hinansho 避難所; sherutā シェルター —— v. (protect) hogo suru 保護する

shelve v. (put on a shelf) tana ni noseru 棚に載せる; (put aside a question) (mondai o) tanaage ni suru (問題を) 棚上げにする

shepard n. hitsujikai 羊飼い

sheriff n. (chief law officer of a country) shū-chō-kan 州長官; hoankan 保安官

shield n. (protective armor) tate 盾; (any protective covering) bōgyo-butsu 防御物

shift v. (move or transfer) ...no ichi o kaeru ...の位置を変える; utsusu 移す —— n. (relay) kōtai 交替; (change) tenkan 転換

shilling n. shiringu シリング

shine v. (be bright) hikaru 光る; (glow) kagayaku 輝く; (polish) migaku 磨く

ship n., v. fune (ni noru) 船 (に乗る); fune (ni tsumu) 船 (に積む)

shipwreck n. nampa (sen) 難破(船) —— v. nampa suru 難破する

shirt n. shatsu シャツ; waishatsu ワイシャツ

shiver v. (tremble) furueru 震える —— n. miburui 身震い

shock n. shōgeki 衝撃; shokku ショック —— v. shōgeki o ataeru 衝撃を与える; (astound) odorokasu 驚かす

shoe *n.* kutsu 靴

shoehorn *n.* kutsu-bera 靴べら

shoemaker *n.* kutsu-ya 靴屋

shoot *v.* (fire a gun) shageki suru 射撃する; utsu 撃つ; hassha suru 発射する; (sprout) me o dasu 芽を出す

shooting *n.* shageki 射撃; hassha 発射; (darting) tosshin 突進

shop *n.* mise 店; kouriten 小売店; (workshop) shigotoba 仕事場; sagyōjō 作業場; (factory) seizōsho 製造所; kōjō 工場

shore *n.* kishi 岸; hama 浜

short *adj.* (little length) mijikai 短い; (not tall) hikui 低い; (brief) kanketsu na 簡潔な; (lacking) kirashite iru 切らしている; (insufficient) fujūbun na 不十分な
(*be*) *short of* …ni toboshii …に乏しい; …ga tarinai …が足りない
in short yōsuru ni 要するに
—— *adv.* (abruptly) kyū ni 急に; kanketsu ni 簡潔に; mijikaku 短く —— *n. pl.* shōto pantsu ショートパンツ
shortly sugu ni すぐに; mamonaku 間もなく

shortage *n.* (lack) fusoku 不足; ketsubō 欠乏

shorten *v.* chijimeru 縮める; mijikaku suru 短くする

shorthand *n.* sokki 速記

short-sighted *adj.* kinshi no 近視の; kingan no 近眼の

shot *n.* (bullet) dangan 弾丸; tama 弾; (shooting) shageki 射撃

should *v. aux.* darō だろう; (if) moshi …sureba もし…すれば; (ought to) subeki de aru すべきである

shoulder *n.* kata 肩 —— *v.* katsugu 担ぐ; ninau 担う

shout *n.* sakebi(goe) 叫び(声) —— *v.* sakebu 叫ぶ

shove v. (push) osu 押す; (thrust) tsuku 突く

shovel n. shaberu シャベル

show vt. (bring in sight) miseru 見せる; shimesu
示す; (make clear) akiraka ni suru 明らかに
する; (explain) setsumei suru 説明する; (point
out) shiji suru 指示する; shiteki suru 指摘する;
(guide) an'nai suru 案内する ―― vi. (appear)
arawareru 現れる; (look) mieru 見える ――
n. (entertainment) shō ショー; misemono 見せ
物; (public exhibition) tenrankai 展覧会
show off misebirakasu 見せびらかす
show the way an'nai suru 案内する

shower n. (brief fall of rain) niwaka-ame にわか
雨; yūdachi 夕立; (shower bath) shawā シャ
ワー

shred n. dampen 断片; kirehashi 切れ端 ――
v. zuta-zuta ni kiru ずたずたに切る; kirisaku
切り裂く

shriek n., v. himei (o ageru) 悲鳴を (を上げる);
kanakirigoe (o dasu) 金切り声 (を出す)

shrimp n. ebi えび

shrine n. jinja 神社; jingū 神宮; yashiro 社

shrink v. (contract) chijimu 縮む; chijimeru 縮め
る; (lessen) heru 減る; (draw back) chūcho
suru ちゅうちょする

shrub n. (bush) kamboku かん木

shuffle v. (walk with feet dragging) ashi o hiki-
zutte aruku 足を引きずって歩く; darashinaku
aruku だらしなく歩く; (mix together) (torampu o) kirimazeru (トランプを) 切り混ぜる

shut v. (close) tojiru 閉じる; shimeru 閉める;
shimaru 閉まる ――adj. shimatte iru 閉まっ
ている *shut out* shimedasu 締め出す

shutter n. shattā シャッター; yoroido よろい戸

shy adj. (bashful) uchiki na 内気な; hazukashi-
gari no 恥ずかしがりの; (timid) okubyō na
おく病な ――v. ojikeru おじける; shirigomi
suru しりごみする

shyly adv. hanikande はにかんで

sick *adj.* (ill) byōki no 病気の; mukatsuku むか
つく; (tired) iyaki ga sashita 嫌気がさした

sickness *n.* byōki 病気; (nausea) hakike 吐き気

side *n.* (surface) men 面; (left or right half) sokumen 側面; yokogawa 横側; (adjacent space) soba
そば; (party) mikata 味方
by one's side …no soba ni …のそばに
from side to side hashi kara hashi e 端から端へ
on all sides shihō-happō ni 四方八方に; itaru-
tokoro ni いたる所に
side by side narande 並んで
take sides mikata suru 味方する

sidewalk *n.* hodō 歩道

sieve *n., v.* furui (ni kakeru) ふるい (にかける)

sigh *n., v.* tameiki (o tsuku) ため息 (をつく);
(yearn) akogare (ru) あこがれ (る)

sight *n.* (ability to see) shiryoku 視力; shikaku 視
覚; (view) kōkei 光景; (act of seeing) miru koto
見ること ―― *v.* miru 見る; mitomeru 認める
at sight mite sugu 見てすぐ
by sight mite (wakaru) 見て (わかる)
in sight of …no mieru tokoro ni …の見える所
に
out of sight me ni mienai 目に見えない

sign *n.* (symbol) kigō 記号; (signboard) kamban
看板; fugō 符号; shirushi 印; (signal) aizu 合図
―― *v.* (write one's name on) shomei suru 署名
する; chōin suru 調印する

signal *n., v.* shingō (suru) 信号 (する); aizu (suru)
合図 (する) ―― *adj.* (remarkable) ichijirushii
著しい

signature *n.* shomei 署名

significant *adj.* (important) jūyō na 重要な; (having a meaning) imi no aru 意味のある; (full of
meaning) imi-shinchō na 意味深長な

signify *v.* (express) shimesu 示す; arawasu 表わす;
(mean) imi suru 意味する

silence *n.* (muteness) chimmoku 沈黙; mugon 無
言; (stillness) seijaku 静寂

in silence damatte 黙って; sotto そっと
—— *v.* damaraseru 黙らせる; chimmoku saseru
沈黙させる

silent *adj.* (still, quiet) shizuka na 静かな; (not
speaking) chimmoku shita 沈黙した
keep silent damatte iru 黙っている

silk *n.* kinu 絹; (raw silk) ki'ito 生糸

silkworm *n.* kaiko 蚕

silly *adj.* baka na ばかな

silver *n.* gin 銀; (silver coin) ginka 銀貨 ——
adj. gin (iro) no 銀 (色) の

similar *adj.* onaji yō na 同じ様な; dōshurui no
同種類の

simple *adj.* (single) tan'itsu no 単一の; (plain)
kantan na 簡単な; shisso na 質素な; (easy) yōi
na 容易な

simplicity *n.* (easiness) kantan 簡単; yōi 容易; (not
complex) tanjun 単純; (plainness) shisso 質素

sin *n.* tsumi 罪, zaiaku 罪悪

since *adv., prep.* (after) sono-go その後; (from the
time that) shite irai して以来 ——*conj.* (from
the time when) irai 以来; (as, because) nanode
なので; ...dakara ...だから

sincere *adj.* (not hypocritical) seijitsu na 誠実な;
(honest) shōjiki na 正直な; (real) hontō no 本
当の

sing *v.* utau 歌う   *singer* kashu 歌手

single *adj.* (only one) tada hitotsu no ただ一つ
の; (unmarried) dokushin no 独身の; (designed
for one person) hitori-yō no 一人用の

singular *adj.* (being only one) tan'itsu no 単一の;
(extraordinary) odorokubeki 驚くべき; (curi-
ous) fūgawari na 風変りな; myō na 妙な ——
n. (*gram.*) tansū 単数

sink *v.* (go down) shizumu 沈む; chimbotsu suru
沈没する; (water basin with a drain) nagashi
流し

sip *v.* susuru すする; su'u 吸う ——*n.* hito-su-
suri 一すすり

sir *n.* anata あなた; sensei 先生; (S-) …kyō …卿

siren *n.* sairen サイレン; kiteki 汽笛

sirup *n.* shiroppu シロップ; mitsu みつ

sister *n.* shimai 姉妹; (elder) ane 姉; (younger) imōto 妹

sit *v.* suwaru 座る; seki ni tsuku 席に着く; koshi o kakeru 腰を掛ける
sit up late yofukashi o suru 夜更しをする
sitting room ima 居間

site *n.* (ground) shikichi 敷地; (location) ichi 位置; (place) basho 場所

situated *adj.* …ni ichi shite iru …に位置している; …ni aru …にある

situation *n.* (place) basho 場所; (position) ichi 位置; tachiba 立場; (circumstances) kyōgū 境遇; (state of affairs) jijō 事情

six *n., adj.* roku (no) 6, 六 (の); muttsu (no) 6つ, 六つ (の)

sixteen *n., adj.* jū-roku (no) 16, 十六 (の)

sixty *n., adj.* roku-jū (no) 60, 六十 (の)

sizable *adj.* kanari ōkii かなり大きい

size *n.* (bigness) ōkisa 大きさ; sumpō 寸法 —— *v.* (measure) hakaru 測る; sumpō o toru 寸法をとる

skate *n.* sukēto-gutsu スケート靴 —— *v.* sukēto o suru スケートをする

skeleton *n.* gaikotsu がい骨; (framework) honegumi 骨組; (outline) gairyaku 概略
skeleton key aikagi 合かぎ

sketch *n.* shitagaki 下書き; suketchi スケッチ

ski *n.* sukī スキー

skill *n.* (proficiency) jukuren 熟練; (expertness) kōmyō 巧妙; (technique) waza 技

skillful *adj.* takumi na 巧みな; jukuren shita 熟練した

skim *v.* (take off by skimming) sukui toru すくい取る *skim milk* dasshi fun'nyū 脱脂粉乳

skin *n.* hifu 皮膚; kawa 皮 —— *v.* kawa o muku 皮をむく

skip *v.* (leap) tobu 跳ぶ; tobasu 飛ばす; haneru はねる; (omit) tobasu 飛ばす —— *n.* karuku tobu koto 軽く飛ぶこと; (omission) shōryaku 省略

skirt *n.* sukāto スカート; (edge, margin) suso すそ; fuchi 縁

sky *n.* sora 空; ten 天

skylark *n.* hibari ひばり

skyscraper *n.* (chō-)kōsō-biru (超)高層ビル; matenrō 摩天楼

slack *adj.* (loose) yurui 緩い; (slow) darashi no nai だらしのない —— *v.* yurumeru 緩める; yurumu 緩む

slam *v.* pishari to shimeru [shimaru] ピシャリと 閉める [閉まる]; batan to shimeru [shimaru] バタンと閉める [閉まる]

slang *n.* zokugo 俗語; surangu スラング

slant *adj.* katamuita 傾いた —— *v.* katamuku 傾く; katamukeru 傾ける —— *n.* keisha 傾斜; (slope) saka 坂

slash *v.* (cut by sweeping strokes) nadegiri suru なで切りする; (cut by random strokes) metta-giri suru めった切りする; (lash with a whip) muchi de utsu むちで打つ

slate *n.* surēto スレート; sekiban 石板

slave *n.* dorei 奴隷 —— *v.* akuseku hataraku あ くせく働く

slay *v.* satsugai suru 殺害する; korosu 殺す

sleep *n.* nemuri 眠り; suimin 睡眠 —— *v.* nemu-ru 眠る *sleeping car* shindai-sha 寝台車

sleepy *adj.* nemui 眠い; (dull) bon'yari shita ぼ んやりした

sleet *n.* mizore みぞれ

sleeve *n.* sode そで; tamoto たもと
turn up one's sleeve ude o makuru 腕をまくる
sleeveless sode-nashi no そでなしの

slender *adj.* (slim) hossori shita ほっそりした; yowai 弱い; (scanty) toboshii 乏しい

slice *v.* usuku kiru 薄く切る —— *n.* (thin flat

piece) usui hito-kire 薄い一切れ; ippen 一片

slide *vi*. suberu 滑べる —— *vt*. suberaseru 滑べらせる —— *n*. suberi-dai 滑り台; suraido スライド

slight *adj*. (inconsiderable) sukoshi no 少しの; (slender) yaseta やせた; (frail) kayowai か弱い —— *v.*, *n*. (disregard) keibetsu (suru) 軽べつ (する); (negligent) mushi suru 無視する

slim *adj*. hossori shita ほっそりした

slip *vi*. suberu すべる —— *vt*. suberaseru すべらせる —— *n*. (underwear) surippu スリップ

slipper *n*. surippa スリッパ

slippery *adj*. suberi-yasui すべりやすい; nameraka na 滑らかな

slit *n*. (long cut) nagai kireme [sakeme] 長い切れ目 [裂け目]; sukima 透き間 —— *v*. (make a long cut in) hosonagaku kiru 細長く切る

slogan *n*. hyōgo 標語; surōgan スローガン

slope *n*. saka 坂; surōpu スロープ —— *v*. keisha suru 傾斜する

slow *adj*. osoi 遅い; noroi のろい; (*watch*) (tokei ga) okurete iru (時計が) 遅れている —— *v*. sokuryoku o yurumeru 速力を緩める

slowly *adv*. osoku 遅く; yukkurito ゆっくりと

slum *n*. himmin-kutsu 貧民くつ; suramu スラム

slumber *n*. suimin 睡眠; nemuri 眠り —— *v*. nemuru 眠る

slump *n.*, *v*. (fall in price) bōraku (suru) 暴落 (する); (remarkable decrease) gata-ochi がた落ち; surampu スランプ

sly *adj*. zurui ずるい; waru-gashikoi 悪賢い

small *adj*. chiisai 小さい; wazukana わずかな
small change kozeni 小銭

smallpox *n*. ten'nentō 天然痘

smart *adj*. sumāto na スマートな; (shrewd) nukeme no nai 抜け目のない

smash *n.*, *v*. (break into pieces) uchi-kowasu 打ち壊す; (shatter) hakai (suru) 破壊 (する); (collide) shōtotsu (suru) 衝突 (する)

smell *v.* nioi o kagu においをかぐ; niou におう; (emit an odor) …no nioi ga suru …のにおいがする; kaori ga suru 香りがする —— *n.* (sense of smelling) kyūkaku きゅう覚; (odor) nioi におい; kaori 香り

smile *v.* nikkori warau にっこり笑う; hohoemu ほほえむ —— *n.* hohoemi ほほえみ

smoke *n.* kemuri 煙 —— *v.* (emit smoke) kemuru 煙る; (smoke tobacco) tabako o suu たばこを吸う; ibusu いぶす　*smoked* kunsei no くん製の
come to [*end in*] *smoke* suihō ni kisu 水泡に帰す
No smoke without fire. Hi no nai tokoro ni kemuri wa tatanu. 火のない所に煙は立たぬ。

smoking *n.* kitsuen 喫煙　*smoking car* kitsuensha 喫煙車　*No smoking.* Kin'en. 禁煙。

smooth *n.* nameraka na 滑らかな; ryūchō na 流ちょうな —— *v.* nameraka ni suru 滑らかにする

smuggle *v.* mitsubōeki suru 密貿易する

snack *n.* karui shokuji 軽い食事; sunakku スナック

snake *n.* hebi 蛇

snap *v.* pokin to oru ポキンと折る; pachin to naru [narasu] パチンと鳴る [鳴らす] —— *n.* (any fastening device) tome-gane 留め金; (snapshot) sunappu (shashin) スナップ (写真)

snare *n.* (trap) wana わな; (tempt) yūwaku 誘惑 —— *v.* wana o kakeru わなをかける; otoshiireru 陥れる

snatch *v.* hittakuru ひったくる; hittsukamu 引っつかむ

sneak *v.* kossori suru こっそりする; uro-uro suru うろうろする; (steal) nusumu 盗む —— *n.* (mean person) hikyō-mono ひきょう者

sneeze *n., v.* kushami (o suru) くしゃみ (をする)

sniff *v.* kun-kun kagu くんくんかぐ; kagitsukeru かぎ付ける

snore *n., v.* ibiki (o kaku) いびき (をかく)

snow *n., v.* yuki (ga furu) 雪 (が降る)

snowfall *n.* kōsetsu 降雪

snowman *n.* yuki-daruma 雪だるま

snowstorm *n.* fubuki 吹雪

snowy *adj.* yuki no o'oi 雪の多い; yuki no furu 雪の降る

so *adj., conj.* sō そう; sono-tōri その通り; (in this or that way) kono yō ni このように; (to such an extent or grade) sorehodo それ程; son'na ni そんなに; (very) taihen 大変; hijō ni 非常に

so and so daresore だれそれ

and so on nado など

so as to suru tame ni するために

so far ima made wa 今までは

so far as ... (suru) kagiri wa ... (する) 限りは

so long sayōnara さようなら

so to speak iwaba いわば

soak *v.* (stay in liquid) hitasu 浸す; (make wet) nurasu ぬらす; (penetrate) shimi-komu 染み込む

soap *n.* sekken 石けん *soap bubble* shabon-dama しゃぼん玉

soar *v.* (rise high) maiagaru 舞い上がる; (tower) sobieru そびえる

sober *adj.* (serious) majime na まじめな; (not drunk) shirafu no しらふの ―― *v.* yoi o samasu 酔をさます; yoi ga sameru 酔がさめる

so-called *adj.* iwayuru いわゆる

social *adj.* shakai no 社会の; shakai-teki na 社会的な *social security* shakai hoshō 社会保障

socialism *n.* shakai-shugi 社会主義

society *n.* (community) shakai 社会; (association) kai 会; dantai 団体

sociology *n.* shakai-gaku 社会学

socket *n.* (hollow) ana 穴; (*electrical*) soketto (no sashikomi) ソケット (の差込み)

socks *n. pl.* sokkusu ソックス

soda *n.* sōda (sui) ソーダ（水）

sofa *n.* sofā ソファー

soft *adj.* (cf. hard) yawarakai 柔らかい；(mild) onwa na 穏和な；(gentle) yasashii 優しい

   soft-boiled (*egg*) hanjuku no (tamago) 半熟の（卵）

   soft drink seiryō inryō 清涼飲料；jūsu ジュース

soften *v.* yawaraka ni suru [naru] 柔らかにする[なる]

soil[1] *n.* (earth) tsuchi 土；dojō 土壌；(ground) to-chi 土地

soil[2] *v.* (make dirty) yogosu 汚す；(become dirty) yogoreru 汚れる

solar *adj.* taiyō no 太陽の

   solar calendar taiyō-reki 太陽暦

   solar eclipse nisshoku 日食

   solar system taiyō-kei 太陽系

soldier *n.* heitai 兵隊；heishi 兵士；gunjin 軍人

sole[1] *adj.* (only) tada hitotsu no ただ一つの；yui-itsu no 唯一の

sole[2] *n.* (bottom of the foot) ashi no ura 足の裏；(bottom of shoe) kutsu no ura 靴の裏

sole[3] *n.* (flat-fish) shitabirame 舌びらめ；shitagarei 舌がれい

solemn *adj.* (sacred) shinsei na 神聖な；(grave) sōgon na 荘厳な；genshuku na 厳粛な

solicitor *n.* bengo-shi 弁護士

solid *n., adj.* (cf. liquid) kotai (no) 固体（の）；ko-kei (no) 固形（の）；(hard) katai 固い；(sound) shikkari shita しっかりした；(firm) kakujitsu na 確実な

solitary *adj.* (living alone) hitori-botchi no 一人ぼっちの；kodoku no 孤独の；koritsu shita 孤立した；(lonely) sabishii 寂しい；(single) tandoku no 単独の；(sole) yuiitsu no 唯一の

solitude *n.* (loneliness) kodoku 孤独；(lonely place) kansei na tokoro 閑静な所

solstice *n.* (taiyō no) shi （太陽の）至

   summer solstice geshi 夏至

winter solstice tōji 冬至

solution *n.* (settlement) kaiketsu 解決; (answer) kaitō 解答; (dissolution) yōkai 溶解; yōeki 溶液

solve *v.* (find answer to) kaitō suru 解答する; (settle) kaiketsu suru 解決する; (explain) setsumei suru 説明する

some *adj.* (a certain amount) ikuraka no 幾らかの; ikutsuka no 幾つかの; aru ある; (about) yaku 約 *some day* itsuka いつか

somebody *n.* aru-hito ある人; dareka 誰か

somehow *adv.* (in some way or other) dōnika shite どうにかして; tomokaku ともかく

someone *pron.* dareka 誰か; aru-hito ある人

something *pron.* aru-mono [-koto] ある物 [事]; nanika 何か; ikuraka 幾らか

sometime *adj., adv.* (former) mae no 前の; itsuka いつか

sometimes *adv.* toki niwa 時には; tokidoki 時々

somewhat *adv.* ikubun ka 幾分か; sukoshi 少し

somewhere *adv.* dokoka e [ni] どこかへ [に]

son *n.* musuko 息子 *son in law* josei 女婿; musume-muko 娘婿

song *n.* uta 歌 *sing a song* uta o utau 歌をうたう

sonic *n.* onsoku 音速

soon *adv.* sugu ni すぐに; mamonaku 間もなく; yagate やがて *sooner or later* osokare-hayakare 遅かれ早かれ

sore *adj.* (sad) kanashii 悲しい; (smarting) hiri-hiri suru ひりひりする; (painful to the touch) (fureru to) itai (触れると) 痛い; (vexed) okotta 怒った

sorrow *n.* kanashimi 悲しみ; hiai 悲哀; (misfortune) fukō 不幸 ── *v.* kanashimu 悲しむ; nageku 嘆く

sorry *adj.* (feeling pity) ki no doku de 気の毒で; (feeling regret) zan'nen de 残念で *I am sorry.* Sumimasen. すみません; Gomen nasai. ごめんなさい.

sort *n.* (kind) shurui 種類; hinshitsu 品質 ──

v. (arrange in order) seiton suru 整とんする

a sort of isshu no 一種の

in a [*some*] *sort* ikubun 幾分; aru teido ある
程度

soul *n.* (person's spiritual element) tamashii 魂;
(mind) seishin 精神

sound[1] *n.* (what is heard) oto 音; onkyō 音響
—— *v.* (make a sound) oto ga suru 音がする;
hibiku 響く; kikoeru 聞こえる *sound wave*
ompa 音波

sound[2] *adj.* (healthy) kenzen na 健全な; (correct)
tadashii 正しい —— *adv.* (thoroughly) fukaku
深く; gussuri ぐっすり

soup *n.* sūpu スープ

sour *adj.* (of acid taste) suppai 酸っぱい; (pee-
vish) kimuzukashii 気難しい; fukigen na 不機
嫌な —— *v.* (make [become] sour) suppaku
suru [naru] 酸っぱくする [なる]

source *n.* (origin) minamoto 源; (first cause)
gen'in 原因; (spring) izumi 泉

south *n., adj.* minami (no, e) 南 (の, へ)

southeast *n., adj.* nantō (no, e) 南東 (の, へ)

southwest *n., adj.* nansei (no, e) 南西 (の, へ)

souvenir *n.* kinen-hin 記念品; miyage-mono み
やげ物

sovereign *n.* (the highest ruler) kunshu 君主;
genshu 元首 —— *adj.* (highest) saikō no 最高
の

sow *n., v.* tane (o maku) 種(をまく)

soybean *n.* daizu 大豆

soy sauce *n.* shōyu しょう油

space *n.* kūkan 空間; (interval) kankaku 間隔;
(room) supēsu スペース; (outer space) uchū
宇宙
space flight uchū-hikō 宇宙飛行
space satellite uchū-eisei 宇宙衛星

spade *n., v.* suki (de horu) すき (で掘る); (*playing card*) supēdo スペード

span *n.* oya-yubi to ko-yubi o hatta nagasa 親指

と小指を張った長さ；(full extent) zenchō 全長；
(length from side to side) sashiwatashi 差渡し；
(short time) tsuka no ma つかの間；(short distance) wazuka na kyori わずかな距離 ——v.
yubi o hirogete hakaru 指を広げて測る；
(*bridge*) (extend across) (hashi o) kakeru (橋を) 架ける；kakatte iru 架かっている

Spanish *n., adj.* Supein-go (no) スペイン語(の)；
Supein-jin (no) スペイン人(の)；Supein-fū no スペイン風の

spare *v.* (be frugal) …o ken'yaku suru …を倹約する；(do without) nashi de sumasu なしで すます；(save) tasukeru 助ける ——*adj.* (reserved) yobi no 予備の；(extra) yobun no 余分の；(scanty) toboshii 乏しい
Spare the rod and spoil the child. Kawaii ko ni wa tabi o saseyo. 可愛い子には旅をさせよ.

spark *n.* hibana 火花；supāku スパーク；senkō せん光；(gleam) hirameki ひらめき ——*v.* (glitter) kirameku きらめく；(shine) kagayaku 輝く；(send out sparks) hibana o dasu 火花を出す

sparrow *n.* suzume すずめ

speak *v.* (talk) hanasu 話す；iu 言う；(make a speech) enzetsu suru 演説する
speak ill of waruku iu 悪く言う
not to speak of …wa iu ni oyobazu …は言うに及ばず；…wa mochiron …はもちろん
roughly [*strictly, generally*] *speaking* zatto [seikaku ni, ippan-teki ni] ieba ざっと [正確に, 一般的に] 言えば
so to speak iwaba いわば
speak to hanashi-kakeru 話し掛ける

speaker *n.* gichō 議長；benshi 弁士；supīkā スピーカー

spear *n.* yari やり

special *adj.* (particular) tokubetsu na 特別な；
tokushu na 特殊な；semmon no 専門の
specially toku ni 特に

specialist *n.* semmon-ka 専門家

specialize *v.* tokushu-ka suru 特殊化する; semmon-ka suru 専門化する; (limit) gentei suru 限定する

specialty *n.* (special study) semmon 専門; (speciality) tokushoku 特色; (detail) tokubetsu no kōmoku 特別の項目; kajō 箇条

species *n.* shu 種; shurui 種類 *the human species* jinrui 人類

specific *adj.* (species) shu no 種の; (special) tokutei no 特定の; (precise) meisai no 明細の; meikaku na 明確な —— *n.* tokkōyaku 特効薬

specify *v.* (name expressly) shitei suru 指定する; (mention definitely) meisai ni kinyū suru 明細に記入する; gutai-teki ni iu 具体的に言う

specimen *n.* (sample) mihon 見本; hyōhon 標本; (pattern) hinagata ひな形

spectacle *n.* kōkei 光景; mimono 見物; *pl.* megane 眼鏡

spectator *n.* (looker-on) kembutsu-nin 見物人; kankyaku 観客; (eyewitness) mokugeki-sha 目撃者

speech *n.* (words) kotoba 言葉; enzetsu 演説

speed *n.* sokuryoku 速力; sokudo 速度; supīdo スピード —— *v.* (hasten) isogu 急ぐ; (make hasten) isogasu 急がす *at full speed* zensokuryoku de 全速力で

speedy *adj.* (rapid) hayai 速い; binsoku na 敏速な

spell *v.* tsuzuru つづる; (mean) imi suru 意味する

spend *v.* (use) tsuiyasu 費やす; tsukau 使う; (stay through) sugosu 過ごす; (exhaust) rōhi suru 浪費する

sphere *n.* (globe) kyū 球; tentai 天体; (heavenly body) chikyū-gi 地球儀 *spherical* kyūkei no 球形の

spice *n.* yakumi 薬味; kōryō 香料; supaisu スパイス

spider *n.* kumo くも

spill *v.* (let run or flow out) kobosu こぼす；koboreru こぼれる

spin *v.* (twist fibers into thread) tsumugu 紡ぐ；(whirl) kaiten suru 回転する；(make a web) (kumo ga) ito o haku（くもが）糸を吐く

spinach *n.* hōren-sō ほうれん草

spinal *adj.* sekitsui no せきついの *spinal column* sekichū せき柱 *spinal marrow* [*cord*] sekizui せき髄

spine *n.* sekitsui せきつい；sebone 背骨；se 背；(thorn) toge とげ

spinning *n.* bōseki 紡績 *spinning mill* bōseki-kōjō 紡績工場 *spinning wheel* ito-guruma 糸車

spiral *n., adj.* rasen(-jō no) ら旋(状の) *spiral stair* rasen-kaidan ら旋階段

spirit *n.* seishin 精神；(soul) rei 霊；kokoro 心；(vigor) genki 元気；(alcohol) arukōru アルコール

spit *n., v.* tsuba (o haku) つば (を吐く)

spite *n.* (ill will) akui 悪意；(grudge) urami 恨み；(malice) tekii 敵意 *in spite of* nimo kakawarazu にもかかわらず

splash *v.* (mizu ya doro o) hane tobasu (水や泥を) はね飛ばす；hanekakeru はねかける ——*n.* (spot, streak) hane はね；tobatchiri とばっちり；shimi しみ

splendid *adj.* (magnificent) rippa na 立派な；(brilliant) migoto na 見事な；(wonderful) subarashii 素晴らしい

splendidly *adv.* rippa ni 立派に；migoto ni 見事に

splinter *n.* kakera かけら；toge とげ ——*v.* saku 裂く；sakeru 裂ける

split *v.* waru 割る；saku 裂く；(divide) bunkatsu suru 分割する ——*adj.* wareta 割れた；saketa 裂けた ——*n.* (crack) wareme 割れ目；(division) bunretsu 分裂；bunri 分離

spoil *v.* (damage, be damaged) sokonau 損なう；sokonawareru 損なわれる；amayakashite dameni suru 甘やかしてだめにする；(decay) kusaraseru 腐らせる；kusaru 腐る

sponge *n.* kaimen 海綿；suponji スポンジ

spontaneous *adj.* (voluntary) jihatsu-teki na 自発的な；mizukara no 自らの

spoon *n.* saji さじ；supūn スプーン

sport *n.* supōtsu スポーツ；(athletic sports) undō kyōgi 運動競技；(amusement) goraku 娯楽 ——*v.* (play) asobu 遊ぶ *make sport of* karakau からかう

spot *n.* (particular place) basho 場所；chiten 地点；(small mark) ten 点；(small stain) hanten はん点；shimi しみ
on the spot sono ba de その場で；sokuza ni 即座に

spout *v.* funshutsu suru 噴出する ——*n.* funshutsu 噴出；(*kettle*) (yakan no) kuchi (やかんの)口；(fountain) funsui 噴水

sprain *v.* teashi o kujiku 手足をくじく ——*n.* kujiki くじき；suji-chigai 筋違い

spray *n.* (water flying in fine drops) shibuki しぶき；mizu-kemuri 水煙；(atomizer) kiri-fuki 霧吹き

spread *vt.* hirogeru 広げる；nobasu 伸ばす ——*vi.* hirogaru 広がる；nobiru 伸びる —— *n.* hirogari 広がり；hirosa 広さ

spring *n.* (*season*) haru 春；(fountain) izumi 泉；(elasticity) zemmai ぜんまい；bane バネ；chōyaku 跳躍 ——*v.* (leap) tobu 飛ぶ；(jump) haneru 跳ねる
hot spring onsen 温泉

sprinkle *v.* furikakeru 振り掛ける；maku まく

sprinkler *n.* jōro じょうろ

sprout *v.* me o dasu 芽を出す

spur *n.* (cf. rowel) hakusha 拍車；(incitement) gekirei 激励；(stimulus) shigeki 刺激 ——*v.* hagemasu 励ます

spurt *v.* (gush out) hotobashiru ほとばしる；ryoku o dasu 全力を出す ——*n.* (jet) fun tsu 噴出; (burst) toppatsu 突発

spy *n.* supai スパイ

square *n., adj.* seihōkei (no) 正方形 (の); shi-kaku (no) 四角(の); (angular) kaku-batta 角張った; (straight) massugu na 真っすぐな; (level) suihei no 水平の; (even) gobu-gobu no 五分五分の; (honest) shōjiki na 正直な; (fair) kōsei na 公正な —— *v.* (*math.*) jijō suru 自乗する

   square root heihō-kon 平方根

squeak *v., n.* chū-chū naku (koe) チューチュー鳴く(声); kī-kī naru (oto) キーキー鳴る(音)

squeeze *v.* (compress) oshi-tsubusu 押しつぶす; (wring) shiboru 絞る; (grip) nigiru 握る —— *n.* (pressure) assaku 圧搾; (grip) nigiri 握り; (hug) dakishimeru koto 抱き締めること

squeezer *n.* assaku-ki 圧搾器

squirrel *n.* risu リス

stab *v.* sasu 刺す; kizu-tsukeru 傷つける —— *n.* hito-tsuki 一突き *stab in the back* chūshō suru 中傷する

stable[1] *adj.* (firm) shikkari shita しっかりした; (steady) antei shita 安定した

stable[2] *n.* umaya 馬屋

stadium *n.* kyōgijō 競技場; sutajiamu スタジアム

staff *n.* (employees) buin 部員; shain 社員

stage *n.* butai 舞台; sutēji ステージ; (step) dan-kai 段階; (period) kikan 期間; ki 期 —— *v.* (perform) jōen suru 上演する

stagger *v.* yoromeku よろめく; yoromekasu よろめかす

stain *v.* yogosu 汚す —— *n.* oten 汚点; yogore 汚れ; shimi しみ

stainless *adj.* shimi no nai しみのない; sabinai さびない *stainless steel* sutenresu ステンレス

stair *n.* (kaidan no) ichi-dan 一段; *pl.* kaidan 階段; hashigo はしご

staircase *n.* kaidan 階段

stake *n.* (pointed stick) kui くい; hashira 柱; (wager) kake かけ; *pl.* kake-kin かけ金 —— *v.* (risk) kakeru かける

stalk¹ *n.* (plant stem) kuki 茎; (axis) jiku 軸

stalk² *v.* (stride haughtily) ibatte aruku 威張って歩く; (track secretly) shinobi-yoru 忍び寄る

stall *n.* (market booth) baiten 売店; (stand) yatai 屋台; (section for one animal in a stable) umaya (no shikiri) 馬屋 (の仕切り)

stammer *v.* domoru どもる; kuchi-gomoru 口ごもる —— *n.* domori どもり

stamp *n.* inshō 印章; sutampu スタンプ; (postage stamp) yūbin-kitte 郵便切手; (revenue stamp) inshi 印紙 —— *v.* kitte o haru 切手をはる

stand *v.* (be set upright) tatsu 立つ; (be) aru ある; (be situated) ichi shite iru 位置している; (bear) taeru 耐える; (endure) jizoku suru 持続する —— *n.* sutando スタンド; baiten 売店
stand for ...o arawasu ...を表わす; imi suru 意味する
stand up tachi-agaru 立ち上がる

standard *n., adj.* (flag) hata 旗; gunki 軍旗; hyōjun (no) 標準 (の); mohan 模範
standard of living seikatsu suijun 生活水準
standard time hyōjun-ji 標準時

standardize *v.* hyōjun ni awaseru 標準に合わせる; tōitsu suru 統一する; kikaku-ka suru 規格化する

staple¹ *adj.* (principal) shuyō na 主要な; jūyō na 重要な —— *n.* (principal article grown in a place) shuyō sambutsu 主要産物; (chief material) shuyō busshitsu 主要物質

staple² *n.* (raw material) genryō 原料; (fiber) sen'i 繊維

stapler *n.* hotchikisu ホッチキス

star *n.* hoshi 星; hoshi-gata 星形; (film star) suta スター; (fixed star) kōsei 恒星; (asterisk) hoshi-gata 星形

the Stars and Stripes seijō-ki 星条旗

starch *n., v.* dempun でん粉; nori (o tsukeru) のり(を付ける); *pl.* kayu かゆ

starchy *adj.* dempun-shitsu no でん粉質の

stare *v.* mitsumeru 見詰める; jiro-jiro miru じろじろ見る

stare one in the face jitto hito no kao o miru じっと人の顔を見る

start *n., v.* (leave) shuppatsu (suru) 出発(する); (begin) hajimaru 始まる; hajimeru 始める; (slight shock) bikkuri suru びっくりする

starting point shuppatsu-ten 出発点

startle *v.* bikkuri saseru [suru] びっくりさせる [する]; gyotto saseru [suru] ぎょっとさせる [する]

starvation *n.* kiga 飢餓

starve *v.* (die of hunger) gashi suru 餓死する; (hunger) ue saseru 飢えさせる

starve for (long for) katsubō suru 渇望する

state[1] *n.* (condition) jōtai 状態; (nation) kokka 国家; shū 州; (rank) chii 地位; kaikyū 階級

State of the Union (daitōryō no) ippan-kyōsho (大統領の) 一般教書

state[2] *v.* (say) hanasu 話す; noberu 述べる

statement *n.* (something stated) chinjutsu 陳述; seimei(sho) 声明(書); (monthly summation of account) keisan-sho 計算書

statesman *n.* seiji-ka 政治家

statesmanship *n.* seiji-teki shuwan 政治的手腕

station *n.* (position) ichi 位置; busho 部署; (railroad station) eki 駅

stationary *n.* bumbō gu 文房具

statistics *n.* tōkei (hyō) 統計(表); tōkei (-gaku) 統計(学)

statue *n.* zō 像; chōzō 彫像; chōkoku-ka 彫刻家

status *n.* (rank) chii 地位; (condition) jōtai 状態; mibun 身分

stay *v.* (remain) todomaru とどまる; (lodge) taizai suru 滞在する; tomaru 泊まる; (continue

to be) (…no) mamade iru [aru] (…の)ままで
いる[ある]
　stay away ikazu ni iru 行かずにいる
　staying power jikyū-ryoku 持久力

stead *n.* kawari 代わり; (place) basho 場所
　in stead of …no kawari ni …の代わりに
　in one's stead hito no kawari ni 人の代わりに

steadily *adv.* chakujitsu ni 着実に; chaku-chaku
to 着々と

steady *adj.* (firm) shikkari shita しっかりした;
(firmly fixed) kotei shita 固定した; (sound)
kenjitsu na 堅実な; (regular) kisoku tadashii
規則正しい
　Slow and steady wins the race. Isogaba ma-
ware. 急がば回れ.

steak *n.* yaki-niku 焼肉; sutēki ステーキ

steal *v.* nusumu 盗む; kossori suru こっそりする;
(*baseball*) tōrui suru 盗塁する

steam *n.* jōki 蒸気; yuge 湯気; suchīmu スチーム

steamship *n.* (steamer) kisen 汽船

steel *n.* kōtetsu 鋼鉄; hagane 鋼

steep *adj.* kewashii 険しい; kyū na 急な ——
n. (steep slope) zeppeki 絶壁

steer *v.* kaji o toru かじを取る; sōjū suru 操縦す
る; ayatsuru 操る
　steering committee un'ei iinkai 運営委員会

stem *n.* (stalk of a plant) kuki 茎; miki 幹; (bow)
senshu 船首; hesaki へさき

stenograph *n.* sokki (moji) 速記 (文字)　*stenog-
rapher* sokki-sha 速記者

step *n.* (pace) hochō 歩調; ippo 一歩; (footstep)
ashi-ato 足跡; (footfall) ashi-oto 足音; (stair)
fumi-dan 踏み段; (degree) dan 段 —— *v.* (walk)
aruku 歩く; (dance) odoru 踊る; (go) susumu
進む
　step by step ippo ippo 一歩一歩
　step aside waki ni yoru 脇に寄る
　step in hairu 入る; jama suru 邪魔する

sterling *adj.* (British money) eika no 英貨の; (genuine) junsui na 純粋な; (reliable) shinrai subeki 信頼すべき

sterling area pondo chiiki ポンド地域

stern *adj*. (harsh) kibishii 厳しい; (severe) genkaku na 厳格な —— *n*. (cf. bow) sembi 船尾

stew *n*. shichū-ryōri シチュー料理 —— *v*. torobi de niru とろ火で煮る *stew pan* shichū-nabe シチューなべ

steward *n*. (one who manages another's property) shitsuji 執事; (purveyor) makanai-kata 賄い方; (waiter) kyūji 給仕; (*airplane*) suchuwādo スチュワード

stewardess *n*. suchuwādesu スチュワーデス

stick *n*. bō 棒; (cane) tsue つえ; sutekki ステッキ; muchi むち —— *v*. (thrust) tsuki-sasu 突き刺す; (cause to adhere) kuttsuku くっつく; haru 張る; (persist) koshu suru 固守する

stiff *adj*. (hard) katai 固い; (rigid) kowabatta こわばった; (not graceful) gigochinai ぎごちない; (beverage) tsuyoi 強い; (hard) kon'nan na 困難な

stifle *v*. (smother) chissoku saseru [suru] 窒息させる [する]; …no iki o tomeru …の息を止める; (put out) kesu 消す

still *adv*. (yet) mada まだ; (even now) imademo 今でも; (nevertheless) yahari やはり; soredemo それでも; (more) issō 一層 —— *adj*. (quiet) shizuka na 静かな; (motionless) seishi shita 静止した —— *v*. (calm) shizumeru 静める

stillness *n*. seijaku 静寂; shizukesa 静けさ; seishi 静止

stimulate *v*. shigeki suru 刺激する; (spur) kakkizukeru 活気付ける; gekirei suru 激励する; (excite) kōfun saseru 興奮させる

sting *v*. sasu 刺す —— *n*. sashi-kizu 刺し傷; (hachi no) hari (ハチの)針; (thorn) toge とげ

stir *v*. (set in motion) ugokasu 動かす; (move) ugoku 動く; (mix a liquid) kaki-mawasu かき回す; (rouse) funki saseru 奮起させる ——

n. (movement) ugoki 動き；(bustle) sawagi 騒
ぎ；(excitement) kōfun 興奮

stitch *n.* hito-hari 一針；hito-nui 一縫い ―― *v.*
nuu 縫う

stock *n.* zaiko(-hin) 在庫(品)；sutokku スト
ック；(stump) kirikabu 切り株；(trunk) miki
幹；(share) kabu(-shiki) 株(式)；(fund) shihon 資本 ―― *v.* shiireru 仕入れる；(store)
takuwaeru 蓄える；(equip) sonae-tsukeru 備え
付ける

livestock kachiku 家蓄
stockbroker kabushiki-nakagai-nin 株式仲買人
stockexchange kabushiki torihikisho 株式取引
所
stockholder kabunushi 株主
stockmarket kabushiki-shijō 株式市場

stocking *n.* sutokkingu ストッキング

stomach *n.* i 胃；hara 腹；(appetite) shokuyoku
食欲　*stomachache* itsū 胃痛

stone *n.* ishi 石；ko-ishi 小石

stool *n.* ashi-dai 足台；koshi-kake 腰掛け；maru-
isu 丸いす

stoop *v.* (bend) kagamu かがむ；koshi o mageru
腰を曲げる

stop *v.* tomeru 止める；yameru やめる；(cease)
yamu やむ；(lodge) tomaru 泊まる；(suspend)
teishi suru 停止する ―― *n.* teishi 停止；(stay)
taizai 滞在；(*bus*) teiryū-jo 停留所；(close) owari
終り；(punctuation mark) kutō-ten 句読点
stop over tochū-gesha suru 途中下車する

storage *n.* chozōsho 貯蔵所；sōko 倉庫
storage battery chikudenchi 蓄電池

store *n.* (supply) takuwae 蓄え；(shop) mise 店；
(abundance) takusan 沢山；(accumulation) chozō 貯蔵；chikuseki 蓄積；(storehouse) sōko 倉庫
―― *v.* shiireru 仕入れる

storey *n.* (floor) (ie no) kai (家の) 階

storm *n.* arashi あらし；bōfū 暴風 ―― *v.* areru
荒れる　*storm-warning* bōfū-keihō 暴風警報

story *n.* (tale) hanashi 話; monogatari 物語; (novel) shōsetsu 小説; (plot) suji 筋; (floor) kai 階

stout *adj.* (strong) tsuyoi 強い; (tough) ganjō na 頑丈な; (brave) yūkan na 勇敢な; (fat) futotta 太った ——*n.* (heavy dark type of beer) kurobīru 黒ビール

stove *n.* sutōbu ストーブ; kitchin renji キッチンレンジ

straight *adj.* (not crooked) massugu na まっすぐな; itchoku-sen no 一直線の; (in order) kichin to shita きちんとした; (honest) shōjiki na 正直な; (neat) junsui na 純粋な *straight away*[*off*] tadachi ni 直ちに

strain *v.* (stretch tightly) pīn to nobasu ぴーんと伸ばす; hipparu 引っ張る; (overtask) karō saseru 過労させる; (filter) kosu こす; (strive hard) kemmei ni doryoku suru 懸命に努力する ——*n.* (stress) kinchō 緊張; (severe effort) hageshii doryoku 激しい努力; karō 過労

strained kinchō shita 緊張した

strainer chakoshi 茶こし; uragoshi 裏ごし

strait *n. pl.* (cf. channel) kaikyō 海峡 ——*adj.* (narrow) semai 狭い

strange *adj.* (not known) mishiranu 見知らぬ; (queer) myō na 妙な; (unfamiliar) minarenai 見慣れない; (foreign) gaikoku no 外国の

stranger *n.* (person unknown to one) mishiranu hito 見知らぬ人; tanin 他人; (person unfamiliar with) fuan'nai na hito 不案内な人; (foreigner) gaikoku-jin 外国人

straw *n.* wara わら; mugi-wara 麦わら

A drowning man will catch at a straw. Oboreru mono wa wara omo tsukamu. おぼれる者はわらをもつかむ.

strawberry *n.* ichigo いちご

stray *adj.* michi ni mayou 道に迷う; mayotta 迷った; hagureta はぐれた

streak *n.* (line of color) suji 筋; shima しま

stream *n.* nagare 流れ; kawa 川; ogawa 小川

streamer *n.* fuki-nagashi 吹流し

streamline *n., adj.* ryūsen-kei (no) 流線型(の)

street *n.* tōri 通り；gairo 街路
   main street ō-dōri 大通り
   street car shigai-densha 市街電車

strength *n.* chikara 力；tsuyosa 強さ

strengthen *v.* tsuyoku suru [naru] 強くする[なる]

strenuous *adj.* (hard) funtō-teki na 奮闘的な；nesshin na 熱心な；mōretsu na 猛烈な

stress *n.* (pressure) appaku 圧迫；kyōchō 強調；jūten 重点；akusento アクセント；(effort) doryoku 努力

stretch *v.* nobasu 伸ばす；(extend) hirogeru 広げる；hirogaru 広がる；(strain) kinchō saseru 緊張させる ―― *n.* (expanse) hirogari 広がり；(extent) han'i 範囲；(tension) kinchō 緊張
   strain oneself nobi o suru 伸びをする

strict *adj.* kibishii 厳しい；genjū na 厳重な

strictly *adv.* kibishiku 厳しく **strictly speaking** gemmitsu ni ieba 厳密に言えば

stride *n., v.* ōmata (ni aruku) 大また(に歩く)；hito-matagi 一またぎ

strife *n.* arasoi 争い；tōsō 闘争；fuwa 不和；kenka けんか

strike *v.* (hit) utsu 打つ；(smite) naguru なぐる；(impress) kanji saseru 感じさせる；(attack) kōgeki suru 攻撃する ―― *n.* (blow) dageki 打撃；(cessation of work by employees) sutoraiki ストライキ；(*baseball*) sutoraiku ストライク
   Strike while the iron is hot. Tetsu wa atsui uchi ni ute. 鉄は熱いうちに打て．

string *n.* himo ひも；ito 糸；gen 弦 ―― *v.* (thread on a string) ito ni tōsu 糸に通す
   string bean saya-ingen さやいんげん

strip *v.* (tear off) hagu はぐ；(deprive of) ubau 奪う；(undress) hadaka ni suru 裸にする
   strip teaser sutorippā ストリッパー

stripe *n.* suji 筋；shima しま；*striped* suji [shima] no aru 筋［しま］のある

strive v. (make great effort) doryoku suru 努力する; honeoru 骨折る; (fight) tatakau 戦う

stroke n. (blow) dageki 打撃; (row) hito-kogi 一こぎ; (light caressing movement) hito-nade 一なで; (fit) hossa 発作; (painting) hito-fude 一筆

stroll v. buratsuku ぶらつく; sampo suru 散歩する *stroller* bebīkā ベビーカー

strong adj. (powerful) tsuyoi 強い; (healthy) jōbu na 丈夫な; (firm) kengo na 堅固な; (severe) hageshii 激しい; (heavy, thick) koi 濃い

strongly adv. tsuyoku 強く; hageshiku 激しく

structure n. (construction) kōzō 構造; kōsei 構成; (organization) soshiki 組織; honegumi 骨組み; (building) tatemono 建物

struggle v. (move one's body in a vigorous effort to get free) mogaku もがく; agaku あがく; (fight) arasou 争う; (strive) doryoku suru 努力する —— n. funtō 奮闘; tatakai 戦い *struggle for existence* seizonkyōsō 生存競争

stub n. (stump of tree) kirikabu 切り株; (remnant of cigar, pencil) (tabako, empitsu no) tsukai-nokori（たばこ，鉛筆の）使い残り

stubborn adj. gōjō na 強情な; ganko na 頑固な; atsukai-nikui 扱いにくい

student n. gakusei 学生

studio n. shigoto-ba 仕事場; sutajio スタジオ

study n. benkyō 勉強; kenkyū 研究 —— v. manabu 学ぶ; kenkyū suru 研究する

stuff n. (substance) mono 物; busshitsu 物質; (material) zairyō 材料; genryō 原料; tsumemono 詰め物; (woolen fabric) keorimono 毛織物 —— v. (cram) tsumeru 詰める

stumble v. (trip) tsumazuku つまずく; yoromeku よろめく; (falter) domoru どもる —— n. tsumazuki つまずき; (failure) shippai 失敗

stump n. kirikabu 切り株; (root) ki no ne 木の根 —— v. (puzzle) nayamasu 悩ます; (walk clumsily) tobo-tobo aruku とぼとぼ歩く

stun v. (make senseless by violence) kizetsu saseru 気絶させる; (stupefy) bōzen to saseru ぼうぜんとさせる; (amaze) bikkuri saseru びっくりさせる

stunt n. (feat) myōgi 妙技; hanare-waza 離れ業; kyokunori-hikō 曲乗り飛行

stupid adj. bakana ばかな; oroka na 愚かな; noroma no のろまの; tsumaranai つまらない

style n. (mode) yōshiki 様式; (pattern) kata 型; (fashion) sutairu スタイル; (way of writing) buntai 文体; (manner) taido 態度

subject adj. (under government) shihai o ukeru 支配を受ける; (owing obedience) fukujū suru 服従する ——n. (people) shimmin 臣民; jimmin 人民; (theme) shudai 主題; kamoku 科目 ——v. shitagawaseru 従わせる; jūzoku suru 従属する

submarine adj. kaitei no 海底の ——n. sensuikan 潜水艦

submerge v. (suichū ni) shizumeru (水中に)沈める; shizumu 沈む; mizu ni hitasu 水に浸す; sensui suru 潜水する

submit v. (yield) shitagawaseru 従わせる; fukujū saseru [suru] 服従させる[する]; shitagau 従う; (present for consideration) teishutsu suru 提出する

subordinate adj. kai no 下位の; kakyū no 下級の ——v. jūzoku suru 従属する; ...no kai ni oku ...の下位に置く; shitagawaseru 従わせる

subscribe v. (sign) shomei suru 署名する; (contribute) kifu suru 寄付する; (undertake to buy periodical regularly) yoyaku suru 予約する; kōdoku suru 購読する

subsequent adj. sono-go no その後の; ato no 後の; tsugi no 次の

subsequently adv. sono-go ni その後に; tsuzuite 続いて

substance n. (matter) busshitsu 物質; (essence)

honshitsu 本質; jittai 実体; (element) yōso 要素

substantial *adj.* (material) jisshitsu-teki na 実質的な; (firm) shikkari shita しっかりした; (important) jūyō na 重要な; (considerable) sōtō na 相当な; (essential) honshitsu-teki na 本質的な

substitute *v.* kaeru 代える; daiyō suru 代用する —— *n.* daiyō-hin 代用品; dairi-nin 代理人

substitution *n.* dairi 代理; daiyō 代用

suburb *n.* kōgai 郊外; machi-hazure 町はずれ

subway *n.* (underground way) chika-dō 地下道; (underground railway) chika-tetsu 地下鉄

succeed *v.* (have success) seikō suru 成功する; (ensue) tsuzuku 続く; (in due course to office) hikitsugu 引継ぐ

success *n.* seikō 成功; jōju 成就; ō-atari 大当たり

successful *adj.* seikō shita 成功した

successfully *adv.* migotoni 見事に; shubi yoku 首尾よく

succession *n.* (series of things following) renzoku 連続; (succeeding to inheritance) sōzoku (-ken) 相続 (権); keishō 継承 *in succession* renzoku shite 連続して

such *adj.* sō iu そういう; son'na そんな; sore hodo no それほどの
such and such kore kore no これこれの
such as ...no yō na ...のような

suck *v.* suu 吸う; susuru すする; shaburu しゃぶる; chichi o suu 乳を吸う

sudden *adj.* kyū na 急な; totsuzen no 突然の; fui no 不意の

suddenly *adv.* totsuzen 突然; niwaka ni にわかに

suffer *v.* (undergo pain) kurushimu 苦しむ; nayamu 悩む; kōmuru 被る; (gai o) ukeru (害を) 受ける; (be subject to) keiken suru 経験する; (endure) taeru 耐える; (allow) yurusu 許す

suffering *n.* kurushimi 苦しみ; kutsū 苦痛; songai 損害; higai 被害

suffice *v.* tariru 足りる; (be enough) jūbun de aru 十分である; (satisfy) manzoku saseru 満足させる

sufficient *adj.* jūbun na 十分な   *sufficiently* jūbun ni 十分に

sugar *n.* satō 砂糖
  granulated sugar zarame ざらめ; guranyūtō グラニュー糖
  lump sugar kaku-zatō 角砂糖

suggest *v.* (hint) honomekasu ほのめかす; anji suru 暗示する; (propose) teian suru 提案する; iidasu 言い出す

suggestion *n.* anji 暗示; teian 提案

suicide *n.* jisatsu(-sha) 自殺 (者)

suit *n.* (lawsuit) soshō 訴訟; (coat and trousers) i-tchaku 一着; sūtsu スーツ; (*playing card*) hito-kumi 一組み ——*v.* (adapt) tekigō saseru 適合させる; itchi saseru 一致させる; (fit) teki suru 適する; niau 似合う

suitable *adj.* tekitō na 適当な

suitcase *n.* sūtsu-kēsu スーツケース; ryokō kaban 旅行かばん

sum *n.* (total amount) gōkei 合計; kingaku 金額; *pl.* keisan 計算; (summary) tairyō 大量 ——*v.* (sum up) gōkei suru 合計する; yakugen suru 約言する; yōyaku suru 要約する
  in sum yōyaku suru to 要約すると

summary *n., adj.* yōyaku (no) 要約 (の); gaiyō (no) 概要 (の)

summer *n.* natsu 夏　*summer resort* hisho-chi 避暑地

summit *n.* chōjō 頂上; itadaki 頂
  summit conference saikō-shunō-kaigi 最高首脳会議

summon *v.* (send for) yobi-dasu 呼び出す; (gikai o) shōshū suru (議会を) 召集する

sun *n.* taiyō 太陽; (sunbeam) nikkō 日光
  sunbeam nikkō 日光

sunburn hiyake 日焼け
sundown nichibotsu 日没
sunrise hi-no-de 日の出
sunset nichibotsu 日没; higure 日暮れ

Sunday *n.* nichiyō-bi 日曜日

sunflower *n.* himawari 日まわり

sunny *adj.* hiatari no yoi 日当りの良い

superintendent *n.* kantoku(-sha) 監督(者)

superior *adj.* (better) sugureta 優れた; (excellent) yūshū na 優秀な

superlative *adj.* saikō no 最高の; (*gram.*) saijō-kyū no 最上級の

supersonic *adj.* chō-onsoku no 超音速の

superstition *n.* meishin 迷信

supervise *v.* kantoku suru 監督する; kanri suru 管理する; kanshū suru 監修する

supper *n.* yūshoku 夕食

supplement *n.* furoku 付録; hosoku 補足

supply *v.* (furnish) kyōkyū suru 供給する; (make up for) oginau 補う; (fill) mitasu 満たす —— *n.* kyōkyū 供給; hojū 補充; (store) taku-wae 蓄え; (stock) zaiko 在庫

support *v.* (hold up) sasaeru 支える; (provide for) iji suru 維持する; yashinau 養う; (back up) shiji suru 支持する; kōen suru 後援する

supporter *n.* shiji-sha 支持者; fuyō-sha 扶養者; sapōtā サポーター

suppose *v.* (imagine) sōzō suru 想像する; (assume) katei suru 仮定する; (think) ...to omou ...と思う; (presuppose) yosō suru 予想する

supposing *prep.* ...to katei sureba ...と仮定すれば

suppress *v.* (restrain) osaeru 押さえる; (put down) dan'atsu suru 弾圧する

supreme *adj.* saikō no 最高の; kono ue nai この上ない

sure *adj.* (certain) tashika na [ni] 確かな[に]; (reliable) shinrai dekiru 信頼できる; kitto...suru きっと...する; (confident) jishin no aru

自信のある　――*adv.* (yes) yoshi よし；tashi-ka ni 確かに；(of course) mochiron もちろん
make sure tashikameru 確かめる

surf *n.* yosenami 寄せ波　*surf riding* nami-nori 波乗り；sāfin サーフィン

surface *n., adj.* hyōmen (no) 表面 (の)；uwabe (no) 上辺 (の)；gaikan 外観

surgeon *n.* geka-i 外科医；gun-i 軍医

surgery *n.* geka 外科；shujutsu 手術

surname *n.* sei 姓；myōji 名字

surplus *adj., n.* zan'yo (kin) 残余 (金)；kajō (no) 過剰 (の)；chōka-gaku 超過額

surprise *v.* odorokasu 驚かす；bikkuri saseru びっくりさせる　――*n.* odoroki 驚き；fuiuchi 不意打ち
by surprise fui ni 不意に
to one's surprise odoroita-koto niwa 驚いたことには
be surprised …ni odoroku …に驚く

surrender *v.* (hand over) hiki-watasu 引き渡す；(yield) kōsan suru 降参する

surround *v.* torikakomu 取り囲む；torimaku 取り巻く　*surroundings* (environment) shūi 周囲；(circumstances) kyōgū 境遇

survey *v.* (look over) miwatasu 見渡す；(measure) sokuryō suru 測量する；(examine) kembun suru 検分する；(review) kentō suru 検討する

survival *n.* iki-nokori 生き残り；seizon-sha 生存者

survive *v.* iki-nokoru 生き残る；…yori nagaiki suru …より長生きする　*survivor* seizon-sha 生存者；ikinokotta hito 生き残った人

suspect *v.* utagau 疑う；ayashimu 怪しむ　――*n.* (suspected person) yōgi-sha 容疑者

suspend *v.* (hang up) tsurusu つるす；kakeru 掛ける；(put off) enki suru 延期する；(stop) teishi suru 停止する；(*school*) teigaku ni suru 停学にする　*suspenders* zubon-tsuri ズボンつり；kutsushita-dome 靴下止め

suspense *n.* mitei 未定；dotchi tsukazu どっちつかず；fuan 不安；kigakari 気がかり；sasupensu サスペンス

suspenseful *adj.* fuan na 不安な；kigakari na 気がかりな

suspicion *n.* utagai 疑い；kengi 嫌疑

suspicious *adj.* utagai-bukai 疑い深い；ayashii 怪しい；utagawashii 疑わしい

sustain *v.* (hold up) sasaeru 支える；(support) yashinau 養う；(stand) taeru 耐える；(keep up) tsuzukeru 続ける；(suffer) kōmuru 被る；(maintain) iji suru 維持する

swallow¹ *n.* tsubame つばめ

swallow² *v.* nomu 飲む；nomikomu 飲み込む —— *n.* hito-nomi 一飲み

swamp *n.* numa 沼；numa-chi 沼地

swan *n.* hakuchō 白鳥

swap *v.* kōkan suru 交換する；torikaekko suru 取り替えっこする

swarm *n.* (large mass of insects) (konchū no) mure (昆虫の) 群れ；takusan 沢山；(throng) ōzei 大勢 —— *v.* (teem) muragaru 群がる

sway *v.* (waver) yusuburu ゆすぶる；yureru 揺れる；(rule over) shihai suru 支配する —— *n.* dōyō 動揺；shihai 支配；tōchi 統治

swear *v.* (make a solemn promise) chikau 誓う；(assent under oath) sensei suru 宣誓する；(declare) dangen suru 断言する；(curse) nonoshiru ののしる；warukuchi o iu 悪口を言う —— *n.* (swear-word) warukuchi 悪口

sweat *n., v.* ase (o kaku) 汗 (をかく)

sweater *n.* sētā セーター

sweep *v.* haku 掃く；sōji suru 掃除する *sweeper* sōji-ki [-nin] 掃除器 [人]

sweet *adj.* (taste) amai 甘い；(fragrant) kōbashii 香ばしい；(melodious) chōshi no ii 調子のいい；(fresh) shinsen na 新鮮な；(dear) kawaii 可愛い；(gentle) yasashii 優しい *sweetly* yasashiku 優しく

sweeten v. amaku suru [naru] 甘くする [なる];
kōbashiku suru [naru] 香ばしくする [なる]

sweetheart n. aijin 愛人; koibito 恋人

sweet potato n. satsumaimo さつまいも

swell v. (dilate) fukureru ふくれる; fukuramaseru
ふくらませる; (expand) hirogaru 広がる; (rise
or raise) ryūki suru 隆起する; bōchō suru 膨張
する

swift adj. (quick) hayai 早い; (prompt) sumiyaka
na 速やかな

swiftness n. jinsoku 迅速; kaisoku 快速

swim v. oyogu 泳ぐ; ukabu 浮かぶ

swimming n. suiei 水泳 *swimming suit* mizu-gi
水着

swindle v. (cheat) damasu だます ——n. (fraud)
sagi 詐欺 *swindler* sagi-shi 詐欺師; peten-shi
ぺてん師

swing v. furueru 震える; yureru 揺れる; (bran-
dish) furi-mawasu 振り回す; buranko ni noru
ぶらんこに乗る ——n. buranko ぶらんこ; fu-
ru koto 振ること; (sweep) han'i 範囲; (tone)
chōshi 調子
in full swing sakan ni 盛んに
swing bridge hane-bashi はね橋

switch n. suitchi スイッチ ——v. (switch on)
(denki o) tsukeru (電気を) つける; (switch off)
kesu 消す

sword n. ken 剣; tsurugi 剣; katana 刀
sword guard tsuba つば

syllable n. onsetsu 音節

symbol n. (emblem) shōchō 象徴; shimboru シ
ンボル; (sign, mark) kigō 記号; fugō 符号

symbolize v. shōchō suru 象徴する; …o arawasu
…を表わす

symmetry n. kinsei 均整; chōwa 調和; shimmeto-
rī シンメトリー

sympathize v. (pity) dōjō suru 同情する; (agree)
kyōmei suru 共鳴する

sympathy n. dōjō 同情; kyōmei 共鳴 *in sympa-*

thy with …ni dōjō shite …に同情して

symphony *n.* kōkyō-gaku 交響楽; shinfonī シンフォニー

symptom *n.* (sign) chōkō 兆候; shōjō 症状; kizashi きざし

synonym *n.* dōgi-go 同義語; shinonimu シノニム

synthetic *adj.* gōsei no 合成の *synthetic resin* gōsei-jushi 合成樹脂

syringe *n.* chūsha-ki 注射器; supoito スポイト —— *v.* chūsha suru 注射する

system *n.* (complex whole) soshiki 組織; (arranged body of ideas, facts, etc.) taikei 体系; (government) seido 制度

systematic *adj.* soshiki-teki na 組織的な; keitō-teki na 系統的な

T

tab *n.* (small flap) tare たれ; (tag) tsuke-fuda つけ札; (label) ラベル

table *n.* tēburu テーブル; shokutaku 食卓; (list) hyō 表; (food) ryōri 料理 *at table* shokuji-chū 食事中

table-spoon *n.* tēburu supūn テーブルスプーン

tablet *n.* (small flat slab) hira-ita 平板; (cf. troche) jōzai 錠剤; hyōsatsu 標札

tabloid *n.* taburoido-ban shimbun タブロイド判新聞 —— *adj.* yōyakushita 要約した

tack *n., v.* (broad-headed nail) byō (de tomeru) びょう（で止める）; tome-gane 止め金; (basting stitch) karinui 仮縫い; (ship's course) shinro 針路; kōro 航路

tackle *n.* (pulley) kassha 滑車; (equipment) dōgu 道具; (*football*) takkuru タックル

tact *n.* kiten 気転; josai-nasa 如才なさ; tegiwa 手際

tactics *n.* senjutsu 戦術; sakuryaku 策略

tadpole *n.* otamajakushi おたまじゃくし

tag *n.* tsuke-fuda 付け札; nifuda 荷札

tail *n.* o 尾; shippo しっぽ; (rear) kō-bu 後部
tail-light bi-tō 尾灯

tailor *n.* yōfuku-ya 洋服屋

taint *n.* (stain) yogore 汚れ; oten 汚点; (dishon-
or) omei 汚名 —— *v.* (become infected) kansen suru 感染する

take *v.* (seize) toru 取る; tsukamu つかむ; (gain)
uru 得る; (accept) ukeru 受ける; (catch) toraeru
捕える; (buy) kau 買う; (carry) motte-iku 持っ
て行く; (eat) taberu 食べる; (drink) nomu 飲む
be taken ill byōki ni naru 病気になる
take after ...ni niru ...に似る
take care of ...ni chūi suru ...に注意する; ...no
sewa o suru ...の世話をする
take charge of ...o hiki-ukeru ...を引き受ける
take up ageru 上げる; mochiageru 持ち上げる
take notice of ...ni chūmoku suru ...に注目す
る
take off nugu 脱ぐ; (*airplane*) (hikōki ga) ririku suru (飛行機が) 離陸する
take out toridasu 取り出す
take over hikitsugu 引き継ぐ
take part in ...ni sanka suru ...に参加する

talent *n.* sainō 才能; giryō 技量 *talented* yūnō
na 有能な *talentless* munō na 無能な

talk *v.* hanasu 話す; kataru 語る; iu 言う; shaberu しゃべる —— *n.* hanashi 話; danwa 談
話
talk back kuchi-gotae suru 口答えする
talk to hanashi-kakeru 話し掛ける; shikaru
叱る
talk over sōdan o suru 相談をする
big talk jiman-banashi 自慢話; hora ほら

talkative *adj.* kuchikazu no ōi 口数の多い ——
n. oshaberi おしゃべり

tall *adj.* sei no takai 背の高い

tame *adj.* (domesticated) nareta 慣れた; (gentle)
otonashii おとなしい; (spiritless) ikuji no nai

意気地のない ── v. narasu 慣らす

tan v. (convert into leather) kawa o namesu 皮を
なめす; (brown by the sun's rays) hi ni yakeru
日に焼ける ── adj. (yellowish) ierō-buraun
イエロー・ブラウン

tangle v. motsureru もつれる; motsure saseru
もつれさせる; karamu 絡む; karamaseru 絡ま
せる ── n. (confused state) konran 混乱;
funkyū 紛糾

tank n. tanku タンク; sui-sō 水そう; sensha 戦
車

tap¹ v. (hit lightly) karuku tataku 軽くたたく

tap² n. (faucet) jaguchi 蛇口; kokku コック;
(plug) sen 栓

tape n. tēpu テープ; (tape measure) makijaku 巻
尺

tar n. tāru タール

tardy adj. noroi のろい; osoi 遅い

target n. (marked object) hyōteki 標的; mato 的;
(aim) mokuhyō 目標

tariff n. (tax on imports) kanzei-ritsu 関税率;
(list of prices) ryōkin-hyō 料金表

tart¹ adj. (sour) suppai 酸っぱい; (bitter) shinra-
tsu na 辛らつな

tart² n. (pastry filled with jam) taruto タルト;
kudamono-iri pai 果物入りパイ

task n. shigoto 仕事; shokumu 職務

taste n. (flavor) aji 味; mikaku 味覚; (hobby)
shumi 趣味 ── v. ajiwau 味わう; aji o mi-
ru 味を見る
 in good [*bad*] *taste* jōhin [gehin] de 上品 [下
品] で; shumi no ii [warui] 趣味のいい [悪
い]

tattoo n. irezumi 入れ墨

tax n. zeikin 税金 ── v. kazei suru 課税する
 tax payer nōzei-sha 納税者
 tax free menzei no 免税の

taxi n. takushī タクシー

tea n. o-cha お茶 *black tea* kōcha 紅茶

teach v. oshieru 教える　**teaching** kyōju 教授;
jugyō 授業

teacher n. kyōshi 教師; sensei 先生

team n. chīmu チーム; kumi 組
team-work kyōdō dōsa 共同動作; chīmuwāku
チームワーク

tear¹ v. hikisaku 引き裂く; chigiru ちぎる; chigi-
reru ちぎれる

tear² n. namida 涙　**burst into tears** watto naki-
dasu わっと泣き出す

tearful adj. namida-gunda 涙ぐんだ; namida-mo-
roi 涙もろい

tease v. (annoy) ijimeru いじめる; nayamasu 悩
ます; (make fun of) karakau からかう

teaspoon n. tīsupūn ティースプーン; cha-saji 茶
さじ

technical adj. gijutsu-teki na 技術的な; (special-
ized) semmon no 専門の; (industrial) kōgyō no
工業の　**technical terms** semmon yōgo 専門用
語

technique n. gikō 技巧; gijutsu 技術

technology n. kōgei (-gaku) 工芸 (学); kōgyō-gi-
jutsu 工業技術

teen-ager n. jūdai no shōnen [shōjo] 10代の少
年 [少女]

teens n. jūdai 10代

telegram n. dempō 電報

telegraph n. denshin (-ki) 電信 (機); dempō 電報
—— v. dempō o utsu 電報を打つ

telephone n. denwa (-ki) 電話 (機) —— v. denwa o kakeru 電話をかける
telephone booth kōshū-denwa 公衆電話; den-
wa-shitsu 電話室
telephone directory denwa-chō 電話帳

telescope n. bōen-kyō 望遠鏡

television n. terebijon テレビジョン

tell v. (narrate) hanasu 話す; (say) iu 言う; tsugeru 告げる; (inform) shiraseru 知らせる; (order)
meijiru 命じる; oshieru 教える; (distinguish)

kubetsu suru 区別する

tell one's fortune mi-no-ue o uranau 身の上を
占う

teller *n.* (one who tells) hanashi-te 話し手; (cashier at a bank) kinsen-suitō-gakari 金銭出納係

temper *n.* (disposition) kishitsu 気質; (mood) kigen 機嫌; (anger) ikari 怒り; (calmness) heisei
平静

in a good [*bad*] *temper* jōkigen [fukigen] de
上機嫌 [不機嫌] で

be in a short temper tanki o okosu 短気を起
こす

keep [*lose*] *one's temper* jitto gaman suru [o-
koridasu] じっと我慢する [怒り出す]

temperament *n.* (disposition) kishitsu 気質;
seikaku 性格

temperate *adj.* (mild) ondan na 温暖な; (moderate) tekido no 適度の; (moderate in opinion)
onken na 穏健な

temperature *n.* (*environment*) ondo 温度; (*body*)
taion 体温

take one's temperature taion o hakaru 体温を
計る

temple[1] *n.* (*Buddhist*) jiin 寺院; tera 寺

temple[2] *n.* (*head*) komekami こめかみ

temporary *adj.* ichiji no 一時の; rinji no 臨時の

tempt *v.* (entice) yūwaku suru 誘惑する; sasou
誘う

ten *n., adj.* jū (no) 10, 十 (の); tō (no) 10, 十
(の) *ten to one* jutchū-hakku 十中八九

tenant *n.* shakuchi-nin 借地人; kosaku-nin 小作
人; shakuya-nin 借家人

tend *v.* (be inclined to) ...no keikō ga aru ...の
傾向がある; ...shigachi de aru ...しがちであ
る; (attend) kyūji suru 給仕する; (look after)
sewa o suru 世話をする

tendency *n.* keikō 傾向; fūchō 風潮

tender[1] *v.* (offer) sashi-dasu 差し出す; (order in
payment) shiharau 支払う

tender[2] *adj.* (kind) yasashii 優しい; (soft) yawarakai 軟らかい; (delicate) kayowai か弱い; (sensible) kanji-yasui 感じやすい

tenderly *adv.* yasashiku 優しく

tennis *n.* teikyū 庭球; tenisu テニス

tense[1] *adj.* (strained) kinchō shita 緊張した; haritsumeta 張り詰めた

tense[2] *n.* (*gram.*) jisei 時制; toki 時

tension *n.* kinchō 緊張; hari 張り

tent *n.* tento テント; temmaku 天幕

tenth *n., adj.* dai-jū (no) 第十 (の); jū-bun no ichi (no) 十分の一 $\frac{1}{10}$ (の)

term *n.* (fixed time period) kikan 期間; (*school*) gakki 学期; (words) yōgo 用語; jōken 条件; *pl.* (personal relationship) aidagara 間柄; naka 仲

terminal *n., adj.* (of or at the end) owari (no) 終り (の); (railroad and bus station) shūten 終点

terminate *v.* oeru 終える; owaru 終る

termination *n.* shūryō 終了; haishi 廃止; manki 満期

terrace *n.* (balcony) terasu テラス; dan 段; (flat mound) takadai 高台; kōchi 高地

terrible *adj.* osoroshii 恐ろしい; hidoi ひどい

terrify *v.* kowagaraseru 怖がらせる; odorokasu 驚かす

territory *n.* ryōdo 領土; ryōchi 領地   *territorial waters* ryōkai 領海

terror *n.* kyōfu 恐怖; osoroshisa 恐ろしさ

test *n.* shiken 試験; tesuto テスト
make a test of ...o tamesu ...を試す
put to the test tamesu 試す
test tube shiken-kan 試験管

testament *n.* (legal will) yuigon 遺言; isho 遺書; (T-) (Bible) seisho 聖書   *the New* [*Old*] *Testament* shin'yaku [kyūyaku] seisho 新約 [旧約] 聖書

testify *v.* shōmei suru 証明する; risshō suru 立証する

testimony *n.* (evidence) shōko 証拠; shōmei 証明; (witness) shōgen 証言

text *n.* hombun 本文; gembun 原文; tekisuto テキスト **text-book** kyōkasho 教科書

textile *n., adj.* orimono (no) 織物 (の)

than *conj., prep.* yori mo よりも; yori wa よりは; mushiro むしろ

thank *v.* kansha suru 感謝する *Thank you.* Arigatō. 有難う。 *No, thank you.* Iie, kekkō desu. いいえ，結構です。

thanksgiving *n.* kansha 感謝; shaon 謝恩 *Thanksgiving day* kansha-sai 感謝祭

that *adj.* sono その; ano あの; sore それ; are あれ ——*conj.* ...to iu koto ...ということ

thaw *v.* (melt) (yuki, kōri ga) tokeru (雪，氷が) 解ける; tokasu 解かす; (become genial) yawaragu 和らぐ; uchitokeru 打ち解ける ——*n.* yuki-doke 雪解け

the *adj.* (*def. art.*) ano あの; sono その

theater *n.* gekijō 劇場; butai 舞台; (plays) shibai 芝居

theft *n.* nusumi 盗み; settō 窃盗

their *pron.* karera no 彼らの *theirs* karera no mono 彼らのもの

them *pron.* karera o [ni] 彼らを [に]

themselves *pron. pl.* karera-jishin o [de] 彼ら自身を [で]

then *adv.* (of that time) sono-toki その時; (after that) sore-kara それから; (next) tsugi ni 次に; (in that case) sore-dewa それでは

theory *n.* gakusetsu 学説; riron 理論; seorī セオリー; (view) ...setsu ...説

therapy *n.* chiryō 治療

there *adv.* soko ni そこに; soko de そこで *There is [are]* ... ...ga aru ...がある

thereafter *adv.* sono-go その後

thereby *adv.* sore ni yotte それによって; sono-tame ni そのために

therefore *adv., conj.* sore-yue ni それ故に; shitagatte 従って；dakara だから

thermometer *n.* kandan-kei 寒暖計 *clinical thermometer* taionkei 体温計

thermos bottle *n.* mahō-bin 魔法びん

these *adj., pron.* korera (no) これら (の)

they *pron.* karera wa [ga] 彼らは [が]

thick *adj.* atsui 厚い；futoi 太い；(dense) koi 濃い；shigetta 茂った；(foggy) kiri-bukai 霧深い

thicken *v.* atsuku suru [naru] 厚くする [なる]；koku suru [naru] 濃くする [なる]

thicket *n.* yabu やぶ；shigemi 茂み

thief *n.* dorobō 泥棒

thigh *n.* futo-momo 太もも；mata また *thigh bone* dai-tai-kotsu 大たい骨

thin *adj.* (cf. thick) usui 薄い；hosoi 細い；(slender) yaseta やせた；(scanty) wazuka na わずかな —— *v.* hosoku naru 細くなる；usuku suru 薄くする

thing *n.* (object) mono 物；(matter) koto 事；*pl.* jōsei 情勢；(circumstances) jijō 事情；(belongings) mochimono 持ち物

think *v.* (consider) omou 思う；kangaeru 考える；(judge) handan suru 判断する *think of* ...no koto o omou ...のことを思う；o omoi tsuku を思い付く

thinking *adj., n.* shikō 思考；kangae (-ru) 考え (る)

third *n., adj.* dai-san (no) 第三 (の)；samban-me (no) 三番目 (の)；sambun-no-ichi (no) 三分の一, ⅓ (の)

thirst *n.* nodo no kawaki のどの渇き；katsu 渇 —— *v.* (feel thirst) katsubō suru 渇望する

thirsty *adj.* nodo no kawaita のどの渇いた；(eager) katsubō suru 渇望する

thirteen *n., adj.* jū-san (no) 十三, 13 (の)

thirty *n., adj.* san-jū (no) 三十, 30 (の)

this *adj.* kono この —— *pron.* kore これ；kon... 今... *this month* kongetsu 今月

for this once (= *for this time*) kondo dake wa 今度だけは

this morning [*afternoon, evening*] kesa [kyō no gogo, komban] けさ [今日の午後, 今晩]

thorough *adj.* kanzen na 完全な; tettei-teki na 徹底的な; mattaku no 全くの

thoroughbred *adj., n.* junketsu-shu no (uma) 純血種の (馬); sarabureddo サラブレッド

thoroughly *adv.* jūbun ni 十分に; sukkari すっかり

those *pron., adj.* sorera (no) それら (の)

though *conj.* nimo kakawarazu にもかかわらず; daga だが; tatoe…demo たとえ…でも *as though* …de aru ka no yō ni …であるかのように

thought *n.* (thinking) shikō 思考; (idea) kangae 考え; shisō 思想; (consideration) kōryo 考慮; (design) ikō 意向

thought control shisō tōsei 思想統制

thoughtful *adj.* shiryo-bukai 思慮深い; (considerate) omoiyari no aru 思いやりのある

thoughtless *adj.* shiryo no nai 思慮のない; fuchūi na 不注意な

thousand *n., adj.* sen (no) 千 (の); (numberless) musū no 無数の; (many) tasū no 多数の

thousands of… sūsen no 数千の

ten [*a hundred*] *thousand* ichi [jū]-man 一 [十]万

thread *n.* ito 糸 —— *v.* ito o tōsu 糸を通す

threat *n.* kyōhaku 脅迫; odoshi 脅し

threaten *v.* odosu 脅す; obiyakasu 脅かす

three *n., adj.* san (no) 三, 3 (の)

threefold sambai no [ni] 三倍の [に]; san-jū no [ni] 三十の [に]

three-quarter(*s*) yombun no san (no) 四分の三, ¾ (の)

thrice *adv.* san-do 三度; (three times) sambai ni 三倍に

thrift *n.* (economy) ken'yaku 倹約

thrill v. (with horror) zotto suru [saseru] ぞっとする [させる]; (with wave of emotion) kandō suru 感動する ── n. (quiver) mi-burui 身震い

thriller n. surirā スリラー

thrilling adj. zotto suru ぞ～とする; mi-no-ke no yodatsu 身の毛のよだつ

throat n. nodo のど

throne n. ōi 王位; ō-za 王座; tei-i 帝位

throng n. (crowd) gunshū 群集 ── v. muragaru 群がる; komi-au 込み合う

through prep., adv. (from end to end or from side to side) hashi kara hashi made 端から端まで; (by reason of) …no tame ni …のために; (by means of) …o hete …を経て; o tōtte を通って; (going through) …o tōshite …を通して; tsura-nuite 貫いて; …made …まで; zutto ずっと ── adj. (with train) chokutsū no 直通の

throw v. (cast) nageru 投げる; (overthrow) kutsu-gaesu 覆す
 throw away suteru 捨てる
 throw oneself on [upon] …ni shinrai suru …に信頼する; mi o makaseru 身を任せる

thrust v. (push) osu 押す; tsuku 突く; (pierce) sa-su 刺す; tsuki-sasu 突き刺す

thumb n. oya-yubi 親指 *thumb tack* ga-byō 画びょう

thunder n. kaminari 雷; raimei 雷鳴 ── v. kaminari ga naru 雷が鳴る

thunderstorm n. raiu 雷雨

Thursday n. mokuyō-bi 木曜日

thus adv. kono-yō ni このように; kōshite こうして; dakara だから
 thus far ima-made 今まで

tick n. (soft click) kachi-kachi iu oto カチカチいう音 ── v. toki o kizamu 時を刻む

ticket n. kippu 切符; (tag) fuda 札; nyūjō-ken 入場券

tickle v. kusuguru くすぐる; (please) ureshiga-raseru 嬉しがらせる ── n. kusuguri くすぐり

tide *n.* shio 潮; (current) chōryū 潮流; (tendency) keikō 傾向; keisei 形勢

tie *v.* (bind) musubu 結ぶ; (fasten) shibaru 縛る —— *n.* (knot) musubi-me 結び目
tie up shikkari kukuru しっかりくくる; (wrap up) tsutsumu 包む

tiger *n.* tora 虎 *tiger cat* yama-neko 山猫
tiger lily oni-yuri 鬼ゆり

tight *adj.* (firmly held) katai 固い; kenrō na 堅ろうな; (closely fastened) kataku musunda 固く結んだ; kitsui きつい; (impermeable) mizu no moranai 水の漏らない —— *adv.* kataku 固く; shikkari to しっかりと

tighten *v.* shimeru 締める; shimaru 締まる; haru 張る

tile *n.* kawara かわら; tairu タイル

till *prep., conj.* made まで

timber *n.* (lumber) zaimoku 材木; mokuzai 木材

time *n.* toki 時; jikan 時間; (period) kikan 期間; (season) kisetsu 季節; (era) jidai 時代; (occasion) kai 回; do 度; (multiplied by) …bai …倍
all the time itsumo いつも
at a time ichi-do ni 一度に
at times tokidoki 時々
by this time imagoro wa 今ごろは
for the time (*being*) tōbun 当分
from time to time tokidoki 時々
in time mani-atte 間に合って
on time jikan-dōri ni 時間通りに
once upon a time mukashi-mukashi 昔々
Time and tide wait for no man. Saigetsu hito o matazu. 歳月人を待たず。

timely *adj.* jiki no yoi 時機のよい; taimurī na タイムリーな

timetable *n.* jikan-hyō 時間表; jikan-wari 時間割

tin *n., adj.* suzu (no) すず (の); buriki (no) ブリキ (の) —— *v.* kanzume ni suru 缶詰めにする
tinfoil suzu-haku すずはく
tin opener kan-kiri 缶切り

tinkle *v.* chirin-chirin to narasu [naru] チリンチリンと鳴らす [鳴る]

tiny *adj.* chippoke na ちっぽけな; goku chiisai ごく小さい

tip[1] *n.* saki 先; sentan 先端

tip[2] *v.* chippu o yaru チップをやる; (overturn) hikkuri-kaesu 引っ繰り返す

tiptoe *n.,* *v.* tsumasaki (de aruku) つま先 (で歩く) *on tiptoe* tsumasaki de つま先で; hissori to ひっそりと

tire[1] *n.* (*for a wheel*) taiya タイヤ

tire[2] *v.* (become weary) tsukareru 疲れる; (make weary) tsukare saseru 疲れさせる; (tire of) akiru 飽きる *tired out* tsukare-hatete 疲れ果てて

tired *adj.* tsukareta 疲れた

tiresome *adj.* hone no oreru 骨の折れる; taikutsu na 退屈な

tissue *n.* usumono 薄物 *tissue paper* tisshu pēpā ティッシュペーパー

title *n.* (subject) dai 題; shomei 書名; taitoru タイトル

to *prep.* ...e ...へ; ...ni ...に; ...made ...まで; no tame ni のために *to and fro* achira-kochira あちらこちら

toast *n.* (toasted bread) tōsuto トースト; (drink in honor) kampai 乾杯 ——*v.* yaku 焼く; aburu あぶる

tobacco *n.* tabako タバコ

today *n.* kyō 今日; honjitsu 本日; gendai 現代

toe *n.* ashi no yubi 足の指; tsuma-saki つま先

together *adv.* issho ni 一緒に; tagai ni 互いに; dōji ni 同時に

toil *v.* (work laboriously) honeoru 骨折る; kurō suru 苦労する ——*n.* honeori 骨折り; kurō 苦労

toilet *n.* (one's grooming) keshō 化粧; semmen-jo 洗面所; (bathroom) yokushitsu 浴室; (lavatory) benjo 便所 *toilet soap* keshō sekken 化粧石けん

token *n.* (sign) shirushi しるし；(evidence) shōko 証拠；(pledge) hoshō 保証

tolerate *v.* (endure) shimbō suru 辛抱する；(allow) ōme ni miru 大目に見る

toll *n.* tsūkō-zei 通行税
   toll call chōkyori-denwa 長距離電話
   toll road yūryō-dōro 有料道路

tomato *n.* tomato トマト

tomb *n.* haka 墓   *tombstone* haka-ishi 墓石

tomorrow *n.* asu 明日；ashita あした；myōnichi
明日
   the day after tomorrow asatte あさって；myō-
gonichi 明後日
   tomorrow morning [*evening*] myōasa [myō-
ban] 明朝［明晩］

ton *n.* ton トン

tone *n.* (musical sound) oto 音；chōshi 調子；
(tint) shikichō 色調

tongue *n.* shita 舌；(language) kokugo 国語

tonight *n.* kom-ban 今晩；kon-ya 今夜

too *adv.* (besides) omake ni おまけに；(also) mata
また；(moreover) sono-ue その上；amari ni…
sugiru 余りに…過ぎる

tool *n.* dōgu 道具

tooth *n.* ha 歯

toothache *n.* haita 歯痛；ha no itami 歯の痛み

toothbrush *n.* ha-burashi 歯ブラシ

toothpaste *n.* neri-hamigaki 練歯みがき

top[1] *n.* (summit) chōjō 頂上；(head) atama 頭；top-
pu トップ ——*adj.* (of, at or being top) saikō
no 最高の

top[2] *n.* (*toy*) koma こま

topic *n.* wadai 話題；topikku トピック

torch *n.* taimatsu たいまつ

tortoise *n.* kame 亀   *tortoise shell* bekkō べっ甲

torture *n., v.* (agony) kunō 苦悩；(torment) gōmon
(suru) 拷問（する）；kurushimeru 苦しめる；naya-
masu 悩ます

toss *v.* (fling) (shita kara ue e) nageru（下から上

へ) 投げる；oshi-ageru 押し上げる

total *adj.* (entire) zentai no 全体の；sōkei no 総計の；(complete) mattaku no 全くの

touch *v.* fureru 触れる；sawaru 触る；(move) kandō saseru 感動させる —— *n.* sesshoku 接触；tatchi タッチ；te-zawari 手触り；(tinge) kimi 気味

touching *adj.* (moving) kandō saseru 感動させる；(pathetic) aware na 哀れな

tough *adj.* (hard to break or cut) katai 固い；(stubborn) ganko na 頑固な；(difficult) kon'nan na 困難な

tour *n., v.* shūyū (suru) 周遊 (する)；ryokō (suru) 旅行 (する)

tourism *n.* kankō 観光

tourist *n.* kankō-kyaku 観光客

tournament *n.* tōnamento トーナメント；shiai 試合

tow *v.* hiku 引く；tsuna de hiku 綱で引く

toward(s) *prep.* …no hō e …の方へ；…ni tai-shite…に対して
towards evening yūgata 夕方；higure-goro 日暮れごろ

towel *n.* taoru タオル

tower *n.* tō 塔；yagura 矢倉 —— *v.* sobie-tatsu そびえ立つ

town *n.* machi 町；tokai 都会 *town planning* toshi-keikaku 都市計画

toy *n.* omocha おもちゃ

trace *n.* ato 跡；(footprint) ashi-ato 足跡 —— *v.* (tracing paper) shiki-utsusu 敷き写す；ato o tsukeru 跡をつける

track *n.* tōtta ato 通った跡；(path) michi 道；(cf. field & track events) torakku トラック —— *v.* (follow) tsuiseki suru 追跡する

trade *n.* (commerce) shōbai 商売；bōeki 貿易 —— *v.* bai-bai suru 売買する；butsu-butsu-kō-kan suru 物々交換する
trade union rōdō-kumiai 労働組合

trademark *n.* shōhyō 商標; torēdo māku トレードマーク

trader *n.* shōnin 商人; bōeki-sen 貿易船

tradition *n.* densetsu 伝説; dentō 伝統

traditional *adj.* dentō-teki na 伝統的な

traffic *n.* kōtsū 交通; ōrai 往来; shōgyō 商業
   traffic signal kōtsū-shingō 交通信号

tragedy *n.* higeki 悲劇

tragic *adj.* higeki no 悲劇の; higeki-teki na 悲劇的な

trail *v.* (drag) hikizuru 引きずる; (track) tsuiseki suru 追跡する; (follow) ato ni tsui te kuru あとについて来る —— *n.* tōtta ato 通った跡

train *n.* (railroad cars) ressha 列車; kisha 汽車; (line) restu 列; (procession) gyōretsu 行列 —— *v.* (instruct) shikomu 仕込む; (drill) kunren suru 訓練する

training *n.* kunren 訓練; yōsei 養成

traitor *n.* hangyaku-sha 反逆者; uragiri-mono 裏切者

tram(**car**) *n.* (shigai) densha (市街) 電車

tramp *v.* (wander) aruki-mawaru 歩き回る; fumu 踏む —— *n.* toho-ryokō 徒歩旅行; ashi-oto 足音

tranquil(**l**)**izer** *n.* chinsei-zai 鎮静剤

transact *v.* (manage) shori suru 処理する; (deal) torihiki suru 取り引きする

transaction *n.* shori 処理; torihiki 取引き; (affair) jiken 事件

transfer *v.* (remove) utsusu 移す; (convey) hakobu 運ぶ; yuzuru 譲る; nori-kaeru 乗り換える

transform *v.* henkei suru [saseru] 変形する [させる]

transfusion *n.* yuketsu 輸血

transistor *n.* toranjistā トランジスター

transit *n.* tsūka 通過; (passage) tsūkō 通行; (conveyance) yusō 輸送
   transit duty tsūkō-zei 通行税

transition *n.* utsuri-kawari 移り変り; henka 変化

translate v. yakusu 訳す; hon'yaku suru 翻訳する

transmission n. dentatsu 伝達; dendō 伝導

transmit v. (pass on) watasu 渡す; (transfer) okuru 送る; (communicate) tsutaeru 伝える

transparent adj. (can be seen through) tōmei na 透明な; (clear) akiraka na 明らかな

transport v. yusō suru 輸送する; unsō suru 運送する

trap n. (snare) wana わな; (pitfall) otoshi-ana 落とし穴

travel n., v. ryokō (suru) 旅行 (する)

travel(l)er n. ryokō-sha 旅行者; tabi-bito 旅人

tray n. bon 盆; sara 皿

treason n. hangyaku 反逆; fushin 不信; muhon 謀反

treasure n. takara 宝; hōmotsu 宝物; zaihō 財宝
treasure house hōko 宝庫

treasurer n. kaikei-gakari 会計係; keiri-buchō 経理部長; shūnyū-yaku 収入役

treasury n. kokko 国庫; kaikei 会計
Treasury Department ōkura-shō 大蔵省

treat v. (behave toward) taigū suru 待遇する; (deal with) atsukau 扱う; (entertain with food and drink) gochisō suru ごちそうする; ogoru おごる; (try to cure) chiryō suru 治療する

treatment n. chiryō 治療; taigū 待遇

treaty n. jōyaku 条約; kyōtei 協定 *be in treaty* kōshō-chū 交渉中

tree n. ki 木; jumoku 樹木

tremble v. buru-buru furueru ぶるぶる震える; (shake) mi-burui suru 身震いする; (quiver) soyogu そよぐ; yureru 揺れる

tremendous adj. (dreadful) osoroshii 恐ろしい; (momentous) taihen na 大変な; (extraordinary) monosugoi ものすごい

trend v. (tend) katamuku 傾く —— n. (tendency) keikō 傾向; katamuki 傾き; (direction) hōkō 方向

trespass n., v. (invade) shin'nyū (suru) 侵入 (す

る); (commit a sin) tsumi o okasu 罪を犯す

trial *n.* (attempt) kokoromi 試み; tameshi 試し;
(test) shiken 試験; (judical examination) saiban
裁判
　on trial …o tameshita ue de …を試した上で
　trial and error shikō sakugo 試行錯誤

triangle *n.* sankaku-kei 三角形

tribute *n.* mitsugi-mono 貢物; kansha [sonkei] no
kotoba 感謝 [尊敬] の言葉

trick *n.* keiryaku 計略; sakuryaku 策略; torikku
トリック —— *v.* (cheat) damasu だます

tricky *adj.* kosui こすい; zurui ずるい

trifle *n.* tsumaranai koto [mono] つまらない事
[物] —— *v.* rōhi suru 浪費する

trifling *adj.* (trivial) tsumaranai つまらない; wazuka no わずかの

trim *adj.* (neat) kichin to shita きちんとした
—— *n., v.* (put in order) seiton (suru) せい
とん (する); (clip) karikomu 刈り込む; (cut)
kiru 切る

trip *n.* (journey) (shō-) ryokō (小) 旅行 —— *v.*
(move with light steps) karui ashidori de aruku
軽い足取りで歩く

triple *adj.* (three times) sam-bai no 三倍の;
(threefold) san-jū no 三重の —— *v.* sam-bai
ni naru [suru] 三倍になる [する]

triumph *n.* (victory) shōri 勝利; (great success)
dai-seikō 大成功 —— *v.* katsu 勝つ

trivial *adj.* sasai na ささいな; tsumaranai つまら
ない

troop *n.* (company) tai 隊; (group) mure 群れ;
(soldiers) heitai 兵隊; *pl.* (army) guntai 軍隊

trophy *n.* senri-hin 戦利品; torofī トロフィー

tropic *n.* kaiki-sen 回帰線; *pl.* nettai-chihō 熱帯
地方
　the Tropic of Cancer [*Capricorn*] kita [mina-
mi] kaiki-sen 北 [南] 回帰線

tropical *adj.* nettai no [-teki na] 熱帯の [的な]

trouble *n.* (distress) kurō 苦労; (care) shimpai

心配; (difficulty) kon'nan 困難; (disease) byōki
病気 —— *v.* (disturb) midasu 乱す; (annoy)
nayamasu 悩ます

troublesome *adj.* yakkai na 厄介な; urusai うる
さい

trousers *n.* zubon ズボン

trout *n.* masu ます

truck *n.* kamotsu-jidōsha 貨物自動車; torakku
トラック

true *adj.* shinjitsu no 真実の; hontō no 本当の;
(faithful) seijitsu na 誠実な; (genuine) hommono no 本物の; (exact) seikaku na 正確な
come true hontō ni naru 本当になる
true to life [*nature*] shin ni semaru 真に迫る

truly *adv.* hontō ni 本当に; tadashiku 正しく
Yours truly. Keigu. 敬具.

trump *n.* (trump card) kiri-fuda 切り札

trumpet *n.* torampetto トランペット; rappa
ラッパ

trunk *n.* (stem) (ki no) miki (木の) 幹; (body)
dō 胴; ryokō kaban 旅行かばん; (proboscis of
an elephant) zō no hana 象の鼻; (trunk line)
tetsudō no kansen 鉄道の幹線

trust *n., v.* shin'yō suru 信用する; shinrai suru
信頼する; (entrust) itaku suru 委託する

trustworthy *adj.* shinrai ni atai suru 信頼に値
する; ate ni naru 当てになる

truth *n.* shinrai 信頼; shinjitsu 真実; (faithfulness) chūjitsu 忠実
to tell the truth jitsu wa 実は
in truth hontō ni 本当に

try *n.* kokoromi 試み —— *v.* kokoromiru 試み
る; yatte-miru やってみる; tamesu 試す; (make
an effort) tsutomeru 努める
try on (*garment*) (fuku o) kite-miru (服を) 着
てみる; (*shoes*) (kutsu o) haite-miru (靴を) は
いてみる

trying *adj.* hidoku hone no oreru ひどく骨の
折れる; kurushii 苦しい

tub *n.* oke おけ; tarai たらい; (bathtub) yubune 湯船

tube *n.* (pipe) kan 管; (cylinder) tsutsu 筒; chūbu チューブ; (*Br.*) (underground railway) chika-tetsu 地下鉄

Tuesday *n.* kayō-bi 火曜日

tug *v.* hiku 引く; hipparu 引っ張る

tulip *n.* chūrippu チューリップ

tumbler *n.* (drinking glass) tamburā タンブラー; (acrobat) karuwaza-shi 軽業師

tuna *n.* maguro まぐろ

tune *n.* (melody) fushi 節; kyoku 曲; chōshi 調子
in [*out of*] *tune* chōshi ga atte [awanai] 調子が合って [合わない]
tune up gakki no chōshi o totonoeru 楽器の調子をととのえる

tunnel *n.* ton'neru トンネル

turf *n.* shibafu 芝生

Turkey *n.* Toruko トルコ

turkey *n.* shichimen-chō 七面鳥

turn *v.* (rotate) mawasu 回す; (go round) mawaru 回る; (change) tenjiru 転じる; (upset) hikkuri-kaesu 引っ繰り返す; (roll) korogaru 転がる; (become) ...ni naru ...になる; (change in direction) magaru 曲がる ── *n.* (rotation) kaiten 回転; (change) henka 変化; (a corner of a street) magari kado 曲り角; (order) jumban 順番
turn against hantai suru 反対する
turn aside sorasu そらす; (kao o) somukeru (顔を) 背ける; yokeru よける
turn away oidasu 追い出す; kao o somukeru 顔を背ける
turn on (sen o hinette) dasu (栓をひねって) 出す; tsukeru つける
turn off kesu 消す; tomeru 止める
turn over hikkuri-kaesu 引っ繰り返す
by turns kawaru-gawaru 代る代る
in turn jumban ni 順番に
take turns kōtai suru 交替する

turning *n.* kaiten 回転; (corner) magari-kado 曲り角; (bend) magari-me 曲り目
  turning point bunki-ten 分岐点; tenki 転機

turnip *n.* kabura かぶら

turtle *n.* umi-game 海亀; (turtledove) yama-bato 山鳩 *turtle shell* bekkō べっ甲

twelve *n., adj.* jū-ni (no) 十二, 12 (の)

twice *adv.* (two times) ni-bai ni 二倍に; (doubly) ni-jū ni 二重に; ni-kai 二回

twig *n.* ko-eda 小枝; kozue こずえ

twilight *n.* tasogare たそがれ

twin *n., adj.* futago (no) 双子(の); sōseiji (no) 双生児 (の); ittsui (no) 一対 (の)

twine *n.* yori-ito より糸; motsure もつれ —— *v.* (twist together) yori-awaseru より合わせる; (entwine) …ni makitsukeru …に巻き付ける; karamaseru 絡ませる; karamaru 絡まる

twist *v.* (wind together) yoru よる; yoreru よれる; nejiru ねじる; (distort) yugameru ゆがめる —— *n.* yore よれ; nejire ねじれ; (distortion) yugami ゆがみ

twitch *v.* (jerk) gui to hiku ぐいと引く; hittakuru ひったくる; (spasmodic motion) pikutto ugoku ぴくっと動く; keiren suru けいれんする —— *n.* hikitsuri ひきつり; keiren けいれん

two *n., adj.* ni (no) 二, 2 (の); futatsu (no) 二つ (の)
  a day or two ichiryō-jitsu 一両日

type *n.* (model) kata 型; taipu タイプ; (symbol) shōchō 象徴; (type face) katsuji 活字 —— *v.* taipu suru タイプする

typewriter *n.* taipuraitā タイプライター

typhoon *n.* taifū 台風

typical *adj.* tenkei-teki na 典型的な; (representative) daihyō-teki na 代表的な

typography *n.* insatsu(gijutsu) 印刷(技術)

tyranny *n.* assei 圧政; bōsei 暴政; sensei 専制

U

ugly *a.* (ill-looking) minikui 醜い; (unpleasant) iyana いやな

ulcer *n.* kaiyō かいよう

ultimate *a.* (last) saigo no 最後の; (final) kekkyoku no 結局の; (fundamental) kompon no 根本の   *ultimately* saigo ni 最後に; kekkyoku 結局

ultimatum *n.* saigo tsūkoku 最後通告

ultra- *pref.* chō- 超-; ka- 過-

umbrella *n.* kōmori-gasa こうもりがさ; kasa かさ   *umbrella stand* kasa-tate かさ立て

umpire *n.* shimpan-sha 審判者; ampaia アンパイア ——*v.* chūsai suru 仲裁する; shimpan suru 審判する

U. N. *n.* (United Nations) Kokusai Rengō 国際連合; Kokuren 国連

unable *a.* dekinai 出来ない

unaccustomed *a.* (not used to) funare no 不慣れの; (unusual) futsū de nai 普通でない

unanimous *a.* manjō-itchi no 満場一致の; igi no nai 異議のない

unavoidable *a.* sake-gatai 避け難い; yamu o enai 止むをえない

unaware *a.* shiranai 知らない; kizukanai 気付かない

unbearable *a.* tae-gatai 耐え難い

unbroken *a.* yaburenai 破れない; (continuous) renzoku shita 連続した; togirenai 途切れない

uncertain *a.* (doubtful) futashika na 不確かな; hakkiri shinai はっきりしない; (untrustworthy) ate ni naranai 当てにならない; (changeable) kawari yasui 変りやすい

uncivilized *adj.* (savage) mikai no 未開の; (barbarous) yaban na 野蛮な

uncle *n.* oji (san) 伯父 (さん)

uncomfortable *a.* fuyukai na 不愉快な; kimochi no yokunai 気持のよくない

uncommon *a.* (unusual) ijō na 異常な; (rare) mezurashii 珍しい; (remarkable) hibon na 非凡な *uncommonly* hijō ni 非常に; ijō ni 異常に

unconcern *n.* (indifference) mukanshin 無関心; heiki 平気 *unconcerned* heiki na 平気な; mukanshin na 無関心な

unconscious *a.* muishiki no 無意識の; ishiki o ushinatta 意識を失った —— *n.* (the u-) senzai-ishiki 潜在意識

unconsciously kizukazu ni 気付かずに; muishiki ni 無意識に

uncover *v.* o'oi o toru 覆いを取る; arawasu 現わす; (disclose) abaku あばく

undecided *a.* mitei no 未定の

under *prep.* ...no shita ni ...の下に; ni motozuite に基づいて; ika no 以下の; ...chū ...中 —— *a., adv.* shita no [ni] 下の[に]; ni motozuite に基づいて; (lower) kabu no 下部の

keep under osae-tsukeru 押え付ける

underdeveloped *adj.* mikaihatsu no 未開発の; hatten-tojō no 発展途上の

underdog *n.* (one who is expected to lose a contest or struggle) kachi-me no usui hito 勝ち目の薄い人; (seizon kyōsō no) haizansha [giseisha] (生存競争の) 敗残者 [犠牲者]

undergo *v.* (be subject to) ukeru 受ける; (suffer) kōmuru 被る; (experience) keiken suru 経験する

undergraduate *n.* daigaku-sei 大学生; zaigaku-sei 在学生

underground *adj.* chika no 地下の —— *n.* (underground railroad) chikatetsu 地下鉄

undergrowth *n.* (mori no) shita-bae (森の)下生え; yabu やぶ

undermentioned *adj.* kaki no 下記の

underneath *adv.* ...no shita ni ...の下に; hikuku

低く

undershirt *n.* hada-gi 肌着; shatsu シャツ

understand *v.* (get the meaning of) rikai suru 理解する; wakaru 分かる; (believe) omou 思う; (be informed) shōchi shiteiru 承知している *understanding* rikai (-ryoku) 理解 (力)

undertake *v.* (attempt) kuwadateru 企てる; (take upon oneself) hiki-ukeru 引き受ける; (set about) chakushu suru 着手する; (promise) yakusoku suru 約束する; (guarantee) hoshō suru 保証する

undertaker *n.* (mortician) sōgi-ya 葬儀屋; hiki-uke-nin 引受人; ukeoi-nin 請負人

undertaking *n.* (enterprise) jigyō 事業; kigyō 企業; (promise) yakusoku 約束

underwear *n.* shita-gi 下着; hada-gi 肌着

underworld *n.* kasō shakai 下層社会; ankoku-gai 暗黒街; (Hades) jigoku 地獄

undesirable *adj.* konomashiku nai 好ましくない; nozomashiku nai 望ましくない

undeveloped *adj.* (immature) mi-hattatsu no 未発達の; (unexploited) mikaihatsu no 未開発の

undo *v.* (reverse) moto-dōri ni suru 元通りにする; (cancel) tori-kesu 取り消す; (unfasten) hodoku ほどく; (untie) toku 解く *leave undone* hōtte oku 放っておく

undoubtedly *adv.* utagai naku 疑いなく; tashika ni 確かに

undress *v.* fuku o nugaseru 服を脱がせる; nugu 脱ぐ

unearned *adj.* rō sezu ni eta 労せずに得た *unearned profit* furō shotoku 不労所得

uneasy *adj.* (anxious) fuan na 不安な; (uncomfortable) fukai na 不快な; (difficult) muzukashii 難しい

unemployed *adj.* shitsugyō shita 失業した; (the u-) shitsugyō-sha 失業者

unemployment *n.* shitsugyō 失業 *unemployment benefit* shitsugyō teate 失業手当

unequal *adj*. hitoshiku nai 等しくない; ichiyō de nai 一様でない; fubyōdō no 不平等の; (not able to) ...ni taenai ...にたえない

uneven *adj*. taira de nai 平らでない; (rough) dekoboko no でこぼこの; (*math*.) (uneven numbers) kisū no 奇数の

unexpected *adj*. omoigakenai 思いがけない; i-gai no 意外の　**unexpectedly** omoigake naku 思いがけなく; fui ni 不意に

unfaithful *adj*. seii no nai 誠意のない; fujitsu na 不実な

unfamiliar *adj*. shitashiku nai 親しくない; narete nai 慣れてない

unfavo(u)rable *adj*. tsugō no warui 都合の悪い; furi no 不利の

unfit *adj*. futekitō na 不適当な

unforeseen *adj*. furyo no 不慮の; fusoku no 不測の; gūzen no 偶然の

unforgettable *adj*. wasure rarenai 忘れられない

unfortunate *adj*. fukō na 不幸な; fu'un na 不運な

unfortunately *adv*. fukō nimo 不幸にも; fu'un nimo 不運にも; ainiku あいにく

ungrateful *adj*. (unthankful) on-shirazu no 恩知らずの

unhappily *adv*. fukō nimo 不幸にも; ainiku あいにく

unhappy *adj*. (sad) fukō na 不幸な; mijime na 惨めな; (unlucky) fukitsu na 不吉な

unhealthy *adj*. (unwholesome) fukenkō na 不健康な; (unsound) fukenzen na 不健全な

uniform *adj*. ichiyō na 一様な; soroi no 揃いの —— *n*. seifuku 制服; gumpuku 軍服; yunifōmu ユニフォーム

unimportant *adj*. (insignificant) jūyō de nai 重要でない; (trifling) tsumaranai つまらない

uninteresting *adj*. omoshiroku nai 面白くない

union *n*. ketsugō 結合; kumiai 組合; rengō 連合 *labor union* rōdō kumiai 労働組合

unique *adj*. dokutoku no 独特の; yunīku na ユニ

ークな

unite v. (combine) ketsugō suru 結合する；(agree) itchi suru 一致する；(join together) gappei suru 合併する　*united* ketsugō shita 結合した；rengō shita 連合した

universal adj. uchū no 宇宙の；zensekai no 全世界の；zempan no 全般の

universe n. (cosmos) uchū 宇宙；(world) sekai 世界

university n. daigaku 大学

unjust adj. fusei na 不正な；(unfair) fukōhei na 不公平な；(wrongful) futō na 不当な

unkind adj. fushinsetsu na 不親切な；(cruel) reikoku na 冷酷な

unknown adj. michi no 未知の；shirarete inai 知られていない

unlawful adj. fuhō na 不法な；ihō no 違法の

unless conj. (if...not) ...de nakere ba ...でなければ

unlike adj. (different) onaji de nai 同じでない；kotonatta 異なった；—— prep. ...to chigatte ...と違って

unlikely adj. arisōmo nai ありそうもない；mikomi no nai 見込みのない

unlock v. ...no jō o akeru ...の錠をあける；(open) hiraku 開く；(disclose) (himitsu o) akasu (秘密を) 明かす

unlucky adj. fukō na 不幸な；fukitsu na 不吉な

unmarried adj. mikon no 未婚の

unnatural adj. fushizen na 不自然な；ijō na 異常な

unnecessary adj. fuhitsuyō na 不必要な；(useless) muyō na 無用な

unofficial adj. hikōshiki no 非公式の

unpack v. (ni o) toku (荷を) 解く；nakami o tori-dasu 中身を取り出す

unpleasant adj. fuyukai na 不愉快な；iyana いやな

unprofitable adj. rieki no nai 利益のない；mōkara nai もうからない

unreasonable *adj.* (irrational) fugōri na 不合理
な; (excessive) tohō mo nai 途方もない; mufumbetsu na 無分別な

unsafe *adj.* anzen de nai 安全でない; abunai
危ない

unselfish *adj.* riko-teki de nai 利己的でない

unsettled *adj.* (changeable) (tenki no) kawari
yasui（天気の）変りやすい; (not fixed) fuantei
na 不安定な

untie *adj.* (musubi o) hodoku（結びを）ほどく;
toku 解く

until *prep., conj.* ...made ...まで

untrue *adj.* hontō de nai 本当でない; fuseijitsu
na 不誠実な

unusual *adj.* ijō na 異常な; mare na まれな

unwell *adj.* kibun ga sugure nai 気分が優れない;
(ill) fukai no 不快の

unwilling *adj.* ki ga susumanai 気が進まない;
iyagaru いやがる　*unwillingly* iya-iya nagara
いやいやながら

up *adj.* jōhō no 上方の; nobori no 上りの ——
adv. ue e 上へ; ue ni 上に; no hō e の方へ
——*prep.* no ue e の上へ; o agatte を上がって
up to ...made ...まで
up train nobori ressha 上り列車
up-and-down jōge ni 上下に; achi-kochi あち
こち
ups and downs tochi no kifuku 土地の起伏;
eiko seisui 栄枯盛衰; (kakaku no) tōki （価格
の）騰貴

uphold *v.* (sustain) yōgo suru 擁護する; (support) shiji suru 支持する; (encourage) hagemasu 励ます

upon *prep.* no ue ni [e] の上に［へ］

upper *adj.* sara ni ue no さらに上の; jōi no 上
位の; jōbu no 上部の; kōi no 高位の
upper jaw [*lip*] uwa-ago [-kuchibiru] 上あご
［唇］

upper-class jōryū no 上流の
Upper House jōin 上院

upright *adj., adv.* (erect) massugu na [ni] 真っすぐな [に]; chokuritsu shita 直立した; (honest) shōjiki na 正直な; (just) kōsei na 公正な

upset *v.* kutsugaesu 覆す; hikkuri-kaesu 引っ繰り返す

upside *n.* jōhō 上方; ue-gawa 上側; jōbu 上部
upside down sakasama ni 逆様に; hikkuri-kaette 引っ繰り返って; (in disorder) konran shite 混乱して

upstairs *adj., adv.* kaijō no [ni] 階上の [に]
——— *n.* nikai 二階; kaijō 階上

upstream *adj., adv.* jōryū no [ni, e] 上流の [に, へ]

up-to-date *adj.* saishin no 最新の; gendai-teki na 現代的な

upward *adj.* ue no hō e 上の方へ; uwa-muki no 上向きの; yori ijō より以上

urban *adj.* toshi no 都市の; tokai ni sumu 都会に住む

urge *v.* (hasten) isogaseru 急がせる; (encourage) hagemasu 励ます; (drive on) kari-tateru 駆り立てる; unagasu 促す ——— *n.* (impulse) shigeki 刺激; shōdō 衝動

urgent *adj.* (pressing) kinkyū no 緊急の; sashi-sematta 差し迫った ——— *v.* kyōyō suru 強要する

urgently *adv.* shikyū ni 至急に; shikiri ni しきりに; setsu ni 切に

us *pron.* wareware o [ni] 我々を [に]; wata (ku)-shi-tachi o [ni] わた(く)したちを [に]

usage *n.* (customary use) kan'yō 慣用; (custom) kanshū 慣習; (way of using) yōhō 用法; (ways of using words) gohō 語法

use *n.* shiyō 使用; riyō 利用; yōto 用途; (usefulness) kōyō 効用 ——— *v.* (employ) shiyō suru 使用する; tsukau 使う; (treat) toriatsukau 取り扱う

make use of ...o shiyō suru ...を使用する; ...o riyō suru ...を利用する

lose the use of ...ga tsukaenaku naru ...が使えなくなる

no use yaku ni tatanai 役に立たない

of [*no*] *use* yaku ni tatsu [tatanai] 役に立つ [立たない]

in [*out of*] *use* shiyō-chū [tsukawarete nai] 使用中 [使われてない]

use up tsukai-hatasu 使い果たす

used¹ *adj.* (accustomed) ...ni narete ...に慣れて

be used to ...ni narete iru ...に慣れている

—— *v.* (used to do) ...suru shūkan ga atta ...する習慣があった; ...suru no ga tsune datta ...するのが常だった; yoku ...shita よく...した

used² *adj.* tsukatta 使った; chūko no 中古の

useful *adj.* yaku ni tatsu 役に立つ; yūeki na 有益な

useless *adj.* yaku ni tatanai 役に立たない; mueki na 無益な

user *n.* riyō-sha 利用者; shōhi-sha 消費者

usual *adj.* (ordinary) itsumono いつもの; (customary) rei no 例の

as usual itsumo no tōri いつもの通り

usually *adv.* tsune ni 常に; itsumo いつも; futsū 普通

utensils *n.* dōgu 道具; kigu 器具

household utensils kateiyō kigu 家庭用器具

cooking utensils kitchin yōgu キッチン用具

writing utensils hikki yōgu 筆記用具

utilizable *adj.* riyō dekiru 利用出来る

utilize *v.* riyō suru 利用する

utmost *adj.* (extreme) kyokudo no 極度の; saidaigen no 最大限の; (furthest) mottomo tōi 最も遠い

do one's utmost zenryoku o tsukusu 全力を尽す

to the utmost kyokudo ni 極度に

utter *adj.* (complete) mattaku no 全くの; kanzen na 完全な *utterly* mattaku 全く; zenzen 全然

V

vacancy *n.* (emptiness) kūkyo 空虚; kara 空; su-kima 透き間; hima 暇; (empty place) akichi 空地; (absent mindedness) hōshin jōtai 放心状態

vacant *adj.* (empty) karano 空の; aite iru 空いている; (stupid) bon'yari shite iru ぼんやりしている

vacation *n.* kyūka 休暇; yasumi 休み

vaccinate *v.* (inoculate) shutō suru 種痘する; yo-bō-chūsha suru 予防注射する

vacuum *n.* shinkū 真空; (vacuum cleaner) denki-sōji-ki 電気掃除機
　vacuum tube shinkūkan 真空管
　vacuum bottle [*flask*] mahō-bin 魔法びん

vague *adj.* (indistinct) aimai na あいまいな; (ill-defined) bakuzen to shita ばくぜんとした

vain *adj.* (futile) muda na むだな; (empty) muna-shii むなしい; tsumaranai つまらない
　in the vain hope hakanai nozomi o idaite はかない望みを抱いて
　in vain kainaku かいなく; munashiku むなしく

valiant *adj.* yūkan na 勇敢な; isamashii 勇ましい; eiyū-teki na 英雄的な

valid *adj.* (sound) kakujitsu na 確実な; seitō na 正当な; datō na 妥当な; (effective) yūkō na 有効な

valuable *adj.* kichō na 貴重な; kachi no aru 価値のある

value *n.* (worth) kachi 価値; neuchi 値打ち; (valuation) hyōka 評価; kakaku 価格 —— *v.* (appraise) hyōka suru 評価する; ne o tsukeru 値を付ける; (esteem) taisetsu ni suru 大切にする

valueless *adj.* mukachi no 無価値の; tsumara-nai つまらない

valve *n.* barubu バルブ; ben 弁; (shell) (mame no) saya (豆の) さや; (vacuum tube) shinkū-kan 真空管

van[1] *n.* (yūgai no) torakku (有蓋の) トラック —— *v.* (nimotsu o) kuruma de hakobu (荷物を) 車で運ぶ

van[2] *n.* sempō 先鋒; sentō 先頭; zen'ei 前衛; sendō-sha 先導車

vanish *v.* (disappear) mienaku naru 見えなくなる; (fade away) kie-useru 消え失せる

vanity *n.* (being conceited) kyoei (-shin) 虚栄(心); (emptiness) munashisa むなしさ

vanquish *v.* seifuku suru 征服する; uchikatsu 打ち勝つ

vapor *n.* (sui-) jōki (水) 蒸気; (mist) kiri 霧; moya もや
 vapor trail hikōki-gumo 飛行機雲

variable *adj.* henka shiyasui 変化しやすい; ittei shinai 一定しない

variety *n.* (diversity) henka 変化; (kind) shurui 種類; baraetī バラエティー *a variety of* shuju no 種々の

various *adj.* iro-iro na 色々な; ikutsu ka no 幾つかの

varnish *n.* wanisu ワニス; nisu ニス; uwagusuri うわぐすり —— *v.* wanisu o nuru ワニスを塗る

vary *v.* (change) kaeru 変える; kawaru 変わる; (modify) shūsei suru 修正する; (differ) koto-naru 異なる

varying *adj.* henka no aru 変化のある; tayō na 多様な

vase *n.* kabin 花びん; tsubo つぼ

vast *adj.* (immense) kōdai na 広大な; (great) hijō na 非常な; (huge) kyodai na 巨大な

vault *n.* (arched ceiling) maru-tenjō 丸天井; (arched roof) maru-yane 丸屋根; (bank vault) kinko-shitsu 金庫室

vegetable *n., adj.* shokubutsu (no) 植物 (の);

yasai (no) 野菜 (の)
green vegetables aomono 青物
vegetable diet sai-shoku 菜食

vehicle *n.* norimono 乗物; kuruma 車; (means)
shudan 手段

veil *n.* bēru ベール; o'oi 覆い; maku 幕; tobari
とばり —— *v.* bēru o kakeru ベールをかけ
る; (cover) o'ou 覆う; tsutsumu 包む

vein *n.* (blood vessel) kekkan 血管; (cf. artery)
jōmyaku 静脈; (*tree*) mokume 木目; (*leaf*) yō-
myaku 葉脈; (*insects*) shimyaku 翅脈

velocity *n.* sokudo 速度

velvet *n., adj.* birōdo (no) ビロード (の)

vengeance *n.* fukushū 復しゅう *take vengeance
with* ...ni fukushū suru ...に復しゅうする

vent *n.* kuchi 口; (hole) ana 穴; tsūki-kō 通気孔
—— *v.* kuchi [ana] o akeru 口 [穴] をあける

ventilate *v.* kaze-tōshi o yoku suru 風通しをよく
する; kanki o suru 換気をする

ventilation *n.* tsūfū 通風; kanki (-sōchi) 換気
(装置); (ventilation fan) kanki-sen 換気扇

venture *n.* (speculation) tōki 投機; (risky undertaking) bōken 冒険 —— *v.* kiken o okasu 危
険を冒す; omoi-kitte suru 思い切ってする
at a venture mukō-mizu ni 向こう見ずに

verb *n.* (*gram.*) dōshi 動詞

verbal *adj.* (of or in words) kotoba no 言葉の;
(oral) kōtō no 口頭の; (of or formed from verb)
dōshi no 動詞の

verdict *n.* (cf. sentence) hyōketsu 評決; hanketsu
判決; (judgment) handan 判断; (opinion) iken
意見

verge *n.* (brink) hashi 端; fuchi ふち; (border-
line) kyōkai 境界
on the verge of no magiwa ni の間際に; ima-
nimo...shiyō to shite 今にも...しようとして
—— *v.* (border) ...to sakai suru ...と境する;
sessuru 接する; mukau 向かう; chikazuku 近
付く

verse *n.* shi 詩; imbun 韻文

version *n.* hon'yaku 翻訳; yakubun 訳文; kyaku-shoku 脚色; setsumei 説明

versus *prep.* ...tai ... 対

vertical *adj.* (standing upright) suichoku no 垂直の; chokuritsu shita 直立した

very *adv.* hijō ni 非常に; totemo とても; taihen 大変; (identical) dōitsu no 同一の; chōdo sono 丁度その; (true) hontō no 本当の; (genuine) makoto no まことの

vest *n.* (waistcoat) chokki チョッキ ── *v.* kiseru 着せる; (give some power or right) kenri o ataeru 権利を与える
vested right [*interest*] kitoku-ken [-shūeki] 既得権 [収益]

veteran *n., adj.* beteran ベテラン; rōren (na) 老練 (な)

veto *n.* (veto power) kyohi-ken 拒否権 ── *v.* kyohi suru 拒否する

via *prep.* ...o keiyu shite ...を経由して

vibrate *v.* shindō suru 振動する; (quiver) furueru 震える

vice[1] *n.* (evil) akutoku 悪徳; zaiaku 罪悪; (defect) kekkan 欠陥

vice[2] *pref.* jiseki no 次席の; fuku- 副...
vice president fuku-daitōryō 副大統領

vicinity *n.* kinjo 近所; fukin 付近

vicious *adj.* (wicked) ja'aku na 邪悪な; (evil) a-kutoku no 悪徳の; (malicious) akui no aru 悪意のある; warui 悪い; (unruly) fu-dōtoku na 不道徳な

victim *n.* gisei-sha 犠牲者; higai-sha 被害者; sō-nan-sha 遭難者
fall a victim to ...no gisei to naru ...の犠牲となる

victor *n.* shōri-sha 勝利者

victory *n.* shōri 勝利

view *n.* (sight) keshiki 景色; nagame 眺め; (range of vision) shikai 視界; (opinion) iken 意見; kenkai 見解; (purpose) mokuteki 目的 —— v. shiraberu 調べる; miru 見る; kansatsu suru 観察する

in view of mieru tokoro ni 見える所に; o kōryo shite を考慮して

point of view kenchi 見地; kenkai 見解

with the [a] view of ...suru mokuteki de ...する目的で

with the [a] view to ...suru tsumori de ...するつもりで

viewpoint *n.* kenchi 見地; kenkai 見解

vigorous *a.* kakki ga aru 活気がある; genki no yoi 元気のよい

villa *n.* bessō 別荘

village *n.* mura 村

villain *n.* warumono 悪者; akkan 悪漢

vine *n.* tsuru-kusa つる草; tsuru つる; (grapevine) budō no ki ぶどうの木

vinegar *n., v.* su (o ireru) 酢 (を入れる)

vineyard *n.* budō-en ぶどう園

violate *v.* (break) (hō o) okasu (法を) 犯す; yaburu 破る; somuku 背く

violence *n.* (fury) mōretsu 猛烈; gekiretsu 激烈; (outrage) buryoku 武力

violent *adj.* (severe) hageshii 激しい; (vehement) mōretsu na 猛烈な; (intense) kibishii 厳しい; rambō na 乱暴な

violet *n.* sumire (-iro) すみれ (色)

violin *n.* baiorin バイオリン

virgin *n., adj.* shojo (no) 処女 (の); otome 乙女; (pure) junketsu na 純潔な

virgin soil shojo-chi 処女地

virgin forest genshi-rin 原始林

virtue *n.* (moral excellence) toku 徳; bitoku 美徳; chōsho 長所; (good quality) biten 美点; (chastity) teisetsu 貞節

by [in] virtue of ...no chikara de ...の力で; ...ni motozuite ...に基づいて

virus *n.* bīrusu ビールス

visible *adj*. (can be seen) me ni mieru 目に見える；(clear) meihaku na 明白な

vision *n*. (sight) shiryoku 視力；(phantom) maboroshi 幻；bijon ビジョン

visit *v., n*. hōmon (suru) 訪問 (する)

visitor *n*. hōmon-sha 訪問者；(o-)kyaku (お)客

vital *adj*. inochi no 命の；(fatal) chimei-teki na 致命的な；(essential) kan'yō na 肝要な；(lively) kakki no aru 活気のある；jūdai na 重大な

vitality *n*. katsuryoku 活力；baitaritī バイタリティー

vitamin *n*. bitamin ビタミン

vivid *adj*. (lively) iki-iki shita 生き生きした；(clear) meikai na 明快な；(bright) azayaka na 鮮やかな

vividly *adv*. iki-iki to 生き生きと

vocal *adj*. koe no 声の；onsei no 音声の　*vocal music* seigaku 声楽

vogue *n*. (fashion) ryūkō 流行；(popular favor) ninki 人気
　bring [come] into vogue hayaraseru [hayaridasu] はやらせる [はやり出す]

voice *n*. koe 声；(*gram.*) (dōshi no) tai (動詞の) 態 ——*v*. (utter) iu 言う；(express) noberu 述べる
　mixed voices konsei 混声
　with one voices manjō-itchi de 満場一致で；ikudōon ni 異口同音に

void *adj*. (empty) kūkyo na 空虚な；kara no 空の；(invalid) mukō na 無効な ——*n*. (empty space) kūkan 空間

volcano *n*. kazan 火山
　active volcano kakkazan 活火山
　dormant volcano kyū-kazan 休火山
　extinct volcano shi-kazan 死火山

volleyball *n*. barē-bōru バレーボール

volume *n*. satsu 冊；kan 巻；(book) hon 本；(amount) ryō 量；(cubic measure) taiseki 体積；(bulk) kasa かさ

voluntary *adj.* (spontaneous) jihatsu-teki na 自発的な; nin'i no 任意の

volunteer *n.* yūshi 有志; shigan-sha 志願者; giyū-hei 義勇兵; borantia ボランティア ── *v.* teikyō suru 提供する; shigan suru 志願する

vomit *v.* tabemono o haku [modosu] 食べ物を吐く[戻す]; funshutsu suru 噴出する ── *n.* ōto おう吐; hedo へど

vote *n., v.* tōhyō (suru) 投票 (する)
vote down hiketsu suru 否決する
vote in tōsen saseru 当選させる

vowel *n., adj.* boin (no) 母音 (の)

voyage *n.* kōkai 航海 ── *v.* kōkō suru 航行する

W

wade *v.* (walk through water) aruite wataru 歩いて渡る; (proceed with difficulty) honeotte susumu 骨折って進む

waffle *n.* waffuru ワッフル *waffle iron* waffuru yaki ワッフル焼き

wag *v.* furu 振る; yureru 揺れる

wage *n.* chingin 賃銀; kyūryō 給料

wagon *n.* ni-basha 荷馬車; (*Br.*) (open railway truck) kasha 貨車

waist *n.* koshi 腰; uesuto ウエスト *waistcoat* chokki チョッキ

wait *v.* (await) matsu 待つ; (serve food at) kyūji suru 給仕する

waiter *n.* kyūji 給仕; ueitā ウエイター

waiting room *n.* machiai-shitsu 待合室

waitress *n.* ueitoresu ウエイトレス

wake *v.* me ga sameru 目が覚める; me o samasaseru 目を覚まさせる; okosu 起す

walk *v.* aruku 歩く; sampo suru 散歩する ── *n.* sampo-michi 散歩道

wall *n.* kabe 壁; hei 塀

wallet *n*. saifu 財布 ; kami-ire 紙入れ

walnut *n*. kurumi くるみ

wander *v*. samayou さ迷う ; aruki-mawaru 歩き回る

want *n*. (lack) ketsubō 欠乏 ; fusoku 不足 ; (necessity) hitsuyō 必要 —— *v*. (need) hitsuyō to suru 必要とする ; (wish) …shitai …したい ; (require) yōkyū suru 要求する ; (desire) nozomu 望む ; (lack) kakete iru 欠けている
 in want of …ga nakute …がなくて ; …ni komatte …に困って
 for want of …ga nai [tarinai] node …がない [足りない] ので

war *n*. sensō 戦争 ; tōsō 闘争
 at war kōsen-chū 交戦中
 declare war sensen suru 宣戦する
 war dead senshi-sha 戦死者

ward *n*. (watch, guard) mihari 見張り ; hogo 保護 ; (city voting division) ku 区 ; (division of a hospital) byōshitsu 病室 ; byōtō 病棟

warden *n*. momban 門番 ; mihari-nin 見張り人

ware *n. pl.* (goods) shōhin 商品 ; seihin 製品
 earthen ware tōki-rui 陶器類
 hardware kanamono-rui 金物類

warehouse *n*. sōko 倉庫

warfare *n*. sensō 戦争 ; kōsen-jōtai 交戦状態

warm *adj*. (moderately hot) atatakai 暖かい ; atsui 暑い ; (hearty) omoiyari no aru 思いやりのある ; (enthusiastic) netsuretsu na 熱烈な ; hageshii 激しい —— *v*. atatameru 暖める ; atatakaku naru 暖かくなる ; (animate) kakkizukeru 活気付ける

warn *n*. keikoku suru 警告する ; chūi suru 注意する

warrant *v*. (guarantee) hoshō suru 保証する ; uke-au 請け合う —— *n*. (justification) seitō na riyū 正当な理由 ; (guaranty) hoshō 保証

was *v*. …de atta …であった ; ita いた

wash *v*. arau 洗う ; sentaku suru 洗たくする

washbasin semmen-ki 洗面器

waste *v.* (use carelessly) rōhi suru 浪費する; muda-zukai suru むだづかいする; (pine away) suijaku suru 衰弱する —— *adj.* (desolate) arehateta 荒れ果てた; (refuse) haibutsu no 廃物の —— *n.* (wilderness) arechi 荒れ地

wastebasket kamikuzu-kago 紙くずかご

wastepaper kami-kuzu 紙くず

wasteful *adj.* rōhi suru 浪費する; muda na むだな

watch *n.* (small clock for wrist) ude-dokei 腕時計; tokei 時計; (act of guarding of observing) mihari 見張り; chūi 注意 —— *v.* (guard) miharu 見張る; (tend) kango suru 看護する; (observe) mimamoru 見守る

water *n.* mizu 水; (liquid) ekitai 液体 *hot water* yu 湯 *boiling water* nettō 熱湯

water-color *n.* suisai enogu 水彩絵具

waterfall *n.* taki 滝

water-fowl *n.* mizu-dori 水鳥

waterlily *n.* suiren すいれん

watermelon *n.* suika すいか

water power *n.* suiryoku 水力

waterproof *adj.* bōsui no 防水の

watt *n.* (unit of electric power) watto-sū ワット数

wave *n.* nami 波; (back and forth movement) hadō 波動 —— *v.* furu 振る; yureru 揺れる; nami-utsu 波打つ *wavelength* hachō 波長

waver *v.* (flicker) yurameku 揺らめく; (fluctuate) dōyō suru 動揺する; (hesitate) tamerau ためらう

wax *n.* rō ろう *wax paper* parafin-shi パラフィン紙

way *n.* (road) michi 道; (means) hōhō 方法; (course) shinro 進路; (manner) shikata 仕方; (distance) kyori 距離; (habit) shūkan 習慣 *all the way* haru-baru はるばる; waza-waza わざわざ; shijū 始終

by the way tsuide ni ついでに; tochū de 途中
で

by way of ...o tōtte ...を通って

give way jōho suru 譲歩する; makeru 負ける

lose one's way michi ni mayou 道に迷う

on the way tochū de 途中で

we *pron.* wareware wa [ga] われわれは [が];
wata(ku)shi-tachi wa [ga] わた(く)したちは
[が]

weak *adj.* yowai 弱い; hakujaku na 薄弱な

weak point jakuten 弱点; yowami 弱み

weaken *v.* (make weaker) yowameru 弱める;
(enfeeble) chikara o sogu 力をそぐ; (dilute)
usumeru 薄める

weakness *n.* yowasa 弱さ; jakuten 弱点

wealth *n.* (riches) tomi 富; (property) zaisan 財
産; (abundance) hōfu 豊富

wealthy *adj.* tonda 富んだ; yutaka na 豊かな

weapon *n.* buki 武器; heiki 兵器

wear *v.* (*on body*) kiru 着る; (*on legs or feet*)
haku はく; (*on head*) kaburu かぶる; (*on
hand*) hameru はめる; (*glasses*) (megane o)
kakeru (眼鏡を)かける *wear out* (exhaust)
hidoku tsukare saseru ひどく疲れさせる ——
n. (*clothing*) ifuku 衣服 *men's wear* shinshi-
fuku 紳士服

weary *adj.* (tired) tsukareta 疲れた; (weary of)
akiru 飽きる; (tedious) taikutsu na 退屈な

weather *n.* tenki 天気; tenkō 天候

weather bureau kishō-chō 気象庁

weather forecast tenki-yohō 天気予報

weave *v.* (interlace threads into cloth) oru 織る;
(knit) amu 編む

web *n.* (*spider*) kumo no su くもの巣

wed *v.* kekkon suru [saseru] 結婚する [させる]

wedding *n.* kekkon(-shiki) 結婚(式)

Wednesday *n.* suiyō-bi 水曜日

weed *n., v.* zassō (o nozoku) 雑草 (を除く)

week *n.* shū 週; isshūkan 一週間

a week ago isshūkan mae 一週間前

every week mai-shū 毎週

last week senshū 先週

next week raishū 来週

once a week isshūkan ni ichi-do 一週間に一度

this week konshū 今週

weekday *adj., n.* heijitsu (no) 平日 (の); uīku-dei ウイークデイ

weekend *n.* shūmatsu 週末; uīkuendo ウイークエンド

weekly *adj., adv., n.* mai-shū (no) 毎週 (の); shūkan (no) 週刊 (の)

weep *v.* (shed tears) naku 泣く; namida o nagasu 涙を流す; (mourn for) kanashimu 悲しむ

weigh *v.* mekata o hakaru 目方を計る; omosa ga...aru 重さが...ある

weight *n.* omosa 重さ; jūryō 重量

welcome *int.* irasshai いらっしゃい; yōkoso ようこそ —— *adj., n.* kangei [kantai] (sareru) 歓迎 [歓待] (される) —— *v.* kangei suru 歓迎する

You are welcome. Yoku irasshai mashita. よくいらっしゃいました; Dō itashimashite. どう致しまして

welfare *n.* (happiness) kōfuku 幸福; han'ei 繁栄; (well-being) fukuri 福利

well *adv.* yoku よく; (fully) jūbun ni 十分に; (much) zuibun ずいぶん; mā まあ; soredewa それでは

as well (equally) dōyō ni 同様に; (besides) sono-ue その上

as well as ...dōyō ...mo ...同様...も

be well off raku ni kurasu 楽に暮らす

get well yokunaru よくなる; naoru 直る

may as well ...shitemo yoi ...してもよい; shita hō ga yoi した方がよい

may well ...suru nomo mottomo da ...するのももっともだ

might as well...as... ...suru nowa ...suru no

mo dōzen da …するのは …するのも同然だ；
…suru kurai nara…shita hō ga mashida …す
るくらいなら …した方がましだ
　　speak well [ill] of …o yoku [waruku] iu …を
よく [悪く] 言う
well *n.* (deep hole dug to obtain water, oil etc.)
ido 井戸；(fountain) izumi 泉
well-being *n.* kōfuku 幸福；fukuri 福利
well-bred *adj.* sodachi no yoi 育ちのよい；jōhin
na 上品な
well-dressed *adj.* minari no yoi みなりのよい
well-educated *adj.* kyōiku no aru 教育のある
well-known *adj.* yūmei na 有名な
well-to-do *adj.* yūfuku na 裕福な
were *v.* …de atta …であった；deshita でした；
ita いた
west *n., adj.* nishi (no) 西 (の)；seibu 西部
western *adj.* nishi no 西の；seibu no 西部の；
(W-) Seiyō no 西洋の
wet *adj.* nureta ぬれた；shimetta 湿った ——
v. nurasu ぬらす
　　wet to the skin bishonure ni naru びしょぬれ
になる
whale *n.* kujira 鯨
what *adj.* (interrogative) nan no 何の；don'na
どんな；(exclamatory) nan to iu 何と言う
　　——*pron.* nani 何；nani goto 何ごと
　　What is this [that] ? Kore [Sore] wa nan desu ka? これ [それ] は何ですか.
　　What do you think about it? Sore ni tsuite dō
omoi masu ka? それについてどう思いますか.
　　What do you want? Nani ga irimasu ka? 何が
いりますか
　　What is your name? Anata no o-namae wa? あ
なたのお名前は.
　　What time is it? Nanji desu ka? 何時ですか.
wheat *n.* ko-mugi 小麦
wheel *n.* wa 輪；sharin 車輪　*steering wheel* handoru ハンドル

when *adv.* itsu いつ —— *conj.* (suru) toki ni (する) 時に; (and then) suruto sono toki するとその時

When are you going? Itsu iki masu ka? いつ行きますか

When does the train start? Kono kisha wa nanji hatsu desu ka? この汽車は何時発ですか.

whenever *adv., conj.* itsu-demo いつでも; (every time that) (suru) toki wa itsu mo (する) 時はいつも

where *adv.* doko ni [e, de] どこに [へ, で]; (in which) suru basho する場所 —— *conj.* (and there) soshite sokode そしてそこで

Where can I buy this? Kore wa doko de kaemasu ka? これはどこで買えますか.

Where can I find a telephone? Denwa wa doko ni arimasu ka? 電話はどこにありますか.

Where do you come from? O-kuni wa doko desu ka? お国はどこですか.

Where do you live? O-sumai wa dochira desu ka? お住居はどちらですか.

wherever *adv.* (tatoe) doko-demo (たとえ) どこでも

whether *conj.* (if) …ka dōka …かどうか

whether…or no izure ni seyo いずれにせよ

which *adj.* dochira no どちらの; dono どの

whichever *adj., pron.* dochira no…demo どちらの…でも; dochira demo どちらでも

while *n.* toki 時; aida 間 —— *conj.* (…suru) aida ni (…する) 間に; (although) (…de aru) noni (…である) のに

for a while shibaraku しばらく

in a little while (soon) mamonaku 間もなく

once in a while tokitama 時たま

whip *n., v.* muchi (utsu) むち (打つ) *whipping cream* nama kurīmu 生クリーム

whirl *v.* (spin rapidly) guru-guru mawaru ぐるぐる回る; (feel dizzy) me ga mawaru 目が回る —— *n.* (spinning) kaiten 回転; sempū 旋風;

(confusion of mind) (kokoro no) konran 心の混乱

whirlwind *n.* sempū 旋風; tsumuji-kaze つむじ風; tatsumaki たつ巻き

whiskey *n.* uisukī ウイスキー

whisper *v.* (speak softly) sasayaku ささやく; (soft, rustling sound) zawa-zawa oto ga suru ざわざわ音がする —— *n.* sasayaki ささやき; uwasa うわさ

whistle *n., v.* kuchibue (o fuku) 口笛 (を吹く); kiteki 汽笛; keiteki 警笛

white *adj.* (color) shiroi 白い; (pale) ao-jiroi —— *n.* (having light skin) hakujin 白人

who *pron.* dareka ga 誰かが; ...suru (tokoro no) ...する (ところの)
Who are you? Donata desu ka? どなたですか.
Who is he [she]? Kare [Kanojo] wa dare desu ka? 彼 [彼女] は誰ですか.

whole *adj.* zentai no 全体の; subete no すべての —— *n.* zembu 全部
as a whole zentai to shite wa 全体としては
on the whole gaishite 概して

wholesale *n., adj.* oroshi-uri (no) おろし売り(の)

wholesaler *n.* oroshiuri-gyōsha おろし売り業者; ton'ya 問屋; toritsugi 取次

whom *pron.* dare ni [o] 誰に [を]

whose *pron.* dare no 誰の

why *adv.* naze なぜ; dōshite どうして; ...suru riyū ...する理由

wicked *adj.* (sinful) yokoshima na よこしまな; fusei no 不正の; (spiteful) ijiwaru na 意地悪な

wide *adj.* (broad) haba no hiroi 幅の広い; (vast) kōdai na 広大な; hiro-biro to shita 広々とした

widely *adv.* hiroku 広く; hijō ni 非常に

widow *n.* mibōjin 未亡人

widower *n.* otoko-yamome 男やもめ

width *n.* haba 幅; hirosa 広さ

wife *n.* tsuma 妻; fujin 夫人

wig *n.* katsura かつら

wild *adj.* (not domescated) yasei no 野生の; (savage) yaban na 野蛮な; (violent) hageshii 激しい; (lawless) rambō na 乱暴な ——*n.* (desert) arechi 荒れ地; kōya 荒野
   grow wild yasei shite iru 野生している
   wild boar inoshishi いのしし
   wild duck kamo かも

wilderness *n.* arechi 荒れ地; kōya 荒野

will[1] *v. aux.* darō だろう; suru-tsumori するつもり

will[2] *n.* (will power) ishi 意志; (determination) ketsui 決意 ——*v.* kokorozasu 志す; (intend) shiyō to omou しようと思う
   good will kōi 好意; shinsetsu 親切
   against one's will fuhon'i nagara 不本意ながら
   free will jiyū-ishi 自由意志

will[3] *n.* (one's last will and testament) yuigon 遺言; isho 遺書

willful *adj.* (intended) kōi no 好意の; (self-willed) wagamama na わがままな

willing *adj.* (yorokonde) …suru (喜んで)…する

willow *n.* yanagi 柳

win *v.* katsu 勝つ; (gain) uru 得る

winner *n.* shōri-sha 勝利者

wind[1] *n.* (air in motion) kaze 風 *windy* kaze no tsuyoi 風の強い

wind[2] *v.* (coil) maku 巻く; (turn) mawasu 回す
   wind up maki-ageru 巻き上げる

windmill *n.* fū-sha 風車

window *n.* mado 窓

wine *n.* budō-shu ぶどう酒; wain ワイン

wing *n.* tsubasa 翼; hane 羽
   on the wing tonde 飛んで
   take wing tobi-tatsu 飛び立つ

wink *n.* (blinking) mabataki まばたき; (instant) isshun 一瞬 ——*v.* mabataki suru まばたきする

winter *n.* fuyu 冬

wipe *v.* (rub) fuku ふく; nuguu ぬぐう   *wipe out*
fukitoru ふき取る

wire *n., v.* (thread of metal) harigane 針金; (electric wire) densen 電線; (telegram) dempō (o utsu) 電報 (を打つ); (telegraph) denshin 電信
by wire dempō de 電報で
send a wire dempō o utsu 電報を打つ

wisdom *n.* chie 知恵; kemmei-sa 賢明さ

wise *adj.* kashikoi 賢い; chie no aru 知恵のある

wisely *adv.* kemmei ni 賢明に

wish *v.* nozomu 望む; …shitai …したい ———
n. negai 願い

wit *n.* kichi 機知; uitto ウイット

witch *n.* majo 魔女; (on'na no) mahō-tsukai (女の) 魔法使い

with *prep.* …to issho ni と一緒に; o mochiite を用いて

withdraw *v.* (draw back) hikkomu 引っ込む; shirizoku 退く

within *adv., prep.* …no han'i nai de …の範囲内で; (indoors) okunai ni 屋内に

without *adv., prep.* …nashi ni …なしに; (outside) …no soto de [ni] …の外で [に]; (out of doors) okugai de 屋外で
go without nashi de sumaseru なしですませる
without fail kitto きっと; kanarazu 必ず

witness *n.* (eyewitness) mokugeki-sha 目撃者; (evidence) shōko 証拠; (testimony) shōgen 証言; (one called upon to testify before a court) shōnin 証人 ——— *v.* mokugeki suru 目撃する; (give evidence) risshō suru 立証する

wolf *n.* ōkami 狼

woman *n.* josei 女性; on'na 女; fujin 婦人

womanly *adj.* on'na no 女の; on'na rashii 女らしい; yasashii 優しい

wonder *n.* (marvel) fushigi 不思議; (amazing thing) kyōi 驚異 ——— *v.* (feel surprise) odoroku 驚く; (question) …kashira to omou …かし

らと思う

wonderful *adj.* (marvelous) subarashii 素晴らしい; fushigi na 不思議な

wonderfully *adv.* subarashiku 素晴らしく; odorokuhodo 驚くほど

woo *v.* kyūkon suru 求婚する; kyūai suru 求愛する

wood *n. pl.* (forest) mori 森; ki 木; mokuzai 木材; (firewood) maki まき

wood block *n.* mokuhan 木版; hangi 版木

woodcut *n.* mokuhan (-ga) 木版 (画)

woodcutter *n.* kikori 木こり; mokuhan-shi 木版師; hanga-ka 版画家

wooden *adj.* ki no 木の; mokusei no 木製の

woodland *n., adj.* shinrin (-chi) no 森林 (地) の

woodpecker *n.* kitsutsuki キツツキ

wool *n.* yōmō 羊毛; ūru ウール; ke-orimono 毛織物

woolen *adj.* ūru no ウールの; ke-ori no 毛織の

word *n.* (speech) kotoba 言葉; go 語; (promise) yakusoku 約束; (talk) danwa 談話; (news) shirase 知らせ
in a word yōsuru ni 要するに
keep [*break*] *one's word* yakusoku o mamoru [yaburu] 約束を守る [破る]

work *n.* (labor) shigoto 仕事; rōdō 労働; (manufacture) sakuhin 作品; (book) chosaku 著作
—— *v.* hataraku 働く; benkyō suru 勉強する
at work hataraite 働いて
out of work shitsugyō shite 失業して
work out kansei suru 完成する; toku 解く

worker *n.* rōdō-sha 労働者

world *n.* (earth, universe) sekai 世界; (the public) seken 世間; (sphere) shakai 社会; kai 界
all over the world zen-sekai de 全世界で
world-wide zen-sekai ni wataru 全世界にわたる

worm *n.* mushi 虫; mimizu みみず
A worm will turn. Issun no mushi ni mo go-

bu no tamashii. 一寸の虫にも五分の魂.

worry *v.* (tease) jirasu じらす; (annoy) nayamasu
悩ます; (be troubled) shimpai suru 心配する;
(be anxious) ira-ira suru いらいらする

worse *adj.* issō warui 一層悪い
　　get worse issō waruku naru 一層悪くなる
　　what is worse (= *to make matters worse*) nao
warui koto niwa なお悪いことには

worship *v., n.* sūhai (suru) 崇拝 (する); reihai
(suru) 礼拝 (する)
　　place of worship reihai-dō 礼拝堂; (church)
kyōkai 教会

worst *adj.* mottomo warui 最も悪い; (the worst)
saiaku 最悪
　　at the worst saiaku no ba'ai demo 最悪の場合
でも
　　have [*get*] *the worst of it* makeru 負ける

worth *n., adj.* (value) kachi ga aru 価値がある
　　worth (*while*) *doing* ...suru kachi ga aru ...す
る価値がある

worthless *adj.* tsumaranai つまらない)

worthy *adj.* kachi no aru 価値のある; fusawashii
ふさわしい

would *v. aux.* ...suru darō ...するだろう; suru
tsumori de aru するつもりである; (used to)
itsumo ...shita いつも ...した; (wish) shitai し
たい
　　would rather suru hō ga mashida する方がま
しだ

wound *v., n.* (injury) fushō (saseru) 負傷 (させ
る); kega けが; (pain) kutsū 苦痛; kizu (tsukeru) 傷 (つける)　　*wounded* kizu-tsuita 傷ついた

wrap *v.* tsutsumu 包む; kurumu くるむ

wrapper *n.* hōsō-shi 包装紙; jaketto ジャケット

wreath *n.* (ring of flowers) hana-wa 花輪; wa 輪;
(curl) (kemuri no) uzumaki (煙の) 渦巻

wreck *n., v.* (shipwreck) nampa (sen) 難破 (船);
(destruction) hakai suru 破壊する; (ruin) hametsu 破滅; (be wrecked) nampa suru 難破する

wrench *v.* (twist) nejiru ねじる; (wrest) mogitoru もぎ取る; (sprain) kujiku くじく ── *n.* nejiri ねじり; (spanner) supana スパナ

wrestle *n., v.* kumiuchi (o suru) 組み打ち(をする); sumō (o toru) 相撲(をとる)

wring *v.* (twist) nejiru ねじる; (squeeze) shiboru しぼる

wrinkle *n.* shiwa しわ; hida ひだ ── *v.* shiwa o yoseru [ga yoru] しわを寄せる[が寄る]

wrist *n.* tekubi 手首

wrist watch *n.* ude-dokei 腕時計

write *v.* kaku 書く; tegami o kaku 手紙を書く
write down kaki-tomeru 書き留める
write a good [*bad*] *hand* ji ga jōzu [heta] da 字が上手[下手]だ

writer *n.* chosha 著者; sakka 作家

writing *n.* kaku koto 書くこと; shūji 習字; (handwriting) hisseki 筆跡; (document) bunsho 文書 *writing brush* fude 筆

wrong *adj.* (evil) warui 悪い; (mistaken) machigatta 間違った; (out of order) koshō no aru 故障のある ── *n.* (unjust) fusei 不正; (injury) gai 害
(be) wrong with guai ga warui 具合が悪い; …ni koshō ga aru …に故障がある
go wrong tsumi o okasu 罪を犯す; akuji o hataraku 悪事を働く

X

X-ray *n.* ekkusu-sen エックス線; rentogen レントゲン

xylophone *n.* mokkin 木琴; shirohon シロホン

Y

yacht *n., v.* yotto (o sōjū suru) ヨット (を操縦
する)

yard *n.* (cf. garden) niwa 庭; (ground around a
building) kōnai 構内; (measure of length) yādo
ヤード

yarn *n.* (spun strand of cotton etc.) ito 糸; (tale)
monogatari 物語

yawn *n., v.* akubi (o suru) あくび (をする)

year *n.* toshi 年; nen 年; sai 歳; *pl.* (age) nenrei
年齢
 all the year round ichi-nen-jū 一年中
 every other year ichi-nen-oki ni 一年置きに
 last year kyonen 去年; sakunen 昨年
 next year rainen 来年
 this year kotoshi 今年
 year after year nen-nen 年々

yearbook *n.* nen-kan 年鑑; nempō 年報

yearly *adj.* mainen no 毎年の; nen ikkai no 年
一回の

yeast *n.* īsuto イースト; kōbo 酵母

yell *v.* (shout) sakebu 叫ぶ; wameku わめく ――
n. sakebi-goe 叫び声; ēru エール

yellow *n., adj.* (color) ki-iro (no) 黄色 (の); (egg)
kimi 黄身

yes *adv.* hai はい; ē ええ; sōdesu そうです
 say yes hai to iu はいと言う; shōchi suru 承知
する

yesterday *n., adv.* kinō 昨日; sakujitsu 昨日
 the day before yesterday issaku-jitsu 一昨日; o-
totoi おととい
 yesterday evening saku-ban 昨晩; yūbe ゆうべ

yet *adv.* mada まだ; mō もう; shikashi しかし
 as yet mada まだ; ima-made no tokoro dewa
今までのところでは

yield *v.* (produce) sanshutsu suru 産出する;

(grant) yurusu 許す; (give) ataeru 与える; (give way) makeru 負ける —— *n.* (product) sanshutsu 産出; (output) sangaku 産額

yolk *n.* tamago no kimi 卵の黄身

you *pron.* (*subjective case*) anata ga [wa] あなたが[は]; kimi ga [wa] 君が[は]; anata-tachi [-gata] ga [wa] あなたたち[方]が[は]; (*objective case*) anata o [ni] あなたを[に]; kimi ni [o] 君に[を]; anata-gata [-tachi] o [ni] あなた方[たち]を[に]; kimi-tachi o [ni] 君たちを[に]

young *adj.* (youthful) wakai 若い; (immature) mijuku na 未熟な

youngster *n.* wakamono 若者; shōnen 少年

your *pron.* (*possessive case*) anata no あなたの; kimi no 君の; anata-gata [-tachi] no あなた方[たち] の; kimi-tachi no 君たちの

yours *pron.* anata no mono あなたのもの; kimi no mono 君のもの; anata-gata [-tachi] no mono あなた方[たち]のもの; kimi-tachi no mono 君たちのもの

yourself *pron.* anata [kimi]-jishin あなた[君]自身

youth *n.* seinen 青年; seishun 青春

youthful *adj.* wakai 若い; waka-waka shii 若々し

Z

zero *n.* zero ゼロ; rei 零

zigzag *adj.* ziguzagu ni ジグザグに; une-une to うねうねと

zinc *n.* aen 亜鉛; (*roofing*) totan トタン

zipper *n.* zippā ジッパー; chakku チャック

zone *n.* chitai 地帯; tai 帯

zoo *n.* dōbutsu-en 動物園

zoology *n.* dōbutsu-gaku 動物学

合図 signal, sign *aizu suru* ～する sig- make a sign

未 taste, savor, flavor *aji ga yoi* [*warui*] がよい [わるい] taste good [bad]

[ajiki]-nai 味気ない wearisome, weary, , wretched

au 味わう taste, appreciate, enjoy

赤 red, crimson, scarlet *akai* ～い red

赤字 red figures, deficit *akaji ni naru* ～ なる show a loss, go into the red

mbō 赤ん坊 baby

ri 明り light, lamp *akari o tsukeru* [*kesu*] をつける [消す] turn on [off] the light

rui 明るい bright, light, cheerful, sunny

ruku naru 明るくなる brighten up

gata 明け方 dawn

eru あける open, unlock, empty (a box), clear (a room)

秋 autumn, fall

bin 空びん empty bottle

iraka na 明らかな clear, plain, evident, obvious

irameru あきらめる give up, resign oneself to

ireru あきれる be amazed, be dumbfounded, be shocked

kiru あきる grow tired (of), become weary (of), lose interest (in)

kisu (nerai) 空巣 (ねらい) sneak-thieving, sneak (thief)

kiya 空家 vacant [empty] house, house to let

kkenai あっけない unsatisfying, too short

kogareru あこがれる long for [after], yearn for

aku 開く open, be vacated, become empty, be free

aku 悪 wrong, vice

akubi あくび yawning, yawn *akubi suru* ～ する yawn

akui 悪意 ill will

JAPANESE-ENGLISH

abareru あばれる act vio
abiru 浴びる pour upon
ふろを～ bathe
abunai 危ない dangerous,
abura 油 oil; 脂 fat
aburae 油絵 oil painting
aburamushi 油虫 cockroacl
achira kochira (=achi ko
[あちこち] here and there
adana あだ名 nickname
adokenai あどけない innoce
aete あえて daringly *aete*
venture
afureru あふれる overflow, b
agaru 上がる rise, enter, eat
ageru あげる raise, elevate,
ago あご jaw, chin
agohige あごひげ beard
ahiru あひる (domestic) duck
ai 愛 love, affection *ai suru* ～
affection for
aida 間 interval, distance, betweer
during, while *aidagara* ～柄 re
aikagi 合鍵 duplicate key
aikawarazu 相変らず as usual, as
aikyō 愛きょう charms *aikyō no*
る charming, attractive
aima 合間 interval, leisure
aimai na あいまいな vague, ambigu
ainiku あいにく unfortunately, unlu
ainoko あいの子 half-blood, mixed bl
aisatsu あいさつ greeting, salutatioı
suru ～する greet, recognize
aite 相手 companion, mate, the oth
opponent

aizu
aizu
nal
aji
～ア
ajike
fla
ajiw
aka
akaj
に
aka
aka
～
aka
aka
ake
ake
c
aki
ak
ak
ak
ak
ak
a
a
a

akuma 悪魔 evil spirit, devil, demon

akunin 悪人 bad [wicked] man, villain

akushu 握手 handshake

ama 海女 woman diver

ama(san) 尼(さん) nun

amaeru 甘える behave like a spoilt child, coax

amagaeru 雨がえる tree frog, green frog

amai 甘い sweet, sugary

ama-no-gawa 天の河 the Milky Way

ama-no-jaku 天のじゃく perverseness, perverse person

amari 余り the remainder, the rest, the surplus

amarini あまりに too, too much

amaru 余る remain, be over

ame 雨 rain *ame ga furu* ～が降る rain falls, it is raining *ame ga yamu [agaru]* ～が止む [上がる] the rain leaves off [stops] *niwaka ame* にわか雨 shower

ame あめ wheat gluten *amedama* ～玉 taffies, toffees

ami 網 net *ami no me* ～の目 meshes (of the net)

amimono 編み物 knitting, crochet

amma あんま massage

amu 編む knit, braid

ana 穴 hole

anata (wa) あなた(は) you *anata no* ～の your *anata o [ni]* あなたを[に] you

ane 姉 elder sister, older sister

angai 案外 unexpectedly, contrary to expectation

angō 暗号 code, cipher

ani 兄 elder brother, older brother

anji 暗示 hint, suggestion *anji suru* ～する hint, suggest

anjiru 案じる be anxious (about, for), worry about

anki suru 暗記する learn by heart, memorize

an'na あんな such, like that, that

an'nai 案内 guidance, invitation *an'nai suru* ～する guide, conduct

ano あの that, those *ano toki* ～時 then

ansei 安静 rest, repose

anshin 安心 peace of mind *anshin suru* ～する feel easy

antei 安定 stability, steadiness, composure

anzen 安全 safety, security *anzen·ni* ～に safely

anzen-chitai 安全地帯 safety zone

anzu あんず apricot

ao(i) 青(い) blue, azure, pale

aoba 青葉 green leaves

aogu あおぐ fan

aogu 仰ぐ look up

aomukeni あおむけに on one's back

aozameru 青ざめる turn pale *aozameta* 青ざめた pale, sallow

aozora 青空 blue sky

apāto アパート apartment

appaku 圧迫 pressure, oppression *appaku suru* ～する oppress

arare あられ hail

arasagashi あら捜し fault finding

arashi 嵐 storm, tempest

arasoi 争い dispute, argument, quarrel

arasou 争う dispute, quarrel, compete

arasuji 荒筋 outline, synopsis

aratana 新たな new, fresh *aratani* 新たに newly, again

arau 洗う wash, cleanse

arawareru 現れる come out, appear

arawasu 現す show, indicate, express

arayuru あらゆる all, every

ari あり ant

arigatō 有難う thank you

aru 有る[在る] there is [are], have

aruku 歩く walk

asa 朝 morning

asagao 朝顔 morning-glory

asahi 朝日 morning sun

asai 浅い shallow, early

asameshi(=**asagohan**) 朝飯[朝御飯] breakfast

asanebō 朝寝坊 late riser

asatte あさって the day after tomorrow

ase 汗 sweat, perspiration *ase o kaku* ～をか
く sweat, perspire

aseru 焦る be hasty, be in a hurry

ashi 足 foot, leg

ashiato 足跡 footprint

ashidai 足代 transportation expenses

ashikubi 足首 ankle

ashioto 足音 sound of footsteps

ashita(=**asu**) あした[あす] tomorrow

asobi 遊び play, game

asobu 遊ぶ play, amuse oneself

asoko あそこ over there, that place

assari あっさり simply, plainly, easily

ataeru 与える give

atama 頭 head

atarashii 新しい new, fresh

atari 辺り neighborhood, surroundings, direction

atarimae 当たり前 proper, right

ataru 当る hit, strike, guess right

atatakai 暖かい warm, mild

atatameru 暖める warm (up)

atchi(=**achira**) あっち[あちら] (over) there

ate 当て aim, end, object
   ate ni suru ～にする expect, look forward to
   ate ga hazureru ～が外れる be disappointed,
   miss one's aim
   ate ni naru [*naranai*] ～になる[ならない]
   [un]reliable, [un]certain

atena(=**atesaki**) 宛名[宛先] address

ateru 当てる apply, hold, place, put on, hit,
strike, touch, guess

ateru あてる address, direct

ato 跡 mark, trace

ato 後 back, rear, next, after **ato de** ～で afterwards, later

atokatazuke suru 後片付けする put in order, clear away

atoshimatsu 後始末 settlement **atoshimatsu suru** ～する settle

atsui 熱い hot, heated

atsui 暑い hot, sultry

atsui 厚い thick, heavy

atsukamashii 厚かましい shameless, unabashed

atsukau 扱う treat, manage, deal with

atsumari 集まり collection, gathering, meeting

atsumaru 集まる gather, come together

atsuraeru あつらえる order (an article)

atsuryoku 圧力 pressure, stress

atsusa 暑さ heat, hot weather

au 会う see, meet with, come across

au 合う agree with, fit, suit, be correct

awa 泡 bubble, foam

aware 哀れ pathos, sorrow, pity **aware na** ～な sad, poor, pitiful, sorrowful

awaseru 合わせる put together, join together, unite, combine, sum up

awasete 併せて all together, all told

awatadashii 慌ただしい busy, bustling, hurried **awatadashiku** 慌ただしく hurriedly, hastily

awatemono 慌て者 flighty person, hasty person

awatete 慌てて confusedly, in a hurry

ayafuyana あやふやな uncertain, vague

ayamachi 過ち fault, error

ayamari 誤り error, mistake

ayamaru 謝る apology, make an apology, beg (one's) pardon

ayamatte 過って by mistake, in error, by accident

ayame あやめ blue iris

ayashii 怪しい doubtful, suspicious, dubious

ayatsuri ningyō 操り人形 marionette, puppet

ayatsuru 操る handle, manage

ayumiyori 歩み寄り mutual concessions

azakeru あざける deride, sneer, ridicule

azayakana 鮮やかな vivid, bright, fine

azukaru 預かる keep, receive in trust, take charge of, take care of, look after

azukeru 預ける place in custody, deposit with, put in charge of *nimotsu o azukeru* 荷物を ～ check one's baggage

azuki 小豆 red beans

B

ba'ai 場合 occasion, time, case ...*no ba'ai (ni) wa* ...の～(に)は in the case of, in the event of

bachi 罰 divine punishment, retribution *bachi ga ataru* ～が当る be punished by Heaven

bai 倍 double, twice, two times

baibai 売買 buying and selling, purchase and sale

baikin ばい菌 bacillus, bacteria

baiten 売店 stand, stall

baiyaku 売約 sales contract *baiyaku-zumi* ～ 済み "SOLD"

baka ばか fool *baka ni* ～に absurdly, terribly *baka na* ～な foolish *bakarashii* ～ら しい ridiculous *baka ni suru* ～にする make a fool of *baka-banashi* ～話 silly talk

bakemono 化け物 ghost, goblin

baketsu バケツ bucket

bakkin 罰金 fine, penalty

bakuchi ばくち gambling

bakudai na ばく大な vast, huge, enormous

bakudan 爆弾 bomb

bakugeki 爆撃 bombing *bakugeki suru* ～す る bomb

bakuhatsu 爆発 explosion *bakuhatsu suru* ～ する explode, burst

bakuzen to shita 漠然とした vague, ambiguous

bamen 場面 scene, situation, place

bammeshi(=**bangohan**) 晩飯[晩御飯] supper, dinner

ban 晩 evening, night

ban 番 turn, order, number, watch, guard

bane バネ spring

bangō 番号 number *bangō-fuda* 〜札 numbered ticket *bangō-jun ni* 〜順に in numerical order

bangumi 番組 program, list *tokubetsu bangumi* 特別〜 feature program

banken 番犬 watch dog, guard dog

bankuruwase 番狂わせ upset, surprise *bankuruwase no* 〜の unexpected

ban'nen 晩年 (in) one's later years, late in life

ban'nin 番人 keeper, watchman

bansan 晩さん dinner, supper

banshū 晩秋 late autumn

banshun 晩春 late spring

bansō 伴奏 accompaniment *bansō suru* 〜する play an accompaniment

bansōkō ばんそうこう adhesive plaster

bara バラ rose

bara-bara ni ばらばらに in drops, in pieces, separately

basha 馬車 carriage, coach, (horse-drawn) cab

basho 場所 place, spot, location

bassuru 罰する punish, penalize

batsu 罰 punishment, penalty

batsugun no 抜群の distinguished

Beikoku 米国 (United States of) America

bekkan 別館 annex

ben 便 convenience, facility

bengi 便宜 convenience, benefit

bengo 弁護 defense, advocacy *bengo suru* 〜する speak in defense of, advocate

bengoshi 弁護士 lawyer, solicitor *komon bengoshi* 顧問〜 legal adviser

beni(-iro) 紅(色) red, crimson

benjo 便所 lavatory, toilet (room), water closet

benkai 弁解 explanation, excuse *benkai suru* 〜する explain, excuse oneself

benkyō 勉強 study, lesson *benkyō suru* 〜する study, work hard

benri 便利 convenience, handiness, facilities *benri na* 〜な convenient, useful

bentō 弁当 portable lunch

bessō 別荘 villa, second house

betsu 別 *betsu no* 〜の another, different, separate *betsu ni* 〜に separately, extra

betsu-betsu 別々 *betsu-betsu no* 〜の separate *betsu-betsu ni* 〜に separately, apart

bi 美 beauty, fineness

bijin 美人 beauty, pretty girl

bijutsu 美術 art, fine arts *bijutsu-kan* 〜館 art museum

bikkuri びっくり surprise *bikkuri suru* 〜する be surprised (at) *bikkuri saseru* 〜させる surprise, astonish

bimbō 貧乏 poverty *bimbō na* 〜な poor

bin 便 chance, opportunity, mail, post

bin びん bottle, jar

biru ビル building

biru ビール beer

bishō 微笑 smile

biyōin 美容院 beauty salon[parlor]

bō 棒 stick, rod, pole

bochi 墓地 graveyard

bōei 防衛 defense *bōei suru* 〜する defend, protect

bōeki 貿易 trade, commerce *bōeki suru* 〜する trade

bōenkyō 望遠鏡 telescope *tentai bōenkyō* 天体〜 astronomical telescope *hansha bōenkyō* 反射〜 reflecting telescope

bōfū 暴風 storm *bōfū-ken* 〜圏 storm zone *bōfū-u* 〜雨 rainstorm

bōgai 妨害 disturbance, obstruction, interruption *bōgai suru* 〜する disturb, interrupt

bōgyo 防御 defense *bōgyo suru* 〜する defend, guard, protect

bōken 冒険 adventure

bokin 募金 fund-raising *bokin suru* 〜する collect contributions

bokō 母校 one's old school, alma mater

bokoku 母国 one's mother country

boku ぼく I *bokura* 〜ら we

bokujō 牧場 stock farm, pasture

bokushi 牧師 pastor, minister, clergyman

bōmei 亡命 *bōmei suru* 〜する flee from one's own country *bōmei-sha* 〜者 refugee, exile

bon 盆 tray, the Buddhist Feast of Lanterns

bōnenkai 忘年会 year end party

bonsai 盆栽 potted plant

bon'yari ぼんやり vacant, stupid, vague, absentminded

boro ぼろ rags *boro no* 〜の ragged

bōru-bako ボール箱 cardboard box

bōru-gami ボール紙 cardboard

bōryoku 暴力 violence *bōryokudan* 〜団 tough gang

bōsan 坊さん Buddhist priest

bōshi 帽子 cap, hat

boshū 募集 levy, invitation, registration *boshū suru* 〜する invite, raise

bōsui no 防水の waterproof

botan ボタン button

botan ぼたん (*tree*) peony

boya ぼや small fire

buai 歩合 rate, ratio, percentage, commission

buaisō na 無愛想な unsociable, inhospitable

bubun 部分 part, portion *dai-bubun* 大〜 a large part (of) *bubun-teki ni* 〜的に partially

bubunhin 部分品 parts, accessories

budō ブドウ grapes

budōshu ブドウ酒 wine

buenryo 無遠慮 unscrupulousness

buji 無事 peace, safety *buji na* ～な safe, peaceful *buji ni* ～に well, safely, in peace

bujoku 侮辱 insult *bujoku suru* ～する insult

buka 部下 subordinate, under-officer

buki 武器 arms, weapons

bukiyō na 不器用な clumsy

bukka 物価 prices

bukkyō 仏教 Buddhism

bumbōgu 文房具 writing materials, stationery *bumbōgu-ya* ～屋 stationer

bummei 文明 civilization, culture *bummeikoku* ～国 civilized country

bumpai 分配 distribution *bumpai suru* ～する distribute

bumpō 文法 grammar

bun 文 writing, sentence, composition

bungaku 文学 literature, letters

bunka 文化 culture, civilization *bunkajin* ～人 cultured man

bunkai 分解 analysis *bunkai suru* ～する analyse

bunryō 分量 quantity, measure

bunshō 文章 sentences, writing, composition

buntsū 交通 correspondence *buntsū suru* ～する correspond (with)

bun'ya 分野 division, field, sphere

buranko ブランコ swing, trapeze *buranko ni noru* ～に乗る swing

burashi ブラシ brush

buratsuku ぶらつく stroll, ramble

burei 無礼 impoliteness

buriki ブリキ tin (plate)

busahō 無作法 bad manners *busahō na* ～な ill-mannered, rude

busshi 物資 goods, resources, material

buta 豚 pig *butaniku* ～肉 pork

butai 舞台 stage *butai-geki* ～劇 stage drama

butsukaru ぶつかる strike, bump

butsurigaku 物理学 physics, physical science
byō 秒 second
byō びょう rivet, tack
byōbu びょうぶ folding screen
byōdō 平等 equality, parity *byōdō no* ～の equal
byōin 病院 hospital, nursing home
byōki 病気 illness, sickness *byōki no* ～の ill, sick
byōnin 病人 sick person, invalid
byōshin 秒針 second hand

C

cha(=**o-cha**) 茶[お茶] tea *cha-no-yu* ～の湯 tea ceremony
cha-iro 茶色 light brown
chakujitsu na 着実な steady, sound
chakuriku 着陸 landing *chakuriku suru* ～する land, make a landing
chakuseki suru 着席する take a seat, sit down
cha-no-ma 茶の間 living-room, sitting-room
chanto ちゃんと quite, perfectly, well
chasaji 茶さじ teaspoon
chawan 茶わん teacup, rice bowl
chi 血 blood *chi ga deru* ～が出る bleed
chian 治安 public peace
chibi ちび tot, kid
chichi 乳 milk, breast
Chichūkai 地中海 Mediterranean Sea
chie 知恵 wisdom, sense, intelligence *chie no aru* ～のある wise, intelligent
chigai 違い difference, distinction *...ni chigai nai* ...に～ない must(be), certainly, surely
chigai-hōken 治外法権 ex(tra)-territoriality
chigau 違う be different (from), differ, change, be mistaken [wrong]
chiheisen 地平線 horizon

chihō 地方 district, the country

chii 地位 status, rank, situation, position, post

chiiki 地域 region, area, zone

chiisai 小さい little, small, tiny, young

chiji 知事 (prefectual, local) governor

chijimu 縮む shrink, contract, be shortened

chijin 知人 acquaintance, friend

chijō 地上 *chijō no* 〜の terrestrial, earthly

chika 地下 *chika no[ni]* 〜の[に] subterranean, underground

chikagoro 近ごろ nowadays, lately, recently

chikai 近い near, close by *chikai uchi ni* 〜うちに shortly, before long

chikai 誓い oath, pledge

chikaku 近く shortly, near

chikamichi 近道 short cut

chikara 力 strength, force, might, power, energy *chikara-zuyoi* 〜強い forcible

chikatetsu 地下鉄 subway, underground, tube

chikau 誓う swear, vow, take an oath

chikazuku 近付く approach, draw near *chikazuki ni naru* 近付きになる make acquaintance, get acquainted with

chikoku suru 遅刻する be late (for school *etc.*), be behind time

chiku 地区 area, region, district, zone

chikyū 地球 the earth, the globe

chimei 地名 place name

chimeishō 致命傷 fatal wound, death blow

chimmoku 沈黙 silence *chimmoku suru* 〜する be silent, hold one's tongue *chimmoku saseru* 〜させる silence

chingin 賃銀 wages, pay

chinō 知能 mental faculties, intellect, intellectual power, intelligence

chinomigo 乳飲み子 suckling (child), infant

chinretsu 陳列 exhibition, show, display *chinretsu suru* 〜する exhibit, display *chinretsudai* 〜台 display stand

chintai(＝**chingashi**) 賃貸 [賃貸し] lease, letting out *chintai suru* 〜する lease, rent, hire out

chintsū no 鎮痛の soothing *chintsū-zai* 鎮痛剤 anodyne

chippoke na ちっぽけな very small, tiny

chirakasu 散らかす scatter, put in disorder

chiri 地理 geography, topography

chiri ちり dust, dirt, rubbish, trash

chirigami ちり紙 toilet paper, bumf

chiritori ちり取り dustpan

chiru 散る fall, scatter, spread

chiryō 治療 medical treatment *chiryō suru* 〜する treat, cure

chisei 知性 intellect, intelligence

chishiki 知識 knowledge, information *chishiki-kaikyū* 〜階級 the educated classes, the intelligentsia

chitsujo 秩序 order, system *chitsujo o tamotsu* 〜を保つ keep order *chitsujo ga midarete iru* 〜が乱れている be in disorder

chittomo ちっとも (not) at all

chizu 地図 map, atlas

chōbo 帳簿 book, register *chōbo ni ki'nyū suru* 〜に記入する enter in a book *chōbo o tsukeru* 〜をつける keep accounts [books]

chochiku 貯蓄 saving *chochiku suru* 〜する save

chōchin ちょうちん (paper) lantern

chōchō ちょうちょう butterfly

chōfuku 重複 repetition, duplication *chōfuku suru* 〜する overlap, repeat

chōgō 調合 compounding, mixing *chōgō suru* 〜する compound, prepare, mix

chōhōkei 長方形 rectangle, oblong

chōin 調印 signature, signing *chōin suru* 〜する sign

chōjo 長女 eldest daughter

chōjō 頂上 top, summit

chōka 超過 excess, surplus *chōka suru* 〜する exceed

chokin 貯金 saving *chokin suru* 〜する save money

chokkaku 直角 right angle

chokkei 直径 diameter

chokkō suru 直行する go direct

chōkō 徴候 sympton, sign

chōkoku 彫刻 carving, sculpture

chokumen suru 直面する face, (be) confronted (with)

chokusen 直線 straight line

chōkyori 長距離 long distance *chōkyori denwa* 〜電話 long distance (call)

chomei na 著名な notable, celebrity

chōmiryō 調味料 seasoning condiments

chōnan 長男 eldest son

chōri 調理 cooking *chōri suru* 〜する cook

chōsei 調整 regulation, adjustment *chōsei suru* 〜する regulate, adjust

chōsen 挑戦 challenge, defiance *chōsen suru* 〜する challenge, defy

chōshi 調子 key, tone, tune, condition

chōshin 長針 minute hand

chōsho 長所 merit, strong good point, virtue

chōshoku 朝食 breakfast

chōshū 聴衆 audience

chōtsugai ちょうつがい hinge

chotto ちょっと just a moment, for a moment, a little

chōwa 調和 harmony *chōwa suru* 〜する harmonize (with), be in harmony

chōyaku 跳躍 spring, jump *chōyaku suru* 〜する jump, leap

chozō 貯蔵 storage, storing *chozō suru* 〜する store, preserve *chozōko* 〜庫 store house

chū 中 middle, average, in, within, during, while, under

chūburu no 中古の used, second-hand

chūcho ちゅうちょ hesitation *chūcho suru* 〜する hesitate

chūdoku 中毒 poisoning *chūdoku suru* 〜する be poisoned

chūgen 中元 the last day of the Lantern Festival, mid year present gift

Chūgoku 中国 China *Chūgoku-go* 〜語 Chinese *Chūgoku ryōri* 〜料理 Chinese dishes

chūi 注意 attention, care *chūi suru* 〜する be careful of, take care of, pay attention to

chūjien 中耳炎 tympanitis

chūjitsu 忠実 faithfulness *chūjitsu na* 〜な faithful *chūjitsu ni* 〜に faithfully

chūkan 中間 middle

chūkoku 忠告 advice, counsel *chūkoku suru* 〜する advise, counsel

chūmoku 注目 attention, observation *chūmoku suru* 〜する pay attention to, watch *chūmoku subeki* 〜すべき remarkable

chūmon 注文 order, request *chūmon suru* 〜する order

chūnen 中年 middle age *chūnen no hito* 〜の人 middle aged person

chūō 中央 center, middle, heart *chūō no* 〜の central, middle

chūritsu 中立 neutrality *chūritsu no* 〜の neutral

chūsan kaikyū 中産階級 bourgeoisie, middle class

chūsei 中世 Middle Ages, medieval times

chūsen 抽選 (lot) drawing, lotterry *chūsen suru* 〜する draw lots

chūsha 注射 injection *chūsha suru* 〜する inject

chūsha 駐車 parking *chūsha suru* 〜する park *chūsha-jō* 〜場 car park, parking lot *chūsha kinshi* 〜禁止 "No Parking"

chūshi 中止 discontinuance, suspension *chūshi suru* 〜する stop, suspend, discontinue

chūshin 中心 center, focus, core *chūshin-ten* ～点 the central point

chūshō 中傷 slander, defamation *chūshō suru* ～する slander, defame

chūshō kigyō 中小企業 minor small enterprises

chūshoku 昼食 lunch, luncheon

chūto de 中途で halfway, midway

D

dai 題 subject, theme, topic

dai 台 stand, rest, rack

daibubun 大部分 majority, greater part

daibutsu 大仏 large image of Buddha

daidokoro 台所 kitchen, cuisine *daidokoro dōgu* ～道具 kitchen utensils

daigaku 大学 university, college

daihyō 代表 representation, representative *daihyō suru* ～する represent

dai-ichi 第一 first, number one *dai-ichi no ~* ～の first, primary

daijin 大臣 minister (government)

daiji na 大事な important, valuable *daiji ni suru* 大事にする think much of

daijōbu 大丈夫 all right, safe, certainly, surely

daikon 大根 large white radish

daiku 大工 carpenter

dai-ni 第二 the second, number two

dairi 代理 procuration, representation, substitute

dai-san 第三 third

daitai 大体 outline, approximately, roughly *daitai ni* ～に generally

daitan 大胆 boldness *daitan na* ～な bold, impudent

daitasū 大多数 large majority (of)

daitōryō 大統領 president

daizu 大豆 soybean

dakara だから so, therefore, because, as, since

-dake …だけ only, no more, merely

daku 抱く hold in one's arms, embrace

damaru 黙る be silent, hold one's tongue *damatte* 黙って without a word, silently

damasu だます deceive, cheat

dambō 暖房 heating

dambōru 段ボール corrugated cardboard

dame 駄目 useless, in vain, *dame ni naru* ～になる fail, fall through *dame ni suru* ～にする spoil, ruin

dan 段 step, stair, terrace, stage

dan-dan だんだん gradually, little by little, step by step

dangan 弾丸 shot, bullet

dangen 断言 affirmation *dangen suru* ～する declare, affirm

danjo 男女 man and woman, both sexes *danjo kyōgaku* ～共学 co-education

danketsu 団結 union *danketsu suru* ～する band, unite

dansei 男性 male, man

dantai 団体 group, organization *dantai kōdō* ～行動 united action *dantai ryokō* ～旅行 group trip

danwa 談話 talk, conversation

dan'yū 男優 actor

-darake …だらけ full of, filled with

daraku 堕落 corruption, degeneration *daraku suru* ～する be corrupted *daraku shita* ～した corrupt, fallen

darashi nai だらしない slovenly, sloppy, loose *darashi naku* だらしなく loosely, sloppily

dare 誰 *dare ga* ～が who *dare no* ～の whose *dare o* ～を whom

dareka 誰か someone, somebody, anyone, anybody

-darō …だろう think [suppose, guess], perhaps, maybe, probably

dassen 脱線 derailment *dassen suru* 〜する (be) derailed

dasu 出す take [put] out

dāsu ダース dozen

datō na 妥当な proper, right, reasonable

deau 出合う meet, come across

deguchi 出口 way out, exit

dekakeru 出かける go out, start, set off

dekiagaru でき上がる finished, completed, ready

dekiai できあい ready-made

dekigokoro でき心 sudden impulse *dekigokoro de* 〜で on the spur of the moment

dekigoto できごと event, accident, affair, happening

dekimono(=odeki) できもの [おでき] boil, swelling

dekiru できる can, be able to *dekiru-dake* 〜だけ as much as possible *dekireba* できれば if possible

dekishi 溺死 drowning *dekishi suru* 〜する be drowned

dekoboko でこぼこ unevenness *dekoboko no* 〜の uneven, rough

demo デモ demonstration

dempō 電報 telegram, wire *dempō o utsu* 〜を打つ send a telegram *shikyū dempō* 至急電報 urgent telegram

demukae 出迎え meeting, reception *demukaeru* 〜る receive, meet

denki 電気 electricity. *denki no* 〜の electric, electrical *denki o tsukeru[kesu]* 〜をつける[消す] put on [off] the light

denki 伝記 life story, biography

denryoku 電力 electric power

densen 電線 electric wire

densen 伝染 contagion, infection *densen-byō* 〜病 communicable disease *densen suru* 〜する be contagious [infectious]

densetsu 伝説 tradition, legend

densha 電車 electric train, streetcar, tram
 densha de iku 〜で行く go by train, take a train
 densha ni noru [kara oriru] 〜に乗る［から降りる］ get on [off] the car
 densha-chin 〜賃 carfare

dentō 電灯 light, electric light

dentō 伝統 tradition *dentō-teki na [ni]* 〜的な［に］ traditional [ly]

denwa 電話 telephone, phone
 denwa o kakeru 〜かける (tele)phone, call, call [ring] up
 denwa o kiru 〜を切る hang up, ring off
 kōshū-denwa 公衆〜 public telephone (booth, box)

denwa-chō 電話帳 telephone book [directory]

denwa-kōkanshu 電話交換手 telephone operator

depāto デパート department store

deru 出る go [come, get] out, be present, leave

deshabaru でしゃばる push oneself forward
 deshabari でしゃばり impertinent fellow

deshi 弟子 pupil, disciple

-deshō …でしょう (I) think [suppose], (I) hope, (I) guess

detarame でたらめ at random, in disorder

dewa では then, in that case, if so

do 度 degree, times

dō 銅 copper

dō 胴 body, trunk

dō どう how *dō attemo* 〜あっても in any case, at all costs *Dō itashi mashite.* 〜致しまして. Not at all; Don't mention it; You are welcome.

dobu どぶ ditch, gutter

dōbutsu 動物 animal *dōbutsu-gaku* 〜学 zoology

dōbutsuen 動物園 zoo

dochira どちら which

dochira ka どちらか either, whichever

dochira mo どちらも both, either, neither

dodai 土台 foundation, basis, base

dōdō to 堂々と imposingly, grandly **dōdō taru** 堂々たる imposing, grand, stately

dōfū suru 同封する enclose **dōfū-butsu** 同封物 enclosure

dōgu 道具 tool, implement, instrument **dōgu-bako** ～箱 tool-box

dōgyōsha 同業者 fellow businessman

dōhan suru 同伴する go with, accompany **dōhan-sha** 同伴者 companion

dōi 同意 consent, assent **dōi suru** ～する consent [agree] to **dōi-go** ～語 synonym

Doitsu ドイツ Germany **Doitsu-go** ～語 German **Doitsu-jin** ～人 German

dōitsu 同一 sameness, identity **dōitsu no** ～の the same

dōji ni 同時に at the same time

dōjō 同情 sympathy, compassion **dōjō suru** ～する sympathize

dōka どうか please, kindly …**ka dōka** …か～ if, whether

dōkan 同感 same opinion, agreement **dōkan de aru** ～である agree with

dōki 動悸 palpitation of the heart **dōki ga suru** (= **doki-doki suru**) ～がする [どきどきする] palpitate, beat, throb

dōki 動機 motive

dokkito suru どきっとする feel a shock, be shocked (at, by), give a start

doko どこ where, what place **dokoka (ni)** ～か(に) somewhere **doko kara** ～から from where **doko to naku** ～となく vaguely

doku 毒 poison **yūdoku no** 有毒の poisonous

dokugaku 独学 self-study, self-education **dokugaku suru** ～する study by oneself

dokuji no 独自の original, personal, unique

dokuritsu 独立 independence *dokuritsu no ~* の independent *dokuritsu suru ~する* be independent *dokuritsu-koku ~国* independent country

dokuryoku de 独力で for oneself, single-handed

dokusen 独占 monopoly, exclusive possession *dokusen suru ~する* monopolize

dokusha 読者 reader, subscriber

dokushin 独身 bachelorhood

dokusho 読書 reading *dokusho suru ~する* read

dokutoku no 独得の peculiar, characteristic, original

dōkyo suru 同居する live together

dōkyūsei 同級生 classmate

dōmei 同盟 alliance, league, union *dōmei suru ~する* ally with, unite

dōnika どうにか somehow, in some way or other

don'na(= **dono yō na**) どんな [どのような] what, what kind of *don'na koto ga atte mo ~ことがあっても* whatever happens, under any circumstances

don'na ni(= **dono kurai**) どんなに [どのくらい] how (much), however, how long, how far, how large

dono どの which, what

dore どれ which *dore demo ~でも* any, whichever *dore hodo* [*dake*] ~ほど [だけ] how much [many] *dore ka ~か* any, some, either *dore mo ~も* any, all, every, neither

dōri 道理 reason, truth *dōri de ~で* indeed, no wonder

doro 泥 mud, mire *doro-darake no ~だらけの* muddy *doro o haku ~吐く* confess (one's crime)

dōro 道路 road, way, street *yūryō-dōro* 有料 ~ toll road

dorobō 泥坊 thief, theft

doru ドル dollar *5 [go] doru shihei* 5 ドル紙幣 five-dollar bill [note]

dōryō 同僚 colleague, comrade

doryoku 努力 endeavor, effort *doryoku suru* ～する endeavor, make efforts

dōsa 動作 action, movement(s), motion

dōsei 同姓 same name

dōsei 同性 same sex

dōseki suru 同席する sit together *dōseki-sha* 同席者 those present, the company

doshaburi 土砂降り pouring rain, downpour

dōshita どうした what *Dōshita no desuka?* ～のですか. What is the matter? *dōshita wake [mono] ka* ～わけ [もの] か somehow

dōshite どうして how, why

dōshite mo どうしても by all means, at all costs

dōsō 同窓 classmate, schoolmate, graduate *dōsō-kai* ～会 alumni association

dosoku de 土足で with one's shoes on

dosshiri shita どっしりした heavily-built, stout, massive

dote 土手 bank

dōtoku 道徳 morality, morals *dōtoku no* ～の moral

dotto どっと suddenly, all together

dōyō 動揺 trembling, quake *dōyō suru* ～する tremble, quake

dōyō 童謡 nursery rhyme

doyō-bi 土曜日 Saturday

dōyō no 同様の the same, similar *dōyō ni* ～に equally, similarly

E

e 絵 picture, painting *e o kaku* ～をかく draw [paint] a picture

e 柄 handle

e へ to, for, into, in

ebi えび *ise-ebi* 伊勢～ lobster, *kuruma-ebi* 車～ prawn *ko-ebi* 小～ shrimp

eda 枝 branch *ō-eda* 大～ bough *ko-eda* 小～ twig

egaku 描く draw, picture, paint

egao 笑顔 smiling face, smile

ehagaki 絵はがき picture post card

ehon 絵本 picture book

eien 永遠 eternity *eien no*[*ni*] ～の[に] permanent, eternal(ly), forever

eiga 映画 cinema, movie *eiga-kan* ～館 movie theater

Eigo 英語 English, English language

eigyō 営業 business, trade

Eikoku 英国 England, Great Britain *Eikoku no* ～の English, British *Eikoku-jin* ～人 Englishman, the English

eikyō 影響 influence, effect *eikyō suru* ～する influence, affect

eikyū 永久 eternity *eikyū no* ～の permanent, eternal *eikyū ni* ～に eternally, forever

eiyō 栄養 nutrition *eiyō no aru* ～のある nutritious *eiyōfuryō* ～不良 undernourishment

eiyū 英雄 hero

eki 駅 (railroad) depot, (railway) station

ekichō 駅長 station-master

ekubo えくぼ dimple

emban 円盤 disk

empitsu えんぴつ pencil *iro-empitsu* 色～ colored pencil *empitsu o kezuru* ～を削る sharpen a pencil

empō 遠方 great, long distance *empō no* ～の distant

en 円 circle, yen

en 縁 relation, connection

enchō 延長 extension *enchō suru* ～する extend, lengthen

endan 縁談 proposal of marriage

endō(mame) えんどう(豆) pea

enjo 援助 assistance   *enjo suru* ～する support, help

enkai 宴会 dinner(party), banquet   *enkai o hiraku* ～を開く hold a dinner party

enki 延期 postponement   *enki suru* ～する postpone

en'nichi 縁日 fair, fete day

enogu 絵具 paints, colors   *enogu o nuru* ～を塗る paint

enryo 遠慮 reserve, hesitation   *enryo suru* ～する hesitate, be reserved   *enryo naku* ～なく without reserve   *enryo-bukai* ～深い modest, shy

enshi(gan) 遠視(眼) long-sightedness

ensō 演奏 performance   *ensō suru* ～する play, perform   *ensō-kai* ～会 concert, recital

ensoku 遠足 excursion, picnic

entotsu 煙突 chimney, (ship's) funnel

enzetsu 演説 speech   *enzetsu suru* ～する make a speech

epuron エプロン apron

erabu 選ぶ choose, prefer

erai 偉い great, grand   *erasō ni* 偉そうに proudly

eri 襟 neckband, collar

erigonomi suru えり好みする be fastidious [particular]

erimaki 襟巻 muffler, scarf

erinuki no えり抜きの picked, choice, select

eru 得る set, have, obtain, earn, gain

esa えさ food, feed, bait

F

fū 封 seal   *fū o suru* ～をする seal   *fū o kiru* ～を切る break the seal

fuan 不安 anxiety, uneasiness   *fuan na* ～な uneasy, anxious

fuben 不便 inconvenience *fuben na* 〜な inconvenient

fubo 父母 parents, father and mother

fubuki 吹雪 showstorm, blizzard

fuchi 縁 edge, bank, margin, rim

fuchi ふち (deep) pool, deep water

fuchō 不調 rupture, failure, bad condition

fuchōwa 不調和 inharmony, discord(ance) *fuchōwa na* 〜な inharmonious, discordant

fuchūi 不注意 carelessness *fuchūi na* [*ni*] 〜な [に] careless [ly]

fuda 札 card, ticket, tag, bill

fudan no ふだんの usual, ordinary

fude 筆 writing brush, pen *fude bushō* [*mame*] 〜不精 [まめ] bad [good] correspondent

fūdo 風土 natural features, climate

fudōsan 不動産 immovable property, real estate

fudōtoku 不道徳 immorality *fudōtoku na* 〜な immoral

fue 笛 flute, whistle, pipe *fue o fuku* 〜を吹く play the flute

fueisei na 不衛生な unhealthy, insanitary

fueru 増える increase, multiply

fuete 不得手 one's weak point

fūfu 夫婦 husband and wife, a married couple

fugō 符号 mark, sign, symbol

fugō 富豪 rich man, millionaire

fugōkaku ni naru 不合格になる be rejected, fail (in the examination)

fugōri na 不合理な irrational, unreasonable

fugu 不具 deformity *fugu-sha* 〜者 cripple, deformed person

fugu ふぐ puffer, blowfish

fugū 不遇 misfortune *fugū na* 〜な unfortunate

fuhai 腐敗 putrefaction *fuhai suru* 〜する rot, addle

fuhei 不平 discontent, complaint *fuhei no aru*

~のある discontented *fuhei o iu* ~を言う grumble, complain

fuhen no 不変の unchangeable, invariable

fui no [ni] 不意の [に] sudden [ly], unexpected [ly]

fuiuchi 不意打ち surprise attack *fuiuchi o kuwasu* ~をくわす take by surprise

fuji 藤 wisteria *fuji-iro* ~色 light purple

fujin 婦人 woman, lady *fujinka-i* ~科医 gynecologist

fujin 夫人 wife, Mrs.

fujiyū 不自由 inconvenience *fujiyū na* ~な inconvenient

fujūbun na 不十分な insufficient, not enough

fukai 深い deep, profound, close *fukaku* 深く deeply

fukai na 不快な unpleasant, disagreeable

fukanō 不可能 impossibility *fukanō na* ~な impossible

fukanzen 不完全 imperfection *fukanzen na* ~な imperfect, incomplete

fukasa 深さ depth

fukasu ふかす steam, puff, smoke

fukazake 深酒 heavy drinking *fukazake suru* ~する drink heavily

fuke ふけ dandruff, scurf

fukei 父兄 parents (and brothers)

fūkei 風景 landscape, scenery

fukeiki 不景気 bad [hard] times, depression *fukeiki na* ~な dull, depressed

fukeizai na 不経済な uneconomical

fukenkō 不健康 unhealthiness *fukenkō na* ~な unhealthy

fukenzen na 不健全な unhealthy, unwholesome

fukeru 老ける grow old, age

fukeru 耽ける be addicted to, be absorbed in

fuketsu na 不潔な uncleanly, dirty

fukidasu 吹き出す begin to blow, burst out laughing, spout

fukidemono 吹き出物 eruption, rash

fukigen 不きげん displeasure, bad humor *fukigen na* ～な ill-humored, displeased

fukin ふきん dish cloth, napkin

fukin 付近 neighborhood, environs *fukin no* ～の neighboring

fukinshin 不謹慎 imprudence *fukinshin na* ～な imprudent

fūkiri 封切り release *fūkiri-kan* ～館 first runner

fukisoku 不規則 irregularity *fukisoku na* ～な irregular

fukitsu 不吉 ill omen *fukitsu na* ～な unlucky

fukitsukeru 吹き付ける spray, blow against

fukkatsu 復活 revival, rebirth *fukkatsu suru* ～する revive *Fukkatsu-sai* ～祭 Easter

fukkō 復興 revival, restoration *fukkō suru* ～する be revived

fukō 不幸 misfortune, ill-luck, disaster, death *fukō na[nimo]* ～な[にも] unfortunate[ly]

fūkō 風光 scenery, views

fukōhei na 不公平な partial, unfair

fukō na 不孝な undutiful, disobedient

fuku 吹く blow, breathe, puff off

fuku 拭く wipe

fuku 服 clothes, dress, uniform

fuku 福 happiness, good luck, fortune *fuku no kami* ～の神 the god of wealth

fuku 副 vice-, sub-, by-

fukuin 福音 the (Christian) gospel *fukuin-sho* ～書 the Gospels

fukuji 服地 cloth, dress material

fukujū 服従 obedience, submission *fukujū suru* ～する obey

fukumu 含む have in one's mouth, bear in mind, include

fukuramaseru 膨らませる swell, bulge

fukureru 膨れる swell, rise, be sulky, pout

fukuro 袋 bag, sack *fukuro no nezumi* ～の ねずみ a mouse in a trap

fukurō ふくろう owl

fukusei 複製 reproduction *fukusei suru* ～する reproduce, reprint

fukusha 複写 reproduction, copy *fukusha suru* ～する copy, reproduce

fukushū 復しゅう revenge, vengeance *fukushū suru* ～する revenge oneself, take vengeance

fukushū 復習 review *fukushū suru* ～する go over one's lesson

fukusō 服装 dress, clothes

fukutsū 腹痛 stomach ache, colic

fukuzatsu 複雑 complexity *fukuzatsu na* ～な complicated *fukuzatsu ni naru* ～になる be complicated, become complex

fukyū 普及 diffusion, spread *fukyū suru* ～する diffuse, popularize *fukyū-ban* ～版 popular [cheap] edition

fumajime na 不まじめな insincere

fumanzoku 不満足 discontent *fumanzoku na* ～な dissatisfied

fumbetsu 分別 discretion, wisdom, good sense

fumei na(=**fumeiryō na**) 不明な[不明瞭な] indistinct, obscure, vague

fumeiyo na 不名誉な dishonorable, disgraceful

fumetsu no 不滅の immortal

fumikiri 踏切り railway crossing

fumoto ふもと foot (of a mountain), foothill

fumu 踏む step on, tread on, go through

fun ふん excrement, feces

fun 分 minute

funanori 船乗り seaman, sailor

funare na 不慣れな inexperienced

funatabi 船旅 sea trip, voyage

funayoi 船酔い seasickness *funayoi suru* ～する get seasick

fune 船 boat, ship, vessel, steamer *fune ni noru* ～に乗る get[go] on board

fungai suru 憤慨する resent, be indignant

fun'iki 雰囲気 atmosphere

funinjō 不人情 unkindness **funinjō na** ～な unkind, unhuman

funka 噴火 eruption **funka suru** ～する erupt **funka-kō** ～口 crater **funka-zan** ～山 volcano

funsō 紛争 trouble, dispute

funsui 噴水 fountain, jet

funsuru 扮する act [play] the part of

funtō 奮闘 fight, struggle **funtō suru** ～する fight, struggle

fureru 触れる touch, refer to, be against, infringe

furi 不利 disadvantage, handicap **furi na** ～な disadvantageous, unfavorable

furikaeru ふり返る turn [look] round, look back

furiko 振り子 pendulum

fūrin 風鈴 wind [hanging] bell

furi o suru ふりをする pretend, affect

furo 風呂 bath, hot-bath **furo-ya** ～屋 bathhouse, public bath

furoku 付録 supplement

furoshiki 風呂敷 wrapping cloth

furu 降る fall, come down, drop

furu 振る wave, shake, reject

furueru 震える shiver, shake, tremble

furuhon 古本 second-hand book **furuhon-ya** ～屋 second-hand bookstore

furui 古い old, ancient, aged, used

furui ふるい sieve **furui ni kakeru** ～にかける sift, screen, weed out

furumau 振舞う behave (oneself), conduct oneself

fūsa 封鎖 blockade, blocking

fusagu 塞ぐ fill, block, occupy

fusagu ふさぐ be depressed, mope

fusai 夫妻 husband and wife, a (married) couple

fusai 負債 debt, loan

fusansei 不賛成 disapproval, disagreement

fusawashii ふさわしい suitable, becoming, worthy

fusegu 防ぐ depend, protect, prevent

fusei 不正 injustice, wrong

fuseikaku 不正確 inaccuracy *fuseikaku na* ～な inaccurate

fuseikō 不成功 failure *fuseikō no* ～の unsuccessful

fūsen 風船 balloon

fuseru 伏せる lie down, turn in, turn down

fushi 節 joint, knuckle, air, tune

fushigi 不思議 mystery, wonder *fushigi na* ～な strange, mysterious *fushigi ni omou* ～に思う wonder

fushinsetsu 不親切 unkindness *fushinsetsu na* ～な unkind

fushizen na 不自然な unnatural, artificial

fushō 負傷 injury, wound *fushō suru* ～する be injured

fushōchi 不承知 disapproval, disagreement

fushōjiki 不正直 dishonesty *fushōjiki na* ～な dishonesty

fūshū 風習 manners, customs

fusoku 不足 shortage, want, discontent

fusuma ふすま sliding door

futa ふた lid, cover

futago 双子 twins

futan 負担 burden, responsibility, charge *futan suru* ～する beat *futan-gaku* ～額 share, allotment

futari 二人 two persons, a pair, a couple

futatabi 再び again, once more

futatsu 二つ two *futatsu to nai* ～とない unique, matchless

futegiwa na 不手際な clumsy, unskillful

futeiki no 不定期の irregular

futei no 不定の unsettled, uncertain

futekitō na 不適当な unfit, unsuitable

fūtō 封筒 envelope

futoi 太い big, thick *futoi koe* 〜声 deep voice

futoji 太字 bold (-face) type

futon 布団 bedding, bedclothes *kake-buton* 掛け〜 quilt *shiki-buton* 敷き〜 mattress

futoru 太る put on weight, grow fat, fatten

futsū 普通 *futsū no [ni]* 〜の [に] common [ly], usual [ly], ordinary [-rily] *futsū ijō [ika]* 〜以上 [以下] above [below] average

futsū 不通 suspension, interruption *futsū ni naru* 〜になる be suspended [stopped]

futsuka-yoi 二日酔い hangover

fu'un 不運 misfortune *fu'un na [nimo]* 〜な [にも] unfortunate [ly]

fuwa 不和 discord, disagreement

fuyasu 増やす increase, add

fuyōi na 不用意な imprudent, careless

fuyō no 不要の useless, of no use

fuyu 冬 winter

fuyukai na 不愉快な unpleasant, disagreeable

fuzoku no 付属の attached, belonging to

G

gabyō 画びょう thumbtack, drawing pin

gai 害 injury, harm, damage *gai suru* 〜する harm, injure *gai no aru* 〜のある harmful, bad

gaibu 外部 the outside, exterior *gaibu no* 〜の outside, exterior

gaika 外貨 foreign currency

gaiken 外見 appearance *gaiken wa* 〜は in appearance, apparently

gaikō 外交 diplomacy *gaikō mondai* 〜問題 diplomatic question *gaikō seisaku* 〜政策 diplomatic policy *gaikō-kan* 〜官 diplomat

gaikoku 外国 foreign country *gaikoku-go* 〜語 foreign language *gaikoku-jin* 〜人 foreigner

gaikotsu がい骨 skeleton

gaimu-daijin 外務大臣 Minister of Foreign Affairs *gaimu-shō* 外務省 the Foreign (Ministry) Office

gairo 街路 street, road

gairon 概論 introduction, outline

gaisan suru 概算する make a rough estimate, estimate roughly

gaishutsu suru 外出する go out

gaitō suru 該当する fall [come] under, correspond to

gaiyū suru 外遊する go on a foreign tour, travel abroad

gaka 画家 painter, artist

gake がけ precipice, cliff

gakka 学課 one's lesson, school work

gakka 学科 subject, course of study, curriculum

gakkari suru がっかりする be disappointed

gakki 楽器 musical instrument

gakki 学期 term, semester

gakkō 学校 school, college *gakkō tomodachi* ～友達 school-mate

gaku 額 tablet, framed picture *gaku-buchi* ～縁 picture frame

gakuchō 学長 president of a school

gakufu 楽譜 score, musical notation

gakuhi 学費 school expenses

gakumon 学問 learning, study

gakunen 学年 school year

gakureki 学歴 school career

gakusei 学生 student *gakusei jidai* ～時代 school days

gakusha 学者 scholar

gaman 我慢 patience, endurance *gaman suru* ～する bear, stand *gaman-zuyoi* ～強い patient

gambaru 頑張る hold out, stand firm

gampeki 岸壁 wharf, quay

gan 雁 wild goose

gan 癌 cancer

gangu 玩具 toy, plaything

ganjitsu 元日 New Year's Day

ganjō na [ni] 頑丈な[に] strong [ly], stout [ly], solid [ly]

ganka 眼科 ophthalmology *ganka-i* ～医 oculist

ganko 頑固 *ganko na* ～な obstinate, stubborn

ganrai 元来 originally, really

gan'yaku 丸薬 pill

gappei 合併 combination *gappei suru* ～する combine, unite, merge

gara 柄 pattern, design, build

garakuta がらくた rubbish, trash, junk

garari to がらりと quite, entirely, suddenly

garasu ガラス glass, pane *mado-garasu* 窓～ windowpane

garō 画廊 picture gallery

gashi 餓死 death from hunger *gashi suru* ～する be starved to death

gasshō 合唱 chorus *gasshō suru* ～する sing together [in chorus]

gatchiri to がっちりと firmly, tightly

gat(t)en 合点 understanding, comprehension *gat(t)en no ikanai* ～のいかない incomprehensible

geijutsu 芸術 art, fine arts

gejun 下旬 the last ten days, latter part of a month

geka-i 外科医 surgeon *geka-iin* ～院 surgery

geki 劇 drama, play

gekirei suru 激励する urge, encourage, cheer up

gekitsū 激痛 acute [sharp] pain

gekiyaku 劇薬 dangerous [powerful] drug

gekkan 月刊 monthly publication, monthly (magazine)

gekkyū 月給 (monthly) salary *gekkyū-bi* ～日 payday

gemmitsu na [ni] 厳密な[に] strict[ly], close [ly]

gendai 現代 present age [day], modern times, today

gendo 限度 limit, limitation

genetsuzai 解熱剤 antifebrile, febrifuge

gengo 言語 language

gen'in 原因 cause, origin *gen'in suru* ～する be caused by, result from

genjitsu 現実 actuality *genjitsu no* [ni] ～の [に] actual [ly], real [ly] *genjitsu-teki na* ～ 的な realistic

genjō 現状 the present state [situation]

genkai 限界 limit, bounds

genkaku na 厳格な strict, stern, severe

genkan 玄関 entrance, entryway

genki 元気 vigor, spirit, energy, vitality *genki na* ～な vigorous *genki o tsukeru* ～をつけ る encourage, cheer up

genkin 現金 cash, ready money *genkin de* ～ で in cash *genkin-barai* ～払い cash payment

genkō 原稿 manuscript, copy

genryō 原料 (raw) material(s)

gensaku 原作 original *gensaku-sha* ～者 original author

genshi 原子 atom *genshi bakudan* ～爆弾 atomic bomb

genshi 原始 beginning, origin *genshi-teki na* ～的な primitive *genshi-jidai* [-jin] ～時代 [人] primitive times [man]

genshoku 原色 primary color

genshō suru 減少する decrease, decline, diminish

genshu suru 厳守する observe [keep] strictly *jikan o genshu suru* 時間を～ be punctual

gensō 幻想 illusion, vision

gensoku 原則 principle, rule *gensoku to shite* ～として as a rule

gentei suru 限定する limit, restrict

genzai 現在 today, the present time

geppu 月賦 monthly installment

geppu げっぷ *geppu ga deru* 〜が出る belch

gesha suru 下車する get off, get out *tochū gesha* 途中下車 stopover

geshuku 下宿 lodging *geshuku suru* 〜する lodge *geshuku-ya* 〜屋 boarding [lodging] house

getsumatsu 月末 end of the month

getsuyō-bi 月曜日 Monday

gichō 議長 president, chairman

gikai 議会 Diet, Parliament, Congress

gikō 技巧 art (ifice), craft

gikyoku 戯曲 drama, play

gimon 疑問 question, doubt *gimon no* 〜の doubtful

gimu 義務 duty, obligation *gimu-kyōiku* 〜教育 compulsory education

gin 銀 silver

ginkō 銀行 bank

ginkonshiki 銀婚式 silver wedding anniversary

ginō 技能 skill, ability

ginzaiku 銀細工 silver work

giri 義理 duty, obligation, justice

giron 議論 discussion, argument *giron suru* 〜する argue, discuss

gisei 犠牲 sacrifice, victim

gishi 技師 engineer

gishiki 儀式 ceremony, rite

gisshiri ぎっしり tight [ly], close [ly] *gisshiri tsumeru* 〜詰める fill up

go 五, 5 five *go-bamme* 〜番目 fifth

gobu-gobu no 五分五分の even, fifty-fifty

goei suru 護衛する guard, escort

gōgai 号外 extra (newspaper)

gogaku 語学 language study, linguistics

go-gatsu 五月 May *go-gatsu no sekku* 〜の節句 Boy's Festival

gogo 午後 afternoon, p. m.

gohan 御飯 boiled rice, meal

gōin ni 強引に by force, in a high-handed way

gōjō na 強情な obstinate, stubborn, stiff

gojū 五十, 50 fifty

gokai 誤解 misunderstanding *gokai suru* ～する misunderstand

gōkaku 合格 success *gōkaku suru* ～する pass, be successful *gōkaku-sha* ～者 successful candidate

gokaku no 互角の even, equal, close

gōka na 豪華な splendid, gorgeous

gōkei 合計 total, sum total *gōkei suru* ～する sum [add] up

goku ごく very, extremely, awfully

gokuraku 極楽 Paradise, heaven

goma ごま sesame

gomakasu ごまかす cheat, deceive

gōman na ごうまんな arrogant, haughty

gomen nasai ごめんなさい Excuse me; I am sorry; I beg your pardon.

gomi ごみ dust, rubbish, trash

gomu ゴム gum, rubber *keshi-gomu* 消し～ eraser

goraku 娯楽 pastime, recreation, amusement

gōrei suru 号令する order, command

gōri-teki na 合理的な rational, logical, reasonable

-goro ～ごろ about, towards, around

gota-gota ごたごた confusion, trouble *gota-gota suru* ～する be in confusion *gota-gota o okosu* ～を起す raise trouble

gōtō 強盗 burglar, robber

gottagaesu ごったがえす be in confusion

gōu 豪雨 heavy rain, downpour

gozen 午前 morning, a. m.

guai 具合 condition, state

gumbi 軍備 military preparations, armaments

gun 軍 army, force

gunshū 群衆 crowd of people

guratsuku ぐらつく totter, shake, waver

gururi ぐるり circumstance, surroundings

gussuri ぐっすり *gussuri neru* 〜寝る sleep soundly

gūsū 偶数 even number

gutai-teki na 具体的な concrete *gutai-teki ni* 具体的に concretely

gūzen 偶然 chance, accident *gūzen no[ni]* 〜の[に] accidental[ly], by chance

guzu-guzu ぐずぐず *guzu-guzu suru* 〜する be tardy, be slowgoing *guzu-guzu iu* 〜いう grumble, complain

gyakkōka 逆効果 counter result, contrary effect

gyaku 逆 opposite, reverse *gyaku no[ni]* 〜の[に] converse[ly] *gyaku ni suru* 〜にする reverse, invert

gyaku-modori 逆もどり relapse, reversion

gyakutai 虐待 ill-treatment *gyakutai suru* 〜する ill-treat, maltreat

gyōgi 行儀 manners, behavior *gyōgi no yoi [warui]* の良い[悪い] well-[ill-] mannered

gyogyō 漁業 fishery, fishing industry

gyōji 行事 regular functions

gyōmu 業務 business

gyōretsu 行列 procession, queue, line

gyorui 魚類 fishes

gyōsei 行政 administration

gyōseki 業績 achievements, results

gyosen 漁船 fishing boat

gyūniku 牛肉 beef

gyūnyū 牛乳 milk

H

ha 歯 tooth *ha no* 〜の dental *haisha* 〜医者 dentist *ha ga itamu* 〜が痛む have a toothache

ha 葉 leaf
ha 刃 edge, blade
haba 幅 width, breadth
habataku 羽ばたく flap the wings, flutter
habuku 省く cut down, abridge, omit
hachi 八, 8 eight
hachi 鉢 bowl, pot
hachi 蜂 bee *hachi no su* ～の巣 (bee)hive
hachi-gatsu 八月 August
hachimitsu 蜂蜜 honey
hachūrui は虫類 reptiles
hada 肌 skin *hada-gi* ～着 underwear, underclothes
hadaka 裸 *hadaka no* ～の bare, naked *ha-*
daka ni naru ～になる strip, become naked
hadashi はだし bare feet
hade na 派手な gay, showy, gaudy
hae はえ fly
hagaki 葉書 postcard *ōfuku-hagaki* 往復～
return postcard
hage はげ baldness
hagemasu 励ます encourage, cheer up
hageshii 激しい violent, furious, severe
haguki 歯茎 gums
hagureru はぐれる lose, get lost
haguruma 歯車 cogwheel, gear
haha 母 mother
hahen 破片 fragment, splinter
hai 肺 lungs
hai 灰 ashes *hai-iro* ～色 gray
haiboku 敗北 defeat, reverse
haibun suru 配分する distribute
haien 肺炎 pneumonia
haifu suru 配布する distribute
haigo 背後 back, rear *haigo ni* ～に behind,
at the back of
haigō 配合 combination, harmony
haikei 背景 background, setting
hairu 入る enter, come in, get in, join

haisen 敗戦 lost battle, defeat

haishi 廃止 abolition *haishi suru* 〜する a-
bolish, abandon

haitatsu 配達 delivery *haitatsu suru* 〜する
deliver, distribute

haitō 配当 allotment *haitō suru* 〜する allot
haitō-kin 〜金 dividend

haiyaku 配役 cast

haiyū 俳優 actor

haizara 灰皿 ash tray

haji 恥 shame, disgrace *haji o kaku* 〜をかく
disgrace oneself *haji o kakaseru* 〜をかかせ
る put (a person) to shame *haji shirazu no* 〜
知らずの shameless

hajiku はじく flip, fillip, snap

hajimaru 始まる begin, start

hajime 初め beginning, origin *hajime no* 〜
の first, initial, early *hajime ni* 〜に at the
beginning, first *hajime wa* 〜は at first *hajimete* 〜て for the first time *hajime kara* 〜
から from the first [beginning]

hajimeru 始める begin, commence, open, start

hajiru 恥じる be ashamed, feel humbled, blush

haka 墓 grave, tomb

hakadoru はかどる progress *hakadoranai* は
かどらない make little progress

hakai 破壊 destruction *hakai suru* 〜する destroy, break *hakai-teki na* 〜的な destructive
hakai-ryoku 〜力 destructive power *hakai-
sha* 〜者 destroyer

hakari はかり balance, scales

hakaru 計る [測る] measure, size, weigh, gauge

hakase 博士 doctor

hakidasu 吐き出す vomit, spit out, puff out

haki-haki shita はきはきした quick, smart *haki-haki shinai* はきはきしない slow, dull, in-
active

hakken 発見 discovery *hakken suru* 〜する
discover, find

hakkiri はっきり *hakkiri shita* 〜した clear, distinct *hakkiri shinai* 〜しない be unsettled

hakki suru 発揮する exhibit, display, show

hakkō 発行 publication, issue *hakkō suru* 〜する publish, issue

hako 箱 box, case, carton

hakobu 運ぶ carry, transport

haku 履く put on, wear

haku 掃く sweep

haku 吐く vomit, spit

hakuchō 白鳥 swan

hakuchū 白昼 broad daylight, the daytime *hakuchū ni* 〜に in broad daylight, in the daytime

hakuhatsu 白髪 gray [white] hair

hakui 白衣 white robe

hakujin 白人 white man

hakujō 白状 confession *hakujō suru* 〜する confess, own, avow

hakujō 薄情 cold-[hard-] heartedness *hakujō na* 〜な unfeeling, heartless, cold-hearted

hakuran-kai 博覧会 exhibition, exposition, fair

hakuryoku 迫力 force *hakuryoku no aru* 〜のある forceful, powerful

hakusha 拍車 spur

hakushi 白紙 white paper

hakushi 博士 doctor

hakushoku 白色 white color *hakushoku-jin-shu* 〜人種 the white race, white people

hakushu suru 拍手する clap (one's hands)

hama 浜 beach, sandy beach

hamaki 葉巻 cigar

hambai 販売 sale, selling

hambun 半分 half

hameru はめる put on, pull on, get in, fix into

hametsu 破滅 ruin, destruction

hami-dasu [**-deru**] はみ出す [出る] protrude, jut out, be forced out

hamigaki 歯みがき tooth-paste, tooth-powder,

dentifrice ***neri-hamigaki*** 練り〜 dental cream

hamono 刃物 edged tool, cutlery

han 判 stamp, seal

hana 花 flower, blossom

hana 鼻 nose

hanabanashii 華々しい splendid, brilliant, glorious

hanabi 花火 fireworks, firecracker

hanahada 甚だ very, greatly

hanaji 鼻血 nosebleed

hanami 花見 flower-viewing, cherry-blossom-viewing

hanamizu 鼻水 snivel, nasal discharge

hanamuko 花婿 bridegroom

hanareru 離れる leave, separate, part from

hanashi 話 talk, conversation, fact, reason

hanashiai 話し合い consultation, negotiation

hanasu 話す talk, converse, tell, state, mention

hanasu 離す part, separate, keep apart

hanasu 放す let go, release, set

hanataba 花束 bouquet, nosegay

hanawa 花輪 wreath

hana-ya 花屋 florist

hanayaka na 華やかな gay, bright, brilliant, gorgeous, colorful

hanayome 花嫁 bride

handan 判断 judgment, decision ***handan suru*** 〜する judge

hane 羽 feather

haneru 跳ねる leap, spring, jump

hanetsukeru はねつける refuse, reject

hanga 版画 print, woodcut [woodblock] print

hangaku 半額 half amount, half price

han'i 範囲 extent, scope, limits, bounds

hanikamu はにかむ shy, bashful ***hanikami-ya*** はにかみ屋 bashful person

hanji 判事 judge, justice

hanjō suru 繁盛する prosper, be prosperous

hankachi ハンカチ handkerchief

hankan 反感 antipathy, ill feeling
hankei 半径 radius, semi-diameter
hanketsu 判決 judgment
hanko 判子 stamp, seal
hankō 反抗 resistance, opposition
hankō 犯行 crime, offence
hankyō 反響 echo, repercussion, influence, reflection
han'nin 犯人 criminal
han'nō 反応 reaction, response
hanran はんらん inundation, flooding *hanran suru* ～する overflow, flood
hansei 反省 reflection *hansei suru* ～する reflect on, reconsider
hansen 帆船 sailing vessel [ship, boat], sailboat
hansha 反射 reflection *hansha suru* ～する reflect
hansū 半数 half
hantai 反対 opposition, resistance, objection, reverse, opposite, contrary *hantai suru* ～する be opposite to, be against *hantai ni* ～に the other way, on the contrary
hantei 判定 judgment, decision *hantei suru* ～する judge, decide
hanten はん点 spot, speck, dot
hantō 半島 peninsula
hanzai 犯罪 crime, guilt
happyō 発表 announcement, publication, statement *happyō suru* ～する announce
hara 腹 abdomen, belly, stomach *hara ga itai* ～が痛い have a stomach ache
hara-hara はらはら *hara-hara ochiru* ～落ちる flutter down *hara-hara suru* ～する feel uneasy, be afraid
haraise 腹いせ revenge *haraise ni* ～に by way of revenge
haran 波らん disturbance, trouble
harappa 原っぱ field
harau 払う pay, clear, sweep, wipe off

harawata はらわた intestines, entrails, guts

hare 晴れ clear [fair, fine] weather

haremono はれもの swelling boil

harenchi 破廉恥 shamelessness, infamy *harenchi na* ～な shameless

hareru はれる swell *hareta* はれた swollen

hareru 晴れる clear(up), become clear

haretsu 破裂 explosion, burning *haretsu suru* ～する burst, erupt

hari 針 needle, pin, hook, hand(of watch or gauge)

hariau 張り合う rival, emulate

harikiru 張り切る be enthusiastic

haru 春 spring *haru-same* ～雨 spring rain

haru 貼る stick, paste, affix

haru 張る stretch, tighten

haru-baru はるばる from afar

haruka ni はるかに far, far away [off], by far, by a long way

hasama-ru [-reru] 挟まる[れる] get between, be caught in, get jammed in

hasami はさみ scissors

hasamu 挟む insert, contain, put between

hasan 破産 insolvency, bankruptcy *hasan suru* ～する become bankrupt, fail

hashi 橋 bridge

hashi はし chopsticks

hashi 端 end, tip, edge *hashi kara hashi made* ～から～まで from end to end

hashigo はしご ladder

hashika はしか measles

hashira 柱 pillar, column

hashiru 走る run, rush, dash

hason 破損 damage, breakdown *hason suru* ～する be damaged, break down

hassei 発生 occurrence, origination *hassei suru* ～する occur, happen

hassha 発射 discharge, firing *hassha suru* ～する discharge, fire, shoot

hassha suru 発車する leave, start, depart

hasshin suru 発信する send a letter [telegram], cable *hasshin-nin* ～人 sender

hassō 発送 sending, forwarding, dispatch, shipping *hassō suru* ～する send out, forward, ship, dispatch

hasu はす lotus

hata 旗 flag, banner

hatachi 二十(歳) twenty years of age

hatake 畑 field, farm

hataku はたく dust, beat, strike

hataori 機織 weaving, weaver

hataraki 働き work, labor, action, working, activity

hataraku 働く work, labor

hatashite 果たして just as one thought, as was expected

hatasu 果たす carry out, accomplish, achieve, attain, finish, discharge

hate 果て end, extremity, limit

hateshinai 果てしない endless *hateshinaku* 果てしなく endlessly

hatoba 波止場 wharf, quay

-hatsu ～発 departure, leaving

hatsu 初 the beginning, the first

hatsubai 発売 sale *hatsubai suru* ～する sell *hatsubai-chū* ～中 be on sale

hatsudenki 発電機 dynamo, generator

hatsuiku 発育 growth, development *hatsuiku suru* ～する grow, develop

hatsukoi 初恋 one's first love, calf love

hatsumei 発明 invention *hatsumei suru* ～する invent

hatsuon 発音 pronunciation *hatsuon suru* ～する pronounce

hattatsu 発達 development, growth, progress, advance *hattatsu suru* ～する develop, grow

hatten 発展 expansion, extension *hatten suru* ～する develop, grow, expand

hau はう crawl, creep

haya-ashi 早足 quick pace, quick steps *haya-ashi de* ～で at a quick pace

hayaga(t)ten 早合点 hasty conclusion

hayai 早い［速い］ quick, fast, speedy, rapid, early

hayaku 早く quickly, fast, rapidly, in haste, soon, immediately

hayakuchi 早口 rapid speaking, quick speaking

hayaoki 早起き early rising *hayaoki suru* ～する get up early

hayaru はやる be in fashion, be popular, prosper, flourish

hayasa 早［速］さ quickness, swiftness, rapidity

hayashi 林 wood, forest, grove

hazubeki 恥ずべき disgraceful, shameful

hazukashigaru 恥ずかしがる be［feel］shy

hazukashii 恥ずかしい be shamed, shy

hazumu 弾む spring, bound

hazureru 外れる be［come］off, be［get］out of place

hazusu 外す take off, remove, unfasten

hebi 蛇 snake, serpent

hei 塀 wall, fence

heibon na 平凡な common, ordinary

heigai 弊害 evil, abuse, vice

heigen 平原 plain, prairie

heijitsu 平日 weekday *heijitsu-dōri* ～通り as usual

heika 陛下 His［Her］Majesty

heikai 閉会 closing *heikai-shiki* ～式 closing ceremony *heikai suru* ～する close

heiki 兵器 arms, weapon

heikin 平均 average *heikin shite* ～して on the average

heikō 平行 parallelism, parallel *heikō-sen* ～線 parallel lines

heikō suru 閉口する be embarrassed

heimen 平面 plane, surface

heisei 平静 calm, quiet, peace *heisei na* 〜な calm, quiet

heishi 兵士 soldier

heiwa 平和 peace *heiwa na[ni]* 〜な[に] peaceful[ly]

heiya 平野 plain

hekomi へこみ dent, hollow, depression

hekomu へこむ sink, become hollow

henji 返事 reply, answer, response *henji suru* 〜する reply, answer

henka 変化 change, variation *henka suru* 〜する change, turn *henka no aru* 〜のある varied

henken 偏見 prejudice

henkyaku 返却 return, repayment *henkyaku suru* 〜する return, give back

hen na 変な strange, odd, funny

henshin 返信 reply, answer

henshū 編集 editing *henshū suru* 〜する edit *henshū-sha* 〜者 editor

herasu 減らす decrease, reduce, shorten, cut

heri へり edge, brink, rim, brim, hem

heru 減る decrease, diminish, lessen, reduce

heru 経る pass, go through *...o hete* ...を経て by the way of, via

heso へそ navel, umbilicus

heta na 下手な unskillful, poor

heto-heto へとへと *heto-heto ni naru* 〜になる be dead[dog] tired, be done up

heya 部屋 room

hi 火 fire, flame

hi 日 day *hibi no* 日々の daily, everyday

hiatari 日当り *hiatari no yoi[warui]* 〜のよい[悪い] [un]sunny

hibari ひばり skylark

hibi ひび crack, chap

hibiki 響き sound, echo

hidari 左 left *hidari-gawa* 〜側 left side *hidari-gitcho[-kiki]* 〜ぎっちょ[利き] left-handed person

hidoi ひどい severe, hard, heavy, violent

hidoku ひどく cruelly, severely, badly

hieru 冷える grow [get] cold

hifu 皮膚 skin

higaeri 日帰り *higaeri suru* ～する go and return in one day

higai 被害 damage, injury

higashi 東 east

hige ひげ *kuchi-hige* 口～ moustache *ago-hige* あご～ beard *hoho-hige* ほほ～ whiskers *hige o soru* ～をそる shave

higeki 悲劇 tragedy

higure 日暮れ nightfall

hihan 批判 criticism *hihan suru* ～する criticize

hihyō 批評 criticism, critique, review *hihyō suru* ～する criticize, comment, review

hiji ひじ elbow

hijō ni 非常に very, so, extremely

hikaeme no 控え目の moderate, temperate

hikaku 比較 comparison *hikaku suru* ～する compare

hikan 悲観 pessimism *hikan suru* ～する be pessimistic

hikari 光 rays, light, beam

hikidashi 引出し drawer

hikiiru 率いる command, lead

hikiniku ひき肉 minced [ground] meat

hikiokosu 引き起す cause, bring about, give rise to

hikitoru 引き取る take over, take care

hikiukeru 引き受ける undertake, take, accept

hikiwatasu 引き渡す deliver, hand over, transfer

hikkaku 引っかく scratch

hikkirinashi ni 引っ切り無しに incessantly, continuously, without a break

hikki suru 筆記する take notes, note down

hikkosu 引っ越す move, remove

hikō 飛行 flying, flight *hikō suru* ～する fly,

make a flight, travel by air

hikōki 飛行機 airplane

hiku 引く draw, pull

hikui 低い low, short, flat

hikyō 卑きょう *hikyō na* ～な cowardly *hikyō-mono* ～者 coward

hima 暇 leisure, time

himawari ひまわり sunflower

hime 姫 princess

himei 悲鳴 scream

himitsu 秘密 secrecy, privacy, secret

himo ひも string, cord

hina ひな chick(en)

hinan 非難 blame, criticism *hinan suru* ～する criticize, blame

hinan suru 避難する take refuge

hinata ひなた sunshine, sunny place *hinata-bokko suru* ～ぼっこする bask, sit in the sun, sun oneself

hineru ひねる twist, twirl, wring

hiniku 皮肉 cynicism, irony *hiniku na* ～な cynical, ironic(al)

hinin 避妊 contraception, birth control

hinkon 貧困 poverty, want, need

hinoki ひのき Japanese cypress

hinshitsu 品質 quality

hipparu 引っ張る pull, draw

hiraku 開く open, begin

hiratai 平たい flat, even

hiraya 平屋 one-storied[-story] house

hirei 比例 proportion, ratio *hirei suru* ～する be proportionate

hirō 疲労 fatigue, exhaustion *hirō suru* ～する be fatigued[tired]

hiroba 広場 open space, square

hirogaru 広がる spread, extend, stretch

hiroi 広い wide, broad

hiroiageru 拾い上げる pick up

hiroku 広く widely, broadly

hirosa 広さ area, extent, width

hirou 拾う pick up, find, pick out

hiru 昼 noon, day

hiruma ・昼間 in the daytime, by day

hirumeshi(＝**hirugohan**) 昼飯［昼御飯］lunch

hirune 昼寝 nap, siesta

hisashiburi ni 久し振りに after a long time [interval, absence]

hisho 秘書 secretary

hiso-hiso ひそひそ secretly, quietly

hisshi no 必死の desperate

hitei 否定 negation, denial *hitei suru* ～する deny, say no

hito 人 man, person

hitogoroshi 人殺し murderer, killer

hito-iki ni 一息に at a breath, at a stretch

hito-kire 一切れ piece (of)

hito-matome 一まとめ *hito-matome ni* ～に in a lump [bunch] *hito-matome ni suru* ～に する put [lump] together

hitome 一目 look, glance

hitonami no 人並の average, ordinary, common

hitori ひとり one (person) *hitori de* 独りで a-lone, by oneself, for oneself *hitori-zutsu* 一人 ずつ one at a time, one by one

hitorigoto 独り言 soliloquy *hitorigoto o iu* ～ を言う talk to oneself, soliloquize

hitorikko 一人っ子 an only child

hitoshii 等しい equal, equivalent

hitotsu 一つ one

hito-tsubu 一粒 grain, drop

hitsuji 羊 sheep, lamb

hitsuyō 必要 necessity *hitsuyō na* ～な neces-sary, essential

hiyasu 冷やす cool, ice, refrigerate

hiyō 費用 expense, expense cost *hiyō no kakaru* ～のかかる costly, expensive

hiyoko ひよこ chicken, chick

hiza ひざ knee, lap *hizamazuku* ひざまずく

kneel

hizashi 日差し sunlight

hizuke 日付 date

hizume ひづめ hoof

hizumu ひずむ warp, be bent

ho 歩 step, pace

ho 帆 sail, canvas

hō(= **hoho**) ほお [ほほ] cheek　*hō* [*hoho*] *o akarameru* 〜を赤らめる blush

hō 法 law, rule

hochō 歩調 step, pace

hōchō 包丁 kitchen knife, cleaver

hodō 歩道 sidewalk, pavement

hōdō 報道 information, report, news

hoeru ほえる bark, bay, howl

hōfu 豊富 abundance, plenty　*hōfu na* 〜な abundant, rich

hōgaku 方角 direction

hogaraka na 朗らかな cheerful, merry

hōgen 方言 dialect

hogo 保護 protection, care　*hogo suru* 〜する protect, look after, preserve

hōhō 方法 method, way, means

hohoemi ほほえみ smile　*hohoemu* ほほえむ smile, beam

hojū 補充 supplement, replacement　*hojū suru* 〜する supplement, replace

hoka ni 外に besides, in addition, but, but except

hoka no 外の other, the other, another

hoken 保険 insurance　*hoken ni hairu* 〜に入る be insured

hoketsu 補欠 substitute, alternate

hōki ほうき broom

hōki suru 放棄する give up, abandon

hokkyoku 北極 the North Pole　*hokkyoku-sei* 〜星 the polestar, the North Star

hōkō 方向 course

hōkoku 報告 report, information　*hōkoku suru* 〜する report, inform

hokori 誇り pride *hokoru* 誇る be proud of

hokori ほこり dust *hokorippoi* 〜っぽい dusty

hokōsha 歩行者 pedestrian, walker

hokuro ほくろ mole

hokusei 北西 northwest

hōmen 方面 direction, district

homeru 褒める praise, admire

hommō 本望 one's wishes, long-cherished desire, satisfaction

hōmon 訪問 visit, call *hōmon suru* 〜する visit, call upon

hōmuru 葬る bury, inter

hon 本 book *hon-bako* 〜箱 bookcase

hone 骨 bone *hone no oreru* 〜の折れる heavy, hard

honjitsu 本日 today, this day

honki no 本気の serious *honki ni* 本気に seriously

hon'nin 本人 the person himself

hon'no ほんの mere, slight, just, only *hon'no sukoshi* 〜少し just a little

hon'nō 本能 instinct

hono'o 炎 flame, blaze

honshitsu 本質 essence, true nature

hontō 本当 truth, reality *hontō no* 〜の true *hontō ni* 〜に truly, indeed *hontō wa* 〜は in fact, really

hon-ya 本屋 bookstore, bookshop

hon'yaku 翻訳 translation *hon'yaku suru* 〜する translate into

hora ほら Look!; There!

hora ほら triton, trumpet shell, conch shell, big talk *hora o fuku* 〜を吹く boast, brag, talk big *hora-fuki* 〜吹き braggart, boaster

hōritsu 法律 law *hōritsu no* 〜の legal

horobiru 滅びる go to ruin, be ruined, be destroyed *horobosu* 滅ぼす ruin, destroy

hōrō suru 放浪する wander

horu 掘る dig, excavate

hōsaku 豊作 good [rich] harvest

hōseki 宝石 jewel, gem

hōsha 放射 radiation *hōsha suru* 〜する radiate *hōsha-nō* 〜能 radio-activity

hoshi 星 star

hōshi 奉仕 service *hōshi suru* 〜する serve

hoshii 欲しい want, desire, wish

hōshin 方針 course, policy, plan, principle

hoshō 保証 guarantee

hōshū 報酬 recompense, reward, fee, pay

hōsō 放送 broadcasting *hōsō suru* 〜する broadcast

hōsō 包装 packing *hōsō suru* 〜する pack, wrap *hōsō-shi* 〜紙 packing [wrapping] paper

hosoi 細い thin, fine, slender

hossuru 欲する desire, wish

hosu 干す dry

hōtai 包帯 bandage, dressing *hōtai suru* 〜する bandage, dress, bind up

hotaru 蛍 firefly, lightning bug

hōtei 法廷 (law)court, tribunal

hotoke 仏 Buddha

hotondo ほとんど nearly, almost, all, but, hardly, scarcely

hotto suru ほっとする be relieved, breathe freely

hozon 保存 preservation *hozon suru* 〜する preserve, keep, conserve

hyakkajiten 百科辞典 encyclopedia

hyakkaten 百貨店 department store

hyaku 百, 100 hundred *hyaku-bai* 〜倍 one hundred times

hyaku-man 百万 million

hyakushō 百姓 farmer, peasant

hyō ひょう hail

hyō 表 list, table, schedule

hyōban 評判 reputation, fame, popularity

hyōdai 表題 title, heading

hyōgen 表現 expression *hyōgen suru* 〜する express, represent

hyōhon 標本 specimen, sample
hyōjō 表情 expression, look
hyōjun 標準 standard, level *hyōjun-go* 〜語 the standard language
hyōka suru 評価する value, estimate
hyōkō 標高 elevation
hyōmen 表面 surface *hyōmen no* 〜の external
hyōron 評論 review *hyōron suru* 〜する review
hyōryū suru 漂流する drift
hyotto shitara ひょっとしたら possibly, by chance
hyōzan 氷山 iceberg

I

i 胃 stomach
ibiki いびき snoring *ibiki o kaku* 〜をかく snore
ichi 位置 situation, position, location *ichi suru* 〜する be located [situated]
ichi 一, 1 one *dai-ichi* 第〜 the first
ichiba 市場 market
ichiban 一番 first, most, best
ichibubun 一部分 part, portion
ichido 一度 once, one time, at a time
ichi-gatsu 一月 January
ichigo いちご strawberry
ichi-ichi 一々 one by one
ichiji ni 一時に simultaneously, at a time
ichijirushii 著しい remarkable *ichijirushiku* 著しく remarkably
ichi-mon nashi no 一文なしの penniless
ichi-nen 一年 one year *ichi-nen-jū* 〜中 throughout the year, all the year round
ichi-nichi 一日 day, one day *ichi-nichi-jū* 〜中 all day (long) *ichi-nichi okini* 〜置きに every other [second] day
ichiryū 一流 first class

idai 偉大 greatness, mightiness *idai na* 〜な great, mighty

idaku 抱く hold, cherish

ido 井戸 well

idō 移動 movement *idō suru* 〜する move

ie 家 house, home

ifuku 衣服 dress, clothes

igai na 意外な unexpected, surprising

igai ni 以外に other than, except, but

igaku 医学 medical science, medicine

igen 威厳 dignity, majesty *igen no aru* 〜のある dignified, majestic

igi 意義 significance, meaning *igi no aru* 〜のある worthy

igi 異議 objection, protest

Igirisu イギリス England, Great Britain

igo 以後 after(that), from now on, since then

igokochi 居心地 *igokochi ga yoi* [*warui*] 〜がよい [悪い] be [un] comfortable

ihan 違反 violation *ihan suru* 〜する violate, disobey, break, be against

ii いい good, nice, fine

iiarawasu 言い表す express, describe

iikagen na いい加減な random, halfway, vague

iin 委員 committeeman *iin-kai* 〜会 committee

iinazuke いいなずけ one's fiancé(e)

iiwake 言い訳 apology, excuse, explanation *iiwake suru* 〜する make an excuse

iji 意地 obstinacy, will, pride *ijippari no* 意地っ張りの stubborn, headstrong

ijimeru いじめる treat badly, bully, tease

ijin 偉人 great man, hero

ijiwaru 意地悪 *ijiwaru no* [*ku*] 〜の [く] cross [ly], perverse [ly], spiteful [ly]

ijō 以上 more than, over, above

ijō na 異常な unusual, abnormal

ika 以下 less than, under, below

ika いか cuttle(fish), squid

ikaga いかが how, what *Ikaga desuka?* 〜で

すか. How are you? How do you feel? How about?

ikaiyō 胃かいよう gastric ulcer

ikameshii いかめしい solemn, stern

ikani いかに how, however, whatever

ikari いかり anchor

ikari 怒り anger, indignation, wrath

ikasu 生かす bring...into full play, keep... alive, revive, let live

ike 池 pond, pool

ikebana 生け花 flower arrangement

ikeiren 胃けいれん gastralgia

iken 意見 opinion, view, idea

ikenai いけない must not, ought not to, bad, be wrong

iki 息 breath, respiration *iki o suru* ～をする breathe, respire

iki-iki shita 生き生きした lively, fresh

ikimono 生き物 living thing, creature

iki na いきな smart, stylish, chic

ikinari いきなり suddenly

ikioi 勢い power, force, spirit, influence

ikiru 生きる live

ikisatsu いきさつ circumstances, state of things

ikizumaru 息詰まる be suffocated, be choked *ikizumaru yōna* ～ような choking, thrilling

ikka 一家 a family

ikko 一個 one, a piece

ikkō 一行 party, company

ikkō ni 一向に (not) at all; (not) in the least

iku 行く go, come, visit

ikubun 幾分 some(thing) *ikubun ka* ～か partly, somewhat

ikudo 幾度 how often [many times] *ikudo mo* ～も (even) so often, frequently, repeatedly

ikuji 意気地 *ikuji no nai* ～のない spiritless, timid, cowardly *ikuji nashi* ～無し coward

ikuji 育児 child care, nursing

ikura 幾ら how many [much] *ikura ka* ～か

some, somewhat, a little

ikutsu 幾つ how many

ima 今 now, the present, this moment　*imagoro* ～ごろ about [by] this time, at this time　*ima made* ～まで until [till] now, up to the present

imi 意味 meaning, sense

imōto 妹 younger sister

inabikari 稲光 lightning

inai 以内 within, less than, inside of

inaka 田舎 the country, the provinces

inaya 否や as soon as..., no sooner...than

inemuri 居眠り doze, nap

ininjō 委任状 power of attorney

inken na 陰険な crafty, treacherous

inki na 陰気な gloomy, dismal

inochi 命 life

inori 祈り prayer　*inoru* 祈る pray

inryō 飲料 drink, beverage, liquor

insatsu 印刷 printing, print　*insatsu suru* ～する print

inshō 印象 impression　*dai-ichi inshō* 第一～ first impression

inshoku 飲食　*inshoku suru* ～する eat and drink　*inshoku-butsu* ～物 food and drink

inshu 飲酒 drinking

intai suru 引退[隠退]する retire from

inu 犬 dog

in'yō 引用 quotation　*in'yō suru* ～する quote, cite

ippai 一ぱい a glass of, a cup of

ippan 一般 generality　*ippan ni* ～に generally, in general

ippo 一歩 step

ippon 一本 one, a piece, a bottle

ippuku 一服 dose, a portion, a smoke　*ippuku suru* ～する have a smoke, rest

iradatsu いらだつ be irritated, be excited

irai 依頼 request, trust

ireru 入れる put in, take in, admit

iriguchi 入口 the entrance

iro 色 color, hue, tinge

irodoru 彩る paint, decorate, color

iro-iro na 色々な various, different

iru 射る shoot, hit

iru 居る be, exist, there is

iru 要る want, need, require

iru いる parch, roast, fire

irui 衣類 clothing, clothes

isagiyoi 潔い manly, brave *isagiyoku* 潔く manfully, bravely

isamashii 勇ましい brave *isamashiku* 勇ましく bravely

isameru いさめる remonstrate, admonish, advise

isan 遺産 inheritance, legacy *isan-sōzokunin* ～相続人 heir, heiress

isasaka いささか little, bit, slightly, rather

ise-ebi いせえび (spiny) lobster

isei 異性 the opposite [other] sex

isha 医者 doctor *isha o yobu* ～を呼ぶ call a doctor

ishi 意志 will

ishi 石 stone, pebble

ishō 衣装 dress, costume

isogashii 忙しい busy

isogu 急ぐ hurry (up), hasten, be in a hurry

isoide 急いで in haste

issai 一切 all, everything

issakujitsu 一昨日 the day before yesterday

issatsu 一冊 a volume, one copy

issei ni 一斉に in chorus, all together

isshin ni 一心に intently, hard

isshō 一生 lifetime, one's life

issho ni 一緒に together, with one, in company with

isshū 一周 round, tour, lap

isshun 一瞬 moment, instant

isu いす chair, bench

ita 板 board, plate, plank

itadaki 頂 top, summit

itai 痛い painful, sore

itami 痛み pain, ache

itamu 痛む be sore, feel painful, ache

itazura いたずら mischief, prank, trick *itazura na* ～な mischievous

itchi 一致 agreement, coincidence, consent *itchi suru* ～する be in accord (with), coincide

iten 移転 removal, transfer *iten suru* ～する remove, move, transfer

ito 糸 yarn, thread, string, cord, line

itoko いとこ cousin

itoshii いとしい dear, beloved

itsu いつ when *itsu demo* ～でも at any time

itsuka いつか someday

itsumo いつも usually, always

itsunomanika いつの間にか before one knows

itsuwaru 偽る lie, feign, pretend

ittai 一体 on earth, in the world

ittō 一等 first grade [class]

iu 言う say, speak, tell, express *iu made mo naku* ～までもなく needless to say, of course

iwa 岩 rock

iwaba 言わば so to speak, as it were

iwai 祝い congratulations, celebration *iwau* 祝う congratulate, celebrate

iya いや *iya na* ～な unpleasant, disagreeable, nasty *iya ni naru* ～になる feel [become] disgusted with

iyagaru 嫌がる dislike, be unwilling

iyo-iyo いよいよ at last, at length, finally

izen 以前 ago, before

izumi 泉 spring, fountain

izure いずれ which *izure mo* ～も any, all *izure ni shitemo* ～にしても anyhow, in any case *izure sonouchi* ～そのうち someday *izure mata* ～また another some other time

J

jagaimo じゃがいも potato

jama 邪魔 obstruction, obstacle, interference *jama na* 〜な obstructive *jama suru* 〜する hinder, obstruct, interfere

jetto-ki ジェット機 jet plane

ji 字 letter, character, ideograph

jibun 自分 self, I, myself

jidai 時代 days, times, era, period *jidaiokure* 〜遅れ out of date

jiden 自伝 autobiography

jidō 児童 child, juvenile

jidō 自動 automatic action, self-motion *jidō no* [*-teki ni*] 〜の［的に］automatic[ally]

jidōsha 自動車 motorcar, automobile, car

jigoku 地獄 hell, inferno

jigyō 事業 undertaking, enterprise

jijitsu 事実 fact, truth

jijō 事情 circumstances, consideration, reasons

jijoden 自叙伝 autobiography

jikan 時間 time, hour *jikan-hyō* 〜表 time-table, schedule

jiken 事件 event, occurrence, matter, affair

jiki 磁器 porcelain, china(ware)

jiki ni 直に directly, immediately, soon, presently

jikken 実験 experiment, laboratory work

jikkō 実行 action, practice *jikkō suru* 〜する put into practice, carry out

jiko 事故 accident, incident, trouble

jikokugo 自国語 one's own language

jiku 軸 axis, axle, spindle, holder

jiman 自慢 pride, self-conceit *jiman suru* 〜する be proud of

jime-jime shita じめじめした damp, dampish, humid, wet

jimen 地面 surface, ground

jimi na 地味な plain, quiet, sober

jimu 事務 business, affairs *jimu-in* ～員 clerk

jinja 神社 Shinto shrine

jinkaku 人格 personality, character

jinken 人権 human rights

jinkō 人口 population

jinkō-eisei 人工衛星 artificial satellite

jinkō no 人工の artificial, man-made

jinrui 人類 mankind, human race, human beings

jinsei 人生 life, human life

jinshu 人種 (human) race

jinzō じん臓 kidney

jirasu じらす irritate

jiriki de 自力で by one's own power, for oneself

jisan suru 持参する take, bring

jisatsu 自殺 suicide *jisatsu suru* ～する kill oneself

jishaku 磁石 magnet

jishin 地震 earthquake

jishin 自信 self-confidence *jishin ga aru*[*nai*] ～がある[ない] be confident[diffident] of

jisho 辞書 dictionary *jisho o hiku* ～を引く consult a dictionary

jissai 実際 truth, fact, indeed *jissai ni* ～に actually

jisshi suru 実施する enforce, execute, carry into effect

jisshitsu 実質 substance, essence *jisshitsu-teki na* ～的な substantial, essential

jitai 辞退 refusal, declination *jitai suru* ～する decline, refuse

jitaku 自宅 one's house[home]

jitensha 自転車 bicycle, bike

jitsubutsu 実物 real thing

jitsugen 実現 realization, materialization *jitsugen suru* ～する realize, materialize

jitsuryoku 実力 real ability, merit *jitsuryoku no aru* ～のある able, capable

jitsu wa 実は really, in fact *jitsu o ieba* ～を言えば to tell the truth

jitsuyō 実用 practical use *jitsuyō-teki na* ～的な practical, useful

jitto じっと fixedly, firmly, patiently, still *jitto shiteiru* ～している keep quiet

jiyū 自由 freedom, liberty *jiyū no* ～の free *jiyū ni* ～に freely

jizen 慈善 charity, benevolence

jobun 序文 preface, foreword

jōbu na 丈夫な strong, well, healthy

jōdan 冗談 joke, jest, fun

jōen suru 上演する (put on the) stage, perform

jogakkō 女学校 girl's school

jogakusei 女学生 girl student

jōge 上下 top and bottom, up and down, high and low

jōgi 定規 rule(r)

jōhatsu suru 蒸発する evaporate, vaporize

jōhin na [ni] 上品な[に] elegant[ly], graceful[ly]

jōho 譲歩 concession *jōho suru* ～する concede

jōhō 情報 information, report, news

joi 女医 lady [woman] doctor

jo-jo ni 徐々に slowly, gradually

jōjun 上旬 the first part [ten days] of a month

jōken 条件 condition, terms, item

jōkyaku 乗客 passenger

jōkyū 上級 high rank *jōkyū-sei* ～生 upperclassman

jōmyaku 静脈 vein

jōnetsu 情熱 passion *jōnetsu-teki na* ～的な passionate

jōriku suru 上陸する disembark, land

jōryū 上流 upper stream *jōryū-shakai* ～社会 the upper classes

josei 女性 woman, feminine

jōsen suru 乗船する go on board

jōsha suru 乗車する take a train [car], get into

idan 階段 steps, stairs *kaidan o agaru*[*oriru*]
~を上がる[下りる] go up[down] stairs, go
upstairs[downstairs]

idan 怪談 ghost story

idō 街道 highway

ifuku 回復 restoration, recovery *kaifuku suru*
~する restore, get better, recover

iga 絵画 pictures, paintings

igai(no) 海外(の) oversea(s), foreign *kaigai
ni* ~に abroad, overseas

igan 海岸 seashore, coast, seaside, beach

igara 貝殻 shell

igi 会議 conference, meeting

igun 海軍 navy *kaigun no* ~の naval, navy

ihatsu 開発 develop, exploit

ihi 会費 (membership) fee, dues

ihō 解放 release, liberation *kaihō suru* ~
する release, liberate

ihō suru 介抱する nurse, tend, care for

ihō suru 開放する open, leave open, open to
the public

iin 会員 member *kaiin ni naru* ~になる become a member

iin 海員 seaman, sailor

ijō 海上 sea *kaijō no* ~の marine, sea *kaijō de*[*ni*] ~で[に] on the sea, at sea

ijō 会場 place of meeting

ijo suru 解除する cancel, release, remove

ikai suru 開会する open, go into session

ikaku 改革 reform, reorganization, improvement *kaikaku suru* ~する reform, reorganize

ikatsu na 快活な cheerful, gay, lively *kaikatsu ni* 快活に cheerfully, gaily

ikei 会計 accounts, finance

iketsu 解決 solution *kaiketsu suru* ~する
solve

iko 回顧 reflection, recollection *kaiko suru*
~する refer *kaiko-roku* ~録 reminiscences,
memoirs

[on] a train

joshi 女子 woman, girl

jōshiki 常識 common sense, mother wit *jōshiki
no aru* ~のある sensible *jōshiki no nai* ~の
ない senseless

joshu 助手 assistant

jōtai 状態 condition, state, situation

jōtatsu 上達 progress, improvement *jōtatsu suru* ~する make progress in, improve in

jōtō no 上等の high-class, superior

joya 除夜 New Year's Eve

joyū 女優 actress

jōzai 錠剤 tablet, pill

jōzō suru 醸造する brew, distill

jōzu 上手 skill, skillfulness *jōzu da* ~だ excel
in, (be) good at

-jū …中 in the course of, through(out)

jū 十, 10 ten

jū 銃 gun

jūbun na 十分な enough, sufficient, full *jūbun
ni* 十分に enough, sufficiently, well, fully

jūdai 十代 teens *jūdai no hito* ~の人 teen-ager

jūdai na 重大な important, serious, grave

jū-gatsu 十月 October

jugyō 授業 school work, lesson

jūji 十字 cross *jūji no* ~の cross-shaped

jūjika 十字架 cross

jūjiro 十字路 crossroads

jūjitsu suru 充実する fill up, complete *jūjitsu
shita* 充実した full, complete

juken suru 受験する take [sit for] an examination, take a test *juken-sei* 受験生 examinee

jukuren 熟練 skill, dexterity *jukuren suru* ~
する become skilled, master *jukuren shita* ~
した skilled, trained

juku suru 熟する ripen, mature, become [get]
ripe *juku shita* 熟した ripe, mellow

jū-man 十万 hundred thousand

jumbi 準備 preparation, arrangements, provision

jumbi suru ～する prepare, arrange, get ready for, provide for

jūmin 住民 inhabitants, residents

jumyō 寿命 life, span of life

jun 順 order, turn

jūni-gatsu 十二月 December

junjo 順序 order, sequence

junsa 巡査 policeman, police officer

jū-oku 十億 thousand millions, milliard, billion

jūsho 住所 dwelling, residence, address

jūtaku 住宅 dwelling

juwaki 受話器 receiver

jūyaku 重役 director (of a company)

juyō 需要 demand, request

jūyō na 重要な important, essential

K

ka 蚊 mosquito

kaban かばん bag, suitcase

kabe 壁 wall

kabi かび mold, mildew, must *kabi-kusai* ～くさい musty *kabiru* かびる get musty

kabin 花瓶 vase

kabocha かぼちゃ pumpkin, squash

kabu 株 stocks, shares, stock speculation, stump, stub

kabu かぶ turnip

kabunushi 株主 stockholder, shareholder *kabunushi-sōkai* ～総会 general meeting of stockholders

kabureru かぶれる be poisoned, be allergic

kaburu かぶる put on, wear

kabuseru かぶせる cover, put on

kachi 勝ち victory, triumph

kachiki na 勝ち気な spirited, unyielding

kadan 花壇 flower bed

kado 角 corner, angle

kaerimichi 帰り道 one's way home

kaerimiru 顧みる look back upon, oneself

kaeru かえる frog

kaeru 変える change, alter, exchan

kaesu 返す return, give back, repa put back

kaesu かえす hatch, incubate

kaette かえって all the more, on instead, rather

kagaku 科学 science *kagaku no* ～

kagaku 化学 chemistry *kagaku* chemical

kagami 鏡 mirror, looking glass

kagamu かがむ stoop, bend

kagayaki 輝き brilliancy, brightne

kagayaku 輝く shine, burn, gleam

kage 影 shadow

kage 陰 shade

kageki na 過激な extreme, excess

kagen 加減 degree, extent *kagen* adjust, regulate

kagi かぎ key *kagi o kakeru* ～を

kagiranai 限らない not always, n

kagiru 限る limit, restrict, fix

kago かご basket

kagu 家具 furniture

kahei 貨幣 coins, coinage, curren

kai 貝 shellfish, shell

kai 会 meeting, party, society

kai 回 time, round

kai 階 story, stairs, grade

kai かい *kai ga aru* ～がある be effective *kai ga nai* ～がな

kaibatsu 海抜 above the sea, ab

kaibutsu 怪物 monster

kaichō 会長 president, chairman

kaichū 懐中 one's pocket *kaic* 灯 electric torch, flashlight

kaikyō 海峡 strait, channel

kaikyū 階級 class, rank

kaimono 買物 shopping, purchase *kaimono suru* ～する buy *kaimono ni iku* ～に行く go shopping

kairan suru 回覧する circulate

kairyō 改良 improvement, reform *kairyō suru* ～する improve, reform

kaisambutsu 海産物 marine products

kaisan suru 解散する break up, disperse, dissolve

kaisatsu suru 改札する examine tickets *kaisatsu-gakari* ～係 ticket examiner [clipper] *kaisatsu-guchi* ～口 (*station*) platform wicket

kaisei 改正 revision, alteration *kaisei suru* ～する revise, reform

kaisei 快晴 fine [clear] weather

kaisetsu 解説 explanation, commentary *kaisetsu suru* ～する explain, comment

kaisha 会社 company, corporation, firm

kaishaku 解釈 interpretation *kaishaku suru* ～する interpret, explain

kaishi 開始 opening, beginning *kaishi suru* ～する start, open, begin

kaishin suru 改心する reform oneself, turn over a new leaf

kaisō 海藻 seaweeds, marine plants

kaisui 海水 sea [salt] water

kaisuiyoku 海水浴 sea bathing

kaisū-ken 回数券 commutation ticket, book of tickets

kaitakusha 開拓者 pioneer, settler

kaitei 海底 bottom of the sea, sea bottom

kaiteki na 快適な comfortable, agreeable

kaiten 回転 revolution, rotation *kaiten suru* ～する revolve, rotate

kaiten suru 開店する open (for business)

kaitō suru 回答する answer, solve

kaiwa 会話 conversation, talk

kaiyaku suru 解約する cancel, call off

kaiyō 海洋 ocean

kaizen 改善 improvement *kaizen suru* ～する improve

kaji かじ rudder, helm, wheel

kaji 家事 household affairs, housework

kaji 火事 fire, conflagration

kajiru かじる gnaw, nibble, bite, munch

kakaeru 抱える hold in one's arms

kakaku 価格 price

kakaru 掛かる take, need, cost, begin, start

kakaru かかる contract, suffer from, get

kakato かかと heel

kakawarazu かかわらず in spite of

kakawaru かかわる concern oneself in, have to do with, affect

kake かけ betting, gambling *kakeru* かける bet

kakedasu 駆け出す run out

kakedokei 掛け時計 wall clock

kakegoe 掛け声 shout, call

kakei 家計 housekeeping

kakeru 掛ける hang, suspend

kakeru 掛ける multiply

kakeru 欠ける lack, be short of, be wanting in

kakezan 掛算 multiplication

kaki かき oyster

kaki 柿 persimmon

kakitome 書留 registration, registered mail [post] *kakitome ni suru* ～にする register

kakki 活気 *kakki no aru* ～のある active, animated, spirited, lively *kakki no nai* ～のない spiritless, dull

kakki-teki na 画期的な epoch-making

kakko 括弧 parenthesis, bracket, brace *kakko ni ireru* ～に入れる parenthesize, bracket

kakkō 格好 shape, figure, appearance

kako 過去 the past, past days

kakō 加工 processing *kakō suru* ～する process

kakomu 囲む surround, enclose

kaku 書く write, compose, describe

kaku 核 nucleus *kaku no* ～の nuclear

kaku かく scrape

kaku 各 each, every

kaku 角 angle, square

kakuchi 各地 every part [place]

kakuchō 拡張 extension, expansion *kakuchō suru* ～する widen, extend, enlarge

kakugo 覚悟 preparedness, resolution *kakugo suru* ～する be prepared

kakujitsu 隔日 every other [second] day

kakujitsu na [ni] 確実な[に] sure [ly], certain [ly]

kakunen 隔年 every other [second] year

kakunin 確認 confirmation, affirmation *kakunin suru* ～する confirm, affirm

kakū no 架空の fictitious, imaginary

kakureru 隠れる hide *kakureta* 隠れた hidden, secret

kakuseiki 拡声器 loudspeaker, megaphone

kakushin 確信 conviction, firm belief *kakushin suru* ～する be convinced of, be sure of

kakushū 隔週 every other week

kakusu 隠す hide, conceal

kakutei 確定 decision, settlement *kakutei suru* ～する decide, confirm, fix

kakutoku suru 獲得する acquire, obtain, get

kakuyaku suru 確約する give a definite promise

kamawanai 構わない do not care [mind], it doesn't matter

kamban 看板 sign (board), billboard

kambashii 芳しい sweet, fragrant, favorable *kambashikunai* 芳しくない unfavorable

kambu 幹部 management, staff

kambyō suru 看病する nurse, care for, attend

kame 亀 tortoise, turtle

kame 瓶 jar, jug

kami 神 god
kami 紙 paper
kami 髪 hair
kamiire 紙入れ pocketbook, purse, wallet
kamikuzu 紙くず wastepaper, paper scraps
　　kamikuzu-kago 〜かご waste(paper) basket
kaminari 雷 thunder
kamisori かみそり razor
kamo かも wild duck
kamome かもめ sea gull
kamotsu 貨物 freight, goods, cargo
kampa 寒波 cold wave
kampai 乾杯 (drinking) toast
kampai 完敗 complete defeat
kampan 甲板 deck
kamu かむ bite, chew
kan 缶 can, tin　*kan-kiri* 〜切り can opener,
　　tin opener
kan 巻 volume, book
kan 寒 cold season, mid-winter
-kan 間 for, during
kana 仮名 Japanese syllabary
kana'ami 金網 wire netting, screen
kanai 家内 family, household, one's wife　*kanai*
　　kōgyō 〜工業 household industry
kanamono 金物 hardware, ironware　*kanamo-*
　　no-ya 〜屋 hardware store
kanarazu 必ず certainly, surely, without fail
　　kanarazu shimo...de nai 必ずしも...でない
　　not always
kanari かなり fairly, pretty, rather, considerably
kanashii 悲しい sad, sorrowful
kanashimi 悲しみ sorrow, sadness, grief
kanashimu 悲しむ grieve, feel [be] sad, be sor-
　　rowful　*kanashimubeki* 〜べき regrettable, sad,
　　pitiable, sorrowful
kanata かなた over there, yonder
kanau かなう suit, measure up to, be fulfilled
kanawanai かなわない be not match for, cannot

stand

kanazuchi 金づち hammer

kanchigai suru 勘違いする mistake, be mistaken

kandai na 寛大な generous, tolerant

kandankei 寒暖計 thermometer

kandenchi 乾電池 dry cell [battery]

kandō 感動 impression, excitement *kandō suru* ~する be impressed, be moved *kandō saseru* ~させる move, impress

kane 金 money, metal

kane 鐘 bell *kane o tsuku* ~を突く strike a bell

kanemochi 金持ち rich man, rich

kangae 考え thinking, thought, ideas *kangae chigai* ~違い misunderstanding

kangaekata 考え方 one's way of thinking

kangaenaosu 考え直す reconsider, think over again

kangaeru 考える think, consider, view, regard ...as

kangei (suru) 歓迎(する) welcome

kangeki 感激 impression, deep emotion *kangeki suru* ~する be deeply moved

kani かに crab

kanja 患者 patient

kanji 感じ feeling, sense, perception, impression *kanjiyasui* ~やすい sensitive

kanjiru 感じる feel, be conscious of

kanjō 感情 feeling, emotion, passion

kanjō 勘定 calculation *kanjō suru* ~する count, calculate, account *kanjō-gaki* ~書 bill

kanjō no 環状の loop, circular *kanjō-sen* ~線 belt line, loop line

kankaku 感覚 sense, sensation, feeling *kankaku-teki na* ~的な sensuous, sensual

kankaku 間隔 interval, space

kankei 関係 relation, concern(ment) *kankei suru* ~する relate to, concern, participate in, be concerned in

kanketsu na [ni] 簡潔な [に] concise [ly], brief [ly], in short

kankō 観光 sightseeing, touring *kankō-kyaku* ~客 tourist

kankoku (suru) 勧告(する) recommendation, recommend, advise

kankyaku 観客 spectator, audience

kankyō 環境 environment, circumstance

kan'nen 観念 idea, sense, resignation, resolution *kan'nen suru* ~する be resigned

kanō 化のう suppuration, purulence *kanō suru* ~する suppurate, fester

kanojo 彼女 she *kanojo no [ni, o]* ~の [に, を] her

kanōsei 可能性 possibility *kanōsei no aru [nai]* ~のある [ない] [im]possible

kanran 観覧 inspection *kanran suru* ~する see, view *kanran-ken [-ryō]* ~券 [料] admission ticket [fee] *kanran-seki* ~席 seat, stand, stadium

kanren suru 関連する be connected with, relate to

kanri 管理 administration, control *kanri suru* ~する manage, control

kanri 官吏 government official, office-holder, civil servant

kansan suru 換算する convert, change

kansatsu 観察 observation *kansatsu suru* ~する observe, watch

kansei 完成 completion, accomplishment *kansei suru* ~する complete, finish, accomplish

kansen suru 感染する be infected, catch

kansetsu no 間接の indirect *kansetsu ni* ~に indirectly

kansha 感謝 thanks, gratitude *kansha suru* ~する thank, feel grateful

kanshin 関心 interest, concern *kanshin o motsu* ~を持つ be interested in

kanshin suru 感心する admire, be impressed

[on] a train

joshi 女子 woman, girl

jōshiki 常識 common sense, mother wit *jōshiki no aru* 〜のある sensible *jōshiki no nai* 〜のない senseless

joshu 助手 assistant

jōtai 状態 condition, state, situation

jōtatsu 上達 progress, improvement *jōtatsu suru* 〜する make progress in, improve in

jōtō no 上等の high-class, superior

joya 除夜 New Year's Eve

joyū 女優 actress

jōzai 錠剤 tablet, pill

jōzō suru 醸造する brew, distill

jōzu 上手 skill, skillfulness *jōzu da* 〜だ excel in, (be) good at

-jū ...中 in the course of, through (out)

jū 十, 10 ten

jū 銃 gun

jūbun na 十分な enough, sufficient, full *jūbun ni* 十分に enough, sufficiently, well, fully

jūdai 十代 teens *jūdai no hito* 〜の人 teen-ager

jūdai na 重大な important, serious, grave

jū-gatsu 十月 October

jugyō 授業 school work, lesson

jūji 十字 cross *jūji no* 〜の cross-shaped

jūjika 十字架 cross

jūjiro 十字路 crossroads

jūjitsu suru 充実する fill up, complete *jūjitsu shita* 充実した full, complete

juken suru 受験する take [sit for] an examination, take a test *juken-sei* 受験生 examinee

jukuren 熟練 skill, dexterity *jukuren suru* 〜する become skilled, master *jukuren shita* 〜した skilled, trained

juku suru 熟する ripen, mature, become [get] ripe *juku shita* 熟した ripe, mellow

jū-man 十万 hundred thousand

jumbi 準備 preparation, arrangements, provision

jumbi suru 〜する prepare, arrange, get ready for, provide for

jūmin 住民 inhabitants, residents
jumyō 寿命 life, span of life
jun 順 order, turn
jūni-gatsu 十二月 December
junjo 順序 order, sequence
junsa 巡査 policeman, police officer
jū-oku 十億 thousand millions, milliard, billion
jūsho 住所 dwelling, residence, address
jūtaku 住宅 dwelling
juwaki 受話器 receiver
jūyaku 重役 director (of a company)
juyō 需要 demand, request
jūyō na 重要な important, essential

K

ka 蚊 mosquito
kaban かばん bag, suitcase
kabe 壁 wall
kabi かび mold, mildew, must *kabi-kusai* 〜くさい musty *kabiru* かびる get musty
kabin 花瓶 vase
kabocha かぼちゃ pumpkin, squash
kabu 株 stocks, shares, stock speculation, stump, stub
kabu かぶ turnip
kabunushi 株主 stockholder, shareholder
kabunushi-sōkai 〜総会 general meeting of stockholders
kabureru かぶれる be poisoned, be allergic
kaburu かぶる put on, wear
kabuseru かぶせる cover, put on
kachi 勝ち victory, triumph
kachiki na 勝ち気な spirited, unyielding
kadan 花壇 flower bed
kado 角 corner, angle

kaerimichi 帰り道 one's way home [back]

kaerimiru 顧みる look back upon, reflect upon oneself

kaeru かえる frog

kaeru 変える change, alter, exchange

kaesu 返す return, give back, repay, pay back, put back

kaesu かえす hatch, incubate

kaette かえって all the more, on the contrary, instead, rather

kagaku 科学 science *kagaku no* ～の scientific

kagaku 化学 chemistry *kagaku no* ～の chemical

kagami 鏡 mirror, looking glass

kagamu かがむ stoop, bend

kagayaki 輝き brilliancy, brightness

kagayaku 輝く shine, burn, gleam

kage 影 shadow

kage 陰 shade

kageki na 過激な extreme, excessive, radical

kagen 加減 degree, extent *kagen suru* ～する adjust, regulate

kagi かぎ key *kagi o kakeru* ～を掛ける lock

kagiranai 限らない not always, not necessarily

kagiru 限る limit, restrict, fix

kago かご basket

kagu 家具 furniture

kahei 貨幣 coins, coinage, currency, money

kai 貝 shellfish, shell

kai 会 meeting, party, society

kai 回 time, round

kai 階 story, stairs, grade

kai かい *kai ga aru* ～がある be worth while, be effective *kai ga nai* ～がない be in vain

kaibatsu 海抜 above the sea, above sea level

kaibutsu 怪物 monster

kaichō 会長 president, chairman

kaichū 懐中 one's pocket *kaichū-dentō* ～電灯 electric torch, flashlight

kaidan 階段 steps, stairs *kaidan o agaru [oriru]* ～を上がる[下りる] go up [down] stairs, go upstairs [downstairs]

kaidan 怪談 ghost story

kaidō 街道 highway

kaifuku 回復 restoration, recovery *kaifuku suru* ～する restore, get better, recover

kaiga 絵画 pictures, paintings

kaigai(no) 海外(の) oversea(s), foreign *kaigai ni* ～に abroad, overseas

kaigan 海岸 seashore, coast, seaside, beach

kaigara 貝殻 shell

kaigi 会議 conference, meeting

kaigun 海軍 navy *kaigun no* ～の naval, navy

kaihatsu 開発 develop, exploit

kaihi 会費 (membership) fee, dues

kaihō 解放 release, liberation *kaihō suru* ～する release, liberate

kaihō suru 介抱する nurse, tend, care for

kaihō suru 開放する open, leave open, open to the public

kaiin 会員 member *kaiin ni naru* ～になる become a member

kaiin 海員 seaman, sailor

kaijō 海上 sea *kaijō no* ～の marine, sea *kaijō de [ni]* ～で[に] on the sea, at sea

kaijō 会場 place of meeting

kaijo suru 解除する cancel, release, remove

kaikai suru 開会する open, go into session

kaikaku 改革 reform, reorganization, improvement *kaikaku suru* ～する reform, reorganize

kaikatsu na 快活な cheerful, gay, lively *kaikatsu ni* 快活に cheerfully, gaily

kaikei 会計 accounts, finance

kaiketsu 解決 solution *kaiketsu suru* ～す solve

kaiko 回顧 reflection, recollection *kaiko ～する refer *kaiko-roku* ～録 reminis memoirs

kaikyō 海峡 strait, channel

kaikyū 階級 class, rank

kaimono 買物 shopping, purchase *kaimono suru* ～する buy *kaimono ni iku* ～に行く go shopping

kairan suru 回覧する circulate

kairyō 改良 improvement, reform *kairyō suru* ～する improve, reform

kaisambutsu 海産物 marine products

kaisan suru 解散する break up, disperse, dissolve

kaisatsu suru 改札する examine tickets *kaisatsu-gakari* ～係 ticket examiner [clipper] *kaisatsu-guchi* ～口 (*station*) platform wicket

kaisei 改正 revision, alteration *kaisei suru* ～する revise, reform

kaisei 快晴 fine [clear] weather

kaisetsu 解説 explanation, commentary *kaisetsu suru* ～する explain, comment

kaisha 会社 company, corporation, firm

kaishaku 解釈 interpretation *kaishaku suru* ～する interpret, explain

kaishi 開始 opening, beginning *kaishi suru* ～する start, open, begin

kaishin suru 改心する reform oneself, turn over a new leaf

kaisō 海藻 seaweeds, marine plants

kaisui 海水 sea [salt] water

kaisuiyoku 海水浴 sea bathing

kaisū-ken 回数券 commutation ticket, book of tickets

kaitakusha 開拓者 pioneer, settler

kaitei 海底 bottom of the sea, sea bottom

kaiteki na 快適な comfortable, agreeable

kaiten 回転 revolution, rotation *kaiten suru* ～する revolve, rotate

kaiten suru 開店する open (for business)

kaitō suru 回答する answer, solve

kaiwa 会話 conversation, talk

kaiyaku suru 解約する cancel, call off

kaiyō 海洋 ocean

kaizen 改善 improvement *kaizen suru* 〜する improve

kaji かじ rudder, helm, wheel

kaji 家事 household affairs, housework

kaji 火事 fire, conflagration

kajiru かじる gnaw, nibble, bite, munch

kakaeru 抱える hold in one's arms

kakaku 価格 price

kakaru 掛かる take, need, cost, begin, start

kakaru かかる contract, suffer from, get

kakato かかと heel

kakawarazu かかわらず in spite of

kakawaru かかわる concern oneself in, have to do with, affect

kake かけ betting, gambling *kakeru* かける bet

kakedasu 駆け出す run out

kakedokei 掛け時計 wall clock

kakegoe 掛け声 shout, call

kakei 家計 housekeeping

kakeru 掛ける hang, suspend

kakeru 掛ける multiply

kakeru 欠ける lack, be short of, be wanting in

kakezan 掛算 multiplication

kaki かき oyster

kaki 柿 persimmon

kakitome 書留 registration; registered mail [post] *kakitome ni suru* 〜にする register

kakki 活気 *kakki no aru* 〜のある active, animated, spirited, lively *kakki no nai* 〜のない spiritless, dull

kakki-teki na 画期的な epoch-making

kakko 括弧 parenthesis, bracket, brace *kakko ni ireru* 〜に入れる parenthesize, bracket

kakkō 格好 shape, figure, appearance

kako 過去 the past, past days

kakō 加工 processing *kakō suru* 〜する process

kakomu 囲む surround, enclose
kaku 書く write, compose, describe
kaku 核 nucleus *kaku no* ～の nuclear
kaku かく scrape
kaku 各 each, every
kaku 角 angle, square
kakuchi 各地 every part [place]
kakuchō 拡張 extension, expansion *kakuchō suru* ～する widen, extend, enlarge
kakugo 覚悟 preparedness, resolution *kakugo suru* ～する be prepared
kakujitsu 隔日 every other [second] day
kakujitsu na [ni] 確実な [に] sure [ly], certain [ly]
kakunen 隔年 every other [second] year
kakunin 確認 confirmation, affirmation *kakunin suru* ～する confirm, affirm
kakū no 架空の fictitious, imaginary
kakureru 隠れる hide *kakureta* 隠れた hidden, secret
kakuseiki 拡声器 loudspeaker, megaphone
kakushin 確信 conviction, firm belief *kakushin suru* ～する be convinced of, be sure of
kakushū 隔週 every other week
kakusu 隠す hide, conceal
kakutei 確定 decision, settlement *kakutei suru* ～する decide, confirm, fix
kakutoku suru 獲得する acquire, obtain, get
kakuyaku suru 確約する give a definite promise
kamawanai 構わない do not care [mind], it doesn't matter
kamban 看板 sign (board), billboard
kambashii 芳しい sweet, fragrant, favorable *kambashikunai* 芳しくない unfavorable
kambu 幹部 management, staff
kambyō suru 看病する nurse, care for, attend
kame 亀 tortoise, turtle
kame 瓶 jar, jug

kami 神 god
kami 紙 paper
kami 髪 hair
kamiire 紙入れ pocketbook, purse, wallet
kamikuzu 紙くず wastepaper, paper scraps
　kamikuzu-kago ～かご waste(paper) basket
kaminari 雷 thunder
kamisori かみそり razor
kamo かも wild duck
kamome かもめ sea gull
kamotsu 貨物 freight, goods, cargo
kampa 寒波 cold wave
kampai 乾杯 (drinking) toast
kampai 完敗 complete defeat
kampan 甲板 deck
kamu かむ bite, chew
kan 缶 can, tin *kan-kiri* ～切り can opener,
　tin opener
kan 巻 volume, book
kan 寒 cold season, mid-winter
-kan 間 for, during
kana 仮名 Japanese syllabary
kana'ami 金網 wire netting, screen
kanai 家内 family, household, one's wife *kanai
　kōgyō* ～工業 household industry
kanamono 金物 hardware, ironware *kanamo-
　no-ya* ～屋 hardware store
kanarazu 必ず certainly, surely, without fail
　kanarazu shimo...de nai 必ずしも...でない
　not always
kanari かなり fairly, pretty, rather, considerably
kanashii 悲しい sad, sorrowful
kanashimi 悲しみ sorrow, sadness, grief
kanashimu 悲しむ grieve, feel [be] sad, be sor-
　rowful *kanashimubeki* ～べき regrettable, sad,
　pitiable, sorrowful
kanata かなた over there, yonder
kanau かなう suit, measure up to, be fulfilled
kanawanai かなわない be not match for, cannot

stand

kanazuchi 金づち hammer

kanchigai suru 勘違いする mistake, be mistaken

kandai na 寛大な generous, tolerant

kandankei 寒暖計 thermometer

kandenchi 乾電池 dry cell [battery]

kandō 感動 impression, excitement *kandō suru* ～する be impressed, be moved *kandō saseru* ～させる move, impress

kane 金 money, metal

kane 鐘 bell *kane o tsuku* ～を突く strike a bell

kanemochi 金持ち rich man, rich

kangae 考え thinking, thought, ideas *kangae chigai* ～違い misunderstanding

kangaekata 考え方 one's way of thinking

kangaenaosu 考え直す reconsider, think over again

kangaeru 考える think, consider, view, regard ...as

kangei(suru) 歓迎(する) welcome

kangeki 感激 impression, deep emotion *kangeki suru* ～する be deeply moved

kani かに crab

kanja 患者 patient

kanji 感じ feeling, sense, perception, impression *kanjiyasui* ～やすい sensitive

kanjiru 感じる feel, be conscious of

kanjō 感情 feeling, emotion, passion

kanjō 勘定 calculation *kanjō suru* ～する count, calculate, account *kanjō-gaki* ～書 bill

kanjō no 環状の loop, circular *kanjō-sen* ～線 belt line, loop line

kankaku 感覚 sense, sensation, feeling *kankaku-teki na* ～的な sensuous, sensual

kankaku 間隔 interval, space

kankei 関係 relation, concern(ment) *kankei suru* ～する relate to, concern, participate in, be concerned in

kanketsu na [ni] 簡潔な [に] concise [ly], brief [ly], in short

kankō 観光 sightseeing, touring *kankō-kyaku* ~客 tourist

kankoku (suru) 勧告(する) recommendation, recommend, advise

kankyaku 観客 spectator, audience

kankyō 環境 environment, circumstance

kan'nen 観念 idea, sense, resignation, resolution *kan'nen suru* ~する be resigned

kanō 化のう suppuration, purulence *kanō suru* ~する suppurate, fester

kanojo 彼女 she *kanojo no [ni, o]* ~の [に, を] her

kanōsei 可能性 possibility *kanōsei no aru [nai]* ~のある [ない] [im]possible

kanran 観覧 inspection *kanran suru* ~する see, view *kanran-ken [-ryō]* ~券 [料] admission ticket [fee] *kanran-seki* ~席 seat, stand, stadium

kanren suru 関連する be connected with, relate to

kanri 管理 administration, control *kanri suru* ~する manage, control

kanri 官吏 government official, office-holder, civil servant

kansan suru 換算する convert, change

kansatsu 観察 observation *kansatsu suru* ~する observe, watch

kansei 完成 completion, accomplishment *kansei suru* ~する complete, finish, accomplish

kansen suru 感染する be infected, catch

kansetsu no 間接の indirect *kansetsu ni* ~に indirectly

kansha 感謝 thanks, gratitude *kansha suru* ~する thank, feel grateful

kanshin 関心 interest, concern *kanshin o motsu* ~を持つ be interested in

kanshin suru 感心する admire, be impressed

kanshin na 感心な admirable   *kanshin shite* 感心して in admiration of

kanshite 関して about, as to, regarding

kanshō 干渉 interference   *kanshō suru* 〜する interfere

kanshō 鑑賞 appreciation   *kanshō suru* 〜する appreciate

kanshō 感傷 sentiment   *kanshō-teki na* 〜的な sentimental

kanshū 慣習 custom, usage

kanshū 観衆 spectators, audience

kansō 感想 thoughts, impressions

kansoku 観測 observation   *kansoku suru* 〜する observe

kanso na 簡素な simple, plain, brief

kansō suru 乾燥する dry (up)

kantan na 簡単な simple, brief, light

kantei 鑑定 judgment, appraisal   *kantei suru* 〜する judge

kantoku 監督 supervision   *kantoku suru* 〜する supervise

kan'yō no 慣用の common, customary   *kan'yō-go* 慣用語 idiom

kanyū 加入 joining, entry   *kanyū suru* 〜する enter, join

kan'yū 勧誘 canvassing, invitation   *kan'yū suru* 〜する canvass, solicit

kanzashi かんざし ornamental hairpin

kanzei 関税 customs, custom duty, tariff

kanzen 完全 perfection, completeness   *kanzen na[ni]* 〜な[に] complete[ly], perfect[ly]

kanzō 肝臓 liver

kanzume 缶詰 tinning, canning   *kanzume ni suru* 〜にする can, tin

kao 顔 face, features, looks   *kao o somukeru* 〜を背ける turn one's face away   *kao o tateru* 〜を立てる save one's face

kaoiro 顔色 complexion, looks

kaori 香り fragrance, aroma

kaoru 香る smell sweet [nice]

kappatsu na [ni] 活発な [に] lively [-lily], active [ly], cheerful [ly]

-kara …から from, (out) of, off, since, after

karada 体 body, physique

karai 辛い hot, salty, strict, severe

karakau からかう banter, tease

karamaru 絡まる coil itself, be twisted, be entangled

kara no 空の empty, vacant

karashi からし mustard

karasu からす crow

kare 彼 he *kare no* ～の his *kare o* [ni] 彼を [に] him

karen na かれんな pretty, lovely

karera 彼等 they *karera no* ～の their *karera o* [ni] ～を [に] them

kareru 枯れる die, wither, be blasted

kari かり wild goose

kari 狩り hunting *kari o suru* ～をする hunt

kari 借り debt, loan *kari ga aru* ～がある be in debt, owe

kari no 仮の temporary *kari ni* 仮に temporarily *kari ni…to shitemo* 仮に…としても even if

kariru 借りる borrow, have the loan of, hire, rent

karō 過労 overwork

karōjite 辛うじて barely, narrowly

karu 刈る cut, crop, mow, reap, clip

karuhazumi na 軽はずみな rash, imprudent

karui 軽い light, slight *karuku* 軽く lightly

kasa 傘 umbrella *kasa o sasu* ～を差す put up [hold] an umbrella *kasa ni kiru* ～に着る make use of another's influence

kasa かさ bulk, volume, size *kasabaru* ～ばる be bulky *kasa ni kakatte* ～にかかって arrogantly, high-handedly

kasanaru 重なる be piled up *kasanatte* 重な

って in piles

kasaneru 重ねる pile up, heap up, put one upon another

kasan suru 加算する add, include

kasegu 稼ぐ earn one's living, win money

kasei 火星 Mars

kashi かし oak tree

kashi 菓子 confectionary, cake

kashi 華氏 Fahrenheit

kashi 河岸 riverside bank, fish market

kashi 貸し loan, lending

kashikoi 賢い clever, wise, smart

kashira 頭 head, leader

kashitsu 過失 fault, mistake, error, accident

kashiya 貸家 house to let

kashu 歌手 singer

kassai かっさい applause, cheers *kassai suru* ～する applaud, cheer

kasshoku 褐色 brown

kasu かす dregs, grounds, refuse, sediment

kasu 貸す lend, advance, hire [let] out, rent

kasuka かすか *kasuka na[ni]* ～な[に] faint [ly], dim[ly], vague[ly], indistinct[ly]

kasumi かすみ haze, mist

kasuri-kizu かすり傷 scratch

kasutera カステラ sponge cake

kata 肩 shoulder *kata o motsu* ～を持つ take part, support, side with *kata o sukumeru* ～をすくめる shrug one's shoulders

kata 形[型] shape, form, model, style, type

katachi 形 shape, form, appearance, figure

katagami 型紙 pattern paper, paper pattern

katagawa 片側 one side

katahō 片方 one side[party]

katai かたい hard, tough, solid, strong, firm

kataki 敵 enemy, foe, rival

katamaru 固まる harden, become hard[firm]

katamukeru 傾ける incline, lean, bend

katana 刀 sword, blade

kataru 語る talk, chat, tell

katate 片手 one hand *katate no* ～の one handed, single-handed

katatsumuri かたつむり snail

katawara 傍ら while, besides *katawara ni* ～に by, beside, near by, aside

katazukeru 片付ける put in order, put back

katei 家庭 home, family, household

katei 仮定 supposition *katei suru* ～する suppose, assume, presume

katei 過程 process, stage

katō na 下等な low, inferior

katsu 勝つ win, beat

katsudō 活動 activity, action *katsudō-teki na* ～的な active, dynamic

katsugikomu 担ぎ込む carry into, take in

katsugu 担ぐ shoulder, carry on one's shoulder

katsuji 活字 type

katsuo かつお bonito

katsura かつら wig

katsuyaku 活躍 activity *katsuyaku suru* ～する be active

katsuyō 活用 practical use, application *katsuyō suru* ～する apply, utilize

katte 勝手 one's own convenience, one's own way, kitchen

katto naru かっとなる fly into a rage, flare up *katto natte* かっとなって in a fit of anger

kau 飼う keep, raise

kau 買う buy, purchase, get

kawa 皮 skin, leather, peel, rind *kawa o muku* ～をむく pare, peel, rind, skin

kawa 川[河] river, stream, brook

kawaigaru かわいがる love, pet, have affection for

kawaii かわいい dear, lovely, pretty, cute

kawaisō na かわいそうな poor, pitiable, miserable

kawaita 乾いた dry

kawaku 乾く dry, dry up

kawaku 渇く be thirsty, feel dry

kawara かわら tile

kawari 代り substitute, deputy *kawari ni* ～に in place of, on behalf of

kawaru 代る take place of, replace

kawaru 変る change, vary, turn into *kawari yasui* 変りやすい changeable, variable

kawase 為替 money order, exchange, bank draft

kawashimo 川下 the lower reaches (of a river)

kawatta 変った different, another

kayaku 火薬 gunpowder

kayō-bi 火曜日 Tuesday

kayou 通う attend, go to and from (a place), commute

kayowai か弱い weak, delicate, tender

kayu かゆ (rice) gruel, porridge

kayui かゆい itch

kazakami 風上 windward

kazamuki 風向き the direction of the wind, the situation

kazan 火山 volcano *kazan-bai* ～灰 volcanic ashes

kazari 飾り decoration, ornament *kazari no* ～の decorative, ornamental

kazaru 飾る decorate, adorn, dress, display

kaze 風 wind, breeze *kaze no* ～の windy

kaze かぜ cold, flu *kaze o hiku* ～をひく catch (a) cold

kazei 課税 taxation *kazei suru* ～する tax, impose

kazoeru 数える count, number *kazoekirenai* 数え切れない numberless

kazoku 家族 family

kazu 数 number, figure

ke 毛 hair

kechi na けちな stingy, mean *kechi-kechi suru* けちけちする be stingy, stint, skimp

kedamono けだもの beast, brute, animal

kega けが injury, wound

kegarawashii 汚らわしい dirty, filthy, disgusting

kegare 汚れ impurity, stain **kegareru** 〜る be polluted, be stained **kegareta** 〜た unclean, filthy

kegasu 汚す make dirty, stain

kegawa 毛皮 fur

kegen けげん **kegen na** 〜な suspicious, dubious **kegen sōni** 〜そうに suspiciously, dubiously

kehai 気配 sign, indication

kei(batsu) 刑(罰) punishment, penalty

keiba 競馬 horse racing

keibetsu 軽べつ contempt, scorn, disdain **keibetsu suru** 〜する despise, disdain, look down upon

keibi suru 警備する defend, guard

keiei 経営 management, administration **keiei suru** 〜する manage, run, keep

keigu 敬具 sincerely yours, yours truly

keihaku na 軽薄な frivolous, flippant, insincere

keihi 経費 expense, cost

keii 敬意 respect, regard

keiji 刑事 (police) detective

keiji 掲示 notice

keika 経過 progress, course, lapse

keikai 警戒 warning, caution **keikai suru** 〜する watch, guard

keikai na 軽快な light, nimble

keikaku 計画 plan, project

keikan 警官 policeman, police officer

keiken 経験 experience **keiken suru** 〜する experience, go through

keiki 景気 the times, things, business conditions

keiko けいこ practice, training

keikō 傾向 tendency, trend, inclination

keikoku 警告 warning, caution **keikoku suru** 〜する warn

keikōtō 蛍光灯 fluorescent lamp

keimusho 刑務所 prison, jail

keireki 経歴 one's career, one's past

keiren けいれん convulsions, spasm

keiri 経理 management, accounting

keisan 計算 calculation, counting, computation *keisan suru* 〜する calculate, count

keisatsu 警察 police *keisatsu-sho* 〜署 police station

keisei 形勢 situation, position, state of things

keiseki 形跡 signs, marks, trace

keisha 傾斜 inclination, slope

keisotsu na [ni] 軽率な [に] rash [ly], hasty [-ily], imprudent [ly]

keitai 形態 form, shape

keitai suru 携帯する carry, take with *keitai-yō no* 携帯用の portable, handy, pocket

keito 毛糸 woolen yarn, wool

keitō 系統 system *keitō-teki na* [ni] 〜的な [に] systematic [ally]

keiyaku 契約 contract, agreement *keiyaku suru* 〜する make a contract *keiyaku-sha* 〜者 contractor *keiyaku-sho* 〜書 contract

keiyō 形容 description *keiyō suru* 〜する describe, modify

keiyu 経由 *keiyu shite* 〜して by way of, via *keiyu suru* 〜する pass through, go by way of

keizai 経済 economy, finance *keizai-teki na* 〜的な economic(al) *keizai-gaku* 〜学 economics

keizoku 継続 continuance, last, renew

kekka 結果 result, consequence, end, fruit

kekkan 欠陥 defect, fault *kekkan no aru* 〜の ある defective, faulty

kekkan 血管 blood vessel

kekkon 結婚 marriage *kekkon suru* 〜する marry

kekkō na 結構な fine, good, nice

kekkyoku 結局 after all, finally, in the end, eventually

kembutsu 見物 sightseeing, visit *kembutsu suru* ～する see, visit

kempō 憲法 constitution

kemuri 煙 smoke, fumes

kemutai 煙たい smoky

ken 剣 sword

ken 県 prefecture

kenasu けなす speak ill of, abuse, run down

kenchiku 建築 architecture, construction, building *kenchiku suru* ～する build, construct

ken'i 権威 authority

kenjū けん銃 pistol, gun

kenka けんか quarrel *kenka o suru* ～をする quarrel, fight

kenkai 見解 opinion, view

kenkō 健康 health

kenkyū 研究 study, research *kenkyū suru* ～する study, investigate

kenri 権利 right, claim, priviledge

kenryoku 権力 power, authority *kenryoku no aru* ～のある powerful, influential

kensa 検査 inspection, test *kensa suru* ～する inspect, examine, check, test

kensetsu 建設 construction, establishment *kensetsu suru* ～する construct, build

kenshō 懸賞 prize

kentō 見当 guess, conjecture, estimate

ken'yaku 倹約 frugality, economy *ken'yaku suru* ～する be frugal, save, economize

kenzen na 健全な sound

keorimono 毛織物 woolen goods [fabrics, textiles]

keredomo けれども but, however, though

keru ける kick

kesa 今朝 this morning

keshigomu 消しゴム eraser, rubber

keshi-in 消印 cancellation stamp, postmark

keshiki 景色 scenery, scene, landscape

keshō suru 化粧する make up one's face, make one's toilet

kessaku 傑作 masterpiece

kessan 決算 settlement of accounts

kesseki 欠席 absence *kesseki suru* ～する be absent, stay away

kesshin 決心 determination, resolution *kesshin suru* ～する determine, be determined

kesshite 決して never, by no means, on no account

kessuru 決する decide

kesu 消す put out, blow out, switch off, turn out

ketatamashii けたたましい noisy, loud

ketsuron 結論 conclusion *ketsuron suru* ～する conclude

kettei 決定 decision *kettei suru* ～する decide

ketten 欠点 defect, fault

kettō 血統 blood

kezuru 削る shave, sharpen, cut down

ki 木 tree, wood

ki 気 heart, mind, spirit, feelings

ki no hayai ～の早い hasty, quick, hot-tempered

ki ga susumanai ～が進まない be unwilling (to do)

ki ga suru ～がする feel, think

ki ni suru ～にする mind, care, be nervous about, worry

ki no yowai[*chiisai*] ～の弱い[小さい] timid, fainthearted

ki no kikanai ～のきかない dull, dull-witted

ki ni iru ～にいる be pleased [satisfied] with

ki ni kuwanai ～にくわない hateful, disagreeable

ki ni naru ～になる feel uneasy about, be anxious about

ki ga tsuku ～が付く notice, become aware

ki o ushinau ～を失う faint, swoon

ki(-iro) 黄(色) yellow

kiatsu 気圧 atmospheric [barometeric, air] pressure

kiba きば tusk, fang

kibarashi 気晴らし pastime, recreation

kibi-kibi shita きびきびした quick, brisk, lively, active

kibin na 機敏な smart, shrewd

kibishii 厳しい severe, strict *kibishiku* 厳しく severely, strictly

kibo 規模 scale, scope

kibō (suru) 希望(する) hope, wish, desire

kibun 気分 feeling, humor, mood

kichi 機知 wit *kichi ni tonda* ～に富んだ witty

kichi 基地 base

kichigai 気違い madman, craziness *kichigai no* ～の mad, crazy

kichinto きちんと accurately, exactly, in good order

kichōmen na きちょうめんな regular, square, punctual

kichō na 貴重な valuable, precious

kidoru 気取る put on airs, be affected

kieru 消える go out, be put out

kifu 寄付 contribution *kifu suru* ～する contribute

kigane suru 気兼ねする feel constrained

kigeki 喜劇 comedy

kigen 期限 period, term, deadline *kigen no kireta* ～の切れた time-expired

kigen 起原 origin, rise, beginning

kigen 機嫌 humor, mood, temper

kigō 記号 sign, mark

kigu 器具 implement, instrument

kigyō 企業 enterprise

kihon 基本 standard, basis *kihon-teki na* ～的な basic

kiji 記事 account, statement, news article

kiji 生地 cloth, suit material, dress material

kijitsu 期日 date, appointed day

kijun 基準 standard, basis

kikai 機械 machine, mechanism　*kikai-ka suru* 〜化する mechanize

kikai 機会 opportunity, chance, occasion

kikan 期間 term, period

kikan 機関 engine　*kikanshi* 〜士 engineer, engine driver

kikazaru 着飾る dress up

kiken 危険 danger, peril, risk　*kiken na* 〜な dangerous

kiki 危機 crisis

kikitoru 聞き取る catch, follow, understand, hear *kikimorasu* 聞き漏らす fail to hear, miss hearing

kikō 気候 climate, weather

kikoku suru 帰国する return to one's country, come [go] home

kiku 聞[聴]く hear, listen to

kiku 菊 chrysanthemum

kiku 利く be effective

kikyō 帰郷 homecoming　*kikyō suru* 〜する go [come] home

kimaru 決る be decided [settled, arranged]

kimben 勤勉 diligence, industry　*kimben na* 〜な diligent, industrious

kimeru 決める decide, settle, arrange

kimi 君 you　*kimi no* 〜の your　*kimi ni [o]* 〜に[を] you

kimi 黄身 yolk

kimijika na 気短な short-tempered, quick-tempered

kimmu 勤務 service, duty, work　*kimmu suru* 〜する serve, work

kimo 肝 liver, courage

kimochi 気持 feeling, sensation, mood　*kimochi no yoi [warui]* 〜のよい[悪い] [un]pleasant, [un]comfortable

kimono 着物 clothes, garments, dress　*kimono*

o kiru 〜を着る put on clothes *kimono o nugu* 〜を脱ぐ take off clothes

kimpaku suru 緊迫する grow strained, become acute

kimpatsu 金髪 blond

kimuzukashii 気難しい hard to please, particular

kimyō na 奇妙な strange, curious

kin 金 gold, money *kin no* 〜の golden

kinchō 緊張 strain, tension *kinchō suru* 〜する become tense, be strained *kinchō shita* 〜した strained, tense, attentive

kindai 近代 the modern age, recent times *kindai no* 〜の modern

kinen 記念 commemoration, memory

kingaku 金額 amount of money, sum

kingan 近眼 short-sightedness *kingan no* 〜の near-sighted

kingyo 金魚 goldfish

kinjiru 禁じる forbid, prohibit

kinjo 近所 neighborhood *kinjo no* 〜の neighboring, nearby

kinka 金貨 gold coin

kinko 金庫 safe, strongbox

kin'niku 筋肉 muscles, sinews

kinō 機能 function, faculty

kinō 昨日 yesterday

kinodoku na 気の毒な pitiable, pitiful

kinsen 金銭 money, cash

kinshi 禁止 prohibition, ban *kinshi suru* 〜する forbid, prohibit

kinu 絹 silk

kin'yō-bi 金曜日 Friday

kinyū 記入 entry *kinyū suru* 〜する enter, make an entry, record

kinzoku 金属 metal

kioku 記憶 memory, remembrance *kioku suru* 〜する remember, bear in mind *kioku-subeki* 〜すべき memorable

kippari きっぱり distinctly, frankly, positively

kippu 切符 ticket *katamichi-kippu* 片道〜 single (ticket), one way ticket *ōfuku-kippu* 往復〜 return ticket *kippu-uriba* 〜売場 ticket office, booking office

kirai 嫌い dislike *kirai na* 〜な hateful, disgusting

kira-kira きらきら glitteringly, brilliantly

kiraku na 気楽な easygoing *kiraku ni* 気楽に comfortably, at ease

kirameku きらめく glitter, sparkle, twinkle

kirau 嫌う dislike, hate, detest

kire きれ cloth, piece, bit, slice, strip, cut

kirei na[ni] 奇麗な[に] beautiful[ly], pretty, clean, lovely *kirei ni suru* 奇麗にする clean, beautify

kireru 切れる cut well, be sharp

kiri 霧 fog, mist *kiri no fukai* 〜の深い foggy

kiri きり gimlet, awl

kiritaosu 切り倒す cut down, fell

kiritoru 切り取る cut off, clip

kiritsu 規律 order, discipline

kiritsumeru 切り詰める shorten, cut down, reduce

kiritsu suru 起立する stand up, rise, come to attention

kiroku 記録 record *kiroku suru* 〜する record, write down

kiru 着る put on, wear, have on, be dressed in

kiru 切る cut, carve, saw

kiryoku 気力 energy, vigor, spirit

kiryū 気流 air current

kisei 気勢 spirit *kisei o ageru* 〜を上げる inspire

kisei no 既製の ready-made

kisei suru 帰省する go [come, return] home, return to one's native place

kiseki 奇跡 miracle, wonder *kiseki-teki na* 〜的な miraculous

kisen 汽船 steamer, steamship

kiseru 着せる dress, clothe

kisetsu 季節 season

kisha 汽車 steam train, carriage, coach

kisha 記者 journalist, reporter

kishi 岸 shore, bank, coast *kishi ni* ～に a-shore, on shore

kishitsu 気質 disposition, nature, temper

kishō 気性 nature, disposition

kishō 気象 weather *kishō-chō* ～庁 the Meteorological Agency

kishō 記章 medal, badge, decoration

kishu 騎手 jockey

kiso 基礎 foundation, basis

kisoku 規則 rule, regulation

kissaten 喫茶店 tearoom

kisū 奇数 odd number

kita 北 north *kita no* ～の north, northern

kitai 期待 expectation, hope *kitai suru* ～する expect, hope for, look forward to

kitai 気体 gaseous body, gas, vapor

kitaku suru 帰宅する come [return] home, go home

kitanai 汚い dirty, foul

kitchiri きっちり punctually, sharp, just, exactly, perfectly

kitsune きつね fox

kitte 切手 (postage) stamp

kitto きっと surely, certainly

kiwamete 極めて very, exceedingly, extremely

kiyō na[ni] 器用な[に] clever[ly], skillful[ly]

kizamu 刻む cut, mince, hash

kiza na きざな affected, conceited, disagreeable

kizetsu suru 気絶する faint away, go faint, lose one's senses

kizoku 貴族 peer, noble

kizu 傷 wound, injury, cut, scar *kizu-guchi* ～口 wound *kizu-gusuri* ～薬 ointment, salve

kizukau 気遣う be [feel] anxious for [about],

be afraid of, worry about

kizuku 気付く notice, become aware of

ko 弧 arc

ko 子 child, baby, infant

kobin 小びん small bottle

kobito 小人 pygmy, dwarf

koboreru こぼれる fall, spill, be spilled, over-flow

kobosu こぼす spill, shed, complain

kobu こぶ wen, swelling, bump, lump

kōbu 後部 rear, back part

kobun 子分 follower, adherent

kobushi こぶし fist

kōbutsu 鉱物 mineral

kōcha 紅茶 black tea

kōchi 高地 high ground, upland

kochira こちら this place, here, this side

kochō 誇張 exaggeration *kochō suru* ～する exaggerate *kochō shita* ～した exaggerated

kōchō 校長 principal, director, schoolmaster, president

kodai 古代 ancient [old] times *kodai no* ～の ancient

kōdai na 広大な vast, great, huge

kodawaru こだわる be particular, stick to

kōden 香典 funeral gift

kōdo 高度 altitude, height

kōdō 行動 action, conduct, deed *kōdō suru* ～する act

kodoku 孤独 solitude, loneliness *kodoku no* ～の solitary, lonely

kōdoku 購読 subscription *kōdoku suru* ～する subscribe *kōdoku-sha* ～者 subscriber

kodomo 子供 child *kodomo o umu* ～を産む bear a child *kodomo-rashii* ～らしい childish, childlike

koe 声 voice, cry

kōei 光栄 honor, glory *kōei ni omou* ～に思う feel honored

kōen 講演 lecture, speech, address *kōen suru* ～する give a lecture, make an address

kōen 公園 park

kōen suru 後援する support, back up

koeru 肥える grow [get] fat, grow fertile [rich] *koeta* 肥えた fat, stout, rich, fertile

koeru 越える go over, jump over, exceed

kofū 古風 old fashion *kofū na* ～な old-fashioned

kōfuku 幸福 happiness, welfare *kōfuku na* ～な happy, blessed, fortunate *kōfuku ni* ～に happily

kōfun 興奮 excitement *kōfun suru* ～する be excited, become warm *kōfun-shiyasui* ～しやすい excitable, be easily excited

kogai 戸外 the open (air) *kogai de* ～で out of doors, outdoors *kogai no* ～の outdoor, open-air

kōgai 郊外 suburbs, outskirts, environs

kogasu 焦がす burn, scorch, singe

kogata no 小型の small-sized, small, miniature, midget

kogecha 焦茶 dark brown

kōgeki 攻撃 attack, assault

kōgen 高原 highland

kogeru 焦げる burn, be scorched

kōgi 講義 lecture

kōgi 抗議 protest, objection *kōgi suru* ～する make a protest, object to

kogitte 小切手 check

kōgo 口語 spoken language, colloquial speech *kōgo no* ～の spoken, colloquial

kogoeru 凍える benumbed, frozen

kogoto 小言 scolding, rebuke, complaint *kogoto o iu* ～を言う scold, rebuke, grumble

kogu こぐ (*boat*) row

kōgyō 工業 industry, industries *kōgyō no* ～の industrial

kōhan 後半 latter half, second half

kōhei na [**ni**] 公平な [に] fair[ly], impartial [ly], just[ly]

kōho 候補 candidate

kōhyō 好評 favorable criticism *kōhyō de aru* 〜である be popular

kōhyō 公表 official [public] announcement

koi 恋 love, tenderness, passion *koi o suru* 〜をする love

koi 濃い dark, deep

kōi 行為 act [action], deed

kōi 好意 kindness, favor

koibito 恋人 lover, love, sweetheart

koishii 恋しい dear(est), darling

kōiu (=**kōyū**) こういう such, (like) this

koji 孤児 orphan

kōji 工事 work(s), construction *kōji-chū* 〜中 under construction

kojiki こじき beggar

kojimmari shita 小ぢんまりした snug, cozy, neat

kojin 個人 individual

kojin 故人 deceased, dead

kōjō 工場 factory, plant, mill

kōka 効果 effect *kōka no aru* 〜のある effective *kōka no nai* 〜のない ineffective

kōka 硬貨 hard money, coin

kōkai 航海 voyage, navigation *kōkai suru* 〜する navigate, sail for

kōkai 後悔 regret, repentance *kōkai suru* 〜する repent of, regret, be sorry for

kōkaidō 公会堂 public hall, town hall

kōkai suru 公開する open (to the public), public

kōka na 高価な expensive, dear, costly

kōkan suru 交換する exchange, make an exchange

koke こけ moss

kōkei 光景 spectacle, sight, scene, view

kokei no 固形の solid

kōken 貢献 contribution, service *kōken suru*

~する contribute to, make a contribution to

kōketsuatsu 高血圧 high blood pressure, hypertension

kōkishin 好奇心 curiosity *kōkishin no tsuyoi* ~の強い curious

kokka 国家 state, country, nation

kokka 国歌 national anthem

kokkai 国会 National Diet, Congress, Parliament

kokkei na こっけいな funny, humorous

kokki 国旗 national flag

kokkyō 国境 frontier, border, boundary

kōkoku 広告 advertisement *kōkoku suru* ~する advertise

kokonotsu 九つ nine

kokoro 心 mind, spirit, heart, will *kokoro-narazumo* ~ならずも against one's will *kokoro ni tomeru* ~に留める bear in mind

kokorobosoi 心細い helpless, hopeless, lonely

kokoroe 心得 knowledge, rules, directions *kokoroeru* ~る know, understand

kokorogakari 心掛り care, anxiety

kokorogakeru 心掛ける intend, mean, keep in mind

kokorogawari 心変り change of mind *kokorogawari ga suru* ~がする change one's heart

kokorogurushii 心苦しい painful, regrettable

kokoromi 試み trial, test, attempt *kokoromiru* ~る try, attempt

kokoroyoi 快い pleasant, agreeable, comfortable *kokoroyoku* 快く pleasantly

kokorozashi 志 will, intention, purpose, ambition *kokorozashi o tateru* ~を立てる aspire, be determined

kōkū 航空 aviation, flying, flight

kokuban 黒板 blackboard *kokuban-fuki* ~ふき eraser

kokufuku 克服 conquest *kokufuku suru* ~する conquer

kokugo 国語 language, national language

kokuhaku 告白 confession *kokuhaku suru ~* する confess

kokuhō 国宝 national treasure

kokujin 黒人 Negro

kokumin 国民 nation, people

kokumotsu 穀物 grain, corn, cereals

kokunai 国内 interior *kokunai no ~の* internal, domestic

kokuren 国連 the United Nations

kokuritsu no 国立の national, state, government

kokusai 国際 *kokusai-teki na ~的な* international *kokusai kankei ~関係* international relations

kokusan 国産 home [domestic] production

kokuseki 国籍 nationality

koku suru 濃くする deepen, thicken, make thick [strong]

kokutetsu 国鉄 national railway [railroad]

kokyō 故郷 one's old home, native place

kokyū 呼吸 breath, breathing *kokyū suru ~* する breathe

kōkyū na 高級な high-class grade

koma こま top

komakai 細かい small, fine, minute, close

komaru 困る suffer, be troubled

komban 今晩 this evening, tonight

kome 米 rice

kommyōnichi 今明日 today or [and] tomorrow *kommyōnichi-jū ni ~中に* in a day or two

kompon 根本 foundation, origin *kompon no ~の* basic, radical

komu 込む be packed, be crowded

kōmuin 公務員 public servant, official

komugi 小麦 wheat *komugi-ko ~粉* flour

kōmuru 被る suffer, receive, get

kōmyō na 巧妙な skillful, clever

kon 紺 dark [deep] blue, navy blue

kona 粉 flour, meal, powder

konchū 昆虫 insect

kondate 献立 bill of fare, menu

kondo 今度 this time, next time

kondō suru 混同する confuse, mix up

kōnetsu-hi 光熱費 heat and light expenses

kongetsu 今月 this month

kongo 今後 after this, in the future *kongo no* ～の future, coming

kongō 混合 mixing, mixture *kongō suru* ～する mix, mingle, compound

konimotsu 小荷物 parcel, packet

kon'in 婚姻 marriage, matrimony

kon'i na 懇意な friendly, familiar, intimate

kōnin suru 公認する authorize, approve *kōnin no* 公認の authorized, approved

konki 根気 patience, endurance *konki ga yoi* ～がよい patient *konki yoku* ～よく patiently

kon'na こんな such, (like) this *kon'na ni* ～に so *kon'na fū ni* ～風に like this

kon'nan 困難 difficulty, trouble *kon'nan na* ～な difficult, hard, troublesome

kon'nichi 今日 today, this day, these days, at present *kon'nichi no* ～の of the days, present-day

konoaida この間 the other day, some time ago

konogoro このごろ now, at present, recently *tsui konogoro* ついこのごろ only the other day, quite recently

konohen ni この辺に near [about, around] here, in this neighborhood

konokurai このくらい about this, about so much [many, big, long]

konomae この前 last, last time, previously *konomae no* ～の last, previous, former

konomashii 好ましい desirable, nice *konomashikunai* 好ましくない undesirable

konomi 木の実 fruits, nuts, berries

konomi 好み taste, liking *konomi no* ～の favorite

konomu 好む like, be fond of

konosai この際 at this juncture, now, under the circumstances

konotabi この度 this time, now

konotoki この時 at this time [moment]

konotsugi この次 next [another] time

konran 混乱 confusion, disorder   *konran suru* 〜する be confused

konsento コンセント electrical outlet, plug receptacle

konshū 今週 this week

kon'ya 今夜 tonight, this evening

kon'yaku 婚約 engagement   *kon'yaku suru* 〜する engage oneself to, be engaged to

kore これ this   *korera* 〜ら these   *koremade* 〜まで so far, until now

kōri 氷 ice   *kōri no yōna* 〜のような icy

koriru 懲りる learn by experience

koritsu 孤立 isolation   *koritsu shita* 〜した isolated, solitary

koro ころ time, about, toward   *sono koro* その〜 in those days, at that time

kōro 航路 sea route, course, line

korobu 転ぶ tumble (down), fall (down)

kōrogi こおろぎ cricket

kōron 口論 dispute, quarrel

korosu 殺す kill, murder

koru 凝る stiffen, be absorbed in

kōru 凍る freeze, be frozen

kōryo 考慮 consideration, thought   *kōryo suru* 〜する consider

kōsai 交際 intercourse   *kōsai suru* 〜する associate with

kosame 小雨 light rain

kōsa suru 交差する cross, intersect

kōsaten 交差点 junction, intersection, crossing

kosei 個性 individual character

kōsei 構成 construction, composition   *kōsei suru* 〜する constitute

kōsei 公正 justice *kōsei na* ～な just, fair

kōsei 校正 proof-reading

koseki 戸籍 (census) register

kōsen 光線 light, beam

kōsha 校舎 schoolhouse, school building

kōsha 後者 latter

koshi 腰 waist, hip

kōshi 講師 lecturer, speaker

koshikake 腰掛 seat, chair, bench

kōshiki 公式 formality, formula

kōshin 行進 march, parade

koshō 故障 accident, defect *koshō suru* ～する get out of order, break down

kōshoku 好色 *kōshoku no* ～の amorous, lewd *kōshoku bungaku* ～文学 pornographic literature, pornography

kōshū 公衆 public *kōshū-denwa* ～電話 public telephone

kōsō (no) 高層(の) many-storied, tall *kōsō-biru* 高層ビル tall [high-rise] buildings

kossori こっそり quietly, secretly

kosu こす filter, strain

kōsui 香水 perfume, scent

kosuru こする rub, scrub

kotae 答え answer, reply, solution *kotaeru* ～る answer, reply

kōtai 交代 turn, relief *kōtai suru* ～する take turns, take place *kōtai de* ～で by turns, in turn

kōtaishi 皇太子 Crown Prince

kōtai suru 後退する retrograde, recede, retreat

kōtei 皇帝 emperor

kōtei 校庭 playgrounds, schoolgrounds

kotei suru 固定する be fixed, settle

koten 古典 classics, classical literature

koto 事 thing, matter, affair, fact

koto 琴 Japanese harp

kōtō (no) 高等(の) high, advanced, high-class *kōtō-gakkō* ～学校 senior high school

kōtō 口頭 *kōtō no* 〜の oral, verbal

kotoba 言葉 speech, language, word, term

kotogotoku ことごとく all, one and all, entirely

kōtokushin 公徳心 public morality

kotonaru 異なる differ from, be different from *kotonatta* 異なった different

kotoni 殊に (e)specially, particularly, in particular, above all

kotori 小鳥 small [little] bird

kotoshi 今年 this year

kotowari 断り refusal, excuse, apology *kotowaru* 断る decline, refuse, apologize

kotowaza ことわざ proverb, maxim

kotozuke 言付け message

kōtsū 交通 communication, traffic

kotsubu 小粒 small grain

kōtsugō na 好都合な favorable, fortunate

kouma 小馬 pony, 子馬 colt

kōun 幸運 good fortune, good luck *kōun na* 〜な fortunate, lucky *kōun nimo* 〜にも fortunately

kouri 小売り retail *kouri suru* 〜する retail

koushi 子牛 calf

kowagaru 怖がる fear, be afraid of, dread

kowareru 壊れる break, be broken, be damaged, break down, get out of order

kowasu 壊す break, destroy, ruin

koya 小屋 cottage, hut, cabin

kōya 荒野 wildness, waste, the wilds

koyagi 子山羊 kid

kōyō 紅葉 red leaves, autumnal foliage

koyomi 暦 calendar, almanac

kōza 講座 chair, course, professorship

kōza 口座 bank account *kōza o hiraku* 〜を開く open an account

kozeni 小銭 change, small change [money]

kōzō 構造 structure, construction

kozue こずえ treetop, twigs

kōzui 洪水 flood, inundation

kozukai 小遣 pocket money

kozutsumi 小包 package, parcel *yūbin kozutsumi* 郵便〜 parcel post

ku 句 phrase, clause

ku 区 ward, district, area

ku 九, 9 nine

kubaru 配る distribute, deal out, deliver

kubetsu 区別 distinction, difference, classfication, division *kubetsu suru* 〜する distinguish

kubi 首 neck

kuchi 口 mouth

kuchibashi くちばし bill, beak

kuchibeni 口紅 rouge, lipstick

kuchibiru くちびる lip

kuchibue 口笛 whistle

kuchi-yakamashii 口やかましい sharp-tongued, nagging

kuchizuke 口付け kiss

kūchū 空中 *kūchū no* 〜の aerial, air *kūchū ni* 〜に in the air [sky]

kuda 管 pipe, tube

kudakeru 砕ける break, go to pieces, be broken

kudamono 果物 fruit, fruits

kudaranai 下らない trifling, worthless, useless

kudaru 下る go down, descend, fall

kudoi くどい tedious, lengthy

kufū 工夫 device, invention, contrive, design

kūfuku 空腹 hunger *kūfuku na* 〜な hungry

ku-gatsu 九月 September

kugi くぎ nail, peg

kugiri 区切り end, stop, pause *kugiru* 区切る divide, mark off

kūgun 空軍 air force *kūgun-kichi* 〜基地 air base

kuguru くぐる dive, pass under

kūhaku 空白 blank

kuichigau 食い違う run counter, collide *kui-*

chigai 食い違い discrepancy

kuisugiru 食い過ぎる eat too much, overeat

kuji くじ lot, lottery

kujikeru くじける be discouraged, lose heart

kujira 鯨 whale

kujō 苦情 complaint *kujō o iu* 〜を言う complain (of), grumble

kūkan 空間 space, room

kukei 矩形 rectangle

kuki 茎 stalk, stem

kūki 空気 air, atmosphere

kukkiri くっきり distinctly, clearly

kūkō 空港 airport

kuma くま bear

kumi 組 class, company, group

kumiai 組合 association, partnership, union

kumiawase 組合せ combination, assortment *kumiawaseru* 組合せる combine, join together, match

kumifuseru 組み伏せる hold down, put under

kumitsuku 組つく grapple with, seize hold of

kumo くも spider *kumo no su* 〜の巣 (cob) web

kumo 雲 cloud

kumoru 曇る become cloudy, become dim *kumori no* 曇りの cloudy

kumoyuki 雲行 sky, weather, situation

kumu 組む braid, plait, unite with

kumu 汲む draw, ladle, dip

kuni 国 country, land, state, nation

kunren 訓練 training, exercise *kunren suru* 〜する train

kura 倉 warehouse, storehouse

kuraberu 比べる compare, make a comparison

kuragari de 暗がりで in the dark (ness)

kurai 位 grade, rank, about, some

kurai 暗い dark, gloomy

kurashi 暮し living, life

kurasu 暮す live, make a living

kure 暮 the end of the year *yūgure* 夕暮 night-fall

kureru 暮れる grow [get] dark

kureru くれる give

kuri くり chestnut

kurikaesu 繰り返す repeat, do...over again *kurikaeshite* 繰り返して repeatedly

kurinuku くりぬく scoop [gouge] out

kuro 黒 black *kuroi* 〜い black

kurō 苦労 troubles, hardships *kurō suru* 〜する go through hardship, suffer hardship

kurōto 玄人 expert, professional

kuru 来る come

kuru-kuru くるくる (turn) round and round

kuruma 車 car, wheel, motor car *kuruma ni noru* 〜に乗る take a car

kurumi くるみ walnut

kurushii 苦しい painful, needy

kurushimeru 苦しめる torment, torture, worry

kurushimi 苦しみ pain

kurushimu 苦しむ feel pain, suffer

kuruu 狂う go mad, be out of order

kusa 草 grass, weed

kusai 臭い bad [foul]-smelling, stinking, offen-sive

kusamura 草むら bush

kusaraseru 腐らせる spoil, rot, addle, be dis-couraged

kusari 鎖 chain

kusaru 腐る rot, go bad, decay, feel blue [gloomy]

kuse 癖 habit *kuse ni naru* 〜になる get into a habit

kūseki 空席 vacant seat, room

kusha-kusha (no) くしゃくしゃ(の) (c)rum-pled, creased *kusha-kusha ni suru* 〜にする crumple up

kushami くしゃみ sneeze, sneezing

kushi 串 spit, skewer *kushi ni sasu* 〜に刺す spit, skewer

kushi 櫛 comb

kushin 苦心 pains, efforts *kushin suru* ～する work hard, take pains

kūsō 空想 fancy, vision, imagination *kūsō suru* ～する fancy, imagine, dream

kusuburu くすぶる smoke

kusuguru くすぐる tickle *kusuguttai* くすぐったい ticklish

kusuri 薬 medicine, remedy *kusuri o nomu* ～を飲む take medicine *kusuri-ya* ～屋 pharmacy *kusuri-yubi* ～指 ring finger

kutō 句読 punctuation *kutō-ten* ～点 punctuation marks

kutsu 靴 shoes, boots *kutsu issoku* ～一足 a pair of shoes *kutsu-bera* ～べら shoehorn *kutsu-himo* ～ひも shoestring, shoelace *kutsu o haku* ～を履く put on one's shoes

kutsū 苦痛 pain, agony, strain

kutsugaesu 覆す upset, overturn, overthrow

kutsurogu くつろぐ make oneself at home, relax, unbend

kutsushita 靴下 socks, stockings

kuttsuku くっつく stick to [together], paste

kuwadate 企て plan, project, plot, attempt

kuwaeru 加える add, add up

kuwaeru くわえる hold [take] in one's mouth

kuwashii 詳しい minute, full, detailed, knew well

kuyami 悔み condolence, sympathy

kuyamu 悔やむ repent, regret, condole

kuyashii 悔しい vexing, regrettable *kuyashigaru* 悔しがる be vexed, regret

kuyo-kuyo suru くよくよする worry, brood

kūyu 空輸 air transport(ation)

kuzu くず waste, refuse, rubbish, scraps *kuzu-kago* ～かご waste basket

kuzureru 崩れる collapse, break, fall

kuzusu 崩す break, destroy, demolish

kyabetsu キャベツ cabbage

kyaku 客 visitor, guest, customer, passenger

kyō 今日 today

kyōbai 競売 auction

kyōchō 協調 cooperation, harmony   *kyōchō suru* ～する cooperate   *kyōchō-teki na* ～的な cooperative

kyōchō suru 強調する emphasize, stress

kyōdai 兄弟 brother, sister

kyōdō 共同 cooperation, association   *kyōdō no* ～の common

kyōfu 恐怖 fear, terror

kyōgaku 共学 coeducation

kyōgi 協議 conference, discussion   *kyōgi suru* ～する talk over, discuss

kyōgū 境遇 circumstances, surroundings, condition

kyōhaku 脅迫 threat, compulsion

kyōi 驚異 wonder   *kyōi no* ～の wonderful

kyōiku 教育 education   *kyōiku suru* ～する educate

kyojin 巨人 giant

kyōju 教授 professor

kyōkai 協会 society, association

kyōkai 教会 church, chapel

kyōkasho 教科書 textbook

kyoku 曲 tune, air, piece, music

kyoku 局 bureau, office

kyokusen 曲線 curved line, curve

kyokutan 極端 extreme, extremity   *kyokutan na [ni]* ～な[に] extreme[ly]

kyōkyū 供給 supply, provision   *kyōkyū suru* ～する supply with, provide with

kyōmi 興味 interest, taste   *kyōmi no aru* ～のある interesting   *kyomi ga aru* ～がある be interested in

kyonen 去年 last year

kyōretsu na 強烈な intense, strong

kyori 距離 distance, range

kyōri 郷里 one's (old) home, native place

kyōryoku na 強力な strong, powerful

kyōsei 強制 compulsion *kyōsei suru* ～する compel, force

kyōshi 教師 teacher, master

kyōshitsu 教室 classroom

kyōshuku suru 恐縮する be grateful [much obliged] to

kyōsō 競争 competition *kyōsō suru* ～する compete with

kyōsō 競走 race, run *kyōsō suru* ～する run a race

kyōtei 協定 agreement, convention *kyōtei suru* ～する agree on, arrange

kyōtsū no 共通の common

kyōwakoku 共和国 republic, commonwealth

kyōyō 教養 culture, education

kyozetsu 拒絶 refusal, rejection *kyozetsu suru* ～する refuse, reject

kyū 球 ball, globe

kyū 九, 9 nine

kyūbyō 急病 sudden illness

kyūden 宮殿 palace

kyūji 給仕 waiter, waitress, steward, stewardess

kyūjitsu 休日 holiday

kyūka 休暇 holidays, vacation *kyūka o toru* ～をとる take a holiday

kyūkei 休憩 rest, recess

kyūkō 急行 express (train), rapid service

kyūkon 求婚 proposal *kyūkon suru* ～する propose

kyūkon 球根 bulb, tuber

kyūkutsu na 窮屈な narrow, strict

kyūkyū 救急 first aid *kyūkyū-sha* ～車 ambulance *kyūkyū-yaku* ～薬 first-aid medicine

kyū na[ni] 急な[に] quick[ly], hasty[-ily], sudden[ly]

kyūryō 給料 pay, salary

kyūshi suru 休止する stop, cease, pause

kyūsho 急所 vital spot, vital point

kyūsoku 休息 rest, relaxation *kyūsoku suru* ～

する rest, take a rest

kyūsoku no [ni] 急速の[に] rapid[ly], swift[ly]

kyūyō 急用 urgent business

kyūyū 旧友 old friend

M

ma 間 space, room, interval

mā まあ Oh!; Dear me!

maatarashii 真新しい fresh, new

mabataki まばたき wink, blink

mabayui まばゆい dazzling, glaring

maboroshi 幻 vision, dream, phantom, illusion

mabushii まぶしい dazzling, glaring

machi 町 town, city *machi-jū* ～中 the whole town

machiaishitsu 待合室 waiting room

machigaeru 間違える make a mistake, mistake

machigai 間違い mistake, error *machigai nai* ～ない unmistakable, right, correct

machigatte 間違って by mistake, by accident

machikaneru 待ち兼ねる wait impatiently for

mada まだ (not) yet, as yet, so far, still

made まで till, until, up to, as far as

madeni までに by, by the time, before, not later than

mado 窓 window *mado-garasu* ～ガラス windowpane

mae 前 front *mae no* ～の former, previous *mae no hi* ～の日 the previous day *mae ni* ～に ago, since, before *mae de* ～で in front of *maemotte* ～もって beforehand, in advance

maeashi 前足 forefoot, foreleg, paw

maeuri 前売り booking, advance sale

mafuyu 真冬 midwinter

magarikado 曲り角 corner, turning

magari suru 間借りする take [rent] a room

magari-nin 間借人 lodger, roomer

magaru 曲る bend, curve

magatte 曲って bent, crooked, winding

mageru 曲げる bend, curve, crook

magirawashii 紛らわしい misleading, confusing

magiwa ni 間際に just before, at the last moment

mago 孫 grandchild, grandson, granddaughter

magokoro 真心 sincerity, true heart *magokoro komete* ~こめて devotedly, earnestly

mago-mago suru(=**magotsuku**) まごまごする [まごつく] get confused, be perplexed, wander [knock] about, hang about, be embarrassed

maguro まぐろ tunny, tuna (fish)

mahō 魔法 magic, witchcraft *mahō-tsukai* ~使い magician, wizard, witch

mahōbin 魔法びん vacuum bottle, thermos (bottle)

mai 舞 dancing, dance

mai 毎 every *maiasa* ~朝 every morning *maiban* ~晩 every night [evening], night after night

maido 毎度 each [every] time, often, frequently, always

maigo 迷子 lost [missing, stray] child

mainen 毎年 every year, yearly, annually *mainen no* ~の annual, yearly

mainichi 毎日 every day, daily

mairu 参る go, come, be beaten, be annoyed

maishū 毎週 every week, weekly

majime まじめ seriousness, earnestness *majime na*[*ni*] ~な[に] serious[ly], earnest[ly]

majinai まじない charm

majiwari 交わり intercourse, association

majiwaru 交わる associate with, come in contact with

majo 魔女 witch, sorceress

majutsu 魔術 conjuring trick, jugglery *majutsu-shi* ~師 juggler, magician

makaseru 任せる leave, commit to a person's care

makasu 負かす defeat, beat, get the better of

make 負け defeat **makeru** 〜る be defeated, be beaten, lose

maki まき (fire)wood

makiba 牧場 pasture, grass

makimono 巻物 scroll, rolled item

makka (na) 真っ赤(な) deep red, crimson

makkuro (na) 真っ黒(な) deep black

maku まく scatter, spread, sprinkle, sow, plant

maku 幕 theater curtain, act or scene (of a play)

maku 巻く wind, roll, coil

makura 枕 pillow

mama (ni) まま(に) as, as it is, with

mamahaha まま母 stepmother

mame 豆 bean, pea

mamonaku 間もなく soon, presently

mamoru 守る keep, defend, protect, observe

man 万 ten thousand

manabu 学ぶ learn, take lessons, study

manaita まな板 chopping board

manatsu 真夏 midsummer

manchō 満潮 high tide

mane まね imitation, mimicry **maneru** 〜る imitate, mimic

maneki 招き invitation

maneku 招く invite, ask

manga 漫画 cartoon, caricature

mangetsu 満月 full moon

maniau 間に合う be in time for, catch, do

man'ichi 万一 by any chance, if...should

man'in (no) 満員(の) jammed, overcrowded

mankai 満開 in full bloom

man'naka 真ん中 the middle, central

man'nenhitsu 万年筆 fountain pen

manugareru 免れる escape, be saved from, avoid

manzoku 満足 satisfaction, gratification, contentment

manzoku suru ～する be satisfied, be gratified, be contènted

manzoku na[ni] ～な[に] satisfactory[-ily]

mare na まれな rare, unusual, uncommon

mare ni まれに rarely, seldom

maru 丸 circle, ring *maruku* ～く round, in a circle *marui* ～い circular, round

marude まるで quite, entirely, perfectly, as if…, as it were, so to speak

masaka まさか by no means, can not be; It is improbable that…

masani まさに just, exactly, certainly, be about to do

masaru 勝る surpass, be superior to

masatsu 摩擦 friction, rub, chafe

mashite まして much [still] more, much [still] less

massaichū 真っ最中 in the midst of, at the height of

massaki ni 真っ先に at the very start, first, first of all

massao na 真っ青な deep blue, deathly pale

masshiro na 真っ白な pure white

massugu na まっすぐな straight, in a straight line

masu ます salmon trout

masu 増す increase, grow, gain

masu-masu ますます more and more, still more

mata また and, again, once more, besides

matagaru またがる ride, mount, sit astride

matagu またぐ step over [across]

mataseru 待たせる keep waiting

matataki 瞬き wink, blink

matataku 瞬く wink, blink, flicker, twinkle

mata wa または or, either…or

mato 的 mark, target

matomeru まとめる settle, arrange

matomete まとめて in a lump, by the lump

matsu 松 pine (tree)

matsu 待つ wait for, look forward to, expect

matsuri 祭 festival

mattaku 全く quite, entirely

mau 舞う dance

maue 真上 right above, overhead

mawari まわり circumference, surroundings, around, tour

mawaru 回る turn round, revolve, rotate

mawasu 回す turn, revolve, spin

mayonaka 真夜中 in the middle of the night, in the dead of night

mayou 迷う be puzzled [perplexed], lose one's way

mayowasu 迷わす perplex, puzzle, mislead

mayu まゆ eyebrow *mayu o hisomeru* ～を ひそめる knit one's brows, frown

maza-maza to まざまざと clearly, vividly

mazeru まぜる mix, mingle

mazu まず first (of all), to begin with

mazushii 貧しい poor

me 目 eye *me ga sameru* ～が覚める awake

me 芽 bud, sprout

meate 目当て aim, purpose

mebaeru 芽生える sprout, bud

medatsu 目立つ stand out, be conspicuous, attract attention

medetai 目出たい happy, joyous

megane 眼鏡 glasses, spectacles

megumi 恵み blessing, mercy, charity

megumu 恵む favor, bless, give money in charity

megusuri 目薬 eye lotion, eyewash

mei めい niece

meibo 名簿 list

meibutsu 名物 special product

meichū 命中 hit *meichū suru* ～する hit, strike

meigetsu 名月 bright moon

meihaku na [ni] 明白な[に] clear[ly], obvious

[ly], evident [ly]

meijin 名人 master, expert

meirei 命令 order, orders, command *meirei suru* ～する order, command

meisei 名声 fame, note, reputation

meishi 名刺 name [calling] card

meishi 名詞 noun

meishin 迷信 superstition

meisho 名所 famous sight, place of interest

meiwaku 迷惑 trouble, bother, annoyance *meiwaku na* ～な troublesome, annoying

meiyo 名誉 reputation, honor

mekata 目方 weight

mekki めっき gilding, plating

mekura めくら blind person

memori 目盛 graduation

men 面 face, surface, mask

mendō 面倒 trouble, difficulty *mendō o miru* ～をみる take care of, look after *mendō-kusai* ～臭い troublesome, tiresome

mendori めん鳥 hen, pullet

menjo 免除 exemption *menjo suru* ～する exempt, remit

menkai 面会 interview, meeting *menkai suru* ～する see, meet, interview

menomae ni 目の前に before one's eyes, in one's presence

menseki 面積 area

mensuru 面する face, front

meshi 飯 cooked rice

meshiagaru 召し上がる eat, help oneself to

mesu 雌 female

metsubō 滅亡 (down)fall, ruin

metta ni めったに seldom, rarely, scarcely

mezamashii 目覚ましい conspicuous, striking, remarkable

mezameru 目覚める wake up, awaken

mezasu 目指す aim at, have an eye on

mezurashii 珍しい rare, curious, uncommon

mezurashiku 珍しく unusually, uncommonly

mezurashisō ni 珍しそうに curiously

mi 実 berry, fruit, nut

miageru 見上げる look up at, look up to

mibōjin 未亡人 widow

mibun 身分 social position

miburi 身振り gesture

miburui 身震い shudder, shiver *miburui suru* ～する shudder, tremble, shiver

michi 道 way, road, street

michibiku 導く lead, guide, show in

michigaeru 見違える (mis)take...for

michi no 未知の strange, unknown

michiru 満ちる be full of, be filled with

midareru 乱れる be disordered, be confused, be in disorder

midashi 見出し title, headline, caption

midasu 乱す put out of order, disturb, disar--range

midori 緑 green

mieru 見える see, be visible, come into sight *(yōni) mieru* (ように)見える look, seem, appear, resemble

migaku 磨く polish, clean, brush

migi 右 right *migi-gawa* ～側 right side

migite 右手 right hand

migoto na 見事な fine, splendid, admirable

migurushii 見苦しい ugly, unbecoming

miharashi 見晴らし view, outlook *miharashi ga yoi* ～がよい command [have] a fine view

mihari 見張り watch, lookout

mihon 見本 sample, specimen, pattern

miidasu 見いだす find, discover

mijikai 短い short, brief

mijikaku suru 短くする make [cut] short, shorten

mijime na 惨めな miserable, pitiable

mijuku na 未熟な unripe, green, poor

mikaiketsu no 未解決の unsolved, unsettled

mikai no 未開の uncivilized, savage

mikake 見掛け appearance, show, look

mikaku 味覚 palate, taste

mikan みかん (mandarin) orange, tangerine (orange)

mikata 味方 friend, supporter *mikata suru ~* する side, take sides with, stand by, support

mikazuki 三日月 new moon, crescent

miki 幹 trunk

mikomi 見込み promise, hope, expectation, chances

mikon no 未婚の unmarried, single

mimai 見舞い inquiry, call

mimamoru 見守る watch, gaze at

miman 未満 under, below, less than

mimi 耳 ear *mimiuchi suru ~* 打ちする whisper in one's ear

mina (= **min'na**) 皆[みんな] all, everything, everyone *min'na de* みんなで in all, all together

minage suru 身投げする drown oneself, throw oneself into

minami 南 south *minami no ~* の southern

minamoto 源 source

minarai 見習い apprenticeship, apprentice

minareru 見慣れる get used to, be familiar with

minasu 見なす regard, consider, look upon

minato 港 harbor, port

minikui 醜い ugly, plain, homely

minogasu 見逃す overlook, pass over

minori 実り crop, harvest

minoru 実る bear fruit, ripen

minoue-banashi 身の上話し story of one's life

minshū 民衆 the people

minshu-shugi 民主主義 democracy

min'yō 民謡 folk song

minzoku 民族 race, people, nation

miokuru 見送る see off, send off

miorosu 見下ろす look down

mirai 未来 future, days to come

miren 未練 regret, attachment *miren ga aru*

　　〜がある feel regret, be still attached to

miru 見る see, look

miryoku 魅力 charm, enchantment　*miryoku no aru* 〜のある fascinating, charming, attractive

misaki みさき cape

mise 店 shop, store

misebirakasu 見せびらかす display, show off, make a show [display] of

miseinen 未成年 (be) under age, minority　*miseinen-sha* 〜者 minor

misemono 見世物 show, exhibition

miseru 見せる show, exhibit

mishin ミシン sewing machine

mishiranu 見知らぬ strange, unknown

miso みそ bean paste

misokonau 見損なう misjudge, make a mistake in

missetsu na [ni] 密接な [に] close [ly], intimate [ly]

misuborashii みすぼらしい shabby, seedy, poor-looking

misugosu 見過ごす overlook, pass over

mitei (no) 未定 (の) undecided, unsettled

mitomeru 認める admit, see, notice, take notice of

mitōshi 見通し perspective, insight, foresight, prospect

mitsu みつ honey

mitsubachi みつばち (honey) bee

mitsukaru 見付かる be discovered, be found

mitsukeru 見付ける find (out), discover

mitsumeru 見詰める gaze [stare] at

miwakeru 見分ける distinguish, recognize　*miwake ga tsukanai* 見分けがつかない indistinguishable, beyond recognition

miwatasu 見渡す look over [out], have a view of

miyage 土産 gift, present, souvenir

mizo 溝 drain, ditch

mizore みぞれ sleet

mizu 水 water

mizugi 水着 bathing [swimming] suit

mizukakeron 水掛け論 endless dispute [argument]

mizukara 自ら (for) oneself, personally

mizutamari 水たまり pool, puddle

mizu'umi 湖 lake

mo 喪 mourning

mo も and, also *mo mata* もまた too, also

mō もう now, soon, already

mochi もち rice cake

mochiageru 持ち上げる raise, lift

mochidasu 持ち出す take [bring] out

mochihakobu 持ち運ぶ carry, convey

mochiiru 用いる use, make use of, utilize

mochiron もちろん of course, needless to say

modoru 戻る go [come] back, return, turn back

modosu 戻す return, give back, restore, put back

moeru 燃える burn, blaze

mōfu 毛布 blanket

mohan 模範 model

mohaya もはや already, now, no more

mōhitsu 毛筆 (writing) brush

mohō 模倣 imitation, copy *mohō suru* ～する imitate, copy

moji 文字 letter, character

moji-moji suru もじもじする fidget, restless, hesitate

mōjū 猛獣 fierce animal

mōkaru もうかる profitable

mōke もうけ profits, gains, earnings

mokei 模型 model, pattern

mōkeru もうける make a profit, earn

mokugeki 目撃 observation *mokugeki suru* ～する observe

mokuhyō 目標 mark, target, object, aim

mokuteki 目的 object, purpose, end

mokuyō-bi 木曜日 Thursday

mokuzai 木材 wood, timber, lumber

mombu-shō 文部省 Ministry of Education

momen 木綿 cotton

momeru もめる have trouble

momiji 紅葉 maple, red leaves

momo もも thigh

momo 桃 peach *momo-iro* ～色 pink

mōmoku 盲目 blindness

momu もむ rub, massage

mon 門 gate *mon-ban* ～番 gate-keeper

mon 紋 crest

mondai 問題 question, problem, subject *mondai ni naranai* ～にならない be out of the question

monku 文句 words, terms, complaint *monku o iu* ～をいう complain, grumble

mono 物 thing, object, matter

mono 者 person, one, people

monogatari 物語 tale, story

monogoto 物事 thing, matter

mono'omoi 物思い meditation *mono'omoi ni fukeru* ～にふける be lost in thought

mono'oto 物音 noise, sound

monoshiri 物知り man of great knowledge, well-informed person

monosugoi 物すごい terrible, hideous

monotarinai 物足りない unsatisfactory

monozuki na 物好きな curious, whimsical

monshō 紋章 crest, coat of arms

moppara 専ら exclusively, entirely, chiefly

morau もらう receive, obtain, get, accept

moreru 漏れる leak, escape

mōretsu na [ni] 猛烈な[に] fierce [ly], violent [ly], strong [ly], furious [ly]

mori 森 woods, grove, forest

moroi もろい frail, fragile

moshi もし if, provided, in case

mōshiawase 申し合せ agreement, arrangement

mōshideru 申し出る propose, offer

mōshikomi 申し込み application

mōshikomu 申し込む apply, request, propose

mō sukoshi もう少し some more, a few more

motareru もたれる lean on, rest against

mōten 盲点 blind spot

moto (no) もと(の) former, one-time　*moto wa* もとは formerly, once, before

motomeru 求める buy, purchase, get, request, demand, ask for

motozuku 基づく be based on, come from, be due to

motsu 持つ have, hold, possess

motsure もつれ tangle　*motsureru* 〜る be tangled

mottaiburu もったいぶる put on airs

motte もって by, through, with

motte no hoka もっての外 unreasonable, out of question

motto もっと more, further

mottomo 最も most, extremely

mottomo もっとも indeed, but, however

mottomo na もっともな reasonable, right, natural

moya もや haze, mist

moyasu 燃やす burn

moyō 模様 pattern, design

moyo'oshi 催し meeting, entertainment

moyo'osu 催す hold, give

mucha na [ni] 無茶な[に] absurd[ly], unreasonable[-bly]

muchi むち whip

muchi 無知 ignorance, stupidity　*muchi na* 〜 な ignorant, uneducated

muchū ni naru 夢中になる be beside oneself, be absorbed in, be crazy about

muda na [ni] 無駄な[に] vain[ly], useless[ly]　*muda ni naru* 無駄になる be wasted, come to nothing

mudan de 無断で without leave [permission]

mufumbetsu na 無分別な thoughtless, indiscreet

mujun 矛盾 contradiction, inconsistency *mujun suru* ～する be contradictory

mukaeru 迎える welcome, greet, (go to) meet

mukai 向かい *mukai no* ～の opposite, across *mukai au* ～合う be opposite to, face each other

muka-muka suru むかむかする feel sick, be annoyed

mukankei na 無関係な unrelated, unconnected

mukanshin na 無関心な indifferent, unconcerned

mukashi 昔 ancient times, old days *mukashi no* ～の old, ancient, past

mukatte 向かって toward(s), for, to

mukau 向かう face, go towards, leave

mukeru 向ける turn [direct] toward

mukiryoku na 無気力な spiritless, nerveless

muko 婿 son-in-law, bridegroom

mukō 無効 invalidity *mukō no* ～の invalid

mukō 向こう over there, the other side, beyond, across

muku 向く turn, look

muku むく peel, pare, skin

mukuiru 報いる return, repay, recompense

mumei no 無名の nameless, anonymous, unknown

munashii むなしい empty, vain *munashiku* むなしく in vain

mune 胸 breast, chest

munō na 無能な incompetent, incapable

mura 村 village

muragaru 群がる crowd, throng

murasaki 紫 purple, violet

mure 群れ group, crowd

muri na 無理な unreasonable, unjust

muryō no 無料の free, free of charge

musebu むせぶ be choked, be stifled

musen 無線 wireless, radio

mushi 虫 insect, bug

mushiba 虫歯 bad tooth

mushiro むしろ rather, sooner, preferably

mushiru むしる pluck, pull, tear off

mushi suru 無視する ignore, disregard

musu 蒸す steam

musubi 結び end, conclusion   *musubi-me* ～目 knot, tie

musuko 息子 son, boy

musume 娘 daughter, girl

musū no [ni] 無数の[に] numberless, innumerable [-bly]

mutto shita [shite] むっとした[して] sullen [ly], angry [-ily]

muyami na [ni] むやみな[に] rash [ly], excessive [ly]

muyō no 無用の useless, of no use, unnecessary

muzai 無罪 innocence   *muzai no* ～の innocent

muzan na [ni] 無残な[に] cruel [ly], pitiless [ly]

muzukashii 難しい difficult, hard

myaku 脈 pulse

myōban 明晩 tomorrow evening

myōchō 明朝 tomorrow morning

myō na 妙な strange, singular, curious

N

nabe なべ pan, pot

nabiku なびく flutter

nadakai 名高い famous

nadameru なだめる soothe, calm

nadare 雪崩 snowslide, avalanche

naderu なでる stroke, pat

nado など and so on, and others

nafuda 名札 name plate

nagagutsu 長靴 rubber boots

nagai 長い long   *nagai aida* ～間 for a long time

nagaiki suru 長生きする live long

nagaku 長く long, for a long time

nagame 眺め view, scene, prospect *nagameru* 〜る look at, see, gaze at

-nagara …ながら as, while, over

nagare 流れ stream, current

nagareru 流れる flow, stream, run

nagasa 長さ length

nagashi 流し sink

nageku 嘆く be grieved, lament, regret

nageru 投げる throw, fling

nagori 名残 parting *nagori o oshimu* 〜を惜しむ be sorry to part from

nagoyaka na 和やかな mellow, ripe

naguru 殴る beat, strike, knock

nagusame 慰め comfort, consolation, entertainment *nagusameru* 〜る comfort, console

naibu 内部 the inside, interior *naibu no* 〜の inside, internal, inner

naika 内科 internal medicine *naika-i* 〜医 physician, internist

naikaku 内閣 cabinet, ministry

naimitsu no [ni] 内密の [に] secret [ly], private [ly], confidential [ly]

naisho 内緒 secret, privacy *naisho no* 〜の secret, private

naishoku 内職 side work, side job, homework

naiyō 内容 content(s), substance

najimi no なじみの familiar, intimate

najimu なじむ become familiar, get intimate

naka 中 interior, inside

naka 仲 relations, terms *naka ga yoi [warui]* 〜がよい [悪い] be on good [bad] terms

nakaba 半ば half, halfway

nakama 仲間 partner, associate, companion

nakanaori suru 仲直りする get reconciled

nakatagai suru 仲たがいする quarrel, fall out, be estranged

-nakattara …なかったら without, but for, if it

were not

nakayoku suru 仲良くする get on very well, be on good terms, make friends

nakigara なきがら corpse, dead body

nakigoe 鳴き声 cry, song

nakigoe 泣き声 tearful voice, cry

naku 泣[鳴]く cry, weep

nakunaru 無くなる be [get] lost, be missing [gone], run short [out]

nakunaru 亡くなる die, pass away

nakusu 無くす lose, miss

namae 名前 name

namaiki 生意気 conceit, impertinence ***namaiki na*[*ni*]** ～な[に] impudent [ly], affected [ly], conceited [ly]

namakeru 怠ける be idle, be lazy, neglect

nama no 生の raw, uncooked, fresh

namari なまり dialect, accent

namari 鉛 lead

Nambei 南米 South [Latin] America

namboku 南北 north and south

nameraka na 滑らかな smooth, even

nameru なめる lick, taste, experience

namesu なめす tan, dress

nami 波 wave

namida 涙 tear ***namida o nagasu*** ～を流す shed tears

namidatsu 波立つ run high, swell

namikimichi 並木道 avenue

nami no 並の common, ordinary

naname no[**ni**] 斜めの[に] oblique [ly]

nanatsu 七つ, 7つ seven

nanda なんだ what!

nandaka なんだか somewhat, somehow

nandemo なんでも any, anything, everything, whatever

nandemonai なんでもない nothing

nando なんど how often ***nando mo*** ～も many times

nani 何 what, which, some, any

naniya-kaya to 何やかやと this and that, one thing and another

naniyori 何より above all (things), before everything, first of all

nanji 何時 what time, when

nankai 何回 how many times, how often

nankō 軟こう ointment, salve

nankyoku 南極 South Pole

nan'nen 何年 how many years

nan'nichi 何日 how many days

nanoru 名乗る give one's name

nao なお still, yet, more

naoru 治る get well, get better, recover, be mended

naosu なおす mend, repair, cure

naraberu 並べる arrange, place in order

narabu 並ぶ stand in line, line up

narasu 慣らす tame, train

narasu 均らす level, make even

narasu 鳴らす ring, sound

narau 習う learn, study, practice

nareru 慣れる get [be] used to, become [grow, get] accustomed to

nareta 慣れた experienced, familiar *narenai* 慣れない new, unfamiliar

naritatsu 成り立つ consist of, be composed of

naru なる become, make grow, result in, turn into

naru 鳴る sound, ring, strike

narubeku なるべく as...as possible, if possible

naruhodo 成る程 indeed, really, it is true, to be sure

nasake 情け sympathy, mercy, kindness *nasake-bukai* ～深い kind, sympathetic *nasakenai* ～ない pitiable, shameful

nashi なし pear

nasu なす eggplant

natsu 夏 summer *sakunen no natsu* 昨年の～

last summer

natsukashigaru 懐かしがる yearn for, long for

natsukashii 懐かしい dear, beloved, old, nostalgic

natsumikan 夏みかん Chinese citron, orange

nattoku suru 納得する consent to **nattoku saseru** 納得させる persuade, convince of

nawa 縄 rope, cord

nayamasu 悩ます annoy, worry, trouble

nayami 悩み trouble, suffering

nayamu 悩む suffer from, be troubled with

naze なぜ why, how, for what reason, what... for

nazo なぞ riddle, puzzle, mystery **nazo o kakeru** 〜を掛ける put a riddle

nazukeru 名付ける name, call

ne 根 root

neagari 値上がり rise in price **neagari suru** 〜する raise, advance, boost

-nebanaranai ...ねばならない must, have to

nebaru 粘る sticky, adhesive

nebiki suru 値引きする reduce price

nedan 値段 price, cost

nedoko 寝床 bed

negai 願い wish, desire

negau 願う wish, hope, ask

negi ねぎ Welsh onion, scallion

negiru 値切る beat down the price, bargain

neiro 音色 sound, tone

neji ねじ screw

nejiru ねじる twist, wrench

nekkyō 熱狂 enthusiasm, excitement, be enthusiastic

neko 猫 cat

nekutai ネクタイ (neck)tie

nemmatsu 年末 the end of the year

nemui 眠い be [feel] sleepy

nemuru 眠る sleep, fall asleep, doze

nen 年 year **nen ni** 〜に yearly

nendai 年代 age, years

nendo 粘土 clay

nenga 年賀 the New Year('s) Greetings

nenjū 年中 all year round *nenjū-gyōji* ～行事 annual events

nenkan 年鑑 yearbook, almanac

nerau ねらう take aim at, watch

neru 寝る go to bed, be in bed, sleep

neru 練る knead

nesshin 熱心 eagerness *nesshin na* ～な eager, earnest *nesshin ni* ～に eagerly

nessuru 熱する heat, make hot

netamu ねたむ be jealous [envious]

netchū suru 熱中する be absorbed in, be enthusiastic

netsu 熱 heat, temperature

nettai 熱帯 tropics

neuchi 値打ち value, worth

nezumi ねずみ rat, mouse

ni 二, 2 two, the second

ni に at, on, in, to

niau 似合う become, suit

nibai 2倍 *nibai no* ～の double, twice

nibun no ichi 2分の1, ½ one [a] half

nichiji 日時 date

nichijō 日常 everyday, usually, always *nichijō no* ～の daily, usual

nichiyō-bi 日曜日 Sunday

nido 2度 twice, two times *nido-me* ～目 the second

nieru 煮える boil, be boiled

nifuda 荷札 label, tag

nigai 苦い bitter

nigami 苦み bitter taste

nigate 苦手 weak point, person hard to deal with

ni-gatsu 二月 February

nigeru 逃げる run away [off], flee

nigiru 握る hold, seize, grasp

nigiwau にぎわう prosperous, crowded

nigiyaka na にぎやかな lively, alive

nigoru 濁る become muddy, become impure

nigotta 濁った muddy, turbid

Nihon 日本 Japan *Nihon-go* ～語 Japanese *Nihon-jin* ～人 Japanese person

niji にじ rainbow

nijimideru にじみ出る ooze out

nijimu にじむ spread, run, blur

nijū 二十, 20 twenty, a score

nijū no 二重の double, twofold, dual

nikai 二階 upstairs, the second floor *nikai-ya* ～家 two-storied house

nikai 二回 twice, two times

nikka 日課 daily lesson [work]

nikkan no 日刊の daily

nikki 日記 diary

nikkō 日光 sunshine, sunlight

nikomu 煮込む boil well, stew

niku 肉 meat, beef, flesh

nikui 憎い hateful, abominable

-nikui …にくい hard, difficult

nikumareru 憎まれる be hated

nikurashii 憎らしい hateful, detestable, spiteful

nikushimi 憎しみ hatred, hate, spite

nikushin 肉親 blood relation

nikutai 肉体 body, flesh

niku-ya 肉屋 meat shop, butcher('s) shop

nimmu 任務 duty, office

nimotsu 荷物 luggage, baggage

ningen 人間 human being

ningyō 人形 doll

ninjin にんじん carrot

ninjō 人情 humanity, sympathy

ninka 認可 approval *ninka suru* ～する approve, authorize

ninki 人気 popularity *ninki no aru* ～のある popular, favorite

nin'niku にんにく garlic

ninshin 妊娠 pregnancy *ninshin suru* ～する

conceive

ninsō 人相 look, features

nintai 忍耐 patience

nioi におい smell, odor, perfume

niou におう smell, be fragrant

niramu にらむ stare hard at, glare at

niru 似る resemble, look like

niru 煮る boil, cook

nisan no 二・三の few, two or three

nisemono 偽物 imitation, fake

nishi 西 west *nishi no* ～の western

nita 似た like, similar

nita 煮た boiled, cooked

niwa 庭 garden, yard

niwatori 鶏 hen, chicken

-ni yoruto …によると according to

no 野 field

-no …の 's, of

nō 脳 brain

nobasu のばす lengthen, stretch, extend, put off, postpone

noberu 述べる state, express

nobiru のびる lengthen, stretch

noboru 登る climb, ascend

noboru 上る rise, go up

nochi ni 後に after, later, in future

-node …ので because, as, since

nodo のど throat *nodo ga kawaku* ～が渇く be [feel] thirsty

nodoka na のどかな traquil, calm, peaceful

nōgyō 農業 agriculture

nohara 野原 field, the green

noki 軒 eaves

nokogiri のこぎり saw

nokori 残り the rest

nokoru 残る remain, be left, stay

nokosu 残す leave, save

nomi のみ chisel

nomikomu 飲み込む swallow, drink in, under-

stand
nomu 飲む drink
-noni …のに (al)though, in spite of, while
noren のれん shop curtain
nori 糊 paste, starch
nori 海苔 laver, edible seaweed
noridasu 乗り出す start, set out
norikaeru 乗り換える change (cars, trains), transfer
norikosu 乗り越す be carried [go] beyond
norikumiin 乗組員 crew
norikumu 乗り組む join (a ship), be on board
noriokureru 乗り遅れる miss, lose
nōritsu 能率 efficiency *nōritsu-teki na* ～的な efficient
noroi のろい slow, tardy
norou のろう curse, imprecate
noru 乗る ride, take
nōryoku 能力 ability, capacity, faculty
noseru 載せる place [put, set, lay] (it) on
nōson 農村 farm [agricultural] village
nozoite 除いて except, save, but
nozoku のぞく look [peep] in
nozoku 除く except, exclude, omit, take off
nozomashii 望ましい desirable, advisable
nozomi 望み wish, desire, hope, expect
nozomu 望む hope, look out, face, front
nugu 脱ぐ take [pull] off, remove
nugu'u ぬぐう wipe, mop
nukarumi ぬかるみ mud, mire
nukemenai 抜け目ない shrewd, smart, careful
nukeru 抜ける come [fall] off, be left [omitted]
nuku 抜く draw [pull] out, outrun
numa 沼 swamp *numachi* ～地 marshy place
nuno 布 cloth *nunogire* ～切れ piece of cloth
nurasu ぬらす wet, moisten, soak, dip
nureru ぬれる wet, drenched
nuri 塗り coating, painting
nuru 塗る paint

nurui ぬるい tepid, lukewarm

nusumu 盗む steal, rob

nusumareru 盗まれる have something stolen, be robbed

nu'u 縫う sew, stitch

nyōbō 女房 wife

nyūbai 入梅 (beginning of) the rainy season

nyūgaku-shiken 入学試験 entrance examination

nyūgaku suru 入学する enter school

nyūin suru 入院する enter [be sent to] hospital

nyūjō 入場 admission, entrance *nyūjō suru* ～する enter, be admitted *nyūjō-ryō* ～料 admission fee *nyūjō-ken* ～券 admission ticket

nyūkin 入金 receipts, money received

nyūkō suru 入港する enter port, arrive in port

nyūshō suru 入賞する win [get] the prize

nyūyoku suru 入浴する take a bath

O

o 尾 tail

ō 王 king

oba 伯母 [叔母] aunt

ōbā オーバー overcoat

obāsan おばあさん grandmother, old woman

Ōbei 欧米 Europe and America

obi 帯 belt, sash

obieru おびえる be frightened, be scared

ōbo 応募 subscription, application *ōbo suru* ～する apply for, make an application

oboeru 覚える remember, keep in mind

oboeteiru 覚えている remember

oboreru おぼれる be drowned, drown

o-cha お茶 tea

ōchaku na 横着な impudent, dishonest

ochiau 落ち合う meet, come together

ochiru 落ちる fall, drop, come down

ochitsuki 落着き composure *ochitsuki no aru*

~のある calm, quiet, self-composed *ochitsu-ki no nai* ~のない nervous, restless

ochitsuku 落ち着く settle (down), keep cool [calm]

ōdan suru 横断する cross, run across *ōdan hodō* 横断歩道 crossing

odateru おだてる instigate, incite, flatter

odayaka na 穏やかな calm, quiet, mild, moderate

odokeru おどける joke, jest, be funny

odo-odo suru おどおどする nervous *odo-odo shite* おどおどして timidly

odori 踊り dancing, dance

ōdōri 大通り main street

odorokasu 驚かす surprise, astonish

odoroki 驚き surprise, astonishment

odoroku 驚く be surprised *odoroku-beki* ~べき wonderful, surprising

odoru 踊る dance, leap

odosu 脅す threaten, scare

ōen suru 応援する aid, help, support

oeru 終える end, finish, complete

ōfuku 往復 going and returning, both ways *ōfuku suru* ~する go and return *ōfuku-kippu* ~切符 round-trip ticket, return ticket

ofukuro お袋 mother

ogamu 拝む worship, bow

ōgata no 大型の large(-sized), big

ogawa 小川 stream, brook

ōgesa na [ni] 大げさな[に] exaggerated [ly]

ōgi 扇 fan

oginau 補う make up, supply

ōgoe de 大声で in a loud voice, loudly

ogori おごり luxury, extravagance

ogoru 傲る be extravagant, be proud

ogoru 奢る treat (a person) to

ogosoka na [ni] 厳かな[に] solemn [ly]

ohayō お早う Good morning!

ōhei na 横柄な arrogant, haughty

oi おい nephew

ōi 多い many, much, lots of, plenty of

oidasu 追い出す expel, turn [send] out

oiharau 追い払う drive [turn] away

oikaesu 追い返す drive back

oikakeru 追い掛ける run [go] after, pursue

oikosu 追い越す pass, outrun, get ahead of

ōini 大いに very, much, greatly

oiru 老いる grow old, age

oishii おいしい delicious, tasty

oitachi 生い立ち one's breeding

oitateru 追い立てる hurry

oitsuku 追い付く overtake, catch up with

oji 伯父[叔父] uncle

ōji 王子 prince

ojigi お辞儀 bow *ojigi o suru* ～をする bow

ōjiru 応じる answer, respond, accept, comply with

ojīsan おじいさん grandfather, old man

ojōsan お嬢さん young lady, daughter

oka 丘 hill, height

okage お陰 assistance, help, favor *okage de* ～で thanks to, by a person's favor

okāsan お母さん mother, ma(mma)

okashii おかしい amusing, funny, comical, strange

okasu 犯す commit, violate

okawari お代り second helping, another cup

okazu おかず (side) dish, relish

oke おけ tub, pail, bucket

okeru おける in, at, on

oki 沖 offing, open sea

ōkii 大きい big, large, great

-okini …おきに at intervals of *ichi-nichi okini* 一日～ every other day

okiru 起きる get up, rise, wake up

ōkisa 大きさ size, dimensions

okite おきて law, rule

okiwasureru 置き忘れる leave, forget

okizari ni suru 置き去りにする desert, leave behind

okonai 行い act(ion), deed, conduct, behavior

okonau 行う do, act, carry out

okoraseru 怒らせる make angry, offend

okori 起り origin, beginning, rise

okorippoi 怒りっぽい touchy, short-tempered

okoru 怒る get angry, get mad

okoru 起る happen, occur, take place

okosu 起す raise [set] up, pick up

okotaru 怠る neglect, be idle

oku 億 one hundred million *jū-oku* 十〜 a thousand million, a billion

oku 奥 interior, heart, depths

oku 置く put, place

okubyō na おく病な cowardly, timid *okubyō-mono* おく病者 coward

okugai 屋外 the open (air)

okujō 屋上 housetop, roof

okunai(no) 屋内(の) indoor

okureru 遅れる late, behind time

okurimono 贈り物 present, gift

okuru 送る send, pass, spend, see off

okuru 贈る give, send, present

okuyukashii 奥床しい refined, graceful

ōkyū no 応急の emergency, temporary *ōkyū-teate* 〜手当 first aid

omake おまけ extra

omamori お守り charm, talisman

omawari おまわり cop, policeman

omedeta おめでた happy event

omedetō おめでとう Congratulations!

ome ni kakaru お目に掛かる see, meet *ome ni kakeru* お目に掛ける show

ōme ni miru 大目に見る overlook, connive

ōmisoka 大みそか New Year's Eve

ōmizu 大水 flood

omocha おもちゃ toy, plaything

omoi 重い heavy

omoidasu 思い出す recollect, recall, be reminded of

omoide 思い出 memories, recollections

omoidōri ni 思い通りに as one likes [pleases]

omoi-gakenai 思いがけない unexpected, casual

omoitsuki 思い付き idea, plan

omoitsuku 思い付く hit, strike upon, think of

omoiyari 思いやり sympathy, consideration *omoiyari no aru[nai]* ～のある[ない] [un]sympathetic, [un]kind

omokage 面影 image

omokurushii 重苦しい heavy, oppressive, gloomy

omomuki 趣 effect, purport, taste, elegance

omomuku 赴く go, proceed

omo na 主な chief, principal, main

omonaga no 面長の long-faced

omoni 重荷 heavy load [burden]

omonjiru 重んじる respect, esteem, think much of

omori 重り weight

omosa 重さ weight *omosa o hakaru* ～を量る weigh

omoshirogaru 面白がる be amused, (take) delight in

omoshiro-hambun ni 面白半分に (half) in fun, partly for amusement

omoshiroi 面白い interesting, amusing, joyful

omoshirokunai 面白くない uninteresting, dull

omote 表 (sur)face, the outside, the front

omote-dōri 表通り main street

omotemuki 表向き openly, officially *omotemuki no* ～の public, official

omou 思う think, believe

omouzombun 思う存分 to one's heart's content, to the full, heartily

omowaku 思惑 thought, opinion

omowareru 思われる seem, appear, look

omowazu 思わず unconsciously, in spite of oneself

ōmu おうむ parrot

ōmukashi 大昔 great antiquity

omuretsu オムレツ omelet

on 恩 favor, obligation, kindness *on ni kiseru* ～に着せる make a favor of it, patronize

on 音 sound, noise, tone

onaji no 同じの the same, equal, similar *onajiku* 同じく in the same way, equally

onaka おなか stomach

ondo 温度 temperature *ondo-kei* ～計 thermometer

ongaku 音楽 music *ongaku-teki na* ～的な musical *ongaku-kai* ～会 concert *ongaku-ka* ～家 musician

oni 鬼 ogre, demon, devil

onjin 恩人 benefactor

onkei 恩恵 favor, benefit

onkyō 音響 sound, noise

on'na 女 woman, girl, female

ono おの axe, hatchet

onozukara おのずから naturally

onsen 温泉 hot spring

onsetsu 音節 syllable

onshirazu 恩知らず ingratitude, ungrateful person

onshitsu 温室 hothouse, green-house

onwa na 穏和な mild, gentle, moderate

o'oshii 雄々しい brave, heroic *o'oshiku* 雄々しく bravely, heroically

ō'otoko 大男 giant

ōppira ni おおっぴらに openly, in public

ōrai 往来 traffic, road, street

Oranda オランダ Holland, the Netherlands *Oranda-go (no)* ～語(の) Dutch *Oranda-jin* ～人 Hollander, Dutchman

oreru 折れる break, give way, give in

ori おり cage, pen

ori 折り occasion, moment, chance

oriai 折り合い compromise, mutual relations

origami 折紙 folded paper, folding paper, paper folding

orikaesu 折り返す turn back

orimageru 折り曲げる bend, double, turn up

orimono 織物 cloth, textile, fabric

oriru 降[下]りる come [go, get] down, get off, leave

oroka na 愚かな foolish, stupid, silly

oroshi 卸 wholesale *oroshi-gyōsha* ～業者 wholesaler

orosoka ni suru おろそかにする neglect, slight

orosu 下[降]ろす take [bring] down, put down, let down, unload

oru 折る break, fold, bend

orugan オルガン organ

osaeru おさえる suppress, control, stop, hold down, keep down

osamaru 納まる contain, put in

osameru 治める rule [reign] over, manage

osanai 幼い young, infant, childish

osarai おさらい review

oseji お世辞 flattery, compliment *oseji o iu* ～を言う flatter, pay a compliment

osekkai na お節介な meddlesome, officious *osekkai o suru* お節介をする meddle

ōsetsu 応接 reception *ōsetsu-shitsu* ～室 drawing room, parlor

oshaberi おしゃべり chatterbox *oshaberi o suru* ～をする talk, chat *oshaberi na* ～な talkative

oshare おしゃれ dandyism, dandy

oshi おし dumb person

oshieru 教える teach, instruct, inform, tell

oshii 惜しい regrettable

oshimu 惜しむ grudge, regret

oshiroi おしろい (cosmetic) powder

oshitaosu 押し倒す knock down

oshitsukeru 押し付ける press [push] against, force

oshoku 汚職 corruption, graft

Ōshū 欧州 Europe　*Ōshū no* 〜の European

osoi 遅い slow, late　*osoku* 遅く slowly, late

osokare-hayakare 遅かれ早かれ sooner or later

osokutomo 遅くとも at (the) latest

osoraku 恐らく perhaps, probably

osore 恐れ fear, terror, horror

osore irimasu 恐れ入ります Much obliged (to you).　*Osore irimasu ga* Pardon [Excuse] me, but … 恐れ入りますが

osoreru 恐れる fear, be afraid of

osoroshii 恐ろしい terrible, dreadful

osou 襲う attack, hit

osu 雄 male

osu 押す push, press

oto 音 sound, noise

otogibanashi おとぎばなし fairy tale

otoko 男 man, male　*otoko no ko* 〜の子 boy

otome 乙女 girl, maiden

otomo suru お供する accompany, go with

otona 大人 adult, grown-up (person)

otonashii おとなしい gentle, obedient, quiet

otoroeru 衰える weaken, decline

otoru 劣る be inferior to, be worse than

otōsan お父さん father, pa(pa)

otoshimono 落し物 lost article, lost property　*otoshimono o suru* 〜をする drop, lose

otosu 落とす drop, lose

otōto 弟 younger brother

ototoi おととい the day before yesterday　*ototoi no asa* [*ban*] 〜の朝 [晩] the morning [night] before last

ototoshi おととし the year before last

otto 夫 husband

ou 負う bear, owe, assure

o'ou 覆う cover, hide, keep off

oushi 雄牛 bull, ox

owari 終り end, close

owaru 終る end, come to an end, be over

oya 親 parents, parent
oyaji おやじ father, dad(dy)
oyako 親子 parent and child
oyasumi(nasai) お休み(なさい) Good night!
oyatsu お八つ tea, (afternoon) refreshments
oyayubi 親指 thumb, big toe
ōyō 応用 application　*ōyō suru* 〜する apply
oyogi 泳ぎ swimming
oyogu 泳ぐ swim
oyoso およそ generally, as a rule, about
ōyuki 大雪 heavy snow
ōzei 大勢 a great number of people　*ōzei de* 〜で in great numbers
ōzora 大空 sky

P

pachinko パチンコ sling(-shot), pinball machine
pāma パーマ permanent (wave)　*pāma o kakeru* 〜をかける have one's hair permed, get a perm
pan パン bread　*pan-ya* パン屋 bakery　*pan-kuzu* 〜くず bread crumbs
panku パンク puncture, blowout, flat　*panku suru* 〜する blow out, be punctured
pantsu パンツ shorts, drawers
para-para furu パラパラ降る patter, sprinkle
pasu パス pass, free ticket
patto パッと suddenly, in a flash
peko-peko ペコペコ be faint with hunger　*peko-peko suru* 〜する cringe, bow to, flatter
penchi ペンチ (cutting) pliers
penki ペンキ paint
pera-pera ペラペラ fluently, glibly
peten ぺてん trickery　*peten ni kakeru* 〜にかける cheat, swindle
pika-pika suru ピカピカする glittering, shining

piku-piku suru　ピクピクする　twitch, jerk
piman　ピーマン　pimiento, bell [green] pepper
pimboke　ピンぼけ　out of focus
pinhane　ピンはね　kickback
pin-pin　ぴんぴん　lively
pinsetto　ピンセット　tweezers, pincers
pinto　ピント　focus
pishari　ぴしゃり　with a bang
pittari　ぴったり　closely, tightly, exactly
poka-poka suru　ぽかぽかする　be [feel] warm
pondo　ポンド　pound
posuto　ポスト　mail-box, post-box
pun-pun niou　ぷんぷん匂う　smell strongly, be
　strongly perfumed
pun-pun okoru　ぷんぷん怒る　be [get] very angry

R

-ra　…ら　and others
raigetsu　来月　next month
raihō　来訪　call, visit
raikyaku　来客　visitor, caller, guest
rainen　来年　next year
raishū　来週　next week
raisukarē　ライスカレー　curry and rice
rajio　ラジオ　radio
rakkan　楽観　optimism　*rakkan suru*　～する
　be optimistic
raku　楽　ease, comfort　*raku na*　～な easy　*ra-*
　ku ni　～に easily
rakuda　らくだ　camel
rakudai suru　落第する　fail in an exam
rakugaki　落書き　scribbling, scrawl, graffiti
rakunō　酪農　dairy farming
raku-raku to　楽々と　easily, in comfort
rambō　乱暴　violence, outrage　*rambō na*　～な
　violent
rampitsu　乱筆　scrawl

ran らん orchid

ranzatsu 乱雑 disorder *ranzatsu na* 〜な confused *ranzatsu ni* 〜に in disorder

rappa らっぱ trumpet

rasen らせん screw, spiral

rashii らしい like, look, be likely

ratai 裸体 nakedness, nude *ratai no* 〜の naked, nude

rei 例 example, instance

rei 霊 soul

rei 零 zero, naught

rei 礼 salutation, bow *rei o suru* 〜をする salute, make a bow, reward *rei o iu* 〜を言う thank

reibō 冷房 cooling, air conditioning

reigai 例外 exception *reigai no* 〜の exceptional

reigi 礼儀 courtesy, politeness, manners, etiquette *reigi tadashii* 〜正しい courteous, polite

reihai 礼拝 worship *reihai-dō* 〜堂 chapel

reijō 礼状 letter of thanks

reikoku na 冷酷な cruel, cold-hearted

reikyaku suru 冷却する cool *reikyaku-ki* 冷却器 freezer, refrigerator

reinen 例年 normal [ordinary] year *reinen no* 〜の annual

reisei 冷静 coolness, calmness

reisei na [ni] 冷静な[に] cool [ly], calm [ly]

reishō 冷笑 sneer, derision

reisui 冷水 cold water

reitan 冷淡 coolness, indifference *reitan na [ni]* 〜な[に] cold [ly], cool [ly]

reitō suru 冷凍する freeze, refrigerate

reizōko 冷蔵庫 refrigerator, icebox

rekishi 歴史 history *rekishi no* 〜の historical *rekishi-ka* 〜家 historian

rekōdo レコード record, disk

ren'ai 恋愛 love

renchū 連中 party

renga れんが brick

rengō 連合 combination, union *rengō suru ～する* combine, union

renketsu 連結 coupling *renketsu suru ～する* connect, join

renraku 連絡 connection, communication *renraku suru ～する* connect

renshū 練習 training, practice *renshū suru ～する* practice

rensō 連想 association *rensō suru ～する* associate, be reminded of

renzoku 連続 continuation *renzoku suru ～する* continue *renzoku-teki na[ni] ～的な[に]* continuous[ly], successive[ly]

ressha 列車 train *ressha de ～で* by train *kyūkō-ressha 急行～* an express

retsu 列 line, row, rank

rettōkan 劣等感 inferiority complex

richi 理知 intellect *richi-teki na ～的な* intellectual

rieki 利益 interest, profit, benefit

rigai 利害 interest

rihatsu 理髪 haircutting *rihatsu-ten ～店* barber shop

rijun 利潤 profit, gain(s)

rika 理科 science

rikai 理解 comprehension, understanding *rikai suru ～する* understand

rikisetsu suru 力説する emphasis, stress

riko 利己 self-interest *riko-teki na ～的な* selfish

rikō na 利口な clever, bright

rikon suru 離婚する divorce

riku 陸 land

rikugun 陸軍 army

rikutsu o iu 理屈を言う argue, quibble

rimen 裏面 the reverse, the back

ringo りんご apple *ringo-shu ～酒* cider

rinji 臨時 special, extra　*rinji no* ～の temporary, provisional

rinjin 隣人 neighbor

rippa na 立派な splendid, fine　*rippa ni* 立派に well, splendidly

rippuku 立腹 anger, offense　*rippuku suru* ～する get angry

rirekisho 履歴書 personal history, curriculum vitae, résumé

ririku suru 離陸する take [hop] off, take to the air

riron 理論 theory　*riron-teki na* ～的な theoretical

risei 理性 reason　*risei-teki na* [*ni*] ～的な [に] rational [ly]

rishi 利子 interest　*rishi ga tsuku* ～が付く yield interest

risoku 利息 interest

risu りす squirrel

ritsu 率 rate

rittai 立体 solid

riyō 利用 use, utilization　*riyō suru* ～する make use of, use

riyū 理由 reason, cause

ro 炉 fireplace

rō ろう wax

roba ろば ass, donkey

rōden 漏電 leakage of electricity

rōdō 労働 labor, toil　*rōdōsha* ～者 laborer

rōdoku 朗読 reading　*rōdoku suru* ～する read

rōdō-kumiai 労働組合 labor union

rōgan 老眼 presbyopia, far-sightedness

rōhi suru 浪費する waste, throw away

roji 路地 alley, lane

rōjin 老人 old man

rōka 廊下 passage, corridor

rokkotsu ろっ骨 rib

rōkō na 老巧な experienced, veteran

rokotsu na [*ni*] 露骨な [に] plain [ly], frank

[ly], suggestive [ly]

roku 六, 6 six, sixth

roku-gatsu 六月 June

rokujū 六十, 60 sixty

rokuon suru 録音する record, make a recording

Rōma ローマ Rome

rombun 論文 treatise, dissertation, thesis, paper

ronri 論理 logic *ronri-teki na*[*ni*] ～的な[に] logical[ly]

ronsetsu 論説 leading article, editorial

ronsō suru 論争する dispute

rōren na 老練な experienced, expert

rōryoku 労力 labor, effort, pains

roshutsu 露出 exposure *roshutsu-kei* ～計 exposure meter

rōsoku ろうそく candle

ruiji 類似 resemblance *ruiji suru* ～する be similar to, resemble

rusu 留守 absence *rusu no* ～の absent

ryaku 略 abbreviation, omission *ryaku suru* ～する abbreviate, abridge

ryō 量 quantity

ryō 寮 dormitory

ryō 猟 shooting, hunting

ryō 漁 fishing *ryō ni iku* ～に行く go fishing

ryōdo 領土 territory

ryōgae suru 両替する exchange

ryōgawa 両側 both sides, either side

ryohi 旅費 traveling expenses

ryōhō 両方 both, both sides [parties]

ryōji 領事 consul *ryōji-kan* ～館 consulate

ryōjū 猟銃 sporting [hunting] gun

ryōkai 了解 understanding *ryōkai suru* ～する understand

ryok(y)aku 旅客 traveler *ryok(y)aku-ki* ～機 passenger airplane

ryoken 旅券 passport

ryōken 猟犬 hunting dog

ryōkin 料金 charge, fee, fare

ryokō 旅行 journey, traveling *ryokō suru* ～する travel, make a trip to

ryōri 料理 cooking, cookery *ryōri suru* ～する cook, prepare

ryōshiki 良識 good sense

ryōshin 両親 parents

ryōshin 良心 conscience

ryōshō suru 了承する understand, acknowledge

ryōshū suru 領収する receive *ryōshū-sho* 領収書 receipt

ryōtan 両端 both ends

ryōte 両手 both hands [arms]

ryū 竜 dragon

ryūchō na[ni] 流ちょうな[に] fluent[ly], eloquent[ly]

ryūgaku suru 留学する study abroad, go abroad for study

ryūkō 流行 fashion, vogue *ryūkō suru* ～する prevail, be prevalent, be in vogue

ryūsenkei no 流線型の streamlined

ryūtsū 流通 circulation *ryūtsū suru* ～する circulate *ryūtsū-kahei* ～貨幣 current money

S

sa 差 difference, variation

sā さあ come, now, well

sabaku 砂漠 desert

sabetsu 差別 distinction, difference *sabetsu suru* ～する distinguish

sabi さび rust *sabiru* さびる rust, get rusty

sabishii 寂しい lonely, lonesome

sabishisa 寂しさ loneliness, lonesomeness

saboten サボテン cactus

sadamaru 定まる be decided, be chosen

sadameru 定める fix, set, decide, establish

-sae …さえ even, only

saegiru 遮る interrupt, cut off, obstruct

saezuri さえずり song, chirp, twitter
saezuru さえずる sing, chirp, twitter
sagaru 下がる fall, drop, hang
sagasu 探す seek, look for
sageru 下げる hang, lower
sageru 提げる carry, take
sagi 詐欺 fraud, cheating
sagi さぎ heron
saguru 探る search for, look for, spy
sagyō 作業 work, operations
sahō 作法 manner
sahodo さほど so (much), much
sai 歳 year, age, years
saiai no 最愛の dearest, beloved
saiaku no 最悪の the worst
saibai 栽培 growing, cultivation *saibai suru*
  ～する cultivate, grow
saiban 裁判 trial, judgment *saiban suru* ～す
  る judge, try
saibō 細胞 cell
saichū 最中 in the midst of, in the course of
saifu 財布 purse, wallet
saigai 災害 disaster, calamity
saigetsu 歳月 time
saigo 最後 the last, the end
saihō 裁縫 sewing, needlework *saihō suru* ～
  する sew
saijitsu 祭日 holiday, festival day
saijō no 最上の the best
saikai suru 再会する meet again
saiken 再建 reconstruction *saiken suru* ～す
  る rebuild, reconstruct
saikin 細菌 bacillus, bacterium, germ
saikin 最近 recently, lately *saikin no* ～の recent, late, up-to-date
saikō no 最高の highest, maximum
saikō suru 再考する reconsider
saiku 細工 work, workmanship
saimatsu 歳末 year end

saimu 債務 debt, obligation

sain サイン sign, signal, signature

sainan 災難 disaster, calamity

sainō 才能 talent, ability, capacity *sainō no aru* 〜のある talented

sairen サイレン siren

sairyō no 最良の best

saisan 再三 again and again, repeatedly

saisan ga toreru 採算がとれる be profitable

saishi 妻子 one's family

saishin no 細心の careful, prudent

saishin no 最新の newest, latest

saisho 最初 first, beginning *saisho no* 〜の first *saisho ni* 〜に in the first place *saisho wa* 〜は at first

saishō(no) 最小(の) smallest, least, minimum

saishū no 最終の last

saishū suru 採集する collect, gather

saitei no 最低の lowest, minimum

saiten 祭典 festival, fete

saiten suru 採点する mark, grade

saiwai 幸い happiness, good fortune *saiwai na[ni]* 〜な[に] fortunate[ly], happy[-ily]

saiyō 採用 adoption *saiyō suru* 〜する adopt

saizen 最善 the best

saji さじ spoon, teaspoon

saka 坂 slope

sakaba 酒場 bar, saloon, public house

sakadaru 酒だる cask, barrel

sakaeru 栄える prosper, flourish

sakai 境 border, boundary

sakana 魚 fish *sakana-ya* 〜屋 fish dealer

sakan na 盛んな prosperous, vigorous, active

sakari 盛り height, peak, bloom

sakariba 盛り場 public [holiday] resort, amusement quarters

sakazuki 杯 cup, (wine) glass

sake さけ salmon

sake 酒 wine, sake *sake o nomu* 〜を飲む

drink *sake ni you* ～に酔う get drunk

sakebi 叫び shout, cry, scream *sakebu* 叫ぶ cry, shout

sakerarenai 避けられない unavoidable, inevitable

sakeru 避ける avoid, keep off

sakeru 裂ける split, rend, burst

saki 先 point, tip, future *saki ni* ～に in advance

sakka 作家 writer, author

sakkaku 錯覚 illusion *sakkaku o okosu* ～を起こす be under an illusion

sakkin suru 殺菌する sterilize, pasteurize

sakkyoku 作曲 composition *sakkyoku suru* ～する compose

saku 柵 fence, paling

saku 策 policy, plan

saku 咲く bloom, open, come out

saku 裂く tear, split

sakuban 昨晩 last night, yesterday evening

sakubun 作文 composition

sakuhin 作品 work

sakujitsu 昨日 yesterday

sakumotsu 作物 crops, farm products

sakura 桜 cherry tree, cherry blossom

sakusen 作戦 operations

sakusha 作者 writer, author

sakuya 昨夜 last night, yesterday evening

sama …様 Mr., Mrs., Miss

samasu 冷ます cool, let…cool

samasu 覚ます wake up, awake, rouse

samatage 妨げ obstruction, disturbance, obstacle *samatageru* ～る obstruct, hinder, disturb, interrupt

samazama na 様々な various, diverse

sambashi 桟橋 pier, wharf

sambutsu 産物 product

same さめ shark

sameru 冷める (get) cool

sameru 褪める fade (away), be discolored

sammaime 三枚目 comic actor, comedian

sammyaku 山脈 mountain range

samo さも just, quite, as if

samonaito さもないと or, otherwise

sampatsu suru 散髪する have one's hair cut

sampo 散歩 walk, stroll *sampo suru* 〜する walk, take a walk

sampuku 山腹 mountainside, hillside

samui 寒い cold, chill(y)

samusa 寒さ cold, coldness

san 産 childbirth, production

san 酸 acid, acids

san 三, 3 three, third

san-gatsu 三月 March

sango さんご coral

sangyō 産業 industry *sangyō no* 〜の industrial

sanjū 三十, 30 thirty

sankaku 三角 triangle

sanka suru 参加する participate, join, take part

sankō 参考 reference, consultation *sankō ni suru* 〜にする refer to, consult *sankō-sho* 〜書 reference book

sanrin 山林 forest

sansei 賛成 approval, agreement *sansei suru* 〜する approve of, agree, support

sanshō 参照 reference *sanshō suru* 〜する refer to

sanso 酸素 oxygen

sanzan ni 散々に severely, terribly, awfully

sao さお pole, rod

sappari さっぱり (not) at all, quite

sappari shita さっぱりした clean, neat, frank, open-hearted

sara 皿 dish, plate

sarainen 再来年 the year after next

sara ni 更に again, anew

sararīman サラリーマン salaried man, office worker

sarasu さらす expose, bleach

sarau さらう carry off, kidnap

saru 猿 monkey

saru 去る go away, leave

sasa ささ bamboo grass

sasae 支え support *sasaeru* 〜る support, hold, dedicate

-saseru …させる make somebody do, let somebody do, have somebody do

sashiageru 差し上げる hold up, give, present

sashiatari 差し当たり for the present, for the time being, at present

sashidashinin 差出人 sender, addresser

sashidasu 差し出す hold [stretch, reach] out, extend

sashie 挿絵 illustration

sashihikaeru 差し控える refrain from, keep from

sashikomu 差し込む insert, put in, come in

sashisematta 差し迫った pressing, urgent

sashitsukae 差し支え objection *sashitsukae nai* 〜ない do not mind, have no objection

sashizu 指図 order, direction *sashizu suru* 〜する direct, order

sasoi 誘い invitation, temptation

sasou 誘う invite, tempt, ask

sassato さっさと quickly, fast, promptly

sassoku 早速 at once, immediately

sassuru 察する guess, feel for

sasu 指す point to, point out, indicate

sasu 差す pour in

sasu 刺す pierce, prick, stab

sasuga ni さすがに indeed, truly

sasurau さすらう wander, roam

sasuru さする rub, chafe

sate さて well, so, now

satō 砂糖 sugar

satoru 悟る see, understand, realize

satsu 札 (bank) note, bill

satsu 冊 volume, copy

satsuei suru 撮影する take a photo(graph), picture

satsujin 殺人 homicide, murder

sattō suru 殺到する rush, pour in

sawagashii 騒がしい noisy

sawagi 騒ぎ noise, uproar, disturbance

sawagu 騒ぐ be noisy, make a noise

sawaru 触る touch, feel

sawayaka na さわやかな refreshing, bracing, fresh

saya さや sheath, scabbard, cap

sayō 作用 action, operation *sayō suru* ～する act, operate on

sayoku 左翼 left wing

sayōnara さようなら Good-by(e); So long.

sayu さゆ (plain) hot water

sayū 左右 right and left *sayū ni* ～に either side, both sides

sazanami さざなみ ripples, wavelets

sebameru 狭める narrow, reduce

sebiro 背広 business suit, lounge suit, sack coat

sebone 背骨 backbone, spine

sechigarai 世知辛い hard to live

sedai 世代 generation

segare せがれ son, my son

sehyō 世評 public opinion, reputation

sei 背 height, stature *sei no takai* [*hikui*] ～の高い [低い] tall [short]

sei 姓 family name

sei 性 sex, gender

sei 精 spirit

sei 聖 holy, sacred, saintly

-sei …せい results, influence, reason

seibi suru 整備する arrange, adjust, maintain

seibo 聖母 Virgin Mary, Holy Mother

seibo 歳暮 end of year, year-end present

seibu 西部 western part(s), the west

seibun 成分 ingredient, component

seibutsu 生物 living thing, creature *seibutsu-gaku* ～学 biology

seichō 成長 growth *seichō suru* ～する grow up

seidai na [ni] 盛大な [に] splendid [ly], grand [ly], successful [ly]

seido 制度 system, institution

seien suru 声援する encourage, cheer

seifu 政府 government, administration

seifuku 制服 uniform

seifuku 征服 conquest *seifuku suru* ～する conquer

seigen 制限 restriction, limitation *seigen suru* ～する restrict, limit

seigi 正義 right, justice

seihantai 正反対 exact reverse, just the opposite

seihin 製品 manufactured goods

seihōkei 正方形 square

seihoku 西北 northwest

seihon 製本 bookbinding

seii 誠意 sincerity *seii no aru* ～のある sincere

seiji 政治 politics, government

seijin 成人 adult *seijin suru* ～する grow up

seijin 聖人 saint, holy man

seijitsu 誠実 sincerity, fidelity *seijitsu na* ～な sincere, faithful

seijōki 星条旗 Stars and Stripes, U. S. flag

seijō na 正常な normal

seijuku suru 成熟する ripen, get ripe *seijuku shita* 成熟した ripe, mature

seikai 政界 political world

seikaku 性格 character, personality

seikaku 正確 accuracy, precision *seikaku na [ni]* ～な [に] correct [ly], exact [ly], accurate [ly]

seikatsu 生活 life, living *seikatsu suru* ～する live, make a living

seiken 政見 political views

seiken 政権 political power, power

seiketsu na 清潔な clean(ly), neat

seiki 世紀 century

seiki 生気 life, vigor, vitality *seiki no aru* ~ のある vital, animated

seiki no 正規の formal, regular, proper

seikō 成功 success *seikō suru* ~する succeed

seikō na[ni] 精巧な[に] elaborate[ly], exquisite[ly]

seikyū 請求 demand *seikyū suru* ~する request, charge *seikyū-sho* ~書 application, bill

seikyū na 性急な quick-tempered, impatient

seimei 姓名 (full) name

seimei 生命 life, soul

seimei 声明 declaration, statement *seimei suru* ~する declare

seimitsu 精密 minuteness, precision *seimitsu na[ni]* minute[ly], accurate[ly]

seinen 青年 youth, young man

seinen 成年 majority, full [adult] age *seinen ni tassuru* ~に達する come of full age

seinen-gappi 生年月日 date of one's birth, birth date

seinō 性能 capacity *seinō no yoi* ~のよい efficient

seireki 西暦 Christian Era

seiretsu suru 整列する line up

seiri suru 整理する put in order, adjust, arrange

seiritsu suru 成立する be formed [effected]

seiryoku 精力 energy *seiryoku-teki na* ~的な energetic

seiryoku 勢力 influence, power *seiryoku no aru* ~のある powerful

seisaku 政策 policy

seisaku suru 製作する manufacture, produce, make

seisan 生産 production *seisan suru* ~する produce *seisan-butsu* ~物 products

seisei-dōdō to 正々堂々と fairly, squarely

seiseki 成績 result, record

seishi 生死 life and death

seishiki na [ni] 正式な[に] formal [ly], regular [ly]

seishin 精神 mind, spirit, soul *seishin-teki na* ～的な spiritual, mental

seishi suru 静止する stand still, rest

seishitsu 性質 nature, character

seisho 聖書 (Holy) Bible

seishōnen 青少年 youth, younger generation

seishun 青春 youth, springtime of life *seishun no* ～の youthful

seisō 清掃 cleaning

seisō suru 盛装する dress up

seiten 晴天 fine [fair] weather

seiton 整とん order, arrangement

seitō na 正当な fair, just, right

seiu 晴雨 fair or rainy *seiu ni kakawarazu* ～にかかわらず rain or shine *seiu-kei* ～計 barometer

Seiyō 西洋 the West *Seiyō no* ～の Western

seizō 製造 making, manufacture

seizon 生存 existence, life *seizon suru* ～する exist, live

seizu 製図 drawing

sekai 世界 world *sekai-teki na* ～的な worldwide, international

seken 世間 world, people *seken-banashi* ～話 gossip

seki せき cough *seki o suru* ～をする cough, have a cough *seki-dome* ～止め cough drop

seki 席 seat, place

sekidō 赤道 equator

sekijūji 赤十字 the Red Cross

sekimen suru 赤面する blush (with shame)

sekinin 責任 responsibility *sekinin aru* ～ある responsible

sekitan 石炭 coal

sekiyu 石油 oil, petroleum

sekkei 設計 plan, design *sekkei suru* ～する plan, design

sekken 石けん soap

sekkin 接近 approach

sekkyoku-teki na [ni] 積極的な [に] positive [ly], active [ly]

semai 狭い small, narrow, limited

sembetsu せん別 parting [farewell] gift

semeru 責める blame, reproach

semeru 攻める attack, assault

semi せみ cicada, locust

semmei na 鮮明な clear, distinct

semmen o suru 洗面をする wash one's face *semmen-ki* ～器 washbowl, basin

semmon 専門 speciality *semmon-ka* ～家 specialist, expert

sempai 先輩 elder, senior

sempūki 扇風機 electric fan

sen 千, 1000 thousand

sen 線 line

sen 栓 stopper, cork, bung

senaka 背中 the back

senchō 船長 captain, skipper, master mariner

senden 宣伝 advertisement *senden suru* ～する advertise

sengen 宣言 declaration *sengen suru* ～する declare

sengetsu 先月 last month

sengo 戦後 after the war, post-war

sen'i 繊維 fiber

sen'in 船員 sailor, seaman

senjitsu 先日 the other day

senkō 専攻 special study *senkō suru* ～する specialize in

senkoku suru 宣告する sentence, proclaim

senkyo 選挙 election *senkyo suru* ～する elect, choose

senren sareta 洗練された polished, refined

senritsu 旋律 rhythm, melody

senro 線路 line, track

senryō 占領 occupation *senryō suru* 〜する occupy

sensei 先生 teacher, master

senshoku 染色 dyeing

senshu 選手 player, champion *senshuken* 〜権 championship, title

senshū 先週 last week

sensō 戦争 war, battle, fight

sensu 扇子 fan

sensui 潜水 diving *sensui suru* 〜する dive *sensui-fu* 〜夫 diver

sentaku 選択 selection, choice *sentaku suru* 〜する select, choose

sentaku 洗濯 wash, washing *sentaku suru* 〜する wash, do washing

sentan 先端 point, tip

sentō 先頭 head, lead

sentō 戦闘 battle, fight

senzai 洗剤 cleanser, detergent

senzen 戦前 prewar days [era]

senzo 先祖 ancestor

seppun suru 接ぷんする kiss

serifu せりふ speech, words

seron 世論 public opinion

sesshi 摂氏 centigrade, Celsius

sesshoku 接触 contact, touch *sesshoku suru* 〜する come into contact [touch] with

sessuru 接する touch, adjoin

setchi suru 設置する establish, set up

setsu 説 opinion, view

setsubi 設備 equipment *setsubi no yoi* 〜のよい well-equipped

setsugō suru 接合する join, unite, connect

setsumei 説明 explanation *setsumei suru* 〜する explain

setsuritsu 設立 establishment, foundation *setsuritsu suru* 〜する establish, set up

setsuyaku 節約 saving, economy *setsuyaku*

suru 〜する economize, save

settai 接待 reception *settai suru* 〜する receive, welcome

settoku 説得 persuasion *settoku suru* 〜する persuade

sewa 世話 care, help *sewa o suru* 〜をする take care [charge] of, look after

-sezaruo o enai …せざるを得ない cannot help doing, cannot but do

shaberu しゃべる chat, chatter, talk

shaburu しゃぶる suck, chew

shachō 社長 company president

shagamu しゃがむ squat down, crouch

shageki 射撃 firing, shooting, shoot

shakai 社会 society, world, public

shakkin 借金 debt, loan *shakkin suru* 〜する borrow money, owe

shakkuri (suru) しゃっくり(する) hiccup, hiccough

shako 車庫 car shed, garage

shakō 社交 social intercourse *shakō-teki na* 〜的な social

share しゃれ joke, jest

sharin 車輪 wheel, cars

shasei suru 写生する sketch

shasen 斜線 oblique line

shasetsu 社説 leading article

shashin 写真 photograph *shashin o toru* 〜をとる take a photograph [picture]

shashō 車掌 (*train*) conductor

shatsu シャツ undershirt, underwear

shazai 謝罪 apology *shazai suru* 〜する apologize

shi 詩 poem, poetry, verse

shi 死 death

shi 市 city, town

shi 四, 4 four, fourth

shi 氏 Mr.

shiageru 仕上げる finish, complete

shiai 試合 match, game

shiawase 幸せ (good) fortune, luck, happiness

shibafu 芝生 lawn

shibai 芝居 play, drama

shibaraku しばらく for a while

shibaru 縛る bind, tie

shiba-shiba しばしば often, frequently

shibire ga kireta しびれがきれた My foot is asleep. *shibire o kirasu* しびれをきらす lose one's patience

shibireru しびれる become numb

shibō 脂肪 fat, grease

shibō 死亡 death, decease *shibō suru* ～する die

shibomu しぼむ fade (away), wither

shibori 絞り variegation, dapple, iris

shiboru 絞る press, wring

shibui 渋い astringent, rough, glum, sour, tasteful

shibu-shibu 渋々 reluctantly, unwillingly

shibutoi しぶとい stubborn, stiff-necked

shichi 七, 7 seven, seventh

shichi-gatsu 七月 July

shichijū 七十, 70 seventy

shichimenchō 七面鳥 turkey

shichō 市長 mayor

shichū シチュー stew

shidai ni 次第に gradually

shiden 市電 streetcar, tram

shidō 指導 guidance, leadership *shidō suru* ～する guide, lead

shigai 市外 suburbs of a city *shigai no* ～の suburban

shigai 市街 streets

shigai-sen 紫外線 ultraviolet rays

shigan 志願 application *shigan suru* ～する apply for *shigansha* ～者 applicant, candidate

shi-gatsu 四月 April

shigeki 刺激 stimulus *shigeki suru* 〜する stimulate

shigen 資源 resources

shigeru 茂る grow thick

shigoto 仕事 work, labor

shigyō-shiki 始業式 opening ceremony

shihai 支配 control, rule *shihai suru* 〜する govern, rule

shiharai 支払い payment, discharge

shiharau 支払う pay, discharge

shihatsu-eki 始発駅 starting station

shihei 紙幣 paper money [currency], a (bank) note, a bill

shihenkei 四辺形 quadrilateral

shihō 司法 administration of justice

shihon 資本 capital, funds

shihō ni 四方に on all sides, in all directions

shiire 仕入れ buying, laying in *shiireru* 〜る lay [buy] in

shiiru しいる force, compel

shiitageru しいたげる oppress

shijin 詩人 poet, poetess

shiji suru 支持する support, back (up), stand by

shiji suru 指示する indicate, point out

shijō 市場 market, fair

shijū 始終 always, all the time, often

shijū 四十, 40 forty

shika 鹿 deer

-shika …しか only, but

shika-i 歯科医 dentist

shikai 視界 sight

shikai-sha 司会者 chairman, master of ceremony, leader

shikake 仕掛 contrivance, mechanism

shikaku 四角 square

shikaku 資格 qualification

shikaku 死角 dead angle

shikameru しかめる frown, (make a) grimace

shikamo しかも moreover, besides

shikarareru 叱られる be scolded

shikaru 叱る scold, chide

shikashi しかし but, however

shikata 仕方 way, method

shike しけ stormy weather, storm

shikei 死刑 capital punishment, death (penalty)

shiken 試験 examination, test *shiken suru ~* する examine, test

shiki 式 ceremony, form, style, type

shiki 指揮 command, orders, direction *shiki suru ~* する command, order, lead

shiki 四季 four seasons, seasons of the year

shikichi 敷地 site

shikimono 敷物 carpet

shikin 資金 capital, funds, a fund

shikiri ni しきりに frequently, repeatedly

shikisai 色彩 color, coloring

shikkaku suru 失格する be disqualified

shikki 湿気 damp, moisture

shikki 漆器 lacquer ware

shikomu 仕込む teach, train

shiku 敷く spread, cover

shikujiri しくじり failure, mistake

shikujiru しくじる fail, blunder

shikyū no [ni] 至急の[に] urgent [ly], pressing [ly], prompt [ly]

shikyū suru 支給する provide, supply

shima 島 island

shima 縞 stripes

shimai 姉妹 sisters

shimai 仕舞い end, close *shimai ni ~* に eventually, finally

shimari 締り tightness, firmness *shimari no nai ~* のない loose

shimaru 締る be shut [closed], tighten, be tight

shimatsu suru 始末する manage, deal with, dispose of

shimatta しまった Heavens!; Dear God!

shima-uma 縞馬 zebra

shimbō 辛抱 patience, endurance *shimbō suru*
~する patient, endure

shimbun 新聞 newspaper

shimei 使命 mission

shimei 氏名 (full) name

shimei suru 指名する nominate, name

shimekiri 締め切り closing, closing date

shimeppoi 湿っぽい damp, moist, wet

shimeru 締める shut, close, tie (up), tighten,
put on

shimeru 絞める wring, strangle

shimeru 湿る become damp [wet]

shimeru 占める occupy, hold

shimesu 示す show, indicate

shimi 染み stain, spot

shimi-jimi しみじみ keenly, fully, heartily

shimin 市民 citizen, townspeople

shimiru 染みる soak [sink] into, penetrate

shimmai 新米 new hand, beginner

shimmi no [ni] 親身の [に] kindly, hearty[-ily]

shimmiri しんみり quietly, seriously

shimmitsu na 親密な intimate, friendly, close

shimo 霜 frost *shimodoke* ~解け thawing

shimon 指紋 fingerprint

shimpai 心配 anxiety, concern *shimpai na* ~
な anxious, uneasy *shimpai suru* ~する be
anxious about, worry about

shimpen 身辺 surroundings

shimpi 神秘 mystery *shimpi-teki na* ~的な
mysterious

shimpo 進歩 progress *shimpo suru* ~する
make progress

shimpu 新婦 bride

shimpu 神父 (Catholic) priest

shin 心 core, wick

shinabiru しなびる wither, shrivel *shinabita*
しなびた withered, shriveled

shinagire 品切れ out of stock

-shinaide …しないで without doing

shin'ai na   親愛な   dear, beloved

-shinai yō ni   …しないように   so as not to do

shinamono   品物   article, merchandise

shinchiku   新築   new building

shinchō   身長   stature, height

shinchō na [ni]   慎重な [に]   careful [ly], cautious [ly]

shinchū   心中   at [in one's] heart

shinchū   真ちゅう   brass

shindai   寝台   bed, berth   *shindai-sha* ～車 sleeping car

shindan   診断   diagnosis   *shindan suru* ～する diagnose

shindō   振動   vibration, shock   *shindō suru* ～する shake, quake

shin'ei   新鋭   fresh, picked

shingō   信号   signal

shinise   しにせ   old store

shinjin   信心   faith, piety   *shinjin suru* ～する believe in   *shinjin-bukai* ～深い pious

shinjiru   信じる   believe, trust

shinjitsu   真実   fact, truth, reality   *shinjitsu no* ～の true, real

shinju   真珠   pearl

shinka   進化   evolution   *shinka suru* ～する evolve, develop

shinka   真価   true [real] value

shinkan   新刊   new publication

shinkan   新館   new building

shinkei   神経   nerves   *shinkei-shitsu na* ～質な nervous

shinken na [ni]   真剣な [に]   serious [ly], earnest [ly]

shinkiroku   新記録   new record

shinkō   信仰   faith, belief

shinkō   進行   progress, advance

shinkoku na   深刻な   serious, severe

shinkon   新婚   newly-married   *shinkon-ryokō ni iku* ～旅行に行く go on a honeymoon

shinkū 真空 vacuum *shinkū no* 〜の vacuous *shinkū-kan* 〜管 tube

shinkyō 心境 state of mind

shinkyū suru 進級する be promoted, win promotion

shin'nen 信念 belief, faith

shin'nen 新年 new year, New Year's Day

shin'nin no 新任の newly-appointed, new

shin'nyū 侵入 invasion *shin'nyū suru* 〜する invade

shin'nyūsei 新入生 freshman, new student

shinobu 忍ぶ bear, endure, put up with

shinrai 信頼 trust, reliance *shinrai suru* 〜する trust, believe

shinri 心理 mental state, mind *shinri-gaku* 〜学 psychology

shinri 真理 truth

shinrin 森林 forest, wood

shinro 進路 course

shinrō 新郎 bridegroom

shinrui 親類 relative, relation

shinryaku 侵略 aggression, invasion *shinryaku suru* 〜する invade

shinryō 診療 medical treatment *shinryō-sho* 〜所 clinic

shinsatsu 診察 medical examination *shinsatsu suru* 〜する examine

shinsei 申請 application *shinsei suru* 〜する apply

shinsei na 神聖な sacred, holy

shinsen na 新鮮な fresh, new

shinsetsu 親切 kindness *shinsetsu na[ni]* 〜な[に] kind[ly]

shinshi 紳士 gentleman

shinshitsu 寝室 bedroom

shinsō 真相 truth, actual fact

shinsui suru 進水する launch (a ship)

shinsui suru 浸水する be flooded

shintai 身体 body

shinu 死ぬ die, pass away
shinwa 神話 myth, mythology
shin'ya ni 深夜に in the dead of the night
shin'yō 信用 confidence, trust *shin'yō suru* ～
する trust, rely on
shin'yū 親友 intimate friend
shinzen 親善 good will, friendship
shinzō 心臓 heart
shinzuru 信ずる believe
shio 潮 tide
shio 塩 salt
shion 子音 consonant
shioreru しおれる droop
shippai 失敗 failure *shippai suru* ～する fail
shippo しっぽ tail
shiraberu 調べる inquire into, investigate
shiraga 白髪 grey [white] hair
shirase 知らせ information, news *shiraseru*
～る inform
shirazu-shirazu 知らず知らず unconsciously
shireikan 司令官 commander
shiri しり buttocks, hips
shiriai 知り合い acquaintance
shiriau 知り合う get acquainted
shirigomi suru しりごみする hesitate, shy
shiro 城 castle
shiroi 白い white
shirōto 素人 amateur
shiru 汁 juice, sap, soup
shiru 知る know, be informed of, be aware of
shirushi 印 sign, symbol, mark *shirushi o tsukeru* ～をつける mark
shiryo 思慮 thought, discretion
shiryo no aru ～のある thoughtful, prudent
shiryo no nai ～のない thoughtless
shiryō 資料 materials, data
shiryoku 視力 eyesight
shisan 資産 fortune
shisatsu suru 視察する inspect, observe

shisei 姿勢 attitude, posture

shiseikatsu 私生活 private life

shiseki 史跡 historic(al) spot

shisetsu 使節 mission, ambassador

shisetsu 施設 establishment

shisha 支社 branch (office)

shisha 使者 messenger, envoy

shisha 死者 dead person

shishōsha 死傷者 casualties

shishū 刺しゅう embroidery *shishū suru* ～する embroider

shishunki 思春期 adolescence

shishutsu 支出 expenses, outgo *shishutsu suru* ～する expend, pay

shisō 思想 thought, ideas

shison 子孫 descendants

shisshin suru 失心する faint

shisso na 質素な simple, plain

shita 舌 tongue

shita 下 lower part, bottom *shita no* ～の under, lower *shita ni* ～に down, below, beneath

shitagatte 従って so that, therefore, as, with, accordingly

shitagau 従う obey, follow

shitagi 下着 underwear, underclothes

shitai 死体 dead body

shitaku 支度 preparations *shitaku suru* ～する prepare

shitamachi 下町 downtown, old business area

shitashii 親しい intimate, friendly

shitashimi 親しみ intimacy, friendship

shitataru 滴る drip, drop

shitateru 仕立てる make, tailor

shitei 指定 appointment *shitei suru* ～する appoint

shiteki 私的 private, personal

shiteki suru 指摘する point out, indicate

shiten 支店 branch (office, shop)

shito-shito しとしと gently, softly

shitoyaka na [ni] しとやかな[に] gentle[-ly], graceful[ly]

shitsu 質 quality

shitsubō 失望 disappointment
  shitsubō suru ～する be disappointed in [at]
  shitsubō saseru ～させる disappoint

shitsudo 湿度 humidity

shitsugen 失言 slip of the tongue

shitsugi 質疑 question, inquiry

shitsugyō 失業 unemployment *shitsugyō suru* ～する lose one's job *shitsugyō-sha* ～者 unemployed workers

shitsuke しつけ breeding, training

shitsu(k)koi しつ(っ)こい obstinate, stubborn

shitsumei 失明 loss of eyesight

shitsumon 質問 question

shitsunai de [ni] 室内で[に] indoors, in the room

shitsurei na 失礼な rude, impolite *Shitsurei shimashita.* ～しました. I am sorry; I beg your pardon. *Shitsurei desuga* ～ですが Excuse me, but…

shitsuren 失恋 disappointed love, broken heart

shittakaburi o suru 知ったか振りをする pretend to know

shitto しっと jealousy *shitto-bukai* ～深い jealous *shitto suru* ～する be jealous

shiwa しわ wrinkles, lines

shiwasu 師走 the year end, December

shiwaza 仕業 action, deed

shiyakusho 市役所 city [municipal] office

shiyō 使用 use, employment *shiyō suru* ～する use, employ

shizen 自然 nature *shizen no* ～の natural *shizen ni* ～に naturally

shizuka na [ni] 静かな[に]   still, quiet[ly], calm[ly]

shizuku 滴 drop

shizumaru 静まる become quiet, calm down

shizumu 沈む sink, go down

shō 賞 prize, reward

shōbai 商売 trade, business

shōben 小便 urine

shōbō 消防 fire fighting **shōbō-fu** ～夫 fireman

shōbu 勝負 game, match **shōbu suru** ～する contest

shobun 処分 disposal, management

shōchō 象徴 symbol

shochū 暑中 summer **shochū-kyūka** ～休暇 summer vacation

shōdaku 承諾 consent, assent **shōdaku suru** ～する consent to

shōdoku 消毒 disinfection **shōdoku suru** ～する sterilize

shōgai 生涯 life, lifetime

shōgai 障害 obstacle, difficulty

shōgai 傷害 injury accident **shōgai-hoken** ～保険 accident insurance

shōgakkō 小学校 primary school

shōgakusei 小学生 school children, schoolboy [-girl]

shōgatsu 正月 New Year('s Day), January

shōgo(ni) 正午(に) (at) noon

shōgyō 商業 commerce, business **shōgyō no** ～の commercial

shōhi 消費 consumption **shōhi suru** ～する consume, spend

shōhin 商品 goods, merchandise

shōhin 賞品 prize

shōji 障子 paper door

shōjiki 正直 honesty **shōjiki na[ni]** ～な[に] honest[ly]

shojo 処女 virgin, maiden

shōjo 少女 girl, young girl

shoka 初夏 early summer

shōka 消化 digestion **shōka suru** ～する digest

shōkai 紹介 introduction **shōkai suru** ～する

introduce, present

shōkai 照会 inquiry *shōkai suru* 〜する inquire

shoki 初期 the early days

shōki no 正気の sane, conscious

shōko 証拠 proof, evidence

shokuba 職場 workshop, one's post

shokubutsu 植物 plant, vegetation *shokubutsu no* 〜の vegetable, plant

shokudō 食堂 dining room, restaurant

shokugyō 職業 occupation, calling, profession

shokuji 食事 meal, dinner, diet *shokuji suru* 〜する take a meal, dine

shokumotsu 食物 food

shokunin 職人 workman

shokupan 食パン bread

shokuryō 食料 food *shokuryōhin-ten* 〜品店 grocery

shokutaku 食卓 (dinner-)table

shokuyoku 食欲 appetite, desire to eat

shōkyoku-teki na[ni] 消極的な[に] negative [ly], passive [ly]

shōkyū 昇給 rise in salary, raise

shombori しょんぼり sadly

shomei 署名 signature *shomei suru* 〜する sign one's name

shomei 書名 title

shōmei 証明 proof *shōmei suru* 〜する prove

shōmei 照明 illumination, lighting

shomen 書面 letter *shomen de* 〜で by letter

shōmen 正面 the front *no shōmen ni* の〜に in front of

shomin 庶民 (common) people

shōmō suru 消耗する consume, exhaust

shomotsu 書物 book

shōnen 少年 boy, lad *shōnen no* 〜の juvenile *shōnen-jidai* 〜時代 one's boyhood (days)

shōnika-i 小児科医 pediatrician

shōnin 商人 merchant

shōnin 証人 witness

shōnin suru 承認する admit, recognize

shōrai 将来 future, in the future

shōrei 奨励 encouragement *shōrei suru* ～する encourage

shōri 勝利 victory, triumph *shōri-sha* ～者 victor *shōri o uru* ～を得る win a victory

shori suru 処理する dispose of, deal with, manage

shorui 書類 papers, documents *shorui-ire* ～入れ briefcase

shōryaku 省略 omission, abbreviation *shōryaku suru* ～する omit, abridge, abbreviate

shosai 書斎 study, library

shōsai 詳細 details, particulars *shōsai ni* ～に in full detail, minutely

shōsan 賞賛 administration, praise *shōsan suru* ～する admire, praise

shōsetsu 小説 novel, story

shoshinsha 初心者 beginner

shōsoku 消息 news, information

shōsū 少数 small number, a few

shōsū 小数 decimal (fraction) *shōsū-ten* ～点 decimal point

shōsuru 称する call, name, pretend

shōtai 招待 invitation *shōtai suru* ～する invite, ask

shoten 書店 bookshop, bookstore

shōten 商店 shop, store

shōten 焦点 focus

shotoku 所得 income, profits

shōtotsu 衝突 collision, conflict *shōtotsu suru* ～する collide with

shoyū 所有 possession *shoyū suru* ～する have, possess

shōzō 肖像 portrait

shozoku suru 所属する belong to, be attached to

shu 主 the Lord, our Lord

shu 朱 cinnabar, vermilion

shū 週 week
shū 州 state, province
shubi 守備 defense
shuchō suru 主張する assert, claim, insist on
shudai 主題 subject
shudan 手段 means, measures, step
shūdan 集団 group, mass
shūdōin 修道院 monastery *joshi-shūdōin* 女子
 ～ convent, nunnery
shudōken 主導権 initiative
shufu 首府 capital, metropolis
shufu 主婦 housewife
shūgeki 襲撃 attack, charge
shugi 主義 principle
shūgiin 衆議院 House of Representative
shugo 主語 subject
shūi 周囲 circumference *shūi no* ～の neighboring
shūji 習字 penmanship, calligraphy
shujin 主人 master, employer, host
shūjitsu 週日 weekday
shuju no 種々の various, diverse
shujutsu 手術 operation *shujutsu suru* ～する
 operate
shūkai 集会 meeting, assembly
shūkaku 収穫 harvest, crop
shūkan 習慣 habit, custom, practice
shūkan 週刊 weekly (publication)
shuki 手記 note, memoirs
shūkin 集金 collection (of money)
shukkin 出勤 attendance *shukkin suru* ～する
 attend one's office
shukudai 宿題 homework, home lessons
shukuhaku suru 宿泊する lodge, stay
shukumei 宿命 fate, destiny *shukumei-teki na*
 ～的な fatal
shukusai-jitsu 祝祭日 public holiday
shukushō 縮小 reduction *shukushō suru* ～す
 る reduce

shūkyō 宗教 religion

shūkyū 週給 weekly pay

shūmatsu 週末 weekend

shumbun 春分 vernal equinox *shumbun no hi* ~の日 Vernal Equinox Day

shumi 趣味 taste, hobby

shunin 主任 chief, manager

shūnin suru 就任する take [assume] office

shunkan 瞬間 moment, instant, second

shūnyū 収入 income

shuppan 出版 publication *shuppan suru* ~する publish, issue

shuppan suru 出帆する leave, sail from

shuppatsu 出発 departure, starting *shuppatsu suru* ~する start, leave for

shūri 修理 repair

shurui 種類 kind, sort

shuryō 狩猟 hunting, shooting

shūryō 終了 conclusion, end

shūsai 秀才 brilliant [talented] man

shūsei suru 修正する amend, revise, modify

shuseki 首席 head, chief

shūsen 終戦 end of the war

shūshi 収支 income and expenditure

shūshi 終始 from beginning to end

shushō 首相 Prime Minister, Premier

shūshoku suru 就職する find [get] employment

shūshū 収集 collection *shūshū-ka* ~家 collector

shussan 出産 childbirth, birth

shussatsu 出札 selling tickets *shussatsu-gakari* ~係 ticket agent *shussatsu-guchi* ~口 ticket window

shusse 出世 success in life *shusse suru* ~する rise in the world

shusshin 出身 graduate *shusshin de aru* ~である come from, be a graduate of *shusshin-kō* ~校 one's Alma Mater

shūten 終点 end, terminus, terminal (station)

shūto しゅうと father-in-law, mother-in-law

shūtoku suru 習得する learn, master, acquire

shu to shite 主として mainly, chiefly

shutsuba suru 出馬する go in person

shutsuen suru 出演する appear, perform

shutsugen suru 出現する appear, come out

shutsujō suru 出場する appear, be present, attend

shuwan 手腕 ability, talent, capacity

shuyaku 主役 leading title [part, role]

shūyō 修養 culture, cultivation, training *shūyō suru* ~する cultivate, train

shuyō na 主要な leading, principal

shūyō suru 収容する accommodate

shūzen suru 修繕する repair, mend, overhaul

soba そば side *soba no* ~の neighboring, nearby *soba ni* ~に by, beside

sōba 相場 speculation, market price

sobakasu そばかす freckles

sōbetsu-kai 送別会 farewell party

sōbi 装備 equipment *sōbi suru* ~する equip

sobieru そびえる soar, rise

sōchi 装置 provision, equipment

sōchō 早朝 early morning

-sōda …そうだ I hear; It is said

sodachi 育ち breeding, growth

sōdan 相談 consultation *sōdan suru* ~する consult, confer with

sodateru 育てる bring up, raise, breed

sodatsu 育つ grow up

sode そで sleeve *sode no shita* ~の下 bribe

sōdō 騒動 riot, disturbance

sofu 祖父 grandfather

sōgaku 総額 total amount

sōgankyō 双眼鏡 binoculars

sōgen 草原 plain, prairie

sōgi 葬儀 funeral

sōgo no [ni] 相互の[に] mutual [ly]

sōgō suru 総合する synthesize, put together

sogu そぐ chip, slice off

sōgū suru 遭遇する encounter, meet with

sohin 粗品 small gift

sōi 相違 difference　*sōi suru* ～する differ

sōji 掃除 cleaning　*sōji suru* ～する clean, sweep

sōji no 相似の similar

sōjū 操縦 management, operation　*sōjū suru* ～する manage, operate

sōjuku na 早熟な precocious

sōkai 総会 general meeting

sōkei 総計 total, sum　*sōkei suru* ～する total, sum up

sōki 早期 early stage

sōkin 送金 remittance　*sōkin suru* ～する remit

sokki 速記 shorthand, stenography

sokkin de 即金で in cash

sokkuri そっくり just as it is, all, altogether, just like

soko 底 bottom, sole

soko そこ there, that place

sokō 素行 conduct, behavior

sōko 倉庫 warehouse, storehouse

sokoku 祖国 fatherland, one's native land

sokonau 損なう hurt, injure, spoil

sokotsu na そこつな careless, rash

-soku …足 pair

sokubaku suru 束縛する restrict

sokudo 速度 speed, velocity　*sokudo-kei* ～計 speedometer

sokujitsu 即日 same day

sokumen 側面 side, flank

sokuryō 測量 surveying, measuring　*sokuryō suru* ～する survey, measure

sokushin suru 促進する hasten, promote

sokutatsu 速達 special delivery

somaru 染まる dye, be dyed

somatsu na 粗末な coarse, crude, poor

sōmei na そう明な wise, intelligent

somuku 背く go [act] against

son 損 loss, damage

sonaeru 備える furnish, provide

sonaeru 供える offer to

sōnan 遭難 disaster *sōnan suru* 〜する meet with a disaster

songai 損害 damage, loss

sonkei suru 尊敬する respect, esteem *sonkei-subeki* 尊敬すべき respectable

son'na そんな such *son'na ni* 〜に so, so far, so much

sono その that, those, its

sonoba de その場で then and there, on the spot

sonogo その後 after that, later, since

sono hi その日 that day

sonokoro そのころ in those days, about that time

sonokurai その位 as much [many], so much

sonomama そのまま as it is, as you find it

sono toki その時 then, at that time

sono-uchi ni その内に soon, by and by, someday

sonzai 存在 existence *sonzai suru* 〜する exist

sō'on 騒音 noise, din

sō'ō no 相応の suitable, proper, reasonable

soppo o muku そっぽを向く look aside, turn away

sora 空 sky, heaven

soramoyō 空模様 the look of the sky, the weather

sore それ it, that *soredake* 〜だけ so much

soredake ni それだけに all the more because

sorede それで so, therefore, and

soredemo それでも nevertheless, but, and yet

soredewa それでは then, in that case, if so

soredokoro ka それどころか on the contrary, far from it

sorehodo それほど so, so much

sorekara それから after that, and then

soremade それまで till then

Soren ソ連 U.S.S.R. (=the Union of Soviet Socialist Republics)

soreni それに besides, moreover

sore ni shitemo それにしても nevertherless, still, though

soreru それる turn away [aside]

soretomo それとも or, or else

soretonaku それとなく indirectly, casually

sorewa-sōto それはそうと by the way, by the by

soreyue それ故 so, therefore

sore-zore それぞれ each, respective

sori そり sleigh, sled

sori 反り curve, bend, warp *sori ga awanai* ～が合わない cannot get along on

sōri 総理 president, premier, prime minister

sōritsu 創立 establishment *sōritsu suru* ～する establish *sōritsu-sha* ～者 founder

soroban そろばん abacus

soroeru そろえる arrange, put in order

soro-soro そろそろ slowly, soon, gradually

sorou そろう be complete, gather

soru そる shave

soru 反る bend, curve, warp

sōryō 送料 carriage, postage

sōsaku 創作 original work, creation, novel *sōsaku suru* ～する create, write (a novel)

sōseiji 双生児 twin

sosen 祖先 ancestor

sōsenkyo 総選挙 general election

soshiki 組織 system, organization *soshiki suru* ～する organize, form

sōshin suru 送信する transmit

soshi suru 阻止する obstruct, hinder

soshitsu 素質 making(s), character, tendency

soshō 訴訟 lawsuit, legal action

sōsho 双書 series, library

sōshoku 装飾 ornament, decoration *sōshoku suru* ～する decorate

sosogu 注ぐ pour into

sosokkashii そそっかしい hasty, careless

sotchoku na[ni] 率直な[に] frank[ly], plain [ly]

soto 外 the outside [exterior] *soto ni*[*de*] ~ に[で] outside, outdoors

sotogawa 外側 the outside *sotogawa no* ~の outer

sōtō no 相当の suitable, proper, fit, equal, fair [ly], considerable

sotsugyō suru 卒業する finish, graduate from

sotte 沿って along, by

sotto そっと softly, gently, quietly

sottō suru 卒倒する faint, swoon

sou 沿う parallel to, lie along

sowa-sowa suru そわそわする be restless, be nervous

soya na 粗野な rough, coarse, rude

soyokaze そよかぜ gentle [light] breeze

soyo-soyo to そよそよと gently, softly

sozei 租税 taxation, taxes

sōzō 創造 creation *sōzō suru* ~する create

sōzō 想像 imagination *sōzō suru* ~する imagine

sōzoku suru 相続する succeed (to), inherit

su 酢 vinegar

su 巣 nest, (honey)comb, wed

sū 数 number, figure

subarashii 素晴らしい splendid, glorious, wonderful

subayai 素早い quick, prompt *subayaku* 素早く quickly, promptly

suberasu 滑らす let slip, slip *kuchi o suberasu* 口を~ make a slip of the tongue

suberidai 滑り台 slide, chute

suberu 滑る slide, glide, slip

sube-sube shita すべすべした smooth, slippery

subete すべて all, all together *subete no* ~の all, every

sudachi suru 巣立ちする leave the nest, fledge out

sudare すだれ bamboo blind

sude de 素手で empty-handed, unarmed

sude ni 既に already

sue 末 end, close

suekko 末っ子 the youngest(child)

sueru 据える set, place

suetsukeru 据え付ける fix, install

sūgaku 数学 mathematics

sugao 素顔 unpainted face

sugaru すがる cling[hold on] to

suga-suga shii すがすがしい refreshing

sugata 姿 figure, form

-sugi …過ぎ past, after

sugi 杉 (Japanese)cedar, cryptomeria

sugiru 過ぎる pass, be over, be gone

sugoi すごい ghastly, gruesome, awful, weird, wonderful, amazing

sugosu 過ごす pass, spend

sugu(ni) すぐ(に) at once, immediately

sugureru 優れる excel in, be superior to *sugureta* 優れた superior, excellent

sūhai suru 崇拝する worship, adore, admire

sūhyaku 数百 hundreds (of)

sui 粋 essence, elegance, best

sui 酸い sour, acid

suiageru 吸い上げる suck[pump] up

suiatsu 水圧 water[hydraulic] pressure

suibun 水分 moisture, water, juice

suichoku no[ni] 垂直の[に] vertical[ly], perpendicular[ly]

suichū ni 水中に in the water, under water

suidō 水道 waterworks, water service

suiei 水泳 swimming, bathing

suigai 水害 flood disaster

suigin 水銀 mercury, quicksilver

suihei na 水平な horizontal, even, level *suihei ni* 水平に horizontally *suihei-sen* 水平線 horizontal line, horizon

suijaku 衰弱 emaciation *suijaku suru* 〜する grow weak

suiji 炊事 cooking

suijun 水準 level, standard

suika すいか watermelon

suimen 水面 surface of the water

suimin 睡眠 sleep

suimono 吸い物 soup

suiri suru 推理する reason, infer *suiri-shōsetsu* 推理小説 mystery story

suiryoku-hatsudensho 水力発電所 hydroelectric [water power] station

suisaiga 水彩画 water color

suisambutsu 水産物 marine products, sea food

suisei 水星 Mercury

suisen 水仙 daffodil

suisen 推薦 recommendation *suisen suru* 〜する recommend

suisha 水車 water wheel

suishō 水晶 crystal

suisō 水槽 water tank

suisō suru 吹奏する blow, play (a wind instrument)

suitchi スイッチ switch *suitchi o ireru* [*kiru*] 〜を入れる[切る] switch on [off]

suiteki 水滴 drop of water

suitō 水筒 canteen

suitorigami 吸取り紙 blotting paper

suitoru 吸い取る absorb, suck up

suitsuku 吸い付く stick [adhere] to

suiyō-bi 水曜日 Wednesday

suizoku-kan 水族館 aquarium

suji 筋 muscle, fiber, reason, logic *suji no tōtta* [*tōranai*] 〜の通った[通らない] [un]reasonable

sūji 数字 figure, numeral

sujigaki 筋書 plot, plan, synopsis

sūjitsu 数日 for several [a few] days

sukareru 好かれる be liked, be popular

sukashi 透かし watermark **sukashi-bori** ～彫り openwork **sukashi-iri no** ～入りの watermarked, openworked

sukasu 透かす look through, hold (something) to the light

sukedachi suru 助太刀する help, assist

suki 好き liking, fondness **suki da** ～だ like, be fond of, love **suki na** ～な favorite

suki すき opening, gap, space

sukikirai 好ききらい one's likes and dislikes **sukikirai no aru** ～のある particular

sukima 透き間 opening, gap **sukima-kaze** ～風 draft

sukitōru 透き通る transparent, clear

sukkari すっかり completely, quite, all

sukkiri shita すっきりした well-formed

sukoshi 少し little, some, few **sukoshi-demo** ～でも any, even a little **sukoshimo** ～も (not) at all, not in the least **sukoshi-zutsu** ～ずつ little by little

suku 好く like, be fond of, love

suku すく comb

sukui 救い help, rescue **sukui o motomeru** ～を求める ask for help

sukumu すくむ crouch, cower

sukunai 少ない few, little, rare

sukunakutomo 少なくとも at least

suku'u 救う save, help, rescue

suku'u すくう scoop (up), ladle

sumai 住い house, dwelling, home

sumasu 済ます finish, get through

sumasu 澄ます put on airs, be affected **sumashita** 澄ました affected, prim

sumi 隅 corner, angle

sumi 炭 charcoal

sumi 墨 India [Chinese] ink

sumigokochi no yoi 住み心地のよい comfortable

sumimasen　すみません　I am sorry; Excuse me.

sumire　すみれ　violet

sumiyaka na[ni]　速やかな[に]　fast, rapid[ly]

sumō　相撲　wrestling

sumpō　寸法　measure, size

sumu　住む　live, dwell

sumu　済む　(come to an) end, be over

sumu　澄む　clear, become clear

suna　砂　sand

suna-dokei　砂時計　hourglass, sandglass

sunahama　砂浜　sandy beach, sands

sunao na[ni]　素直な[に]　gentle[-tly], obedient[ly]

sunawachi　すなわち　that is, namely

sunda　澄んだ　clear

sunzen　寸前　immediately, before

suppai　酸っぱい　sour, acid

suppanuku　素っ破抜く　expose, disclose

suppokasu　すっぽかす　leave(it) work undone, neglect(one's duties), break one's word, give(a person) the slip

-sura　…すら　even

surari to shita　すらりとした　slender, slim

sura-sura to　すらすらと　smoothly, easily, fluently

surechigau　擦れ違う　pass each other

sureru　擦れる　rub, be rubbed

suri　すり　pickpocket

surigarasu　すりガラス　frosted glass

surikireru　擦り切れる　wear out　*surikireta*　擦り切れた　threadbare, worn-out

surikizu　擦り傷　graze, scratch

suritsubusu　すりつぶす　grind, mash

suru　する　do, try, act

suru　掏る　steal, pick pockets

surudoi　鋭い　sharp, keen

susamajii　すさまじい　terrific, terrible

suso　すそ　skirt, bottom, base

susu　すす　soot

susumeru 薦[勧]める recommend, advise

susumeru 進める advance, put forward

susumu 進む advance, go forward, gain, be fast

susuri-naki すすり泣き sobbing *susuri-naku* すすり泣く sob, weep silently

suteki na[ni] 素敵な[に] splendid[ly], wonderful[ly]

suteru 捨てる throw away, abandon

su'u 吸う breathe in, inhale, smoke, absorb

suwaru 座る sit down, take a seat

suya-suya すやすや quietly, gently

suzu 鈴 bell

suzume すずめ sparrow

suzuri すずり ink stone

suzushii 涼しい cool, refreshing *suzushii kao o suru* ～顔をする look serene [unconcerned]

suzushisa 涼しさ cool(ness)

T

ta 田 rice field

taba 束 bundle, bunch

tabako タバコ tobacco *tabako o su'u* ～を吸う smoke (tobacco) *tabako-ya* ～屋 cigar store

taberu 食べる eat, take, have

tabi 旅 traveling, travels, tour, trip

-tabi ni …度に every time, whenever

tabisaki de 旅先で while traveling, on a journey

tabi-tabi 度々 often, many times, frequently

tabō na 多忙な busy

tabun 多分 probably, perhaps, maybe

tachiagaru 立ち上がる stand [get] up, rise

tachiau 立ち会う be present at, attend, be witness to

tachiba 立場 position, situation

tachidomaru 立ち止まる stop, halt, pause

tachigiki suru 立聞きする overhear, eavesdrop

tachiiru 立ち入る enter, come [go] into

tachimachi たちまち in a moment, at once, suddenly

tachimukau 立ち向かう fight (against), face, proceed to

tachinaoru 立ち直る recover (oneself), improve, pick up

tachiōjō suru 立往生する come to a standstill, be stalled

tachiyoru 立ち寄る drop in, stop at, call at

tada ただ only, merely, simply *tada no* 〜の common, ordinary

tada ただ free, no charge

tadachi ni 直ちに at once, immediately

tadaima ただ今 now, at present, soon; I am here [home]; Hello!

tadashi 但し provided *tadashi-gaki* 〜書 provisional clause, proviso

tadashii 正しい right, proper, correct *tadashiku* 正しく rightly, properly, correctly

tadasu 正す correct, rectify, reform

tadayou 漂う drift about, float

tadoru たどる follow, trace

tado-tado shii たどたどしい faltering, unsteady

taegatai 耐え難い unbearable, intolerable

taema nai [naku] 絶え間ない [なく] continual [ly], incessant [ly]

taeru たえる endure, bear, stand

taezu 絶えず constantly, always

tagai no [ni] 互いの [に] mutual [ly], each other, one another

tagaku no 多額の large, large sum of

tagayasu 耕す till, plough, cultivate

tahata 田畑 farm, fields

tai 鯛 sea bream, red snapper

tai 対 versus, against, between

tai 隊 party, company

tai 体 body *tai o kawasu* ～をかわす dodge, parry

-tai …たい wish [want] to do, should [would] like to do

taibō no 待望の long-awaited

taibyō 大病 serious illness *taibyō-nin* ～人 serious case

taichō 隊長 commander, leader

taida 怠惰 idleness, laziness *taida na* ～な idle, lazy

taidan 対談 talk, conversation

taido 態度 attitude, manner

taifū 台風 typhoon, hurricane

taigū 待遇 treatment, salary, pay *taigū suru* ～する treat, pay

taihan 大半 greater part, majority

Taiheiyō 太平洋 the Pacific (Ocean)

taihen na 大変な serious, grave, terrible

taihō 大砲 gun, cannon

taiho suru 逮捕する arrest

taii 大尉 captain

taiiku 体育 physical training [culture]

taiin suru 退院する leave hospital

taijū 体重 weight

taikai 大会 mass meeting, convention

taikaku 体格 build, physique

taiken 体験 experience *taiken suru* ～する go through, experience

taiki 大気 atmosphere, air

taiki 大器 great talent, genius

taiko 太鼓 drum

taikutsu na 退屈な tiresome, wearisome *taikutsu suru* ～する be bored, be tired of *taikutsu-shinogi ni* ～しのぎに by the way of diversion, for a change

taikyaku 退却 retreat, withdrawal *taikyaku suru* ～する retreat, fall back

taikyūryoku 耐久力 durability

taiman 怠慢 negligence, neglect *taiman na* ～

な negligent

taimen 体面 honor, reputation, appearance

taimō 大望 great ambition

taion 体温 temperature of the body *taion o hakaru* ～を計る take one's temperature *taion-kei* ～計 (clinical) thermometer

taira na [ni] 平らな[に] level, even[ly] *taira ni suru* 平らにする flatten, level

tairiku 大陸 continent *tairiku-teki na* ～的な continental

tairitsu suru 対立する be opposed to each other

tairyō 大量 large quantity

taisaku 対策 policy

taisei 体制 system, organization

Taiseiyō 大西洋 the Atlantic (Ocean)

taiseki 体積 (cubic) volume, capacity

taisetsu na 大切な important, valuable *taisetsu ni suru* 大切にする take good care of, make much of, value

taishaku 貸借 loan, debt and credit *taishaku-kankei* ～関係 (loan) accounts, financial relations *taishaku-taishōhyō* ～対照表 balance sheet

taishi 大使 ambassador *taishi-kan* ～館 embassy

taishite 対して against, to, towards

taishō 大将 general, admiral, leader

taishō 対照 contrast, comparison *taishō suru* ～する contrast, compare

taishō 対象 object

taishoku 退職 retirement *taishoku suru* ～する retire from office

taishū 大衆 the masses

taisō 体操 gymnastics, exercise

taisuru 対する face, confront, oppose

taitei no 大抵の most, general, usual

taitō 対等 equality *taitō no* ～の equal *taitō de* ～で on equal terms

taiwa 対話 conversation, dialogue

taiya タイヤ tire

taiyaku 大役 important task [duty], important part [role]

taiyō 太陽 sun *taiyō no* ～の solar

taizai 滞在 stay, visit *taizai suru* ～する stay at

taji-taji to naru たじたじとなる stagger, flinch

taka たか hawk

taka-daka 高々 at the highest, at most *taka-daka to* ～と high

takai 高い high, tall, expensive *takaku* 高く high, aloft

takamaru 高まる rise, go up, be raised

takameru 高める raise, lift

takara 宝 treasure

takaru たかる swarm, gather, sponge on (a person), blackmail (a person)

takasa 高さ height

take 丈 height, stature, length

take 竹 bamboo

taki 滝 waterfall, falls

takkyū 卓球 ping-pong

tako 蛸 octopus

tako 凧 kite

takoku 他国 foreign country

taku 炊く burn, kindle

takuetsu suru 卓越する excel *takuetsu shita* 卓越した superior, distinguished

takujisho 託児所 day nursery, baby farm

takumashii たくましい stout, strong

takumi na [ni] 巧みな [に] skillful [ly]

takurami たくらみ plot, trick, design

takuramu たくらむ conspire, design, plan

takusan 沢山 enough, sufficient *takusan no* ～の a lot of, many, much

takuwae 蓄え savings, store, stock

takuwaeru 蓄える save, lay by, store

tama 玉 [球] ball, globe

tamago 卵 egg

tamanegi 玉ねぎ onion

tama no [ni] たまの[に] occasional[ly], rare[ly]

tamaranai たまらない intolerable, unbearable

tamaru たまる accumulate, collect

tamashii 魂 soul, spirit

tama-tama たまたま accidentally, casually

tambo たんぼ (rice) field

tame ni ために in order to (do), so as to (do), because of, owing to

tamerai ためらい hesitation

tamerau ためらう hesitate *tamerau koto naku* ～ことなく without hesitation

tameru ためる save, lay up

tameshi 試し trial, attempt

tamesu 試す try, attempt

tamoto たもと sleeve

tamotsu 保つ keep(up), maintain, preserve

tampen 短編 short piece [story]

tampopo たんぽぽ dandelion

tana 棚 shelf

tanabata 七夕 the Festival of the Weaver Star

tanchō na 単調な monotonous

tandoku no [de] 単独の [で] independent [ly], alone

tane 種 seed, stone (of fruit)

tango 単語 word, vocabulary

tango no sekku 端午の節句 Boy's Festival

tani 谷 valley, ravine

tan'i 単位 unit

tanin 他人 stranger, another

tanjikan ni 短時間に in a short time

tanjō 誕生 birth *tanjō suru* ～する be born *tanjō-bi* ～日 birthday

tanjun 単純 simplicity *tanjun na* ～な simple, plain *tanjun-ka suru* ～化する simplify

tanken 探検 exploration *tanken suru* ～する explore

tanki 短気 short [quick] temper, impatience *tanki na* ～な short-tempered

tanki 短期 short term

tankō 炭坑 coal mine

tankyū 探究 search, investigation **tankyū suru**
～する search for, seek for

tan naru 単なる simple, mere **tan ni** 単に only

tan'nen na [ni] 丹念な [に] careful [ly], consci-
entious [ly]

tan'nin suru 担任する take [be in] charge of,
teach

tan'nō na たん能な skillful, good at

tanomi 頼み request, reliance, trust

tanomoshii 頼もしい reliable, trustworthy

tanomu 頼む ask, entreat

tanoshii 楽しい pleasant, cheerful **tanoshiku**
楽しく pleasantly, cheerfully

tanoshimi 楽しみ pleasure, delight, joy

tanoshimu 楽しむ enjoy, amuse

tanren suru 鍛錬する temper, train, discipline

tansho 短所 weak point, fault, defect

tanshuku suru 短縮する shorten, reduce

tansū 単数 singular (number)

tantei 探偵 detective **tantei-shōsetsu** ～小説
detective story

tanuki たぬき badger, racoon dog

taoreru 倒れる fall, break down

taoru タオル towel

tappuri たっぷり fully, plenty of, enough

tarai たらい (wash) tub, basin

tarasu 垂[滴]らす hang (down), suspend, drop,
drip

-tarazu …足らず less than…, nearly, almost

tareru 垂[滴]れる hang down, droop, drip

tarinai 足りない not enough, insufficient

tariru 足りる enough, sufficient

taru 樽 cask, barrel

tarumu たるむ slacken, sag, be loose

taryō 多量 large quantity

tasatsu 他殺 murder

tashikameru 確かめる ascertain, make sure,
confirm

tashika na [ni] 確かな [に] certain[ly], sure[ly]

tashinami たしなみ taste, prudence *tashinami no yoi* ～のよい prudent, well-mannered

tashinamu たしなむ like, be fond of

tashō 多少 more or less, some, in some degree, a little

tasogare たそがれ dusk, twilight *tasogare-doki ni* ～時に at dusk, in the twilight

tassei suru 達成する accomplish, achieve

tassha na 達者な healthy, expert, skillful

tassuru 達する reach, arrive, attain

tasu 足す add (to)

tasū 多数 a large [great] number, the majority

tasukaru 助かる be saved, be rescued

tasuke 助け help, aid, assistance *tasukeau* ～合う help each other

tasukeru 助ける help, assist

tatakai 戦い war, battle, fight

tatakau 戦う fight (with), make war, struggle

tataku たたく tap, strike, knock

tatamu 畳む fold (up)

tate 縦 length, height *tate no* [ni] ～の [に] vertical [ly]

tategami たてがみ mane

tategu 建具 fittings, fixtures

tatemono 建物 building, structure

tateru 建てる build, construct, establish

tatetsuku たて突く oppose, set oneself against

tatetsuzuke ni 立て続けに in succession

tateyakusha 立て役者 leading actor [actress]

tateyoko 縦横 length and breadth, warp and woof *tateyoko jūmonji ni* ～十文字に crosswise

tatoe たとえ proverb, saying

tatoe...demo たとえ...でも even if, even though, if, (al)though

tatoeba 例えば for example, for instance

tatoeru たとえる compare (to)

tatsu 立つ rise, stand up

tatsu 建つ be built [established]

tatsu 発つ start, leave

tatsu 断つ cut (off), break (off)

tatsu 経つ pass (by), go by

tatsumaki 竜巻 tornado, whirlwind

tatta たった only, merely, just, no more than *tatta hitori de* ～一人で all alone, by oneself *tatta ima* ～今 just now, at once

tawainai たわいない silly, absurd, trifling

tawamure 戯れ play, sport, flirtation

tawamureru 戯れる play, joke, flirt

tayasu 絶やす exterminate, wipe out

tayasui たやすい easy, simple *tayasuku* たやすく easily

tayori 便り news, tidings, word, letter

tayori 頼り reliance *tayori ni naru* ～になる reliable, dependable

tayoru 頼る rely on, depend on

tazuna 手綱 bridle, reins

tazuneru 訪ねる call at, call on, visit

tazuneru 尋ねる ask, inquire

tazusaeru 携える have, carry, take, bring

te 手 hand *te ni ireru* ～に入れる get, obtain *te ni toru yōni* ～にとるように quite clearly *teatari-shidai (ni)* 手当たり次第(に) at random

teami no 手編みの hand-knit

tearai 手洗 hand washing *o-tearai* お～ washroom, lavatory

teate 手当 allowance, aid, treatment

tebanasu 手放す part with, dispose of

tebiroi 手広い extensive *tebiroku* 手広く extensively

tebukuro 手袋 glove

tebura de 手ぶらで empty-handed

tegakari 手掛り clue

tegami 手紙 letter

tegara 手柄 exploit, merit

tegata 手形 bill, promissory note

tegatai 手堅い firm, steady　*tegataku* 手堅く firmly, steadily

tegiwa yoi 手際よい skillful, clever　*tegiwa yoku* 手際よく skillfully, cleverly

tegoro na 手ごろな handy, moderate

tegowai 手ごわい tough, formidable

tehai 手配 arrangement(s)　*tehai suru* 〜する arrange

tehazu 手はず plan, program

tehon 手本 copy, copybook

teian 提案 proposal, suggestion　*teian suru* 〜する propose

teibō 堤防 embankment, dike

teichō na[ni] 丁重な[に] polite[ly]

teiden 停電 stoppage of electric current

teido 程度 degree, grade

teien 庭園 garden

teigi 定義 definition

teihyō aru 定評ある of established reputation, recognized

teiin 定員 the full number

teiji suru 提示する present, bring up

teika 定価 fixed price

teika suru 低下する fall, drop, go down

teikei suru 提携する act in concert (with), join hands

teikiatsu 低気圧 low (atmospheric) pressure

teiki no[ni] 定期の[に] regular[ly], periodical[ly]　*teiki kankōbutsu* 定期刊行物 periodical (publication)　*teiki-ken* 定期券 season ticket, commuter pass

teikō 抵抗 resistance, opposition　*teikō suru* 〜する oppose

teikoku 帝国 empire

teikoku ni 定刻に at the appointed time, on time, punctually

teikyō 提供 offer　*teikyō suru* 〜する offer, make an offer

teikyū-bi 定休日 regular [fixed] holiday

teikyū na 低級な low-grade

teinei na [ni] 丁寧な [に] polite [ly], civil [ly]

tei-no-yoi 体のよい disguised, plausible

teion 低温 low temperature

teire 手入れ care, repairing ***teire suru*** ～する repair, care for

teiryūjo 停留所 stop, depot

teisai 体裁 form, style, appearance ***teisai no yoi*** [***warui***] ～のよい [悪い] [un] seemly, [un] becoming

teisei 訂正 correction ***teisei suru*** ～する correct

teishi suru 停止する stop, suspend

teishu 亭主 master, host, husband

teishutsu suru 提出する present, bring forward

tejika no [ni] 手近の [に] close by, near

teki 敵 enemy, foe

tekido no [ni] 適度の [に] moderate [ly]

tekipaki てきぱき promptly, quickly

tekisetsu na 適切な suitable, fit

tekishite iru 適している be suited to [for]

tekiyō suru 適用する apply to

tekkaku na [ni] 的確な [に] accurate [ly], precise [ly], exact [ly]

tekkyō 鉄橋 iron bridge

teko てこ lever

tema 手間 time, labor

tēma テーマ theme, subject matter

temane 手まね gesture

temawari-hin 手回り品 personal effects

temawashi ga yoi 手回しがよい be fully prepared

tembai suru 転売する resell

tembō 展望 view ***tembō suru*** ～する have a view of ***tembō-sha*** ～車 observation car

temmondai 天文台 astronomical observatory

temmon-gaku 天文学 astronomy

temoto ni 手元に on [at] hand, have (something) by [near] one

tempi 天火 oven

tempuku suru 転覆する overthrow, capsize
tempu suru 添付する attach, annex
temukai suru 手向かいする resist, oppose
ten 天 sky, heaven
ten 点 spot, point, mark, run, score
　ten ga yoi[*warui*] 〜がよい[悪い] have good [bad] marks
　ten o tsukeru 〜をつける mark, give marks
　yoi[*warui*] *ten o toru* よい[悪い]〜をとる get good [bad] marks
　ten o kasegu 〜を稼ぐ work hard for better marks
　ko no ten de[*ni oite*] この〜で[において] in this regard [respect]
　ten-ten to 点々と here and there, sporadically, scattered
tenazukeru 手懐ける tame, domesticate
tenchi 天地 heaven and earth
tengoku 天国 heaven, paradise
tengu てんぐ long-nosed goblin
tenimotsu 手荷物 baggage, luggage
ten'in 店員 shop clerk
tenji 展示 exhibition, display　*tenji suru* 〜する exhibit　*tenji-kai* 〜会 show, exhibition
tenjō 天井 ceiling
tenkai suru 転回する revolve, rotate
tenkan suru 転換する convert, change
tenka suru 点火する ignite, light
tenkei 典型 type, model　*tenkei-teki na* 〜的な typical, model
tenken 点検 inspection　*tenken suru* 〜する inspect
tenki 天気 weather
tenki-yohō 天気予報 weather forecast
tenkyo suru 転居する remove, move
ten'nen 天然 native　*ten'nen no*[*ni*] 〜の[に] natural[ly]　*ten'nen kinembutsu* 〜記念物 natural monument
ten'nō 天皇 emperor　*Ten'nō Heika* 〜陛下

His Majesty the Emperor

tenraku suru 転落する fall, roll down

tenran-kai 展覧会 exhibition, show

tensai 天才 genius

tensai 天災 (natural) calamity

tensen 点線 dotted line, perforated line

tenshi 天使 angel

tensū 点数 marks, grade

tenugui 手ぬぐい (hand) towel

tenurui 手ぬるい slow, sluggish

teochi 手落ち omission, slip

teori no 手織の hand-woven

teppen てっぺん top, summit

teppō 鉄砲 gun, rifle

tera 寺 temple

terasu 照らす shine, light, illuminate

terebi テレビ television *terebi-hōsō* ～放送 television broadcast, telecast

tereru 照れる be shy, be abashed

teru 照る shine, be fine

teryōri 手料理 home-made dish

tesaguri suru 手探りする feel [grope, fumble] for

tesei no 手製の hand-made, home-made

tesū 手数 trouble, pains, care *tesū no kakaru* ～のかかる troublesome *tesū-ryō* ～料 fee, charge, commission

tetsu 鉄 iron, steel

tetsudai 手伝い help, assistance, assistant, helper

tetsudau 手伝う help, assist, aid

tetsudō 鉄道 railway, railroad

tetsugaku 哲学 philosophy *tetsugaku-teki na* [*ni*] ～的な[に] philosophical[ly] *tetsuga-ku-sha* ～者 philosopher

tetsuya de 徹夜で all night *tetsuya suru* 徹夜する sit up all night

tetsuzuki 手続き procedure, process, proceedings *tetsuzuki o toru* ～をとる go through formalities, take steps

tettei suru 徹底する be thorough (going) [consistent] ***tettei-teki na*** [***ni***] 徹底的な [に] thorough [ly]

tettori-bayai [**bayaku**]　手っ取り早い [早く] quick [ly], prompt [ly]

tezawari　手触り feel, touch

tezukami de　手づかみで with one's fingers

to　戸 door

tō　十, 10 ten　***tō-ka***　～日 ten days

tō　塔 tower, pagoda

tō　党 (political) party

tōan　答案 paper, examination paper

tobaku　とばく gambling

tōban　当番 duty, watch

tobasu　飛ばす (let) fly

tobiagaru　飛び上がる fly up, jump

tobikomi　飛込み diving, dive

tobioriru　飛び降りる jump down, jump off

tobira　とびら door

tobisaru　飛び去る fly away

tobitsuku　飛び付く jump at, fly at

tobokeru　とぼける pretend not to know

toboshii　乏しい scarce, scanty, short

toboshiku naru　乏しくなる run short, get scarce

tōbō suru　逃亡する flee, run away

tobu　飛ぶ fly, spring

tōbun　当分 for the present, for some time

tōbun suru　等分する divide equally

tōchaku　到着 arrival　***tōchaku suru***　～する arrive at, reach, get to

tochi　土地 land, ground, soil

tōchi　統治 rule, government　***tōchi suru***　～する rule, reign over

tōchi　当地 this place, here

tochū de　途中で on the way

tōdai　灯台 lighthouse

todana　戸棚 cupboard, closet

todokeru　届ける report, notify, forward, send

todoku　届く reach, get to

todomaru　とどまる stop, stay, put up

todoroku とどろく roar, peal

togameru とがめる find fault, flame, challenge

tōgarashi 唐辛子 red [cayenne] pepper

togarasu とがらす sharpen, make sharp

togatta とがった pointed, sharp

toge とげ thorn, prickle

tōge 峠 (mountain) pass, the height *tōge o ko-su* ～を越す pass the crisis, get out of danger

togeru 遂げる accomplish, attain, achieve, carry out

togireru 途切れる break, be interrupted

togu 研ぐ sharpen, grind

tōhō 東方 east *tōhō no* ～の eastern

toho de 徒歩で on foot

tōhoku 東北 northeast

tohō ni kureru 途方に暮れる be at a loss, be at one's wits' end, be puzzled, be quite embarrassed

tōhyō 投票 vote *tōhyō suru* ～する vote, ballot (for)

toi 樋 drain pipe, rain gutter

tōi 遠い far, distant, remote

toiawase 問い合せ inquiry, enquiry *toiawaseru(= toiawasu)* 問い合せる [問い合す] inquire, refer

tōitsu 統一 unify, unification

tōji 当時 (in) those days, (at) that time

tojikomeru 閉じ込める confine, keep indoors, shut in

tojiru 閉じる shut, close

tōjō suru 登場する enter, appear *tōjō-jimbutsu* ～人物 the characters

tokai 都会 city, town

tokei 時計 watch, wrist watch, clock

tōkei 統計 statistics *tōkei(-jō) no* ～(上)の statistical

tokeru 溶ける melt, dissolve

tokeru 解ける get loose, come untied

toki 時 time, hour, the times

tōki 陶器 earthenware, china, pottery

tokidoki 時々 sometimes, at times, from time to time

-(no)toki ni …(の)時に when, while, as

tokka 特価 special price *tokka-hin* ～品 bargain

tokken 特権 privilege

tokkumiai 取っ組み合い grapple

tokkyo 特許 patent

tokkyū 特急 limited express

toko 床 bed *toko ni tsuku* ～につく go to bed

tokonatsu 常夏 everlasting summer

tokoro 所 place, spot, district *tokoro-dokoro* 所々 here and there *tokoro-kamawazu* ～構わず everywhere

tokoro de ところで by the way, now, well

toko-ya 床屋 barber shop, barber, hairdresser

toku 解く untie, solve, answer

toku 説く explain, state

toku 徳 virtue, morality

toku 得 profit, benefit *toku na* ～な profitable *toku o suru* ～をする benefit, profit, gain

tōku 遠く far away, in the distance

tokubai 特売 special [bargain] sale

tokubetsu no 特別の special, particular *tokubetsu ni* 特別に particularly, specially

tokuchō 特徴 mark, characteristic

tokuhain 特派員 (special) correspondent

tokui 得意 pride, triumph, one's strong point, customer, client *tokui-gao* ～顔 triumphant look *tokui ni natte* ～になって triumphantly

toku ni 特に specially

tokushu no 特殊の special, particular

tōkyū 等級 class, grade

tomaru 止まる stop

tomaru 泊まる stop in, put up at

tōmawari 遠回り detour, roundabout way *tōmawari suru* ～する make a detour, take a long way about

tōmei na 透明な transparent, limpid, clear

tōmen no 当面の present, urgent **tōmen no mondai** 〜問題 the matter in hand, urgent question

tomeru 止める stop

tomi 富 riches, wealth, fortune

tomodachi 友達 friend, companion

tomokaku ともかく at any rate, in any case

tomonau 伴う be followed by, be attended with, accompany

tomo ni 共に both, together with

tōmorokoshi とうもろこし (Indian) corn, maize

tomoru ともる burn

tomoshibi ともしび light

tomurau 弔う mourn

tonaeru 唱える recite, chant

tōnan 東南 southeast

tōnan 盗難 robbery, theft

tonari no 隣の next, next-door

tonikaku とにかく at any rate, in any case

ton'neru トンネル tunnel

tonosama 殿様 lord, prince

ton'ya 問屋 wholesale store

toppa suru 突破する break through, overcome

toppatsu suru 突発する break out, happen

tora とら tiger

toraeru 捕える catch, seize, arrest

torampu トランプ (playing) cards

torawareru 捕われる be caught, be captured

tori 鳥 bird

toriaezu 取りあえず in haste, just, for the time being

toriageru 取り上げる take [pick] up, adopt

toriatsukai 取り扱い treatment, handling

toriatsukau 取り扱う treat, handle, deal with

toriawase 取り合せ assortment, combination **toriawaseru** 〜る assort, combine

toridasu 取り出す take out, pull out

toride とりで fort(ress)

torie 取り柄 merit, value, worth

torihakarai 取計い arrangement(s), discretion

torihazusu 取り外す remove, detach

torihiki 取引 trade, business *torihiki suru* ~ する transact business, deal with

toriire 取入れ harvest

torikaeru 取り替える change for

torikaesu 取り返す get back, recover *torikaeshi no tsukanai* 取返しのつかない irrevocable, irretrievable

tori-kago 鳥かご (bird) cage

torikakaru 取り掛る set to, begin, set about

tōrikakaru 通り掛る happen to pass

torikeshi 取消 cancellation, withdrawal

torikesu 取消す cancel, withdraw, recall

torikime 取り決め arrangements *torikimeru* ~る arrange, settle

toriko とりこ captive, prisoner

tōrikosu 通り越す go [walk] beyond, pass

torikumi 取組 match, bout

torimaku 取り巻く surround, encircle

torimidasu 取り乱す be agitated [confused]

torimodosu 取り戻す take [get] back

tōri ni 通りに as, like

torishimari 取締り regulation, control *torishimaru* 取り締る regulate, control

toritsugi 取次 agency, agent, usher *toritsugi-ten* ~店 agency

toritsukeru 取り付ける fit up, install

toriyoseru 取り寄せる get, obtain

tōrō 灯ろう lantern

tōroku 登録 registration *tōroku suru* ~する register

tōron 討論 discussion *tōron suru* ~する debate, discuss

toru 取る take

toru 採る pick, catch

tōru 通る pass (by), pass through, go along

toryō 塗料 paint, coating

tōsen suru 当選する be elected, win the prize

toshi 都市 cities, towns

toshi 年 year, age *toshi o toru* ～をとる grow old

tōshi 投資 investment *tōshi suru* ～する invest

toshigoro 年ごろ age, marriageable age

toshishita no 年下の younger, junior

-toshite ...として as, by way of

toshitsuki 年月 years

toshiue no 年上の older, senior

toshiyori 年寄 old man, the old

tōsho 投書 contribution, anonymous letter

toshokan 図書館 library

tōsō 闘争 fight, struggle *tōsō suru* ～する fight, struggle

tōsō suru 逃走する escape, flee

tossa ni とっさに in an instant, at once

tosshin suru 突進する rush, dash

tōsu 通す pass through, pierce, show

totan トタン zinc *totan-ita* ～板 galvanized iron

totan ni 途端に just as, at the moment

tōtatsu suru 到達する arrive, reach, get to

tōtei 到底 at all, possibly

totemo とても very, so, awfully

tōtō 到頭 at last, after all

tōtobu 尊ぶ respect, hold dear, make much of

tōtoi 貴い valuable, precious, holy

totonoeru 整える arrange, adjust

totsugu 嫁ぐ be [get] married

totsuzen 突然 suddenly, all of a sudden, all at once

totte 取手 handle, knob

totte-oku 取って置く keep, reserve, put aside, save

tou 問う ask, question, inquire

tōwaku suru 当惑する be perplexed, be puzzled

Tōyō 東洋 the East, the Orient *Tōyō no* ～の

Eastern, Oriental

tōyu 灯油 lamp oil, kerosene

tōzai 東西 east and west

tōzakaru 遠ざかる keep away, keep aloof, become more distant, go away (from), withdraw from, go far from

tozan 登山 mountain-climbing *tozan-ka* ～家 alpinist

tōzen 当然 naturally, of course *tōzen no* ～の right, proper, natural

tsuba 唾 spittle *tsuba o haku* ～を吐く spit

tsuba 鍔 sword-guard, brim

tsubaki つばき camellia

tsubame つばめ swallow

tsubasa 翼 wings

tsubo つぼ jar

tsubomeru つぼめる close, shut, get narrower, pucker up, shrug

tsubomi つぼみ bud

tsubu 粒 grain, drop

tsubusu つぶす crust, smash, mash, ruin, pass, waste

tsubuyaku つぶやく mutter, murmur, grumble

tsuchi 土 earth, soil, ground

tsūchi 通知 notice, information *tsūchi suru* ～する inform

tsudo 都度 every [each] time, whenever

tsudoi 集い meeting

tsue 杖 (walking) stick, cane

tsugai つがい pair, couple

tsūgaku suru 通学する attend [go to] school

tsugeru 告げる tell, inform

tsugi 次 the next *tsugi no[ni]* ～の[に] next, following, coming

tsugime 継目 joint, juncture *tsugime-nashi no* ～無しの jointless, seamless

tsugi-tsugi ni 次々に one after another

tsugō 都合 convenience, circumstances, condition *tsugō no yoi* ～のよい convenient

tsugu 次ぐ come [rank] next (to)

tsugu 継ぐ succeed (to), inherit

tsugu 接ぐ join, put together

tsugu 注ぐ pour (in), fill (with)

tsugumu つぐむ keep silent *kuchi o tsugumu* 口を～ shut [close] one's mouth

tsugunai 償い compensation *tsugunau* 償う compensate for

tsui つい just, only, quite, carelessly, by mistake *tsui imashigata* ～今し方 just now

tsuide ついで apropos, occasion *tsuide ni* ～に by the way

tsuihō 追放 exile, purge *tsuihō suru* ～する expel, banish

tsuika 追加 addition, supplement

tsuikyū 追求 pursuit *tsuikyū suru* ～する pursue

tsui ni ついに at last

tsuiraku 墜落 fall, drop *tsuiraku suru* ～する fall, crash

tsuiseki 追跡 pursuit, chase

(ni) tsuite (に)ついて about, of, on, as to

tsuitotsu 追突 rear-end collision *tsuitotsu suru* ～する bump, collide (with a car) from behind

tsūjiru 通じる run [lead] to, be understood, be familiar with

tsūjō 通常 normally, usually

tsukaeru つかえる be obstructed, be choked

tsukaeru 仕える serve, be in service

tsukai 使い errand, messenger *tsukai ni iku* ～に行く go on an errand

tsukai-hatasu 使い果たす use up, exhaust, squander

tsukaikata 使い方 how to use

tsūkai na 痛快な delightful, thrilling

tsukamaeru 捕まえる seize, catch, take hold of

tsuka-no-ma つかの間 brief space of time, moment *tsuka-no-ma no* ～の brief, momentary

tsūkan suru 痛感する feel keenly

tsūkan suru 通関する pass customs **tsūkan-tetsuzuki** 〜手続き customs clearance

tsukare 疲れ fatigue, exhaustion **tsukareru** 〜る get tired from, get weary from

tsukaru つかる soaked, steeped, flooded

tsūka suru 通過する pass (through), go through

tsukau 使う use, make use of, spend (money) on

tsuke 付け bill **tsuke de kau** 〜で買う buy on credit

tsukekaeru 付け替える renew, replace, change

tsukemono 漬物 pickles

tsukeru つける set [put] on, fix [attach] to, apply, light, follow, wear

tsuki 月 moon, month

tsukiataru 突き当る run against, collide, come to the end of

tsukiau 付き合う associate with, keep company with

tsukihanasu 突き放す thrust [push] aside, give up

tsukihi 月日 months and days, time, days

tsukikaesu 突き返す thrust [send] back, refuse to accept

tsukimatou 付きまとう follow (a person) about

tsukinami na 月並な conventional, common

tsūkin suru 通勤する attend office

tsukiotosu 突き落す push [shove] off

tsukiru 尽きる be exhausted [consumed, used up], end **tsukinai** 尽きない inexhaustible, endless

tsukisasu 突き刺す thrust, pierce

tsukisoi 付添い attendant, chaperon, bridesmaid

tsukitaosu 突き倒す knock down

tsukitobasu 突き飛ばす thrust away

tsukitomeru 突き止める ascertain, make sure of, locate, trace

tsukiyo 月夜 moonlight night

tsukizuki 月々 every month

tsukkomu 突っ込む thrust in, pierce

tsūkō 通行 passing, traffic　*tsūkō suru* 〜する pass (by), go along

tsuku 着く reach, arrive

tsuku 付く stick [adhere] to, be smeared

tsuku 突く thrust, pierce

tsukue 机 desk

tsukuriageru 作り上げる make, build, complete

tsukurikata 作り方 way of making, directions

tsukuroi 繕い repair, mending　*tsukurou* 繕う mend, repair

tsukuru 作る make, create, compose

tsukusu 尽くす do one's best

tsuku-zuku つくづく intently, intensely, over and over

tsuma 妻 wife

tsumami つまみ pinch, knob, (simple) relish

tsumami-dasu つまみ出す pick [drag] out, turn out

tsumamu つまむ pick, pinch

tsumaranai 詰らない trifling, worthless, useless

tsumari つまり after all, in the end, in short

tsumaru 詰まる be stopped [blocked] up, be fully packed, be hard up

tsumazuku つまずく stumble (over), lose one's footing, fail

tsumbo no つんぼの deaf, hard of hearing

tsume つめ (finger-, toe-) nail, claw

tsumeawase 詰合せ assortment　*tsumeawase no* 〜の assorted

tsumekaeru 詰め代える refill, repack

tsumekiri つめ切り nail scissors, nail clippers

tsumeru 詰める cram, stuff, fill

tsumetai 冷たい frigid, cold, chilly

tsumi 罪 crime, sin

tsumiageru 積み上げる heap [pile] up, accumulate

tsumidashi 積出し shipment, consignment　*tsumidasu* 積み出す ship, send　*tsumidashi-kō*

~港 port of shipment

tsumikasaneru 積み重ねる pile, heap

tsumiki 積木 building blocks [bricks]

tsumini 積荷 load, freight

tsumitateru 積み立てる save, lay aside

tsumoru 積もる accumulate, lie (on)

tsumu 積む pile, load, ship

tsumu 摘む pick, pluck, clip, trim, cut

tsumuji つむじ cowlick (hair), the whirl of hair *tsumuji-magari no* ～曲がりの perverse *tsumuji o mageru* ～を曲げる get cranky, become perverse

tsuna 綱 rope, line, cord

tsunagari つながり connection, relation

tsunagu つなぐ tie, fasten, chain

tsunawatari 綱渡り tight rope walking

tsune no 常の usual, customary, ordinary *tsune ni* 常に always, usually

tsuneru つねる pinch

tsuno 角 horn, antler

tsunoru 募る raise, collect

tsunto つんと primly *tsunto suru* ～する be prim, be sullen

tsuppaneru 突っぱねる reject, refuse

tsupparu 突っ張る stretch, hold out

tsurai つらい hard, bitter

tsuranaru 連なる stand [stretch] in a row, be present

tsurara つらら icicle

tsure 連れ company, companion

tsuredasu 連れ出す take [bring] out

tsurenai つれない cold, hard *tsurenaku* つれなく coldly

tsureru 連れる take, bring, be accompanied *tsurete* 連れて with, accompanied by

tsuri 釣 fishing

tsuri(sen) 釣(銭) change (money)

tsuriai 釣合い balance, proportion

tsuriau 釣り合う balance, be in harmony with

tsuribari 釣針 fishing hook

tsuriito 釣糸 fishing line

tsūro 通路 passage, way

tsuru 鶴 crane

tsuru 蔓 vine, runner

tsuru 弦 (bow)string, chord

tsuru 吊る angle, hang, suspend

tsurushi-age 吊るし上げ kangaroo court *tsurushi-ageru* 〜る impeach, persecute with question

tsuru-tsuru suru つるつるする be smooth [slippery]

tsūsan suru 通算する sum [add] up, total

tsūsetsu na [ni] 痛切な [に] keen [ly], acute [ly]

tsūshin 通信 correspondence, communication *tsūshin suru* 〜する correspond (with)

tsūshō 通商 commerce, trade

tsuta つた ivy

tsutaekiku 伝え聞く hear, learn, learn by hearsay

tsutaeru 伝える communicate, tell

tsutanai つたない poor, clumsy

tsutawaru 伝わる be handed down, come down, be transmitted, spread

tsute つて connection, influence

tsutome 勤 [務] め duty, service, business

tsutomeru 努める try hard, make an effort

tsutomeru 勤める be in the employ of

tsutsu 筒 pipe, tube

tsutsuji つつじ azalea

tsutsuku つつく pick, peck

tsutsumashii つつましい modest *tsutsumashiku* つつましく modestly

tsutsumi 堤 embankment

tsutsumi 包み parcel, package

tsutsumu 包む wrap up, pack up

tsutsushimi 慎み discretion, prudence *tsutsushimi-bukai* 〜深い discreet

tsutsushimu 慎む be careful, be cautious

tsūwa 通話 (telephone) call

tsuwamono つわ者 warrior

tsuya つや gloss, luster, polish *tsuya no aru* 〜のある glossy, polished

tsūyaku 通訳 interpretation, interpreter *tsūyaku suru* 〜する interpret

tsuyogari 強がり bluff(ing), show of courage *tsuyogari o iu* 〜を言う bluff

tsuyoi 強い strong, powerful

tsuyoki 強気 bull *tsuyoki no* 〜の strong

tsuyoku 強く strongly, hard

tsuyomeru 強める strengthen, make strong

tsuyosa 強さ strength, power

tsūyō suru 通用する pass, circulate

(o-)tsuyu （お）つゆ soup, gravy, juice

tsuyu 露 dew, dewdrop

tsuyu (= **baiu**) 梅雨 the rainy spell in early summer *baiu-ki* 〜期 the rainy season

tsuzukeru 続ける continue, keep up *tsuzukete* 続けて continuously, without break, in succession

tsuzuki 続き continuation, sequel

tsuzuku 続く continue, go on, follow

tsuzuri つづり spelling, orthography

tsuzuru つづる spell, bind

U

uba 乳母 nurse *uba-guruma* 〜車 baby carriage

ubau 奪う snatch, rob (someone) of

uchiakeru 打ち明ける confide, confess

uchigawa 内側 inside *uchigawa no* 〜の inside

uchikatsu 打ち勝つ conquer, overcome

uchikesu 打ち消す deny, contradict

uchiki na 内気な shy, bashful, reserved

uchikiru 打ち切る close, discontinue

uchikomu 打ち込む drive in, strike into

uchiwa うちわ (round) fan

uchiwa 内輪 family (circle) *uchiwa no* ～の private, informal *uchiwa de* ～で privately, in private

uchōten ni naru 有頂天になる be enraptured, go into ecstasies

uchū 宇宙 universe [cosmos] space *uchū no* ～ の universal

ude 腕 arm *ude-dokei* ～時計 wrist watch

ue 上 upper part, surface *ue no* ～の up, upper *ue de [ni]* ～で [に] on, above, over, up

ue 飢え hunger *ueru* ～る be hungry

ueki 植木 (garden) tree, potted plant *ueki-bachi* ～鉢 flowerpot *ueki-ya* ～屋 gardener

ueru 植える plant

ugai suru うがいする gargle

ugokasu 動かす move, remove

ugoki 動き movement

ugoku 動く move, stir

uguisu うぐいす (Japanese) nightingale

ukaberu 浮べる float, set afloat

ukabu 浮ぶ float

ukagau うかがう watch, see, look at, peep

ukagau 伺う call, visit, ask, inquire

ukai suru う回する detour, go round

ukanukao o suru 浮かぬ顔をする look gloomy

ukeau 請け合う undertake, guarantee

ukeireru 受け入れる accept, receive

ukemi 受身 passive *ukemi no* ～の defensive

ukemotsu 受け持つ take charge (of), be in charge

ukeru 受ける receive, accept

uketamawaru 承る hear, listen, understand

uketori 受取 receipt *uketori-nin* ～人 receiver

uketsugu 受け継ぐ inherit

uketsuke 受付 reception, usher, receptionist

uketsukeru 受け付ける receive, accept, take up *uketsukenai* 受け付けない refuse, reject

ukkari うっかり carelessly, absent-mindedly

uku 浮く float, be refloated

uma 馬 horse *uma ni noru* ～に乗る ride a horse

umai うまい delicious, good, nice, skillful

umaku うまく skillfully, well, cleverly

umare 生れ birth, origin *umareru* ～る be born *umaretsuki* ～つき by nature

ume 梅 plum (tree) *ume-boshi* ～干し pickled plum

umeru 埋める bury, inter

umi 海 sea, ocean

ummei 運命 destiny, fate, fortune

umu 有無 existence, presence *umu o iwasazu* ～を言わさず forcibly

umu うむ become septic, fester

umu 産む bear, be delivered of, lay (egg)

un 運 destiny, fortune *un no yoi[warui]* ～の よい[悪い] [un]fortunate, [un]lucky

unadareru うなだれる hang one's head

unagasu 促す urge, press, spur

unagi うなぎ eel

unaru うなる groan, roar, growl

unasareru うなされる have a nightmare

unazuku うなずく nod

unchin 運賃 freight, rates, fare

undō 運動 sports, exercise, motion, movement *undō suru* ～する take exercise, move *undō-kai* ～会 athletic meet

un'ei 運営 management, operation *un'ei suru* ～する manage, operate

unga 運河 canal

unsō 運送 transport(ation)

untenshu 運転手 driver

unten suru 運転する drive (a car), operate

unubore うぬぼれ (self-)conceit, vanity *unuboreru* ～る be conceited

unzari suru うんざりする be disgusted

uo 魚 fish *uo-na-me* ～の目 corn

ura 裏 back, reverse, opposite side

uragiru 裏切る betray, turn against *shinrai o uragiru* 信頼を〜 betray a person's confidence *kitai o uragiru* 期待を〜 disappoint one's expectation(s)

urameshii 恨めしい resentful, bitter

urami 恨み grudge, ill feeling, hostility

uraomote 裏表 both sides

uraraka na うららかな bright, beautiful, fine

urayamashii うらやましい enviable

urayamu うらやむ envy, be envious

urei 憂い grief, sorrow, anxiety

urekko 売れっ子 popular person

urenokoru 売れ残る remain, unsold

ureru 売れる sell, be sold

ureshii うれしい happy, delightful, glad

ureshisa うれしさ joy, delight

ureshisō na [ni] うれしそうな[に] delightful [ly], joyful [ly], happy [-ily]

ureyuki 売行き sale *ureyuki ga yoi[warui]* 〜がよい[悪い] [do not] sell well

uri うり melon *uri-futatsu* 〜二つ be as like as two peas (eggs)

urikireru 売り切れる be sold out, go out of stock

uroko うろこ scale

urotaeru うろたえる be confused, lose one's head

urotsuku うろつく loiter, wander

uru 得る get, have, gain, obtain

uru 売る sell, deal in

urumu 潤む be wet [moist], be dim

uruoi 潤い moisture, dampness

uruosu 潤す wet, moisten

urusai うるさい annoying, tiresome *urusaku* うるさく annoyingly, tiresomely

urushi 漆 lacquer, japan

uryō 雨量 rain(fall), precipitation

usa 憂さ gloom, melancholy *usa-barashi ni* 〜晴らしに for amusement

usagi うさぎ rabbit

useru うせる disappear, vanish, be lost

ushi 牛 cow, bull, ox

ushinau 失う lose, miss

ushiro 後ろ back *ushiro no* 〜の back *ushiro ni* 〜に behind

uso うそ lie, falsehood *uso no* 〜の false *uso o tsuku* 〜をつく tell a lie

usugurai 薄暗い dim, gloomy

usui 薄い thin, light

uta 歌 song *uta o utau* 〜を歌う sing (a song)

utagai 疑い doubt, question *utagai naku* 〜なく without doubt

utagau 疑う doubt, suspect

utagawashii 疑わしい doubtful, uncertain

utau 歌う sing, chant

uto-uto suru うとうとする doze, feel drowsy

utsu 打つ beat, strike, hit

utsukushii 美しい beautiful, fair, pretty

utsukushiku 美しく beautifully, charmingly, prettily

utsukushisa 美しさ beauty

utsumuku うつむく look down, bend one's head *utsumuke ni* うつむけに on one's face, prone

utsurigi na 移り気な fickle, capricious

utsurikawari 移り変り change, transition

utsuru 移る remove, move into

utsusu 移す (re)move, transfer

utsusu 映す reflect, mirror

utsusu 写す copy, imitate, photograph, take

utsuwa 器 vessel, utensil

uttae 訴え (law)suit, charge *uttaeru* 〜る go to the law, appeal

uttori suru うっとりする be entranced [enraptured]

uttōshii うっとうしい gloomy, dull

uwabe 上辺 exterior surface, outside *uwabe no* 〜の outward, apparent *uwabe wa* 〜は on the surface

uwagi 上着 coat

uwaki 浮気 inconstancy *uwaki na* ～な fickle *uwaki o suru* ～をする be false to (him), have a love affair *uwaki-mono* ～者 inconstant lover, coquette

uwasa うわさ rumor *uwasa o suru* ～をする talk of, gossip

uyamau 敬う respect, honor

uyauyashii 恭しい respectful, reverent *uyauyashiku* 恭しく respectfully, reverently

uyo-uyo うようよ in swarms *uyo-uyo shite iru* ～している swarm

uzuku うずく ache, smart, tingle

uzukumaru うずくまる crouch, squat down

uzumaki 渦巻 whirlpool, vortex, eddy, scroll *uzumaki-gata no* ～形の spiral *uzumaki-moyō* ～模様 scrollwork

uzumaku 渦巻く whirl, eddy, swirl

uzumeru うずめる bury, fill

uzu-uzu suru うずうずする be impatient [itching] (to do)

W

wa 輪 circle, ring

wabi わび apology *wabiru* ～る apologize, make an apology

wabishii わびしい miserable, unhappy

wadai 話題 subject, topic

wadakamari わだかまり cares, ill-feeling, reserve

waga 我が my, our

wagamama 我がまま selfishness, egoism *wagamama na* ～な selfish, wilful *wagamama o suru* ～をする be selfish

wagiri 輪切り (cut in) round slices

wairo わいろ bribery, bribe

waisetsu na わいせつな obscene, indecent

wakai 若い young, youthful, younger

wakai 和解 reconciliation, compromise *wakai suru* ～する compromise with, make peace with

wakare 別れ farewell, separation *wakareru* ～る separate from

wakari-nikui 分りにくい difficult [hard] to understand *wakari yasui* 分りやすい easy, plain

wakaru 分る understand, see

wakasa 若さ youth(fulness)

wakasu 沸かす boil, heat

wakawakashii 若々しい youthful, young

wake 訳 meaning, why, reason, cause

wakemae 分け前 share, portion

wakeru 分ける divide, distinguish, share

waki わき side *waki ni* ～に aside by, beside

wakitatsu 沸き立つ boil up, seethe

waku 枠 frame

waku 沸[湧]く gush out, spring, boil

wameku わめく yell, shout, scream

wampaku na 腕白な mischievous, unruly

wan 湾 bay, gulf

(o-)wan (お)わん bowl

wana わな trap *wana o kakeru* ～を掛ける set a trap *wana ni kakeru* ～に掛ける entrap

wani わに crocodile, alligator

wara わら straw

warai 笑い laugh, smile, laughter

warau 笑う laugh, smile, ridicule

wareme 割れ目 crevice, crack, fissure

wareru 割れる be broken, be smashed, be split

wareware 我々 we *wareware no* ～の our *wareware ni* [*o*] ～に[を] us

wariai 割合 proportion, rate *wariai ni* ～に rather, comparatively

wariate 割当 assignment, allotment *wariateru* ～てる assign, divide, allot

waribiki 割引 discount, reduction *waribiki suru*

～する discount, reduce

waru 割る divide, cut, break

warui 悪い bad, evil, wicked

warukuchi 悪口 abuse, sarcasm *warukuchi o iu* ～を言う speak ill

washi 和紙 Japanese (handmade) paper

washi わし eagle

washoku 和食 Japanese food

wasuremono 忘れ物 something forgotten *wasuremono o suru* ～をする leave a thing

wasureru 忘れる forget, leave behind *wasurerarenai* 忘れられない unforgettable

wata 綿 cotton batting [wool]

watakushi(= watashi) 私 I, myself *watakushi wa* ～は I *watakushi no* ～の my *watakushi ni[o]* ～に[を] me

watakushi-goto 私事 privacy, private

watari-dori 渡り鳥 bird of passage, migratory bird

wataru 渡る cross, go over, pass over

watashi 渡し ferry *watashi-bune* ～船 ferry-boat

watasu 渡す take over, ferry, carry across

waza to わざと purposely, on purpose

wazawai 災い disaster, calamity

waza-waza わざわざ especially, on purpose

wazuka わずか only, slight, (a) little *wazuka no* ～の few, little *wazuka ni* ～に only, merely, barely

wazurawashii 煩わしい troublesome, annoying

wazurawasu 煩わす trouble, worry, annoy

Y

ya 矢 arrow

yaban na 野蛮な savage, barbarous *yaban-jin* 野蛮人 barbarian

yabu やぶ bush

yabun 夜分 night, evening

yabureru 破れる be torn, be broken

yaburu 破る tear, break

yado 宿 hotel, inn

yagai no 野外の field, open-air, out-door *yagai de* 野外で in the open

yagate やがて soon after, before long, in due time

yagi やぎ goat

yahari やはり too, also, as well

yajiuma 野次馬 mob, rabble, spectators

yajū 野獣 (wild) beast

yakamashii やかましい noisy, clamorous

yakan 夜間 at [by] night

yake やけ desperation, despair
  yake o okosu 〜を起こす become desperate
  yake ni natte 〜になって desperately

yakedo やけど burn, scald

yakei 夜景 night view [scene]

yakeru 焼ける burn, be burned, be (well) done

yakimochi 焼きもち jealousy *yakimochi o yaku* 〜を焼く be jealous

yakkai 厄介 trouble, worry *yakkai na* 厄介な troublesome, annoying *yakkai ni naru* 厄介になる depend on, stay with

yaku 訳 translation, version

yaku 約 about, approximately

yaku 役 office, post, service
  yaku ni tatsu 〜に立つ serve, be useful
  yaku ni tatanai 〜に立たない be useless

yaku 焼く burn, roast

yakudatsu 役立つ be useful, be good

yakuhin 薬品 medicines, pharmaceuticals

yakumi 薬味 spices, condiments

yakunin 役人 official, public servant

yakusha 役者 actor, actress

yakushin suru 躍進する rush, make rapid progress

yakusho 役所 public office

yakusoku 約束 promise, engagement *yakusoku suru* ～する promise *yakusoku o mamoru* ～を守る keep one's promise

yakusu 訳す translate

yakuwari 役割 role, part

yakuyō no 薬用の medical

yakuza やくざ good-for-nothing, gambler, hoodlum

yakyū 野球 baseball

yama 山 mountain, hill

yamabiko 山びこ echo

yamaguni 山国 mountainous district

yamamori 山盛り heap *yamamori ni suru* ～にする heap up

yama-no-te 山の手 hilly section, residential area

yamaoku 山奥 far up (in) the mountains, in the heart of the mountains

yamashii やましい have a guilty conscience *yamashikunai* やましくない have an easy conscience

yameru やめる stop, cease, finish, give up

yami やみ darkness, the dark

yamu やむ stop, end, be over

yamu-o-enai やむを得ない unavoidable *yamu-o-ezu* やむを得ず unavoidably

yanagi 柳 willow

yane 屋根 roof *yane-gawara* ～がわら roof tile *yane-ura* ～裏 attic

yanushi 家主 landlord, owner of the house

yanwari やんわり softly, quietly

yaochō 八百長 put-up job, double-cross, set-up

yao-ya 八百屋 vegetable store, greengrocer

yari やり spear, lance

yarikaketa やりかけた unfinished, half-done

yarikirenai やり切れない cannot bear [stand], be intolerable

yarikomeru やり込める talk down, refute

yarō 野郎 fellow, rascal

yaru やる give, present, do

yasai 野菜 vegetables, greens

yasashii 優しい gentle, tender *yasashiku* 優しく gently, tenderly

yasashii 易しい easy, plain, simple *yasashiku* 易しく easily, plainly, simply

yasei no 野生の wild

yaseru やせる become thin, lose flesh

yaseta やせた thin, lean

yashiki 屋敷 mansion, residence

yashin 野心 ambition *yashin no aru* ～のある ambitious

yashinau 養う cultivate, bring up, support

yasui 安い cheap, low *yasuku* 安く at a low cost

yasumi 休み vacation, rest, holiday

yasumono 安物 cheap article

yasumu 休む take (a) rest

yasuraka na [ni] 安らかな [に] peaceful [ly], quiet [ly]

yasuri やすり file *kami-yasuri* 紙～ sandpaper

yatoi-nin 雇人 employee

yatoi-nushi 雇主 employer

yatou 雇う employ

yatsuatari suru 八当りする be cross with everybody

yatsugibaya ni 矢継ぎ早に rapidly

yatsureru やつれる become thin *yatsureta* やつれた worn-out, careworn, emaciated

yatto やっと at last, barely

yattsukeru やっつける beat, finish

yawarageru 和らげる soften, lessen

yawaraka na [ni] 柔 [軟] らかな [に] soft [ly], gentle [-tly], tender [ly]

yo (no naka) 世 (の中) the world, society

yo (ru) 夜 night, evening *Yo ga akeru.* ～が明ける. The day breaks; It dawns.

yō 用 business, engagement *yō ga aru* ～がある have something to do

yoake 夜明け daybreak, dawn

yobi 予備 preparation *yobi no* ～の preparatory

yōbi 曜日 day of the week

yobigoe 呼び声 call, cry

yobikakeru 呼び掛ける call to, appeal

yobirin 呼び鈴 bell, doorbell

yobō 予防 prevention, protection *yobō suru* ～する prevent *yobō-chūsha* ～注射 preventive injection

yōbō 容ぼう face, looks, features

yōbō 要望 demand

yobu 呼ぶ call

yobun 余分 excess, extra *yobun no* ～の extra

yochi 余地 room, space

yōchi na 幼稚な infantile, childish

yōchien 幼稚園 kindergarten

yōdateru 用立てる lend, advance

yodōshi 夜通し all night, whole night

yōfu 養父 foster [adoptive] father

yōfū 洋風 foreign style, Western style

yofukashi suru 夜更しする sit up till late

yofuke ni 夜更けに late at night

yōfuku 洋服 foreign clothing *yōfuku o tsukuru* ～を作る have a suit made *yōfuku-ya* ～屋 tailor, tailor shop

yōga 洋画 Western painting, foreign film

yogen 予言 prophecy, prediction *yogen suru* ～する prophesy, foretell

yogore 汚れ dirt, filth, stain *yogore-mono* ～物 soiled [dirty] things, washing, laundry

yogoreru 汚れる become dirty, be soiled *yogoreta* 汚れた dirty

yogosu 汚す stain, soil

yōhin-ten 洋品店 dry-goods [clothing] store

yohō 予報 forecast *tenki-yohō* 天気～ weather forecast

yoi 良[好]い good, fine, nice

yoi 酔 intoxication *yoi ga mawaru* ～が回る get drunk [tipsy] *yoi ga sameru* [*o samasu*] ～がさめる[をさます] get sober, sober up

yoi 宵 early evening

yōi 用意 preparation *yōi suru* ～する prepare

yōiku suru 養育する bring up, rear

yōi na [ni] 容易な[に] easy [-ily], ready [-ily]
yōi-naranu 容易ならぬ serious, grave

yoitsubureru 酔いつぶれる be dead drunk

yōji 幼児 baby, infant

yōji 用事 business, engagement

yōjin 用心 carefulness *yōjin suru* ～する be
careful *yōjin-bukai* ～深い careful, cautious

yōjō suru 養生する take care of one's health

yoka 予科 preparatory course

yoka ni 余暇に in spare moments, at one's leisure

yokei na [ni] 余計な[に] abundant [ly], more,
excessive [ly], too many, very much

yōken 要[用]件 important matter, business

yokeru よける avoid, shun

yoki 予期 expectation *yoki suru* ～する expect

yōki 容器 container, vessel

yōki 陽気 liveliness, gaiety, season, weather
yōki na ～な cheerful, merry, gay

yokin 預金 deposit, account

yokkyū 欲求 desire, urge

yoko 横 side, width *yoko ni naru* ～になる
lie (down), recline

yōkō 洋行 going [traveling] abroad *yōkō suru*
～する go abroad

yokodori suru 横取りする usurp, seize

yokogiru 横切る cross, go across

yokoku 予告 (advance) notice *yokoku suru* ～
する announce [inform] beforehand

yokome de miru 横目で見る look sideways (at),
look askance, cast sheep's eye

yokosu よこす send, forward, hand over

yokotaeru 横たえる lay (down), put across

yokotawaru 横たわる lie (down), lay oneself
down

yoku 良[好]く well, nicely

yoku 欲 avarice, greed *yoku no fukai* 〜の深い greedy

yokuasa 翌朝 next morning

yokubō 欲望 desire, wants

yokugetsu 翌月 next month

yokujitsu 翌日 next day

yokunaru よくなる recover, become better, improve

yokunen 翌年 next year

yokusei 抑制 control

yokushitsu 浴室 bathroom, bath

yōkyū 要求 request, demand *yōkyū suru* 〜する request

yome 嫁 bride, (young) wife *yomeiri* 〜入り wedding *yomeiri suru* 〜入りする get married

yomigaeru よみがえる come to oneself, be brought to life

yomimono 読物 reading (matter), book

yōmō 羊毛 wool *yōmō no* 〜の woolen

yomu 読む read

yonaka 夜中 midnight

-yoreba …よれば according to

yoreru よれる get twisted

yore-yore no よれよれの worn-out, threadbare

-yori …より from, out of, since, than

yorinuki no より抜きの picked, choice

yori o modosu よりを戻す get reconciled with, make up with

yorisou 寄り添う draw close [near]

yoritsuku 寄り付く get [come] near *yoritsuka-nai* 寄り付かない keep away

yoriwakeru より分ける sort out, assort

yoroi よろい armor

yorokobashii 喜ばしい joyful, glad, happy

yorokobi 喜び joy, delight

yorokonde 喜んで joyfully, gladly, with pleasure

yoromeku よろめく stagger, totter

yoron 輿論 public opinion

Yōroppa ヨーロッパ Europe *Yōroppa tairiku* ～大陸 the Continent

yoroshiku よろしく well; Give my best regards.

yoru 夜 night, evening

yoru よる depend [rely] on, be based on

yoru 寄る call at, drop in, draw near

yōryō 要領 (main) point, essentials *yōryō o enai* ～を得ない pointless *yōryō no yoi* ～のよい sensible, sharp

yōsai 洋裁 dressmaking *yōsai-shi* ～師 dressmaker

yosan 予算 estimate, budget

yose 寄席 vaudeville theater

yoseatsumeru 寄せ集める gather, collect

yosei 余生 the rest of one's life

yōsei 妖精 fairy

yōsei 陽性 positive, active

yōsei suru 養成する cultivate, train

yōseki 容積 capacity, volume, bulk

yōshi 要旨 point, substance

yōshi 容姿 figure, form *yōshi-tanrei* ～端麗 graceful figure

yōshi 用紙 blank, form

yōshiki 様式 style, way

yōsho 洋書 foreign book

yōshoku 洋食 Western food

yōshu 洋酒 foreign wine [spirits]

yoshū suru 予習する prepare (for) lessons

yoso よそ another place, somewhere

yōso 要素 factor, element

yōsō 予想 expectation, forecast *yosō suru* ～する expect, foresee *yosōgai* ～外 beyond all expectations *yosō ni hanshite* ～に反して unexpectedly

yoso'ou 装う wear, dress oneself

yoso-yoso-shii よそよそしい cold, distant *yoso-yoso-shiku* よそよそしく coldly, distantly

yōsu 様子 condition, state of affairs, circumstances, looks, appearance, air

yōsuru 要する require, need, want, take *yō-suru ni* ～に in short, in a word

yotei 予定 plan, program, schedule

yōten 要点 (main) point

yotsukado 四つ角 street corner

yotte よって according to, therefore, owing to, by

yottsu 四つ four

you 酔う get drunk, feel sick

yowai 弱い weak, delicate, faint

yowami 弱み weakness

yowane 弱音 complaints *yowane o haku* ～を吐く make complaints

yowaru 弱る weaken, grow weak, fail

yoyaku 予約 booking, reservation, subscription *yoyaku suru* ～する reserve, subscribe

yōyaku ようやく at last, at length, barely

yōyaku 要約 summary *yōyaku suru* ～する summarize, condense

yoyū 余裕 surplus, reserve, room *yoyū ga aru* ～がある afford

yu 湯 hot water

yū 言う say, talk, tell *yūmademonaku* 言うまでもなく needless to say

yūben 雄弁 eloquence, fluency *yūben na[ni]* ～な[に] eloquent[ly]

yūbin 郵便 mail, post
yūbin-hagaki ～葉書 post card
yūbin-haitatsunin ～配達人 mailman
yūbin-kitte ～切手 postage stamp
yūbin-kyoku ～局 post office

yūbi na 優美な graceful, elegant

yubiori no 指折りの leading, prominent

yubisaki 指先 finger tip

yubisasu 指さす point to, indicate

yubiwa 指輪 finger ring

yūbō na 有望な promising, hopeful

yūchō na 悠長な leisurely, slow

yūdachi 夕立 shower

yūdai na 雄大な grand, magnificent

yudan 油断 inattention, negligeance **yudan suru** ～する be careless

yudaneru ゆだねる entrust with

Yudaya ユダヤ Judea **Yudaya no** ～の Jewish **Yudaya-jin** ～人 Jew

yuderu ゆでる boil

yūdō suru 誘導する induce, conduct, lead

yūeki na 有益な profitable, useful

yūenchi 遊園地 recreation ground, amusement park

yūetsukan 優越感 sense of superiority, superiority complex

yūfuku na 裕福な rich, wealthy

yūgai na 有害な harmful

yugameru ゆがめる distort, bend

yugami ゆがみ bend, strain

yugamu ゆがむ be crooked, warp

yūga na 優雅な elegant, graceful

yūgata 夕方 evening, dusk

yuge 湯気 steam, vapor

yūgū 優遇 warm reception, hospitality, good treatment

yūhi 夕日 evening sun, setting sun

yuigon 遺言 will, one's dying wish

yuiitsu no 唯一の only, sole

yūjin 友人 friend, companion

yūjō 友情 friendship

yuka 床 floor

yukai na 愉快な pleasant, merry, joyful

yūkai suru 誘かいする kidnap, abduct

yūkan 夕刊 evening newspaper

yūkan 勇敢 bravery **yūkan na[ni]** ～な[に] brave[ly]

yūkan-kaikyū 有閑階級 leisure class

yukashii 床しい sweet, charming

yūken-sha 有権者 holder of a right, voter

yuki 雪 snow, snowfall **yuki no** ～の snowy

-yuki …行き for, bound for

yūki 勇気 courage, bravery *yūki no aru* 〜の ある courageous

yuki-daruma 雪だるま snow man

yukidoke 雪解け thaw, melting of snow

yukisugiru 行き過ぎる go past, go too far, go to extremes

yukitodoku 行き届く be careful, be complete

yukizumaru 行き詰まる stand still, come to a deadlock

yukkuri ゆっくり slowly, leisurely *yukkuri suru* 〜する take one's time

yūkō 友好 friendship *yūkō-kankei* 〜関係 friendly relations

yūkō na[ni] 有効な[に] effective[ly], valid[ly] *yūkō ni suru* 有効にする validate, make valid

yuku 行く go, visit

yukue 行方 one's whereabouts
yukue o kuramasu 〜を暗ます disappear
yukue-fumei no 〜不明の missing, lost

yukusaki 行く先 destination, address

yume 夢 dream, vision

yūmei 有名 reputation, fame *yūmei na* 〜な famous, well-known, celebrated

yumi 弓 bow, archery

yūmoa ユーモア humor

yunyū 輸入 import

yuragu 揺らぐ swing, sway, flicker

yurai 由来 origin, history, source

yūran 遊覧 excursion, sightseeing *yūran-basu* 〜バス sightseeing bus

yūrei 幽霊 ghost, apparition

yureru 揺れる shake, sway, roll

yuri ゆり lily

yūri na 有利な profitable, favorable

yurui 緩い loose *yuruku* 緩く loosely

yurumeru 緩める loosen, unfasten, relax

yurumu 緩む become loose, relax

yurushi 許し permission, approval

yurusu 許す permit, allow, approve

yūryoku na 有力な powerful, influential
yūryō na 優良な superior, excellent
yūsei 優勢 superior power
yūsei 郵政 postal administration **yūsei-shō ~**
省 the Ministry [Minister] of Postal Services
yūsen-teki ni 優先的に preferentially
yushi 油脂 oils and fats
yūshi 勇士 hero, brave man
yūshi 有志 volunteer, sympathizer
yūshi 融資 financing, accommodation
yūshoku 夕食 supper, dinner
yūshoku no 有色の colored **yūshoku-jinshu**
有色人種 colored race
yūshō suru 優勝する win the championship
yūshō-ki 優勝旗 champion flag
yūshū na 優秀な superior, excellent
yushutsu 輸出 export(ation)
yusō 輸送 transportation **yusō suru ~する**
transport, carry
yūsō na 勇壮な brave, heroic
yusugu ゆすぐ wash, rinse
yūsū no 有数の prominent, leading
yusuri ゆすり extortion, blackmail
yusuru ゆする extort
yutaka na 豊かな abundant, plentiful, rich
yuttari shita ゆったりした easy, calm, composed
yū'utsu 憂うつ melancholy, low spirits **yū'utsu**
na ~な melancholy, gloomy
yūwaku 誘惑 temptation **yūwaku suru ~する**
tempt, lure
yūyake 夕焼け evening glow, sunset colors
yūyami 夕やみ dusk, twilight
yūzai no 有罪の guilty
yūzei no 有税の taxable
yuzu ゆず citron
yūzū 融通 accommodation, advance **yūzū suru**
~する accommodate, lend
yuzuriau 譲り合う compromise, meet halfway,

concede

yuzuriukeru 譲り受ける take over, obtain by transfer

yuzuriwatasu 譲り渡す hand over, transfer

yuzuru 譲る give to, hand over, transfer, give way, concede

Z

za 座 seat *za ni tsuku* ～に着く take one's seat, be seated *za o hazusu* ～を外す leave one's seat, excuse oneself

zabuton 座布団 cushion

zai 財 money, wealth

zaigaku suru 在学する in [at] school [college] *zaigaku-sei* ～生 student body

zaigen 財源 source of revenue, funds

zaikohin 在庫品 goods in stock, stock on hand

zaimoku 材木 wood, timber

zainin 罪人 criminal

zairyō 材料 material(s)

zaisan 財産 property, fortune, assets, wealth

zaisei 財政 finance, financial affairs *zaisei-jōtai* ～状態 financial affairs

zaitaku suru 在宅する be at home

zakka 雑貨 miscellaneous goods, general merchandise *zakka-ya* ～屋 general store [shop]

zakkubaran no ざっくばらんの outspoken, frank

zankoku na [ni] 残酷な[に] cruel [ly]

zan'nen 残念 pity, regret, repentance *zan'nen na* ～な regrettable *zan'nen sōni* ～そうに regretfully *zan'nen garu* ～がる regret, be sorry

zarani aru ざらにある quite common, met with everywhere

zara-zara suru ざらざらする be [feel] rough *zara-zara shita* ざらざらした rough, coarse

zaru ざる basket

zaseki 座席 seat

zashiki 座敷 room, drawing room

zasshi 雑誌 magazine, journal *gekkan-zasshi* 月刊〜 monthly

zasshu 雑種 mixed breed, cross-bred

zassō 雑草 weeds

zatsudan 雑談 gossip, chat

zatsuzen to 雑然と in disorder [confusion]

zatto ざっと roughly, approximately, about

zattō 雑踏 congestion *zattō suru* 〜する be crowded

zawameku ざわめく be noisy, bustle

zehi 是非 by all means, without fail

zeikan 税関 customhouse, customs

zeikin 税金 tax, duty

zeitaku ぜい沢 luxury, extravagance *zeitaku na* 〜な luxurious *zeitaku o suru* 〜をする be extravagant *zeitaku-hin* 〜品 luxury

zekkō no 絶好の capital, splendid

zekkō suru 絶交する break (off) with, cut (a friend)

zembu 全部 all, the whole, in all

zemmen-teki na 全面的な general, overall

zemmetsu suru 全滅する be annihilated, be wiped out

zempan 全般 the whole *zempan no* 〜の whole, general

zen 善 good, goodness, virtue

zen 禅 religious meditation

zen 全 all, whole, total

zen 前 former

zenchishi 前置詞 preposition

zenchō 全長 total length

zengaku 全額 full amount

zengo 前後 order, sequence, before and behind, about

zenhan 前半 first half

zen'i 善意 good faith *zen'i ni* 〜に in good part, favorably

zen'in 全員 all the members

zenkai 前回 last [previous] time

zenkai suru 全快する recover (completely) from one's illness, get quite well

zenki no 前記の the above(-mentioned), the preceding

zenkoku 全国 the entire country *zenkoku-teki no* 〜的の national, nation-wide *zenkoku-teki ni* 〜的に all over the country

zen'nen 前年 preceding [previous] year, last year

zen'nin 善人 good man

zenrei 前例 precedent, previous example

zenryō na 善良な good, honest

zensei 全盛 height of prosperity *zensei-jidai* 〜時代 one's best days

zensha 前者 the former

zenshin 前進 advance, march *zenshin suru* 〜する advance

zenshin 全身 whole [entire] body

zenshū 全集 complete works

zensokuryoku de 全速力で at full speed

zentai 全体 the whole, all *zentai de* 〜で in all *zentai to shite* 〜として as a whole

zento 前途 future, prospects

zen'ya 前夜 the previous night, night before, the eve

zenzen 全然 entirely, completely, never, not... at all

zetsubō 絶望 despair, hopelessness

zettai ni 絶対に absolutely, positively

zō 象 elephant

zō 像 image, figure, statue

zōdai suru 増大する enlarge, increase

zōen 造園 landscape gardening

zōge 象牙 ivory

zōhei 造幣 coinage *zōhei-kyoku* 〜局 the Mint

zōka 増加 increase, rise

zōkin ぞうきん dustcloth, mop

- **zokkō suru** 続行する continue, resume
- **zokugo** 俗語 slang, colloquialism
- **zokuhen** 続編 sequel, second volume
- **zoku ni** 俗に commonly, popularly
- **zokusuru** 属する belong to
- **zoku-zoku** ぞくぞく in succession
- **zōsen** 造船 shipbuilding
- **zōshin** 増進 promotion　*zōshin suru* ～する promote
- **zōsho** 蔵書 collection of books
- **zōtei** 贈呈 presentation　*zōtei suru* ～する present
- **zōtōhin** 贈答品 presents, gifts
- **zotto suru** ぞっとする shudder, shiver, thrill
- **zōwai** 贈賄 bribery　*zōwai suru* ～する bribe
- **zu** 図 drawing, picture, map, plan　*zu ni ataru* ～にあたる hit the mark
- **zuan** 図案 design
- **zubanukete** ずば抜けて by far, exceptionally
- **zubon** ズボン trousers, pants
- **zubora na** ずぼらな slovenly, loose
- **zubunure ni naru** ずぶぬれになる get wet to the skin, be wet through
- **zuga** 図画 drawing, picture
- **zuhyō** 図表 chart
- **zuibun** 随分 pretty, fairly
- **zujō ni [no]** 頭上に [の] above one's head
- **zuki-zuki suru** ずきずきする throb
- **zunguri shita** ずんぐりした thickset, squat
- **zunō** 頭脳 head, brains
- **zun-zun** ずんずん rapidly, fast
- **zurari to** ずらりと in a row [line]
- **zureru** ずれる slip, lag
- **zurui** ずるい sly, cunning
- **zutsū** 頭痛 headache　*zutsū ga suru* ～がする have a headache
- **zutto** ずっと all the time, through(out), direct, straight
- **zūzūshii** ずうずうしい impudent, bold, shameless